Lecture Notes in Computer Science   12980

Lucio Tommaso De Paolis · Pasquale Arpaia ·
Patrick Bourdot (Eds.)

Augmented Reality, Virtual Reality, and Computer Graphics

8th International Conference, AVR 2021
Virtual Event, September 7–10, 2021
Proceedings

 Springer

Editors
Lucio Tommaso De Paolis ⓘ
University of Salento
Lecce, Italy

Pasquale Arpaia
University of Naples Federico II
Naples, Italy

Patrick Bourdot ⓘ
University of Paris-Sud
Orsay, France

ISSN 0302-9743   ISSN 1611-3349 (electronic)
Lecture Notes in Computer Science
ISBN 978-3-030-87594-7   ISBN 978-3-030-87595-4 (eBook)
https://doi.org/10.1007/978-3-030-87595-4

LNCS Sublibrary: SL6 – Image Processing, Computer Vision, Pattern Recognition, and Graphics

This Springer imprint is published by the registered company Springer Nature Switzerland AG
The registered company address is: Gewerbestrasse 11, 6330 Cham, Switzerland

Preface

In recent years, there has been a huge research interest in virtual reality (VR), augmented reality (AR) and mixed reality (MR) technologies, which now play a very important role in various fields of application such as medicine, industry, cultural heritage, and education.

The boundary between the virtual and real worlds continues to blur, and the constant and rapid spread of applications of these technologies makes it possible to create shortcuts that facilitate the interaction between humans and their environment and encourage and facilitate the process of recognition and learning.

Virtual reality technology enables the creation of realistic looking worlds and enables users to completely isolate themselves from the reality around them, entering a new digitally created world. User inputs are used to modify the digital environment in real time and this interactivity contributes to the feeling of being part of the virtual world.

Augmented reality and mixed reality technologies, on the other hand, allow the real-time fusion of digital content into the real world to enhance perception by visualizing information that users cannot directly detect with their senses. AR and MR complement reality rather than replacing it completely and the user has the impression that virtual and real objects coexist in the same space.

This book contains the contributions to the 8th International Conference on Augmented Reality, Virtual Reality and Computer Graphics (SALENTO AVR 2021) held during September 7–10, 2021, and organized by the Augmented and Virtual Reality Laboratory (AVR Lab) at the University of Salento, Italy. This year the event was rescheduled as a virtual conference to ensure the welfare of the community.

SALENTO AVR 2021 brought together the community of researchers, scientists, and innovators to discuss key issues, approaches, ideas, open problems, innovative applications, and trends in virtual and augmented reality, 3D visualization, and computer graphics in the areas of medicine, cultural heritage, arts, education, entertainment, military, and industrial applications.

We cordially invite you to visit the SALENTO AVR website (www.salentoavr.it) where you can find all relevant information about the event.

We are very grateful to the members of the Program Committee for their support and time spent in reviewing and discussing the submitted papers and doing so in a timely and professional manner.

We would like to sincerely thank the keynote speakers who gladly accepted our invitation and shared their expertise through enlightening speeches, helping us to fully meet the conference objectives. In this edition of SALENTO AVR we were honored to have the following invited speakers:

- Aldo Franco Dragoni – Università Politecnica delle Marche, Italy
- Matija Marolt – University of Ljubljana, Slovenia
- Volker Paelke – University of Applied Science of Bremen, Germany

SALENTO AVR 2021 attracted high-quality paper submissions from many countries. We would like to thank the authors of all accepted papers for submitting and presenting their works, making SALENTO AVR 2021 an excellent forum on virtual and augmented reality, facilitating the exchange of ideas, and shaping the future of this exciting research field.

We hope the readers will find in these pages interesting material and fruitful ideas for their future work.

July 2021

Lucio Tommaso De Paolis
Pasquale Arpaia
Patrick Bourdot
Marco Sacco

Organization

Conference Chair

Lucio Tommaso De Paolis   University of Salento, Italy

General Chairs

Patrick Bourdot   CNRS/LIMSI, University of Paris-Sud, France
Pasquale Arpaia   University of Naples, Italy
Marco Sacco   STIIMA-CNR, Italy

Program Committee

Andrea Abate	University of Salerno, Italy
Giovanni Aloisio	University of Salento, Italy
Giuseppe Anastasi	University of Pisa, Italy
Pasquale Arpaia	University of Naples, Italy
Selim Balcisoy	Sabanci University, Turkey
Vitoantonio Bevilacqua	Polytechnic University of Bari, Italy
Monica Bordegoni	Polytechnic University of Milan, Italy
Davide Borra	NoReal.it, Italy
Andrea Bottino	Polytechnic University of Turin, Italy
Pierre Boulanger	University of Alberta, Canada
Patrick Bourdot	CNRS/LIMSI, University of Paris-Sud, France
Andres Bustillo	University of Burgos, Spain
Massimo Cafaro	University of Salento, Italy
Bruno Carpentieri	University of Salerno, Italy
Sergio Casciaro	IFC-CNR, Italy
Marcello Carrozzino	Scuola Superiore Sant'Anna, Italy
Mario Ciampi	ICAR-CNR, Italy
Pietro Cipresso	Istituto Auxologico Italiano, Italy
Arnis Cirulis	Vidzeme University of Applied Sciences, Latvia
Mario Covarrubias	Polytechnic University of Milan, Italy
Rita Cucchiara	University of Modena, Italy
Egidio De Benedetto	University of Naples, Italy
Yuri Dekhtyar	Riga Technical University, Latvia
Giorgio De Nunzio	University of Salento, Italy
Francisco José Domínguez Mayo	University of Seville, Spain
Aldo Franco Dragoni	Polytechnic University of Marche, Italy
Italo Epicoco	University of Salento, Italy
Ben Falchuk	Perspecta Labs Inc., USA

Contents

Augmented Reality

Mixed Reality

Applications of VR/AR/MR in Cultural Heritage

Applications of VR/AR/MR in Medicine

Applications of VR/AR/MR in Education

Applications of VR/AR/MR in Industry

Virtual Reality

Virtual Scene Components for Data Visualization

Bruno Ježek$^{(\boxtimes)}$ ⓘ, Ondřej Šimeček ⓘ, and Antonín Slabý ⓘ

University of Hradec Králové, Rokitanského 62, 50002 Hradec Králové, Czech Republic
{bruno.jezek,ondrej.simecek,antonin.slaby}@uhk.cz

Abstract. The article describes selected components and connected procedures applied in virtual reality scene which emphasize quality and quantity of perception of visualized information and at the same time improve comfort for the user. Firstly, perception of space, movement and interaction are identified as key aspects of virtual reality in visualization. To fulfill these three aspects, the components of the virtual scene, such as the floor, the horizon, the origin of the space coordinate system, the hands, and others, are defined. The methods of their use is demonstrated through typical examples and advanta ges and gained experience is added.

Keywords: Data visualization · Information visualization · Virtual reality · Interaction

1 Introduction

Data visualization is the transformation of information or data to the form of visual representation. This transformation, usually computer-supported, generates a visual and interactive representation of data to amplify human cognition [1]. The purpose of visualization is not just pictures but insight [2] and information about the data must be represented effectively and accurately [3]. These are the best-known definitions of the data visualization process that can be expressed even very briefly „Above all else show the data" [4].

However, classical two-dimensional static methods of data visualization have a number of limitations which make it difficult to understand the information for the average user. Modern methods and devices of virtual reality bring the possibilities of extended natural user interaction, the use of large 3D space, and thus deeper immersion into virtual space [5–7].

Although the deployment of virtual reality (VR) in the field of visualization brings a number of new possibilities, the mere use of spatial sensors and the 3D display may not yet bring the desired quality of experience, level of immersion, and subsequent perception of the presented phenomenon or information. The aim is to understand the depicted phenomenon and the possibility of interaction by the presented entities. The user interface of systems (UI) enabling user interaction with the environment is nowadays not only menus and buttons, but all the interface through which it is communicated with the virtual environment. These can be hand gestures, head or eye movements, or just

© Springer Nature Switzerland AG 2021
L. T. De Paolis et al. (Eds.): AVR 2021, LNCS 12980, pp. 3–16, 2021.
https://doi.org/10.1007/978-3-030-87595-4_1

moving within a scene and interaction with individual objects. A subset of the UI is the so-called User Experience (UX) used mainly in connection with virtual and mixed reality. It indicates the quality of the experience and the usability of the program or system. The UX issue does not address whether the program does its job properly, but rather how user-friendly the whole system is and how it affects the user. The key elements of UX can significantly affect the user comfort and quality of the experience [8].

In our publication, we search for and try to find partial answers to the following basic question. What components of the virtual reality scene help to understand the visually presented information? What makes it easier for the user to immerse in the virtual space and bring the quality of the user experience? On selected tasks, we demonstrate elements of interaction and visualization helping the user with UX in VR.

The article text is organized as follows. After a brief introduction in chapter 1, chapter 2 describes the basic aspects of virtual reality that are examined in the next text, which includes a perception of space, movement and interaction and states technical limits of virtual reality. The following chapter 3 lists the virtual scene components for data visualization in virtual reality having the key role in strengthening friendliness due to human experience. It shows the role of hands, space limits, the existence of the origin of the coordinate system, and the ability to focus user attention. The following chapter 4 demonstrates practical experience with the perception of movement, space, and interaction. Selected other general tools are briefly mentioned too. The experiments have been implemented using the Unity engine and then tested based on the views of specific users. A brief conclusion closes the text.

2   Aspects of VR in Visualization

Today, virtual reality systems are commonly equipped with a stereoscopic display that allows direct visualization of 3D space, sensors that monitor the movement of the head or the entire user, and controllers that allow interaction within the virtual scene. The interaction and 3D visualization allow user a new way of perception, which can take the visualization of information to a higher level and make it more effective. In this article, we will deal with three aspects, the perception of space, movement, and interactions.

2.1   Perception of Space

Until the 20th century, most visualization methods were limited to two-dimensional space, often in paper form. Later, computers made it possible to create data views containing depth and thus achieve a certain form of 3D, but it was still a matter of rendering the image using 2D displays and similar technologies. Rendering techniques such as perspective projection, visibility, lighting, and surface shading, or cast shadows were used afterwards to support the representation of 3D space.

Despite these techniques, however, there was no reliable way to display information so that the human mind really thought it was inside a three-dimensional environment. Virtual reality has made it possible to convey a real spatial experience and thus differs significantly from all other ways of data visualization.

The use of advanced algorithms and 3D visualization techniques used regularly in virtual reality are already a great benefit in themselves. The emphasis on realism is the main reason why the development of imaging technologies is leading to ever better mediation of spatial perception. The included graphics are becoming more realistic, especially through improved technologies for rendering, working with light, shading, and the like. The closer the simulated environment is to the real one, the less the human mind becomes confused and focuses on the perception of the data contained rather than the way it is displayed. The quality of the mediation of spatial perception is a key component for many technical fields. This fact is evident in a number of types of software with applications in the field of technical design. For example, until recently, an architect had to use a certain degree of imagination when working in a CAD tool to be able to determine that an element placed in this way would serve its purpose really well. Thanks to virtual reality, there is no longer required a high degree of imagination for performing many technical professions. The perception of space mediates the natural perception of perspective, object size, symmetry, and other key factors. These benefits are of great benefit to architects, engineers, and designers in a variety of application areas. Wherever larger objects are used, there is no need to create expensive disposable prototypes to validate the concept.

2.2 Perception of Movement

During the process of developing virtual reality techniques, the creators responded to the software equipment and especially the ways of controlling popular computer games. They also took over the most common way of movement, where the player uses the arrows or joystick to determine the direction in which the character is walking. This option was often used with the first versions of the Oculus Rift [9]. However, right after the initial user tests, it was clear that this method was not optimal. After a few minutes, a large number of people felt severe nausea and could not continue to use the device. The reason was a significant detachment of movement in the visualization from the real world. The situation was least pleasant for the users if they were moving in a direction they could not see, i.e. to the sides or backwards. Another iteration of this method was to limit the movement only forward according to the direction of view when the player determined his direction by turning his head. For most individuals, this method is more acceptable and better captures the way people really move, making it one of the optional solutions for movement in many visualizations.

A significant competitor to smooth movement is the so-called teleportation. Although there are several slightly different versions of teleportation, all versions have a common feature. The user points to the selected location with his hand or other pointer and is immediately moved to the specified position after pressing the button. This method does not cause nausea even to the most sensitive people. On the other hand, the user loses the natural perception of movement, so it may be a certain ecstasy from the experience.

Another solution may be to limit the movement to the size of the user's real space only. This method was made possible by the implementation of motion sensing directly into a virtual reality device. Here a person can move in free space similarly as in reality, but it is limited by virtual reality to stay in the same place where there are real obstacles. It is used by many popular games such as Beat Saber [10] or Job Simulator [11]. In this experience, no form of nausea occurs, but the amount of user-accessible space is limited to some extent.

The possibilities of natural free movement in the virtual scene also include significant differences from standard visualization methods. The human body is very sensitive to the perception of movement and balance. People can determine with sufficient accuracy whether a visual perception corresponds to a movement perception. As soon as inaccuracies occur, feelings of nausea are almost immediately evoked.

2.3 Perception of Interaction

Perception of space and motion perception gives the virtual environment realism but puts the user in the simple role of a passive observer. The perception of interaction and the ability to interact with the environment allows user activities and turns virtual reality into a tool that is really useful for working with more complex simulations and visualizations.

Let us mention the conceptual apparatus in the context of interactions and their development. In this context, the term degree of freedom (DoF) is introduced for motion about an axis or along an axis. 3 DoF means that the rotations of the three main axes are monitored at the controller. When using 6 DoF, position data in space are added to this data. 3 DoF drivers are often used in mobile VR and are gradually disappearing over time due to their limitations. In contrast, 6 DoF drivers are becoming a natural part of all major representatives of virtual reality devices. If it is possible to reliably monitor all parameters of the controller, such as position and rotation, in virtual reality they can be used in roles and functions similar to the use of a real human hand. The hand thus becomes an important element of the virtual scene.

As already mentioned, the interaction allows the observer to become an active participant in the visualization. Many other features and possibilities of interaction make virtual reality a powerful tool. One example of the use of interaction can be the integration of various tools directly into a virtual hand. In this way, it is possible to turn a common hand into a 3D brush, which can draw information directly into the scene, an optical device for a detailed survey of the environment, a sword, a bow, or another weapon with one click, wave or another movement. Another useful feature of the interaction is its ability to directly simplify the operation of the visualization. For example, the Interactive Map application described in Sect. 4.3 shows that virtual reality combined with natural interaction can become a quality tool for visualizing more complex data. The controls are intuitive and easy to use even for inexperienced users. In addition, we managed to present the data in a simple but effective form.

3 Components of Virtual Scene for Data Visualization

The main component of virtual reality is the computer-simulated environment itself, sometimes called the virtual scene. Generally, this is the entire space of which the user is a part. Here, the designer of the visualization can create almost any illusion that the technical limitations allow. The goal of the procedures mentioned in this section is to increase the quality of the usability of the program or system, usually expressed as the user experience. It is therefore necessary to follow certain principles that ensure the correct transfer of presented information.

One of the important principles is to keep the user's orientation in the virtual spatial scene. This is aided by some basic visual components, which should be placed in the three-dimensional space as is the ground, horizon, or space origin, visualization of hands, and focus of attention.

Floor

An important task in the virtual scene is to create the illusion of a solid surface in the part of the space where the user expects the ground. This element, which we call the floor, respects the traditional human experience. The movement of a person in a virtual scene is limited by the bond to the substrate to which he is attracted in the direction of gravitational acceleration. If the user's feeling of solid ground under his feet is removed, nausea and discomfort appear almost immediately.

Limited Space and Existence of the Horizon

An important feature of the virtual scene is also the spatial limitation of all objects in the scene. The existence of the horizon is a related element in this context - The horizon forms a symbolic boundary between the sky and the earth, where large objects end, as well as an imaginary scene. When the horizon is removed or a sufficient illusion of the final space is not created, the user feels confused and, as a result, is unable to determine the basic orientation in the space, such as the upward direction.

Existence of the Origin of Space Coordinate System

Another key element in the virtual scene is the origin point. Although this element does not exist in the real world, it is quite important in virtual reality because it is perceived by the user as the origin of an imaginary coordinate system in a virtual environment that does not allow the user to see his body in the scene and thus determine his position - the implicitly understood origin. Many creators of virtual experiences have therefore decided to place this point in a simulated environment in various forms. It often takes the form of a circle or footprints on the floor, according to which the user can orient himself and possibly return to the correct position. This element also contributes to a better experience in the virtual scene and reduces the nausea or confusion of the user.

Hands

Hands are a basic human tool for interacting with the environment. In virtual reality, controllers are often used for this purpose. In many virtual reality applications, it has proven successful to replace the virtual representation of controllers with a simplified model of human hands. As a result, users have a stronger feeling of seeing and working with their real hands, and to some extent forget that they are using a VR device instead.

Focus of Attention

Focussing attention is another basic, important and at the same time problematic process of virtual reality. Visualization procedures of classic non-virtual applications do not solve the problem of whether the user is currently watching what is happening on paper or the screen because the display area is usually limited and the user is well oriented. In contrast, virtual reality offers unlimited 3D display space surrounding users. It can easily happen that the user is turned in a different direction at a key moment, or pays attention to another part of the visualized scene. This problem must be addressed when designing a virtual scene. Distractions or objects capable of obscuring the user's field of view should not be included in the scene. In addition, key components of the environment can be highlighted with lighting, colors, or animations. Sound can also help direct attention.

There is other appropriate information to support the real-world experience, giving the user more confidence in the movement and clarifying his awareness of the surrounding space. They include restricting the user's movement to a free part of the real space and preventing unwanted impacts, equipment damage, or injuries. This information can be realized, for example, by displaying a virtual wall in places where the real wall is located. Many other elements have a similar function.

4   Practical Tests of Visualization Techniques in Virtual Reality Scene

The three mentioned key aspects of the perception of visualization in virtual reality will be demonstrated in this part on specific practical examples aimed at emphasizing a selected specific area - the perception of space, movement, and interaction. For each demonstration following aspects will be presented: purpose and principle, scenario and procedure, development issues and benefits.

In the process of design and implementation of visualizations, some limitations and problems were revealed, but often new benefits were also found. Thanks to the creative process, it was also possible to confirm or refute the assumed principles and assumptions and at the same time to prove the reality of the statement from the theoretical part. Emphasis is placed on highlighting the key features of virtual reality which are the perception of space or movement and the use of interaction. The size of the virtual environments used in this publication has been limited to the size of a normal room for time and technical reasons. The goal of each of the demonstrations was to provide the user with a 3–10 min experience.

The testing was performed on HTC Vive, which has accurate tracking of the position of the headset and hand controls. The size of the real space was around 4 square meters most of the time. The designed tests were implemented using the Unity engine. This technology provides ease of use, variability in scene design and interaction, has high-quality documentation available [12], an available license, and most importantly is compatible with HTC Vive [13].

4.1   Perception of Movement

Analytical data is often displayed statically by displaying a static graph. The purpose of this demonstration is to test the dynamics of visualization represented by user movement. The visualization shows changes in the exchange rate of the virtual currency in Bitcoin during the period 05/2020 to 05/2021. The current exchange rate is shown as a roller coaster, the height of which changes according to the price of the currency in dollars. In addition to the classic tour of the roller-coaster trajectory as a 3D model, the user can experience movement on the path of the roller coaster, mediating changes in the course over time.

Fig. 1. The shape of the path used for movement along the Bitcoin roller-coaster visualization.

The first step in the process was to obtain the necessary data. The Bitcoin exchange rate at daily intervals was obtained from the Coinbase online exchange office in CSV data format. Subsequently, using the created script, the necessary virtual path was automatically generated from the data, i.e., the curve that served as the basis of the path for the user's movement (Fig. 1).

The user is placed in a virtual reality scene in a seat that moves according to price fluctuations. Thanks to the inserted information boards, the user always has an overview of the time period in which he is moving and what the current exchange rate is. Thus, changes in price are not only perceived as a curve in the graph but also directly affect the movement of the person.

Minor deficiencies began to appear during user testing deficiencies. Sharp fluctuations in the course caused nausea and loss of user orientation. It was necessary to proceed to smooth the generated route. The implementation of elements aimed at reducing or eliminating confusion has also been added into the scene. One of the most important improvements was the addition of the artificial horizon (Fig. 2). From the movement along the roller-coaster in this visual scene, the user gained an adequate idea of what is the direction upwards and at the same time, his ability to orient himself in space has significantly improved. The constant speed of movement has been adjusted so that the seat and the user slow down its movement when ascending, and conversely gaining speed when descending.

The necessary adjustments also took place on the track itself. The curve was originally realized as only a gray stripe leading forward. A texture resembling train rails and sleepers was subsequently added to the curve to improve the perception of movement (Fig. 2). The user could subsequently better perceive the magnitude of the forward speeds. A minor modification that also proved successful was the addition of flying particles. Tiny white particles appeared over the roller-coaster in a small amount. If the user moved, he got the impression that the particles were heading against him, similarly to the situation when a car is driving in a blizzard. All these elements significantly contributed to the reduction of disorientation and led to the improvement of the feeling of movement.

Fig. 2. Components of the roller-coaster virtual scene: the horizon, flying particles, the textured solid ground floor, cast shadows, train rails, and sleepers.

Although the main goal of this particular visualization was to demonstrate the use of motion perception, the perception of interaction and the perception of space could not be neglected either. Although the user climbed high along the course, there was no element that would clearly show him how high he is above the ground. Thus, a textured area was added to the visualization to achieve a solid ground floor (Fig. 2). Thanks to the regular texture, the user at higher altitudes clearly recognized that he was no longer moving just above the ground. Furthermore, the light in the scene was adjusted so that the track cast its shadow on the surface. As a result, the feeling of perception of space, and therefore of height, was greatly enhanced (Fig. 3).

As part of the interaction implementation, the user could influence his own movement along the path. The user was allowed to adjust the speed of forward movement using a control lever attached to the seat (Fig. 3, Fig. 4). If any part of the visualization of the path was judged by the user to be particularly interesting, he could stop using the lever.

Interesting associations were discovered in the field of perception of movement and space. Very important was the finding that it is necessary to work with movement in virtual reality scenes very carefully, as otherwise the user very soon becomes sick. However, by inserting an artificial horizon, a feeling of solid ground, and other elements, these feelings can be almost eliminated.

Fig. 3. The final Bitcoin roller-coaster visualization with the user seat.

Fig. 4. The user seat of the roller-coaster scene. The labels show the actual date and exchange rate of Bitcoin. The model of hands helps to interact with the speed lever.

4.2 Perception of Space

The second visualization, called Animal Exposure, concerns the perception of space and is focused on the perception of natural size and perspective. It allows the user to compare closely the real size of a dog, horse, and giraffe. When tested, this scene proved to be one of the most impressive. The ability to convey spatial perceptions is easily and extensively used in the professional field, such as design or architecture.

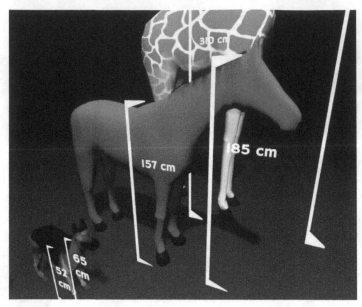

Fig. 5. The Animal Exposer virtual scene. Viewing several animals side by side along with a scale helps with relative size perception.

The essence of the visualization is the space of the virtual scene, in which several well-known animals are placed, in our example, it is a dog, a horse, and a giraffe. Everyone can easily imagine the size of a dog, but because we do not often come into contact with a horse or even a giraffe, it can be difficult to determine what their real dimensions are. Animal Exposure virtualization seeks to address this issue. It allows the user to see these creatures in their real size using virtual reality and easily compare them with each other and thus clarify the idea of their dimensions and size.

The horse model was placed in an empty room in the first version of the visualization. The user was able to move freely around the model and perceive the individual proportions of this creature. However, the scene seemed empty and did not attract user interest enough. Giraffe and dog models created in the Blender 3D modeling tool were then added to the horse model to improve the impression (Fig. 5).

The scene then looked much more effective and the user was clearly fascinated by the possibility of an unusual comparison. However, the visualization still lacked sufficient benefit in terms of information and data received. To mitigate this problem, some improvements were made. The important part was adding a chair as an origin point and object of well-known size, thanks to this comparing and illusion of size were greatly improved (Fig. 6). Also, individual size indicators were added to the scene for this purpose. The user could thus remember specific values.

4.3 Perception of Interaction

The aim of the third demonstration focused on interaction, was to provide an experience of the educational-cognitive nature of data visualization of a special kind, in which the

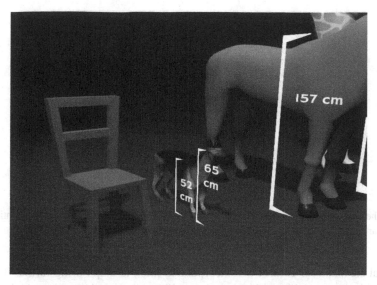

Fig. 6. The chair in the virtual scene defines the origin point and is another comparison object.

user is the one who controls the visualization. The use of the map proved to be a suitable option for displaying a larger set of statistical data of economic nature.

As a third proposal, the Interactive Map scene was created to display selected data. The user can use the slider to change the year that the visualization displays. The data is presented to the user in a pleasant and easy-to-understand form, while the user can have control over the visualization all the time thanks to easy operation.

Data on timber harvesting in regions of the Czech Republic between 2000 and 2017 were selected. The main reason for this choice was observable fluctuations in certain regions, as a result of the bark beetle calamity. The next step was to create a map. The area of the Czech Republic was divided into parts according to regions (Fig. 7). The Blender tool was used for modeling again.

This made it possible to work with each region separately. To show the extent of logging, a tree model was placed on each of the regions, the size of which indicated the extent of the logging in a given year. The accompanying programmed script allowed reading data from source files and their transfer for visualization purposes and also enabled easy data editing.

As a last part of the visualization, elements for visualization control were created and included. The slider used consists of 18 pieces, one for each year (Fig. 7). The user can further move the needle, which points to the currently selected year. The visualization on the map changes continuously according to the movement of the needle. It was necessary to highlight the needle with a different color so that it was possible to use an important 3D highlighter element in the virtual scene, which we will mention in the following text.

Visualization has proven that even more complex data can be displayed in an efficient and easy-to-use form. The interactive slider has also proven to be a simple and useful tool for controlling visualization. Emphasis was placed on efficient data transmission without unnecessary distractions, and this goal was achieved. A large amount of data with

Fig. 7. The Interactive Map scene. The highlighted needle on the slider allows you to continuously set the year for which the harvest is visualized by the size of the trees.

additional elements for control was incorporated into the map during further iterations in the development of this application. A specific territorial choice, by which the user can highlight and examine only a specific region and information about it is an example of this procedure.

4.4   Other Significant Components of Virtual Scene

Models of chairs and hands became important elements contained in most of the presented virtual scenes. The chair, which also served as the origin point of the space (see chapter 3), helped the user to compare unknown objects with an object he knew better, and consequently to perceive the presented dimensions better (Fig. 4, Fig. 6). The hands allowed more natural interactions and also served the purpose of comparing objects (Fig. 4, Fig. 8). It has been shown that if suitable data is available, VR visualization can provide the user with a much more powerful experience than information perceived through a standard form of display.

The 3D highlighter is a special object that has been implemented in all of the virtual reality scene samples mentioned in this article. It proved to be a great solution when used, for example, in the role of a notepad, or in the area of highlighting important objects in the scene. The basic idea of this tool, which allows recording in 3D space, is based on publication [14].

In our scenes, the implementation of this tool is performed using the LineRenderer component of the Unity engine. The purpose of this component is only to draw a line between the specified points and thus create the desired shape. At the same time, it performs so-called billboarding, where the lines are always turned perpendicular to the user. As a result, a person in virtual reality can look at the recording from any angle and always see a full line. The interaction is created by pressing the joystick button. The model of the hand changes at the moment of pressing so that the index finger is raised in the palm, at the end of which the user "writes". In this way, better visual contact is achieved and the accuracy of the recording is relatively high. An example of one of the possible uses of this tool in the scene is shown in figure (Fig. 8).

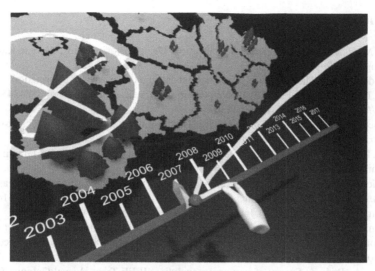

Fig. 8. The 3D highlighter allows focusing the user's attention.

5 Conclusion

The aim of the publication was to demonstrate the advantages of using virtual reality compared to standard forms of display. It was shown that techniques are suitable for data visualization in virtual scene, what are the necessary components of the simulated environment, what perceptions virtual reality can convey, and whether the interaction is at a sufficient level for professional use. The principles and benefits of virtual reality in this area have been defined. The main benefits were found in the areas of space perception, movement perception, and interaction. The output of the publication is a demonstration of the benefits of using virtual reality to visualize information using these three aspects. To fulfill these aspects, the key components of the virtual scene, such as the floor of the 3D space, the limited space, existence of the horizon and the origin of the space coordinate system, the model of user's hands, and focus of user's attention, are defined. The aspects of VR and scene components defined in the theoretical part of the work were shown on a practical example, with emphasis on the acquired effect and highlighting their role of visualization in virtual reality environment.

Several discoveries were made during the design process. Among the most interesting belong the use of hand models to improve the quality of the experience, the chair as the origin in the scene and an object that can serve as a standard for comparing sizes, and the use of 3D highlighter as an effective element for recording information into the scene. It was also found that current software and hardware technologies are able to provide a quality experience and can be used in the commercial sphere. Unity or Blender visualization tools have shown that they provide enough functionality to create a wide class of visualizations.

Acknowledgments. This work and the contribution were supported by a project of Students Grant Agency (SPEV 2021) - FIM, University of Hradec Kralove, Czech Republic.

References

1. Card, M.: Readings in Information Visualization: Using Vision to Think. Morgan Kaufmann, Burlington (1999)
2. Shneiderman, B.: The eyes have it: a task by data type taxonomy for information visualizations. In: Proceedings 1996 IEEE Symposium on Visual Languages, pp. 336–343 (1996). https://doi.org/10.1109/VL.1996.545307
3. Schroeder, W., Martin, K., Lorensen, W.: The Visualization Toolkit, An Object-Oriented Approach To 3D Graphics (2006)
4. Tufte, E.R. The visual display of quantitative information / Edward R. Tufte. Graphics Press, Cheshire, Conn. (Box 430, Cheshire 06410) (1983)
5. Donalek, C., et al.: Immersive and collaborative data visualization using virtual reality platforms. In: 2014 IEEE International Conference on Big Data (Big Data), pp. 609–614. IEEE, Washington, DC, USA (2014). https://doi.org/10.1109/BigData.2014.7004282
6. Dalton, J.: 5 Reasons to Use Virtual Reality for Data Visualisation. https://towardsdatascience.com/5-reasons-to-use-virtual-reality-for-data-visualisation-86cd37d5c1ee. Accessed 26 Apr 2021
7. Fonnet, A., Prié, Y.: Survey of immersive analytics. IEEE Trans. Visual Comput. Graphics 27, 2101–2122 (2021). https://doi.org/10.1109/TVCG.2019.2929033
8. Rebelo, F., Noriega, P., Duarte, E., Soares, M.: Using virtual reality to assess user experience. Hum Factors. 54, 964–982 (2012). https://doi.org/10.1177/0018720812465006
9. Oculus Rift History - How it All Started - Rift Info. https://riftinfo.com/oculus-rift-history-how-it-all-started. Accessed 13 May 2021
10. Beat Saber - VR rhythm game. https://beatsaber.com/. Accessed 13 May 2021
11. Owlchemy Labs: Job Simulator: the 2050 Archives. https://jobsimulatorgame.com/. Accessed 13 May 2021
12. Unity Technologies: Unity Manual. https://docs.unity3d.com/Manual. Accessed 13 May 2021
13. VIVE United States: Discover Virtual Reality Beyond Imagination. https://www.vive.com/us/. Accessed 13 May 2021
14. Keefe, D.F., Laidlaw, D.H.: Virtual reality data visualization for team-based STEAM education: tools, methods, and lessons learned. In: Shumaker, R. (ed.) VAMR 2013. LNCS, vol. 8022, pp. 179–187. Springer, Heidelberg (2013). https://doi.org/10.1007/978-3-642-39420-1_20

Developing a Gesture Library for Working in a Virtual Environment

D. D. Tsoy, Ye. A. Daineko$^{(\boxtimes)}$, M. T. Ipalakova, A. M. Seitnur,
and A. N. Myrzakulova

International Information Technology University, Almaty, Kazakhstan
y.daineko@iitu.edu.kz

Abstract. From year-to-year virtual reality conquers more and more IT market share and according to the forecasts, it will continue further. Except for virtual reality itself, there is also a need for the creation of new interaction ways. The specific feature of the VR requires special methods and tools that will provide users with comfort, efficiency, fast response. Also, it is important to make these tools native and understandable to answer the needs of consumers.

In the following paper, the authors present an analysis of works that suggest new types of human-computer interaction. The necessity in searching for new methods in communication between users and the virtual environment, and the need for their inclusivity and accessibility are shown.

Besides, the self-developed product and the process of a gesture library creation are reflected in the paper. It is assumed that the approach will improve the perception of information, shorten the training time for the user, which together will increase the efficiency of the application in which the product will be implemented.

Keywords: Virtual environment · Gesture · Human-computer interaction · Program application

1 Introduction

Human-computer interaction is one of the main aspects that appeared with the creation of the personal computer. Since then, people have been tending to ease the process of computer control. Nowadays we have plenty of types of different manipulators and controllers but almost all of them require specific skills to work with. From this point of view, the most interesting approach in the field of human-computer interaction is gesture control because it does not need additional effort or equipment. Also, this approach is available for a broad group of people and can be used in different areas. The reason is gestures are simple and natural, even for people with some impairments.

So, one of the most popular devices of this type is Leap Motion Controller (LMC). It tracks the movement of hands without any physical contact. There are two infrared cameras and three LEDs within Leap Motion which collect the data that is then processed by software.

Many researchers use the controller in their studies that demonstrates the versatility of the device. For example, [1] provides a study and its results in the development and

© Springer Nature Switzerland AG 2021
L. T. De Paolis et al. (Eds.): AVR 2021, LNCS 12980, pp. 17–24, 2021.
https://doi.org/10.1007/978-3-030-87595-4_2

definition of gestures based on American Sign Language. The authors pointed out the lack of such studies, justified using a single sensor, which leads to low-quality data and, as a result, to an incorrectly trained neural network. For this reason, the researchers used a multi-sensor system. Then, by overlaying the extracted data, a set was obtained for training a neural network based on a hidden Markov model. The results of the work demonstrate the effectiveness of this approach compared to existing systems.

In [2], the authors also used a neural network to process data obtained with the Leap Motion controller. Since the study is based on the determination of a combination of gestures, the SVM algorithm was used. The full process consisted of three parts. In the end, the authors obtained 63.57% of the accuracy of gesture recognition in real-time, and the system determined gestures shown not only by hands but also by fingers.

Another trend in the natural user interface world is the use of the Leap Motion controller as a means of authorization and authentication. So, according to the [3], the controller can be used equally with traditional means of information input: a mouse and a keyboard. The paper also provides information on the uniqueness of the behavior of each user during the execution of a given gesture. The results of the work demonstrated high accuracy rates, which confirmed the authors' assumption about the effectiveness and high potential of using the Leap Motion controller.

The following work [4] describes a study on the use of Leap Motion as a video player control device. The authors have created a framework for blind and visually impaired people, based on the definition of gestures for performing video operations. Their results demonstrate the effectiveness of this approach to interacting with software for people with vision problems. Thus, according to the respondents of the study, control with the help of gestures in 35% of cases was assessed as "very easy" and "easy" in 65%.

Another interesting example of implementing gesture recognition to interact with a program is the Scratch extension [5]. It allows the user to implement the controller's functionality into his project and, for example, control the movement of the character through the movement of his fingers. Figure 1 shows an example of the interface of this program. However, the extension only allows you to use standard Leap Motion gestures.

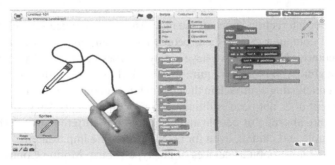

Fig. 1. Scratch app interface.

There is also an extension that allows managing the elements of the Google Chrome browser using Leap Motion [6]. A user, after the controller is connected, can scroll pages (vertically and horizontally), refresh pages, zoom in/out, navigate through history, and switch tabs. Also, it is possible to configure the controller parameters for personalization, when the user can change the set of gestures, notifications mode and sensitivity coefficient.

The authors in [7] demonstrated results of the project on dynamic gesture recognition approach in medicine. To define gestures, the SVM algorithm also was used. In result authors got the library with eleven dynamic gestures and overall performance of the model 80%. Within the work they described each of the gesture definition step. In general, the paper shows how LMC can ease the work of the stuff in areas where contactless control is required.

The following work [8] describes gesture elicitation study during which participants used some gestures and evaluated their difficulties for different tasks of TV control. The authors have given a list of commands, tasks, and results of research where different features of gesture performance were tracked. This project allows better understanding of features that are important in gesture recognition and execution.

2 Prerequisites for Development

The authors' work on virtual physical laboratories raised the problem of user interaction with objects within the virtual environment. One of the main tasks during the development of these laboratories is to choose the way of material presentation. It is important because users should get certain experience and knowledge about experiments after the execution of a laboratory work. In the case of a virtual laboratory, the quality of interaction between application and the user depends on the naturalness of the interface. Thus, an experiment conducted with one's hands improves the perception of the material being studied and makes the experience of working with the program brighter and more memorable.

Based on these features the Leap Motion controller was chosen as an alternative to a mouse and keyboard and other types of joysticks. The virtual physics laboratory works were created within the Unity game engine. Thus, Leap Motion integration was done easily and quickly because of the special module.

However, further work with the controller revealed several drawbacks. Although operations with virtual objects are performed without intermediaries, that is, directly with the help of hands, they are not so easy to implement due to various conditions: insufficient lighting, its excess, lack of feedback from the controller, especially for people who had no previous experience working with Leap Motion.

This prompted the authors to create a library that expands the set of standard Leap Motion gestures, and, thereby, speeds up the work inside the virtual laboratory for performing experiments and facilitates the interaction between the user and virtual elements. The aforementioned drawbacks have been mitigated by the recognition of the implemented gestures. In addition, the new introduction mode within the virtual laboratory have been introduced, in which a user can learn these new gestures and receive the feedback from the system as screen messages with the information about a device, the hand that is tracked and the recognized gesture.

3 Project Description

The Leap Motion Controller is a new consumer-grade sensor. It is primarily designed to detect hand gestures and finger positions in interactive software applications.

According to its API [9], the controller recognizes four gestures (Fig. 2):

- TYPE_SWIPE – quickly move fingertip across the screen to the right and left;
- TYPE_CIRCLE – fast circular motion of fingertip across the screen;
- TYPE_SCREEN_TAP – quickly push or tap the screen;
- TYPE_KEY_TAP – quickly move fingertip from down to up on the screen surface.

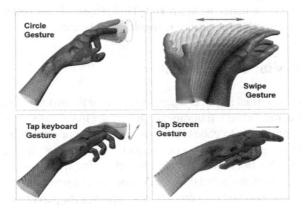

Fig. 2. API's gestures graphical representation.

Initially, it was planned to create an additional set of gestures that would allow controlling the virtual laboratory work. However, it was decided to create a library that could be used in other applications with ability to change the gestures set and redefine their functionality. Now, the authors have implemented the following gestures:

- TYPE_FLIP – flip the palm with outstretched fingers;
- TYPE_BLOOM – transition from a palm with fingers, the tips of which are gathered together, to a palm with spread fingers;
- TYPE_FIST – fist, all fingers of the hand are clenched;
- TYPE_PINCH – the tips of the index and thumb are brought together.

A graphic demonstration of the implemented gestures is shown in Fig. 3 a, b, c, and d. The gestures were selected based on their prevalence among existing analogs, as well as considering the ease of execution and ease of memorization.

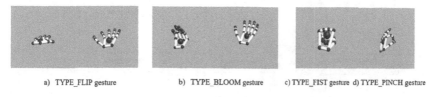

a) TYPE_FLIP gesture   b) TYPE_BLOOM gesture   c) TYPE_FIST gesture d) TYPE_PINCH gesture

Fig. 3. Graphical representation of new gestures.

4 Project Structure

The library was developed in C#, Fig. 4 shows an activity diagram that demonstrates how the library can be used in an application. The user launches an application using a library. Then he or she can override given gestures or to customize them to suit user's needs.

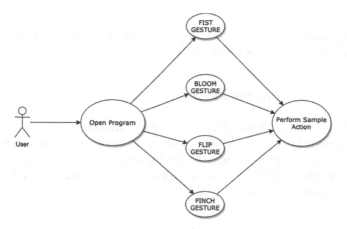

Fig. 4. Activity diagram.

Figure 5 shows the relationship between the classes that were implemented in the library. There are four classes on the diagram: PinchGesture, FlipGesture, FistGesture, and BloomGesture, which are based on the FrameworkGestures class. FrameworkGestures class defines their basic parameters. Thus, they are in a generalizing relationship. Then, each class describes its conditions to track a particular gesture. Finger Class, Arm Class, Hand Class are in an association relationship.

The classification of a human hand bones corresponds to the classification in Leap Motion. Bones are identified as:

- metacarpal bone – the bone within the hand that connects the finger to the wrist (excluding the thumb).
- proximal phalanx – the bone at the base of the finger, connected to the palm.
- intermediate phalanx – the middle bone of the finger between the tip and the base.
- distal phalanx – the terminal bone at the end of the toe.

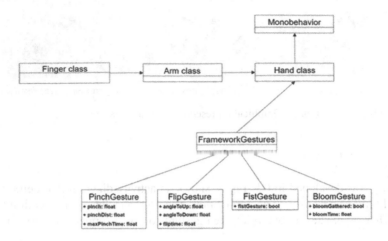

Fig. 5. Class diagram.

Depending on the gesture and the bones required to define it, the angles between the bones and the duration of the gestures are calculated.

5 Pinch Gesture Implementation

To define the gesture, the Hand class and its pinchStrength attribute are used, which returns a float value from 0 to 1 and indicates the pressure between the thumb and one of the four remaining fingers. Since in the library the Pinch gesture is defined as squeezing the index and the thumb, in the function we calculate the distance between them to make sure that the definition is correct.

6 Bloom Gesture Implementation

Bloom gesture tracking is done by calculating the distance between the knuckles. Having set a value for the maximum allowable distance, we track its change and, if it is done, we check the implementation of the palm gesture. Thus, the gesture consists of two sequential actions: bringing the fingertips together and then opening the palm. If the second stage is not performed, then the gesture is not considered as executed. Therefore, the duration of these movements one after another in a certain period is also important.

7 Fist Gesture Implementation

Leap Motion has a built-in boolean function isExtended, which determines whether the finger is extended. If it is, the return value is true. The finger will not be extended when it is bent towards the palm. The palm containing the instruments will always return a positive value. We count the fingers that are not extended, and if all fingers are bent, the gesture is regarded as Fist.

8 Flip Gesture Implementation

To implement this function, the Vector3 structure was used, which allows to operate with vectors and points in three-dimensional space. This structure is used to convey 3D positions and directions. It also contains functions for performing general vector operations and has many pre-defined properties for specifying direction, tilt, and rotation, and transforming vector points. In this example, the angle of rotation of the palm is calculated at a certain time, which allows tracking the rotation of the palm with outstretched fingers. As with the Bloom gesture, the sequence of movements is important in the current one. Therefore, we first track the palm with the fingers outstretched, turned back down, and then turned up. If the actions are performed sequentially, then the gesture is considered as completed.

Thus, now there is an implementation of the definition of four gestures that you can override and perform the actions necessary to work in the virtual world. It is planned to expand the library and create an interface, as well as write documentation to involve stakeholders and improve the project.

Now, the framework has been implemented in the virtual laboratory work on the topic "Investigation of the flight range of the body from the throwing angle". Its use helped to simplify the placement of the ball in the gun tray for throwing, as well as the user interface interaction required to launch the gun and reload the application to invoke reference materials. Thanks to the ability to override gesture functions, the framework becomes more flexible and easily customizable for an individual user. To assess and determine the effectiveness, it is planned to compare the results of users using the application without and with the framework.

9 Conclusion

Every year, more and more new projects appear that help various groups of users to simplify the work with the software, making it native and accessible. This article describes the latest developments in gesture control. The work presents the gesture library developed by the authors, which is an extension of the existing functionality of the Leap Motion controller.

Further work includes expanding the list of possible functions based on raw data from Leap Motion sensors, as well as analyzing two-handed gestures and dynamic gestures. This will greatly increase the intuitiveness of the system. Also, this functionality is planned to be implemented in augmented reality learning systems to automatically detect gestures and the user's actions. In the course of work on the project, the need for a survey to identify the most frequent and simple gestures was identified. This will increase the stability of the system and supplement it with many available movements.

Acknowledgment. This research has been funded by the Science Committee of the Ministry of Education and Science of the Republic of Kazakhstan (Grant No. AP08857146).

References

1. Fok, K.Y., Ganganath, N., Cheng, C.T., Chi, K.T.: A real-time ASL recognition system using leap motion sensors. In: International Conference on Cyber-Enabled Distributed Computing and Knowledge Discovery, pp. 411–414. IEEE (2015)
2. Kumar, P., Saini, R., Behera, S.K., Dogra, D.P., Roy, P.P.: Real-time recognition of sign language gestures and air-writing using leap motion. In: Fifteenth IAPR International Conference on Machine Vision Applications (MVA), pp. 157–160. IEEE (2017)
3. Chan, A., Halevi, T., Memon, N.: Leap motion controller for authentication via hand geometry and gestures. In: Tryfonas, T., Askoxylakis, I. (eds.) HAS 2015. LNCS, vol. 9190, pp. 13–22. Springer, Cham (2015). https://doi.org/10.1007/978-3-319-20376-8_2
4. Funes, M.M., Trojahn, T.H., Fortes, R.P.M., Goularte, R.: Gesture4All: a framework for 3D gestural interaction to improve accessibility of Web videos. In: Proceedings of the 33rd Annual ACM Symposium on Applied Computing, pp. 2151–2158 (2018)
5. Scratch Leap Motion Extension. https://khanning.github.io/scratch-leapmotion-extension/. Accessed 18 Feb 2021
6. Leap of Faith Chrome Extension. https://github.com/Issam-b/leap-faith. Accessed 21 Feb 2021
7. Ameur, S., Khalifa, A.B., Bouhlel, M.S.: A comprehensive leap motion database for hand gesture recognition. In: 2016 7th International Conference on Sciences of Electronics, Technologies of Information and Telecommunications (SETIT), pp. 514–519. IEEE (2016)
8. Zaiți, I.A., Pentiuc, Ș.G., Vatavu, R.D.: On free-hand TV control: experimental results on user-elicited gestures with leap motion. Pers. Ubiquitous Comput. **19**, 821–838 (2015)
9. Leap Gesture. https://developer-archive.leapmotion.com/documentation/python/api/Leap.Ges ture.html. Accessed 14 Mar 2021

Large-Scale 3D Web Environment for Visualization and Marketing of Household Appliances

Paweł Sobociński[1]([✉]) [ID], Dominik Strugała[1] [ID], Krzysztof Walczak[1] [ID], Mikołaj Maik[1] [ID], and Tomasz Jenek[2]

[1] Poznań University of Economics and Business, Poznań, Poland
{sobocinski,strugala,walczak,maik}@kti.ue.poznan.pl
[2] Amica S.A., Wronki, Poland
tomasz.jenek@amica.com.pl
http://www.kti.ue.poznan.pl/

Abstract. Manufacturers are continually looking for new methods to present their products to a broader range of customers in order to increase the selling numbers and brand recognition. Furthermore, with the quickly developing e-commerce market, there is a strong need for efficient and user-friendly methods of online product visualization for both wholesale and retail customers. In this paper, we describe and evaluate a method of products visualization using 3D web technologies. The visualization encompasses a large virtual showroom with a number of high-detail product models. In the showroom, customers can see an entire collection of products and can inspect particular products. The visualization has been designed to reflect as much as possible the real experience, including high detail architecture and furniture, photographs, videos, and music. The virtual environment has been prepared using AutoCAD, SketchUp, 3ds Max and Unity, and exported to WebGL. In the paper, we describe the design of the environment and evaluate its performance on different hardware and software platforms.

Keywords: 3D Web · Marketing · Visualization · WebGL · Unity

1 Introduction

Marketing is one of the critical activities that manufacturers need to perform to boost their selling numbers and gain more recognition among customers. However, recent studies concerning human perception show that most recipients developed resistance towards traditional visual media, which are the primary sources of information these days [10]. As a result, there is a need to find new innovative ways to influence customers. This need can be fulfilled by 3D web visualization. Constant progress in 3D web technology offers new possibilities of transferring various physical spaces into virtual spaces accessible online to a wide range of recipients. By using the 3D web, potential customers may be able to

© Springer Nature Switzerland AG 2021
L. T. De Paolis et al. (Eds.): AVR 2021, LNCS 12980, pp. 25–43, 2021.
https://doi.org/10.1007/978-3-030-87595-4_3

experience a virtual reality space being a digital counterpart to a real exhibition, possibly located in a distant place. This way of presenting goods may positively influence the customer's decision process and create proper expectations on the later experience in reality [13].

Another important use of 3D visualization of product exposition spaces is to perform merchandising studies. Such studies verify how different product arrangements in the modeled physical space influence customers' perception of the products. It can increase a store's selling numbers by influencing the customers or promoting a particular product or a group of products. Currently, such merchandising research is typically performed with the use of physical mock-ups of real stores [3]. However, the use of virtual spaces has significant advantages comparing to traditional physical spaces. It allows fast, easy, and well-controlled rearrangement of products. Moreover, there is no need to possess physical versions of all different kinds of products, which may quickly become unusable because of their expiration date.

Building realistic 3D virtual stores is a significant step in the process of moving daily shopping to the virtual world. This process already began with creating the first online stores and is still gaining importance in the modern economy—shopping is one of the most popular online activities worldwide. In 2016, retail e-commerce sales worldwide amounted to 1.86 trillion US dollars, and e-retail revenues are projected to grow to 4.48 trillion US dollars in 2021 [25]. Today, commonly used 2D shopping websites have their natural limitations; for example, lack of interaction with products, limited perception of the products' sizes and properties, and lack of social interaction between people, which can be a significant aspect of shopping for some groups of customers. The use of 3D avatars to navigate and communicate in a virtual environment introduces a social aspect into this activity, which is not achievable in traditional forms of e-commerce. These aspects can have a significant impact on the popularity of new forms of shopping [16].

To reach an average customer, a widely accessible visualization is required. It should be possible to reach the visualization using typical customers' equipment without installing additional software. The best platform for this kind of visualization is the web. In this paper, we present and evaluate a 3D web application that enables users to experience a virtual showroom of Amica S.A., which is a leading kitchen appliances manufacturer in Poland. To make the visualization as user-friendly as possible, and also to maximize the marketing impact, the application covers the whole physical showroom, which is used by Amica S.A. to expose their series of products, mainly for wholesale marketing.

The remainder of this paper is structured as follows. First, in Sect. 2, an overview of the state of the art is provided. Next, in Sect. 3, we present the 3D web application developed for Amica S.A. Then, in Sect. 4, we provide an evaluation of the application that measures its performance in various hardware and software environments. In the last section, we conclude the paper and indicate directions for future works.

2   Related Works

2.1   Designing 3D Virtual Environments

Geometry and appearance of real objects can be acquired using automatic and semi-automatic 3D scanning. There are several methods of achieving this goal. For example, static 3D objects can be precisely digitized using active scanners based on laser ToF measurement, triangulation, and structured light. There are also less precise, but more affordable methods—software tools enabling reconstruction of 3D objects from a series of images, such as Autodesk 123D and 3DSOM. 3D scanning can be combined with other content creation methods, allowing designers to influence the digitization process and the created content.

Both existing and non-existing objects can be modeled with the use of visual 3D content design environments. Software packages that enable modeling or sculpting 3D content include Blender, 3ds Max, Modo, Maya, ZBrush, and 3D-Coat. Professional environments like these offer advanced modeling capabilities of various content elements, but their complexity requires high expertise. Narrowing the application domain and the set of available operations enables the development of tools that are easier to use by domain experts. Examples of such environments include AutoCAD Civil 3D, Sweet Home 3D, and Ghost Productions. These tools enable relatively quick and efficient modeling without requiring users' extensive experience in 3D content creation. It is achieved, however, at the cost of reduced generality of the content creation process.

The high structural complexity of 3D content, combined with the requirement of adjusting specific content parameters, implicates the development of content models—well-defined structures, which describe the content organization and parameterization [30]. Based on such models, the final form of 3D content can be generated by content generation software—either fully automatically or semi-automatically in an interactive process. Content models offer data structures that are better organized and easier to maintain than typical 3D content representations. They also permit automatic verification of data consistency and elimination of redundancy. Content patterns provide an additional conceptual layer on top of content models, defining roles of specific elements in the model [20, 22].

Instead of fixed content models, rules of content composition can be used. Such rules describe how different types of content elements should be combined to form the final 3D model. Rules permit flexible composition of content from predefined building blocks—components [5, 28–30]. Components may represent geometrical objects, sounds, interaction elements, scenarios, and others. Content creation based on the configuration of predefined components constrains possible forms of the final created content. However, in many application domains, this approach is sufficient, while the process is much more straightforward and more efficient than creating content from scratch.

To further simplify content modeling, separation of concerns between different categories of users is required. Different users may have different expertise and may be equipped with different modeling tools. A non-expert designer may use ready-to-use components and assemble them into virtual scenes. Composing a scene in such a way is relatively simple, but the process is constrained. New content creation capabilities can be introduced by programmers or 3D designers, who can add new components and new ways of combining them.

Another aspect that can simplify the process of 3D content creation is the use of semantic web techniques [1,24,27,35]. These techniques enable the use of high-level domain-specific concepts in the content creation process instead of low-level concepts specific to 3D graphics. Content creation may be also supported by knowledge inference. The use of semantic modeling enables the creation of content that is platform-independent. Several approaches have been proposed to enable 3D content modeling with the use of semantic web techniques [4,6,9,14, 32,33].

The availability of easy-to-use and efficient content creation methods, in particular based on the semantic web techniques, enables social 3D content creation [31]. In this approach, content can be collaboratively created by users who both produce and consume the content (prosumers). 3D content sharing portals, such as Unity Asset Store, Highend3D, Turbosquid, 3D ContentCentral, and many others (e.g., CG People Network, Creative Crash, 3d Export, Evermotion, The 3D Studio and 3D Ocean) allow access to vast libraries of 3D content. However, the available content largely differs in style and quality, and is not suitable for applications requiring detailed models of specific products.

2.2   Interaction in 3D Virtual Environments

Choosing proper user interaction methods within a virtual environment is essential to offer a user-friendly 3D experience. The methods should be easy to use and intuitive to new users. This is not an easy task, because such users have often problems even with simple navigation in 3D environments. This section describes different approaches to the interaction of users in 3D/VR environments.

The first approach is based on classic input devices, such as a mouse and a keyboard. The possibility of translating 2D mouse movements to a 3D space [19] and the high degree of technological adoption make this approach preferred by many users in 3D environments. However, due to natural limitations of these devices (low number of degrees of freedom and the requirement to use key combinations), such navigation and interaction can often be non-intuitive and complicated, especially in VR environments.

The next approach consists in the use of specific equipment, such as gaming input devices (joysticks and pads) or dedicated VR devices (tracked controllers and haptic arms) for interaction with a virtual environment. The key advantage of this solution is user's comfort and efficient and accurate control of virtual elements in adequately configured environments [8,12]. However, low availability of such devices, quickly changing standards and—in some cases—high cost of specific equipment, results in limited use of this approach. In the case of more specialized devices, adapting them to environments other than those for which they were initially designed is difficult. Nevertheless, the approach based on specialized devices is often the basis for further research [2,26].

Another quickly developing approach for interaction in 3D environments is the analysis of natural human behavior. It includes techniques such as motion capture (e.g., with marker tracking or directly like in case of the Microsoft Kinect sensor system [23]), gesture recognition [15], eye tracking [21], and verbal/vocal input [36]. These techniques focus on providing intuitive, natural interfaces, which are user friendly even for non-experienced users. However, this kind of interaction is not suitable for web environments.

The context-based approach is an interaction technique popular in computer games, in particular in simulations (e.g., "The Sims" and "SimCity" series by Maxis) and in adventure games. This approach is not based on specific input devices, but focuses on the use of available devices to interact with the use of a contextual interface. The set of operations available in the interface depends on the current state of the environment and its objects (e.g., time, position, current object state). The context-based approach is also often used in modern VR environments [11]. However, users may find this approach uncomfortable due to the mismatch between classic UI elements (buttons, menus, charts) and the 3D virtual environment. Also, this technique is not convenient for entering data (such as text or numbers). This is an important limitation, especially when the interface is used for modification of content.

Another way to enable users' interaction within VR environments is to use devices with their own CPUs and screens for controlling the environment. Mobile devices, such as smartphones and tablets, are often used for this purpose due to their widespread availability and advanced user-interface features, including high-resolution touch screen displays and various types of built-in sensors, such as gyroscope and accelerometer. In this approach, a user has a specific predefined interface located on the client device to control the environment. This interface can be generated with the use of specialized software (e.g., PC Remote application by Monect [17]), or it can be dedicated to a specific environment and released in the form of an independent application. However, developing dedicated client applications is a time-consuming and costly activity, and the applicability of such an interaction interface is often limited to a single VR environment, making it unsuitable for the web.

3   Showroom 3D Web Application

The possibility to visualize 3D products over the web has a great value for marketing and presentation of a company's offer. Users are able to access the visualization of products directly from a web browser. There is no need for any extra devices like HMD or other specific VR hardware. Such a presentation can provide the capabilities of navigating, rotating, moving, and zooming depending on the user's needs. Moreover, there can be the possibilities to interact with the environment and the products themselves, including such operations as opening, closing, removing particular elements, and switching on/off a product. This kind of interaction is crucial for convincing visualization and proper demonstration of product's features and functionality [7,34].

In this section, we describe a 3D web application that has been implemented for visualization of products of Amica S.A. – a leading Polish manufacturer of kitchen appliances. To make the visualization as user-friendly as possible, and also to maximize the marketing impact, the application provides digital reconstruction of the whole real physical showroom, which is used by Amica S.A. to expose their series of products, mainly for wholesale marketing. The showroom space also contains other elements, such as screens with slide-shows and movies describing the company, a collection of historical products, and an entire cooking area. The physical showroom serves also as a place for business meetings.

3.1   Architectural Design

A virtual showroom, like any other space, requires a certain representation of real architectural objects. The representation depends on the technology in which the space is to be presented and whether the space is a visualization of a real place or just a sample generated environment. A model designed for a 3D presentation on a computer can be a very detailed reconstruction of the reality. However, not every platform allows for such a level of detail, mainly due to technical limitations. An example of such a platform is the web. Due to the limited capabilities of popular web browsers and typical consumer hardware, the level of details must be strictly controlled. The goal is to provide the highest user experience possible, while limiting the size of the visualization—both in terms of the number of polygons and the size of textures. These features greatly impact the loading time and the performance of a 3D visualization. In some cases, loading a large model may not be possible at all.

Regardless of the technology in which a given architectural space is presented, selected architectural design patterns should be used. For example, when designing computer games, urban design principles should be taken into account when creating urban spaces. The urban structure of buildings in such a case should draw from the basic methods of urban shaping in order to increase the realism and immersion. In turn, in architectural interiors, these rules are less formalized at the stage of spatial visualization and are based mostly on common sense, e.g., objects should not be placed in places that disturb the navigation or obstruct the view. When building a virtual representation of an architectural space, apart from the design patterns, it is important to maintain its correct structure. Such structure divides the space into separate areas, which can be then filled with furniture, equipment, and minor design elements.

The process of designing and creating architectural spaces can be accomplished in several ways. It is possible to fully prepare a 3D space in a modeling program. However, this approach requires specialized knowledge and skills to use 3D content creation tools efficiently. Users have more freedom in designing, but the process is more time consuming. The second possibility for this type of space is to use ready-made tools that support the creation process. Thanks to such tools, which use either artificial intelligence or assistance functions to support the design process, a designer can prepare a given space in a much easier and faster way. Instead of looking for semantic links or specific design patterns, thanks to the use of this type of tool, a designer automatically gains feedback on possible mistakes or solutions. Most often, these tools have component libraries that additionally facilitate the creation process [18]. It is also possible to use generators of architectural spaces, but currently these tools are still in an early stage of development and do not allow for a great amount of freedom in the design process.

3.2 Amica Showroom Design

In the case of the Amica 3D showroom application, the intention was to reproduce the real environment as accurately as possible. Original construction designs were provided by Amica S.A. in the *.dwg format. To avoid losing information, they were again imported into AutoCAD, where all redundant drawing elements usually found in architectural projects were removed. The drawings prepared in this way were then imported into SketchUp. This program was chosen due to the possibility of representation of the real dimensions with an accuracy of millimeters. At this stage, the general outline of the architectural space was prepared in the form of walls, floors, ceilings, and doors. The prepared model was then exported to the COLLADA format. In parallel, elements of decor were designed in 3ds Max. The difference between 3ds Max and SketchUp is essential. In SketchUp, it is easier to operate on real dimensions, while 3ds Max is much better suited for modeling elements of decor, as it provides a much larger set of tools for creating curves and complex shapes. The elements of the decor prepared in this way were then exported to the *.fbx format. Finally, these models were imported into Unity, where they were placed properly on the scene, and appropriate textures were assigned to them.

3.3 Web Application Design

The Unity environment (v. 2018.3.12f1) was used to program all elements of navigation and user interaction. Many optimizing processes were also carried out to boost the application's performance, so that it can be displayed quickly and smoothly in web browsers. To compile the application, we used Unity WebGL build option, which allows Unity to publish content as a JavaScript program that uses HTML5 technologies and the WebGL rendering API to run 3D content in a web browser. The deployment architecture of the web application is presented in Fig. 1.

In the case of web applications, the client hardware is not known. Users may run such applications on laptops or other computers with limited computing and graphical capabilities. To reduce possible fluctuations in the application's performance, post-processing methods in the form of motion blur and chromatic aberration were used. These effects reduce the impression of a sudden drop in frames per second. The compiled project's size was reduced from 30 GB, which was the size of the original compiled Unity project, to 118 MB in the case of the binary web application.

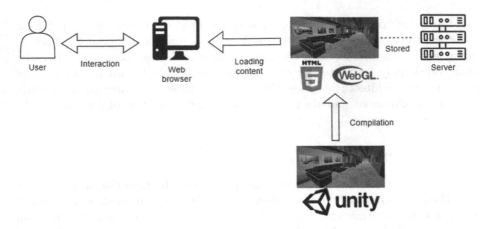

Fig. 1. Deployment architecture of the showroom 3D web application

The optimizations used for the creation of the web version of the application include:

1) striping unused engine code;
2) applying occlusion culling, which disables the rendering of objects not currently visible by the camera;
3) using the Brotli compression format, which significantly reduces the size of the final build;
4) pre-baking collision data into the meshes at the build time;
5) reducing the resolution of all textures and optimizing mesh data;
6) reducing the size of embedded movies.

The Unity WebGL support and performance varies among the major desktop web browsers. Unity WebGL content is not fully supported on mobile devices, although in many cases, it works, especially on high-end smartphones and tablets. The problem is that many mobile devices are not powerful enough and do not have enough memory to support Unity WebGL content well. For this reason, the browser shows a warning message when trying to load content on a mobile browser.

Interaction and navigation in 3D applications can be accomplished using traditional computer input devices (i.e., a mouse and a keyboard). Indirect mapping of the movement of a 2D mouse (having 2 or 3 degrees of freedom) to 3D space (requiring 6 degrees of freedom) can be done using additional buttons on the mouse or keyboard. The keyboard allows relatively rich interaction. It is used by most 3D web applications and games where the camera is positioned in the first-person perspective (FPP). A user moves by pressing the WSAD buttons or the arrow buttons on the keyboard and rotates the camera by moving the mouse. Additionally, by holding the Shift key, a user can move faster around the showroom. On mobile devices navigation is accomplished with the use of the touchscreen.

3.4   Functional Design

The showroom 3D web application's primary goal is to allow every customer to get familiar with the products and the brand itself. The virtual showroom is a detailed reconstruction of the real exhibition. The space is filled with kitchen appliances produced by Amica (Fig. 2). Users can freely walk around the space and view products from all directions. The experience resembles walking a real exposition, but customers are able to view the products without leaving their homes. An alternative way of gaining more information about products is by watching short movie clips with the visualization of products' operation. Such movies—embedded in the 3D environment—are an efficient way of presenting features and additional information that are hard to visualize in the form of 3D models.

Fig. 2. Area of the showroom with kitchen appliances displayed for view

The visualization of the offered products is not the only purpose of the application. Another critical aspect is the possibility of getting to know the company better. While walking around the showroom, a user can watch and listen to movie clips that explain the production processes. Other movie clips present the history of the company (Fig. 3). There is also an exhibition of historical products together with a high-resolution graphic that shows the most critical events in the company's history (Fig. 4). These elements are a significant part of the Public Relations strategy that builds trust in the brand and can increase sales numbers in the future.

4   Evaluation

The goal of building a web application is to make it accessible to most users on most devices. However, the level of support for WebGL varies among browsers

Fig. 3. Movie presenting history of the company

and operating systems. Therefore we tested the functionality and the performance of the application on all major browsers. In Mozilla Firefox, Google Chrome, MS Edge and Opera web browsers, the application runs without problems. In the case of Apple Safari, at the time of testing, the browser did not support WebGL 2.0, but only the older version of WebGL 1.0, so the application could not run.

4.1 Design of the Experiment

To check the application's performance, we tested it on three different computers, including two with different graphics cards, four browsers, and three selected spots in the virtual showroom. The following configurations of computers were used for testing:

1) Device I: Intel Core i5-4210H processor, 8 GB RAM, graphics cards: Intel HD Graphics 4600 (Device I*) and NVIDIA GeForce GTX 960M (Device I**)
2) Device II: Intel Core i5-9300H processor, 8 GB RAM, graphics cards: Intel UHD Graphics 630 (Device II*) and NVIDIA RTX 2060 (Device II**)
3) Device III: Intel Core i7-5930K processor, 32 GB RAM, graphics card: NVIDIA RTX 2080

The tests were performed in the following browsers:

1) Opera Browser version: 69.0.3686.95
2) Google Chrome version: 84.0.4147.105
3) Microsoft Edge version: 84.0.522.44
4) Mozilla Firefox version: 78.0.2 (64 bits)

Fig. 4. Historical products area in the showroom

The following spots in the virtual showroom were used as testing areas:

1) Spot I – the lobby area (Fig. 5)
2) Spot II – the comfort area (Fig. 6)
3) Spot III – the display area (Fig. 7)

The key to choosing these spots was the complexity of the 3D models in these areas. Starting with the first area, the complexity of the models increases: spot I has the smallest complexity (59K visible triangles and 95.2K vertices), spot II has the medium complexity (720K visible triangles and 863.7K vertices), and spot III has a very high complexity of the models (3.7M visible triangles and 3.4M vertices). In each experiment in a given spot, the user's viewpoint had the same location and direction in space.

The first goal of the experiment was to measure the performance of the application by checking the average number of frames per second (FPS) for every spot, device, and browser. To check the performance, we used FPS meters that are built into the browsers.

The second goal of the experiment was to check the time it takes to load the application into the browser. We compared the times by using network monitoring tools available in the browsers in the developer mode. We compared the loading times in four different browsers on all test devices. All client devices and the servers were running in the same campus network (1 Gb/s).

4.2   Experiment 1 – Rendering Performance

The results of the first experiment measuring the average number of FPS for every device, spot, and browser are shown in Table 1. Every value in the table represents the average number of FPS in a given spot. Overall, the results are good, indicating that even very complex 3D applications can be effectively used

Fig. 5. Spot I – the lobby

in their web versions. The highest scores were about 60 FPS (which is the maximum for the browser). Such scores were achievable in spot I and—in some cases, spot II—but only on devices with more advanced graphics cards. The weakest performance could be noticed in spot III, where some devices could not deal properly with the complexity of models. In Opera, Chrome, and MS Edge, they reach there only about 6 FPS on low-end devices.

In Fig. 8, a comparison of rendering speed in different browsers is presented. Based on the experiment, it can be observed that Mozilla Firefox provides the fastest rendering. It clearly stands out from the rest. In our case, it had almost twice the average FPS of the rest of the browsers. Opera, Chrome, and MS Edge did not differ significantly.

The next comparison (Table 2) presents the average number of FPS for every spot grouped by browsers. As can be expected, spots with higher complexity of models have a smaller average number of FPS. The highest differences are noticeable when comparing both spots I and II to spot III and the Firefox browser to the others.

The next figure (Fig. 9) shows the performance comparison between devices. As expected, the choice of the graphics card had a significant impact on the performance. The highest difference is noticeable between the graphics cards from the RTX series and the others, especially when we look at the performance of device II with the two different graphics cards.

Fig. 6. Spot II – the comfort area

Table 1. Performance results (FPS by device and browser)

		Spot I	Spot II	Spot III
Device I*	Opera	20	17	11
	Chrome	15	14	10
	Edge	16	13	11
	Firefox	40	32	13
Device I**	Opera	16	13	6
	Chrome	15	13	6
	Edge	16	13	6
	Firefox	54	45	21
Device II*	Opera	22	15	7
	Chrome	26	16	8
	Edge	20	17	8
	Firefox	57	28	13
Device II**	Opera	34	35	21
	Chrome	34	32	20
	Edge	35	32	22
	Firefox	60	56	30
Device III	Opera	59	32	17
	Chrome	59	34	15
	Edge	59	37	16
	Firefox	59	59	33

4.3   Experiment 2 – Loading Times

The average loading times for different devices and browsers are shown in Fig. 10. It can be noticed that the loading times are high, which is partially due to the large size of the content (118 MB), and partially due to the content processing time in the browser. Nevertheless, they are all below 30 s and in most cases below 20 s, which means that with appropriate warning message users should accept it.

Figure 11 presents average loading times in four different browsers. The most noticeable is the difference between Mozilla Firefox and other browsers. On the Firefox browser, the average loading time is higher in all cases. The differences between Opera, Google Chrome, and MS Edge are not large.

Fig. 7. Spot III – the display area

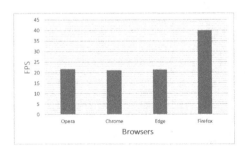

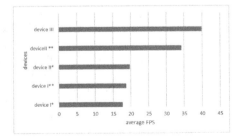

Fig. 8. Comparison of the performance in different browsers

Fig. 9. Comparison of the performance on different devices

Table 2. Performance results (FPS by spot and browser)

	Spot I	Spot II	Spot III	*Average*
Opera	30.2	22.4	12.4	*21.7*
Chrome	29.8	21.8	11.8	*21.1*
Edge	29.2	22.4	12.6	*21.4*
Firefox	54	44	22	*40*
Average	*35.8*	*27.65*	*14.7*	***26.05***

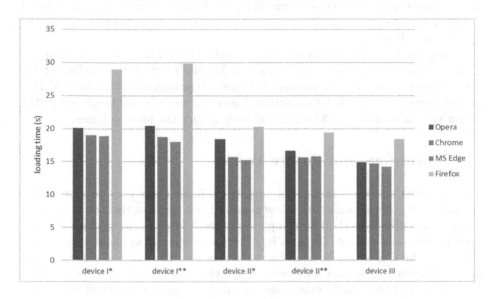

Fig. 10. Comparison of the loading times for different devices and browsers

The last comparison (Fig. 12) presents the average loading time on three different devices. The results indicate that devices with better performance have lower loading times, yet the differences are not significant.

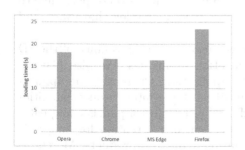

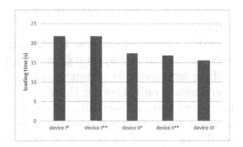

Fig. 11. Comparison of the average loading times in different browsers

Fig. 12. Comparison of the average loading times on different devices

4.4 Discussion

The results of the first experiment clearly indicate that each of the three elements: the equipment, the browser, and the complexity of models influenced the application's performance. The most important impact had the level of detail in the 3D models. For users with slower devices, it can be a significant obstacle to use the application conveniently. Even devices with much better specifications had a noticeable decrease in performance in places with a high number of triangles in the 3D models. This indicates that during the creation of a virtual space like a showroom, it is essential to find the right balance between models' level of detail and rendering capabilities to enable as many users as possible to use the application efficiently.

The second experiment shows that both the browser and the type of device influence the loading times. In the case of Mozilla Firefox, the loading of the application is longer than in the case of the rest of the browsers (but the rendering performance is the highest). Comparing different devices, it can be observed that better specification of the device can slightly reduce the loading times.

5 Conclusions and Future Works

The use of 3D web applications can have a significant impact on promotion and marketing. It gives manufacturers new possibilities to present their products, and it can be an efficient method for companies to reach large numbers of people with their promotional content. Unlike VR/AR technologies, an application that uses 3D web technologies can be used by customers regardless of the place and the device. However, designing a 3D web application is a complicated process that requires many factors to be taken into account, e.g., proper design of the virtual space, conveniently implemented interaction, complexity of models, and devices used by users, which can influence the performance of the application.

In this paper, we described a 3D web application implemented for promoting kitchen appliances and the Amica brand. The application permits visualization of products and presentation of information about the manufacturer. We have also conducted an evaluation of the application's performance by testing it with different devices and browsers. The evaluation indicates what level of performance is achievable, and how much it depends on the used 3D models, hardware, and software.

Future works encompass further improvement of the performance of the 3D web application by applying other optimization techniques. We also plan on adding new methods of interaction in the application. Currently, the application enables only viewing the products in 3D. Adding interaction capabilities like opening ovens, switching them on/off, and using control panels can greatly increase the customers' immersion level and keep their attention for longer. It would also permit to present more information about the products. Moreover, we plan to test users' perception and interest in the developed application to gain more knowledge about the application's usefulness for marketing purposes.

Acknowledgment. The authors would like to thank Amica S.A. for supporting this research work and providing 3D models of products and graphics.

References

1. Alpcan, T., Bauckhage, C., Kotsovinos, E.: Towards 3D internet: why, what, and how? In: International Conference on Cyberworlds, 2007. CW 2007, pp. 95–99. IEEE (2007)
2. Alshaer, A., Regenbrecht, H., O'Hare, D.: Investigating visual dominance with a virtual driving task. In: 2015 IEEE Virtual Reality (VR), pp. 145–146, March 2015. https://doi.org/10.1109/VR.2015.7223337
3. Borusiak, B., Pierański, B., Strykowski, S.: Perception of in-store assortment exposure. Studia Ekonomiczne **334**, 108–119 (2017)
4. Chaudhuri, S., Kalogerakis, E., Giguere, S., Funkhouser, T.: Attribit: content creation with semantic attributes. In: Proceedings of the 26th Annual ACM Symposium on User Interface Software and Technology, pp. 193–202. ACM (2013)
5. Dachselt, R., Hinz, M., Meissner, K.: CONTIGRA: an xml-based architecture for component-oriented 3D applications. In: Proceedings of the Seventh International Conference on 3D Web Technology, pp. 155–163. Web3D 2002. ACM, New York, NY, USA (2002). https://doi.org/10.1145/504502.504527
6. De Troyer, O., Bille, W., Romero, R., Stuer, P.: On generating virtual worlds from domain ontologies. In: Proceedings of the 9th International Conference on Multi-Media Modeling, pp. 279–294. Taipei, Taiwan (2003)
7. Dziekoński, J., Walczak, K.: A configurable virtual reality store. In: Web3D 2018 Proceedings of the 23rd International ACM Conference on 3D Web Technology, p. Article 29; Best Poster. ACM New York, NY, USA (2018). https://doi.org/10.1145/3208806.3208831
8. Flotyński, J., et al.: An immersive service guide for home appliances. In: 2018 IEEE 8th International Conference on Consumer Electronics - Berlin (ICCE-Berlin), pp. 370–375. IEEE Xplore (2019). https://doi.org/10.1109/ICCE-Berlin47944.2019.8966215, https://ieeexplore.ieee.org/document/8966215
9. Flotyński, J., Walczak, K.: Ontology-based creation of 3D content in a service-oriented environment. In: Abramowicz, W. (ed.) BIS 2015. LNBIP, vol. 208, pp. 77–89. Springer, Cham (2015). https://doi.org/10.1007/978-3-319-19027-3_7
10. Fransen, M., Verlegh, P., Kirmani, A., Smit, E.: A typology of consumer strategies for resisting advertising, and a review of mechanisms for countering them. Int. J. Advertising **34**, 6–16 (2015). https://doi.org/10.1080/02650487.2014.995284
11. Gebhardt, S., et al.: flapAssist: how the integration of VR and visualization tools fosters the factory planning process. In: 2015 IEEE Virtual Reality (VR), pp. 181–182, March 2015. https://doi.org/10.1109/VR.2015.7223355
12. Kitson, A., Riecke, B.E., Hashemian, A.M., Neustaedter, C.: NaviChair: evaluating an embodied interface using a pointing task to navigate virtual reality. In: Proceedings of the 3rd ACM Symposium on Spatial User Interaction, pp. 123–126. SUI 2015. ACM, New York, NY, USA (2015). https://doi.org/10.1145/2788940.2788956, http://doi.acm.org/10.1145/2788940.2788956
13. Klein, L.R.: Creating virtual product experiences: the role of telepresence. J. Interact. Mark. **17**(1), 41 – 55 (2003). https://doi.org/10.1002/dir.10046, http://www.sciencedirect.com/science/article/pii/S1094996803701285
14. Latoschik, M.E., Blach, R., Iao, F.: Semantic modelling for virtual worlds a novel paradigm for realtime interactive systems? In: VRST, pp. 17–20 (2008)

15. LaViola, Jr., J.J.: Context aware 3D gesture recognition for games and virtual reality. In: ACM SIGGRAPH 2015 Courses, pp. 10:1–10:61. SIGGRAPH 2015. ACM, New York, NY, USA (2015). https://doi.org/10.1145/2776880.2792711, http://doi.acm.org/10.1145/2776880.2792711

16. Lee, K.C., Chung, N.: Empirical analysis of consumer reaction to the virtual reality shopping mall. Comput. Hum. Behavior **24**(1), 88–104 (2008). https://doi.org/10.1016/j.chb.2007.01.018, http://www.sciencedirect.com/science/article/pii/S0747563207000155

17. Monect: Monect pc remote. https://www.monect.com/ (2017). Accessed 27 Sept 2017

18. Neufert, E., Neufert, P.: Architects' Data. Wiley (2012). https://books.google.pl/books?id=6N68sMtqXSUC

19. Nielson, G.M., Olsen, Jr., D.R.: Direct manipulation techniques for 3D objects using 2D locator devices. In: Proceedings of the 1986 Workshop on Interactive 3D Graphics, pp. 175–182. I3D 1986. ACM, New York, NY, USA (1987). https://doi.org/10.1145/319120.319134, http://doi.acm.org/10.1145/319120.319134

20. Pellens, B., De Troyer, O., Kleinermann, F.: CoDePA: a conceptual design pattern approach to model behavior for X3D worlds. In: Proceedings of the 13th International Symposium on 3D Web Technology, pp. 91–99. Web3D 2008. ACM, New York, NY, USA (2008). https://doi.org/10.1145/1394209.1394229, http://doi.acm.org/10.1145/1394209.1394229

21. Piumsomboon, T., Lee, G., Lindeman, R.W., Billinghurst, M.: Exploring natural eye-gaze-based interaction for immersive virtual reality. In: 2017 IEEE Symposium on 3D User Interfaces (3DUI), pp. 36–39, March 2017. https://doi.org/10.1109/3DUI.2017.7893315

22. Polys, N., Visamsetty, S., Battarechee, P., Tilevich, E.: Design patterns in componentized scenegraphs. Shaker Verlag, Proceedings of SEARIS (2009)

23. Roupé, M., Bosch-Sijtsema, P., Johansson, M.: Interactive navigation interface for virtual reality using the human body. Comput. Environ. Urban Syst. **43**(Supplement C), 42–50 (2014). https://doi.org/10.1016/j.compenvurbsys.2013.10.003, http://www.sciencedirect.com/science/article/pii/S0198971513000884

24. Spagnuolo, M., Falcidieno, B.: 3D media and the semantic web. IEEE Intell. Syst. **24**(2), 90–96 (2009)

25. Statista: Retail e-commerce sales worldwide from 2014 to 2021 (2018). https://www.statista.com/statistics/379046/worldwide-retail-e-commerce-sales/

26. Thomann, G., Nguyen, D.M.P., Tonetti, J.: Expert's Evaluation of Innovative Surgical Instrument and Operative Procedure Using Haptic Interface in Virtual Reality, pp. 163–173. Springer International Publishing, Cham (2014). https://doi.org/10.1007/978-3-319-01848-5-13

27. Van Gool, L., Leibe, B., Müller, P., Vergauwen, M., Weise, T.: 3D challenges and a non-in-depth overview of recent progress. In: 3DIM, pp. 118–132 (2007)

28. Visamsetty, S.S.S., Bhattacharjee, P., Polys, N.: Design patterns in X3D toolkits. In: Proceedings of the 13th International Symposium on 3D Web Technology, pp. 101–104. Web3D 2008. ACM, New York, NY, USA (2008). https://doi.org/10.1145/1394209.1394230, http://doi.acm.org/10.1145/1394209.1394230

29. Walczak, K.: Flex-VR: configurable 3D web applications. In: Proceedings of the Conference on Human System Interactions, pp. 135–140. IEEE (2008)

30. Walczak, K.: Structured design of interactive VR applications. In: Proceedings of the 13th International Symposium on 3D Web Technology, pp. 105–113. Web3D 2008. ACM, New York, NY, USA (2008). https://doi.org/10.1145/1394209.1394231, http://doi.acm.org/10.1145/1394209.1394231

31. Walczak, K.: Semantics-supported collaborative creation of interactive 3D content. In: De Paolis, L.T., Bourdot, P., Mongelli, A. (eds.) AVR 2017. LNCS, vol. 10325, pp. 385–401. Springer, Cham (2017). https://doi.org/10.1007/978-3-319-60928-7_33

32. Walczak, K., Flotyński, J.: On-demand generation of 3D content based on semantic meta-scenes. In: De Paolis, L.T., Mongelli, A. (eds.) AVR 2014. LNCS, vol. 8853, pp. 313–332. Springer, Cham (2014). https://doi.org/10.1007/978-3-319-13969-2_24

33. Walczak, K., Flotyński, J.: Semantic query-based generation of customized 3D scenes. In: Proceedings of the 20th International Conference on 3D Web Technology, pp. 123–131. Web3D 2015. ACM, New York, NY, USA (2015). https://doi.org/10.1145/2775292.2775311, http://doi.acm.org/10.1145/2775292.2775311

34. Walczak, K., et al.: Virtual and augmented reality for configuring, promoting and servicing household appliances. In: Trojanowska, J., Ciszak, O., Machado, J.M., Pavlenko, I. (eds.) MANUFACTURING 2019. LNME, pp. 368–380. Springer, Cham (2019). https://doi.org/10.1007/978-3-030-18715-6_31

35. Zahariadis, T., Daras, P., Laso-Ballesteros, I.: Towards future 3D media internet. NEM Summit, pp. 13–15 (2008)

36. Zielasko, D., Neha, N., Weyers, B., Kuhlen, T.W.: A reliable non-verbal vocal input metaphor for clicking. In: 2017 IEEE Symposium on 3D User Interfaces (3DUI), pp. 40–49, March 2017. https://doi.org/10.1109/3DUI.2017.7893316

Users' Evaluation of Procedurally Generated Game Levels

Riccardo Galdieri[1]([⊠]) [iD], Alessandro Longobardi[1] [iD], Michele De Bonis[2],
and Marcello Carrozzino[1] [iD]

[1] Scuola Superiore Sant'Anna, Pisa, Italy
[2] Università di Pisa, Pisa, Italy

Abstract. Iterative design is an expensive yet necessary task in the creation of coherent game levels. However, it often requires many resources, something that many projects, especially in the academic field, are usually lacking. This paper discusses the results of a test performed on EscapeTower, a pre-existing customer-ready research game where hand-crafted levels have been replaced by procedural ones to speed up the development process. A custom room generator has been developed and used to procedurally generate several levels for the EscapeTower project. A User Study was subsequently conducted to assess how the procedurally generated levels affect the user experience within the game and how they compared to the original levels designed by professionals. Results are in line with current literature, showing that players have a significant preference over manually designed spaces. However, data also shows that procedurally generated environments did not impact users' ability to navigate the spaces, leading to the possibility to use such systems in early prototyping and designing phases.

Keywords: Procedural content generation · HCI · Game studies

1 Introduction

In the world of game development, one of the most time-consuming activities is the creation of coherent, dynamic and believable environments where players can freely roam, interact, and essentially live. To create such scenarios, a designer must balance elements like narrative, gameplay mechanics and visual appeal, carefully tweaking many individual parameters to produce something that fits a broader game context. To save time and costs, many attempts have been made to automate this process by using Procedural Content Generation (PCG), with mixed results.

PCG has been widely used in game development since its infancy, from the generation of 3D structures to the creation of game levels, but it is also known to have a degree of artificiality that distinguish it from hand-tailored environments. For this reason, it is often used as a support tool to add variation to pre-designed environments, as it is helpful to add elements of variation into structures that would otherwise be too similar to each other. Another fruitful area of application for procedural content generation is the creation of urban environments such as facades, buildings, houses, streets, and their

L. T. De Paolis et al. (Eds.): AVR 2021, LNCS 12980, pp. 44–52, 2021.
https://doi.org/10.1007/978-3-030-87595-4_4

arrangement on the terrain map in an organic manner and the decoration of such spaces with visual and sound effects, music, and even game logic.

This paper describes an attempt to use procedural level creation in support of a pre-existing research project. Following the success of game-based research, multiple new instances of the same environment were needed to expand the experiment further, and procedural generation was the only feasible option that matched both budget and creation time. With a plethora of potential application fields to dwell into with PCG, this paper focuses on one particular aspect of procedural level generation: creating a non-supervised game-ready closed environment to personalise and make unique every user experience [1]. Internal testing showed that despite being able to guide players through the experience as intended, procedural generation was not advanced enough to create believable market-ready buildings that could be compared with the original design.

2 Previous Literature

PCG is a macro-category that comprehend many computational techniques used to algorithmically produced contents that would otherwise require a human to be created. PCG has been applied to several contents especially when a high degree of repetitiveness is present, like for instance urban environments [13] or vegetation [14]. PCG has also been applied to game development, with PCG-G (Procedural Content Generation for Games) being the subset of PCG techniques that can help create procedural elements in gaming contexts. A first attempt to create a taxonomy of PCG-G was published by Hendrikx et al. [2], who identified six classes in which PCG can be applied: game bits, game space, game systems, game scenarios, game design, and derived content. This taxonomy is structured in a pyramidal shape, with the top elements built upon those presented at the lower levels.

A different classification has instead been proposed by [5], who classified PCG based on several non-mutually exclusive independent parameters. These can be distinguished into:

- online vs offline approach: Whether it is necessary to generate content while playing (e.g., endless running games). In the first case, it is necessary to use algorithms that are not too computationally heavy and very efficient in terms of time. In the case of offline generation, human (non-aware) control can improve or make the resulting content more usable.
- Generation of optional or necessary content: A distinction is made between content that is essential for the continuation of the video game or simply decorative and whose incorrect generation does not affect the continuation of the adventure.
- Random or parametric vectors: If the generation of contents is fully randomised or is influenced by some sort of seeding. This distinction is crucial in the case of algorithms such as those based on cellular automata.
- Deterministic or stochastic generation: Whether given an initial default parameter, the obtained result is deterministic or stochastic.
- Constructive or generate-and-test approaches: a constructive generation is guaranteed to have a result that fit the desired parameters because the model is already established

and integrated into the algorithm, and a generate-and-test approach, in which content is generated and verified in two different stances.

Another distinction, suggested by Gillian Smith [4], uses different criteria to catalogue PCG techniques. It defines:

- Building blocks: how design knowledge is represented in a content generator.
- Game Stage: whether if the contents are generated before the game or at runtime.
- Interaction Type: how much input is required by the player to interact with the generator.
- Player Experience: how much player experience is vital in relation to content creation.

The taxonomies mentioned above are helpful to explain where PCG-G is used but do not specify how. Most real implementations have often been developed behind closed doors by gaming companies, and it is hard to draw a line between what is current technology and what is not.

While not being taken by actual commercial games, various implementations of PCG-G have been explored in academic work [2]. Among the newly developed trends, in recent years, the use of evolutionary algorithms, inspired by biological concepts of reproduction, crossover, has gained popularity [11]. The starting point is a subset initialised with a population (usually an array with random values), that undergo several randomised transformations that are subsequently evaluated by a carefully tailored fitness function. Ashlock et al. [6] experimented with similar methods for generating mazes, a system that heavily inspired the one described in this paper.

Evolutionary algorithms also offer vast opportunities in content customisation. Modern trends are concerned with making automatically generated contents more in line with the player's expectations and thus more adjustable, and search-based algorithms have been extensively used for this purpose. There have been attempts to generate levels based on an algorithm that tried to assess the degree of enjoyment of the players [3]. Those algorithms have proven to be so successful that they have been used to write a generator that produces generators for other contexts [12].

3   The Experiment

This experiment was developed in the framework of EscapeTower (Fig. 1), a research project aiming to investigate players' behaviour in unknown environments and their adaptability to non-standard game commands [7, 8].

EscapeTower is a puzzle game where the player must solve a series of puzzles, placed on multiple levels, to reach the final room and escape the maze. Each floor has a different sequence of puzzles, and to move from one floor to the others, players could either use ladders or jump from heights. Players are encouraged to search for the right tools by themselves, finding the objects that grant access to the final puzzle without any guidance from the game.

Following EscapeTower's initial releases, the project needed to test more research questions, but it was soon realised that fast iterations were hardly possible, as players

Fig. 1. The EscapeTower game environment (from the editor)

would be facing the same environments over and over, knowing the puzzles and the levels' topology. With the project aiming to expand, procedural generation of puzzles and mazes was the only feasible solution to reduce development costs while producing significantly different environments.

A common criticism that is usually made to procedurally generated environments is that they can sometimes feel too artificial and repetitive, making in-game situations not as enjoyable as ones designed by hand. It does not matter how complex the generation is, in the long term, monotony and repetition often seem to set in. However, players of the EscapeTower project only played one session of approximately 15–20 min, and repetition of contents would not be an issue in such a (relatively) short time span. Still, the procedural generation of a structure posed a risk: players should not get stuck in the EscapeTower, and puzzles should always have specific visual cues that can help players to solve them. For these reasons, while generating levels at runtime, procedural generation of contents in the EscapeTower project was executed offline, within the Unreal Engine editor, giving designers complete control over the results.

3.1 Procedural Level Generation

The first version of the EscapeTower was designed by professional designers and featured a precise structure, with an initial linear tutorial section and a vertical structure for the main game. The main block has a slightly increased level of difficulty as the game progressed, a feature that had to be maintained in the procedural version.

Given the experimental nature of this project, the level generator was conceived both as an additional tool within the UE4 Editor, one that could be used to create in-editor contents that could be further tweaked by designers, but also as a tool that could automate the whole procedure directly within the game at runtime if needed.

The level generator processed levels separately, receiving the initial level number as input parameter and following an approximation of the original structure:

- The first level of the game has a rectangular base, with two corridors arranged in a cross. The generator inserts the corridors within a predefined grid size and then place each of the four rooms of the level in the four spaces that have been formed.
- On the second floor, the location of the rooms and, as a consequence, the corridors leading to them are always variable. At least one of the corridors must be connected to the central ladder. Otherwise, it will not be possible to access the floor.
- The second and third floors are not as determined as the first one. Their peculiarity is that they can have the rooms randomly arranged, connected all together by corridors. When created, the rooms are arranged on a grid with their dimensions defined by parameters.
- On the third floor, there is a particular middle floor that could only be accessed through a trapdoor that will be placed in one of the possible random locations.

A module performs the level generation with three major blocks that are executed consequentially:

1. the first block deals with creating the rooms and arranging them on a grid-based matrix. The size of the matrix can be specified as input parameter.
2. The second block finds paths to connect the rooms. The paths must connect one room to another and ensure that all rooms are connected, i.e. that each room can be accessed without having to enter another. The paths between the rooms are not stochastic. Given the exact position of two rooms, the same path will always be determined.
3. the third part organises the rooms' orientation so that the side with the door corresponds to the side connected to the corridor, and the corridor does not have to have a wall on this side because the wall of the room is already there.

The module provides a mechanism for adding constraints to avoid creating rooms and corridors in unwanted places. Having a separate module for the procedural generation leaves open the possibility of future expansions to create more and dynamic environments, as the number of rooms is not fixed but regulated by a dedicated parameter.

4 Methods

A user study has been proposed to evaluate the differences between playing with a human-designed level and a procedurally generated one. Two groups of users were created: one playing procedurally generated levels and one playing the original game as control group. Choosing the procedural level, two versions were available, randomly picked by the game: one version was pre-generated by the room generator during the design process, in which the level designer had only tweaked minor aesthetic details, and another version was real-time generated, just before the player started playing. After the game session with either type of level, each user was asked to fill out a questionnaire. The questionnaire consisted of 10 questions ranging from 1 to 5, the first half about users' impressions of the game environment, the second half about their game experience. Demographic data instead was collected in-game during the tutorial section.

Fig. 2. A few procedurally generated environments

A website was created to present the game to as many users as possible, containing basic information regarding the project, a download page, and a page to upload questionnaires. The questionnaire was inserted at the end of the game and then saved to a file on the user's desktop. The game executable was designed to automatically send the survey to a collection web page, informing the user in advance and asking him to disable the Windows Firewall or any other anti-virus for the application. Alternatively, the generated file containing the answers to the questionnaire could be uploaded by hand to a specific prepared page. Besides, there was another link leading to the questionnaire on Google Forms. All these measures were intended to ensure that all users would fill in the questionnaire, even if they did not finish the game.

To reach users who had problems with installation or did not have a Windows operating system, a browser version was subsequently implemented so that the players had not to download or install any software on their machines. This version was developed using Pixel Streaming, a cloud gaming technology supported by version 4.25 of Unreal Engine, through a plug-in currently in beta. The only requirement is a reliable Internet connection. Furthermore, this approach allowed any user connected to the page to watch the player's gameplay.

5 Results

The game was downloaded 126 times, but only 32 players completed it and filled a questionnaire.

14 were assigned the procedural environment, while 18 played using the manually designed one.

The survey showed that 5% of the participants were older than 50 years, 20% between 27–32, 50% between 21–26 and 25% aged between 15–20.

In terms of gender 61.9% of the players identified as males, 33.3% as females and 4,8% preferred not to declare.

76,2% of users were playing from Europe, 19% from Asia and 4,8% from America.

In terms of experience, 14,3% of the players said that they had been playing video games for more than 20 years, 9,5% between 15–20, 19% between 11–15, 42,9% between 6–10 and 14,3% between 1–5.

46,7% of the players declared that they play most days, 9,5% often but not every day, 4,8% regularly with very long breaks, 14,3% Few times per month, 19% almost never, 1,8% never.

Looking at the questionnaire, data shown in Fig. 3a and Fig. 3b show that, on average, players had a better experience with the manually designed levels, with the procedural levels failing to become a believable environment. In terms of visual appearance, more than 1 point of difference was found between the two groups, but the procedural level had a lower average when players were asked to judge the environment's naturalness. On the contrary, players got stuck less often in the manually designed environment.

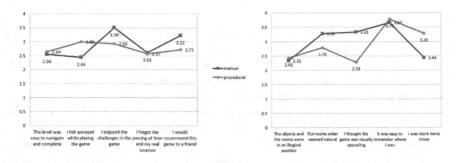

Fig. 3. a (Left) and b (right): questionnaire data

6 Discussion

The survey showed that most participants had a WEIRD profile [10] and clearly represented a young and active sample of videogame players.

From a spatial point of view, procedural generation does not seem to affect the users' perception of their overall position within the level, but it does affect their spatial perception throughout the game. The player's orientation ability remains the same both in manually and procedurally generated levels, seemingly depending on the player himself. However, looking at the data, it is clear how users gave a clear preference for the manually designed level: the visual appeal seems to be impacted because, in the random generator, the structural generation of the level had more relevance than paying attention to detail, the last one is very often perceived positively, even subconsciously, by the players.

The other aspect that emerges from the comparison of the graphs is the greater propensity for players to get stuck in the exploration of procedural levels, which may be due to two reasons:

- procedurally generated rooms are not distributed in a rational order within the floor (two rooms, that have to be visited consecutively, have the same probability of being either very close to each other or on the opposite side of the floor, very far from each other);
- there may be actual errors in generation (one user reported finding a staircase placed in front of a door, preventing access to a room).

From the point of view of the gaming experience, the data confirms what was already predicted: manually generated levels are on average more pleasant than procedurally generated ones and are slightly more playable. On average, it appears that procedural levels do not impact the possibility to complete the level, and the degree of immersion remains the same compared to the handmade level. So, these factors are not primarily influenced by the structure of game level.

A more significant difference is found in the degree of annoyance measured in the players and their appreciation of the challenges offered in the game. While the degree of annoyance, and, in a complementary way, that of enjoyment seems to depend more on the type of player than on anything else (σ relatively high for both hand-drawn and procedural levels), the appreciation for the game's challenges varies a lot from user to user in the case of procedural levels. This seems to be due to the fact that they change each time they are played, arousing alternating reactions in the players (σ higher for procedural levels than for hand-drawn ones). This affects the overall enjoyment to a certain degree and makes a user more likely to recommend the game to others if the handmade version has been played.

All measures confirm what has already been verified with commercialised video game titles, even those developed by large software companies [9]: procedural level generation does not enjoy an excellent reputation and is not used as extensively as it could be because it involves many risks, which can affect the degree of user satisfaction and consequently affect the number of sales and profit margin. Moreover, part of the time saved in the creation phase has to be reused in the testing phase, which is necessary when using PCG techniques. Overall, PCG has demonstrated not to be a sufficiently reliable tool, not even in a simple scenario as the one presented in the EscapeTower project.

7 Conclusions and Further Applications

In this paper, an example of virtual environment generator was presented, enabling the automatic realization of levels for the video game EscapeTower. While more dynamic environments are still required for such projects, the preliminary user study presented in this work has shown that the development costs and the overall quality of the generated level make such solution not completely suitable in all circumstances. The doubts in the game industry about the widespread use of PCG have been fully confirmed in the user test. The temptation to take risks associated with PCG use is not very strong, even in the face of the time savings that can be expected, especially if profit margins can be significantly affected. However, procedural generation tools remain an excellent aid in creating three-dimensional environments, as they involve considerable time savings (what the room generator does in a few seconds would require several hours if manually done by a level designer). The best scenario is therefore probably not the completely automatic generation of entire levels but the combined use with the supervision of a level designer, whose work can be considerably accelerated and simplified. The room generator here presented is still a valuable tool for speeding up the design phases of three-dimensional rooms. Possible future developments could include the extension of the game EscapeTower, to procedurally generate not only the levels of the game but also other content, such as objects within the rooms and their arrangement.

References

1. Yannakakis, G.N., Togelius, J.: Experience-driven procedural content generation. IEEE Trans. Affect. Comput. **2**(3), 147–161 (2011)
2. Hendrikx, M., Meijer, S., Van Der Velden, J., Iosup, A.: Procedural content generation for games: a survey. ACM Trans. Multimedia Comput. Commun. Appl. **9**(1), 1–22 (2013)
3. Togelius, J., Yannakakis, G.N., Stanley, K.O., Browne, C.: Search-based procedural content generation: a taxonomy and survey. IEEE Trans. Comput. Intell. AI Games **3**(3), 172–186 (2011)
4. Smith, G.: Understanding procedural content generation: a design-centric analysis of the role of PCG in games. In: CHI 2014, pp. 917–926 (2014)
5. Shaker, N., Togelius, J., Nelson, M.J.: Procedural Content Generation in Games: A Textbook and an Overview of Current Research. Springer, Cham (2016). https://doi.org/10.1007/978-3-319-42716-4
6. Ashlock, D., Lee, C., McGuinness, C.: Search-based procedural generation of maze-like levels. IEEE Trans. Comput. Intell. AI Games **3**(3), 260–273 (2011)
7. Galdieri, R., Haggis-Burridge, M., Buijtenweg, T., Carrozzino, M.: Exploring players' curiosity-driven behaviour in unknown videogame environments. In: Paolis, L.T.D., Bourdot, P. (eds.) AVR 2020. LNCS, vol. 12242, pp. 177–185. Springer, Cham (2020). https://doi.org/10.1007/978-3-030-58465-8_13
8. Galdieri, R., Haggis-Burridge, M., Buijtenweg, T., Carrozzino, M.: Users' Adaptation to Non- standard Controller Schemes in 3D Gaming Experiences, pp. 411–419. Springer, Cham (2020). https://doi.org/10.1007/978-3-030-58465-8_30
9. Korn, O., Lee, N., (eds.): Game dynamics. In: Best Practices in Procedural and Dynamic Game Content Generation. Springer (2017). https://doi.org/10.1007/978-3-319-53088-8
10. Arnett, J.J.: The neglected 95%: why American psychology needs to become less American. Am. Psychol. **63**(7), 602–614 (2016)
11. Raffe, W.L., Zambetta, F., Li, X.: A survey of procedural terrain generation techniques using evolutionary algorithms. In: 2012 IEEE Congress on Evolutionary Computation. IEEE (2012)
12. Kerssemakers, M., et al.: A procedural procedural level generator generator. In: 2012 IEEE Conference on Computational Intelligence and Games (CIG). IEEE (2012)
13. Carrozzino, M., Tecchia, F., Bergamasco, M.: Urban procedural modeling for real-time rendering. In: Proceedings of the 3rd ISPRS International Workshop 3D-ARCH (2009)
14. Togelius, J., Shaker, N., Dormans, J.: Grammars and L-systems with applications to vegetation and levels. In: Procedural Content Generation in Games, pp. 73–98. Springer, Cham (2016). https://doi.org/10.1007/978-3-319-42716-4_5

A Preliminary Investigation on a Multimodal Controller and Freehand Based Interaction in Virtual Reality

Nicola Capece[✉], Monica Gruosso, Ugo Erra,
Rosario Catena, and Gilda Manfredi

Dipartimento di Matematica, Informatica ed Economia,
Università degli Studi della Basilicata, Potenza, Italy
{nicola.capece,monica.gruosso,ugo.erra}@unibas.it
{rosario.catena,gilda.manfredi}@studenti.unibas.it

Abstract. In the last years, the synergy between VR and HCI has dramatically increased the user's feeling of immersion within virtual scenes, improving VR applications' user experience and usability. Two main aspects have emerged with the evolution of these technologies concerning immersion in the 3D scene: locomotion within the 3D scene and interaction with the components of the 3D scene. Locomotion with classical freehand approaches based on hand tracking can be stressful for the user due to the need to keep the hand still in a specific position for a long time to activate the locomotion gesture. Likewise, using a classic Head Mounted Display (HMD) controller for the interaction with the 3D scene components could be unnatural for the user, using the hand to pinch and grab the 3D objects. This paper proposes a multimodal approach, mixing the Leap Motion and 6-DOF controller to navigate and interact with the 3D scene to reduce the locomotion gesture stress based on the hand tracking and increase the immersion and interaction feeling using freehand to interact with the 3D scene objects.

Keywords: User interaction · Locomotion · HCI · Virtual reality · Visualization · Freehand · 3D graph

1 Introduction

Today, one of the main challenges concerns the development of new approaches to interact with 3D environments in Virtual Reality that overcome the traditional techniques based, for example, on controllers [17,18]. For this reason, more and more approaches have been investigated in this direction [21,22] in addition to new methods and studies of locomotion [3,19,23] to increase the level of user immersion in the virtual environment, trying to reduce as much as possible the interference feelings of the real environment. Freehand through hand tracking indeed represents one of the innovations that in recent years is

© Springer Nature Switzerland AG 2021
L. T. De Paolis et al. (Eds.): AVR 2021, LNCS 12980, pp. 53–65, 2021.
https://doi.org/10.1007/978-3-030-87595-4_5

becoming increasingly popular in the field of human-computer interaction applications [5] and VR [1,16,27]. Indeed, several new technologies and devices such as omnidirectional treadmill (ODT) [12] and integrated hand tracking [28] with HMD such as Oculus Quest [10] are emerging to increase the user's feeling of immersion in the virtual scene. However, some of them, such as ODT, also need very efficient support technologies, such as harness and haptic devices, allowing users to achieve a sufficiently comfortable and low-stress experience.

One of the main limitations of the hands tracking and gesture recognition is the muscle fatigue and tired arm, also called the gorilla-arm effect, due to keeping for long time hands and fingers visible to the tracking devices [8] such as Depth Cameras, Leap Motion, Webcam, and so on. In our previous study [3], we analyzed the different type of freehand-steering locomotion techniques by providing an empirical evaluation and comparison with the use of HTC Vive controllers. One of the issues emerging from this study is that fatigue can affect the user when a hand gesture must be reproduced continuously to perform the movement.

Although virtual object interaction through hand gestures certainly increases the users' immersion feeling in the virtual scene, the use of freehand for the locomotion forces them to keep the arm still for a long time, consequently increasing fatigue and stress. [29]. For this reason, we introduced a multimodal approach allowing users to move through the virtual scene with a 6-DOF controller and contextually interact with the virtual object using well-defined hand gestures detected through the Leap Motion controller. To the best of our knowledge, it is the first approach that combines natural user hand interaction and navigation through a controller. A 3D graph visualization in VR, where the user can explore and interact with a 3D graph and its nodes, was used as a case study for our multimodal approach.

The remainder of this paper is structured as follow: some related work is reported in Sect. 2; some implementation details and used developing tools are reported in Sect. 3; Sect. 4 shows our proposed system and its architecture; Sect. 5 shows the case study dealt, and finally Sect. 6 reports the conclusions and future works.

2   Related Work

Performing locomotion in the scene and interacting with its virtual objects using hand tracking and gesture recognition requires a high user effort [7,11,13,15,25]. Moreover, freehand locomotion techniques with continuous controlling constrain the user to keep his hands in the same position for the entire movement time [3,30]. This limitation is also highlighted in [3], which proposed an empirical evaluation study of three freehand-steering locomotion techniques compared with each other and with a controller-based approach. Indeed, this study aimed to evaluate the effectiveness, efficiency, and user preference in continuously controlling the locomotion direction of palm-steering, index-steering, gaze-steering, and controller-steering techniques. In [30], authors proposed a locomotion technique based on double-hand gestures, in which the left palm was used to control the forward and backward movement, and the right thumb was used to perform the left or right turning. The users reported a low level of perceived fatigues, reasonable satisfaction, and learning and operating efficiently. An interesting approach was proposed in [26] that focused on AR intangible digital map navigation with hand gestures. The authors conducted a well-structured study in which they explored the effect of handedness and input mapping by designing two-hybrid techniques to transit between positions smoothly. From this study, the authors reported that input-mapping transitions could reduce arms fatigue, increasing performance. A novel 3D interaction concept in VR was proposed in [21], which integrated eye gaze to select virtual objects and indirect freehand gestures to manipulate them. This idea is based on bringing direct manipulation gestures, such as two-handled scaling or pinch-to-select, to any virtual object target that the user looks at. For this purpose, the authors implemented an experimental UI system consisting of a set of application examples. The gaze and pinch techniques were appropriately calibrated to the needs of the task. Since freehand input often could invoke different operation respect the user intention, showing an ambiguous interaction effect. This problem was faced in [6], who proposed an experimental analysis to evaluate a set of techniques to disambiguate the effect of freehand manipulations in VR. In particular, they compared three input methods (hand gaze, speech, and foot tap), putting together three-timing (before, during, and after an interaction) in which options were available to resolve the ambiguity. The arm fatigue problem was faced by authors in [13] that proposed an approach based on a combination of feasible techniques called "ProxyHand" and "StickHand" to reduce this problem. The "ProxyHand" enabled the user to interact with the 3D scene in VR by keeping his arm in a comfortable position through 3D-spatial offset between his real hands and his virtual representation. "StickHand" was used where "ProxyHand" was not suitable. The gorilla-arm effect was also faced in [25], who proposed a VR low-fatigue travel technique hand-controller-based useful in a limited physical space. In this approach, the user can choose the travel orientation through a single controller, the average of both hand controllers, or the head. Furthermore, the speed can be controlled by changing the frontal plane controller angle. The gorilla-arm effect was dealt with by also estimating some useful metrics, e.g., the "Consumed Endurance" proposed in [11]. In the same way, this paper [15] developed a method to estimate the maximum shoulder torque through a mid-air pointing task. However, to the best of our knowledge, there are no specific hand-and-controller-based studies where hand and controller were used to interact and locomote in 3D scenes to reduce the user arm fatigue.

3   Background

The proposed approach, which consists of the 3D scene and the case study (see Sect. 5), was developed using the Unity 3D game engine. In addition, Unity 3D allowed us to integrate the Steam VR frameworks for the integration of the HMD, its controllers, and the Leap Motion SDK for hand tracking and gesture recognition (see Fig. 2). Users can immerse in VR scene through the HTC Vive HMD (first version), which consists of a 3.6 inch AMOLED with 2160×1200 pixels (1080×1200 per eye), a refresh rate 90 Hz, and 110 degrees as a field of view. Thanks to the *Eye Relie* technology HTC Vive allows users to adjust the interpupillary distance and the distance of the lens to better adapt to its specifications. The locomotion of the user inside the 3D scene was performed through a single HTC Vive controller (see Fig. 2), which is based on a 6-DOF and is associated with a specific hand (left and right). HMD and the controller are tracked from the base stations defining a room scale [20] in which the user can move freely. Leap Motion is a well-known infrared-based device useful to track the user's hands and perform gesture recognition from them. The compact size of the Leap Motion device allows it to be mounted directly on the HMD, enabling the users to visualize their hands in the virtual scene and increasing their VR immersion feeling. As explained in Sect. 5, our multimodal interaction approach was tested on the 3D Graph visualization. To generate and export the graph structure for the proposed application, we used a well-known software called Gephi [2]. In particular, through Gephi, we defined the colors, the sizes, the positions of the nodes, and the adjacents nodes that define edges. Furthermore, we used the Force Atlas 2 [14] to assign a 3D layout to the graph. The next operation consists of exporting the graph description as *.gexf*, which is the standard Gephi format based on XML. Subsequently, the *.gexf* file was imported in our 3D scene through a specially developed parsing function. We also used a random graph generation Gephi function to create large graphs to test the robustness of our 3D application with a growing variable number of edges and nodes. The 3D Graph scene was created starting from the *.gexf* file, which was scanned from a *PlacePrefabPoint* component, a particular Unity 3D component (prefab) we developed. For each node found, it creates a specific prefab to which the graphic features are associated (*e.g.*, sphere, color, position, *etc.*). Furthermore, *PlacePrefabPoint* creates an empty adjacency list for each node, which will be filled from another prefab called *PlacePrefabEdge* with the connected nodes defined in the *.gexf* file, and creating the edges.

4   Interaction System

VR immersion in our developed 3D scene is allowed through the HTC Vive HMD. The locomotion is performed through one of its controllers, which is kept in one user's hand. Instead, the interaction with the 3D scene components is allowed through the other user's hand tracked from the Leap Motion controller, as shown in Fig. 1. In this section, we describe the fundamental part of our multimodal approach.

4.1   Locomotion

HTC Vive 6-DOF controller allows the user locomotion through the 3D scene. As can be seen in Fig. 2, the user has to interact with the trackpad of the

Fig. 1. The image shows the rendering of a 3D graph with its devices used to interact with the scene. The controller and the tracked hand work jointly. When a node is selected, its color changes to purple and the ray becomes red. (Color figure online)

controller to provide the locomotion direction. In particular, the user can move along the horizontal axis: forward, backward, left and right in flight mode. The vertical movement is possible through the HMD forward direction by pointing and pressing the forward trackpad button. Furthermore, the Grip button (see left part of Fig. 2) allows the user to increase the locomotion speed.

The buttons of the controller are used to activate and interact with the application menu, which allows changing the option setting (*e.g.*, max user speed movement and max graph plot scale) of the application. Furthermore, the menu allows the user to visualize and navigate the list of nodes, select one node and teleport in front of it. Another menu feature concerns the possibility to view details of the selected nodes, i.e., their labels.

4.2   Interaction

The interaction was implemented through the ray casting technique [24] by setting the ray collision distance as inf. In particular, to select one or more desired nodes of the 3D Graph, we used a simple pinch gesture by considering the thumb and the index fingers (see Fig. 2). In particular, the node selection feature is activated whether the distance between the index and thumb fingers is between 2 cm and 2.5 cm. To select multiple nodes, the user can use the same gesture and look at the desired nodes while keeping the hand performing the pinch gesture in the HMD field of view because losing track of the hand will deactivate this function. The ray is cast from the HMD position in the same direction as the camera. For ease of use' sake, the ray is rendered using hand position instead of HMD

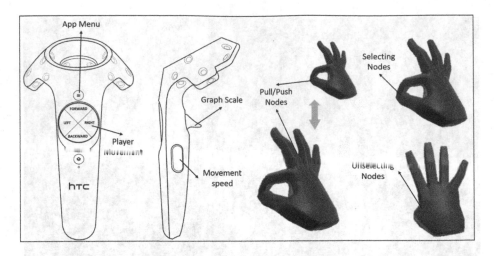

Fig. 2. The scheme of the multimodal approach. On the left, the features associated with the HTC Vive controller helpful to interact with the menu and for the locomotion in the scene. On the right, the gestures associated with hand tracking using the leap motion controller to interact with the scene components (the nodes).

position, as can be seen in Fig. 1. To ensure a good level of stability and accuracy of both the displayed and used ray, we included a queue that keeps track of the average of the last 15 positions. If the user must deselect the nodes, the tracked hand has to be fully opened with fingers toward the up direction, except the thumb finger, which has to be closed towards the palm. When the nodes are selected, their color change to purple. (see Fig. 3). For simplicity, when the ray points to an unselected node, the color of the ray changes from green to red. Selected nodes can be moved and placed in other scene positions. To move the nodes, the user has to activate the node selection feature. Furthermore, when the ray is directed toward the already selected node (purple), the ray color change to yellow and node follow the HMD position until the user releases the pinch. The last feature concern the graph scale, which can be activated from the user, holding down the trigger button of the HMD controller (see Fig. 2) and move the tracked hand and the HMD controller away from each other.

5 Case Study

The proposed navigation and interaction system finds fertile ground in virtual scenes characterized by complex data structures, such as 3D graphs. Indeed, interacting and navigating these 3D structures in VR requires a massive user effort, primarily when they represent highly interconnected data.

5.1 Graph Visualization

To explore the 3D graph, the user has to fly through the scene, and he can move in 6 directions (left, right, up, down, forward, and backward) (see Sect. 4.1).

Fig. 3. When the ray hits one or more nodes already selected, the ray color becomes yellow, and the user can move the nodes. (Color figure online)

As often happens in 3D graph visualization [4], nodes are displayed by spheres and edges through rendered lines (see Fig. 4). The use of the physical object as a sphere to represent nodes is required to allow user interaction. Instead, the edges are non-physical object because not allow user interaction. In this way, we reduced the polygonal complexity of the edges, increasing performance and allowing the system to represent in 3D as many nodes as possible. The graph and its structure (node colors, sizes, positions, labels and edges) were defined in a *.gexf* XML-based format (Fig. 5), which is a standard file format of the well-known Gephi [2] graph visualization software.

When all nodes are visible from the VR camera, the worst performances are obtained in terms of rendering time. This situation occurs when the user is placed in the center of the 3D graph or looks at the whole graph from the outside of it. To solve this problem, we applied a common computer graphics approach called Level Of Details (LOD) (see the blue block in Fig. 5). This approach adapts the geometric complexity of the 3D objects automatically based on their distance from the camera. In our application, we defined 3 LODs and an occlusion culling level. This last level allows preventing the rendering for all nodes that are completely hidden from view. In this way, we further improved the rendering time performance.

With the LOD 0, the sphere mesh is high poly and very heavy. A label is associated with each node as a child of the sphere. To allow the user to visualize such labels, we rotate the node hierarchy (sphere and label) toward the VR camera. At LOD 0, the rotation is computationally expensive, and for this reason, we allow the rotation every 4 seconds to reduce the GPU workload. In the LOD 1, the node hierarchy is not present because we assumed the label

Fig. 4. Graph 3D view: nodes are represented from spheres (colors, sizes, positions, and edges are defined in the *.gexf* file); edges are represented from rendered lines. (Color figure online)

was not visible beyond a certain distance from the user. For this reason, we consider only a simplified sphere with fewer polygons and to retrieve further computing resources, for this LOD 1 and the LOD 2, we removed the rotation of the sphere toward the user. In particular, in the LOD 2, we foresee using a low poly sphere because the distance between the user and the nodes makes this simplification unnoticeable. Finally, the last is a culling level, in which the nodes are completely hidden, decreasing the GPU workload. LOD activation distance was identified based on the percentage of the camera portion occupied from each node. Based on empirical evidence, we established that the LOD 0 was activated when the percentage is between 100% and 15%, the LOD 1 was activated when the percentage is between 15% and 3%. Finally, the LOD 2 was triggered when the percentage is between 3% and 1%, and the culling level is activated when the percentage is less than 1%. Furthermore, we increased our application performance by considering the edges' behaviour during the nodes' movement. Indeed, when a node is selected and moved by the user, the edges are not rendered but are hidden until the selected node is released in its final position. Only at the end of the movement will the edges' length be recomputed, and next, they will be displayed again. This decrease the recomputing positions

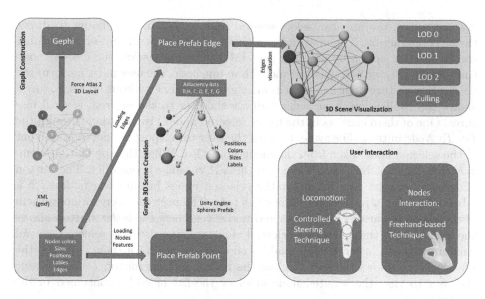

Fig. 5. The workflow design. Orange block shows the graph features definition using Gephi and storing it in an XML document. The green block shows the 3D graph building using Unity 3D and two developed prefabs. The blue block shows the 3D scene optimization, and finally, the yellow block shows the user HCI and locomotion techniques. (Color figure online)

effort for the edges in real-time by carrying out this operation only when the node movement was done. We reported two experiments with two different graph configurations in terms of nodes and edges in Table 1.

Table 1. These tests are performed using a workstation equipped with an Intel 8700k CPU, a RAM with 16 GB memory, and one NVidia GTX 1080 Ti GPU.

Nodes	Edges	VR FPS	Desktop FPS
1800	8000	50	71
6000	60000	45	57

5.2 Application Features

When starting the application, the user selects the *.gexf* that contains the information of the graph structure, as discussed in Sect. 5.1. The user can move freely in the 3D graph using the flight mode, increasing or decreasing the movement speed, and without direction and distance constraint. To select the desired nodes, the user can use a viewfinder and performs the pinch gesture to activate the ray casting, as mentioned in Sect. 4.2. By continuously keeping the pinch gesture active, the user can select several nodes using the viewfinder to direct the selection action. The viewfinder is also activated when the user performing the deselection action by pointing the HMD direction toward the desired node (previously selected). To deselect more than one node, the user must perform the deselection gesture pointing towards an area of the scene without nodes. Figure 6 shows the application menu, which allows the user to choose from several features. One of them consists in the list of selected nodes visualization through the *Go To Node* button. The system allows the user to teleport his position in front of the selected node taken from the menu nodes list. When the application menu is active, four buttons are rendered on the VR visualized controller. The button *Cluster* allows the user to gather the selected nodes in only one node with a label containing a progressive number as text. The user can merge among them also clusters of clusters or clusters and nodes together. *Uncluster* button allows the user to split the nodes of a selected cluster. If the user has selected several clusters, the *Uncluster* button enables the user to separate them. Finally, the button *Menu* allows the user to close the menu, and the button *Details* enable the user to view the selected node label or the list of nodes contained in the cluster.

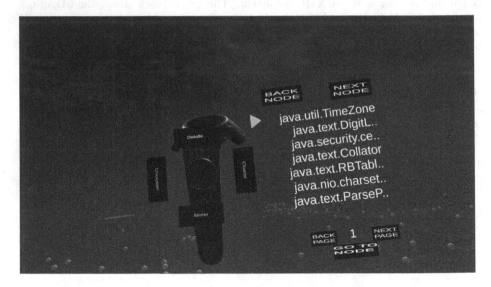

Fig. 6. The application menu. On the controller mesh the *Cluster*, *Uncluster*, *Details*, and *Menu* buttons appeared. The user can interact with them to perform the clustering, unclustering, view node or cluster details, and close the menu. The image on the right shows how to consult the list of selected nodes. The user can select a node from the list and teleport in front of the desired node through the *Go To Node* button.

6 Conclusions and Future Works

We presented a multimodal approach in VR to allow the users to interact with the virtual scene using hands gestured tracked by the Leap Motion controller and locomote through the virtual 3D scene using a 6-DOF controller. As a case study, we implemented a VR 3D Graph Visualization application developed with Unity 3D game engine and provided a description of hand-based methods to interact with the nodes, visualize their details, and locomote in the 3D Graph scene using the controller. Furthermore, we proposed an optimization strategy to render as many as possible nodes and edges by preserving the computational performances. To the best of our knowledge, the proposed work is the first to evaluate the combination of natural interaction through hand gesture recognition and controller-based navigation mode to decrease user arm fatigue. The next step consists of experimentation through comparison among several HCI techniques. In particular, we are working on an extension of the proposed application, which includes combining different types of devices to interact and locomote with and in a virtual scene.

In addition, the hand tracking could be improved using an end-to-end deep learning-based system, which replaces the Leap Motion controller [9]. For example, a deep neural network for RGB camera image analysis could be used to overcome the infrared devices' well-known lighting problems.

References

1. Virtual Reality Applications: Guidelines to Design Natural User Interface, International Design Engineering Technical Conferences and Computers and Information in Engineering Conference, vol. Volume 1B: 38th Computers and Information in Engineering Conference (2018). https://doi.org/10.1115/DETC2018-85867, v01BT02A029
2. Bastian, M., Heymann, S., Jacomy, M.: Gephi: an open source software for exploring and manipulating networks (2009). http://www.aaai.org/ocs/index.php/ICWSM/09/paper/view/154
3. Caggianese, G., Capece, N., Erra, U., Gallo, L., Rinaldi, M.: Freehand-steering locomotion techniques for immersive virtual environments: a comparative evaluation. Int. J. Hum. Comput. Interact. **36**(18), 1734–1755 (2020). https://doi.org/10.1080/10447318.2020.1785151
4. Capece, N., Erra, U., Grippa, J.: GraphVR: a virtual reality tool for the exploration of graphs with HTC Vive system. In: 2018 22nd International Conference Information Visualisation (IV), pp. 448–453 (2018)
5. Capece, N., Erra, U., Gruosso, M., Anastasio, M.: Archaeo puzzle: an educational game using natural user interface for historical artifacts. In: Spagnuolo, M., Melero, F.J. (eds.) Eurographics Workshop on Graphics and Cultural Heritage. The Eurographics Association (2020)
6. Chen, D.L., Balakrishnan, R., Grossman, T.: Disambiguation techniques for freehand object manipulations in virtual reality. In: 2020 IEEE Conference on Virtual Reality and 3D User Interfaces (VR), pp. 285–292 (2020)

7. De Chiara, R., Di Santo, V., Erra, U., Scarano, V.: Real positioning in virtual environments using game engines, vol. 1, pp. 203–208 (2007), https://www.scopus.com/inward/record.uri?eid=2-s2.0-84878192833&partnerID=40&md5=83a6d6543f0358d6bd23a9882c42a65f, cited By 12

8. Falcao, C., Lemos, A.C., Soares, M.: Evaluation of natural user interface: a usability study based on the leap motion device. Procedia Manuf. **3**, 5490–5495 (2015), https://www.sciencedirect.com/science/article/pii/S2351978915006988, 6th International Conference on Applied Human Factors and Ergonomics (AHFE 2015) and the Affiliated Conferences, AHFE 2015

9. Gruosso, M., Capece, N., Erra, U., Angiolillo, F.: A preliminary investigation into a deep learning implementation for hand tracking on mobile devices. In: 2020 IEEE International Conference on Artificial Intelligence and Virtual Reality (AIVR), pp. 380–385 (2020)

10. Hillmann, C.: Comparing the Gear VR, Oculus Go, and Oculus Quest, pp. 141–167. Apress, Berkeley, CA (2019). https://doi.org/10.1007/978-1-4842-4360-2_5

11. Hincapié-Ramos, J.D., Guo, X., Moghadasian, P., Irani, P.: Consumed endurance: a metric to quantify arm fatigue of mid-air interactions, pp. 1063–1072. CHI 2014. Association for Computing Machinery, New York, NY, USA (2014). https://doi.org/10.1145/2556288.2557130

12. Hooks, K., Ferguson, W., Morillo, P., Cruz-Neira, C.: Evaluating the user experience of omnidirectional VR walking simulators. Entertainment Comput. **34**, 100352 (2020). https://www.sciencedirect.com/science/article/pii/S1875952119301284

13. Iqbal, H., Latif, S., Yan, Y., Yu, C., Shi, Y.: Reducing arm fatigue in virtual reality by introducing 3D-spatial offset. IEEE Access **9**, 64085–64104 (2021)

14. Jacomy, M., Venturini, T., Heymann, S., Bastian, M.: ForceAtlas2, a continuous graph layout algorithm for handy network visualization designed for the Gephi software. PLOS ONE **9**(6), 1–12 (2014). https://doi.org/10.1371/journal.pone.0098679

15. Jang, S., Stuerzlinger, W., Ambike, S., Ramani, K.: Modeling cumulative arm fatigue in mid-air interaction based on perceived exertion and kinetics of arm motion. In: Proceedings of the 2017 CHI Conference on Human Factors in Computing Systems, pp. 3328–3339. CHI 2017. Association for Computing Machinery, New York, NY, USA (2017). https://doi.org/10.1145/3025453.3025523

16. Lee, P.W., Wang, H.Y., Tung, Y.C., Lin, J.W., Valstar, A.: Transection: hand-based interaction for playing a game within a virtual reality game. In: Proceedings of the 33rd Annual ACM Conference Extended Abstracts on Human Factors in Computing Systems, pp. 73–76. CHI EA 2015. Association for Computing Machinery, New York, NY, USA (2015). https://doi.org/10.1145/2702613.2728655

17. Li, Y., Huang, J., Tian, F., Wang, H.A., Dai, G.Z.: Gesture interaction in virtual reality. Virtual Reality Intell. Hardware **1**(1), 84–112 (2019). https://www.sciencedirect.com/science/article/pii/S2096579619300075

18. McMahan, R.P., Lai, C., Pal, S.K.: Interaction fidelity: the uncanny valley of virtual reality interactions. In: Lackey, S., Shumaker, R. (eds.) VAMR 2016. LNCS, vol. 9740, pp. 59–70. Springer, Cham (2016). https://doi.org/10.1007/978-3-319-39907-2_6

19. Metsis, V., Smith, K.S., Gobert, D.: Integration of virtual reality with an omnidirectional treadmill system for multi-directional balance skills intervention. In: 2017 International Symposium on Wearable Robotics and Rehabilitation (WeRob), pp. 1–2 (2017)

20. Peer, A., Ponto, K.: Evaluating perceived distance measures in room-scale spaces using consumer-grade head mounted displays. In: 2017 IEEE Symposium on 3D User Interfaces (3DUI), pp. 83–86, March 2017
21. Pfeuffer, K., Mayer, B., Mardanbegi, D., Gellersen, H.: Gaze + pinch interaction in virtual reality. In: Proceedings of the 5th Symposium on Spatial User Interaction, pp. 99–108. SUI 2017. Association for Computing Machinery, New York, NY, USA (2017). https://doi.org/10.1145/3131277.3132180
22. Piumsomboon, T., Lee, G., Lindeman, R.W., Billinghurst, M.: Exploring natural eye-gaze-based interaction for immersive virtual reality. In: 2017 IEEE Symposium on 3D User Interfaces (3DUI), pp. 36–39 (2017)
23. Pyo, S.H., Lee, H.S., Phu, B.M., Park, S.J., Yoon, J.W.: Development of an fast-omnidirectional treadmill (F-ODT) for immersive locomotion interface. In: 2018 IEEE International Conference on Robotics and Automation (ICRA), pp. 760–766 (2018)
24. Roth, S.D.: Ray casting for modeling solids. Comput. Graph. Image Process. 18(2), 109–144 (1982). https://www.sciencedirect.com/science/article/pii/0146664X82901691
25. Sarupuri, B., Chipana, M.L., Lindeman, R.W.: Trigger walking: A low-fatigue travel technique for immersive virtual reality. In: 2017 IEEE Symposium on 3D User Interfaces (3DUI). pp. 227–228 (2017)
26. Satriadi, K.A., Ens, B., Cordeil, M., Jenny, B., Czauderna, T., Willett, W.: Augmented reality map navigation with freehand gestures. In: 2019 IEEE Conference on Virtual Reality and 3D User Interfaces (VR), pp. 593–603 (2019)
27. Szabó, B.K.: Interaction in an immersive virtual reality application. In: 2019 10th IEEE International Conference on Cognitive Infocommunications (CogInfoCom), pp. 35–40 (2019)
28. Voigt-Antons, J.N., Kojic, T., Ali, D., Möller, S.: Influence of hand tracking as a way of interaction in virtual reality on user experience. In: 2020 Twelfth International Conference on Quality of Multimedia Experience (QoMEX), pp. 1–4 (2020)
29. Wiedemann, D.P., Passmore, P.J., Moar, M.: An experiment design: investigating VR locomotion & virtual object interaction mechanics (2017)
30. Zhang, F., Chu, S., Pan, R., Ji, N., Xi, L.: Double hand-gesture interaction for walk-through in VR environment. In: 2017 IEEE/ACIS 16th International Conference on Computer and Information Science (ICIS), pp. 539–544 (2017)

Replacing EEG Sensors by AI Based Emulation

Fabio Genz[1]([✉])[iD], Clemens Hufeld[1][iD], Simone Müller[2][iD], Daniel Kolb[2][iD], Johannes Starck[1][iD], and Dieter Kranzlmüller[1,2][iD]

[1] Ludwig-Maximilians-Universität München, Munich, Germany
fabio.genz@nm.ifi.lmu.de
[2] Leibniz Supercomputing Centre, Garching near Munich, Germany

Abstract. Electroencephalography (EEG) has become a widely used non-invasive measurement method for brain-computer interfaces (BCI). Hybrid BCI (hBCI) additionally incorporate other physiological indicators, also called bio-signals, in order to improve the decryption of brain signals evaluating a variety of different sensor data. Although significant progress has been made in the field of BCI, the correlation of data from different sensors as well as the possible redundancy of certain sensors have been less frequently studied. Based on deep learning our concept presents a theoretical approach to potentially replace one sensor with the measurements of others. Hence, a costly or difficult to sensor measurement could be left out of a setup completely without losing its functionality. In this context, we additionally propose a conceptual framework which facilitates and improves the generation of scientifically significant data through their collection within a corresponding VR application and set-up. The evaluation of these collected sensor data, which is described in five consecutive steps, is to cluster the data of one sensor and to classify the data from other sensors into these clusters. Afterwards, the sensor data in each cluster are analysed for patterns. Through the predictive data analysis of existing sensors, the required number of sensors can be reduced. This allows valid statements about the output of the original sensor with no need to use it effectively. An artificial intelligence (AI) based EEG emulation, derived from other directly related bio-signals, could therefore potentially replace EEG measurements which indirectly enables the use of BCI in situations where it was previously not possible. Future work might clarify relevant questions concerning the realisation of the concept and how it could be further developed.

Keywords: Hybrid brain-computer-interfaces · Computational intelligence · Sensor-sensor interaction · Sensor replacement

1 Introduction

Through the considerable progress of the last decades, the technology of Head Mounted Displays (HMD) has improved significantly. In addition to including

© Springer Nature Switzerland AG 2021
L. T. De Paolis et al. (Eds.): AVR 2021, LNCS 12980, pp. 66–80, 2021.
https://doi.org/10.1007/978-3-030-87595-4_6

improved display technologies [7], the number of sensors, for different measurements based on physiological indicators, increased. The manufacturer HP for example, announced the *HP Reverb G2 Omnicept Edition* for May 2021 [13]. This HMD device intergrates sensors for eye tracking, pupillometry, heart rate, pulse rate variability and even a face camera. In addition to sensory hardware integration, the first software solutions for measuring near-real-time cognitive load are already being developed. However, these solutions are often insufficient in their precision and quality because only individual sensors are interpreted. Due to sensor characteristics and software misinterpretations the number of errors increases whereas the quality of measurements decreases at the same time. By using more precise sensors or fusing sensor data, the quality of measurement can be increased.

In addition to sensor fusion, the interpretation of sensor data is a key discipline. Here, human computer interaction (HCI) forms the interface between humans and computers. The previously collected sensor data is processed in a special machine language. For this purpose, the signals are interpreted and evaluated in the form of logical relationships. These evaluated data sets can be visualised and converted into a human-understandable language.

The next step of HCI on the way to further connect humans and technology is seen in the creation of interfaces between the human brain and computers through so-called BCIs [9]. BCIs are basically intended to translate signals from the human brain into directly commands for interactive applications [18]. Methods for measuring brain activity can be divided into two groups: invasive and non-invasive [27].

Invasive measurement methods such as electrocorticography (ECoG) record signals directly from the cortical surface or from inside the brain [24,34]. In this context, the decoding of bio-mechanical parameters has already been successfully used for monkeys and humans to control prostheses [12,16,31–33]. However, the high risk of the associated necessary surgical intervention and the gradual degradation of the recorded signals over time, entail considerable disadvantages, which is why non-invasive approaches such as functional magnetic resonance imaging (fMRI), magnetoencephalography (MEG), near-infrared spectroscopy (NIRS), and EEG are increasingly used in context of human users [1]. Although fMRI, for example, offers higher spatial resolution, EEG has become the most popular method due to its direct measurement of neuronal activity, comparative ease of portability and low cost [27].

Although significant progress has been made in this field of research. BCIs still face a number of challenges due to inaccuracy, unreliability and latency, as it is difficult to obtain and accurately process the information from the brain. For this reason, the inclusion of other signals in order to decode data for BCI user is becoming increasingly important. A BCI system that additionally uses other physiological indicators, also called bio-signals, is referred to as hBCI [5]. Several works [6,22] have already shown improvements for BCI, e.g. in accuracy and information transfer, rate by incorporating other bio-signals such as electromyography, electrooculography or electrocardiography (ECG). Nevertheless, the search for valid and reliable hBCI systems remains a serious challenge [4, 23].

In this context, we propose a conceptual framework which facilitates and improves the generation of meaningful measurement data through their collection within a corresponding VR application and set-up. Furthermore, the measured sensor data should also be used in order to analyse other sensors in the same setup for ultimately being able to replace one sensor with the measurements from others. Therefore AI based EEG emulations, derived from other directly related biosignals, could potentially replace EEG measurements which indirectly enables the use of BCI in situations where it was previously not possible.

In addition to a comprehensive concept proposal, our contribution also provides valuable information of the potential procedure in the context of an expected subsequent implementation.

The presented work is structured as follows. In Sect. 2, we discuss the currently relevant fields of literature. Section 3 describes the general conceptual framework, as well as the detailed theoretical procedure in five consecutive steps, followed by a discussion of the presented approach in Sect. 4. Here the potential advantages and expected difficulties, especially in the interaction of the measurement data collected in the context of the VR application were addressed. While Sect. 5 summarizes our approach and intentions, Sect. 6 furthermore gives an outlook on the potential next steps and further work.

2   Related Work

We identified three areas of relevant related work. The first is the machine learning based analysis of BCI data, often with a focus on deep learning. The second is concerned with the connection of BCIs and the VR ecosystem while the third addresses the idea of analysing the correlation of sensor data from existing sensor data. The amount of research in the three areas decreases as far as we have observed. Hence, there is currently no research that creates a connection between these three aspects, namely an analysis of sensor correlation for hBCIs and HMDs. Some relevant work on these three areas will be highlighted in turn.

The use of physiological measurements for emotion detection has been a research subject for a longer time. While in many papers emotion detection is performed using one or two individual measurements, recently there have been more publications where a multi-modal sensor-set has been used. Ali et al., for example, created an emotion recognition system where multiple physiological signals like ECG, EDA and skin temperature were studied and most commonly used statistical features extracted [3]. A public HCI tagging database "MAH-NOB" was used for training, testing and initial validation while own data was used for final validation. The study also compared the results of using the same sensor brands in training and testing to the results when using different brands in order to generalize the findings.

Regarding the use of deep learning in EEG-signal analysis Zhang et al. give a comprehensive review over the advancements in this field [38]. Here the different deep learning methods for EEG-analysis are explained, reviewed and discussed and a selection of applications in different fields are listed. In particular, [14] Kanjo et al. 2019 are using an approach that is similar to our approach, where they take data from multiple sensors and process the input from all sensors at the same time using deep learning models. The use case for classifying the sensor data is emotion detection. Kanjo et al. differ by using over twenty sensors, providing a wide range of data types and sensor types such as physiological and environmental sensors and using deep learning models to enhance the predictive capabilities of the sensor data rather than analysing the sensors themselves.

For the practical implementation of EEG-sensor measurement while wearing VR-Headsets Tauscher et al. examine how VR-Headsets and EEG-Caps can be physically combined for parallel measurements so that signal quality from both is preserved [29]. Weibel et al. furthermore present a framework for conducting physiological experiments in VR-environments where standardized modules for data collection using questionnaires, the synchronization of physiological measurements, and data storage are included as well as tools for data visualization and evaluation [35]. A reproducible protocol for conducting experiments with this framework is also provided.

Although literature already mentioned certain improvements for BCI by integrating other bio-signals [6, 22], the variety of additional integrated bio-signals and the previous amount of research yet remain limited. Besides potential correlations of data from different sensors, possible redundancies of certain sensors have been less frequently studied so far. In addition, these research topics are not interconnected across disciplines, suggesting that there is a need for a general concept across research disciplines. [2] Agarwal et al. directly address the idea of replacing sensors with the help of other sensor data. Their goal is to use existing sensors more prudently in order to improve energy management. Although the basic idea of sensor replacement is present, there is no analysis of the sensor data itself.

[37] Yan et al. and [11] Gao et al. take multiple sensor data and perform correlative analysis on the sensors to address data loss in wireless sensor networks. Yan et al. propose a multiple linear regression model to recover data, while Gao et al. propose an approach to find the spatial-temporal correlation in the sensor data. This approach is also used by [30] Tayeh et al., who follow the data reduction and energy saving paradigm for environmental sensors in wireless sensor networks. Yan et al. attempt the same thing as the model in this paper. Instead of making one sensor redundant because other sensors contain the same information, it attempts to find this information because it may be missing for a specific use case. Even though Yan et al. and our approach share the idea of enhancing sensor networks, they differ in the type of sensors (environmental sensors in green houses), the reason for analysing the sensors, and the machine learning tools used. Gao et al. and Tayeh et al. use the approach even more similar, but the premise is different. Both papers focus on data reduction in systems with many identical sensors distributed across a region rather than an array of different sensors at the same location.

Thus, this paper fills multiple gaps in the current research. Not only by sensor data correlation analysis using deep learning models but specifically since this analysis is done in order to analyse the used sensors themselves. The gained knowledge of sensor correlation can thereby be applied to a large number of use cases.

3   Conceptual Framework

In this chapter we describe the conceptual Framework Fig. 1 of EEG sensor replacement by AI based emulation.

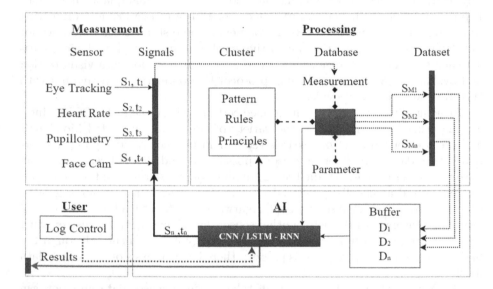

Fig. 1. Concept: The time-dependent signals (S,t) of different sensors (eye tracking, heart rate, pupillometry, face cam) are detected in the course of measurement. The signals are further evaluated in process and read into a buffer as a data set (S_M). Various AI methodologies are used to analyse the data from buffer. A cluster analysis based on patterns, rules, and principles takes place. If a data modification is made, the parameters are stored again. Furthermore, new data sets are deposed in the buffer. As a result of the AI analysis, a temporal and signal-based adjustment is made to the actual number of sensors required as well as temporal query of signals. During the entire measurement, a user machine communication takes place via log control. The user can intervene in the system at any time. The concept can be divided into five steps of measurement, cluster, user control, dataset and AI/Results.

Contrary to the previous literature on sensor-sensor interaction, the goal of the presented concept is to replace one sensor with the measurements from other sensors. Thus, sensors are not investigated for their ability to predict certain use cases like emotion or stress but rather used to analyse the data of other sensors in the same setup. If the concept is successful, a costly or difficult to measure sensor could be left out of a setup completely without losing its functionality. The basic idea of the concept is to cluster the sensor data from one sensor and to classify the data from the other sensors into these clusters. Afterwards, the sensor data in each cluster is analysed for pattern that make statements about the output of the original sensor possible. The individual steps of the concept are each described below, followed by a discussion of the potential uses and the significance of the concept.

Step 1: Measurement of Sensor Data in a VR Setup. The experimental setup consists of a VR environment in which a test person plays a game or is exposed to specific different situations that trigger different emotions. Physiological sensors measure the user's responses throughout the experiment and the results are logged. As long as there is a time stamp attached to the data, the concept is agnostic to the origin of the data. As mentioned above, some retail HMDs already provide several sensors to measure bio-signals, including eye tracking, ECG, gyroscope and electro-dermal activity. The impractical headcaps used for EEG measurement represent both, a physical constraint to the experimental setup as well as an inspiration for the concept. Even though the literature has shown the possibility of combining an EEG headcap and HMDs [29], it is desirable to ultimately lose the need for a headcap with the successful implementation of our concept.

The main challenge for this step is the elusive nature of emotions. Research on emotions is at the intersection of philosophy, linguistics, sociology, anthropology, psychology and neuroscience. One approach is to look at emotions as a discrete variable and to define certain basic emotions that participants can chose from as a response. For this, a prominent model is the differentiation by Ekman, in which the six well-established basic emotions anger, disgust, fear, happiness, sadness, and surprise are proposed as distinguishable across cultures [10]. A different approach looks at emotions on a continuous scale between pleasant-unpleasant and between low and high intensity [20]. Although breaking up emotions into a small set of discrete categories is appealing for an experimental study, a number of problems are associated with this approach: Taking the six basic emotions as the basis for an experiment would be a misapplication of Ekman's research. Even though the basic emotions might be distinguishable for humans across cultures, there is no claim that these are the only emotions or building blocks of other emotions. In fact, Ekman identifies candidate emotions like relief, guilt, embarrassment or excitement that are not as easily distinguishable. Ignoring emotions that are not part of the six basic emotions because of their unclear boundaries is to simplify the concept of emotions beyond recognition. At the same time, there might be a disconnection between what humans feel, the signals their brains produce and the way that they transport the feelings in words or physical movement. The dimensional model may avoid the problem of oversimplification of the available labels but introduces an element of subjectivity that is more difficult to measure and control in an experimental setup. Because of the complexity and ambiguity of the term "emotions", an experimental setup should attempt to investigate specific emotions rather than emotions in general.

Beyond the problem of emotion classification there is the problem of emotion elicitation in VR, which is equally challenging for the experimental setup proposed here. Even if Ekman's six basic emotions are taken as a basis of what the term "emotions" means, the setup needs to trigger at least one of the six emotions reliably, in order to deliver reliable quality data. To achieve this, common techniques are active and passive in nature [17]. In the passive version, participants are faced with stimuli with no interaction beyond the sensory experience. The International Affective Picture System and the International Affective Digitalised Sound System, for example, are databases that can be consulted for visual and auditory passive elicitation of emotions and have been used in VR setups as well [25]. In the active version of emotion elicitation, a participant could, for example, interact with a situation or an avatar in a VR environment to elicit emotions [26]. Even though the passive elicitation poses a lower threshold to the experimental setup, VR is uniquely suited for the active elicitation of emotions and has been shown to be more effective than 2D elicitation [28]. For a systematic literature review of emotion elicitation using VR, see Marin-Morales et al. [21]. Also, emotion elicitation has to remain ethical, so an experimental setup that elicits strong negative emotions would have to be designed prudently and would have to be conducted with prior knowledge of the participants. Experiments that use jump scares (e.g. [36]) have to be weighed carefully for the benefits of the jump scare in emotion elicitation on the one hand and the biases that prior proper information of the risks introduces on the other hand. As a word of caution for the interpretation of results of any VR based emotion elicitation study, there is more research needed on the relatedness of emotions triggered in real world situations and emotions triggered in artificially created VR setups [19,21].

There are several consequences for an experimental design for the concept proposed here. Firstly, a choice has to be made as to which emotions should be induced. Secondly, a decision should be made between active (interaction based) or passive (consumption of content based) methods of elicitation. This paper does not propose a right way for either of these design choices, as the concept proposed here engages with the results of sensor data. These results are in principle independent from the design choices of the underlying experiment. With regard to the emotions chosen in an experimental setup, the next step of the concept is to cluster the measured sensor data. It may seem contradictory to first classify emotions for the experimental setup but to disregard this classification in the next step, but the significance becomes clear in the third step, where the researchers are then able to check, whether the clustering has produced results that are similar to the results envisioned from the experimental setup. This may not only lead to an adjustment of the clustering algorithm, but also to an adjustment in the experimental design if some emotional triggers appear to produce ambiguous results.

For a larger setup, a higher number of participants as well as a control group would be needed. A control group in sensor measurements would have to provide a baseline of EEG data. Here, providing no stimulus would probably not enable good control groups, as participants' wandering minds would cause unforeseen sensor data. We rather propose an easy task or games like light Sudoku puzzles or Solitaire while wearing the same HMD and sensor cap to be appropriate for a control group.

Step 2: Clustering of Sensor Data. Even though the data is time series data, on stream clustering is not necessary. Recording and storing of the data makes it possible to work with the data at will and without the constraint of processing in real time. Here, one sensor is chosen as a possible replacement candidate. The data from this sensor has to be broken up into different clusters representing one emotional category each. To achieve this, several approaches can be used. In the vein of deep learning, autoencoders could be used as feature extractors. It is possible that the experimental setup does not yield enough data for clustering to be useful or necessary. If labelling by hand is feasible, there is the option of labelling the experimental data outright. This has the downside of being labour intensive and costly. A middle ground would be to either take one occurrence as a prototype and classify the rest of the data by similarity or to create pseudo-labelled data with a semi-supervised machine learning algorithm.

Regardless of the model used, the time series data could be approached with a sliding window strategy, in which the step size is smaller than the window size. The resulting clusters contain lists of timestamps at which certain significant events occur. These lists of timestamps have to be controlled for their meaningfulness as they are the basis for further processing.

Step 3: Labelling of Clusters and Reassessment. If a clustering mechanism is used, the clusters in and of themselves are not meaningful. Instead, the clusters have to be controlled for how well a certain human-understandable label can be connected to them. If, for example, a cluster contains time stamps from EEG data that were all connected to joyful moments in the VR clues, the cluster may safely be labelled as a positive emotional category. This not only depends on the experimental setup, but also on the use case that is envisioned. A more or less fine-grained approach will yield different amounts and qualities of clusters. If the clusters do not represent the clues in the VR simulation, the clustering parameters such as bias, learning rate or the loss function of the algorithm can be changed until a useful clustering is achieved.

As a last resort, if the clusters do not seem to produce comprehensible groupings, the VR simulation can be tagged for timestamps at which certain emotions are cued. These timestamps can be used for manual classification or a semi-supervised deep learning based model.

Step 4: Synchronization and Operationalisation of the Other Sensor Data. Each cluster will correspond to a certain type of emotion or set of emotions, depending on the label that it is assigned in step 3. Each of the clusters contains a list of timestamps at which the clustered data points occurred. Now the sensor data from all other sensors are taken into account. The list of timestamps from a cluster is used as the index of a relational database. Each column represents the data from a different sensor, each row represents a point in time. As a first approach, each cell could contain the measurement for one sensor at one point during the experiment.

Taking the raw sensor measurements at the exact timestamp would not be fine-grained enough for some sensors, however. Rather, each sensor has to be taken into account individually. For example, the value from a sensor measuring electro-dermal activity may be taken at face value. Heart rate data or ocular movement on the other hand would be better represented by a gradient of change. Ideally, each sensor's data is preprocessed using recurrent neural networks to look for patterns around each timestamp. This preprocessing transitions into data analysis seamlessly, as patterns in the data of one sensor sampled by timestamps already indicate a correlation between the cluster results and the sensor results. The cell values of the resulting table would contain single values of the sensor or short periods of sensor data depending on what has the highest information density.

It is possible, that during analysis, the sensor produces data that is very different from the originally clustered data. In order to prevent false classification in the analysis stage, data that is considered to be an outlier will be captured by a buffer that is fed back into the clustering stage. In this way, not all the data is classified immediately by brute force. Rather the data that is easily classified will be passed through, while some data will await processing later on. The concept can even run in soft real time after an initial setup period.

Step 5: Analysis of the Sensor Data and Interpretation. Statistical analysis of the table data can be done using household statistical methods or machine learning models. This requires a machine learning based pipeline, which includes preprocessing, feature selection and adjusting of weights. This pipeline can be bypassed using a deep learning approach. While an artificial neural network could take the form of any neural network for pattern recognition, of which there is a large choice of different types [8], a promising approach in the area of emotion classification based on input from multiple sensors has been to use a hybrid approach of a convolutional neural network together with a long short term memory recurrent neural network [14], although any other deep learning approach could be used as well, depending on which model produces the best result.

The most basic analysis of the table would be to look for patterns within a single column, denoting one sensor. If all data points in a single column are similar, there might be a correlation between this sensor and the one to be replaced. Yet the similarity may only be assessed when compared to the rest of that sensor's data that is not in the table. If, for example, a sensor has the value 0.75 for all occurrences in the table, the meaningfulness is determined by the values of the sensors outside of the selected timestamps. If all values are 0.75, there is no meaning. If all other values are 0.50, there is a strong correlation between that sensor and the EEG data. Therefore, the analysis has to find patterns within a column as a first step and compare these to the rest of the data produced by that sensor.

The more interesting and more intricate approach is to look for patterns in the combined data of multiple sensors. Even though there might not be a pattern within one sensor, the relationship between multiple sensors might be distinctive. These patterns could be found through regular machine learning models or using deep learning models again. The advantage of deep learning models is that the required domain knowledge is reduced drastically. It is, however, not eliminated, as the assessment of a model still requires human evaluation of the results.

The result of the concept would be a list of correlations between the sensors. If sensor A is investigated, there would be individual correlation values of sensor A's data with the other individual sensors but also values for sensor A's data with all possible combinations of the other sensors. This table would allow insights into how much the information content from the input sensor A could be gleaned from any combination of the other sensors. In the following exemplary Table 1, the combination of sensors A, B and C together contain 90 % of the information content of sensor A.

Table 1. Each cell contains an exemplary value of how closely the combined sensor data of the sensors named in row and column correlate with the target sensor A's data

Target sensor A	Sensor B	Sensor C	Sensor D
Sensor B	0.2	0.4	0.3
Sensor C	0.4	0.1	0.5
Sensor D	0.3	0.5	0.0
Sensor BC	0.4	0.4	0.9

4   Discussion

There are several underlying assumptions attached to the concept. The first is that it is beneficial for certain use cases to use multiple sensors at the same time. The interaction of sensors, which the concept in this paper seeks to investigate, can only be relevant if multiple sensors provide a benefit in the first place. This assumption is backed up by the related work, in which many papers utilize multiple sensors. The authors consider this assumption to be reasonable in the face of the complexity of use cases.

Another assumption is that there is overlap in the information content each sensor measures with regard to a use case. Again, interaction can only take place if the data measured has some significance for the use case. If, for example, heart rate measurements and EEG measurements are completely disconnected, investigating overlap in their respective information content would be futile. This possibility should not be considered as a shortcoming but as a justification of the very model proposed here. Ultimately, knowing that heart rate and EEG measurements in emotion detection are disconnected is a result that is as relevant as finding a strong connection. In this way, there is a strong connection between possible shortcomings of the concept and opportunities for further research.

Overall, the results of the concept would be percentages, not absolute answers. If overlap in the sensors' information content is found, the overlap would not be binary (yes/no) but rather on a scale between 0 for no correlation and 1 for a total correlation. This result not only depends on the efficacy and the error margin of the models used but also to a large extend on the quality of the input data. It might be that some sensors do not produce data reliable enough for repeatable measurements. It could also be that the categories chosen per use case (e.g. emotional categories such as fear, joy, etc.) do not correspond to measurable physiological phenomena. Here, setting up the experimental design with specialists for the specific use case is crucial to prevent spurious research. Also, a strict ethical review of the experimental setup is advisable for two reasons. Firstly, a simulation triggering strong emotions repeatedly can cause harm to participants without the right oversight. Secondly, physiological sensor data is amongst the most sensitive of personal data that has to be strictly protected.

If the experimental setup is sufficient, the concepts holds great potential to fill a research gap on the interaction between sensors in VR applications. In a best-case scenario, sensors could be replaced outright because their information content can be taken from a combination of other sensors. This could lead to cheaper devices, a reduction of data transfer or increase the hardware lifecycle, as individual sensor failures would not result in a broken device. In a worst case scenario, the concept can enhance our knowledge on the information content of sensors in specific use cases. This has immense scientific value, which is further described in the section on opportunities for future work.

5   Conclusion

The aim of this work was to propose a theoretical concept for potentially replacing one sensor with the measurements from other sensors. Hence, costly or difficult to measure sensors could be left out of a setup completely, without losing its functionality. An AI based EEG emulation, derived from other directly related bio-signals, could therefore potentially replace EEG measurements which indirectly enables the use of BCI in situations where it was previously not possible.

The conceptual framework thereby builds upon the generation of meaningful measurement data through the collection within a corresponding VR application and set-up. The evaluation of the collected sensor data is processed in five consecutive steps, by clustering the data of one sensor and classifying the data from other sensors into these clusters. Afterwards, the sensor data in each cluster are analysed for regularities that make statements about the output of the original sensor possible.

Although the concept presented has not yet been implemented, the detailed description of the individual processing steps enables a targeted and comprehensible implementation. Nevertheless, the success of the possible implementation of the concept stands and falls with the validity of a number of assumptions. One is that it is advantageous for certain use cases to use several sensors simultaneously. Secondly, that there is overlap in the information content that each sensor measures in relation to a use case. However, it must be fundamentally emphasised that the results of the concept are in any case statistical probability values and not absolute answers.

In the best case, sensors, not limited to EEG, could be indirectly integrated or completely removed based on the findings. In turn this could lead to a reduction in the size of devices, a reduction in data transfer or an extension of the life cycle of the hardware in general. In the worst case, the concept can at least expand the general knowledge about the information content of sensors for specific use cases.

Therefore, the proposed approach offers considerable added value in any case, especially in the results of the literature research carried out and the relevance in the field of BCI established in the process. A successful implementation could also be used for a number of use cases in which the measurement of brain activity could not be used or could not be used in a practicable way for interaction between the user and the application.

6   Future Work

There are two main avenues of future work. The first is the realisation of the setup described in this paper, the other is how the idea presented here can be developed further. The first question, how this concept could be realised, requires a good VR application to trigger emotions. An issue here is that most VR applications have the goal of eliciting some kind of emotion at some point during the use of the application. A more direct approach to investigating emotion would be to create a simulation that produces certain emotions repeatedly in a controlled manner. The data is most distinctive if the patterns occur repeatedly and the relevant events in the data are not outliers. A good VR application for this experiment would therefore seek to produce similar emotions reliably. Here, working with neuroscientists is imperative, as the concept of emotions in natural language understanding can be at odds with a scientific meaning of what is being measured.

Another area of research is how well the parameters of a clustering algorithm and the patterns found in the data can be transferred between participants. A study here would take one person's patterns and apply them to other participants' data to control for individual differences in the sensor data that is to be replaced.

The second avenue for future work, the further development of the concept, is an open ended field of research. Here, the idea of a sensor hierarchy could be developed for each use case. Since the results would be percentage based, a final result might be a large venn diagram per use case in which sensors are represented as circles and overlap by the amount they correlate. If one sensor can be replaced by others outright, that sensor would be represented as lying inside of an overlapping area.

Additionally, more sensors and different types of sensors could be added to the analysis. The close connection between emotional and environmental data in emotion detection [15] begs the question whether there is a correlation between environmental sensors measurements and physiological sensor measurements when testing for emotion.

Acknowledgement. We would like to thank Thomas Odaker, Elisabeth Mayer and Lea Weil who supported this work with helpful discussions and feedback.

References

1. Abiri, R., Borhani, S., Sellers, E.W., Jiang, Y., Zhao, X.: A comprehensive review of EEG-based brain-computer interface paradigms. J. Neural Eng. **16**(1) (2018). https://doi.org/10.1088/1741-2552/aaf12e
2. Agarwal, A.A., Munigala, V., Ramamritham, K.: Observability: replacing sensors with inference engines. In: Proceedings of the Seventh International Conference on Future Energy Systems Poster Sessions, pp. 9:1–9:2. ACM (2016)
3. Ali, M., Al Machot, F., Haj Mosa, A., Jdeed, M., Al Machot, E., Kyamakya, K.: A globally generalized emotion recognition system involving different physiological signals. Sensors **18**(6) (2018). https://doi.org/10.3390/s18061905
4. Allison, B., Dunne, S., Leeb, R., Millán, J., Nijholt, A.: Towards Practical Brain-Computer Interfaces: Bridging the Gap from Research to Real-World Applications. Biological and Medical Physics, Biomedical Engineering. Springer, Heidelberg (2012). https://doi.org/10.1007/978-3-642-29746-5
5. Alonso-Valerdi, L., Gutiérrez-Begovich, D., Argüello-García, J., Sepulveda, F., Ramírez-Mendoza, R.: User experience may be producing greater heart rate variability than motor imagery related control tasks during the user-system adaptation in brain-computer interfaces. Front. Physiol. **7** (2016). https://doi.org/10.3389/fphys.2016.00279
6. Amiri, S., Fazel-Rezai, R., Asadpour, V.: A review of hybrid brain-computer interface systems. Adv. Hum.-Comput. Interact. **2013**, 1–8 (2013). https://doi.org/10.1155/2013/187024
7. Anthes, C., García-Hernández, R., Wiedemann, M., Kranzlmüller, D.: State of the art of virtual reality technology. In: 2016 IEEE Aerospace Conference, pp. 1–19. IEEE (2016). https://doi.org/10.1109/AERO.2016.7500674
8. Bishop, C.: Neural Networks for Pattern Recognition. Oxford University Press, Oxford (1995)
9. Deller, A.: Brain-computer interfaces: The next step in human evolution: The merging of humanity with the technology we have created has begun... (2020). https://www.wevolver.com/article/brain-computer-interfaces-the-next-step-in-human-evolution. Accessed 31 May 2021

10. Ekman, P.: Basic emotions. In: Handbook of Cognition and Emotion, vol. 98, pp. 45–60 (1999)
11. Gao, Z., Cheng, W., Qiu, X., Meng, L.: A missing sensor data estimation algorithm based on temporal and spatial correlation. Int. J. Distrib. Sensor Netw. **11**(10) (2015). https://doi.org/10.1155/2015/435391
12. Hochberg, L., et al.: Reach and grasp by people with tetraplegia using a neurally controlled robotic arm. Nature **485**(7398), 372–375 (2012). https://doi.org/10.1038/nature11076
13. HP Development Company, L.P.: HP omnicept & HP reverb G2 omnicept edition (2021). https://www8.hp.com/us/en/vr/reverb-g2-vr-headset-omnicept-edition.html. Accessed 31 May 2021
14. Kanjo, E., Younis, E.M., Ang, C.S.: Deep learning analysis of mobile physiological, environmental and location sensor data for emotion detection. Inf. Fusion **49**, 46–56 (2019). https://doi.org/10.1016/j.inffus.2018.09.001
15. Kanjo, E., Younis, E.M., Sherkat, N.: Towards unravelling the relationship between on-body, environmental and emotion data using sensor information fusion approach. Inf. Fusion **40**, 18–31 (2018). https://doi.org/10.1016/j.inffus.2017.05.005
16. Kim, S., Simeral, J., Hochberg, L., Donoghue, J., Friehs, G., Black, M.: Point-and-click cursor control with an intracortical neural interface system by humans with tetraplegia. IEEE Trans. Neural Syst. Rehabil. Eng. **19**(2), 193–203 (2011). https://doi.org/10.1109/TNSRE.2011.2107750
17. Kory, J., D'Mello, S.: Affect elicitation for affective computing. In: The Oxford Handbook of Affective Computing, pp. 371–383. Oxford Library of Psychology (2015)
18. Lotte, F., Nam, C., Nijholt, A.: Introduction: evolution of brain-computer interfaces. In: Brain-Computer Interfaces Handbook: Technological and Theoretical Advance, pp. 1–11. Taylor & Francis (CRC Press) (2018)
19. Marín-Morales, J., et al.: Real vs. immersive-virtual emotional experience: analysis of psycho-physiological patterns in a free exploration of an art museum. PloS One **14**(10) (2019). https://doi.org/10.1371/journal.pone.0223881
20. Marín-Morales, J., et al.: Affective computing in virtual reality: emotion recognition from brain and heartbeat dynamics using wearable sensors. Sci. Rep. **8**(1), 1–15 (2018)
21. Marín-Morales, J., Llinares, C., Guixeres, J., Alcañiz, M.: Emotion recognition in immersive virtual reality: from statistics to affective computing. Sensors **20**(18), 5163 (2020). https://doi.org/10.3390/s20185163
22. Müller-Putz, G., et al.: Principles of hybrid brain-computer interfaces. In: Allison, B., Dunne, S., Leeb, R., Del, R., Millán, J., Nijholt, A. (eds.) Towards Practical Brain-Computer Interfaces. BIOMEDICAL, pp. 355–373. Springer, Heidelberg (2012). https://doi.org/10.1007/978-3-642-29746-5_18
23. Müller-Putz, G., et al.: Towards noninvasive hybrid brain-computer interfaces: framework, practice, clinical application, and beyond. Proc. IEEE **103**(6), 926–943 (2015). https://doi.org/10.1109/JPROC.2015.2411333
24. Nicolas-Alonso, L., Gomez-Gil, J.: Brain computer interfaces, a review. Sensors **12**(2), 1211–1279 (2012). https://doi.org/10.3390/s120201211
25. Orefice, P.-H., Ammi, M., Hafez, M., Tapus, A.: Design of an emotion elicitation tool using VR for human-avatar interaction studies. In: IVA 2017. LNCS (LNAI), vol. 10498, pp. 335–338. Springer, Cham (2017). https://doi.org/10.1007/978-3-319-67401-8_42

26. Roberts, N., Tsai, J., Coan, J.: Emotion elicitation using dyadic interaction tasks. In: Handbook of Emotion Elicitation and Assessment, pp. 106–123. Oxford University Press, New York (2007)

27. Slutzky, M.W., Flint, R.D.: Physiological properties of brain-machine interface input signals. J. Neurophysiol. **118**(2), 1329–1343 (2017). https://doi.org/10.1152/jn.00070.2017

28. Susindar, S., Sadeghi, M., Huntington, L., Singer, A., Ferris, T.: The feeling is real: emotion elicitation in virtual reality. In: Proceedings of the Human Factors and Ergonomics Society Annual Meeting, vol. 63, pp. 252–256. SAGE Publications Sage CA, Los Angeles (2019). https://doi.org/10.1177/1071181319631509

29. Tauscher, J., Schottky, F., Grogorick, S., Bittner, P., Mustafa, M., Magnor, M.: Immersive EEG: evaluating electroencephalography in virtual reality. In: IEEE Conference on Virtual Reality and 3D User Interfaces (VR), pp. 1794–1800. IEEE (2019). https://doi.org/10.1109/VR.2019.8797858

30. Tayeh, G., Makhoul, A., Perera, C., Demerjian, J.: A spatial-temporal correlation approach for data reduction in cluster-based sensor networks. IEEE Access **7**, 50669–50680 (2019). https://doi.org/10.1109/ACCESS.2019.2910886

31. Taylor, D.M., Tillery, S.I.H., Schwartz, A.B.: Direct cortical control of 3D neuroprosthetic devices. Science **296**(5574), 1829–1832 (2002). https://doi.org/10.1126/science.1070291

32. Velliste, M., Perel, S., Spalding, M., Whitford, A., Schwartz, A.: Cortical control of a prosthetic arm for self-feeding. Nature **453**(7198), 1098–1101 (2008). https://doi.org/10.1038/nature06996

33. Vogel, J., et al.: An assistive decision-and-control architecture for force-sensitive hand-arm systems driven by human-machine interfaces. Int. J. Robot. Res. **34**(6), 763–780 (2015). https://doi.org/10.1177/0278364914561535

34. Waldert, S., Pistohl, T., Braun, C., Ball, T., Aertsen, A., Mehring, C.: A review on directional information in neural signals for brain-machine interfaces. J. Physiol. **103**(3–5), 244–254 (2009). https://doi.org/10.1016/j.jphysparis.2009.08.007

35. Weibel, R., et al.: Virtual reality experiments with physiological measures. J. Visualized Exp. JoVE (138) (2018). https://doi.org/10.3791/58318

36. Wilkinson, M., Pugh, Z., Crowson, A., Feng, J., Mayhorn, C., Gillan, D.: Seeing in slow motion: manipulating arousal in virtual reality. In: Proceedings of the Human Factors and Ergonomics Society Annual Meeting, vol. 63, pp. 1649–1653. SAGE Publications Sage CA, Los Angeles (2019)

37. Yan, X., Xie, H., Tong, W.: A multiple linear regression data predicting method using correlation analysis for wireless sensor networks. In: Proceedings of 2011 Cross Strait Quad-Regional Radio Science and Wireless Technology Conference, vol. 2, pp. 960–963. IEEE (2011). https://doi.org/10.1109/CSQRWC.2011.6037116

38. Zhang, X., Yao, L., Wang, X., Monaghan, J., McAlpine, D., Zhang, Y.: A survey on deep learning-based non-invasive brain signals: recent advances and new frontiers. J. Neural Eng. **18**(3) (2021). https://doi.org/10.1088/1741-2552/abc902

A Preliminary Study on Virtual Reality Tools in Human-Robot Interaction

Sara Kaszuba(iD), Francesco Leotta(✉)(iD), and Daniele Nardi(iD)

Department of Computer, Control, and Management Engineering (DIAG),
Sapienza University of Rome, via Ariosto 25, Rome, Italy
{kaszuba,leotta,nardi}@diag.uniroma1.it

Abstract. Choosing the best interaction modalities and protocols in Human-Robot Interaction (HRI) is far from being straightforward, as it strictly depends on the application domain, the tasks to be executed, the types of robots and sensors involved. In the last years, a growing number of HRI researchers exploited Virtual Reality (VR) as a mean to evaluate proposed solutions, focusing in particular on safety and correctness of collaborative tasks. This allows to prove the effectiveness and robustness of a certain approach in a simulated environment, thus permitting to converge more easily to the best solution, also avoiding to experiment potentially harmful actions in a real scenario. In this paper, we aim at reviewing existing VR based approaches targeting or embodying HRI.

Keywords: Human-robot interaction · Virtual Reality · Speech acts · Communication modalities

1 Introduction

Both technical and societal drivers are pushing a vision of robotics where machines work together with people [14], thus making the study of *Human-Robot Interaction* (HRI) fundamental. One of the prevalent forms this interaction happens if by having robots and humans collaborating together in executing a specific task, which is one of the key elements in recently developed systems. In particular, in such solutions, researches have proved that a joint effort of people and androids in a shared workspace, would significantly reduce the time of executing certain tasks, by improving the efficiency of the overall architecture [13]. In particular, robots can support and relieve human operators, enable versatile automation steps and increase productivity by combining human capabilities with the efficiency and precision of machines [20].

HRI can rely on single sensory channels such as hearing, sight, speech and gestures [38] or through the combination of two or more of them in order to obtain a more robust system [5]. Signals that are exchanged along these channels must be coherent, since a clear understanding of their meanings is resuired to enable communication [25] and to establish a more solid relationship between people and machines. Additionally, human safety is an aspect to be taken into

L. T. De Paolis et al. (Eds.): AVR 2021, LNCS 12980, pp. 81–90, 2021.
https://doi.org/10.1007/978-3-030-87595-4_7

account in robotics systems, in which human workers and androids need to share the same workspace with different degrees of proximity avoiding risks [39].

Development and validation of HRI solutions still lacks to a large extent fast and effective approaches, typically undergoing a long trial-and-error expensive cycle. Recently, *Virtual Reality* (VR) has been employed in variety of ways to replace preliminary validation of HRI approaches, which often requires hard to implement experimental settings where the interaction between humans and robots takes place [8]. Indeed, a VR environment may allow users to perform multiple evaluations in sequence by observing and manipulating virtual objects in a simulated immersive scenario. Hence, VR has the advantage to support the validation of costly solutions in a safe and cheap artificially replicated world [21]. Since the interaction between people and androids requires an in depth analysis of the communication modalities, type and position of sensors on the robot, human-machine distance and the application domain where the relationship will take place, a virtual world seems to be very suitable to conduct such tests.

Our goal is to adopt a VR environment to carry out the experimental activity planned in the CANOPIES project (see https://canopies.inf.uniroma3.it/), where the collaboration between humans and robots takes place in an agriculture scenario, for grape harvesting and branch pruning operations, with the aim of combining people and machines skills. In order to design and implement our collaborative framework, we look at the interaction from an agent communication perspective, which identifies different message types (speech acts) and characterizes their meaning to allow for a proper understanding of each other. Hence, we have investigated the literature in order to distinguish the VR solutions that have been proposed to support in manifold ways the exchange of information between humans and robots. While we are still trying to identify the basic principles to develop the aforementioned system, our analysis shows interesting findings in terms of the design space to be explored.

In this paper we aim at reviewing existing VR solutions targeting or embodying HRI. The remainder of this study is structured as follows: Sect. 2 provides a general view of the topic, while Sect. 3 presents a scheme for the examination of the literature that is centered on the notion of communication act and Sect. 4 elaborates on the interaction modalities that are associated with different types of speech acts. We conclude the paper with a discussion of the findings for exploring the design space of our application.

2   Related Works

In order to define a first taxonomy, we analyzed recent surveys in the area of HRI, focusing on works where VR is used for the evaluation purposes. In particular, we identified three studies targeting this topic from different points of view.

Authors in [8] classify papers according to the goal of the interaction. In particular, four main categories have been identified, namely operator support, simulation, instruction and manipulation.

Papers belonging to the *operator support* category focuses on interaction modalities helping operators in controlling predicting and monitoring robots' actions through, for example, acoustic and visual feedback methods [4]. Moniri et al. [28] introduce an additional dimension to existing HRI scenarios, involving two participants in different physical locations: one shares the robot's workspace to perform a collaborative task, while the other monitors the process of the area through a VR system. The necessity of increasing human safety awareness [33] and providing more information of the surrounding environment through the use of Augmented Reality (AR) are other relevant aspects that are emerging in some studies belonging to this category.

The *simulation* category explores solutions using simulation software to enhance the users' understandability of the working ambient. In particular, the virtual space allows the human to interact either with a robot or with objects.

Papers in the *instruction* category focus on providing the human user with a hierarchy of tasks that are proposed in the virtual environment. Here, the distinction of the workspace in safe and dangerous zones is essential where the presence of both, humans and robots is a prerequisite. Virtual buttons, to confirm or change the next robot task, allow the user to exploit a gesture-based interaction by pointing with the finger to the desired instruction.

Finally, papers in the *manipulation* category focus on teleoperating and supervising robots remotely.

Authors of the survey [39] stress instead the importance of *human safety* as a critical factor when HRI is applied in collaborative environments, and provide an in depth analysis of safety aspects in systems involving a close collaboration with people. In particular, based on the existing articles on safety features that minimize the risk of HRI, provide a classification of the works into five main categories, i.e., robot perception for safe HRI, cognition enabled robot control in HRI, action planning for safe navigation close to humans, hardware safety features and societal and psychological factors.

Robot perception has a profound impact on safety aspects in Human-Robot Collaboration tasks. Human-in-the-loop systems are developed, for example, for human assistance provision through teleoperation. In this case, VR is used to test several abilities of the robots (e.g., the effectiveness of grasping strategies), or to teach the robot new skills for collaborative work. Vision-enabled methods play a key role in the perception-based safety approaches, in which real-time modeling of the operating workspace through accurate RGB-D and lidar sensors [11] allow fast robot planning, obstacle avoidance [27] and increase human presence understanding [19], leading to more predictable and safe robot behaviors [29].

Human aware robot navigation, actions prediction and recognition, together with the understanding of a shared workspace, are essential in the development of novel systems where collaboration between people and machines is required, thus allowing a safe human-robot coexistence. Human behavior understanding should be also integrated into robots' navigation mechanisms [18] allowing, for example, to adapt action execution to velocity, speed and proximity distances [35].

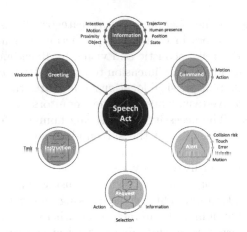

Fig. 1. The identified taxonomy

Safe system degradation also plays an important role in HRI, since it can avoid uncomfortable situations in HRI tasks by informing the person about robots current abilities, while at the same time retaining fail-safe mechanisms.

Finally, in a recent survey [6], authors focus on AR instead of VR solutions. Despite this important difference, authors provide a list of application domains that are relevant to our case including manufacturing and assembly, pick and place, search and rescue, medical, space, and restaurants. Noticeably, agriculture is not covered by any of the analyzed papers.

Despite the availability of these recent surveys, at the best of our knowledge, there is no work that classifies studies of HRI performed in VR based on the information exchanged between humans and robots. For this reason, we propose an innovative way of analyzing the topic based on the speech act theory [15].

3 Taxonomy of Content Information

A clear and exhaustive definition of the term *speech act* is provided by the philosopher Kent Bach, that explained this concept by saying that "almost any speech act is really the performance of several acts at once, distinguished by different aspects of the speaker's intention: there is the act of saying something, what one does in saying it, such as requesting or promising, and how one is trying to affect one's audience" [3]. Generally, such term identifies a set of classes differing according to the information exchanged in a Human-Human, Robot-Robot or, as in our case of study, HRI. Another relevant aspect is the selected interaction channel (e.g. voice, gesture, text, visual feedbacks, audio signals).

Our aim in this paper is to present a preliminary study in which two fundamental concepts are highlighted: **what** is the informative content exchanged and **how** the communication takes place in a virtual world. The first aspect is discussed in this section, whereas the second one is presented in Sect. 5.

By reviewing papers concerning VR evaluation for HRI, we identified the following speech act categories: information, command, alert, request, instruction and greeting. In addition, a further subdivision, based on the specific message type, is performed as shown in Fig. 1.

Information is the most frequently adopted speech act, allowing to notify a teammate about: an intention [1,23], the current activity, the measured distance from the target [23] or from the human [36], object properties [37] or trajectory [2]. Human presence (awareness of the person in the environment) is another relevant element considered in different studies [31], together with information about position with respect to an object [10,22] or a teammate [32], current status [36] and achieved performance [26,36].

An unidirectional speech act category, expressing the commands given by the human to the robot, is represented by the *command* speech act class, in which two sub-classes have been identified: motion, in which the android must reach a new position [22,23], change its velocity, or stop its operation [7,23], and action, that consists of performing specific activities, such as following a person [16,32], picking up [7] or positioning an object [17].

A notification of a dangerous situation is a fundamental aspect that emerges from different works and for this reason, the *alert* speech act category is provided. Collision risk (higher probability of human-robot collision [31]), touch (the collision is verified, hence the person and the android are in contact [12]), error (about task execution), velocity (reduction or increase of robot's speed [24]) and motion (change in machine's motion trajectory [24]) belong to this classification.

Another relevant class, which has not to be confused with the already introduced command category, is *request*. The difference is straightforward: in the last case, the human is asking the teammate to perform a specific action [37], select an object [30] or provide information [22,26], but the robot can refuse while, when a command is issued, the android must follow the person's requirements.

A further unidirectional speech act class is represented by *instructions*, by which the machine provides instructions [9] or hand motion suggestions [24,31] to be performed by the human worker to complete the assignment.

Finally, a category that emerges when interacting with social robots is *greeting*. In particular, the robot can welcome the user to increase human's trust, which is fundamental in collaborative tasks [34].

4 Taxonomy of Delivery Modality

Starting from the aforementioned speech act categories and their classification based on the informative content, we devote this section to examine the modalities adopted in the analyzed articles for performing information exchange between humans and robots in virtual environments. The following discussion mainly concerns robot-human communication, but some categories can be employed also to allow the exchange of information from human to robot. In any case, we present the most relevant interaction channels for each speech act, together with an explanation of their use in the analyzed studies.

Voice and *visual feedbacks* are the preferred interaction channels for the *information* category. The first modality is exploited, for example, by a social robot tour guide in the virtual museum, with the aim of showing and talking about existing artworks of the Metropolitan Museum of Art of New York [37]. Moreover, vocal communication allows the exchange of mission details between humans and robots in marine [32] and military [7] scenarios; to update the teammate about processes, so to increase awareness of system's features and to improve performances, by clarifying ambiguous situations, giving suggestions to correctly complete a task [34] and communicating the final outcome [26]

Light signals, as visual feedbacks, are employed on industrial robots to notify the human about their proximity to the goal or intention, as presented in [23], in which a filled circle with higher intensity indicates that the robot is far from its target position, while the empty shape identifies the zero distance. Such interaction channel is described by [2] as an immediate and efficient way of communicating the android's future trajectory in a shared environment, where multiple robots collaborate with humans and each of the autonomous driving workers is able to re-plan its motion based on the teammates intentions. Human presence detection is introduced in [31] through the usage of different colors, exploited to categorize three zones: green, yellow and red. The green one is a completely safety area, a medium risk is associated to the yellow region, while a higher hazard is assigned to the red sector, in which the human and the industrial robot perform the collaborative task very close to each other. Visual feedbacks are exploited to increase awareness of robot's workspace, represented as a toroidal red semitransparent surface and its projection on the floor through a red line circle, as developed in [24]. In addition, the authors of this work, introduce a yellow semitransparent wedge to specify the robot movement volume in an industrial scenario. Interesting is the combination of visual and audio signals to exchange information from robots to humans, as shown in [36] and [17]. In the first study, the authors associate a particular beeping frequency to one of the eight colored rings (one for each zone), distinguished based on human-robot distance in a collaborative nut screwing task, that allows the user to understand the android's state by considering the sound wave together with different shapes and colors of the signs on the machine. In the second article instead, researchers focus on the advantages related to the simultaneous reproduction of a yellow warning light (positioned in the bottom part of each of the two robotic arms) and a sound. In this case, a reduction of mental workload of industrial operators and increment of the final performance and awareness have been observed.

Gestures are the preferred communication modality for the *command* speech act category. In [23] and [7], such interaction channel is exploited by the human to stop robot's activity in an immediate way by showing his/her opened hand to the mobile vehicle, but also indication of the next position to reach by the android is covered in the first aforementioned study. This is not the only work that uses gestures as a way of communicating a new location to a mobile teammate; in effect this concept is also emphasized in [26], in which the authors highlight the power of their system for the presence of a robot able to translate a non-verbal behavior into an understandable action. Pointing is not only employed to provide a specific position to reach, but also to indicate an object, as presented in [16]. The authors of this article stress the importance of such interaction channel in commanding a robot to follow someone, by only pointing the person [32].

From the analyzed studies, one can see that *visual feedbacks* are more suitable for the *alert* category. Generally, such communication modality is combined with audio signals in order to provide an imminent warning of a dangerous situation to the person, as in [24] where a sound is used to notify the contact between the human and the robot's motion volume. Furthermore, in this work, a visual and audio information are provided when a reduction/increment of robot's speed is verified or a change in motion is performed to avoid a risky condition. Therefore, when a human and a robot touch each other, a red and blurred vision is displayed, together with a simultaneous haptic vibration, as described in [12].

Voice is obviously the modality adopted in all studies that belong to *request* category. For example, the description and properties of a certain object, are asked by a teammate to the other one, as in [26] and [30]. In this last work, other important concepts emerge, such as the request of performing an action [16,37], select a certain object or ask information to other teammates about their tasks [32]. Such interaction channel is also used to provide notifications coming from an industrial robotic platform to the human [22].

Visual feedbacks are displayed to the user to perform a specific action by following a semitransparent palm that appears in the immersive industrial VR scenario [24] or to follow assembly instructions slides, illustrating how to complete the collaborative task [9].

The sole work belonging to the greeting category [34] employs *voice* as interaction modality to welcome the person in the virtual environment.

5   Discussion

In this paper, a preliminary study about the deployment of VR as an evaluation mean for HRI solutions has been presented. This aspect is fundamental for us to define the most suitable delivery channels to be adopted for developing the interaction in the CANOPIES project, with the aim of discovering the most frequently employed communication modalities for exchanging the different informative contents between humans and robots.

Noticeably, none of the considered studies targeted the agriculture scenario, with most of the proposed solutions focusing on industrial application domains. As a consequence, our future work will address the evaluation of identified techniques in a smart agriculture environment modeled using VR.

To summarize the outcome of our first investigation, some general conclusions can be drawn about modalities to be employed to exchange a specific informative content, and to emphasize the importance of considering each of the presented speech act categories in creating a complex robotic system. From our analysis emerges that *(i)* rarely, *all* speech act categories are examined in designing an elaborated interaction; so to develop a more robust and efficient robotic architecture, they should all be taken in consideration, *(ii)* the most used communication channels adopted for messages belonging to *information* speech act category are voice and visual feedbacks, *(iii) commands* are mainly based on gestures, e.g., by pointing an object to pick up, *(iv) alert* and *instruction* notifications employ visual feedbacks as the way of interaction, because such modality generates information easily understandable by the human, *(v) voice* is preferred for the *request* and *greeting* categories to ask a robot/person to perform specific tasks, but also to make the human feel comfortable and safe in executing the collaborative assignment with the android in a VR scenario.

In order to avoid issues associated to the employment of a single communication channel, it could be interesting to combine more modalities to increase awareness and facilitate the interaction. For example, considering that in an outdoor scenario, as in our case in an agriculture environment, noise or sounds in the background are frequent, the preferred choice would be to exploit voice together with other modalities such as *(i)* visual feedbacks, to notify the human about particular events or situations, and *(ii)* gestures, to provide commands or request information to the robot, but also to greet a person in a more natural way. Investigating multimodality to alert the human about dangerous situations by using visual and audio feedbacks, would surely improve both human safety and the performances of a collaborative task. Hence, an efficient and clear way to show instructions about a specific assignment to the user, would be the combination of visual feedbacks and voice/gesture.

As anticipated at the beginning of this article, our goal relies on developing a robust system, in which humans and robots can collaborate on a shared task by overcoming issues associated to a single communication channel to interact with each other. Therefore, in a future work, we plan to better investigate and discuss this topic by also considering AR solutions in HRI.

Acknowledgements. The work of S. Kaszuba, F. Leotta and D. Nardi has been partly supported by the H2020 EU project CANOPIES - A Collaborative Paradigm for Human Workers and Multi-Robot Teams in Precision Agriculture Systems, Grant Agreement 101016906.

References

1. Arntz, A., Eimler, S.C.: Experiencing AI in VR: a qualitative study on designing a human-machine collaboration scenario. In: Stephanidis, C., Antona, M., Ntoa, S. (eds.) HCI International 2020 - Late Breaking Posters, pp. 299–307 (2020)
2. Aschenbrenner, D., Tol, D.v., Rusak, Z., Werker, C.: Using virtual reality for scenario-based responsible research and innovation approach for human robot co-production. In: 2020 IEEE International Conference on Artificial Intelligence and Virtual Reality (AIVR), pp. 146–150 (2020)
3. Bach, K., Harnish, R.M.: Linguistic Communication and Speech Acts. MIT Press, Cambridge (1979)

4. Bolano, G., Juelg, C., Roennau, A., Dillmann, R.: Transparent robot behavior using augmented reality in close human-robot interaction. In: 28th IEEE International Conference on Robot and Human Interactive Communication (RO-MAN), pp. 1–7 (2019)
5. Bonarini, A.: Communication in human-robot interaction. In: Current Robotics Reports, pp. 1–7 (2020)
6. Chang, C.T., Hayes, B.: A survey of augmented reality for human-robot collaboration (2020)
7. Cockburn, J., Solomon, Y.: Multi-modal human robot interaction in a simulation environment (2013)
8. Dianatfar, M., Latokartano, J., Lanz, M.: Review on existing vr/ar solutions in human-robot collaboration. Procedia CIRP **97**, 407–411 (2021)
9. Dimitrokalli, A., Vosniakos, G.C., Nathanael, D., Matsas, E.: On the assessment of human-robot collaboration in mechanical product assembly by use of virtual reality. Procedia Manuf. **51**, 627–634 (2020)
10. Etzi, R., et al.: Using virtual reality to test human-robot interaction during a collaborative task. In: International Design Engineering Technical Conference and Computers and Information in Engineering Conference. ASME Digital Collection (2019)
11. Flacco, F., Kröger, T., Luca, A.D., Khatib, O.: A depth space approach for evaluating distance to objects. J. Intell. Rob. Syst. **80**, 7–22 (2015)
12. Fratczak, P., Goh, Y.M., Kinnell, P., Soltoggio, A., Justham, L.: Understanding human behaviour in industrial human-robot interaction by means of virtual reality. In: Proceedings of the Halfway to the Future Symposium 2019, pp. 1–7 (2019)
13. Galin, R., Meshcheryakov, R.: Review on human-robot interaction during collaboration in a shared workspace. In: Ronzhin, A., Rigoll, G., Meshcheryakov, R. (eds.) Interactive Collaborative Robotics, pp. 63–74 (2019)
14. Goodrich, M., Schultz, A.: Human-robot interaction: a survey. Found. Trends Human-Comput. Interact. **1**, 203–275 (2007)
15. Hidayat, A.: Speech acts: force behind words (2016)
16. Inamura, T., Mizuchi, Y.: Sigverse: a cloud-based vr platform for research on multimodal human-robot interaction. Front. Rob. AI **8**, 158 (2021)
17. Kaufeld, M., Nickel, P.: Level of robot autonomy and information aids in human-robot interaction affect human mental workload - an investigation in virtual reality, pp. 278–291 (06 2019)
18. Khambhaita, H., Alami, R.: Assessing the social criteria for human-robot collaborative navigation: A comparison of human-aware navigation planners. In: 2017 26th IEEE International Symposium on Robot and Human Interactive Communication (RO-MAN), pp. 1140–1145 (2017)
19. Kostavelis, I., Gasteratos, A.: Semantic maps from multiple visual cues. Expert Syst. Appl. **68**(C), 45–57 (2017)
20. Kurth, J., Marcel Wagner, A.: New planning methods for systems with human-robot collaboration. Carl Hanser Verlag Munich **115**, 698–702 (12 2020)
21. Liu, D., Bhagat, K.K., Gao, Y., Chang, T.W., Huang, R.: The potentials and trends of virtual reality in education (2017)
22. Malik, A.A., Masood, T., Bilberg, A.: Virtual reality in manufacturing: immersive and collaborative artificial-reality in design of human-robot workspace. Int. J. Comput. Integr. Manuf. **33**(1), 22–37 (2020)
23. Mara, M., et al.: Cobot studio vr: A virtual reality game environment for transdisciplinary research on interpretability and trust in human-robot collaboration (2021)

24. Matsas, E., Vosniakos, G.C., Batras, D.: Prototyping proactive and adaptive techniques for human-robot collaboration in manufacturing using virtual reality. Rob. Comput.-Integr. Manuf. **50** (2017)
25. Mavridis, N.: A review of verbal and non-verbal human-robot interactive communication. Rob. Auton. Syst. **63**, 22–35 (2015)
26. Milliez, G., Ferreira, E., Fiore, M., Alami, R., Lefèvre, F.: Simulating human-robot interactions for dialogue strategy learning. In: Brugali, D., Broenink, J.F., Kroeger, T., MacDonald, B.A. (eds.) SIMPAR 2014. LNCS (LNAI), vol. 8810, pp. 62–73. Springer, Cham (2014). https://doi.org/10.1007/978-3-319-11900-7_6
27. Mohammed, A., Schmidt, B., Wang, L.: Active collision avoidance for human-robot collaboration driven by vision sensors. Int. J. Comput. Integr. Manuf. **30**(9), 970–980 (2017)
28. Moniri, M.M., Valcarcel, F.A.E., Merkel, D., Sonntag, D.: Human gaze and focus-of-attention in dual reality human-robot collaboration. In: 2016 12th International Conference on Intelligent Environments (IE), pp. 238–241 (2016)
29. Morato, C., Kaipa, K.N., Zhao, B., Gupta, S.: Toward safe human robot collaboration by using multiple kinects based real-time human tracking. J. Comput. Inf. Sci. Eng. **14**, 011006 (2014)
30. Murnane, M., Higgins, P., Saraf, M., Ferraro, F., Matuszek, C., Engel, D.: A simulator for human-robot interaction in virtual reality. In: 2021 IEEE Conference on Virtual Reality and 3D User Interfaces Abstracts and Workshops, pp. 470–471 (2021)
31. Nikolakis, N., Maratos, V., Makris, S.: A cyber physical system (cps) approach for safe human-robot collaboration in a shared workplace. Rob. Comput.-Integr. Manuf. **56**, 233–243 (2019)
32. Novitzky, M., Semmens, R., Franck, N.H., Chewar, C.M., Korpela, C.: Virtual reality for immersive human machine teaming with vehicles. In: Chen, J.Y.C., Fragomeni, G. (eds.) HCII 2020. LNCS, vol. 12190, pp. 575–590. Springer, Cham (2020). https://doi.org/10.1007/978-3-030-49695-1_39
33. Palmarini, R., del Amo, I.F., Bertolino, G., Dini, G., Erkoyuncu, J.A., Roy, R., Farnsworth, M.: Designing an ar interface to improve trust in human-robots collaboration. Procedia CIRP **70**, 350–355 (2018)
34. Schmitz, N., Hirth, J., Berns, K.: A simulation framework for human-robot interaction. In: 2010 Third International Conference on Advances in Computer-Human Interactions, pp. 79–84. IEEE (2010)
35. Shi, D., Collins Jr, E.G., Goldiez, B., Donate, A., Liu, X., Dunlap, D.: Human-aware robot motion planning with velocity constraints. In: 2008 International Symposium on Collaborative Technologies and Systems, pp. 490–497 (2008)
36. Shu, B., Sziebig, G., Pieters, R.: Architecture for safe human-robot collaboration: multi-modal communication in virtual reality for efficient task execution, pp. 2297–2302 (2019)
37. Wijnen, L., Bremner, P., Lemaignan, S., Giuliani, M.: Performing human-robot interaction user studies in virtual reality*. In: 29th IEEE International Conference on Robot and Human Interactive Communication (RO-MAN), pp. 794–794 (2020)
38. Yan, H., Ang, M.A., Poo, A.: A survey on perception methods for human-robot interaction in social robots. Int. J. Soc. Rob. **6**, 85–119 (2014)
39. Zacharaki, A., Kostavelis, I., Gasteratos, A., Dokas, I.: Safety bounds in human robot interaction: A survey. Saf. Sci. **127**, 104667 (2020)

Gaze-Based Interaction for Interactive Storytelling in VR

Heiko Drewes$^{(\boxtimes)}$ ⓘ, Evelyn Müller, Sylvia Rothe ⓘ, and Heinrich Hussmann ⓘ

LMU Munich, Munich, Germany
{heiko.drewes,sylvia.rothe,hussmann}@ifi.lmu.de,
Mueller.Evelyn@gmx.de

Abstract. Interactive stories in Virtual Reality need a way of making decisions that influence the further progress of the story. The decision making should be easy and should not disturb the feeling of presence in the virtual world. As many virtual reality glasses come with an integrated eye tracker, it suggests itself to use gaze for making the decisions. We created an interactive story and implemented three different gaze interaction methods, which we evaluated in a user study with 24 participants. The three interaction methods used a dwell-time mechanism, one with a gaze button, one with a texture change of the object looked at, and one method without any feedback. The texture change was the favorite of the users, however, the choice of the interaction method may also depend on the intended dramaturgy and aesthetic aspects of the story.

Keywords: Interactive story telling · Gaze interaction

1 Introduction

Virtual Reality (VR) is a highly immersive technology which aims on giving the users a strong feeling of presence in a virtual world. Interactive storytelling is a method of involving the listener into the story by giving her or him the possibility to make decisions which influence the ongoing of the story. Both, VR and interactive storytelling, have the goal to create a strong, preferably realistic, illusion of being part of a fictional world. Telling an interactive story in VR seems to be a perfect match.

VR and interactive storytelling need ways to interact with the fictional world, which do not destroy the illusion. Among all possible forms of interaction such as with a controller device, voice, or body movements, gaze seems to be a good candidate for this demand. Additionally, many of the newer head-mounted devices (HMDs) come along with an integrated eye tracker.

Therefore we explored how to utilize gaze for decisions in interactive stories told in a VR environment. Within a user study we tested three different interaction methods. All three methods used gaze, either in a more subtle way by interpreting at what participants looked, or actively by requiring them to look at

© Springer Nature Switzerland AG 2021
L. T. De Paolis et al. (Eds.): AVR 2021, LNCS 12980, pp. 91–108, 2021.
https://doi.org/10.1007/978-3-030-87595-4_8

an interaction object for a certain time to trigger a decision. The first method, the *button method*, used labeled buttons, while the other methods used an object from the story world to look at. With the second method the interactive object changes its texture while the user is looking at it and consequently we called this method the *texture method*. The third method, the *invisible method*, interprets the user's gaze, without giving feedback by changing the texture.

Although our research aims for an application in cinematic VR (CVR), a story told in pre-rendered or prerecorded parts, we created an interactive story as animation rendered in real-time and implemented three gaze-based interaction methods. However, to keep the constraints of cinematic VR, the users' position was fixed in one location. We invited 24 participants to our study, where each participant tried all interaction methods and filled questionnaires after the trials.

The user study results show that the button method is easy to understand, but weakens the illusion. The invisible method does not affect the illusion, but is irritating because of loss of control. The texture method seems to be a good compromise between keeping the illusion and keeping control.

2 Related Work

Interactive stories existed already in the analog times, for example as role-playing games[1], there the story progress depends on a process of structured decision-making. In the digital world computer adventure games can be seen as an interactive story. Such adventure games typically have a very high degree of interactivity, which often depends on reaction time, and maybe more a game of skill than an interactive story.

Since the 1960s, filmmakers and researchers have been investigating how films can interact with cinema screens and different types of displays [15]. Interactive stories on the web uses game elements such as solving tasks, collecting points, and giving feedback [1]. The interaction is closely related to engagement: the audience changes their lean-back attitude to a lean-forward attitude. Vosmeer and Schouten introduced the term lean-in medium for CVR [23]: In lean-in media, the direction of view, and thus the seen part of the image, is freely chosen. As a result the user is more active than in classic lean-back media, but remains a spectator.

2.1 Story Structures

Different story structures can be used to create interactive stories [19,20]. The simplest of them, the linear structure, can also be implemented without any interaction and corresponds to the traditional film. However, a linear structure can also be implemented interactively. In contrast to a conventional film, the viewer's interaction determines the speed of the story progress. By expanding the interaction options to include additional interactive regions, non-linear storylines are possible. If the viewer looks at a certain region, the film continues with a connected scene.

---

[1] https://www.goodreads.com/genres/role-playing-games.

2.2 Interaction

The term interaction is used in different fields with different meanings. This paper looks at interactions between people and a digital story that is implemented for using a HMD. The selection of the image section by looking around is a very natural type of interaction: the user's head movements are analyzed by the sensors of the HMD and the corresponding image section is displayed, just as the user is used to from the real world.

Interaction techniques in VR are divided into navigation (change of location), selection (selection of objects), manipulation (change of objects) [2]. In CVR the user cannot walk, move or modulate objects. The main interactions in CVR are looking around and selecting areas. Most CVR films are currently linear, even if the additional spatial component is predestined for non-linear story structures. Interactive stories depending on the direction of view can be a natural interaction without restricting the freedom of the viewer. This requires selection techniques with which the viewer can intentionally or unintentionally select regions [16,17].

2.3 Selection Techniques in VR

Various studies have been carried out in recent years on the selection of objects in VR environments. Head and eye movements, gestures and sensor data can be used for selection processes. Most of these methods have been developed for VR environments with six degrees of freedom (DoF) and require careful examination of whether they are also suitable for CVR where only three DoFs exist. Some of these techniques focus on the accuracy of pointing or on performing tasks. Such criteria are often less important for CVR, since the focus is a pleasant film experience.

Nukarinen et al. [11] compared raycasting (using a beam emanating from the controller as a pointer) with two gaze-based selection techniques. In their experiments, the ray cast method followed the controller direction and pressing the controller button triggered the event. The two gaze-based methods differ in the release technique, one method being triggered by the controller button and the other by dwell time. In their study, the beam performed better than the gaze methods and the gaze with additional button better than the dwell time.

Kallioniemi et al. [9] examined different types of selection for hotspots: dwell time and immediate fade in. The immediate fade-in of the next scene started automatically when the head pointed in the direction of a hotspot. In their experiments, the fade-in with large symbols performed best. Qian and Teather [12] compared gaze- and head-based techniques. The head-based selection was faster, more accurate, and offered a better user experience.

2.4 Eye-Based Interaction

There are different ways to use the eyes in human-computer communication. Jacob [7,8] examined gaze-based interaction techniques using dwell-time. The user has to look at an interaction object for a certain time, the dwell-time.

With a short dwell-time this interaction method carries the risk of accidentally triggering events, e.g. when a viewer inspects an area for a long time. Jacob called this effect, the unwanted activation of commands, the Midas Touch effect [7,8].

Further gaze interaction methods like gaze gestures [4] or smooth pursuit eye movements [22] seem not suitable for gaze interaction in interactive storytelling. Both methods do not need calibration, but this advantage is not important for a personal HMD. Gaze gestures are far away from being intuitive, need instructions, and are much less natural than looking at something. Smooth pursuits are a natural eye movement, but need moving interaction objects. Moving objects are not a problem in a movie, however, reliable smooth pursuit detection requires a minimum speed of 5°/s [3], which is relatively high. Our experiments with smooth pursuit detection in 2D videos were discouraging, mostly because there are not many moving targets in a 2D video as typically the camera follows moving objects. Although this might be different for CVR content we decided to stick on the dwell-time method for our study.

3   Prototype

3.1   Story

We created an interactive story to test different interaction methods for the decisions within the story. We implemented the story in Unity[2] with C# scripts, Blender, Photoshop, and Audacity[3]. As this research aims on cinematic virtual reality, the viewer of the story stays in a fixed location. Within a 3D animation solution it is easy to identify at which object the user looks. With a real video it would be necessary to provide a mapping of the interactive objects to regions over time.

The story plays on a spaceship where an one-eyed alien wants to do a coffee break and gets interrupted by an alarm caused by the cat (see Fig. 1). In the story progress the alien has to make decisions on how to deal with the problem.

Everything happens in the alien's relaxation room (see Fig. 2), where the character has access to two vending machines (coffee and strawberry milkshakes), various monitors, a maintenance hatch, an alarm, some objects for the cat and a cozy corner. Figure 2 also shows the positions of buttons, which were used for the button interaction method.

The story consists of six sections with a decision at the end of the first five sections and three possible ends - the alien finds the cat as the source of the problem (end 1), the alien calls the break-down service (end 2), the alien heads for a space ship garage (end 3). There are seven different paths through the story which lead to seven different comments (a–g) from the alien at the end (see Fig. 3).

---

[2] https://unity.com.
[3] https://www.audacity.de/.

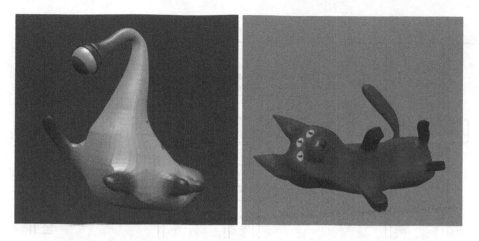

Fig. 1. An alien (left) is the main character of the interactive story. The cat (right) caused a malfunction of the spaceship.

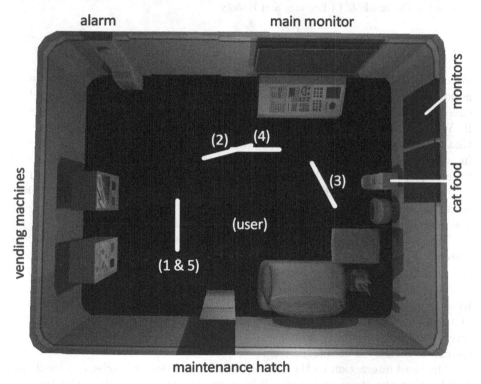

Fig. 2. Positions of objects, user and (if chosen) buttons for all decisions (1–5)

The story has a branching structure with optional scenes. All links occur between narrative nodes and are therefore external according to Reyes [13]. There is no exploratorium in the sense of Vesterby et al. [21].

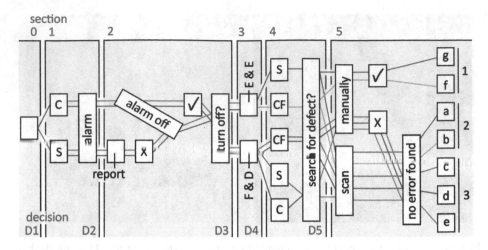

Fig. 3. Structure of the interactive story. S: Strawberry, C: Coffee, CF: Cat food, F & D: Food & Drinks, E & E: Engines and Energy

3.2 Interaction Methods

We decided to use three different gaze-based interaction methods. The first interaction method is a typical gaze button using the dwell time method and therefore called *button method*. For feedback the button fills with color while looking at it. While blinking with the eyes the filling stops for at most 150 ms, and after that, or when looking somewhere else, the button drains. A complete fill without interruption needs two seconds, which is quite long for a dwell time. A long dwell time helps to avoid the Midas Touch effect [7]. Ia a CVR context, and in contrast to eye typing, the users have to interact only few times and a long dwell time seems to be justified. Additionally, we placed a button label as a caption above the button. The appearance of the gaze button is depicted in Fig. 4.

The second interaction method works similar to the gaze button, however instead of looking at a button the users have to look at an object. We realized the feedback by a changing texture of the interactive object and therefore call the method *texture method*. In our prototype we changed the colors of the objects to blue or red (see Fig. 5). In contrast to the button method there is no labeling of the possibilities, and consequently it is not obvious to the users what the interaction objects are. A user has to look at an object and wait for a texture change to identify it as interactive.

The third interaction method is very subtle, as it does not offer any feedback, besides that the story progresses differently. Therefore we call it the *invisible method*. During a decision period this method measures for how long the user looks at each decision object. If they look at an object multiple times, all duration measurements are added up. The decision period ends, if either the gaze has been on relevant objects for at least three seconds, or if the elapsed time exceeded the maximum duration of five seconds. After that, the object with a higher gaze

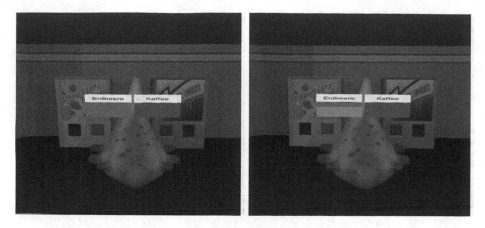

Fig. 4. Button method: The gaze button fills from the bottom while looking at it, in this case the left button. When the button is filled completely the decision is done.

duration during the decision period gets selected. If the user did not look at any interaction object, the invisible method selects the object at which the user looked the most since the story started.

3.3   Hard- and Software

The hardware for the prototype consisted of a laptop (Acer Aspire A715-74G), headphones (VIVANCO 34877 COL 400) and a VR head-mounted display (FOVE[4]).

4   User Study

4.1   User Study Design

We decided to use a within-group design for the study so that every participant tested all of the three interaction methods and we could ask everybody about her or his opinion on every method. The participants watched the story three times and therefore had the opportunity to try different paths through the story.

We designed a questionnaire with questions on demographic data and possible debility of sight, experiences with virtual reality similar to the IFcVR questionnaire of Reyes et al. [14], questions on the interaction method, and a selection of questions from commonly accepted questionnaires. These questionnaires were the igroup presence questionnaire IPQ[5] with one question each for spatial presence, involvement, and experienced realism, the user experience

---

[4] https://fove-inc.com/product/.
[5] http://igroup.org/pq/ipq/download.php.

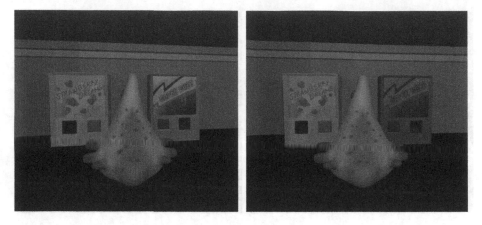

Fig. 5. Texture method: While looking at an object, the object's texture changes. Here it is the coffee vending machine in the right picture.

questionnaire UEQ-S[6], subjective task workload NASA-TLX [5,6], and simulator sickness questionnaire [10]. Additionally, inspired by Reyes et al. [14], we asked about autonomy, effectance, and believability. This part of the questionnaire had to be filled after each experienced interaction method and this was the reason why we used only a shortened version of the standard questionnaires.

4.2   Conducting the User Study

On arrival every participant got a printed information on the study and were told that their gaze will have influence on the ongoing of the story. Then the FOVE was calibrated on the participant and the calibration success was checked with a sample scene supplied by FOVE. After this the participants filled a consent form and the demographic part of the questionnaire.

In the next step the participants watched the story three times, each time with a different interaction method and a new calibration. We changed the six possible orders of interaction methods from participant to participant to eliminate possible learning effects. After each round the participants filled the questionnaire. Finally we asked the participants which interaction method they liked best.

5   Results

5.1   Demographic Data

We recruited 24 participants, 18 (75%) female and 6 (25%) male persons, in the age from 19 to 63 years (Mean: 28.6) for the user study. Eleven (45.8%) persons

---

[6] https://www.ueq-online.org/.

wore glasses or contact lenses. One third of the participants stated that they have no experiences with virtual reality, two persons were experienced in VR, and the rest stated that they have little experiences. Three quarters of the participants had no experience with eye trackers and the remaining quarter had only little experience.

5.2 Paths Through the Story

The average story time including the time for interaction was 4 min and 20 s. The story had three possible ends as explained in Sect. 3.1. Random decisions lead to end 3 with 50% and with 25% to end 1 or end 2. Figure 6 shows the distribution of reached ends for all three runs and Fig. 7 for the first run only.

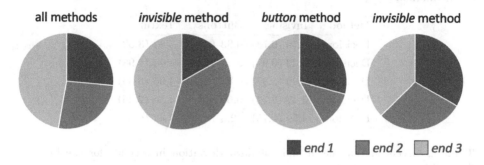

Fig. 6. Reached story end over all participants for three runs.

Table 1 shows the mean decision times and standard deviations for each inter-action method for all runs and Table 2 only for the first run. The mean decision times for the first run are longer than the mean decision times for all runs. This means there is a learning effect, however this might be by learning the story and not necessarily by learning the interaction method.

5.3 Questionnaire

The questionnaire used Likert scales for the answers. As this scale is non-parametric we used Friedman tests with a post-hoc Conover squared ranks test to calculate whether there are significant differences between the interaction methods (with a significance level $\alpha = 0.05$). The calculation where done with JASP[7].

Presence. Figure 8 shows the results for presence on a 7-point Likert scale. We could not find significant differences for presence. It seems that the interaction method does not affect the feeling of presence.

---

[7] https://jasp-stats.org/.

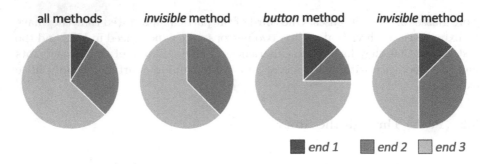

Fig. 7. Reached story end over all participants in the first run.

Table 1. Decision time mean and standard deviation in seconds for all runs depending on the method

Method	Invisible	Buttons	Texture
Decision 1	3.79 (0.73)	6.83 (6.32)	5.82 (3.62)
Decision 2	4.32 (0.95)	8.23 (12.7)	6.48 (4.98)
Decision 3	3.90 (0.87)	4.87 (2.71)	4.95 (6.39)
Decision 4	4.47 (0.73)	9.68 (14.2)	4.56 (2.35)
Decision 5	4.59 (0.75)	12.4 (8.33)	7.44 (6.35)

Table 2. Decision time mean and standard deviation in seconds for the first run depending on the method

Method	Invisible	Buttons	Texture
Decision 1	3.87 (0.79)	8.89 (9.87)	7.02 (4.25)
Decision 2	4.82 (0.59)	6.65 (2.21)	11.5 (5.46)
Decision 3	4.16 (0.83)	4.96 (2.47)	3.37 (0.97)
Decision 4	4.60 (0.58)	6.96 (4.02)	3.89 (1.40)
Decision 5	5.01 (0.09)	16.5 (11.7)	9.14 (8.61)

User Experience. We evaluated the shortened version of the user experience questionnaire with the data analysis tools provided by the UEQ website[8]. Figure 9 shows the results on the 7-point Likert scales. In total the invisible method (Mean: 4.82—SD: 0.97) was significantly worse than the texture method (Mean: 5.69—SD: 0.81—$p_{Conover} < 0.001$) and the button method (Mean: 5.39—SD: 0.97—$p_{Conover} = 0.010$).

The UEQ's data analysis tools distinguish pragmatic and hedonic qualities, The first four questions in our shortened questionnaire were pragmatic and the last four questions were hedonic. All interaction methods got positive values

---

[8] https://www.ueq-online.org.

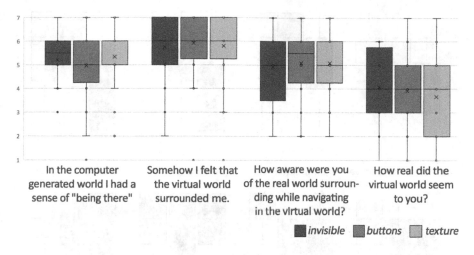

Fig. 8. Results of the presence questionnaire (1: negative, 7: positive).

for both qualities, except the pragmatic quality of the invisible method, which evaluated to neutral.

Workload. We used the NASA-TLX [5,6] to measure the participants' work-load. Figure 10 shows the results. The evaluation with a Friedman and a Conover Post Hoc test on a 5% significance level did not reveal any significant difference for the three interaction methods, except for frustration. The users' frustration for the invisible method (Mean: 35.21—SD: 27.63) was significantly bigger for the texture method (Mean: 18.96—SD: 17.26—$p_{Conover} = 0.032$) and for the button method (Mean: 15.0—SD: 14.14—$p_{Conover} = 0.001$).

Further Questions. Further questions on a Likert scale from 1 to 7 aimed on how users experienced the study. Figure 11 summarizes the results. Again we used a Friedman and a Conover post hoc test for the analysis.

There were no significant differences for the three methods for the question whether the story was comprehensible, and also for the question whether the users would like to watch further stories using this interaction method.

For the question whether the participants felt they had control over the story we found significant worse judgment for the invisible method (Mean: 4.13—SD: 2.01) against the button method (Mean: 5.83—SD: 1.57—$p_{Conover} = 0.003$) and the texture method (Mean: 5.96—SD: 1.21—$p_{Conover} = 0.002$).

Also for the question on whether the system correctly registered the users' decisions the invisible method (Mean: 5.0—SD: 2.31) was significantly judged worse than the button method (Mean: 6.63—SD: 1.22—$p_{Conover} = 0.001$) and the texture method (Mean: 6.63—SD: 1.25—$p_{Conover} < 0.001$).

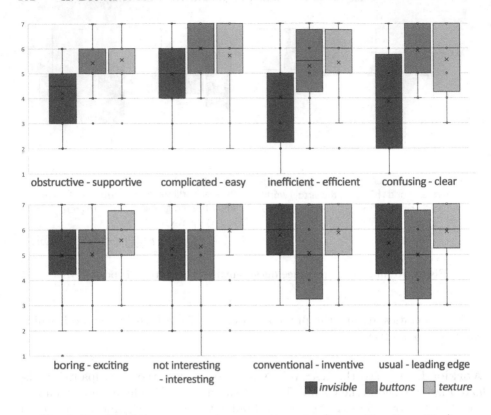

Fig. 9. Results of the user experience questionnaire (1: negative, 7: positive)

The question whether the users are always aware of all possible choices showed a significance for the button method (Mean: 6.46—SD: 1.29—$p_{Conover}$ = 0.002) against the invisible method (Mean: 4.88—SD: 2.13) but not for the texture method (Mean: 6.13—SD: 1.30).

Finally the users perceived the texture method (Mean: 6.42—SD: 0.76—$p_{Conover}$ < 0.001) and the button method (Mean: 6.41—SD: 0.81—$p_{Conover}$ < 0.001) as more intuitive than the invisible method (Mean: 4.29—SD: 1.95).

We evaluated the results for the first run with a Kruskal-Wallis test with Dunn post hoc test as this test works for unpaired data. Already for the data from the first run only we found significant differences for the question on whether the system correctly registered the users' decisions, where the invisible method (Mean: 4.88—SD: 2.37) was rated lower than the button method (Mean: 6.88—SD: 0.33—p_{Dunn} = 0.009) and the texture method (Mean: 7.00—SD: 0—p_{Dunn} = 0.007) and for the question how intuitive are the methods, where the texture method (Mean: 6.75—SD: 0.43—p_{Dunn} = 0.021) was judged significantly more intuitive than the invisible method (A: 4.875—SD: 1.83).

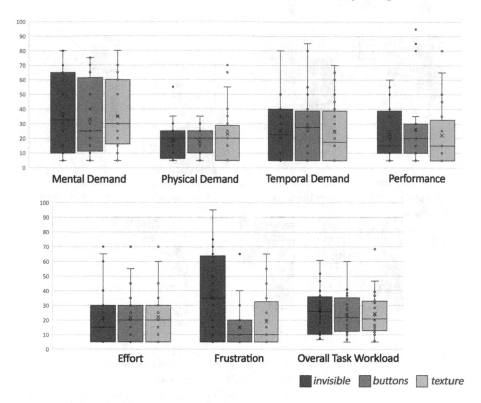

Fig. 10. Results of the NASA-TLX questionnaire for the three interaction methods.

User Opinion. In the last questionnaire after the users tried all interaction methods we asked the users which method they liked best, which method was least interrupting, and which method was the easiest interaction. Figure 12 shows the results.

6   Discussion and Limitations

We found several differences between the methods. The button method is easiest to understand for the users. It reveals all possible choices for a decision, has explanatory texts, and it is clear that the story waits for a decision. The texture method has no explanatory texts and the story has to communicate that it expects a decision. The possible options have to be discovered by the user by searching for objects which give feedback. The invisible method is confusing for the user.

The result that the form of interaction does not significantly influence the feeling of presence was surprising in the first moment. The reason is that there is a difference between the feeling of being present in a virtual world and the illusion of being in a real world. The appearance of a button levitating in space

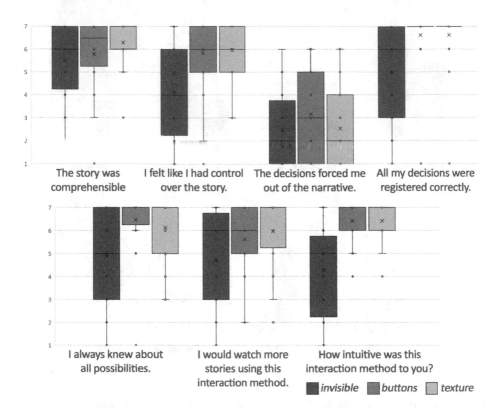

Fig. 11. Results of further questions on how users experienced the study.

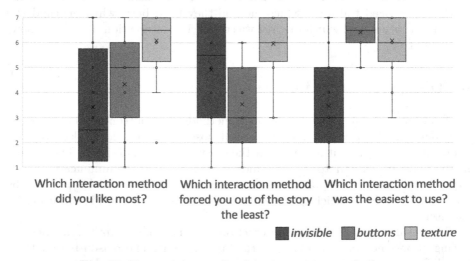

Fig. 12. User opinion on the three interaction methods.

contradicts experiences from the real world, but does not affect the perception of the three-dimensional space. The user still feels to be present in a virtual world, but not in a real world.

The button method interrupts the story and destroys the feeling of being in a real world. To mitigate the effect the button design should match the style of the story, what is very common in 3D computer games, or could even be a part of the storyworld (diegetic). In the user study's story, buttons could be on the spaceship's control console. However, depending on the story, such solution is not always possible, especially as it is not possible to move inside cinematic VR.

The invisible method does not disturb the story at all and consequently keeps the illusion, but for the price that the user may not even be aware of her or his decision. Within a user study, where the users have the feeling that they have to fulfill a task, the invisible method creates a feeling of failure. However, if the story maker sells the story as a sequence of riddles, the perception will be different. It will lead also to a more exploratory way of looking at the scenes.

The texture method seems to be a good compromise for keeping the illusion and at the same time enables control over decisions. However, a changing texture is something that does not happen in reality and therefore still flaws the illusion. A form of feedback which does not contradict real world experiences is preferable. For example an actress or actor could turn towards the observer when looking long enough at her or him, or an indicator light could start blinking when looking at the coffee vending machine. However, such solutions for feedback depends heavily on the story and are hard to generalize.

The texture method is only one representative for a more general class of interaction methods. In this class the interaction takes place by an diegetic object that belongs to the story, which gives feedback. There are many possible ways to provide this feedback. For example instead of changing the texture it is also possible to let the object glow or give it a halo. The answer to the question which feedback works best depends on the story and the context.

Our results are in accordance with the research of Vesterby et al. [21] for stories presented on a 2D screen. However, in the context of VR the loss of the illusion weights much more. It can be seen as a limitation of our study, that the story was a rendered animation and not a real video. A real video creates a more realistic illusion and the button method may destruct the illusion even more than in an animation.

7 Future Work

The interaction objects in our study did not move. It is unclear whether moving objects or subjects are suitable for interaction. On one hand following a character leaving the scene with the gaze is natural, signals interest in this character, and could be taken as a decision. On the other hand such a situation limits the time to make the decision. Alternatively, the movement of an interactive object could stay within the scene of a 360° movie but leave the field of view. Following the object by turning the head to keep the object in the view could be the required action for decision making. It is also possible to have a moving interaction object which stays in the field of view and the viewer makes the decision by following the moving object. Questions on the speed range and the predictability of the movement trajectory and their influence on the user experience are not answered yet.

New HMDs have integrated trackers which report the exact position of all fingers. This allows to control an interactive story with hand gestures such as pointing with the index finger. Such gestures are as natural as gaze movements and open further possibilities which needs further research

With volumetric video [18] a new media technology is already on the horizon. With this technology the borders between 3D computer games and interactive stories dissolve. In a volumetric video the watching person can move within the presented world, which is not possible in cinematic VR. This has consequences for interaction design. For the button method it means that the buttons have to be placed within the proximity of the spectator. For the texture and the invisible method the diegetic interaction object changes the (angular) size depending on the user's position. It may be necessary to be close to the object to interact with it and make a decision for the story that way. Additionally, it may make a difference from which direction, means from the front or the backside, a user looks at the interaction object.

8   Conclusion

The work analyzes the behavior of viewers and shows different aspects that should be taken into account in interactive stories. We compared three gaze-based methods, which do not require any additional devices for input. For the investigated scenario, the viewers preferred to be informed about the decision possibilities. They favored methods in which they can actively influence the decision-making process. If possible, the feedback should be embedded in the story, e.g. by changing the texture, which was used in this work. The opportunities for interaction that remain hidden from the user and are triggered due to their gaze behavior, without the viewer being actively involved in this decision, led to lower acceptance.

This work is a first step to find methods to facilitate the realization of interactive stories in VR that support the user in exploring the story in such a way that the story is not disturbed.

References

1. Argyriou, L., Economou, D., Bouki, V., Doumanis, I.: Engaging immersive video consumers: challenges regarding 360-degree gamified video applications. In: 2016 15th International Conference on Ubiquitous Computing and Communications and 2016 International Symposium on Cyberspace and Security (IUCC-CSS), pp. 145–152 (2016). https://doi.org/10.1109/IUCC-CSS.2016.028

2. Bowman, D.A., Kruijff, E., LaViola, J.J., Poupyrev, I.: An introduction to 3-d user interface design. Presence Teleoperators Virtual Environ. **10**, 96–108 (2001). https://doi.org/10.1162/105474601750182342. http://www.mitpressjournals.org/doi/10.1162/105474601750182342

3. Drewes, H., Khamis, M., Alt, F.: Smooth pursuit target speeds and trajectories. In: Proceedings of the 17th International Conference on Mobile and Ubiquitous Multimedia, MUM 2018, pp. 139–146. ACM, New York (2018). https://doi.org/10.1145/3282894.3282913. http://doi.acm.org/10.1145/3282894.3282913

4. Drewes, H., Schmidt, A.: Interacting with the computer using gaze gestures. In: Baranauskas, C., Palanque, P., Abascal, J., Barbosa, S.D.J. (eds.) INTERACT 2007. LNCS, vol. 4663, pp. 475–488. Springer, Heidelberg (2007). https://doi.org/10.1007/978-3-540-74800-7_43   http://dl.acm.org/citation.cfm?id=1778331.1778385

5. Hart, S.G.: Nasa-Task Load Index (NASA-TLX); 20 years later. In: Proceedings of the Human Factors and Ergonomics Society Annual Meeting, vol. 50, no. 9, pp. 904–908 (2006). https://doi.org/10.1177/154193120605000909

6. Hart, S.G., Staveland, L.E.: Development of NASA-TLX (Task Load Index): results of empirical and theoretical research. In: Hancock, P.A., Meshkati, N. (eds.) Advances in Psychology: Human Mental Workload, vol. 52, pp. 139–183. North-Holland (1988). https://doi.org/10.1016/S0166-4115(08)62386-9. http://www.sciencedirect.com/science/article/pii/S0166411508623869

7. Jacob, R.J.K.: What you look at is what you get: eye movement-based interaction techniques. In: Proceedings of the SIGCHI Conference on Human Factors in Computing Systems, CHI 1990, pp. 11–18. Association for Computing Machinery, New York (1990). https://doi.org/10.1145/97243.97246. https://doi.org/10.1145/97243.97246

8. Jacob, R.J.K.: The use of eye movements in human-computer interaction techniques: what you look at is what you get. ACM Trans. Inf. Syst. **9**, 152–169 (1991). https://doi.org/10.1145/123078.128728. http://portal.acm.org/citation.cfm?doid=123078.128728

9. Kallioniemi, P., et al.: Hotspot interaction in omnidirectional videos using head-mounted displays. In: Proceedings of the 22nd International Academic Mindtrek Conference, Mindtrek 2018, pp. 126–134. Association for Computing Machinery, New York (2018). https://doi.org/10.1145/3275116.3275148. https://doi.org/10.1145/3275116.3275148

10. Kennedy, R.S., Lane, N.E., Berbaum, K.S., Lilienthal, M.G.: Simulator sickness questionnaire: an enhanced method for quantifying simulator sickness. Int. J. Aviat. Psychol. **3**(3), 203–220 (1993). https://doi.org/10.1207/s15327108ijap0303_3

11. Nukarinen, T., Kangas, J., Rantala, J., Koskinen, O., Raisamo, R.: Evaluating ray casting and two gaze-based pointing techniques for object selection in virtual reality. In: Proceedings of the 24th ACM Symposium on Virtual Reality Software and Technology, VRST 2018. Association for Computing Machinery, New York (2018). https://doi.org/10.1145/3281505.3283382. https://doi.org/10.1145/3281505.3283382

12. Qian, Y.Y., Teather, R.J.: The eyes don't have it: an empirical comparison of head-based and eye-based selection in virtual reality. In: Simeone, A.L. (ed.) Proceedings of the 5th Symposium on Spatial User Interaction, Brighton, UK, pp. 91–98. ACM (2017). https://doi.org/10.1145/3131277.3132182

13. Reyes, M.C.: Screenwriting framework for an interactive virtual reality film. In: Online proceedings of the 3rd Immersive Learning Research Network, Coimbra, Portugal (2017). https://doi.org/10.3217/978-3-85125-530-0-15
14. Reyes, M.C.: Measuring user experience on interactive fiction in cinematic virtual reality. In: Rouse, R., Koenitz, H., Haahr, M. (eds.) ICIDS 2018. LNCS, vol. 11318, pp. 295–307. Springer, Cham (2018). https://doi.org/10.1007/978-3-030-04028-4_33
15. Roth, C.: Experiencing interactive storytelling. Ph.D. thesis, Vrije Universiteit Amsterdam, January 2015. http://dare.ubvu.vu.nl/handle/1871/53840
16. Rothe, S., Hussmann, H.: Spaceline: a concept for interaction in cinematic virtual reality. In: Cardona-Rivera, R.E., Sullivan, A., Young, R.M. (eds.) ICIDS 2019. LNCS, vol. 11869, pp. 115–119. Springer, Cham (2019). https://doi.org/10.1007/978-3-030-33894-7_12
17. Rothe, S., Pothmann, P., Drewes, H., Hussmann, H.: Interaction techniques for cinematic virtual reality. In: Teather, R., Itoh, Y., Gabbard, J. (eds.) Proceedings, 26th IEEE Conference on Virtual Reality and 3D User Interfaces, Osaka, Japan, pp. 1733–1737. IEEE (2019). https://doi.org/10.1109/VR.2019.8798189
18. Schreer, O., et al.: Lessons learned during one year of commercial volumetric video production. SMPTE Motion Imaging J. **129**(9), 31–37 (2020). https://doi.org/10.5594/JMI.2020.3010399
19. Tanak, N.: Interactive Cinema. MediaLAB Amsterdam (2015)
20. Verdugo, R., Nussbaum, M., Corro, P., Nuñnez, P., Navarrete, P.: Interactive films and coconstruction. ACM Trans. Multimedia Comput. Commun. Appl. **7**, 1–24 (2011). https://doi.org/10.1145/2043612.2043617. http://dl.acm.org/citation.cfm?doid=2043612.2043617
21. Vesterby, T., Voss, J.C., Hansen, J.P., Glenstrup, A.J., Hansen, D.W., Rudolph, M.: Gaze-guided viewing of interactive movies. Digital Creativity **16**(4), 193–204 (2005). https://doi.org/10.1080/14626260500476523
22. Vidal, M., Bulling, A., Gellersen, H.: Pursuits: spontaneous interaction with displays based on smooth pursuit eye movement and moving targets. In: Proceedings of the 2013 ACM International Joint Conference on Pervasive and Ubiquitous Computing, UbiComp 2013, pp. 439–448. ACM, New York (2013). https://doi.org/10.1145/2493432.2493477. http://doi.acm.org/10.1145/2493432.2493477
23. Vosmeer, M., Schouten, B.: Interactive cinema: engagement and interaction. In: Mitchell, A., Fernández-Vara, C., Thue, D. (eds.) ICIDS 2014. LNCS, vol. 8832, pp. 140–147. Springer, Cham (2014). https://doi.org/10.1007/978-3-319-12337-0_14

An Automatic 3D Scene Generation Pipeline Based on a Single 2D Image

Alberto Cannavò[1]([✉]) [ID], Christian Bardella[1], Lorenzo Semeraro[1],
Federico De Lorenzis[1], Congyi Zhang[2] [ID], Ying Jiang[2],
and Fabrizio Lamberti[1] [ID]

[1] Politecnico di Torino, Corso Duca degli Abruzzi 24, Torino, Italy
{alberto.cannavo,christian.bardella,lorenzo.semeraro,federico.delorenzis,
fabrizio.lamberti}@polito.it
[2] The University of Hong Kong, Pokfulam Road, Hong Kong, China
cyzhang@cs.hku.hk, yingjiang@connect.hku.hk

Abstract. In the last years, solutions were proposed in the literature to alleviate the complexity of using sophisticated graphic suites for 3D scene generation by leveraging automatic tools. The most common approach based on the processing of text descriptions, however, may not represent the ideal solution, e.g., for fast prototyping purposes. This paper proposes an alternative methodology able to extract information about the objects and the layout of the scene to be created from a single 2D image. Compared to previous works, experimental results reported in this work show improvements in terms of similarity between the 2D and 3D scenes.

Keywords: Image-based modelling · Scene-object modelling · Machine learning

1 Introduction

Today, the commonly used software to generate graphics assets are suites, such as Blender[1], and Autodesk Maya[2], since they provide a number of functionalities and tools that allow users to produce 3D animated scenes [10]. Although these suites are generally characterized by a higher degree of flexibility in terms of available features, they also present a very steep learning curve [8]. Difficulties in learning such software prevent unskilled users to operate with them or, more in general, make the generation of 3D contents a time-consuming task requiring a lot of effort even for professional users [2].

One of the most common operation being performed with such suites is represented by the objects' layout. Although the commands to move and rotate objects are generally simple to activate, the standard input interfaces to control

---

This work has been supported by VR@POLITO initiative.
[1] Blender: https://www.blender.org/.
[2] Autodesk Maya: https://www.autodesk.com/products/maya/overview.

L. T. De Paolis et al. (Eds.): AVR 2021, LNCS 12980, pp. 109–117, 2021.
https://doi.org/10.1007/978-3-030-87595-4_9

the transformations are based on mouse and keyboard. Therefore, users can handle only two degrees of freedom at a time, resulting in an increase of the users' mental effort [3]. As a consequence, the scenes generated by unskilled users are generally unrealistically simple [14]. However, operating with such software is becoming inescapable for non-professional users [5], e.g., to share a prototypical idea of 3D scenes that can be later used by experts to build the ultimate version.

In order to overcome these limitations, the literature proposed a number of solutions able to automatically reconstruct 3D scenes by processing, e.g., text [4], images [1] and audio clips [19]. The high number of works based on text descriptions (e.g. [4,5]) suggests that this approach represents the most common solution. However, in the case of fast prototyping, it may not be the ideal solution, since the need to write the entire description of the scenes can slow down the process [1]. Leveraging a simple 2D image (e.g. a sketch or a photo) of the desired scene could be significantly faster than writing a text description. Image-based approaches introduce a number of new challenges in the understanding of the input regarding, for example, the need to infer/detect objects to model them individually, solve the depth ambiguity to correctly place objects, recognize relationships among objects, etc. To cope with the above issues, this paper proposes a methodology that breaks down the complexity of the overall process into a number of simpler steps. The main idea is to leverage information regarding the camera framing the scene (e.g. point of view, perspectives cues, relative positions of the objects in the view, etc.) to generate a similar layout in the reconstructed environment. Machine learning algorithms complement this methodology to infer the number and types of objects as well as determining the distance from the camera.

Moreover, differently from solutions presented in the literature, which were usually implemented as standalone applications, the proposed pipeline is integrated within a traditional graphics suite. Besides the possibility to improve the quality of the generated scene by leveraging the sophisticated methods embedded in the software, the integration allows users to explore scenes into an immersive environment using virtual reality technologies, thus helping them to better understand the scene layout. The integration within a traditional software suite was made possible by developing a dedicated add-on that can be installed into the open-source 3D graphics software named Blender. The add-on is also released as open-source at https://github.com/logicesecutor/3D_scene_generator.

In order to assess the effectiveness of the proposed system it was compared with a previous work [1]. Results showed promising improvements in terms of scene similarity.

2   Related Works

Different solutions have been proposed to solve the problem of generating 3D graphics assets from 2D images. For example, in [13] perspective cues, such as perspective lines or distorted planes, identified within a single 2D image, are leveraged to reconstruct both indoor and outdoor environments as a combination of flat textured planes represent walls, floor, and ceiling. Another example is reported in [6], which describes a number of tools developed for Matlab to reconstruct a 3D environment from multiple calibrated images. With respect to the previous work in [6] the shapes of the objects identified in the images are preserved. However, the resulting 3D scene is built as a single high-poly mesh. This approach, named photogrammetry, may be considered not the ideal solution for fast prototyping, since the high number of vertices in the resulting mesh could make it difficult to apply changes or further operate with it. In [11] a neural network was introduced for recognizing and reconstruct boxes and spheres identified into the 2D image provided as input to the network. Although this approach partially solves the issue regarding the shape of the objects, the poor flexibility related to the limited set of recognized objects could represent a weakness for general-purpose applications.

The works reviewed so far described systems and tools developed as standalone applications not integrated into existing 3D graphics software. However, in the context of fast prototyping, the integration with such software can allow expert developers to further edit on the generated scenes seamlessly without the need for additional import/export operations.

To the best of the authors' knowledge, a few works were reported in the literature that are able to generate 3D scenes from single 2D images that is already integrated into a graphics suite. An example is the add-on for Blender proposed in [1]. The environment automatically built with this tool can be explored and modified into an immersive environment. However, in this work, the positions of the objects in the source image and their relations were not considered in the generation of the scenes. The layout was generated automatically through a probabilistic method, that could introduce significant differences in the objects positioning.

Moving from the above review, a system is proposed able to automatically generate 3D scene from its 2D representation. The idea was to leverage information extracted from the source image not only to infer the number and types of objects but also to understand their positions and relations in the environment. The tool is integrated within a well-known suite for enabling further editing.

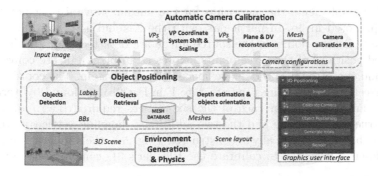

Fig. 1. System architecture.

3 System Overview

The overall architecture of the system is illustrated in Fig. 1. The expected work-flow starts with the selection of the source image used as input to the following steps. By analyzing this image, a number of data are inferred, i.e., information of the camera framing the environment represented in the 2D image and the objects identified in the scene. These data are then combined in order to recon-struct the 3D environment (more details on each step will be provided in the remaining part of this section).

The entire workflow is integrated within the well-known 3D computer graph-ics software (Blender). After the installation of the proposed add-on, a graphical user interface is shown in Blender's 3D Viewport Editor to let users select images and start the elaboration as shown in Fig. 1. Once the 3D scene has been gener-ated, the user can apply further changes by using the functionalities of Blender and explore the scene into an immersive environment by means of Blender's native add-on that enables the VR visualization.

3.1 Automatic Camera Calibration

The main objective of this step is to calibrate the Blender's camera to match as much as possible the external and internal parameters of the camera framing the scene represented in the 2D image. In particular, the main idea behind the camera calibration is to look at the scene with the same camera setting used to obtain the source image in order to extract the relative positions of the objects in the scene and their relationship. To this aim, the add-on Camera Calibration PVR[3] was used. The add-on matches the Blender's 3D Camera to the perspec-tive observed in the source image. As requirements, the user has to manually shape the mesh of a plane to match the perspective lines and add two dangling vertices corresponding to perpendicular lines observed in the image. An exam-ple of a valid input is shown in Fig. 2a. In order to automate this process, the Camera Calibration PVR add-on was integrated within the proposed system and its functionalities were combined with a further library, i.e., XiaohuLuVPDetec-tion[4], that implements the algorithm for the automatic vanishing points esti-mation proposed in [9]. In particular, with the XiaohuLuVPDetection library, the three vanishing points in the source image are detected (Fig. 2b). Then the computed positions of the three points, expressed in pixel unit are converted in meters and expressed into the image space reference system. The coordinates of the intersection between lines (points A to F in Fig. 2b) are found by iteratively solving a linear system for each of the six vertices required (i.e., four vertices for constructing the plane and the two additional dangling vertices). Once the plane has been automatically reconstructed (Fig. 2c), the Camera Calibration PVR add-on is executed to calibrate the Blender's 3D camera. The operations

---

[3] Camera Calibration PVR: https://github.com/mrossini-ethz/camera-calibration-pvr.

[4] XiaohuLuVPDetection: https://github.com/rayryeng/XiaohuLuVPDetection.

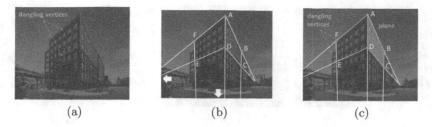

(a)   (b)   (c)

Fig. 2. Automatic camera calibration: a) dangling vertices, b) vanishing points, c) reconstructed plane.

described above are totally transparent to the user, who is only asked to click on the "Calibrate Camera" button Fig. 1 to automatically execute the entire calibration process.

3.2 Object Positioning

By clicking on the "Object Positioning" button, the system automatically extracts objects from the source image and places them into the environment according to a number of rules detailed in the following. A Convolutional Neural Network (CNN) is used to extract from the source image the labels and the bounding boxes (BBs) of the objects detected in the environment. To this aim, the open-source python library Image AI[5] was considered, since it offers a number of reproducible machine learning algorithms for image prediction, object detection, video object tracking, etc. Object detection is supported using three models, i.e., RetinaNet, YOLOv3 and TinyYOLOv3, trained on COCO dataset[6]. The YOLOv3 model was selected for its performance in terms of computation time, however, in the future, more advanced or custom models could be leveraged to improve the quality of the recognition. Moreover, fine-tuning on a specialized custom dataset could be applied to reduce the error-rate and increase the number of labels extracted from the source image. The labels are leveraged to search corresponding 3D models in the mesh database. The mesh database contains 50 models, covering all the possible labels that can be extracted from the source image with the considered CNN. Besides the 3D geometry, the database also memorizes materials, textures, physical properties, and baked animations. A number of alternative models are also provided in the database to avoid repetitions in case of labels recognized multiple times. The BBs are leveraged by the Object Retrieval block to extract from the source image the RGB color picked at the center of the BB. The RGB values are used to edit the default shader of the 3D objects to make it assume a base color similar to that observed in the source image.

Once all the models are retrieved from the database, their positions are adjusted in the 3D environment to match the center of the BB detected in the

---

[5] Image AI: https://github.com/OlafenwaMoses/ImageAI.
[6] COCO dataset: https://cocodataset.org/#home.

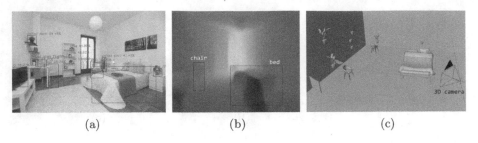

(a)   (b)   (c)

Fig. 3. Objects' depth estimation: a) source image with recognized objects and DDs, b) depth maps with two sample BBs mapped in.

source image with that observed by looking at the object from the calibrated 3D camera. To compute the BB of an object observed by the 3D camera, all the 3D coordinated of the vertices are mapped into a 2D plane and then converted to pixel coordinates in the camera viewport. This operation can take time for high poly meshes. For this reason, the geometry of the mesh is first simplified by using a Blender's modifier that automatically reduces the number of vertices.

From a perspective point of view, bringing an object closer to the camera or scaling it, makes no difference in the projected image. Moreover, the coordinates of the BBs retrieved by the object detection components are 2D and do not contain indications about the depth. To solve this issue, a principal assumption was made, i.e., the proportions among the objects are fixed (according to the sizes defined in the database) and coherent among the objects. Under these hypotheses, it is possible to use a depth prediction algorithm to extrapolate the depth value of the objects in the image. To this aim, the CNN models trained for depth prediction from a single RGB image proposed in [7] and available at https://github.com/iro-cp/FCRN-DepthPrediction are leveraged. Depth prediction network predicts depth map for the source image as shown in Fig. 3b. Pixel coordinates of the BBs detected in the source image are then mapped to the depth map and the depth value at the center of the BB is used to set the distance of the object from the 3D camera. The result of this process is depicted in Fig. 3c. Finally, the orientation of each object is adjusted with a successive approximation method with the goal of minimizing the difference between the aspect ratio of the BB detected in the source image and that observed in the scene from the 3D camera.

3.3 Environment Generation and Physics

This step, executed by clicking on the "Generate room" button, generates a plane with grass in case of outdoor settings or a complete room with walls, floor and ceiling for indoor settings. Then, physics constraints are applied to the scene, i.e., gravity force, to avoid floating elements and correctly place objects on the surface below. Examples of 3D scenes generated by the proposed system are shown in Fig. 4.

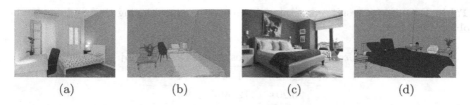

| (a) | (b) | (c) | (d) |

Fig. 4. Considered use cases: a) source image n.1 (source: https://www.aluna.it), b) result obtained from image n.1, c) source image n.2 (source: https://www.wattpad.com), and d) result obtained from image n.2.

4 Experimental Setup

With the aim to assess the performance of the proposed system a user study was conducted by involving 31 volunteers (24 males and 7 females), aged between 22 and 55 ($\mu = 31.45$ and $\sigma = 10.55$). Participants can be considered as non-professional users, since only a limited number of them had experience with graphics suites. Participants' background was evaluated through a demographics questionnaire filled in before the experiment. Collected data revealed the following statistics on the usage of graphics suite: never: 51.6%, sometimes: 25.8%, once a week: 9.7%, everyday: 12.9%. To evaluate the proposed system, both objective and subjective measurements have been collected for generating three representative indoors settings. The objective measurements consider the completion time needed to infer the objects from the image (inference time), the time required to create the scene layout (position time), and the number of objects detected in the image. The subjective metrics have been used to compare the proposed system with the automatic scene generation tool proposed in a previous work [1]. The subjective observations were based on a questionnaire aimed at evaluating the scene similarity. In particular, participants were requested to judge the similarity of the generated scenes in terms of number and types of objects, overall scene layout, as well as applied materials and textures. A within-subject approach was used in this study to compare the two tools. The questionnaire is available at https://bit.ly/3akDFbk.

4.1 Results

The results in terms of inference and position time, as well as the number of detected objects, are reported in Table 1

It is worth noticing that the most time-consuming task is represented by the inference time, which on average covers the 76.14% of the overall process. The flexibility of the proposed architecture makes it possible, in the future, to replace the block in charge of inferring objects in order to speed up this process and increase the number of detectable objects.

Average scores regarding scene similarity are reported in Fig. 5. Paired samples t-test with 5% significance ($p < 0.05$) was used to analyze statistically significant differences. Participants found that the proposed system was able to

Table 1. Objective results concerning: inference time, positioning time and number of objects detected.

Use case	Inf. time	Pos. time	Detected obj
1	22.32 s	4.35 s	4
2	25.20 s	12.59 s	13
3	26.20 s	7.37 s	6

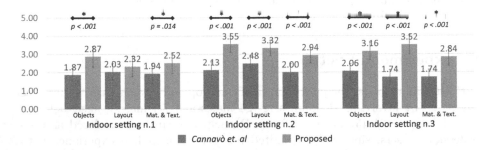

Fig. 5. Subjective results concerning scene similarity: average scores (bars height) and standard deviation (errors bars). Statistically significant differences ($p < 0.05$) are marked with the '*' symbol.

generate a better reconstruction of the source image compared with the previous work in the majority of the considered use cases, as confirmed by the higher values obtained in all the considered metrics (except for the first use case, in which no significant differences were found for the layouts).

5   Conclusions and Future Work

This paper presented a system that allows non-professional users to quickly create 3D scenes for fast prototyping. A methodology was introduced that combines the advantages of automatic 3D scene generation with traditional graphics suites through the development of an add-on target to a well-known graphics suite. The system proposed in this paper was not meant to replace the traditional graphics suites, but rather to support non-professional users in the quick prototyping of 3D scenes by leveraging a single 2D image as input. The scene generated automatically by the proposed system can be considered as a draft that expert developers can take as reference or starting point to obtain the ultimate version. A user study performed by involving participants with limited skills in using graphics suites. Results showed promising improvements in terms of scene similarity with respect to a previous work.

Currently, the system presents limitations in terms of flexibility, i.e., possible scenes that can be created, due to the limited number of objects in the database and labels that can be inferred by the selected library. Besides solving the above limitations, which can be faced with the development of new models and the introduction of alternative tools for inferring objects from images, possible evolution will consider the introduction of techniques, to further improve the capacity of the system of preserving the relationship among objects.

References

1. Cannavò, A., D'Alessandro, A., Maglione, D., Marullo, G., Zhang, C., Lamberti, F.: Automatic generation of affective 3D virtual environments from 2D images. In: Proceedings of the International Conference on Computer Graphics Theory and Applications, pp. 113–124 (2020)
2. Cannavò, A., Demartini, C., Morra, L., Lamberti, F.: Immersive virtual reality-based interfaces for character animation. IEEE Access **7**, 125463–125480 (2019)
3. Cannavò, A., Lamberti, F.: A virtual character posing system based on reconfigurable tangible user interfaces and immersive virtual reality. In: Proceedings of the Smart Tools and Applications for Graphics - Eurographics Italian Chapter Conference, pp. 1–11 (2018)
4. Chang, A., Savva, M., Manning, C.: Interactive learning of spatial knowledge for text to 3D scene generation. In: Proceedings of the Workshop on Interactive Language Learning, Visualization, and Interfaces, pp. 14–21 (2014)
5. Chang, A.X., Eric, M., Savva, M., Manning, C.D.: SceneSeer: 3D scene design with natural language. arXiv preprint arXiv:1703.00050 (2017)
6. Esteban, I., Dijk, J., Groen, F.C.: From images to 3D models made easy. In: Proceedings of the 19th ACM International Conference on Multimedia, pp. 695–698 (2011)
7. Laina, I., Rupprecht, C., Belagiannis, V., Tombari, F., Navab, N.: Deeper depth prediction with fully convolutional residual networks. In: 4th International Conference on 3D Vision, pp. 239–248 (2016)
8. Lu, J., Li, C., Yin, C., Ma, L.: A new framework for automatic 3d scene construction from text description. In: Proceedings of IEEE International Conference on Progress in Informatics and Computing, vol. 2, pp. 964–968 (2010)
9. Lu, X., Yaoy, J., Li, H., Liu, Y., Zhang, X.: 2-line exhaustive searching for real-time vanishing point estimation in Manhattan world. In: Proceedings of the IEEE Winter Conference on Applications of Computer Vision, pp. 345–353 (2017)
10. Oliveira, B., Azulay, D., Carvalho, P.: GVRf and blender: a path for android apps and games development. In: Proceedings of the International Conference on Human-Computer Interaction, pp. 329–337 (2019)
11. Payne, B.R., Lay, J.F., Hitz, M.A.: Automatic 3D object reconstruction from a single image. In: Proceedings of the ACM Southeast Regional Conference, p. 31 (2014)
12. Sra, M., Maes, P., Vijayaraghavan, P., Roy, D.: Auris: creating affective virtual spaces from music. In: Proceedings of the 23rd ACM Symposium on Virtual Reality Software and Technology, p. 26 (2017)
13. Vouzounaras, G., Daras, P., Strintzis, M.G.: Automatic generation of 3D outdoor and indoor building scenes from a single image. Multimedia Tools Appl. **70**(1), 361–378 (2011). https://doi.org/10.1007/s11042-011-0823-0
14. Xu, K., Stewart, J., Fiume, E.: Constraint-based automatic placement for scene composition. Proc. Graph. Interface **2**, 25–34 (2002)

Overcoming the Limits of a Neural Network for Character-Scene Interactions

Marco Mameli[(⊠)], Dario De Carolis, Emanuele Frontoni, and Primo Zingaretti

Dipartimento di Ingegneria dell'Informazione (DII), Università Politecnica delle Marche, Via Brecce Bianche, 60131 Ancona, Italy
m.mameli@pm.univpm.it,{e.frontoni,p.zingaretti}@univpm.it

Abstract. The motor synthesis of humanoid characters is one of the main problems in data-driven animations, with applications in robotics, entertainment and game development. Both in the commercial and academic fields there is a strong interest in developing new synthesis techniques. The attention of researchers in this field has recently turned to artificial intelligence techniques with the use of neural networks, in particular recurrent neural networks (RNN) that are well suited to predict data sequences, such as animations. The use of RNNs for the generation of animations despite the high success in the scientific field and the excellent results in real development, still has limitations that prevent its use on a larger scale. In this work, therefore, the need to overcome these limits has required to focus on the phase following the generation of interactions by the network. In particular, starting from a work present in the literature, the limitations were analyzed and solutions were proposed that made it possible to improve the visual rendering of the Carry and Sit operations. The results obtained are positive and did not require any intervention on the neural network. New items and characters have been successfully introduced. Both pre-existing characters and imported characters are able to interact with all objects with greater effectiveness, responsiveness and visual fidelity.

Keywords: Computer graphics · Animations · Recurrent neural network

1 Introduction

In recent years, the interest in virtual character animation has rapidly grown. Application areas that benefit from advances in motor synthesis include robotics, virtual reality, video games, and non-interactive animation [6]. The advances in this field are strongly linked to the development of artificial intelligence, especially deep learning [11,15].

Examples of synthesis of human animations aimed at precision interactions can be found in commercial games such as *Gears of War 4* [1], *For Honor* [4] and *Star Citizen* [8] and underline the strong interest of large companies to research in the sector. The main component of the games is immersion, or the

© Springer Nature Switzerland AG 2021
L. T. De Paolis et al. (Eds.): AVR 2021, LNCS 12980, pp. 118–134, 2021.
https://doi.org/10.1007/978-3-030-87595-4_10

user's illusion of not being in front of a machine but of interacting with a real and coherent world. Artificial intelligence plays a fundamental role in this mechanism, not only in the more direct application of creating adversaries and more skilled allies. In particular, the 10 categories identified are: *Non-player character (NPC) behavior learning* [14], *Search and planning* [7], *Player modeling* [22], *Games as AI benchmarks* [20], *Procedural content generation* [18], *Computational narrative* [2], *Believable agents* [13], *AI-assisted game design* [21], *AI in commercial games* [3]. Concerning this last point, in academic field, there is a strong emphasis on the use of Recurrent Neural Network (RNN) for the synthesis of novel animations and transitions starting from Motion Capture (MoCap) data. RNN has good performance to classify sequential data as natural speech recognition, handwriting recognition and animation synthesis. The attempts to increase generality are based on the variety of character actions, the variety of objects they can interact with, and transitions. To do this, it is often proposed to retrain the network with novel data. This process is very expensive for two reasons: first of all, novel data with the same structure as the pre-existing ones are necessary. Tools and methods for acquiring MoCap data are not easily accessible. Data must be cleaned and augmented before being inserted into the training set. Then, the training of the network requires much more time how much more data are available.

This research aims to propose a non invasive method to generalize the techniques of motor synthesis in terms of diversity of build and variety of objects. Departing from the solution proposed by [19], the purpose is to test the introduction of new assets. Through the definition of import rules and the introduction of components in the post-processing phase, the problems of compatibility, visual fidelity and responsiveness have been solved. The components are non-invasive as they do not modify the original structure and are activated only when a correction is needed. Furthermore, the results were obtained without modifying the neural network.

The main contributions of this paper are summarized as follows:

- Visual fidelity: the gap between the hands and the objects carried by the character must be eliminated.
- Effectiveness and responsiveness: characters must lift objects without blocking and without lingering in the lift transition.
- No intervention on the network: the neural network must be unaffected, so corrections cannot be based on introducing novel data or retraining the network.
- Control: activation of fixes must be under the control of the developer.

The remainder of the paper is organized as follows. In Sect. 2, a comparative analysis with other motor synthesis techniques is proposed. Section 3 describes the specific objectives, the problems encountered and the techniques adopted. The results obtained are described in Sect. 4. Finally, Sect. 5 describes the degree of achievement of the objectives and the ideas for future developments.

2   Related Works

Several approaches have been adopted to generate realistic animations for humanoid characters. These methods are mainly divided into [10,16,23]:

- *Simulation based*: aims to create animations that respect physical constraints.
- *Data driven*: aims to create animations that can be managed in real time starting from unstructured data.

Since the solution adopted in this paper concerns the data-driven based models with phase-labeled deep-learning, we present literature works for the second approach and the differences with our solution.

2.1   Data Driven Models

The purpose of data driven models is the creation of animations and transitions that can be controlled in real time, starting from MoCap data. A classic approach to data driven animation has been proposed by [9] and based on "motion graph". It is possible to control a character by selecting the task, sketch of a path in a maze or by imitating a person in front of a camera. The effectiveness of this solution depends on the quality and the quantity of the available MoCap data. The data are organized in a 2-level structure (motion graph). The top level is a probabilistic mode which groups character states into clusters and serves as an interface for user control. The lowest level is a Markov model which handles the transition between animations. At the lowest level, data are organized in trees, with frame precision. By traversing the trees, the smoothest transition to the next frame is determined. This solution works when the character slowly moves and for a database of comparable size to that used in the experiment.

The work of [17] proposes a motor for the synthesis of constrained movements, offline (not interactive) based on motion graph. The user can specify a high level goal. The engine is capable of generating a realistic offline animation. The traversing of the motion graph is performed through an algorithm that allows to specify an inflation factor for the heuristic that decreases the traversal times of the tree, to find sub-optimal solutions. By compressing and pruning the shaft, the difference between suboptimal and optimal solutions decreases. Animations of 15 s were successfully created by specifying 2d trajectories and applying various constraints.

In time, data driven models have shown encouraging results by adopting machine learning techniques, in particular reinforcement learning.

In [12], the authors developed a controller based on reinforcement learning, powered by a first-person environmental sensor and a motion graph containing MoCap data. The sensor organizes the data in a hierarchical structure and does not require parameterization. The character is able to perceive the depth of the scene and the obstacles that surround it. Planning is formulated as a Markov decision problem. For training, a reinforcement learning algorithm is used, adapted to benefit from the hierarchical structure of the data. At the end of the training, the controller is able to manage the animations of the character in real time and avoid obstacles.

Deep learning techniques have shown an excellent scalability and ability to create credible unpublished animations. In particular, the RNNs have proved to be very efficient in managing animations. The RNNs in fact take into account the previous states in the prediction phase, for this reason they present good performances for sequential tasks such as natural language processing, speech recognition, handwriting recognition or animation synthesis [5,19]. In [5], the authors have proposed a prediction and classification technique of humanoid poses based on Encoder-Recurrent-Decoder, a particular implementation of RNN. This model operates on two domains: MoCap data and video footage.

The reference solution adopted [19] belongs to data driven models based on deep learning. This model, based on a novel architecture called NSM, allows to start from MoCap data to obtain a character that can be controlled in real time. Novel transitions not present on the original data are generated, precise interactions can be made, and the character can be controlled through high-level tasks. The functioning of NSM consists of two main components. i) Gating Network generates weights (experts) used to modify the value of the internal weights of the Motion Prediction Network. It receives a subset of the Motion Prediction Network inputs. ii) Motion Prediction Network is the main component that deals with the prediction of the position to the next frame.

Similar to the [12] technique, the character is equipped with sensors. The interaction sensor activates when the character has to sit or lift an object and detects the geometry of the target. It is shaped like a parallelepiped and is centered on the object. The environmental sensor is centered on the character, has a cylindrical shape, is always active and informs the network about all the near obstacles. The advantages of this solution compared to the previous ones are: interactions of precision, generalization and response and control times.

The solutions shown are often specific to a certain character model. In some cases, no mesh is assigned to the characters. Attempts to extend generality are oriented towards the environment, the tasks that can be performed and the variety of objects to interact with. The expansions are carried out upstream, affecting the variety and quality of the training data, and thus retraining the network. No attempts have been made to expand the solutions to characters of different sizes.

This research has showed an increase in generality compared to the solution of [19] without intervening on the training of the network. The solution adopted is based on the addition of non-invasive components in the post-processing phase. This approach has 2 advantages: non-invasiveness and no training.

3   Materials and Methods

This section shows the solution approaches adopted for the 2 main procedures:

- Adaptation of the Carry task;
- Adaptation of the Sit task and positional corrections.

For each approach we describe the problems occurred in the original design and the adopted solution. The common purpose is to augment the generality of the solution, allowing the use of novel objects and characters and to increase the visual fidelity of the interactions.

Import of Custom Assets. During the analysis of the demo, the need derived to import a custom character, as the included character had display problems. The import of custom characters, such as the import of objects to interact with, is a relevant aspect if the intent is to evaluate the versatility of the animation tool in adapting it to different projects. Moreover, the solutions adopted in this study provide good performance also when the characters have been imported.

3.1   Adaptation of the Carry Task

One of the actions that the character can perform once it is set up is to carry objects. For that regard, this section highlights the defects, describing and showing the problems related to the transport and their respective causes. In addition, in order to understand the corrections, the steps of the algorithm of lifting at threshold, which manages lifting and transport, was analyzed. Changes of thresholds are also shown to improve effectiveness and responsiveness. Finally, two approaches were used to eliminate the empty space between the hands and the object, the first modifies the rotations of the character's bones while the second modifies the geometry of the object.

The imported character has some problems:

- Effectiveness: some failures in lifting objects. In some cases, when the character is preparing to lift the object, it remained in the position for a very long time before starting the lifting or in the worst cases it blocked without success.
- Efficiency: unacceptable response times. Since the project is intended for interactive applications, such a lack of responsiveness is unacceptable.
- Visual fidelity: the hands are too far from the raised object. The cause of the distance of the hands is given by the difference between the skeletons of the default character and the imported character. The network performs better with the default character, as because it also has longer arms and a mesh that hides the defects when present.

Algorithm of Lifting at Threshold. The algorithm of lifting at threshold is structured in 5 main phases.

1. Approaching the object: if the character is not close to the object, he proceeds by walking to a target position.
2. Lifting: the character is in the target position and is ready to lift the object. Bending down, he grabs the object with his hands, then stands up to carry it.

3. Movement with object in hands: it is possible to control the character to make him walk while carrying the object.
4. Positioning transition: when the transport signal is interrupted, the transition is started to place the object on the ground.
5. Positioning of the object on the ground: the object is placed on the ground and the Carry task ends.

In the approaching phase, at each iteration the character continues walking towards the object. The interaction sensor is constantly updated.

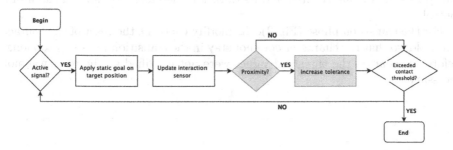

Fig. 1. The modified approaching phase (changes are highlighted in blue). (Color figure online)

To solve the problem in the approaching the object, the proposed approach acts on the contact threshold (Fig. 1). The lock of the character occurred at the check on the contact threshold. Even if the character was close enough to the object with the hands in the correct position, the neural network did not assign contact values such as to allow him to exit the cycle. The introduced tolerance increase mechanism is triggered only if the character is already bent to lift the object and the tolerance increases with each iteration both towards the hand-object distance and the contact values.

Even if there are no changes in the lifting phase, the updates of the threshold values affect the stability of the cycle, when checking the contact values. At each iteration, the time elapsed from the beginning of the lift, the position of the object, the static goal and the interaction sensor are updated. Once the lift limit time is exceeded, the next phase begins. It is possible that this phase prematurely ends due to a lack of contact or interruption of the signal. In this case the character drops the object to the ground.

The modify in the movement phase (Fig. 2) provides that before entering the main loop it is signaled that the character is standing and carrying the object. This allows to isolate when the change in the position of the hands is necessary.

For each iteration, the destination of the object is calculated, i.e. the middle position between the hands, which is then assigned to it. Following the application of the dynamic goal, the character can be made to move through movement signals. Finally, the interaction sensor is updated. This phase ends only when the

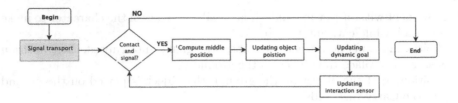

Fig. 2. The modified movement phase.

transport signal is interrupted and its duration therefore depends on the user's control.

For the transition phase (Fig. 3), the modify concerns the reset of the contact threshold, so that the character does not stay in the transition phase for too long. Before the change, the threshold values were not modified so the reset was not necessary.

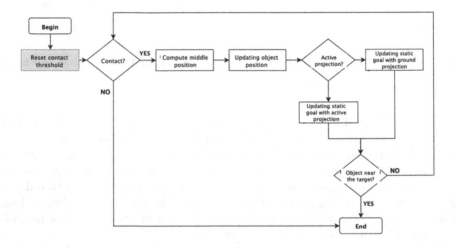

Fig. 3. The modified transition phase.

For the final phase of the repositioning of the object on the ground (Fig. 4), the modify concerns the control of the distance of the object from the final position. If it is close enough then the transition phase ends.

Wrist Correction. In some cases the character's hands are too far from the transported object. This defect was both in the imported character and the one included in the demo. To contextualize the change it is necessary to understand the logic of assigning the character's posture (Fig. 5). The network is powered for each frame, in order to be able to predict the values.

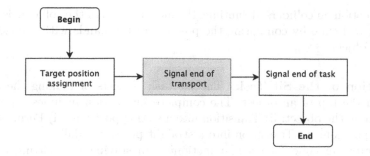

Fig. 4. The modified repositioning phase.

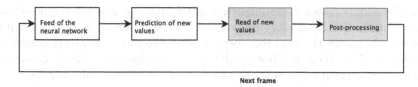

Fig. 5. The modified update phase for each frame.

During the read of new values, the positions and rotations of the bones for the current frame are assigned. In the Postprocess phase corrections are made to the skeleton through assignments and calculation of inverse kinematics. Figure 6 shows the Read phase. After updating the time series and the trajectory, the posture is assigned. A check has been added that allows to disable the network control on the skeleton, in order to facilitate tests and isolate conflicts.

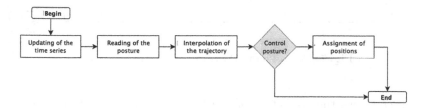

Fig. 6. The modified reading phase.

Three strategies have been adopted to correct the position of the wrists.

1. Intervention on transformations: in the postprocessing phase the transformations of the wrists were modified. The first attempt was to intervene directly on the positions of the wrists, then on the rotation of the elbows.
2. Intervention on colliders in the editor: by intervening on the objects transported incorrectly and modifying the geometry of the colliders, the network is influenced to bring the hands closer to the object.

3. Intervention on colliders at runtime: the modification of the colliders is carried out in real time by comparing the position of the hands with the extension of the object.

Adaptation of the Sit Task. The Sit task consists of making the character sit on the top of an object. The complete interaction includes 4 phases: i) Approaching the object; ii) Transition into a sitting position; iii) Permanence in a sitting position; iv) Transition into a straight position (Idle).

The problem concerned a malfunctioning in staying in a sitting position. In particular, the ankles were not positioned correctly and interpenetrations between the mesh of the character and the object were visible. The different length of the legs creates an inconsistency at the moment of arbitrary positioning of the ankles in the Read and Postprocessing phase. Since the network expects longer legs, it places the hips too deep, causing the mesh to interpenetrate. To solve the problem, there has been a change in the algorithm. By intervening in the algorithm it is sufficient that the modification is carried out after the inverse kinematics so that the old position is overwritten (the final position is the one that counts for rendering).

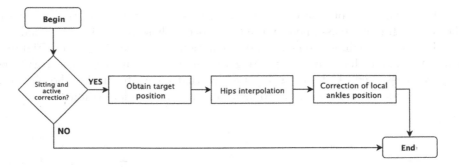

Fig. 7. Correction in Post-process of the task Sit.

Figure 7 shows the correction of the Sit task. The correction is activated only if the character is seated and if it is activated for the object with which he is interacting. All objects that the character can sit on have a contact point for the hips. To allow a smooth correction, an interpolation is performed with the desired position. Finally, we intervene on the local position of the ankles to eliminate graphic artifacts.

Positional Corrections. The default potion is also a task. If the character did not receive any assignment to the skeleton positions while standing still, she would initially remain in T-pose. The animation in the Idle condition gives the character a natural look.

The problem is that even without receiving any input, the character tends to move around the scene. The skeleton remains motionless while the entire character moves along the surface creating a sliding effect. The movement of the character is given by the assignment to each frame of the new position of the bones. The position at each frame is determined by the neural network. For each bone there are two network outputs that directly affect its new position, the positions of the bones and their speeds (Fig. 8).

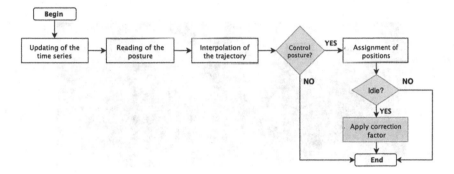

Fig. 8. Modified post-process phase to correct sliding.

When the posture reading is taken, position and speed are calculated for each bone.

The calculation of the actual position is $pos_f = \frac{(pos_{f-1}+velocity \cdot time)+pos}{2}$, where pos_f is the position in the current frame, pos_{f-1} the position in the previous frame, $velocity$ the speed obtained from the network and $time$ the elapsed time. Sliding is corrected by applying a "correction factor" to the speed of each bone, only when the character should be standing still.

4   Results

This Section shows the results obtained for the 2 areas of improvement: adaptation of the Carry task and adaptation of the Sit task and positional corrections.

4.1   Adaptation of the Carry Task

The success criterion is given by the correct lifting of all objects (pre-existing and new) both by the original character and the imported ones. By applying the appropriate correction method it was possible to make all the characters lift all the objects without creating gaps.

The 3 methods adopted were:

- Intervention on the transformations;
- Intervention on the colliders in the editor (sensor);
- Intervention on the colliders at runtime (sensor).

Intervention on the Transformations. The first intervention on the transformations was on the position of the wrists. The effect of this correction can be seen in Fig. 9. Although the hands are in a believable position relative to the carried object, the mesh associated with the elbow has an incorrect rotation. By forcing arbitrary positions in the skeleton, it is possible to create errors of this type, as inconsistencies in terms of lengths and rotations can occur. The network's assignment of global positions takes the wrists away from the correct local position.

Fig. 9. Effect of direct positioning.

The intervention on the rotation is the most solid, as it help to position the hands correctly and partially returns control of the skeleton to the developer. This aspect allows more freedom in the positioning of the bones, but can generate conflicts with the network. These conflicts can show as graphic imperfections in some characters. For the conflicts with the positioning of the neural network, we have decided to intervene directly on the values detected to influence the rotation of the arms, and therefore leave the network for posture complete control again. Visual problems can also be related to the character skinning process. To solve these problems it is therefore necessary to go back to the "weight painting" phase, uniform the weights of the mesh and then re-import the character.

Intervention on the Colliders in the Editor. Figures 10 and 11 shows the effects of the resizing of bounds and colliders along the X-axis. The objects are always raised considering the forward direction, which coincides with the Z-axis (in blue). The space between the hands and the object is eliminated after the modification.

To determine if and when to apply the scaling, the same control considered for the rotation of the elbows was used. It is then checked that the character is actually being transported and that the object contains the contact points of the wrists. The intervention on the colliders in the editor allows to have a good control for a specific object, leaving unchanged the interactions with the other objects. Since the positions and rotations of the bones are not arbitrarily changed, no conflicts with the network are generated. This method requires more

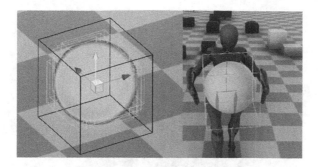

Fig. 10. Collider, bounds and effect on transport before the modification. (Color figure online)

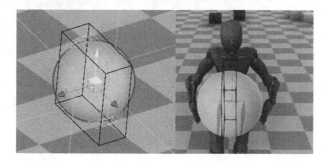

Fig. 11. Collider, bounds and effect on transport after the modification. (Color figure online)

effort on the part of the developer who has to test the transport of the object and make any changes to the colliders. Another disadvantage is the specificity, as the modification to the colliders is static, it may be correct for a certain character but not for others. With multiple characters this approach may not work. Another limitation of this approach compared to direct intervention is that it fails to correct the transport of smaller objects (Fig. 12).

Intervention on the Colliders at Runtime. Figure 13 shows the result of this operation equal to that obtained through the modification in the editor. The intervention on colliders at run-time, exploiting the difference between the distance of the hands and the extension of the object, can automatically adapt to different characters and geometries. It therefore has a good generality and automaticity. The intervention on the sensor does not generate conflicts with the neural network, but could have conflict with corrections made offline. For this reason, an option has been added in the Interaction component that allows to disable corrections for certain objects.

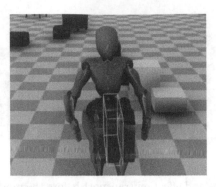

Fig. 12. Example of inefficiency with too small objects.

Fig. 13. Effect of the fix at runtime on a new character. The size of the bounds (in blue) is restricted with respect to the mesh.

Comparison. The comparison among the 3 described methods can be summarized in the Tables 1 and 2.

Thanks to a selector, it is possible to easily change the correction method.

4.2 Adaptation of the Sit Task and Positional Corrections

In the Sit task, the visual fidelity is increased thanks to the correct positioning of the ankles and the elimination of interpenetrations. The autonomous sliding has been minimized and the character has been brought back to the ground via the height correction.

Table 1. Summary table of the 3 correction methods (1).

Method	Generality (Characters)	Generality (Objects)	Control	Conflict with the neural network
Rotation of the elbows	High	High	Medium	Yes
Offline modification	Low	Low	High	No
Run-time modification	High	Low	Medium	No

Table 2. Summary table of the 3 correction methods (2).

Method	Automaticity	Integrity	Problems
Rotation of the elbows	Yes	High	Problems with the mesh of the character
Offline modification	No	Media	Does not manage good little objects
Run-time modification	Yes	Low	Does not manage good little objects

Sit Task. The results are shown in Fig. 14. The detachment with the ankles was canceled. In the chair, the contact points have been changed to allow the character to sit further forward. The knees are positioned at the edge of the chair avoiding interpenetration. However, this translation is in a less natural arm position. Another defect is the loss of fluidity in the transition: in the most serious cases it is possible to notice a sort of teleportation of the character to the target position. Finally, as in the case of the transport, the corrections are specific to the character and mainly depend on the length of the legs. In many cases, the fix to the Sit task is unnecessary and the control can be left to the network. Multiple touch-points can also be defined for different characters.

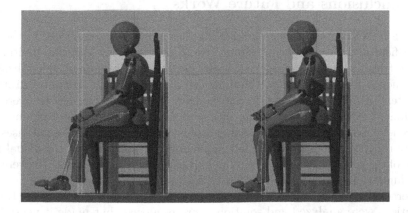

Fig. 14. Comparison before (left) and after (right) the correction.

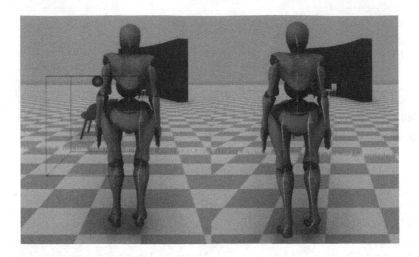

Fig. 15. Timelapse of 30 s without input with corrective factor.

Table 3. Comparison of translation in the absence of input and in the absence or presence of the correction factor in 30 s.

	Translation X	Translation Z	Absolute translation
Without correction	−0.5	+1.4	1.49
Active correction	−0.2	−0.1	0.22

Sliding. The sliding correction by acting on the speeds greatly improves the stability of the character (Fig. 15). A more solid (and more invasive) solution would be an integral modification of the system by which the translation in the scene is established. The effect of the correction is shown in Table 3.

5   Conclusions and Future Works

The use of RNNs to generate animations despite the high success in the scientific field and the excellent results in real development still has limitations that restrict its use on a larger scale. In particular, the lack of generalization of the networks and therefore the difficulty of their use on computer graphics characters of different nature or composition, studies are needed to overcome this limit. Furthermore, the composition of animations and interactions with the scene, based on the data, presents graphical-visual renders in some cases not exactly realistic which prevent their application in areas where the visual rendering of the result is of fundamental importance, such as in games. To overcome these limitations, this work has focused on the phase following the generation of interactions by the network. In particular, starting from the work of [19], its limitations were analyzed and solutions were proposed that made it possible to improve the visual rendering of the Carry and Sit operations.

The proposed correction method is non-invasive. Corrective factors have been added, both in the logic of the task and in Postprocess, which improve visual fidelity, effectiveness and response times. In addition, new characters and new objects have been successfully introduced to make them interact. The new objects are compatible with the existing solution. The improvements made are also reflected in the starting assets. The original character is more responsive and can correctly lift all objects. Additional components have a good tradeoff between automaticity and control. Thanks to the introduction of control variables, they can be easily activated, calibrated and tested during execution. The results have been obtained without modifying the neural network. This is important as it demonstrates that it is possible to make minor changes to some network inputs without creating conflicts. It is also possible to avoid the operations of new data acquisition, preparation and training. The objectives have been fully reached and an increase in the generality of the solution has been achieved.

Possible future developments may concern two aspects:

- Collision management: the character can avoid obstacles thanks to the environmental sensor. He can pass through cracks by bending over or sit on a chair behind a desk by moving his legs appropriately.
- Importing IK characters: by resolving IK constraints at runtime, offset errors between the bones can be corrected. To obtain this advantage, the imported character must have been configured with inverse kinematics. It is therefore interesting to study the behaviour of IK characters in lifting objects and sitting down. The application of inverse kinematics has been included in the correction by rotation of the elbows and in the Sit task.

References

1. Bollo, D.: High performance animation in gears of war 4. In: ACM SIGGRAPH 2017 Talks. SIGGRAPH '17, Association for Computing Machinery, New York, NY, USA (2017). https://doi.org/10.1145/3084363.3085069
2. Burelli, P., Yannakakis, G.: Combining local and global optimisation for virtual camera control, pp. 403–410 (2010). https://doi.org/10.1109/ITW.2010.5593328
3. Buro, M.: Real-time strategy games: a new AI research challenge. IJCAI **2003**, 1534–1535 (2003)
4. Clavet, S.: Motion matching and the road to next-gen animation. GDC Vault, New York, NY, USA (2016). https://www.gdcvault.com/play/1023280/Motion-Matching-and-The-Road
5. Fragkiadaki, K., Levine, S., Felsen, P., Malik, J.: Recurrent network models for human dynamics. In: 2015 IEEE International Conference on Computer Vision (ICCV), pp. 4346–4354 (2015)
6. Frontoni, E., Loncarski, J., Pierdicca, R., Bernardini, M., Sasso, M.: Cyber physical systems for industry 4.0: towards real time virtual reality in smart manufacturing. In: De Paolis, L.T., Bourdot, P. (eds.) AVR 2018. LNCS, vol. 10851, pp. 422–434. Springer, Cham (2018). https://doi.org/10.1007/978-3-319-95282-6_31
7. Hazim, N., Al-Dabbagh, S.S.M., Naser, M.A.S.: Pathfinding in strategy games and maze solving using a* search algorithm. J. Comput. Commun. **04**, 15–25 (2016). https://doi.org/10.4236/jcc.2016.411002

8. Herzog, I.: Teaching a character how to walk with procedural assisted animations. CitizenCon (2017). http://youtube.com/watch?v=ZMgHhu7XT78

9. Lee, J., Chai, J., Reitsma, P.S.A., Hodgins, J.K., Pollard, N.S.: Interactive control of avatars animated with human motion data. ACM Trans. Graph. $21(3)$, 491–500 (2002)

10. Li, Z., Zhou, Y., Xiao, S., He, C., Huang, Z., Li, H.: Auto-conditioned recurrent networks for extended complex human motion synthesis (2017)

11. Liciotti, D., Paolanti, M., Frontoni, E., Zingaretti, P.: People detection and tracking from an RGB-D camera in top-view configuration: review of challenges and applications. In: Battiato, S., Farinella, G.M., Leo, M., Gallo, G. (eds.) ICIAP 2017. LNCS, vol. 10590, pp. 207–218. Springer, Cham (2017). https://doi.org/10.1007/978-3-319-70742-6_20

12. Lo, W.Y., Knaus, C., Zwicker, M.: Learning motion controllers with adaptive depth perception. In: Proceedings of the ACM SIGGRAPH/Eurographics Symposium on Computer Animation, SCA '12, Eurographics Association, Goslar, DEU, pp. 145–154 (2012)

13. Loyall, A.B.: Believable agents: Building interactive personalities. CARNEGIE-MELLON UNIV PITTSBURGH PA DEPT OF COMPUTER SCIENCE, Technical report (1997)

14. Lucas, S.M., Kendall, G.: Evolutionary computation and games. Comp. Intell. Mag. $1(1)$, 10–18 (2006)

15. Paolanti, M., Frontoni, E.: Multidisciplinary pattern recognition applications: a review. Comput. Sci. Rev. 37, 100276 (2020)

16. Park, S., Ryu, H., Lee, S., Lee, S., Lee, J.: Learning predict-and-simulate policies from unorganized human motion data. ACM Trans. Graph. 38(6) (2019). https://doi.org/10.1145/3355089.3356501

17. Safonova, A., Hodgins, J.K.: Construction and optimal search of interpolated motion graphs. ACM Trans. Graph. $26(3)$, 106-es (2007). https://doi.org/10.1145/1276377.1276510

18. Shaker, N., Togelius, J., Nelson, M.J.: Procedural Content Generation in Games. Springer, Heidelberg (2016). https://doi.org/10.1007/978-3-319-42716-4

19. Starke, S., Zhang, H., Komura, T., Saito, J.: Neural state machine for character-scene interactions. ACM Trans. Graph. $38(6)$ (2019). https://doi.org/10.1145/3355089.3356505

20. Xia, B., Ye, X., Abuassba, A.O.: Recent research on ai in games. In: 2020 International Wireless Communications and Mobile Computing (IWCMC), pp. 505–510. IEEE (2020)

21. Yannakakis, G.N., Togelius, J.: A panorama of artificial and computational intelligence in games. IEEE Trans. Comput. Intell. AI Games $7(4)$, 317–335 (2015)

22. Yannakakis, G.N., Spronck, P., Loiacono, D., André, E.: Player modeling (2013)

23. Zhang, H., Starke, S., Komura, T., Saito, J.: Mode-adaptive neural networks for quadruped motion control. ACM Trans. Graph. $37(4)$ (2018). https://doi.org/10.1145/3197517.3201366

Immersive Insights: Virtual Tour Analytics System for Understanding Visitor Behavior

Roberto Pierdicca[1]([✉]), Michele Sasso[2], Flavio Tonetto[3], Francesca Bonelli[3], Andrea Felicetti[1], and Marina Paolanti[1]

[1] Dipartimento di Ingegneria Civile, Edile e dell'Architettura (DICEA), Università Politecnica delle Marche, Via Brecce Bianche, 12, 60131 Ancona, Italy
r.piedicca@staff.univpm.it
[2] Ubisive Srl, Via Luigi Einaudi, 280, 62012 Civitanova Marche Macerata, Italy
michele.sasso@ubisive.it
[3] Sinergia srl, Via Luigi Einaudi, 74c, 61032 Fano Pesaro-Urbino, Italy
ftonetto@sinergia.it, francesca.bonelli@isiday.it

Abstract. Virtual tours are gaining increasing importance especially in the last year, when emerged the need to make develop new products and strategies due to the COVID-19 pandemic, in which people where obliged to stay at home or, however, with strong limitations. To increase visibility and attraction of the users towards many kinds of services, virtual tours are used in different contexts: mainly tourism, but also universities and schools, real estate agencies and commercial activities. Then, virtual tours are communication tools that allow the visitor to navigate in an immersive and interactive way inside a website thanks to the integration of multimedia contents, so to live a real experience. Therefore, it has become mandatory the definition of a standard method for the creation of virtual tours and also a tool for evaluating their effectiveness related to the context in which they operate. In this context, this paper aims at proposing a standard data layer as a baseline to develop serialized virtual tours. Moreover, it presents an analytic tool able to evaluate the performance of a specific virtual tour. The case study taken into exam is the Open Days in a University located in the Marche region, in the center of in Italy. However, the approach can be extended in several context and can be generalised.

Keywords: Virtual tour · Standardization · Analytic · Virtual reality · Editor

1 Introduction

The spread of digital technologies implies that they are increasingly perceived as the most effective means to communicate ideas, concepts, aspirations, news, and research results. The perception of information technology as a privileged

L. T. De Paolis et al. (Eds.): AVR 2021, LNCS 12980, pp. 135–155, 2021.
https://doi.org/10.1007/978-3-030-87595-4_11

means of transmitting information is related to the immediateness with which it allows to reach a large audience, the reproducibility, the apparent simplicity of implementation and the infinite availability of products such as videos, images, up to three-dimensional models. Information technology effectively removes this distance through the possibility of reproducing and recreating objects distant in time and space, even those that no longer exist.

The use of Virtual Reality (VR), the last frontier of new media that allows raising communication to an experiential level, has led to the birth of virtual tours [4], an evolution of the static image, which makes the user protagonist of the scene and navigation within it. Virtual tours [11] are communication tools consisting of images or videos that can be intuitively navigated and allow the user to make an immersive and interactive visit thanks to the integration of multimedia content such as audio, video, images, texts, etc., for recreating the real experience [1,17]. In this way, virtual tours, together with the use of high-definition 360° images or videos, are able to recreate a greatly realistic response to visual stimuli, appearing a highly informative and simultaneously engaging tool for the visitor. Virtual tours can be used in different areas. In particular, as well as in tourism [15], they are frequently used by universities and schools, real estate agencies and commercial activities of various kinds, in order to increase visibility and attract new users to the services offered. Compared to a simple web page containing texts, images or videos, the advantages associated with the use of virtual tours come from the ability to better emphasize the particularities of a place and capture the attention of the visitor, who will be completely involved in the experience and will have time to explore further. The increased visibility will produce an immediate image return and an increase in the number of visitors and customers [18]. Thus, there will be the possibility of transforming virtual visits into real visits [12]. Moreover, due to the huge spread of the coronavirus pandemic and the continuous directive of "stay at home" the movements of people have been restricted and many places are not accessible [20]. So, the introduction of virtual tours can produce similar feelings to a real experience since it stimulates the human senses such as images and sounds to trick the brain which is responding to virtual stimuli [8].

One of the main characteristics that a virtual tour must have is the accessibility to different places, through different devices and heterogeneous communication tools. For these reasons, one of the best solutions for their implementation turns out to be a web application for which the use of a web browser is required without the use of additional components.

In general, and regardless of ambit, the elements that must necessarily be included in a virtual tour are: i) informative and descriptive contents of the environments and activities that can be carried out; ii) multimedia content, such as photo and video galleries; iii) a map with the route of the tour; iv) menu with the steps of the tour for the quick selection of the environments; v) a virtual guide properly integrated into the environment; vi) a 360-degree video to introduce the dynamism of the environments or provide useful instructions.

Nowadays, there are two main bottlenecks that researchers and practitioners are facing: the first one is related to the lack of existing tools to speed up the creation of Virtual Tours. Indeed, despite the acquisition phase is more straight-forward than in the past, the editing tools are complex, very time consuming and not licence free [14]; a brief examination of the existing tools will be given in the following section. The second one is the lack of well-established methods to monitor the performances of users' usage. In other words, Virtual Tours are not designed with a user-centered approach, but still relies on the developer choices. Instead, it would be useful to share analytic able to provide developers with a data-driven design. To evaluate the performance of a virtual tour, five are the areas can be investigated [13]:

- Storytelling: the tour must tell a true and identifiable story about the location, with the aim of creating an emotional relation with users.
- Engagement: the tour must combine the right content in the right positions in order to keep users engaged.
- User-experience: the tour must be user-friendly, intuitive and easy to explore.
- Accessibility: a user should access to the tour anytime and everywhere. The access must be available in all device and for all people to the same extent.
- Analytics: the tour should offer not only a personal and dedicated experience to the visitor, but also acquire data on the behavior of the visitor (visit time, visited areas, completion time of tasks, number of clicks, etc.).

The works of the literature neglects all these areas, but evaluate the perfor-mance of a virtual tour by limiting the investigation only to a limited number of areas, mainly depending on the context. In fact, some areas are of interest independently by the field of application, while others are strictly related to the context.

Given the above, this work has the twofold aim of, on one hand, i) proposing a standard data layer which could become the baseline for a serialized development of virtual tours. The data schema has been developed in *.json* format to manage a huge amount of spherical images (more than 300) and all the elements for the users' interaction. Thanks to this data layer, the development of the tour is easier and agile. On the other ii) developing an analytics tool to monitor the performances of the virtual tour. The analytics have been set up in Google Analytics, considering the previously mentioned data layer so that developers and managers can understand the real potential of the tool in term of usability and usefulness of the virtual tour.

The remainder of the paper is organized as follows: Sect. 2 describes the state of art for virtual tour evaluation. Section 3 is focused on the description of the workflow and in particular the details of phases that compose the overall system. Some insights about the potential given by the analytic tool set up for this virtual tour are discussed in Sect. 4. Finally, the Sect. 5 closes the paper, presenting also future developments.

2   Related Works

According to [7], is currently limited the number of researches that measure the effectiveness of virtual tours, by evaluating the measure to which they can replace site visits and the real benefit of users. Therefore, the role of virtual tours as a provisional tool associated to a crisis, such as the one we are undergoing [20], and as promotional tools [9] and also the improvement of quality based on user experience [3], requires further research works.

However, in this section, we present works that propose evaluation tools of virtual tours in different contexts. Concerning the cultural heritage context, the work of [5] aims to propose a study that creates an online platform (Cultural Tourism Digital Guiding Platform, CTDGP) and also evaluates the performance of the user-experience. They based their model on an unified theory of acceptance model of [19], to highlight the relations among the elements that influence the use of the platform. After the virtual tour, a web-based questionnaire to collect data concerning the user perception and usability was administrated. Moreover, the validity of the questionnaire was examined by two experts in the sector. Then, several metrics are used to quantitatively validate the platform.

Another work that evaluates the efficiency of a virtual tour in terms of the user-experience is presented by [2]. The virtual tour is hosted in a University website. The aim of the study is to evaluate the needs and expectations of visitors, mostly students. The participants of the test were 6 students with different technological skills. They must complete seven tasks, and the indicators taken into consideration were how many tasks was completed and the time of completion. In particular, the research wants to estimate how the virtual tour provides the requirements of the students, how this last engage with the virtual tour, and finally to recognise any problems that users meet by clicking link during the virtual tour.

Another research that involves students is proposed by [6]. The authors have studied the perception of the students (two males and four female) that have tested a virtual tour application in an educational context. The study consisted of usability analysis, a user-experience evaluation, and two questionnaires (using a five-point scale) to verify if there were changes in the attitude of students, before and after the experience. The questionnaire concerned engagement, accessibility and user-experience areas. As in [2], the participants had to complete the assigned tasks and a parameter of evaluation was the time of completion.

The evaluation of a 360° virtual tour application in a University website is made in the study proposed by [16]. The tour was constructed through a collection of 3600 images of offices and structures, and shows the location and directions to go to the building. After the tour, a questionnaire, quantified using five-point scale values, was administered to 100 participants, to assess the effectiveness, efficiency, and satisfaction of users. A quantitative evaluation was made: an equation is used to calculate both effectiveness and efficiency, and another for satisfaction. The usability is the mean value in percentage terms of the three previous parameters.

A complex framework of a virtual tour evaluation is proposed in the study of [10]. The case study is a virtual tour of Italian museums. The authors combine two multi-criteria decision making theories: the analytic hierarchy process (AHP) implemented to estimate the weights of the heuristics and the fuzzy technique for order of preference by similarity to ideal solution (TOPSIS) to evaluate the virtual tours of museums. Unlike previous approaches, the evaluators of virtual tour in museums considered are four experienced researchers in VR, pattern recognition, software engineering and in cultural heritage conservation. During the evaluation of the virtual tour of different museums, they assigned a score (using a five-point linguistic scale) transformed then into fuzzy numbers.

3   Materials and Methods

3.1   Methodology of Data Acquisition

Prior to describe the core contributions of the paper, namely the data layer and the analytics tool, it is worth mentioning the data acquisition phase. Nowadays, to achieve the best resolution and image quality for 360° images, the most widespread practice is that of collecting single pictures with a spherical head and stitching the images in post-processing. This process, albeit allowing to achieve the best result, is very time consuming and might not result affordable in cases, like the one here presented, where the rapidity of acquisition is a must. The images used for the virtual tour have been acquired with the Insta360 Pro 2 camera (see Fig. 1). It is a six-eye panoramic camera, whose wide-angle fish-eye lens is parallel to one turn of the camera itself. The Insta360 Pro 2 has an accurate stitching parameter that can be used in most shooting situations, which can vary due to the differences between specific shooting situations. Moreover, the stitching effect calibration on the camera or on the control app can be used.

Fig. 1. Frontal view of Insta360 Pro 2 camera.

It offers different camera connection modes which can be divided into three types: Farsight, Wired Connection and Wi-Fi Connection. The connection can occur through a computer, an Ipad or a smartphone, and thus have remote control of the camera. Among these modes, the wired connection has been achieved via a network cable or a local area network (LAN). Connecting via Farsight has a more stable signal and farther communication distance.

Fig. 2. Image of the entrance of faculty of Engineering.

Fig. 3. Image of break room of Engineering Faculty.

Summarizing, the special functions of this camera are:

1. FlowState stabilization: the Pro 2's hardware has 9-axis gyroscopes and implements a super FlowState stabilization to counteract moving scenes.
2. Photography with Auto Exposure Bracketing (AEB), which allows to choose to take 3, 5, 7, 9 photos at equal intervals for high dynamic range photos for post production synthesis.
3. All photo modes can be photographed in Raw + Jpg formats (generic single shot, AEB shot, groups of 10 burst photos, delayed timelapse photography). The images are stored in dng and jpg formats.

Fig. 4. Image of auditorium of Engineering Faculty.

4. HDR video: Some video modes allow to shoot high dynamic range HDR effect videos and are suitable for shooting scenes with a large illumination.
5. Multi-channel shooting, higher frequency, wider color gradation and better quality: Pro 2 has 7 cards stored inside, which include 6 TF (MicroSD) cards plus one SD card. When storing in the SD card of the real-time stitching with low bitrate proxy video, it can store the original high bitrate chip in 6 TF (MicroSD) cards up to 120 MBps, with more detail in the image quality. Pro 2 uses YUVJ420P, a color gamut that displays brighter and darker colors.
6. Dual antenna, more distant and stable signals: It has an external antenna to ensure smooth control preview from 0 to 20 m. The antenna and the GPS module have been added to the same camera, so as to avoid the clutter of external accessories and signal interference when shooting for Street View.
7. Onboard Farsight system support: the latest graphics transmission system introduced by Insta360, which can achieve smooth handling of long distances. The communication distance can be up to 300 m in open ground-to-ground environments without shelter.

3.2   Editing Tool for Virtual Tour

To the best of our knowledge, since there is not in literature a standard procedure to produce virtual tours, our idea is to create a standard data structure for this purpose. Nowadays, in fact, we can divide the tools for Virtual Tour Creation into two categories. Commercial software, like the more famous Pano2VR[1], that allow the user to manage the digital contents; the intuitive interfaces is at the expenses of costs, since an expert operator is needed and the number of panoramic images that can be managed is limited. Free of licenes web-tools like Marzipano[2], on the counterpart, have very limited and basic functions

---

[1] https://ggnome.com/pano2vr/.
[2] https://www.marzipano.net.

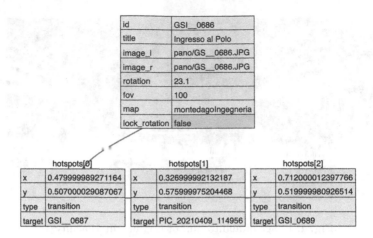

Fig. 5. JSON scheme of entrance of Engineering Faculty.

Data structures in Figs. 5, 6 and 7 are some examples of JSON diagrams of three different scenes belonging to the virtual tour. These diagrams have the same structure. That is, each scene is univocally identified by an ID code. Within each scene there is a number of hotspots, that represent interactable points linked to a list of contents available for users. Through the hotspot it is possible:

- to move towards another scene;
- to show contents in the form of: text, image, audio, and video.

The hotspots can be useful to track the path of visitors with the aim to obtain a quantitative evaluation of the most visited and attractive locations.

Moreover, the virtual tour has one or more maps. The map aims to provide a spatial positioning of different locations and a fast navigation. Then, the map is formed by an image with different locations, each of them associated with a scene. The tour is shown on a normal screen and the interaction occurs through a mouse or touch.

Some example of images belonging to the virtual tour of the Polytechnic University of Marche are presented in the Fig. 2, 3 and 4.

4   Data Analytics of the Virtual Tour

In this section, it is our aim to provide some insights about the potential given by the analytic tool set up for this virtual tour. Of course, the statistics here shown are limited to a specific monitoring period (1st of May to 01st of August). It is worth to note that the tour was not yet advertised at the time of the submission of this manuscript, even if the virtual tour is available in the University web-site [3].

---

[3] https://www.orienta.univpm.it/virtual-tour/.

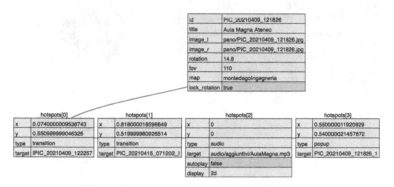

id	PIC_20210409_123944
title	Sala Ristoro
image_l	pano/PIC_20210409_123944.jpg
image_r	pano/PIC_20210409_123944.jpg
rotation	-152.4
fov	100
map	montedagoIngegneria
lock_rotation	true

hotspots[0]		hotspots[1]		hotspots[2]		hotspots[3]	
x	0.556999981403351	x	0.0939999967813492	x	0.416999995708466	x	0.163000002503395
y	0.50900000333786	y	0.510999977588654	y	0.524999976158142	y	0.513000011444092
type	transition	type	transition	type	transition	type	transition
target	IPIC_20210409_122257	target	PIC_20210415_063656	target	PIC_20210409_131558	target	PIC_20210409_132301

Fig. 6. JSON scheme of break room of Engineering Faculty.

id	PIC_20210409_121826
title	Aula Magna Ateneo
image_l	pano/PIC_20210409_121826.jpg
image_r	pano/PIC_20210409_121826.jpg
rotation	14.8
fov	110
map	montedagoIngegneria
lock_rotation	true

hotspots[0]		hotspots[1]		hotspots[2]		hotspots[3]	
x	0.0740000009536743	x	0.818000018596649	x	0	x	0.550000011920929
y	0.550999999046326	y	0.519999980926514	y	0	y	0.540000021457672
type	transition	type	transition	type	audio	type	popup
target	IPIC_20210409_122257	target	PIC_20210415_071202_l	target	audio/aggiuntivi/AulaMagna.mp3	target	PIC_20210409_121826_1
				autoplay	false		
				display	2d		

Fig. 7. JSON scheme of auditorium of Engineering Faculty.

Figure 8 shows that in total 1070 users access to the tour of which 1066 had never accessed the tour before that time. 1339 are the sessions started for a total of 1720 accesses to all pages. The averages are 1.25 sessions per user and 1.28 pages per session. The average duration of a session is 3 min and 1 s.

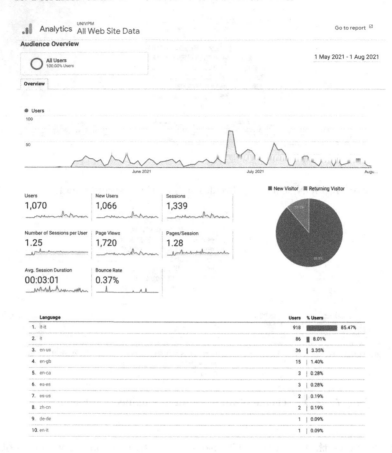

Fig. 8. Data Audience Overview in period from 2021/05/01 to 2021/08/01

Figure 9 shows a list of the visited pages in the considered period. In total, the different pages were opened 1720 times, but actually, for each session they were visited 1357 times.

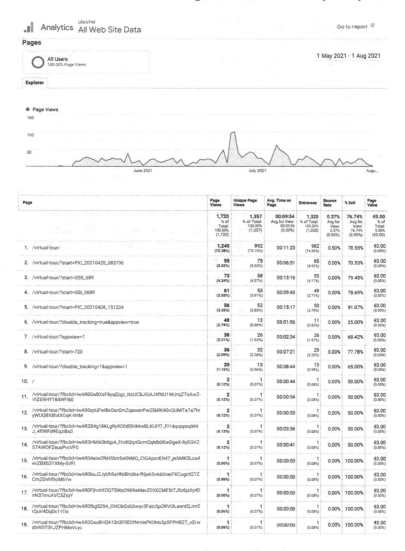

Fig. 9. Data pages. List of visited pages.

Figure 10 presents a list of pages with which the session began started; while Fig. 11 in detail considers the list of the exit pages from the session.

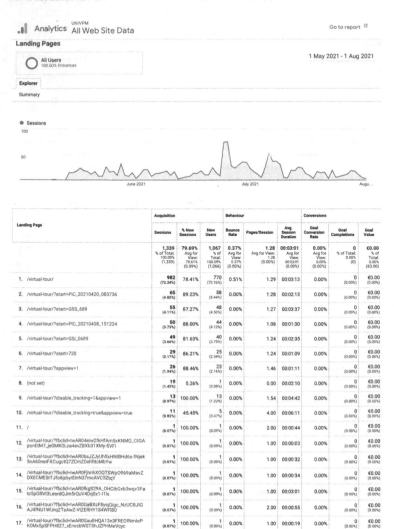

Fig. 10. Data landing pages.

Figures 12 and 13 respectively present the list of nation and the list of city from which the tour was accessed.

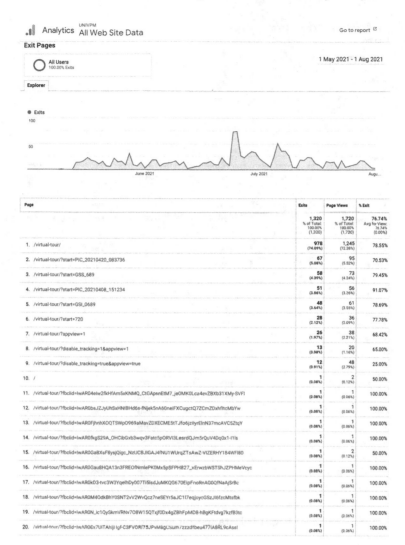

Fig. 11. Data exit pages.

A list of devices from which the tour was accessed is presented in Fig. 14. There are smartphone, tablet and computer.

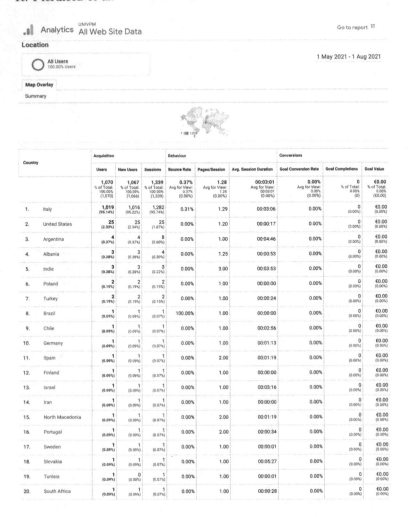

Fig. 12. Data nation location.

Interesting is the information concerning the way with which users have accessed the tour. Figure 15 indicates that the access occurred mainly through a direct link, and minimally reference on the web, search engine. A more detailed description on the way and sources of access to the tour is highlighted in Fig. 16.

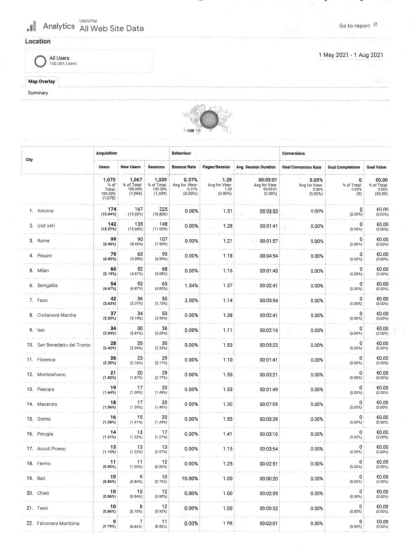

Fig. 13. Data city location.

Figure 17 shows the events generated by clicking on buttons during the tour. In particular, there were a total of 14828 interactions (user-button). Figure 18 shows a detail of the action generated by the event: 3880 times the "ing" button was clicked, while only 10 times the "MODE" button was clicked. Figure 19 shows a detail of the label associated to the event. Figure 20 represents the flow of the events departing from the page of access the tour.

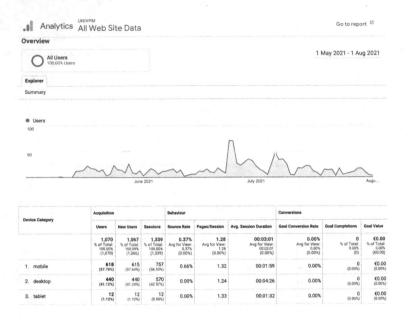

Fig. 14. Mobility. List of devices (mobile, tablet, desktop) used to access the tour.

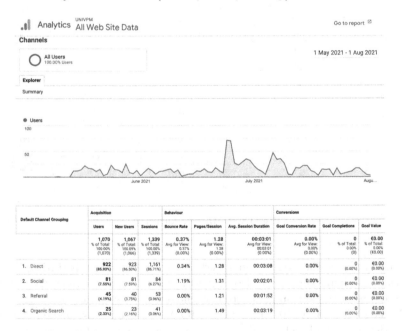

Fig. 15. Access Mode.

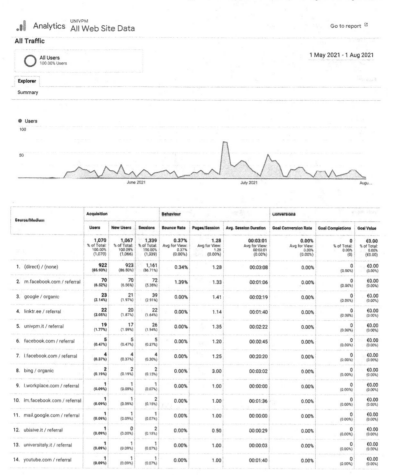

Fig. 16. Access source.

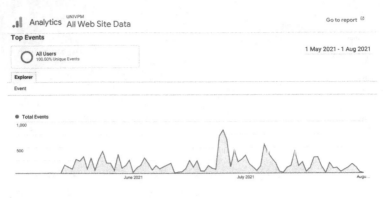

Fig. 17. Top event category.

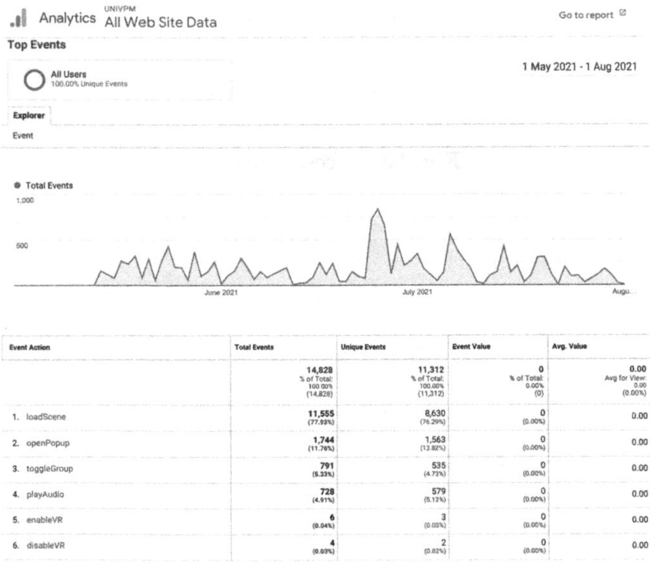

Event Action	Total Events	Unique Events	Event Value	Avg. Value
	14,828 % of Total: 100.00% (14,828)	11,312 % of Total: 100.00% (11,312)	0 % of Total: 0.00% (0)	0.00 Avg for View: 0.00 (0.00%)
1. loadScene	11,555 (77.93%)	8,630 (76.29%)	0 (0.00%)	0.00
2. openPopup	1,744 (11.76%)	1,563 (13.82%)	0 (0.00%)	0.00
3. toggleGroup	791 (5.33%)	535 (4.73%)	0 (0.00%)	0.00
4. playAudio	728 (4.91%)	579 (5.12%)	0 (0.00%)	0.00
5. enableVR	6 (0.04%)	3 (0.03%)	0 (0.00%)	0.00
6. disableVR	4 (0.03%)	2 (0.02%)	0 (0.00%)	0.00

Fig. 18. Top event action.

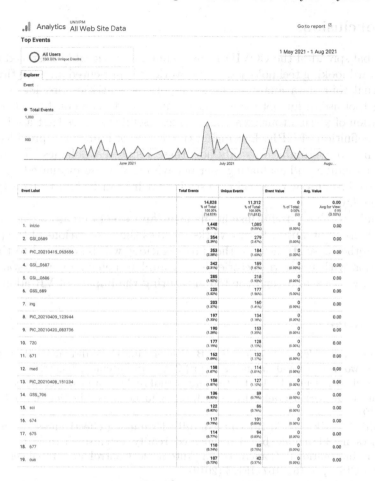

Fig. 19. Top event label.

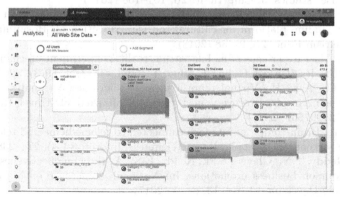

Fig. 20. Events flow detail.

5   Conclusions

The global spread of the COVID-19 pandemic has noticeably hastened the testing forward-looking technologies. In this work, it is presented an analytics system for virtual tour data analysis. These important statistics provide a decision-making tool useful for both the manager and the developers. In fact, the standardization of virtual tour creation provides useful statistics that are important for the definition of KPIs. Leveraging the degree of immersion provided by virtual tours, we were able to study how these rising technologies can contribute to understanding and evaluating user behaviour. We also evaluated and defined immersive insights, with a real case study which is an Italian University during the open days.

Thanks to these useful insight manager and events creators can define the virtual journey of a user. Future works involves the applications of the proposed tools to other case studies. Further investigations will be devoted to the to the integration with users' trajectories for a complete behaviour understanding. In addition, we seek to extend the tool measuring the impact of VR adoption.

References

1. Aguilera, J., Alonso, F., Gomez, J.B.: Generating three-dimensional virtual tours from two-dimensional images, 22 April 2014, uS Patent 8,705,892
2. Alenazi, M., Demir, F.: Understanding virtual reality tours: a user experience study with the princess Norah University. Int. J. Current Res. Life Sci. 8(10), 3248–3253 (2019)
3. Andri, C., Alkawaz, M.H., Waheed, S.R.: Examining effectiveness and user experiences in 3d mobile based augmented reality for msu virtual tour. In: 2019 IEEE International Conference on Automatic Control and Intelligent Systems (I2CACIS), pp. 161–167. IEEE (2019)
4. Barbieri, L., Bruno, F., Muzzupappa, M.: Virtual museum system evaluation through user studies. J. Cult. Herit. 26, 101–108 (2017)
5. Chiao, H.M., Chen, Y.L., Huang, W.H.: Examining the usability of an online virtual tour-guiding platform for cultural tourism education. J. Hospitality Leisure Sport Tourism Educ. 23, 29–38 (2018)
6. Dirin, A.: User experience of mobile virtual reality: experiment on changes in students' attitudes. Turkish Online J. Educ. Technol. -TOJET 19(3), 80–93 (2020)
7. El-Said, O., Aziz, H.: Virtual tours a means to an end: An analysis of virtual tours' role in tourism recovery post covid-19. Journal of Travel Research, p. 0047287521997567 (2021)
8. Hsu, W.Y.: Brain-computer interface connected to telemedicine and telecommunication in virtual reality applications. Telematics Inform. 34(4), 224–238 (2017)
9. JS, R., Reddy, T.N., Ghouse, S.M., Reddy, K.S.: A study on effectiveness of google virtual tour on business promotions. In: National Conference on Marketing and Sustainable Development, vol. 13, p. 14 (2017)
10. Kabassi, K., Amelio, A., Komianos, V., Oikonomou, K.: Evaluating museum virtual tours: the case study of Italy. Information 10(11), 351 (2019)
11. Mohammad, A.O.N.A.W., Ismail, H.: Development and evaluation of an interactive 360 virtual tour for tourist destinations (2009)

12. Ortiz, J.L.: A case study in the roi of online virtual tours (2003)
13. Pagano, A., Palombini, A., Bozzelli, G., Nino, M.D., Cerato, I., Ricciardi, S.: Arkae-vision vr game: user experience research between real and virtual paestum. Appl. Sci. **10**(9), 3182 (2020)
14. Pierdicca, R., Frontoni, E., Zingaretti, P., Mancini, A., Loncarski, J., Paolanti, M.: Design, large-scale usage testing, and important metrics for augmented reality gaming applications. ACM Trans. Multimed. Comput. Commun. Appl. **15**(2) (2019). https://doi.org/10.1145/3311748
15. Pierdicca, R., Paolanti, M., Frontoni, E.: etourism: Ict and its role for tourism management. J. Hospitality Tourism Technol. (2019)
16. SETIAWAN, Y., ERLANSHARI, A., Mochammad, Y., Purwandari, E.P., et al.: Usability testing to measure real perception generation level in introduction of bengkulu university building based on virtual tour with 360° object modelling. In: Sriwijaya International Conference on Information Technology and Its Applications (SICONIAN 2019), pp. 645–648. Atlantis Press (2020)
17. Spielmann, N., Mantonakis, A.: In virtuo: how user-driven interactivity in virtual tours leads to attitude change. J. Bus. Res. **88**, 255–264 (2018)
18. Stewart, S., Warburton, F., Smith, J.D.: Cambridge international AS and A level travel and tourism coursebook. Cambridge University Press (2016)
19. Venkatesh, V., Thong, J.Y., Xu, X.: Consumer acceptance and use of information technology: extending the unified theory of acceptance and use of technology. MIS quarterly, pp. 157–178 (2012)
20. Yang, T., Lai, I.K.W., Fan, Z.B., Mo, Q.M.: The impact of a 360° virtual tour on the reduction of psychological stress caused by covid-19. Technol. Soc. **64**, 101514 (2021)

Immersive VR as a Promising Technology for Computer-Supported Mindfulness

Lucio Tommaso De Paolis[1]([✉]), Pasquale Arpaia[2], Giovanni D'Errico[2], Carola Gatto[3], Nicola Moccaldi[2], and Fabiana Nuccetelli[4]

[1] Department of Engineering for Innovation, University of Salento, Lecce, Italy
lucio.depaolis@unisalento.it
[2] Department of Electrical Engineering and Information Technology,
University of Naples, Federico II, Naples, Italy
{pasquale.arpaia,nicola.moccaldi}@unina.it,
giovanni.derrico@unisalento.it
[3] Department of Cultural Heritage, University of Salento, Lecce, Italy
carola.gatto@unisalento.it
[4] Department of Health Psychology, Nursing Home "Prof. Petrucciani", Lecce, Italy
fabiana.nuccetelli@libero.it

Abstract. Therapeutic effects of Mindfulness meditation practices in clinical interventions, specifically in the treatment of stress, anxiety, depression, chronic and acute pain are scientifically well founded. Mindfulness is increasingly being supported by technology and among various interventions immersive VR seems rather peculiar due to its ability to improve decentering and interoceptive awareness. A systematic review on Virtual Reality supported Mindfulness is currently being published. In this paper, some preliminary results of this review are presented, also providing a brief discussion about a possible evolutionary technological trend, on the basis of the input and output perceptual domains exploited.

Keywords: Virtual Reality · Mindfulness · Meditation · Biofeedback · Neurofeedback

1 Introduction

In the neuroscience literature [1,2], meditation is described as a set of complex training strategies aimed to perform a regulation of attention and emotions, and oriented to foster general well-being and emotional balance. The term refers to a wide variety of practices, such as techniques to promote relaxation and exercises performed to reach a greater sense of well-being.

The most common forms of meditation can be classified as Focused Attention (FA) or Open Monitoring (OM) Meditation [1]. In the former, selective attention is focused on a specific object (e.g., localised sensation of breathing) in a sustained way. The latter involves non-reactive and continuous monitoring of the events occurring during the meditation experience to promote a non-judgemental awareness.

© Springer Nature Switzerland AG 2021
L. T. De Paolis et al. (Eds.): AVR 2021, LNCS 12980, pp. 156–166, 2021.
https://doi.org/10.1007/978-3-030-87595-4_12

Most of the recent scientific interest in meditation has focused on Mindfulness meditation [2,3], which often directly refers to OM meditation [4,5], but actually includes both the previous categories, with the underlying implicated psychological processes [1]. According to Kabat-Zinn, Mindfulness is *"the awareness that emerges through paying attention on purpose, in the present moment, and non-judgmentally to the unfolding of experience moment by moment"* [6]. It promotes a peculiar attention regulation, which refers to the *"non elaborative awareness of thoughts, feelings, and sensations as they arise"* [7].

A huge interest has grown towards both therapeutic effects in clinical interventions, with a peculiar focus on stress-related problems, leading to several consolidated Mindfulness-Based Interventions (MBIs), and, more in general, to non formal wellness promotion programs. Over the years, an important support to Mindfulness has come from the ICT world, which provided several technological solutions oriented to support users to approach the meditation practice and to increase retention, affection and motivation to it.

In the first computer-supported Mindfulness era, computers were used to deliver and teach Mindfulness techniques, simply presenting them to users without providing interactive practices and immersive solutions [8]. Initially, the clinical field was the most explored, including the treatment of stress syndrome [9], chronic pain [10,11], irritable bowel syndrome [12], and depression in epileptic subjects [13]. Several papers begin to point out the increase in the effectiveness of computer-supported Mindfulness compared to traditional strategies. In [14], one of the first simple interactive exercises is proposed, by offering a tool for emotion labeling and disidentification from recurring thoughts. In a non-judgmental way, the user labels a passing cloud on a blue sky background with his or her emerging thoughts. Then, he/she simply watches his/her thoughts drift away with the cloud.

A further upgrade of computer-supported Mindfulness was achieved through the concept of an embodied conversational agent: in [15], a virtual coach is proposed to support the patient's Mindfulness training via the web.

Immersive Virtual Reality (VR) emerges as a peculiar technology to improve the practice of Mindfulness meditation, thanks to the immersion feature provided and the following sense of presence. It can offer an isolation from outer distractors, also allowing the practitioner to live a multisensory connection with nature-inspired environments and by offering the chance for customized and user-tailored experiences.

In a previous work, an innovative ICT technologies based methodology was discussed in order to protect the vulnerable population in the context of Covid-19 emergency [16]. In particular, the feasibility of a combination of Cross Reality (XR) and therapeutic methods of Mindfulness and Art Therapy was evaluated.

According to Moseley et al. [17], the brain constantly generates and updates a *body matrix*, a predictive representation of the body and the surrounding space, based on all individual's perceptual channels (sensory, interoceptive, proprioceptive and vestibular). Immersive Virtual Reality has in common with the brain the same predictive mechanism, and whether enhanced by neuro/biofeedback, it can act at both exteroceptive (sensory) and interoceptive level in order to provide vivid and believable experiences [18]. It could then promote and alteration of the body matrix, by correcting dysfunctional body representations.

A systematic review was recently published, focusing more generally on immersive technologies to support Mindfulness meditation [19]. This work highlights body-based innovations specifically provided by Extended Reality (XR) but does not adequately emphasize why XR is so peculiar in supporting Mindfulness in terms of immersion and alterations of the body matrix.

The lack of a specific survey covering exhaustively studies on VR-supported Mindfulness, stimulated us to produce a currently being published systematic review, aimed at assessing appropriately the scientific relevance of the reviewed researches. A framework-background, useful to position future studies on this topic, has also been produced according to Kitchenham's guidelines [20].

In this paper, some preliminary results of the aforementioned review are presented, also providing a brief discussion about a possible evolutionary technological trend, according to the perceptual input and output channels considered by the multimodal immersive VR systems.

In the following, the methods and the preliminary survey results are presented in Sects. 2 and 3, respectively, by dedicating two different subsections to mobile apps (Sect. 3.1) and VR-based solutions (Sect. 3.2) separately. Then, Sect. 4 will be reserved to Conclusions.

2   Methods

A systematic review about immersive VR-supported Mindfulness solutions is currently being published and it has been produced following PRISMA reccomendations in order to report paper extraction process transparently. The literature research has been performed in the period until December 2020, considering Computing Machinery (ACM), Science Direct, Web of Science, Scopus, IEEE (Institute of Electrical and Electronics Engineers) Xplore and PubMed as databases. The included articles were required to have a peer review, published in journal or conference proceedings, and written in English.

The research query applied was: (VR OR Virtual Reality) AND Mindfulness.

Taking into account some exclusion criteria, studies referring to Mindfulness as a dispositional trait or considering non-immersive VR solutions not specifically based on 3D computer graphics or first-person perspective (1PP) were kept out.

A quality assessment of the reviewed papers has been carrying on, by also clustering them according to specific research goals.

In this paper a preliminary results selection is provided, highlighting some technological emerging perspectives.

3   Preliminary Results

Analyzing the preliminary results of the ongoing survey from a technological point of view, interesting evidences emerge which allow us to make some exploratory considerations on the future trend of computer-supported Mindfulness.

A first general consideration is that the combination of ICT and Mindfulness technologies is having a great impact on the wellness market, leading to a proliferation of companies offering digital Mindfulness solutions on several app stores. Therefore, a first important use of technological solutions to support meditative practice is oriented to the free time of users, having a significant relevance also on the consumer market. Despite their market relevance which is an index of the social impact of the phenomenon, these solutions still appear far from representing a consolidated and well-structured protocol for the promotion of well-being.

At the same time, there is a clinical/therapeutic use of computer-supported Mindfulness solutions, which requires some particular technological conditions. In this context, immersive VR-based solutions take place, offering greater levels of immersion and sense of presence and acting on the interoceptive awareness and the body matrix.

The collected papers generally present VR-based solutions in the context of Computer supported Mindfulness, focusing the phenomenon of mobile apps. Thus, the phenomenon of mobile apps, representing the subset with the greatest impact on the market, are discussed (Subsect. 3.1). Subsequently, VR-based solutions are focused (Subsect. 3.2), considering also the integration of bio/neurofeedback. In this subsection, a perspective table, useful to critically classify current available studies, is provided.

3.1   The Mobile App Invasion

The feasibility of computer supported Mindfulness is made evident by the now disruptive spread of mobile apps. Referring, for example, to the Google Play Store, over 250 Mindfulness and meditation apps were downloadable during December 2020. Nevertheless, the effectiveness of the majority of these applications is not proved yet. A recent study [21] shows the benefits of distributing Mindfulness sessions through mobile apps, suggesting that short guided Mindfulness meditations provided via smartphone and practiced several times a week may improve results related to stress and well-being at work, with potentially long-lasting effects.

In many of the papers collected in the survey, references to smartphone apps appear. Given the economic and social importance of the phenomenon, the cited apps were classified by identifying five main categories (Fig. 1):

- *General support to the practice:* apps offering guided meditations and timer tools to remember or timing the practice [22–27];
- *Thought Distancing Techniques:* working on reaction to thoughts, teaching to become aware and simply observing them as they go away [8, 28–31];
- *Breathing Techniques:* the user is asked to pay attention to his own breathing, for example, touching the screen with each breathing cycle [32];

- *Neurofeedback Support:* used in combination with the EEG Muse headset and offering the mental state feedback for modulating the meditation experience [33];
- *Mindfulness Therapy* explicitly dedicated to the clinical/therapeutic field including (i) an app for stress syndrome management by Acceptance and Commitment Therapy (ACT) [34], and (ii) two apps where a generic mobile app-based Mindfulness protocol is implemented, for light depression treatment [35], and stress reduction [36], respectively.

Year	Mobile APP	Interactive	Category	Available on the Store	Appl. Field
2010	Mindfulness Meditation [23]	✗	General Support to the Practice	✗	Ed
2011	Just Let Go [27]	✓	Thought Distancing Techniques	✗	Ed
2011	The Shredder [28]	✓	Thought Distancing Techniques	✗	Ed
2011	Throw Your Worry Away! [29]	✓	Thought Distancing Techniques	✗	Ed
2011	Worrydoll Lite [30]	✓	Thought Distancing Techniques	✓	Ed
2012	Lotus Bud Mindfulness Bell [21]	✗	General Support to the Practice	✓	Ed
2012	Zazen Suite - Mindfulness Bell [22]	✗	General Support to the Practice	✓	Ed
2012	The Mindfulness App [24]	✗	General Support to the Practice	✓	Ed
2012	Mindfulness TS [31]	✓	Breathing Techniques	✗	Ed
2013	OIVA [33]	✓	ACT Therapy	✗	Th
2014	AEON Mindfulness App [8]	✓	Thought Distancing Techniques	✓	Ed
2014	Mindfulness [34]	✗	General Guided Meditation	✓	Th
2014	Muse Meditation Assistant [32] (**)	✓	Neurofeedback	✓	Ed
2015	It's time to relax! [35]	✗	General Guided Meditation	✗	Th
2019	HeadSpace [25]	✗	General Guided Meditation	✓	Ed
2019	Buddhify [26]	✗	General Guided Meditation	✓	Ed

Fig. 1. Mobile apps for Mindfulness cited in the scientific literature [Education (Ed), Therapy (Th)].

3.2   VR Based Mindfulness

The growing interest of the clinical world towards computer-supported Mindfulness requires to deeply discuss about specific technological requirements. Two of the most important mechanisms at the base of Mindfulness are body awareness and decentering [37]. The first has to do with the ability to correctly access and appraise body signals [38]. The second refers to the adoption of an objective and non-judgmental attitude towards one's self [39]. When these mechanisms appear dysfunctional, they generate pathological implications: a poor interoceptive awareness is often linked to anxiety, chronic pain and eating disorders, a high decentering is often connected to depressive symptoms. Mindfulness already prevents and treats these dysfunctional forms in itself [40,41]. By creating a presence in a virtual body and in the surrounding virtual space, VR provides the building of a new vision of the self [42]. Furthermore, through the use of neuro/biofeedback, immersive VR proposes experience able to intervent on body matrix, and on interoceptive awareness.

All the input and output channels considered by a multimodal immersive VR-supported Mindfulness system are shown in Fig. 2. It seems very useful for evaluating which perceptual domains are used by VR-supported Mindfulness and which are not.

	Perceptive Domain	Channel	Technology	A representative study
Input	Sensorial	Visual	Camera	(Room et al. 2017)
		Acoustic	Microphone	(Cikajlo et al. 2016)
		Tactile	Pressure sensors	(Gromala et al. 2011)
		Olfactory	Chemical sensors (aeriform)	(Keller et al. 1995)
		Gustatory	Chemical sensors (liquid and solid)	
	Vestibular		Accelerometer, gyroscope, magnetometer	(Blum et al. 2019)
	Proprioceptive		Optical, acoustic and microwave sensors	(Chessa et al. 2016)
	Interoceptive	Brain	EEG	(Kosunen et al. 2016)
		Other organs	Biosignal	(Seol et al. 2017)
ouput	Sensorial	Visual	Display	(Navarro Haro et al. 2017)
		Acoustic	Speakers	(Navarro Haro et al. 2017)
		Tactile	Haptic Interface	(Seol et al. 2017)
		Olfactory	Aeriform Synthesizer	(Micaroni et al. 2019)
		Gustatory	Chemical, electrical and acoustic actuators	(Vi et al. 2017)
	Vestibular		Vibro-tactile actuators	(Paredes et al. 2018)
	Proprioceptive		Vibro-tactile actuators	(Riva et al. 2017)
	Interoceptive	Brain	Acoustic actuators	(Sas and Chopra 2015)
		Other organs	Vibro-tactile actuators	(Riva et al. 2017)

Fig. 2. Perceptual input and output channels considered by the multimodal immersive VR-supported Mindfulness systems. Grey-coloured references refer to non-Mindfulness studies.

Despite this general overview, only a part of these channels have been already taken into account by the reviewed literature. As regards outputs, most of the solutions consider only visual and acoustic sensory channels. This is the case, for instance, of Navarro-Haro and colleagues [43]. In accordance with Attention Restoration Theory (ART), the authors proposed a nature-inspired virtual scenario aimed at treating Borderline Personality Disorder, by implementing Dialectical Behavior Therapy (DBT) (see Fig. 3.A). The study hightlights the long-term benefits in patients, who gain higher levels of acceptance with a better therapeutic outcome.

Seol et al. [44] extends multimodality also to haptic channel: the proposed system feeds back the heart rate information by means of an haptic physical model of the user's heart beating in his/her hand (see Fig. 3.B). This represents a peculiar example of how concentration on the present moment could be improved through an augmented virtuality strategy. Dramatically lower is the number of studies which consider interoceptive and vestibular outputs. Regarding the former, Paredes and colleagues [45] proposed a mindful in-car virtual reality intervention in order to adequately stimulate the vestibular system: the use of relaxing VR content in a dynamic context like a moving car, can lead to lower autonomic arousal levels. The only reviewed paper that works with interoceptive feedbacks is [46]. The authors stress the advantages of using EEG-based binaural feedback in order to reach deeper meditative states. The interoception is oriented to the brain directly, and the brain activity modulation is induced on a physiological level. None of the collected papers exploit other interoceptive, proprioceptive or alternative sensory channels (e.g. olfactory and gustatory), even though a consistent literature in a more general VR context has been consolidating [18,47,48].

As regards input, sensory channels are sometimes exploited: the visual information captured by a camera has received in input in augmented reality scenarios [49], while acoustic data can be acquired by using a microphone and sent to the meditation platform, like in [50] which proposes a web-based delivered VR Mindfulness. An interesting case study about the haptic input is [51], where a virtual meditative walk is implemented and the movement of the user into the virtual environment is allowed by a treadmill.

Neuro/biofeedback enhanced system are characterized by exploiting interoceptive input: in [52] alpha and theta waves activity are both involved during meditation and they are connected to relaxation and concentration respectively (see Fig. 3.C). Vestibular input is quite exploited by all systems using HMD equipped by inertial sensors [53].

Immersive VR-supported Mindfulness has not been used in many perceptual domains: therefore it is not yet used to its full potential to support Mindfulness. Generally, the higher will be the number of perceptive channels considered, the more VR tool will be well exploited to support Mindfulness. The overall use of all channels will lead scientists to broaden the discussion not limiting it only to immersive VR, by including all the possibilities in the XR spectrum.

Fig. 3. A. A virtual reality world watched by the participant through the Oculus Rift; B. A biofeedback based VR-haptic system; C. A neurofeedback based immersive VR solution.

4   Conclusions

Immersive virtual reality turns out to be one of the most peculiar technologies in support of Mindfulness meditation, due to some specific technological features. In particular, immersion is defined as the ability to actively stimulate the user through a wide set of perceptual channels, both external (sensory) and internal (e.g. interoceptive). Immersion and its psychological product, the sense of presence, make the immersive VR system capable of altering the body matrix and intervening on decentralization and interoceptive awareness.

Until now, there are no literature surveys specifically focused on virtual reality assisted Mindfulness. In this paper, some preliminary results of an ongoing review on VR supported Mindfulness are presented. In particular, a brief discussion is developed on possible evolutionary technological trends, according to the perceptive input and output VR channels.

Immersive Mindfulness supported by virtual reality still appears to be underused in many perceptual domains. Researchers are supposed to consider the most of the perceptual domains properly, in order to get the highest potential by VR in supporting Mindfulness meditation.

References

1. Lutz, A., Slagter, H.A., Dunne, J.D., Davidson, R.J.: Attention regulation and monitoring in meditation. Trends Cogn. Sci. **12**, 163–169 (2008)
2. Lomas, T., Ivtzan, I., Fu, C.H.: A systematic review of the neurophysiology of mindfulness on eeg oscillations. Neurosci. Biobehav. Rev. **57**, 401–410 (2015)
3. Chiesa, A., Calati, R., Serretti, A.: Does mindfulness training improve cognitive abilities? a systematic review of neuropsychological findings. Clin. Psychol. Rev. **31**, 449–464 (2011)
4. Raffone, A., Srinivasan, N.: The exploration of meditation in the neuroscience of attention and consciousness (2010)
5. Cahn, B.R., Polich, J.: Meditation states and traits: Eeg, erp, and neuroimaging studies. Psychol. Bull. **132**, 180 (2006)
6. Kabat-Zinn, J.: Mindfulness-based interventions in context: past, present, and future. Clin. Psychol. Sci. Pract. **10**, 144–156 (2003)
7. Bishop, S.R., et al.: Mindfulness: a proposed operational definition. Clin. Psychol. Sci. Pract. **11**, 230–241 (2004)
8. Chittaro, L., Vianello, A.: Computer-supported mindfulness: Evaluation of a mobile thought distancing application on naive meditators. Int. J. Hum. Comput. Stud. **72**, 337–348 (2014)
9. Krusche, A., Cyhlarova, E., King, S., Williams, J.M.G.: Mindfulness online: a preliminary evaluation of the feasibility of a web-based mindfulness course and the impact on stress. BMJ open 2 (2012)
10. Gardner-Nix, J., Backman, S., Barbati, J., Grummitt, J.: Evaluating distance education of a mindfulness-based meditation programme for chronic pain management. J. Telemed. Telecare **14**, 88–92 (2008)

11. Kristjánsdóttir, Ó.B., et al.: Written online situational feedback via mobile phone to support self-management of chronic widespread pain: a usability study of a web-based intervention. BMC Musculoskelet. Disord. **12**, 51 (2011)
12. Ljótsson, B., et al.: Internet-delivered exposure and mindfulness based therapy for irritable bowel syndrome-a randomized controlled trial. Behav. Res. Ther. **48**, 531–539 (2010)
13. Thompson, N.J., et al.: Distance delivery of mindfulness-based cognitive therapy for depression: project uplift. Epilepsy Behav. **19**, 247–254 (2010)
14. Glück, T.M., Maercker, A.: A randomized controlled pilot study of a brief web-based mindfulness training. BMC Psychiatry **11**, 175 (2011)
15. Hudlicka, E.: Virtual training and coaching of health behavior: example from mindfulness meditation training. Patient Educ. Couns. **92**, 160–166 (2013)
16. Gatto, C. et al. Xr-based mindfulness and art therapy: Facing the psychological impact of covid-19 emergency. In International Conference on Augmented Reality, Virtual Reality and Computer Graphics, 147–155 (Springer, 2020)
17. Moseley, G.L., Gallace, A., Spence, C.: Bodily illusions in health and disease: physiological and clinical perspectives and the concept of a cortical 'body matrix'. Neurosci. Biobehav. Rev. **36**, 34–46 (2012)
18. Riva, G., Serino, S., Di Lernia, D., Pavone, E.F., Dakanalis, A.: Embodied medicine: mens sana in corpore virtuale sano. Front. Hum. Neurosci. **11**, 120 (2017)
19. Döllinger, N., Wienrich, C., Latoschik, M.E.: Challenges and opportunities of immersive technologies for mindfulness meditation: a systematic review. Frontiers Virtual Reality **2**, 29 (2021)
20. Kitchenham, B.: Procedures for performing systematic reviews. Keele, UK, Keele University **33**, 1–26 (2004)
21. Bostock, S., Crosswell, A.D., Prather, A.A., Steptoe, A.: Mindfulness on-the-go: effects of a mindfulness meditation app on work stress and well-being. J. Occup. Health Psychol. **24**, 127 (2019)
22. Sager. Lotus Bud Mindfulness Bell (Version 1.0) [Mobile application software] (2012)
23. Hangen. Zazen Suite - Meditation Timer & Mindfulness Bell (Version 1.13) (2012)
24. Inc., M. W. Mindfulness Meditation (Version 3.0) [Mobile application software] (2010)
25. The Mindfulness App (Version 1.5) [Mobile application software] (2012)
26. Headspace. Headspace - Your guide to health and happiness (2015). https://www.headspace.com/
27. Ltd, M. E. Buddhify: Meditation & Mindfulness App. (2019). https://buddhify.com/
28. Wolffram, J.T.: Just Let Go (Version 1.0) [Mobile applicationsoftware] (2011)
29. Bowers. The Shredder (Version 1.0) [Mobile application software] (2011)
30. Keru. Throw your worry away! (Version 1.2) [Mobile application software] (2011)
31. Dontworrycompany. Worrydoll lite (Version 1.01) [Mobile applicationsoftware] (2011)
32. Mindfulness TS (Version 2.1) [Mobile application software] (2012)
33. Interaxon. Muse (2014). https://choosemuse.com/
34. Ahtinen, A., et al.: Mobile mental wellness training for stress management: feasibility and design implications based on a one-month field study. JMIR Mhealth Uhealth **1**, e11 (2013)
35. Ly, K.H., et al.: Behavioural activation versus mindfulness-based guided self-help treatment administered through a smartphone application: a randomised controlled trial. BMJ open 4 (2014)

36. Carissoli, C., Villani, D., Riva, G.: Does a meditation protocol supported by a mobile application help people reduce stress? suggestions from a controlled pragmatic trial. Cyberpsychol. Behav. Soc. Netw. **18**, 46–53 (2015)
37. Fresco, D.M., et al.: Initial psychometric properties of the experiences questionnaire: validation of a self-report measure of decentering. Behav. Ther. **38**, 234–246 (2007)
38. Farb, N., et al.: Interoception, contemplative practice, and health. Front. Psychol. **6**, 763 (2015)
39. Kessel, R., et al.: Exploring the relationship of decentering to health related concepts and cognitive and metacognitive processes in a student sample. BMC psychology **4**, 1–10 (2016)
40. Hanley, A.W., Mehling, W.E., Garland, E.L.: Holding the body in mind: Interoceptive awareness, dispositional mindfulness and psychological well-being. J. Psychosom. Res. **99**, 13–20 (2017)
41. Hölzel, B.K., et al.: How does mindfulness meditation work? proposing mechanisms of action from a conceptual and neural perspective. Perspect. Psychol. Sci. **6**, 537–559 (2011)
42. Riva, G., Wiederhold, B.K., Mantovani, F.: Neuroscience of virtual reality: from virtual exposure to embodied medicine. Cyberpsychol. Behav. Soc. Netw. **22**, 82–96 (2019)
43. Navarro-Haro, M.V., et al.: Meditation experts try virtual reality mindfulness: A pilot study evaluation of the feasibility and acceptability of virtual reality to facilitate mindfulness practice in people attending a mindfulness conference. PLoS ONE **12**, e0187777 (2017)
44. Seol, E., et al.: Drop the beat: virtual reality based mindfulness and cognitive behavioral therapy for panic disorder–a pilot study. In: Proceedings of the 23rd ACM Symposium on Virtual Reality Software and Technology, pp. 1–3 (2017)
45. Paredes, P.E., et al.: Driving with the fishes: towards calming and mindful virtual reality experiences for the car. Proc. ACM Interactive, Mobile, Wearable Ubiquitous Technol. **2**, 1–21 (2018)
46. Sas, C., Chopra, R.: Meditaid: a wearable adaptive neurofeedback-based system for training mindfulness state. Pers. Ubiquit. Comput. **19**, 1169–1182 (2015)
47. Micaroni, L., Carulli, M., Ferrise, F., Gallace, A., Bordegoni, M.: An olfactory display to study the integration of vision and olfaction in a virtual reality environment. J. Comput. Inf. Sci. Eng. **19**, 031015 (2019)
48. Vi, C.T., Ablart, D., Arthur, D., Obrist, M.: Gustatory interface: the challenges of 'how'to stimulate the sense of taste. In: Proceedings of the 2nd ACM SIGCHI International Workshop on Multisensory Approaches to Human-Food Interaction, pp. 29–33 (2017)
49. Roo, J.S., Gervais, R., Frey, J., Hachet, M.: Inner garden: connecting inner states to a mixed reality sandbox for mindfulness. In: Proceedings of the 2017 CHI Conference on Human Factors in Computing Systems, pp. 1459–1470 (2017)
50. Cikajlo, I., Čižman-Štaba, U., Vrhovac, S., Larkin, F., Roddy, M.: Recovr: realising collaborative virtual reality for wellbeing and self-healing. In: Proceedings of the 3rd IASTED International Conference Telehealth Assistive Technology TAT, pp. 11–17 (2016)

51. Gromala, D., et al.: Immersive vr: a non-pharmacological analgesic for chronic pain? In: CHI'11 Extended Abstracts on Human Factors in Computing Systems, pp. 1171–1176 (2011)
52. Kosunen, I., et al.: Relaworld: neuroadaptive and immersive virtual reality meditation system. In: Proceedings of the 21st International Conference on Intelligent User Interfaces, pp. 208–217 (2016)
53. Blum, J., Rockstroh, C., Göritz, A.S.: Heart rate variability biofeedback based on slow-paced breathing with immersive virtual reality nature scenery. Front. Psychol. 10, 2172 (2019)

Augmented Reality

AR Scribble: Evaluating Design Patterns for Augmented Reality User Interfaces

Ingo Börsting[✉][iD], Bastian Fischer, and Volker Gruhn[iD]

University of Duisburg-Essen, Essen, Germany
{ingo.boersting,bastian.fischer,volker.gruhn}@uni-due.de

Abstract. The virtual enhancement of the physical world through Augmented Reality (AR) has an enormous potential in its application, but faces challenges in its development. The lack of standards and the increased complexity of interaction opportunities complicate the definition of suitable User Interfaces (UIs). Several principles and patterns have been formulated to simplify UI design for AR applications, but their joint contribution to a positive usability as well as the influence of individual patterns remain unclear. In this paper we merged design principles for AR to formulate a comprehensive pattern model. Based on this model, we developed AR Scribble, a mobile AR application which imitates a physical spray can to virtually sketch within a real environment. In a user-based study, we evaluated the usability of AR Scribble as well as the role of individual patterns for the overall usability. We found promising indications that the pattern model implementation is related to a positive usability. The individual pattern analysis showed that AR users particularly desire a consistent and structured UI. A consistent appealing design and multimodal interaction concepts were also found to positively correlate with the overall usability.

Keywords: Augmented reality · User interface · Design patterns

1 Introduction

The novel technology Augmented Reality allows the extension of the physical world by virtual information and is already used in many application areas. AR has an enormous potential and enables novel interaction possibilities, but faces challenges in the development process, including the complex modeling of 3D content and interactions [17]. Furthermore, the relevance of the physical world requires AR user interfaces to comprise virtual and physical artifacts, resulting in a particularly complex development process [1]. Since no standards for AR UI engineering have yet been established [18,20], each UI concept has to be considered individually. Thus, Ashtari et al. [3] name the lack of concrete design guidelines as one of the key barriers to AR development.

Current AR usability research often focusses on the adaption of established UI engineering methods to AR requirements. For example, sketching has been

© Springer Nature Switzerland AG 2021
L. T. De Paolis et al. (Eds.): AVR 2021, LNCS 12980, pp. 169–177, 2021.
https://doi.org/10.1007/978-3-030-87595-4_13

applied for the conception of AR UIs, especially regarding virtual objects [13,16] or as a foundation for interaction prototyping [12]. Prototyping itself is applied to iterate and evaluate interaction concepts in order to foster design decisions [14], even using related technologies like Virtual Reality [6].

Only few approaches have focused on the core objective, the formulation of usability guidelines for the creation of AR UIs. Here, most approaches formulate best practices by performing meta analyses of AR applications. In a few cases, this results in usability principles [15], pre-patterns [22] or design heuristics [11], which are often focused on a specific domain, such as educational video games [7], kindergarten applications [21] or industry 4.0 [2]. However, it remains unclear whether a joint set of principles and pre-patterns is actually accompanied by a positive usability and, in addition, which of the defined patterns play a particularly crucial role for the usability. As a first step, this paper evaluates the implementation of a joint pattern model as well as the role of of individual UI patterns for the usability of an AR application.

In Sect. 2, related work of current AR usability research is highlighted. A derived design pattern model is defined in Sect. 3, followed by the presentation of an AR application implementing this model (see Sect. 4). The user-based study evaluating the AR application in Sect. 5 contributes to AR usability research by providing recommendations for AR UI engineering in Sect. 6.

2   Related Work

AR usability research is often concerned with adapting existing design heuristics to AR requirements. These design heuristics are usually a collection of best practices [9] that simplify recurring problems [4]. For instance, Dünser et al. [10] linked user-centered design principles to AR requirements and derived challenges to be considered by researchers. This results in recommendations for AR UI design, like the reduction of cognitive overhead. Nevertheless, the design principles are limited to a small set and remain rather general. As Dünser et al. state, their work should be seen more as a research encouragement and less as a holistic pattern model.

Tuli and Mantri [21] conducted a promising meta-analysis of existing usability guidelines through research exploration, expert evaluation, and the derivation of mobile AR design principles for kindergarten children. The resulting patterns include aspects of cognition, orientation, design, and support. However, this research has a strong focus on a specific target group, so that a transfer of findings to other domains needs to be evaluated.

Our research especially builds on the work of Ko et al. [15] and Xu et al. [22] (see Sect. 3). Ko et al. [15] define AR usability principles by analyzing existing research on mobile applications, tangible UIs and heuristic evaluation methods, resulting in new guidelines to solve AR usability problems. Based on this research, 22 AR usability principles, such as *Enjoyment* or *Learnability*, were defined and classified. Xu et al. [22] analyzed academic and commercial AR games and generated best practices for AR UI engineering. Based on this, Xu et al. formulate nine design pre-patterns, such as *World Consistency* or *Landmarks*.

Although research regarding the definition of AR design principles exists, approaches are often focused on individual design artifacts or application domains. Consequently, the definition and evaluation of a joint pattern model is an essential first step towards applicable AR usability standards.

3   AR Design Pattern Model

In order to investigate the role of of existing design patterns for the usability of AR systems, design principles were identified and then transformed into a joint model. As shown in Table 1, design principle categories formulated by Ko et al. [15] were adopted. We also distinguish between *Usage*, dealing with the application operation and environment, *Interaction*, comprising interaction possibilities within the virtual and physical world, *Information*, covering the configuration, structure and visibility of information, *Cognition*, affecting users' cognitive abilities, as well as *Support*, including patterns that support the application usage.

Table 1. AR design pattern model

Usage

Pattern	Type	Description
Control Mapping (2)	Core	Map control elements to unique actions
	Impl.	Voice command & haptic input mapped to unique actions
Context-based (1)	Core	Cover relevant contextual situations
Seamful Design (2)	Core	Address limitations (e.g., tracking)
Device Metaphors (2)	Core	Ensure the device feels like a familiar object
	Impl.	Shaking device refills paint; sound resembles spray can
World Consistency (2)	Core	Adapt the virtual world to the real world
	Impl.	Adoption of ambient light to virtual artifacts

Interaction

Pattern	Type	Description
Feedback (1)	Core	Communicate the current state of processes
	Impl.	Constant visualization of current configuration; Visual prompt when refill is required; Acoustic feedback while painting
Physical Effort (1)	Core	Minimize tiredness due to physical effort
	Impl.	Applicable through simple hand movements
Personal Presence (2)	Core	Users should have direct influence on the virtual world
Body Constraints (2)	Core	Users' actions should influence conditions of others
Landmarks (2)	Core	Spatial navigation points should be provided

Information

Pattern	Type	Description
Defaults (1)	Core	Ensure an intuitive usage through initial configuration
	Impl.	Default values for line width and color
Enjoyment (1)	Core	Offer a consistent appealing UI design
	Impl.	Corporate Design
Hierarchy (1), Navigation (1) & Availability (1)	Core	Structured information, free navigation and stable states
	Impl.	Structured and organized user interface
Multimodality (1) & Hidden Information (2)	Core	Include enhancing modalities and non-visible information
	Impl.	Voice command to change color; Haptic input to refill paint & when refill is required; Acoustic output while painting
Visibility (1)	Core	Ensure visible content within the field of view
	Impl.	Minimalistic, non-overloading interface design
Consistency (1)	Core	Provide a consistent design to prevent confusion
	Impl.	Corporate Design

Cognition

Pattern	Type	Description
Learnability (1) & Recognition (1)	Core	Ensure applicable, learnable and rememberable interactions
	Impl.	Users learn and remember the refill functionality
Predictability (1)	Core	Ensure predictable reactions to executed actions

Support

Pattern	Type	Description
Help & Documentation (1)	Core	Provide appropriate and easy to understand instructions
	Impl.	Help menu with instructions
Personalization (1)	Core	Applications should be adaptable to individual preferences
	Impl.	Configuration of line width and color
User Control (1) & Responsiveness (1)	Core	Applications should run stable and meet user expectations
	Impl.	Stable application through extensive testing

Specific patterns were collated from Xu et al. [22] and Ko et al. [15], then reviewed and consolidated into shared patterns based on their core objectives. Here, the patterns *Learnability* and *Predictability* were merged, since they both essentially concern the explicitness of UI artifacts. The joint pattern *Hierarchy, Navigation & Availability* was defined, which determines the structuring of and navigation through information. The pattern *Multimodality & Hidden Information* was consolidated since the transmission of hidden information is usually tied to the consideration of multiple modalities. Furthermore, *User Control* and

Responsiveness were merged, since they relate to the system's uninterrupted response to user input and the resulting sense of control for the user. In addition, only those patterns from Xu et al. [22] were extracted which were evaluated as transferable from their AR game origin to general AR applications. All extracted and merged patterns can be found in Table 1, where their origin from Ko et al. (1) or Xu et al. (2) is highlighted[1]. The pattern implementation listed in Table 1 is explained in the following chapter.

4   AR Scribble

In order to evaluate the defined pattern model, the smartphone application *AR Scribble* was developed, which imitates a physical spray can, allowing users to virtually paint within the real environment (see Fig. 1). Since the feasibility of design patterns depends on the application use case, not all, but as many patterns as possible were implemented (15 out of 21, see Table 1).

Fig. 1. AR scribble

A consistent appealing UI design was implemented by following Apple's corporate design, allowing to reuse empirically evaluated artifacts throughout the application. Within the UI, a centered marker constantly visualizes the currently configured line width and color. By default, the color and line width are set to appropriate values (a well visible yellow tone in a medium line width), but can be configured by the user. Although touch input serves as the primary interaction form, color changing can be performed using a voice command

---

[1] Patterns have been reduced to their core objectives within Table 1. Full explanations can be found in the corresponding literature.

as well. Besides mentioned functionality, only two additional UI buttons were implemented (speech recognition, help menu), ensuring a well organized and non-overloading design. As shown in Fig. 1, the help menu offers further functionality explanations. To simulate the use of a real spray can, the virtual fill level decreases while painting and users are prompted to shake the smartphone to refill the can. Prompts are visually displayed as well as haptically transmitted by vibration and disappear as soon as the paint is refilled. Since this frequently occurs while painting, users develop a feeling for when to refill the can. Besides haptic signals, acoustic output has been integrated, which imitates the sound of painting with a real spray can. As soon as the painting button is released, the acoustic signal stops. Furthermore, painted virtual artifacts are illuminated through adopting ambient light from the real world. The whole application was tested extensively in several iterations, resulting in a stable application.

5 Empirical Study

The application presented in Sect. 4 was analyzed within a user-based study, evaluating the overall usability as well as the role of individual patterns for the usability. In this chapter, we first introduce our research questions, experimental design, and sample, followed by the presentation and discussion of results.

5.1 Research Questions, Experimental Design, and Sample

As stated in Sect. 2, current AR usability research often focusses specific domains or individual UI artifacts. In our study, we wanted to evaluate whether a bundling of design patterns and their implementation are related to a positive usability. Thus, the following research question was formulated: *Does the consideration of joint AR design patterns correlate with a positive usability (RQ1)?*

In order to identify particularly influencing patterns and thus derive explicit recommendations for AR UI engineering, the role of individual patterns for the overall usability needs to be considered. This results in the following research question: *Which of the design patterns play a particularly crucial role for the overall usability (RQ2)?*

To investigate these research questions, an empirical study was conducted with $N = 18$ participants of which 13 were male and 5 female. Participants were on average $M = 29$ $(SD = 7.27)$ years old. Within our study, several tasks were performed that guided participants through the full feature range of *AR Scribble* to ensure that all implemented patterns were noticed. First, participants were asked to paint their initials into the real environment with free choice of color and line width. Next, participants outlined their painted initials with a thick red and a thin blue line. These tasks were performed under controlled conditions, within the same physical room under identical lighting conditions using the same device.

Afterwards, the System Usability Scale (SUS, see [5]) was surveyed to evaluate the overall usability of the application, rating statements like *"I think that I would like to use this system frequently.*" on a 5-point Likert scale ranging from 1 (*"Strongly disagree"*) to 5 (*"Strongly agree"*), resulting in a cumulative SUS score on a scale of 0−100. To evaluate the role of individual patterns for the SUS, the individual pattern implementation was evaluated (e.g., *"I think the pattern 'Default' in AR Scribble is well implemented (initial color and line width)"*) on a 5-point Likert scale ranging from 1 (*"Strongly disagree"*) to 5 (*"Strongly agree"*). Finally, the prior AR experience was surveyed (*"How much experience do you have in operating AR applications?"*) on a 5-point Likert scale ranging from 1 (*"None"*) to 5 (*"Very much"*) in order to consider an influence of previous AR experience on the usability evaluation.

5.2 Results

The overall usability was calculated and results in a total SUS score of $M = 80.56$ ($SD = 11.26$), with a minimum single score of 47.5 and a maximum of 97.5. The relationship between individual patterns and the overall SUS score was evaluated through correlation analyses, based on the individual implementation ratings. As shown in Table 2, the patterns *Enjoyment* ($M = 4.50, SD = 0.51$), *Consistency* ($M = 4.50, SD = 0.62$) and *User Control & Responsiveness* ($M = 4.50, SD = 0.62$) were rated as particularly well implemented, whereas *Physical Effort* ($M = 3.83, SD = 1.09$), *Device Metaphors* ($M = 3.94, SD = 1.06$) and *World Consistency* ($M = 3.94, SD = 0.99$) were rated slightly lower. The correlation values indicate, that *Control Mapping* ($r = .497, p = .036$) and *User Control & Responsiveness* ($r = .486, p = .041$) show a significant positive correlation with a small effect size[2] with the SUS. The patterns *Enjoyment* ($r = .558, p = .016$), *Hierarchy, Navigation & Availability* ($r = .521, p = .022$) and *Multimodality & Hidden Information* ($r = .521, p = .027$) show a significant positive correlation with a medium effect size. Finally, the pattern *Consistency* ($r = .718, p = .001$) shows a highly significant positive correlation and a large effect size.

In order to assess a possible influence of prior AR experience on the usability evaluation, the AR experience was correlated with the SUS score. Participants reported a prior AR experience of $M = 2.54$ ($SD = 1.25$) and the correlation of the SUS score with the prior AR experience showed no significant result ($r = -.199, p = .429$).

5.3 Discussion

The usability evaluation of AR Scribble resulted in a SUS score of 80.56. Since meta studies found that a SUS score between 78.9 and 80.7 is considered as a "grade *A-*" usability (based on the american school grading system, see [19]), the usability of AR Scribble was rated as particularly good. Thus, underlying assumptions of *RQ1* were confirmed, since the consideration of a joint model of current design patterns was positively related to a positive usability.

---

[2] The classification of effect sizes is based on Cohen [8].

Table 2. Correlation results regarding pattern implementation and SUS

		M	SD	SUS	
				r	p
Usage	Control Mapping	4.00	0.84	.497*	.036
	Device Metaphors	3.94	1.06	.213	.396
	World Consistency	3.94	0.99	.186	.460
Interaction	Feedback	4.28	0.90	.057	.823
	Physical Effort	3.83	1.09	.317	.200
Information	Defaults	4.22	0.88	.269	.280
	Enjoyment	4.50	0.51	.558*	.016
	Hierarchy, Navigation & Availability	4.28	0.46	.535*	.022
	Information	4.17	0.79	.521*	.027
	Visibility	4.28	0.67	.095	.707
	Consistency	4.50	0.62	.718**	.001
Cognition	Learnability & Recognition	4.44	0.78	.170	.499
Support	Help & Documentation	4.17	0.71	.338	.169
	Personalization	4.39	0.78	.377	.123
	User Control & Responsiveness	4.50	0.62	.486*	.041

Note. *p < .05, **p < .01

Analyses regarding individual patterns showed a strong significant correlation between *Consistency* and the overall usability. It is conceivable that users seek consistency in order to master an application, especially when familiarizing with novel technologies. This assumption is supported by the significant correlation coefficients for the patterns *Hierarchy, Navigation & Availability*, *Control Mapping* and *User Control & Responsiveness*, since their objectives also promote clear structures, well-organized interfaces and uninterrupted use. The significant effects for the pattern *Enjoyment* strengthens this assumption, since an appealing design thrives on clear structures and well organized information. Additionally, the results implicate that AR UIs should integrate multiple modalities, since the pattern *Multimodality & Hidden Information* was significantly positive related to the SUS score, likely facilitated by the increased freedom of use. Thus, the underlying assumptions of *RQ2* were confirmed by revealing particularly crucial patterns.

Nevertheless, some limitations of the empirical study need to be mentioned. Although it can be assumed that the implementation of individual patterns had a positive influence on the SUS, the causality could also be reversed. Future research should investigate causality effects by means of long-term studies or more complex experimental designs. Additionally, the design pattern model focused on two main sources and was evaluated through a single smartphone application. Subsequent studies should extend the pattern model with further research (e.g., [2,11,21]) and evaluate additional AR interfaces to exclude influencing effects as well as to investigate non-evaluated patterns.

6   Conclusion

We explored design patterns for AR systems by evaluating a joint design pattern model, implemented through an AR application. A conducted user-based study indicates that the implementation of these design patterns lead to a positive usability. The examination of individual patterns revealed that patterns concerning the consistency, structure and organization of UI artifacts were particularly influential, emphasizing users' need for clear structures and interactions in new technologies like AR. Our results further indicate that users seek freedom in their choice of interaction methods.

For future work, several interesting research options remain. We plan on extending the defined pattern model through including further AR usability publications. Additional AR applications will be developed to evaluate our findings. Finally, other related research questions will be addressed, such as the transfer of results to other device groups, as well as the consideration of UI complexity and application domains as influencing factors.

References

1. Abawi, D.F., Dörner, R., Haller, M., Zauner, J.: Efficient mixed reality application development. In: 1st European Conference on Visual Media Production, CVMP 2004, pp. 289–294 (2004)
2. Agati, S.S., Bauer, R.D., Hounsell, M.d.S., Paterno, A.S.: Augmented reality for manual assembly in industry 4.0: gathering guidelines. In: 2020 22nd Symposium on Virtual and Augmented Reality (SVR), pp. 179–188 (2020). https://doi.org/10.1109/SVR51698.2020.00039
3. Ashtari, N., Bunt, A., McGrenere, J., Nebeling, M., Chilana, P.K.: Creating augmented and virtual reality applications: current practices, challenges, and opportunities. In: Proceedings of the 2020 CHI Conference on Human Factors in Computing Systems, pp. 1–13. Association for Computing Machinery, New York (2020). https://doi.org/10.1145/3313831.3376722
4. Billinghurst, M., Clark, A., Lee, G.: A survey of augmented reality. Found. Trends® Human-Comput. Interact. 8(2–3), 73–272 (2015). https://doi.org/10.1561/1100000049
5. Brooke, J.: SUS: a 'quick and dirty' usability scale. In: Usability Evaluation in Industry, p. 189 (1996)
6. Burova, A., et al.: Utilizing VR and gaze tracking to develop AR solutions for industrial maintenance. In: Proceedings of the 2020 CHI Conference on Human Factors in Computing Systems, CHI '20, pp. 1–13. Association for Computing Machinery, New York (2020). https://doi.org/10.1145/3313831.3376405
7. Chang, A., Paz, F., Jesús Arenas, J., Díaz, J.: Augmented reality and usability best practices: a systematic literature mapping for educational videogames. In: 2018 IEEE Sciences and Humanities International Research Conference (SHIRCON), pp. 1–5 (2018). https://doi.org/10.1109/SHIRCON.2018.8592976
8. Cohen, J.: A power primer. Psychol. Bull. 112(1), 155–159 (1992). https://doi.org/10.1037//0033-2909.112.1.155
9. Dearden, A., Finlay, J.: Pattern languages in HCI: a critical review. Human-Comput. Interact. 21(1), 49–102 (2006). https://doi.org/10.1207/s15327051hci2101_3

10. Dünser, A., Grasset, R., Seichter, H., Billinghurst, M.: Applying HCI principles to AR systems design. In: Mixed Reality User Interfaces: Specification, Authoring, Adaptation (MRUI '07) Workshop Proceedings, Charlotte, NC, USA, pp. 37–42 (2007)

11. Endsley, T.C., Sprehn, K.A., Brill, R.M., Ryan, K.J., Vincent, E.C., Martin, J.M.: Augmented reality design heuristics: designing for dynamic interactions. In: Proceedings of the Human Factors and Ergonomics Society Annual Meeting, vol. 61, no. 1, pp. 2100–2104 (2017). https://doi.org/10.1177/1541931213602007

12. Gasques, D., Johnson, J.G., Sharkey, T., Weibel, N.: What you sketch is what you get: quick and easy augmented reality prototyping with PintAR. In: Extended Abstracts of the 2019 CHI Conference on Human Factors in Computing Systems, CHI EA '19, pp. 1–6. Association for Computing Machinery, New York (2019). https://doi.org/10.1145/3290607.3312847

13. Hagbi, N., Grasset, R., Bergig, O., Billinghurst, M., El-Sana, J.: In-place sketching for content authoring in augmented reality games. In: Proceedings of the 2010 IEEE Virtual Reality Conference, VR '10, pp. 91–94. IEEE Computer Society, USA (2010). https://doi.org/10.1109/VR.2010.5444806

14. Kang, S., et al.: ARMath: augmenting everyday life with math learning. In: Proceedings of the 2020 CHI Conference on Human Factors in Computing Systems, CHI '20, pp. 1–15. Association for Computing Machinery, New York (2020). https://doi.org/10.1145/3313831.3376252

15. Ko, S.M., Chang, W.S., Ji, Y.G.: Usability principles for augmented reality applications in a smartphone environment. Int. J. Hum.-Comput. Interact. **29**(8), 501–515 (2013). https://doi.org/10.1080/10447318.2012.722466

16. Langlotz, T., Mooslechner, S., Zollmann, S., Degendorfer, C., Reitmayr, G., Schmalstieg, D.: Sketching up the world: in situ authoring for mobile augmented reality. Pers. Ubiq. Comput. **16**, 1–8 (2011). https://doi.org/10.1007/s00779-011-0430-0

17. MacIntyre, B., Gandy, M., Dow, S., Bolter, J.D.: DART: a toolkit for rapid design exploration of augmented reality experiences. In: Proceedings of the 17th Annual ACM Symposium on User Interface Software and Technology, UIST '04, pp. 197–206. ACM, New York (2004). https://doi.org/10.1145/1029632.1029669

18. Martinez, H., Skournetou, D., Hyppölä, J., Laukkanen, S., Heikkilä, A.: Drivers and bottlenecks in the adoption of augmented reality applications. J. Multimedia Theory Appl. **2**, 27–44 (2014). https://doi.org/10.11159/jmta.2014.004

19. Sauro, J., Lewis, J.R.: Quantifying the User Experience: Practical Statistics for User Research, 2nd edn. Morgan Kaufmann, Cambridge (2016)

20. de Sá, M., Churchill, E.: Mobile augmented reality: exploring design and prototyping techniques. In: Proceedings of the 14th International Conference on Human-computer Interaction with Mobile Devices and Services, MobileHCI '12, pp. 221–230. ACM, New York (2012). https://doi.org/10.1145/2371574.2371608

21. Tuli, N., Mantri, A.: Usability principles for augmented reality based kindergarten applications. Procedia Comput. Sci. **172**, 679–687 (2020). https://doi.org/10.1016/j.procs.2020.05.089

22. Xu, Y., et al.: Pre-patterns for designing embodied interactions in handheld augmented reality games. In: 2011 IEEE International Symposium on Mixed and Augmented Reality - Arts, Media, and Humanities, pp. 19–28 (2011)

Interdisciplinary Collaboration in Augmented Reality Development - A Process Model

Ingo Börsting[✉][iD], Evgenia Shulikina, and Volker Gruhn[iD]

University of Duisburg-Essen, Essen, Germany
{ingo.boersting,evgenia.shulikina,volker.gruhn}@uni-due.de

Abstract. The development of Augmented Reality (AR) applications still poses several challenges for research and development. Apart from the complex modeling of interaction concepts comprising physical and virtual objects, the collaboration of different actors within the development process is particularly demanding. In AR development, authoring tools facilitate the modeling of User Interfaces (UI) and special frameworks simplify the implementation of AR-specific functionalities, but collaborative processes between UI designers and software developers are still underrepresented. We present a process model for interdisciplinary collaboration in AR development, based on several components which convert modeled UIs into collated artifacts that facilitate a shared understanding of the desired application. A conducted empirical study demonstrated the suitability of generated artifacts for the process model, since no specialized prior knowledge was needed to correctly interpret process artifacts, which thus serves the cross-role understanding of the desired application as a basis for interdisciplinary collaboration.

Keywords: Augmented reality · Collaboration · Process model

1 Introduction

The novel technology Augmented Reality enables the enrichment of the physical world with virtual content [5], which already serves several application areas. Unfortunately, the novelty and the core characteristics of the technology lead to challenges, which span over every phase and role within the development process. When considering development phases individually, it becomes apparent that, for example, the UI design process is hindered by a lack of standards and explicit guidelines [16,23] as well as by the complex modeling of 3D content and interactions [15,20]. The implementation phase poses further challenges, such as non-standardized hardware [20] or the complex integration of tracking methods that usually lack localization accuracy [16]. In previous AR research, approaches have been presented that address specific challenges in individual phases. Here, approaches to simplify UI design usually result in conceptual approaches or

© Springer Nature Switzerland AG 2021
L. T. De Paolis et al. (Eds.): AVR 2021, LNCS 12980, pp. 178–194, 2021.
https://doi.org/10.1007/978-3-030-87595-4_14

authoring tools that support the creation of UIs and integrated interaction concepts (e.g., [1,4,6]). On the implementation side, several frameworks and libraries have been released, mostly from the commercial sector, which aim to simplify the AR implementation.

However, AR-specific challenges multiply when development phases are considered as an aggregated process. Here, the transition between development phases as well as the interdisciplinary collaboration between actors have not been adequately addressed in research, resulting in an underrepresentation of collaboration in AR, especially regarding asynchronous collaboration [19]. In detail, the transition between engineering activities is hindered by the limited compatibility between design and implementation tools [9], as these usually address a specific domain problem [14]. Based on related work, it can be assumed that an interdisciplinary AR process is needed that aggregates isolated activities and roles into a shared model, enabling cross-competency collaboration, since individual competences and objectives of different collaborators need to be considered [10].

In our paper, we present an aggregated process model for collaborative development of AR applications that integrates activities from UI design and implementation and considers the expertise and goals of involved actors. The basis for this interdisciplinary process is the transformation of modeled UIs into artifacts that are exchanged between roles and phases. In an empirical study, we evaluate the manageability of these artifacts, especially with regard to required prior experience in order to demonstrate their suitability for cross-competence collaboration.

Within our paper, we first present related approaches that address collaborative aspects in AR development in Sect. 2. We then introduce our collaboration process model in Sect. 3 by presenting core components and their prototypical implementation. The empirical evaluation of process artifacts is described in Sect. 4, which is followed by a conclusion and outlook on future research in Sect. 5.

2 Related Work

In current research on AR collaboration, related work mainly focusses on user-specific variables, such as user experience or awareness. For example, Piumsomboon et al. [21] investigate user-awareness and the role of natural interaction in a collaborative environment that combines aspects of AR and Augmented Virtuality. Within AR research, aspects of user experience extend from network impairments that influence remote AR collaboration [2] to comparing user experience variables between AR- and VR-based collaboration [17].

Collaborative AR systems are widely applied and investigated in many fields, i.e. for the training of emergency personnel [18], in the immersive exploration of data [13], or in remote assistance [12]. However, this use case-driven research focuses less on the development process itself but more on the supporting application of AR collaboration.

An approach for utilizing collaborative elements to support AR development is formulated by Zhang et al. [25], who present *CARS*, a collaborative framework for cloud-based AR applications, which allows to share environmental recognition data between devices to increase the quality of experience. However, Zhang et al. focus on the improvement of user experience and not on the development process itself.

With their established authoring tool *Studierstube*, Schmalstieg et al. [22] present an approach to collaborative modeling of AR UIs, which are created within an immersive 3D environment. Here, the collaboration focuses on actors of the same discipline who jointly create and organize virtual objects. Nevertheless, the transition to the implementation phase or the support of interdisciplinary aspects are underrepresented.

Aoyama and Iida [3] present a collaborative design system that enables designers and engineers to remotely participate in product design. Here, these interdisciplinary actors can view and edit shared virtual objects and discuss results. Again, the focus is on modeling virtual UI artifacts and less on software development itself. Additionally, this approach addresses Virtual Reality systems, so a transfer to AR would need to be investigated.

Finally, Zhang et al. [24] formulate a component-based process model for designing AR applications. The authors distinguish between a modeling component, predefined libraries and different roles in the design flow. Here, designers are able to model an AR UI, which can be transferred to a simulation tool, where it can be evaluated by users. Thus, the interdisciplinarity in this process refers to the users' evaluation of artifacts produced by designers, and not to the collaborative development of applications. Furthermore, the process model seems to be domain-specific, an adaption to further AR projects thus needs to be validated.

Our work contributes to the current AR research landscape by approaching AR development as a collaborative interdisciplinary process in which the transition from the design to the implementation phase is particularly considered.

In the following chapter, we present a process model for interdisciplinary collaboration in AR development, which was defined and prototypically implemented.

3   Process Model for Interdisciplinary Collaboration

In this chapter, we introduce a process model for interdisciplinary collaboration in AR development. As shown in Fig. 1, we distinguish between the roles *UI Designer* and *Developer*, which are associated with the *User Interface Designer* module, the *GUI Configurator* module and the *Code Generator* module within a collaborative process.

Within this process, the UI designer primarily interacts with the *User Interface Designer* component, an authoring tool used to model an AR UI with predefined GUI elements. The *GUI Configurator* module transforms this UI into a configuration file, which serves as an exchange artifact between actors and components and thus supports the communication between actors. Based on this transformation, a template-based source code is generated within the *Code*

Generator module. Here, the developer enriches the modeled UI with dynamic data or adds further code snippets for required interactions or events and thus provides them to the *User Interface Designer* module to establish an iterative development process.

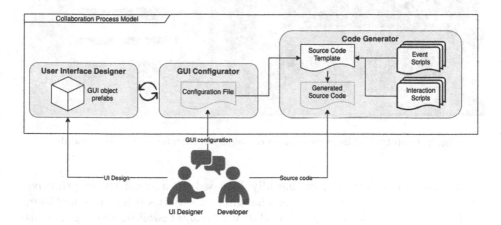

Fig. 1. Interdisciplinary collaboration process model

Following this high-level analysis of our process model, individual process components are considered in detail below, with a special consideration of roles and the information exchanged between actors.

3.1 User Interface Designer

The *User Interface Designer* module serves as an GUI abstraction layer used for the actual UI modeling by the UI designer. As already mentioned, AR research supporting UI modeling usually results in authoring tools and conceptual approaches (see Sect. 1). Thus, we decided to integrate the device-independent conceptual approach of Börsting and Gruhn [7] for the implementation and validation of our process model. Here, AR UIs are defined as a set of modular interaction sequences (*Interaction Stories*), specified by UI designers within an AR authoring tool. These *Interaction Stories* consist of a precondition that queries the execution context or history (through pre-defined conditions, e.g., like *OnStart* or *wasActive*), an interaction (e.g., gesture input or object detection), and resulting actions, such as the fading in and out of virtual objects at defined positions.

Within the current work, we implemented a working prototype of this conceptual approach for Head-mounted displays (i.e. Microsoft Hololens) using Unity (see Fig. 2). Here, the UI designer is able to organize and modify predefined virtual objects and associate them with interactions and resulting actions[1]. Pre-

---

[1] Referred to as "events" in the further course of the work for the purpose of clarification.

conditions affecting *Interaction Stories*, as defined by Börsting and Gruhn [7], have not been considered so far and will be integrated in future work.

Fig. 2. Prototypical implementation of the *User Interface Designer* module

For validation purposes, we initially focussed on a small set of primitive objects and possible events, such as changing an object's color (*ChangeColor*, see Fig. 2a) or switching objects' visibility (*ChangeVisibility*, see Fig. 2a), as well as four basic forms of interaction (*gesture, speech, gaze* and *detectObject*). Additionally, virtual objects can be provided with individual identifiers (*Object-Name*, see Fig. 2b) and comments (*ObjectDescription*, see Fig. 2b) to communicate key points in the UI concept. In an exemplary UI, it is conceivable that the UI designer integrates a dummy text field whose content is to be replaced by dynamic data in the later implementation, e.g., with the username of the currently logged-in user or with sensor data fed into an industrial application. The according instruction to the software developer can thus either be instructed in a personal conversation by naming the *ObjectName* (e.g., "myPrimitiveCube", see Fig. 2b), or can be realized by directly storing the instruction in the *Object-Description*, since all object attributes are shared between roles as exchange artifacts (see Sect. 3.2).

Within our process model, modeled interactions collectively define the UI concept of the desired AR application. The transition to the implementation phase as well as the generation of exchange artifacts is enabled by further process model components, which are explained in the following.

3.2   GUI Configurator

The *GUI Configurator* module is the essential link between the modeled UI and the applications business logic. For this purpose, all UI artifacts from the modeling tool are transferred into a configuration file based on the JSON format, which is both machine and human readable and hence serves for communication between actors.

Within this configuration file, all virtual objects are listed individually with the parameters that were assigned to them within the *User Interface Designer* module. In the excerpt of an exemplary configuration file displayed in Fig. 3, a text element was defined (*"objectType": "Text"*, line 1) with an individual identifier (*"objectName:" "Welcome_Greeting"*, line 2), displaying the specific content *Hello World!* (*"text:" "Hello World!"*, line 4) at a defined position (*"objectPosition": { "x":0, "y":0, "z:":-3}*, line 6) in relation to the user's current position (*"positionInRelationTo": "User"*, line 7). Additionally, this text element was annotated with a comment for the developer (*"objectDescription": "personalize with username"*, line 3). As described in the example in Sect. 3.1, it is conceivable that the UI designer defined a dummy text element within the *User Interface Designer* and deposited a direct instruction to the developer to replace the dummy text with the logged-in user's name. This information could alternatively be provided in a direct conversation with the developer by mentioning the individual identifier of this text element (*"Welcome_Greeting"*). Since JSON is human-readable format, this configuration file thus contributes to shared communication as UI artifacts can be labeled and customizations named and discussed.

Events take a special role in the configuration file, resulting in an accumulated listing of all assigned interaction-event pairs (*"eventData"*, line 11–14). In our simple example (see Fig. 3), we want the color of the text element to change to white (line 13) when an *AirTap*[2] gesture is performed (line 12).

```
1    "objectType": "Text",
2    "objectName": "Welcome_Greeting",
3    "objectDescription": "personalize with username",
4    "text": "Hello World",
5￬   "recTransformData": [{
6        "objectPosition": {"x": 0,"y": 0,"z": -3},
7        "positionInRelationTo": "User",
8        "objectScale": {"x": 0.05999,"y": 0.05999,"z": 0.05999},
9        "objectRotation": {"x": 0,"y": 0,"z": 0}
10   }],
11￬  "eventData": [{
12       "interaction": {"type": "Gesture","subtype": "AirTap"},
13       "event": {"name": "ChangeColor","parameter": "White"}
14   }]
```

Fig. 3. Excerpt from an exemplary configuration file

Here, many other events are conceivable (see Fig. 4), such as the fading in (line 4) of a specific virtual object (line 7) at a defined position next to a QR code marker (line 8–9) when the QR code marker is detected (line 2). The set of interactions and events that are applicable in the *User Interface Designer* and configurable through the configuration file is defined by interaction and event scripts, which are part of the *Code Generator* module (see Sect. 3.3).

---

[2] Standard confirmation gesture when using the Microsoft Hololens.

```
 1 ▾ "eventData": [{
 2        "interaction": {"type": "detectObject", "subtype": "QR", "ID": "1234"},
 3 ▾      "event": {
 4          "name": "show",
 5 ▾        "item": {
 6            "type": "Virtual",
 7            "ID": "mySpecificObject",
 8            "Coordinates": {"x": 50, "y": 10, "z": 0},
 9            "positionInRelationTo": {"type": "Marker", "ID": "1234"}
10          }
11        }
12 }]
```

Fig. 4. Alternative conceivable interaction event pair

Within the *GUI Configurator* module, possible changes to the UI, which are usually implemented via the *User Interface Designer*, can also be realized directly in the configuration file and transferred back into the modeling tool, allowing for a quick iteration and direct evaluation of design artifacts. The *Air-Tap* gesture as the interaction form in our example in Fig. 3 could easily be exchanged to a *gaze* interaction by simply modifying the corresponding line in the configuration file (e.g., *"interaction":* { *"type": "Gaze", "subtype": "focus"*}, line 12). The re-import of the updated configuration file allows the direct verification of the new interaction form in the *User Interface Designer*, where e.g., a user-based evaluation of the interaction can be performed.

As described, the *GUI Configurator* module acts as a communication vehicle and as an essential link between the modeled UI and the applications business logic, which is implemented by the *Code Generator* module and explained in the following chapter.

3.3 Code Generator

Within our process model, the *Code Generator* module is based on the generated configuration file (see Sect. 3.2) and consists of several components, like a preprocessing template engine (*Source Code Template*) formatting the resulting code base in a recurring structure, as well as predefined *Interaction Scripts* and *Event Scripts*. In our process model, the *Code Generator* is under the responsibility of the developer and intended to simplify the UI modification on code level as well as to define artifacts (i.e. interactions and events) that are applicable within the UI modeling tool.

```
1  GameObject Text2 = setObjectType("Text");
2  setObjectProperties(Text2, 2, "Text", "Welcome_Greeting", "personalize with username");
3  setObjectPosition(Text2, new Vector3(0 f, 0 f, -3 f));
4  setObjectPositionInRelationTo(Text2, "User");
5  setObjectScale(Text2, new Vector3(0.06 f, 0.06 f, 0.06 f));
6  setObjectRotation(Text2, new Vector3(0 f, 0 f, 0 f));
7  setUIText(Text2, "Hello World!");
8
9  Text2. < Event > .Add(new Interaction("Gesture", "AirTap"), new Event("ChangeColor", "White"));
```

Fig. 5. Excerpt from the generated source code of the exemplary UI

Here, the formatted source code instantiates all modeled UI artifacts with defined attributes and their association with required interaction and event scripts. The replacement of static UI artifacts with dynamic data, such as overwriting a dummy text with the logged-in user's name (as described in the example in Sect. 3.1), can be realized at this point, e.g., through replacing the dummy text *"Hello World* (see Fig. 5, line 7) with a code like *setUIText (Text2, loggedUser.username)*. Of course, many other use cases for replacing static placeholders through dynamic data are conceivable within the *Code Generator*.

As shown in Fig. 5, pre-defined event and interaction scripts are referenced in the generated source code and can either be added, edited or removed during application development. Separating these scripts from the actual source code enables the dynamic adaptation to requirements, like device groups or use cases. Here, a set of possible interactions can be pre-defined as scripts on code level, e.g., to pre-define individual interactions for different device-groups, like head-mounted displays (e.g., *AirTap* gesture) or smartphones (e.g., *single-touch* event) in order to quickly adapt UI concepts to different devices. Within our example, only the reference to the script would need to be modified in order to change the interaction form (e.g., [..]*(new Interaction("Touch", "Single")*[...], Fig. 5, line 9). All interaction forms stored as scripts within the *Code Generator* can thus either be integrated at code level by the developer or selected in the *User Interface Designer* by the UI Designer.

The same applies to events, allowing for storing individual scripts and specify required parameters, so that developers and UI designers can define these events as resulting actions on executed interactions within their assigned process components. An example of a simple *ChangeColor* event script is shown in Fig. 6. Here, the color of the affected virtual object is updated to the color handed over to the code snippet. In our example, the UI designer defined the color *"White"* as the target color, as seen in the configuration file (Fig. 3, line 13) and in the resulting source code (Fig. 5, line 9). Following this concept, any events and interactions can be defined within the *Code Generator* and applied within our other process components.

```
1  public void ChangeColor(string color) {
2      gameObject.GetComponent < Renderer > ().material.SetColor("_Color", color);
3  }
```

Fig. 6. Exemplary event script of the *ChangeColor* event

In summary, our collaboration process model enables UI designers to model AR UIs using the *User Interface Designer* module, from which the *GUI Configurator* module derives a configuration file, which serves as a communication vehicle between actors and as the foundation for the *Code Generator* module. In this component, a template-preprocessed code basis is generated, which can be modified by the developer and enriched with additional events and interactions.

We assume that the collaborative manipulation of UI artifacts leads to an iterative interdisciplinary process, respecting the competencies of individual actors by assigning them to specific components while ensuring communication via exchange artifacts. Nevertheless, the fundamental precondition for cross-competence collaboration in our process model is that automated generated artifacts must be manageable. In order to investigate the suitability of the generated artifacts for our formulated process model, an empirical study was conducted, which is presented in the following chapter.

4   Empirical Study

We see the manageability of our generated process artifacts (configuration file, source code, interaction/event scripts, see Sect. 3) as a prerequisite for the collaboration concept, as these automatically generated artifacts either serve as a communication tool or as a basis for UI manipulation and thus need to be understood and editable. We evaluated these artifacts within an empirical study, which is reported in the present chapter. Here, we first introduce our research questions, followed by the experimental design and sample. Finally, we present and discuss our results.

4.1   Research Questions

In our research, we see prior experience needed to correctly interpret and manage our process artifacts as a relevant indicator for their general manageability. We thus aim to investigate whether different levels of prior experience, from general software development experience to specialized AR-specific knowledge, have an impact on whether the code is manageable, indicated by task performance in different tasks. This leads to the following research question: *Does the prior experience correlate with the task performance (RQ1)?*

It is further of relevance to evaluate whether the task type is related to the manageability of generated artifacts. It is conceivable that the code base is easy to understand for simple tasks, such as interpreting the mere positioning of objects, but poses challenges for more difficult tasks. From this, we derive the following research question: *Does the task type correlate with the task performance (RQ2)?*

We further assume that the complexity of a modeled UI has a negative effect on the manageability of the transformed code base, since the UI complexity is reflected in generated artifacts. To address this, the following research question is derived: *Does the UI complexity correlate with the task performance (RQ3)?*

In the following chapter, we describe our experimental design as well as the study sample.

4.2   Experimental Design and Sample

In order to investigate the stated research questions, participants performed a series of tasks. For each task, participants were provided with a generated code base, which could be inspected during the entire task performance and which differed for each new task. Each code base contained a configuration file describing GUI objects and their parameters, the generated source code, and the predefined event and interaction scripts. Participants were able to click through files via different tabs, as shown in Fig. 7.

Fig. 7. Excerpt of a generated code basis as provided in our empirical study

Within our study, tasks were varied in type and UI complexity. The task types were classified by difficulty between: the simple interpretation of GUI objects and their parameters (type I), the comprehension of interactions, events and their effects on the GUI (type II) as well as the GUI manipulation on code level (type III). In task type I, participants selected a screenshot of the GUI generated by the provided code basis from a list of alternative GUIs (*"Which GUI is generated by the code above?"*), as highlighted in Fig. 8. In task type II, a GUI was displayed from which a specific event is triggered. Participants were asked to determine the correct GUI state following the triggered event (*"How does the GUI change when the user interacts with the element 'New Text'?"*). In task type III, the code basis was to be modified following a formulated scenario (*"Modify the source code so that the visibility of objects can be manipulated using voice commands only."*). In order to ensure comparable results, participants were asked to determine a specific code line in one of the provided files that would need to be adjusted in order to fulfill the scenario. Within our tasks, the UI complexity was varied based on the number of comprised elements. Here, a UI with a maximum of two elements is considered *Low*, a UI comprising three to four elements as *Medium* and a UI including a minimum of five elements as *High* (see Fig. 8). Each of the three task types were processed in the three different UI complexity levels, so that every participant completed a total of nine tasks.

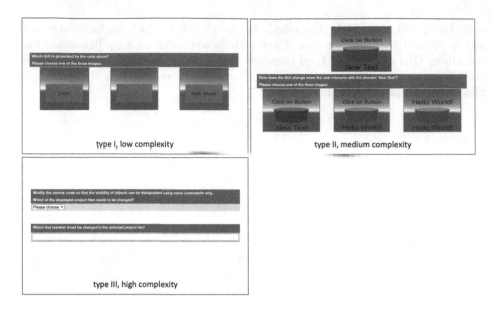

Fig. 8. Sample task types and UI complexities as provided in our empirical study

Our empirical online study was conducted with $N = 19$ participants of which 17 were male and 2 female. Participants were on average $M = 36$ ($SD = 10.14$) years old. Within our study, nine tasks in varying type and UI complexity were performed. After each task, participants were asked to rate their decision confidence (*"How confident are you in your decision?"*) on a five-point Likert scale from 1 (*"not certain"*) to 5 (*"very certain"*). We assume that a decrease in decision confidence indicates that the increasing UI complexity and task difficulty were actually experienced. At the end of the online study, participants were asked to rate their prior knowledge (*"Please indicate below how you rate your prior experience in the listed categories."*) in different categories (*"General software development"*, *"Object-oriented programming"*, *"Usage of augmented reality applications"*, *"Development of augmented reality applications"*) on a 5-point Likert scale from 1 (*"low or none"*) to 5 (*"above average"*).

4.3   Results

In our empirical study, task performance was measured by the number of correctly solved tasks. For this purpose, the number of correct answers was cumulated for each participant. In task type III, various correct answers were possible and thus evaluated manually. The overall correctness of task performance resulted in a mean value of $M = 6$ ($SD = 1.63$) out of nine tasks, with a minimum score of 3 and a maximum of 9. Correctness considering task types and UI complexity was examined applying an analysis of variance (ANOVA). As presented in Table 1, there was no significant difference in task correctness between task types (after significance level correction, see Holm

Table 1. Overview of ANOVA results

		Correctness				Confidence			
		M	*SD*	*F*	*p*	*M*	*SD*	*F*	*p*
	Type I	2.37	.68			3.70	.99		
Task Type	Type II	1.95	.91	3.261	.046	3.09	1.09	2.750	.073
	Type III	1.68	.89			3.04	.85		
	Low	2.42	.69			3.54	.86		
UI Complexity	Medium	2.21	.79	7.200	**.002**	3.54	.86	2.887	.064
	High	1.37	1.17			2.93	1.01		

Note. *p < .01, significance level was corrected using the Holm-Bonferroni method

[11]). Nevertheless, the mean values show that task correctness decreases from type I ($M = 2.37, SD = .68$) to type II ($M = 1.95, SD = .91$) to type III ($M = 1.68, SD = .89$). Furthermore, although decision confidence between task types shows no significant difference, the mean values indicate decreasing confidence as task difficulty increases.

In addition, we observed a significant difference between correctness and UI complexity, $F(11.79, 44.21) = 7.2, p = .002$. Again, the mean values indicate that task correctness decreases with increasing UI complexity from *Low* ($M = 2.42, SD = .69$) to *Medium* ($M = 2.21, SD = .79$) to *High* ($M = 1.37, SD = 1.17$). Even though the decision confidence does not differ significantly between UI complexity levels, the mean values indicate that decision confidence decreases with increasing UI complexity.

In order to evaluate the role of prior experience for task performance, it was surveyed in four different categories. Here, participants reported prior knowledge in *general software development* ($M = 3.05, SD = 1.13$), *object-oriented programming* ($M = 2.89, SD = 1.10$), *usage of augmented reality applications* ($M = 1.58, SD = .90$), and *development of augmented reality applications* ($M = 1.32, SD = .67$). The relationship between prior experience and task performance was evaluated through correlation analyses. After the significance level correction (see Holm [11]), a marginal significant correlation ($p = .023$) with a large effect size ($r = .518$)[3] was observed between prior experience in *general software development* and task performance in task type III. No further significant correlations between prior experience and task performance were observed (Table 2).

---

[3] The classification of effect sizes is based on Cohen [8].

Table 2. Correlation results regarding prior experience and task performance

		Prior Experience						
		Software Development		Object-Oriented Programming		Usage of AR Application		Development of AR Application	
Performance		r	p	r	p	r	p	r	p
Total correctness		.271	.261	.155	.527	-.038	.878	.101	.680
Task Type	Type I	.015	.857	-.019	.937	-.185	.449	-.025	.918
	Type II	-.051	.835	-.061	.803	.107	.664	.210	.387
	Type III	.518	.023	.363	.126	-.037	.882	-.010	.968
UI Complexity	Low	.183	.453	-.012	.963	-.234	.335	-.302	.209
	Medium	.362	.128	.284	.239	.445	.056	.498	.030
	High	.027	.914	.032	.897	-.214	.378	-.015	.952

Note. *p < .02, significance level was corrected using the Holm-Bonferroni method

4.4 Discussion

Our empirical study aimed at evaluating the interpretability of process model artifacts, especially regarding required prior experience, UI complexity and task type.

First, we investigated the relationship between prior knowledge and task correctness considering different experience levels, task types and UI complexities (*RQ1*). Since no significant correlations between prior experience and task performance were observed, we can assume that no specialized knowledge or technical experience is required to accurately interpret the generated code basis. This conclusion is supported by the overall high task correctness with rather low prior experience in AR utilization and development. Here, only a marginal significant correlation was found between prior experience in *general software development* and the code manipulation task (type III). It is not surprising that prior experience in software development is necessary to perform code manipulation. As stated in our process model, we do not see code manipulation as an interdisciplinary task, but as the developer's responsibility, so this result does not contradict our process model. In sum, our observations suggests that generated artifacts are indeed manageable and thus employable within our process model.

Furthermore, we could not observe a significant relationship between task type and task performance (*RQ2*). Although mean values suggest that task correctness decreases with increasing task difficulty, this seems to be a minor aspect in our process model.

We further investigated the relevance of the UI complexity for the interpretability of process artifacts (*RQ3*). We found the UI complexity to have a significant impact on task correctness. Here, the task correctness decreases with increasing UI complexity. It can thus be assumed that the UI complexity is a driving factor within our process model and should be focused in future work (see Sect. 5).

Furthermore, the decision confidence values indicate that the task types were indeed perceived as increasingly difficult and the UIs as increasingly complex, which supports the accuracy of our task classification.

Nevertheless, some limitations of the empirical study need to be mentioned. We conducted an online study and could therefore not ensure controlled conditions, which may have influenced task performance. We further surveyed a rather homogenous participant group, in which little prior AR experience was available. So far, we have not distinguished between UI designers and developers within our sample. To support and further investigate our findings, we will consider these actors individually in further studies and selectively analyze influencing factors.

5   Conclusion and Future Work

In our paper, we presented a process model for interdisciplinary collaboration in AR development. In this model, we consider the UI designer and the developer as actors and bring them together in a joint process, especially with regard to the transition between the design and the implementation phase. Here, different model components aim for the simplified UI modeling (*User Interface Designer*) or the generation of exchange artifacts as a communication vehicle (*GUI Configurator*), which serves as a basis for UI manipulation in a formatted code base (*Code Generator*). The interplay of actors utilizing these components is intended to lead to an iterative AR development process, respecting individual competencies and supporting interdisciplinary communication.

In an empirical study, we investigated the interpretability of automatically generated process artifacts, which need to remain manageable in order to serve communication or code manipulation. We defined prior experience required to master given interpretation and manipulation tasks as an indicator of the comprehensibility of our artifacts. As a result, we could not observe a significant relationship between prior experience and the interpretation of generated artifacts, demonstrating the suitability of our artifacts for the formulated process model. Nevertheless, the UI complexity was found to be a significant factor in the interpretability of generated artifacts and should therefore be focussed on in future studies.

Finally, some exciting research topics remain for future work. First, the UI complexity will be focused considering realistic AR applications in varying complexity, which requires an extension of the prototypically implemented process modules. After the initial validation of generated artifacts, we further aim to validate the process model itself, considering the interplay of designers and developers using our process components in realistic development settings.

With our work, we defined an interdisciplinary process model, considering UI design and implementation as well as the transition between phases through exchange artifacts. We encourage other researchers to build on our findings and further investigate influencing process variables to eventually define solutions for collaborative processes in AR software engineering.

References

1. Abawi, D.F., Dörner, R., Haller, M., Zauner, J.: Efficient mixed reality application development. In: 1st European Conference on Visual Media Production, CVMP 2004, pp. 289–294 (2004)
2. Ahsen, T., Dogar, F.R., Gardony, A.L.: Exploring the impact of network impairments on remote collaborative augmented reality applications. In: Extended Abstracts of the 2019 CHI Conference on Human Factors in Computing Systems, CHI EA 2019, pp. 1–6. Association for Computing Machinery, New York, May 2019. https://doi.org/10.1145/3290607.3312774
3. Aoyama, H., Iida, R.: Collaboration design system using internet and virtual reality technology. In: Shumaker, R. (ed.) VMR 2009. LNCS, vol. 5622, pp. 513–521. Springer, Heidelberg (2009). https://doi.org/10.1007/978-3-642-02771-0_57
4. Arnd, V., Hussmann, H.: Modeling augmented reality user interfaces with SSIML/AR. J. Multimed. 1, June 2006. https://doi.org/10.4304/jmm.1.3.13-22
5. Azuma, R.T.: A survey of augmented reality. Presence: Teleoperators Virtual Environ. 6(4), 355–385 (1997). https://doi.org/10.1162/pres.1997.6.4.355
6. Broll, W., Lindt, I., Ohlenburg, J., Herbst, I., Wittkamper, M., Novotny, T.: An infrastructure for realizing custom-tailored augmented reality user interfaces. IEEE Trans. Visual Comput. Graphics 11(6), 722–733 (2005). https://doi.org/10.1109/TVCG.2005.90
7. Börsting, I., Gruhn, V.: Towards efficient interdisciplinary authoring of industrial augmented reality applications. In: Conference Companion of the 4th International Conference on Art, Science, and Engineering of Programming, Programming 2020, pp. 65–68. Association for Computing Machinery, New York, March 2020. https://doi.org/10.1145/3397537.3398474
8. Cohen, J.: A power primer. Psychol. Bull. 112(1), 155–159 (1992). https://doi.org/10.1037//0033-2909.112.1.155
9. Dünser, A., Grasset, R., Seichter, H., Billinghurst, M.: Applying HCI principles to AR systems design. In: Mixed Reality User Interfaces: Specification. Authoring, Adaptation (MRUI'07) Workshop Proceedings, pp. 37–42, Charlotte, NC, USA (2007)
10. Gandy, M., MacIntyre, B.: Designer's augmented reality toolkit, ten years later: implications for new media authoring tools. In: Proceedings of the 27th Annual ACM Symposium on User Interface Software and Technology, UIST 2014, pp. 627–636. ACM, New York (2014). https://doi.org/10.1145/2642918.2647369
11. Holm, S.: A simple sequentially rejective multiple test procedure. Scand. J. Stat. 6(2), 65–70 (1979)
12. Hoppe, A.H., Westerkamp, K., Maier, S., van de Camp, F., Stiefelhagen, R.: Multi-user Collaboration on Complex Data in Virtual and Augmented Reality. In: Stephanidis, C. (ed.) HCI International 2018 - Posters' Extended Abstracts. pp. 258–265. Communications in Computer and Information Science, Springer International Publishing, Cham (2018). https://doi.org/10.1007/978-3-319-92279-9_35

13. Jing, A., Xiang, C., Kim, S., Billinghurst, M., Quigley, A.: SnapChart: an augmented reality analytics toolkit to enhance interactivity in a collaborative environment. In: The 17th International Conference on Virtual-Reality Continuum and its Applications in Industry, VRCAI 2019, pp. 1–2. Association for Computing Machinery, New York, November 2019. https://doi.org/10.1145/3359997.3365725

14. Kulas, C., Sandor, C., Klinker, G.: Towards a development methodology for augmented reality user interfaces. In: Proceedings of the International Workshop exploring the Design and Engineering of Mixed Reality Systems - MIXER 2004, Funchal, Madeira, CEUR Workshop Proceedings (2004)

15. MacIntyre, B., Gandy, M., Dow, S., Bolter, J.D.: DART: a toolkit for rapid design exploration of augmented reality experiences. In: Proceedings of the 17th Annual ACM Symposium on User Interface Software and Technology, UIST 2004, pp. 197–206. Association for Computing Machinery, New York (2004). https://doi.org/10.1145/1029632.1029669

16. Martínez, H., Skournetou, D., Hyppölä, J., Laukkanen, S., Heikkilä, A.: Drivers and bottlenecks in the adoption of augmented reality applications. J. Multimed. Theory Appl. **2**, 27–44 (2014). https://doi.org/10.11159/jmta.2014.004

17. Müller, J., Zagermann, J., Wieland, J., Pfeil, U., Reiterer, H.: A qualitative comparison between augmented and virtual reality collaboration with handheld devices. In: Proceedings of Mensch und Computer 2019, MuC 2019, pp. 399–410. Association for Computing Machinery, New York, September 2019. https://doi.org/10.1145/3340764.3340773

18. Nilsson, S., Johansson, B., Jönsson, A.: Design of augmented reality for collaboration. In: Proceedings of The 7th ACM SIGGRAPH International Conference on Virtual-Reality Continuum and Its Applications in Industry, VRCAI 2008, pp. 1–2. Association for Computing Machinery, New York, December 2008. https://doi.org/10.1145/1477862.1477920

19. Pidel, C., Ackermann, P.: Collaboration in virtual and augmented reality: a systematic overview. In: De Paolis, L.T., Bourdot, P. (eds.) AVR 2020. LNCS, vol. 12242, pp. 141–156. Springer, Cham (2020). https://doi.org/10.1007/978-3-030-58465-8_10

20. Piekarski, W., Thomas, B.H.: An object-oriented software architecture for 3D mixed reality applications. In: The Second IEEE and ACM International Symposium on Mixed and Augmented Reality, 2003. Proceedings, pp. 247–256 (Oct 2003). https://doi.org/10.1109/ISMAR.2003.1240708

21. Piumsomboon, T., Day, A., Ens, B., Lee, Y., Lee, G., Billinghurst, M.: Exploring enhancements for remote mixed reality collaboration. In: SIGGRAPH Asia 2017 Mobile Graphics & Interactive Applications, pp. 1–5. SA 2017. Association for Computing Machinery, New York, November 2017. https://doi.org/10.1145/3132787.3139200

22. Schmalstieg, D., Fuhrmann, A.L., Hesina, G.: Bridging multiple user interface dimensions with augmented reality. ISAR (2000). https://doi.org/10.1109/ISAR.2000.880919

23. de Sá, M., Churchill, E.: Mobile augmented reality: exploring design and prototyping techniques. In: Proceedings of the 14th International Conference on Human-computer Interaction with Mobile Devices and Services, MobileHCI 2012, pp. 221–230. ACM, New York (2012). https://doi.org/10.1145/2371574.2371608

24. Zhang, F., Zhao, L., Liang, X., Qi, Y., Shen, X.: The augmented reality research progress in collaboration environment of CAR-CA. In: Proceedings of the 9th ACM SIGGRAPH Conference on Virtual-Reality Continuum and its Applications in Industry, VRCAI 2010, pp. 229–236. Association for Computing Machinery, New York, December 2010. https://doi.org/10.1145/1900179.1900229
25. Zhang, W., Han, B., Hui, P., Gopalakrishnan, V., Zavesky, E., Qian, F.: CARS: collaborative augmented reality for socialization. In: Proceedings of the 19th International Workshop on Mobile Computing Systems & Applications, HotMobile 2018, pp. 25–30. Association for Computing Machinery, New York, February 2018. https://doi.org/10.1145/3177102.3177107

Interoperable Dynamic Procedure Interactions on Semantic Augmented Reality Browsers

Martín Becerra[1]([✉]) [iD], Jorge Ierache[1] [iD], and María José Abasolo[2,3] [iD]

[1] Engineering Department, Applied Augmented Reality Team, National University of La Matanza, 1754 San Justo, Buenos Aires, Argentina
{mabecerra,jierache}@unlam.edu.ar

[2] School of Computer Sciences, National University of La Plata, III-LIDI, 1900, La Plata, Buenos Aires, Argentina
mjabasolo@lidi.info.unlp.edu.ar

[3] Commission for Scientific Research of Buenos Aires, 1900 La Plata, Buenos Aires, Argentina

Abstract. This article presents a framework that aims to assist users in their daily tasks by creating and exploiting reusable procedures for semantic augmented reality browsers using the ontology of our research. The contribution aims to fill the gap in current semantic augmented reality browsers to allow users to interact dynamically with virtual content through the performance of procedures or sequence of steps in the real environment. These capabilities will have an impact in several areas, for example, in Industry 4.0 contexts, such as the creation of a sequence of tasks to be performed by an intelligent operator in a Smart factory or in the increase of tasks to be done with an IoT device/equipment in the plant, as well as its potential use in massive contexts such as the growth of IOT devices in augmented home contexts.

Keywords: Augmented reality · AR browsers · Semantic web · Linked data · Linked Data Cloud

1 Introduction

Augmented reality (AR) allows to enrich the perception of reality with virtual information by merging virtual data with the physical environment [1]. In the last decade, AR has expanded to different fields of application such as tourism, entertainment, industry, health and marketing. Nowadays in the marketing application field, users have at their disposal augmented reality browsers such as LayAR [2] which grew in popularity under the premise of facilitating the creation of basic virtual content such as images, buttons to open web content to encourage product promotion by augmenting brochures, business cards and product packages. CamOnApp [3] is an application that allows the user with its AR browser to consume augmented reality content created by different advertising agencies using its Studio editor to augment different media, paper, objects. Meanwhile, Wikitude [4] is considered a general purpose browser which has grown as a service to develop general purpose applications where the user passively consumes information provided by the creators of the applications.

© Springer Nature Switzerland AG 2021
L. T. De Paolis et al. (Eds.): AVR 2021, LNCS 12980, pp. 195–208, 2021.
https://doi.org/10.1007/978-3-030-87595-4_15

Augmented reality browsers such as Layar and Wikitude have become a well-known way of delivering AR experiences. However, these can be seen as isolated silos of information, designed specifically for the application in which they have been generated.

Analyzing [5] the advantages of using semantic web technologies, the main one is the separation between models and applications, as well as others: the use of vocabulary to describe data, universal data access, thanks to the semantic interoperability achieved using a standardized base data model called RDF (Resource Description Framework) [6] and ontologies. An ontology is an explicit, formal specification of a shared conceptualization [7]. In this article, the term Semantic AR Browser is equivalent to Augmented Reality (AR) browsers that integrate linked data using semantic web technologies. In this line, different works can be mentioned for example, ARCAMA3D [8], T. Matuszka et. al. [9] and SmartReality [10], these are prototypes that particularly present virtual content about different points of interest (POI) geolocated in the real world, e.g., a user is near a POI uses this type of application that provides access to information of interest of this place, mainly extracted from the Linked Data Cloud [11]. However, the applications described above, although they allow the creation of contents, these are consumed in a passive and static way. The user only reads information of interest without being able to exploit it for any particular purpose. It is very useful for the user to be able to use these contents under a dynamic interaction, defined by a set of actions to be performed in an environment enriched by augmented reality technologies. In this order, a framework is presented as a result of the research that provides this dynamic interaction to users through semantic interoperable procedures applied to augmented objects through AR applications that use semantic web technologies. These capabilities will have an impact in several areas, for example, in Industry 4.0 contexts, such as the creation of a sequence of tasks to be performed by an intelligent operator in a Smart factory or in the increase of tasks to be done with an IoT device/equipment in the plant, as well as its potential use in mass contexts such as the growth of IOT devices in augmented home contexts.

This paper presents the architecture of the experimental framework, the overview of the ontology product of our research and the implementation of two of the three components, the augmented reality browser and the web service that we call Semantic middleware (Sect. 2). This service performs all the semantic operations necessary for the procedures to be interoperable with other third-party applications that use semantic web technologies. In Sect. 3, one of the application cases where the proposed framework could be used will be described. In Sect. 4, a discussion is made comparing the contribution made so far by other proposals and emphasizing the features that distinguish our AR browser. In Sect. 5 the conclusions and future lines of research are presented.

2 Framework

2.1 Architecture

The proposed framework aims to assist users in their tasks by creating and exploiting procedures that can be reused by other AR applications which implements semantic web technologies. The general architecture is composed of three parts (Fig. 1) a semantic middleware, which represents a set of services which maintains the Semantic AR Procedure Ontology, receives http requests from the different parts of the system and manages the RDF triplestore to store the published procedures. The procedures are created using an editor called Semantic Procedure Editor and an augmented reality browser is used to exploit the created contents.

Two flows were designed in the proposed framework. The content creator user performs the creation flow (CF) using the Semantic Procedure editor to create a procedure, adding the steps to be performed in its physical environment. Relevant information can be associated to each of these steps to be shown at the moment they are performed. Once this edition is finished, it is uploaded through an http request (Operation CF 1 Fig. 1) to the Gateway web which publishes the procedure (Operation CF 2 Fig. 1) in the Public Semantic AR Procedure RDF Triple store so that it is ready to be consumed by other applications through a SPARQL [12] endpoint. The user of the augmented reality browser of the proposed framework performs the content exploitation (EF) flow, starting with a search of previously created procedures (Operation EF 1 Fig. 1) to select and download the one they want to consume (Operation EF 2 Fig. 1), once their data is obtained, they perform the step-by-step as guided by the augmented reality browser.

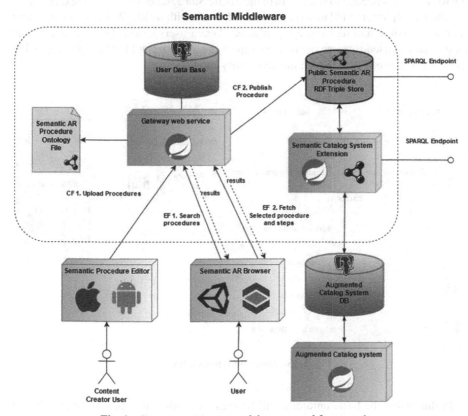

Fig. 1. General architecture of the proposed framework.

2.2 Semantic Middleware Implementation

The Semantic middleware is a set of web services which provides different capabilities, which receives data requests from the AR browser and the semantic procedure editor; structures procedures with the Semantic AR Procedure Ontology and coordinates their publication through its Gateway service component. This is composed of different layers (Fig. 2), a Postgres database layer [13] that stores the users registered in the platform so that they can be authenticated to use both the editor and the browser. This database layer is connected through Hibernate [14] which acts as a framework to map an object-oriented model to a relational database. These layers are used only to manage users accessing the system. The Gateway web service was developed using Java [15] and Spring framework [16]. This service runs in a Tomcat instance [17] in charge of managing the lifecycle of the whole system. The semantic Middleware was divided in different layers. The Data Access Objects (DAO) is the layer which has the responsibility to access to the database entities. The user session service maintains the user's session data needed to attend the http request received. The procedure provider service uses the DAO layer to obtain the SPARQL queries needed to send them to the Triple Store Access service for execution. It uses the RDF4j library [18] to serialize data to be sent with its Rio Writer subcomponent when a procedure and its steps are published. When users search for procedures, this same library is used to parse the response from the Anzograph [19] triplestore to RDF JSON for transmission to the augmented reality browser.

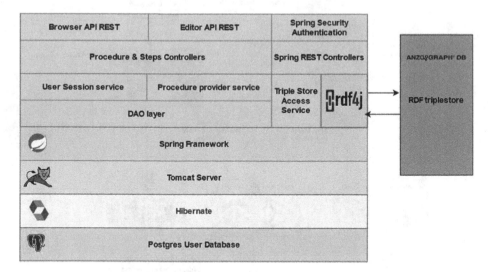

Fig. 2. Semantic middleware layers.

In this order, the basic ontology will be presented, allowing the interoperability of augmented web browsers.

2.3   Semantic AR Procedure Ontology Basic Schema

The proposed framework uses a basic ontology called Semantic AR Procedure Ontology to be used by the Gateway service (Fig. 1) to structure the procedures to be published in the RDF triple store for consumption. This ontology can be visualized in Fig. 3, where users have a username and a profile image to have visibility as an author at the moment of consuming a procedure. The procedure has the properties title and description to indicate what it is about and the first step that will start the sequence. Each step has the properties title and description, which will have the corresponding instruction to follow when it is enabled. The sequence of steps of the procedure is expressed as a double linked list with the properties nextStep and previousStep in which each one indicates the previous and next step until the last one is reached. The chosen scheme allows an easy creation and edition of the chain of steps. Finally, external entities can be linked using the relatedEntity property. These entities can allude to real objects or instruments involved in the instruction described in the step or entities from other data sources, e.g. DBPedia [20].

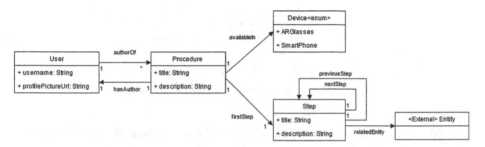

Fig. 3. Semantic AR procedure ontology basic schema.

2.4   Semantic Augmented Reality Browser Implementation

The Augmented Reality Browser allows users to search for procedures and their exploitation through augmented reality technologies. This prototype was implemented by using Unity3D [21] and Vuforia [22] as Augmented Reality SDK to present virtual contents on physical markers. For the design of the system, we chose the architecture MVC to define the different components of the augmented reality browser. The components the Browser Controller and Search Controller perform the fine-grained operations using tasks classes. They encapsulate the details of the operations, so the controllers are only responsible for their invocation and configuration of the view components. The next subsections will explain the functionalities that strongly contribute to achieve a dynamic interaction with AR contents to integrate them in their daily tasks. In this order, Procedure search by text, selection of procedures to perform, and the advance of steps of the selected procedure with the classes involved in each of these cases will be described.

Procedure Search by Text

This Procedure Search scenario involves objects instances from the classes in the diagram shown in Fig. 4, Search View represents the search bar which receives the writing events and triggers the procedure search event when the user performs any of these actions. Search Controller has the logic to receive the different actions and execute the Search Procedure Task to make the http request to request procedures to the Gateway service of the Semantic middleware (Fig. 1) using the Network Layer.

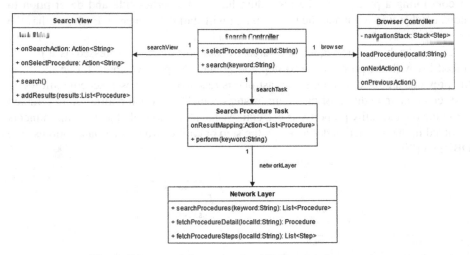

Fig. 4. Diagram of classes involved in the procedure search.

In this order, it will be described the sequence of events presented in Fig. 5, once the user types in the search textfield, he presses the search button to trigger the initial search event that is received by the search view. Once received, the onSearchAction message is sent so that the search controller executes the Search Procedure Task to communicate with the Gateway service (Fig. 1) to find procedures whose titles match the keywords sent through the Network Layer. The gateway service receives this request and provides the browser with the requested procedures to be loaded in the Search View results.

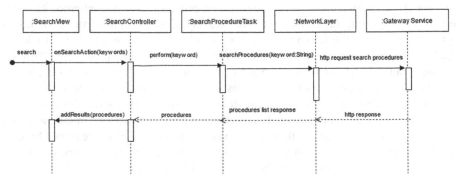

Fig. 5. Procedure search sequence diagram.

The next section will detail the interaction when selecting a procedure to perform.

Selection of Procedure to Perform

This Procedure Search scenario involves object instances from the classes in the diagram shown in Fig. 6. The Search View class receives the procedure selection event, Search Controller sends the selection action to the Browser Controller. This performs the tasks of searching for procedure detail and steps to be loaded in the AR browser, by using the Fetch Procedure Detail Task and Fetch Steps Task classes. The Network Layer is used to communicate with the Gateway service (Fig. 1) of the Semantic middleware.

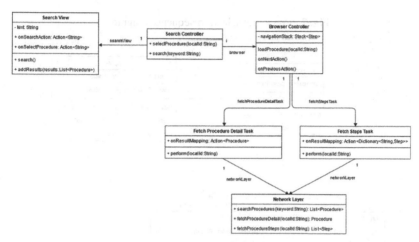

Fig. 6. Diagram of classes involved in the procedure selection.

In this order, the sequence of events presented in Fig. 7 will be described, where the steps are triggered by the initial event "select result". This scenario occurs when the user selects a procedure resulting from the search previously performed. Once the initial event is triggered, it is received by the Search View that will trigger the execution of the onSelectResult action. This action will allow the Search controller to send the id of the procedure to be loaded to the Browser controller. Once the procedure identifier is received, the FetchProcedureDetailTask and FetchStepsTask tasks are executed to request the detail and the steps associated with the procedure to the Gateway Service of the Semantic middleware (Fig. 1) using the NetworkLayer. When the response from the web service is received, it will be loaded on the browser screen.

Selected Procedure Step Advance

In this scenario, the user advances steps in the procedure, so this interaction has the classes shown in Fig. 8. The ProcedureListView class allows user to visualize the progress and has the forward and previous step buttons. The Browser Controller coordinates the general operation of the navigation of steps using a stack to maintain the state of the navigated steps. The top of the stack is the current step which the user is performing.

In this order, the interaction of the sequence diagram in Fig. 9 will be described, which is initiated when the user presses the button to advance one step of the loaded procedure.

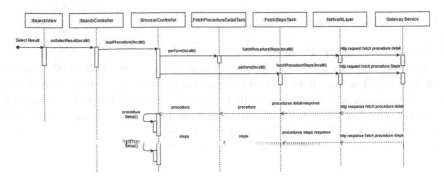

Fig. 7. Procedure selection sequence diagram

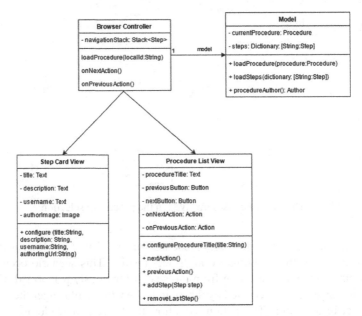

Fig. 8. Diagram of classes involved in the step advance of the selected procedure.

Once the ProcedureListView receives the initial forward event, it proceeds to perform onNextAction, so the Browser Controller looks for the local ID of the next step indicated in the current top-of-stack step. The Browser controller tells ProcedureListView to check the current step as finished and with the id of the next step it uses it as a key to obtain the object that represents it from the step dictionary. Once obtained, the Browser Controller proceeds to push it on the stack to maintain the state of the current navigation. Once this is done, it proceeds to load the step in ProcedureListView and in the StepCardView to show the name and description of the step.

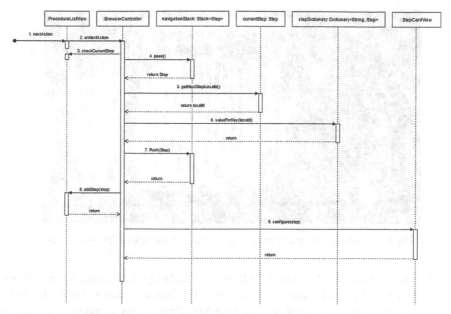

Fig. 9. Step advance of the selected procedure sequence diagram.

2.5 Augmented Catalog System Integration

The proposed framework needs to incorporate augmented virtual contents appropriately organized for their consumption in the procedures generated by using the Semantic Procedure Editor. For this purpose, an authoring tool called Augmented Virtual Catalog System [23, 24] allows the generation and exploitation of Augmented Reality content. Some works are currently being performed to extend this catalog system (Fig. 1) to structure the access to data by using ontologies that allow the system to be semantically interoperable so that it works as a universal data repository for the proposed framework. The catalogs created with this tool are composed of a set of markers that are augmented with information provided by users at the time of their creation, which is visualized using a smartphone application connected to the internet. The virtual catalog system allows the creation of virtual content such as text, images, audio and 3D models for each marker along with their geometric transformations (position, rotation, scale) and their order of appearance in the editor.

In [25], the user workflow was simplified to build and generate augmented content without the need for specific AR domain knowledge by using templates, which provides great flexibility to generate AR content for the proposed framework.

3 Application Case

In this application case a user wants to follow a cooking recipe. This example wants to illustrate the framework Exploitation flow for procedures created with the semantic procedure editor, triggered by object detection. Figure 10 simulates the search for recipes by detecting one of the instruments, e.g., a grill that can be found in a kitchen.

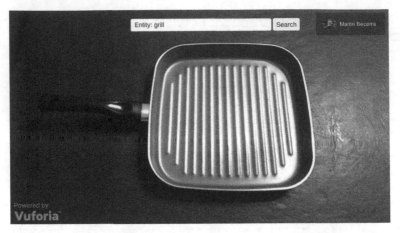

Fig. 10. Cooking instrument to be detected to start the search for procedures

Once the instrument is detected, the AR browser will trigger the search for procedures that have the searched entity in any of their steps. The Semantic web technologies make it easy to search for related entities, since the knowledge representation is a directed graph (a set of nodes interconnected by directed edges), so it explores the related Entity property of the Procedure Steps (see ontology Sect. 2.3) to retrieve it. Figure 11 shows the procedures found so that the user can select the one he wants to do.

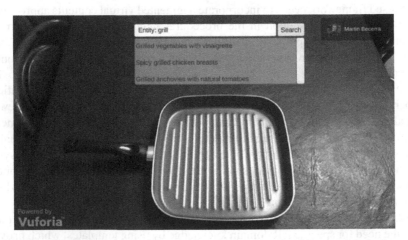

Fig. 11. Procedures that have the cooking element associated in one of their steps.

Once the user selects one of the results obtained (Spicy Grilled chicken breasts), the procedure is loaded as shown in Fig. 12. The user observes on the left the loaded procedure and its progress. At that moment he is in the first step where in order to advance he has to follow the instructions shown in the box in the lower right corner. Once this is done, the user selects the next button to advance to the next steps. At each step, a green check is made to indicate that the step has been completed.

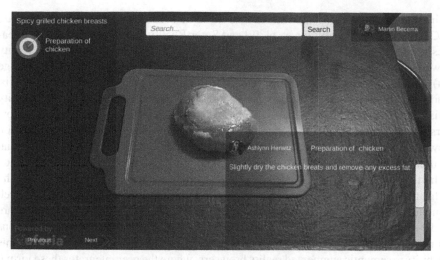

Fig. 12. First step of the cooking recipe

Once the user makes a progress through the steps, this one will be displayed in the left panel as shown in Fig. 13.

Fig. 13. Visualization of the Procedure progress.

4 Discussion

This article cites Layar [2] and Wikitude [4] and CamOnApp [3] as augmented reality browsers which cannot integrate external information sources. Different augmented reality browser proposals emerged that integrate semantic web technologies to achieve the integration of different information sources to be used in their prototype, which are ARCAMA3D [8], T. Matuszka et. al. [9] and SmartReality [10]. Table 1 shows the features evaluated in each of them in terms of the capabilities that an augmented reality browser can offer. In this order, the evaluated aspects will be explained: (a) Knowledge (Kn) that a user needs to operate the prototype, this aspect can be general or specific, (b) Readable content indicates that they are applications that offer the user the possibility to visualize descriptions of entities, (c) Editable content refers to applications that allow users to create content, together with the reading feature indicates that the application allows to exploit and edit virtual contents (d) Interactive content refers to the ability that the user can perform actions with the content, in all proposals are basic actions such as sharing content, opening URLs in traditional browsers or playing videos within the application, e) Interoperable Content indicates that the applications apply semantic web technologies to share application models, integrate data from different sources and share the data generated. f) Dynamic Procedural Interactions, so far none of the applications mentioned above provide dynamic procedural interactions. Our architecture brings this capability to semantic augmented reality browsers, where the user integrates these virtual contents in the routines of their daily tasks.

Table 1. Summary of state of the art proposals and our particular contribution.

Projects	a) Kn	b)Read	c)Edit	d)Interact	e)Interop	f)Proc
Layar	General	X	–	X	–	–
Wikitude	General	X	–	X	–	–
CamOnApp	General	X	–	X	–	–
Arcama 3D	General	X	X	–	X	–
T. Matuszka et. al	General	X	X	–	X	–
Smart Reality	General	X	–	–	X	–
Proposed framework	General	X	X	X	X	X

Works are being performed on presenting metrics that are useful for measuring the viability of the architecture. This paper focuses on the current development of the architecture that allows the addition of dynamic interaction through procedures that seek to contribute to the direction of semantic augmented reality browsers. The results obtained are encouraging.

5   Conclusions and Future Lines of Research

This article presents the architecture of the proposed framework which allows user to interact dynamically with virtual content in real environments through a semantic augmented reality browser. The implementation of the key actors of the proposed framework are presented, the semantic middleware which receives data requests, structures procedures by using the ontology of our research and coordinates the publication of procedure in the RDF triplestore and the semantic augmented reality browser allows users to exploit virtual contents and procedures. Then, an application case is exemplified where it is useful to have procedures to perform tasks in the daily life of users. Finally, the capabilities offered by state of the art prototypes are evaluated and it is emphasized the main contribution of the proposed framework, the ability to allow users to interact dynamically with augmented reality content. The future lines of research are the integration of the virtual catalog system as a data repository for augmented reality applications by using a semantic layer to the current system and the proposed framework adaptation for augmented reality glasses.

Acknowledgements. This research was funded by PROINCE C231. We would like to thank the Engineering and Technological Research Department (DIIT - Departamento de Ingeniería e Investigaciones Tecnológicas) of UNLaM for supporting research.

References

1. Yee C., Abásolo M.J., Más Sansó R., Vénere M.: Realidad virtual y realidad aumentada. Interfaces avanzadas (2011). ISBN 978-950-34-0765-3
2. LayAR. https://www.layar.com/. Accessed 2 May 2021
3. CamOnApp. https://camonapp.com/. Accessed 2 May 2021
4. Wikitude. https://www.wikitude.com/. Accessed 2 May 2021
5. Vert, S., Vasiu, R.: Integrating linked data in mobile augmented reality applications (2014). https://tinyurl.com/5ebe577s. Accessed 2 May 2021
6. Resource Description Framework (RDF). https://tinyurl.com/2ch64tu7. Accessed 2 May 2021
7. Gruber, T.: A translation approach to portable ontology specifications. Knowl. Adquisition 5(2), 199–220 (1993)
8. Aydin, B., Gensel, J., Genoud, P.: Extending augmented reality mobile application with structured knowledge from the LOD cloud. https://tinyurl.com/3x87c6ss. Accessed 2 May 2021
9. Matuszka, T., et al.: The design and implementation of semantic web-based architecture for augmented reality browser. https://tinyurl.com/nf5jxswx. Accessed 2 May 2021
10. Nixon, L., Grubert, J., Reitmayr, G.: SmartReality: integrating the web into augmented reality. https://tinyurl.com/46hzw8b9. Accessed 2 May 2021
11. Linked Data Cloud. https://lod-cloud.net/. Accessed 2 May 2021
12. SPARQL. https://tinyurl.com/2fstac94. Accessed 2 May 2021
13. Postgres. https://tinyurl.com/35z2euyz. Accessed 2 May 2021
14. Hibernate. https://tinyurl.com/94wy58n4. Accessed 2 May 2021
15. Java. https://tinyurl.com/f8kp2b4w. Accessed 2 May 2021
16. Spring Framework. https://spring.io/. Accessed 2 May 2021
17. Tomcat. https://tomcat.apache.org/. Accessed 2 May 2021
18. RDF4j. https://rdf4j.org/. Accessed 2 May 2021
19. AnzoGraph. https://tinyurl.com/t9asru6f. Accessed 2 May 2021
20. DBPedia. https://www.dbpedia.org/. Accessed 2 May 2021
21. Unity3D. https://unity.com/. Accessed 2 May 2021
22. Vuforia. https://www.ptc.com/en/products/vuforia. Accessed 2 May 2021
23. Ierache, J., Mangiarua, N., Verdicchio, N., Becerra, M., Duarte, N., Igarza, S.: Sistema de Catálogo para la Asistencia a la Creación, Publicación, Gestión y Explotación de Contenidos Multimedia y Aplicaciones de Realidad Aumentada. CACIC 2014 Red UNCI (2014). ISBN 978-987-3806-05

24. Ierache J., et al.: Development of a catalogs system for augmented reality applications. Int. J. Comp. Electr. Autom. Control Inf. Eng. **9**(1), 1–7 (2015). ISSN 1307:6892. World Academy of Science, Engineering and Technology, International Science Index 97
25. Mangiarua, N., Ierache, J.S., Becerra, M.E., Maurice, H., Igarza, S., Spositto, O.: Templates Framework for the Augmented Catalog System. CACIC 2018 Red UNCI (2018). ISBN 978-3-030-20786-1

Creating Immersive Play Anywhere Location-Based Storytelling Using Mobile AR

Gideon Raeburn[✉], Laurissa Tokarchuk, and Martin Welton

Queen Mary, University of London, Mile End Road, Bethnal Green,
London E1 4NS, UK
g.raeburn@qmul.ac.uk

Abstract. Map Story is an Augmented Reality (AR) location-based storytelling app for smartphones, that directs users to nearby real-world locations whilst following a new story. Some of the locations are augmented with virtual content visible on users phones, in order to bring the locations closer in line with those described in the story. In addition to developing the app, a preliminary user study is described, with participants using the app at their own choice of starting location, with data collected through a combination of in-app feedback and questionnaires, alongside post interviews with a selection of those who took part. As well as developing guidelines for such an experience, there is evidence that the real sites visited were reported as being a closer match to the story events, and more believable in terms of the story events playing out there than the AR locations, but with the AR sites potentially beneficial in encouraging a greater focus on the story.

Keywords: Location-based storytelling · Augmented reality · User experience

1 Introduction

Digital story experiences including some immersive theatre productions and escape rooms have grown in popularity in recent years, though are often site specific, since it is easier to connect a narrative to the features and layout of a known location, rather than one which cannot be guaranteed to contain all the elements required for the story. This often limits these experiences to having short runs for a limited audience, due to the cost of props, actors and orchestration [35]. This research aims to develop a location based story experience that can be experienced anywhere using the technology in a personal smartphone. To bring a user's location closer in line with that described in the story, the app makes use of Augmented Reality (AR), allowing virtual content to be overlaid on the real world and combined with a camera view, visible on the display of the mobile phone. The public have largely been put off by the discomfort and

© Springer Nature Switzerland AG 2021
L. T. De Paolis et al. (Eds.): AVR 2021, LNCS 12980, pp. 209–226, 2021.
https://doi.org/10.1007/978-3-030-87595-4_16

cost of current AR headsets, so mobile AR still provides various opportunities to discover how AR can enrich a user experience [4,27].

Providing an engaging experience at an unknown location is challenging, given that makers of site specific experiences often emphasise a location's unique atmosphere to aid both seamless and ethical design, sometimes providing insight into the area [13,34,37]. AR is adopted here as an approach to solving some of the unknown aspects of a location, with the added advantage that a blended AR environment offers unique opportunities for agency and immersion that can potentially feel more authentic than a purely virtual environment [32,44]. Immer sion is a commonly used subjective measure to gauge the quality of a mixed reality experience, with varying definitions existing in AR and Virtual Reality (VR), given that being fully sensory immersed and present in the environment is often desired in VR, whilst in AR a user will need to retain some awareness of their real surroundings, such as for safety reasons [39].

The research described produced the app Map Story, which aims to provide a solo interactive story at a location of the user's choosing, through a suitable iOS or Android mobile phone. Mobile AR enables the user to both discover hidden items at real-world locations to progress the story, as well to overlay buildings and other features referenced in the story on top of the user's real-world surroundings, when no real-world equivalent exists. The app incorporates GPS to locate the user, identifying suitable story locations or *Points Of Interest* (POIs) through the Mapbox API. A preliminary user study was conducted using the app, where participants were asked to submit feedback whilst taking part in terms of a pre-questionnaire, a short questionnaire completed at each POI site visited, and a post immersion questionnaire, where they could also supply additional thoughts and comments. The open feedback collected was analysed alongside post interviews with some of those who took part, in order to gain a deeper understanding of the benefits and limitations of the current app, in relation to its use of AR content alongside real-world locations.

The feedback are also aims to identify the challenges posed by real-world distractions to discover how Map Story might be improved. A further area investigated is how different users responded to the experience. This has been studied in video games in terms of player models, in VR with Witmer and Singer's *Immersive Tendency Questionnaire* (ITQ), and in literary narratives using *Reader Response Theory* [5,9,17,51]. However, little prior research exists in relation to AR, so the preliminary approach adopted here compares a subset of the *Big-5 Personality Inventory* in relation to users reported immersion [20]. This personality questionnaire has previously been applied in related fields, such as to adapt a video game narrative based on players' interests [10]. Another factor considered is the amount of walking users might be willing to do, particularly for those without a predilection to it as a pastime. Popular apps like *Zombies Run!* (2012) also offered a story alongside localisation features, but this app was promoted as an exercise tool, whilst Map Story is designed primarily to offer an immersive story experience [21].

2   Related Work

Location-based experiences have grown with the improved sensors found in modern smartphones. GPS gave rise to early experiences such *Geocaching* (2000) treasure hunts and work by Blast theory, such as *Can You See Me Now* (2006) [14]. AR has also been used in heritage projects such *The SPIRIT project* (2001), encouraging new types of visitors by connecting tour sites to an overarching narrative [42]. The inaccuracy of GPS requiring the use of physical markers, alongside faster battery drain were commonly reported issues in such experiences. However modern AR libraries include *Simultaneous Localisation and Mapping* (SLAM), a machine vision algorithm that can accurately align content to the real world without the need for physical markers, whilst phones collect ever more data about the user and their location, giving the potential for greater personalisation of experiences and new opportunities to immerse users [1,18,23].

Location-based experiences aim to generate perceptual immersion though the events closely relating to the user's surroundings, with popular AR game *Pokémon Go* (2016) also demonstrating how real-world locations can gain new significance as a result of the virtual content discovered there [2,30,41]. Research into location-based storytelling has highlighted the benefits in creating moments of ambiguity, such that the user might implicate passers-by in the experience, tied to what Reid refers to as *magic moments* [36]. These result in high immersion when the user perceives a suitably close match between the fictional events and their real surroundings. Karapanos et al. similarly found that watching a short video narrative in the real location corresponding to the narrative offered greater immersion and mental imagery, compared to one where the surroundings did not match or have a similar atmosphere [22]. Artificial Intelligence (AI) and Natural Language Processing (NLP) have been used to try and connect the available information about an area to generate a story, though such approaches have often struggled to make the story engaging and coherent [8,47]. A further approach is to transpose a site-specific experience to new locations by finding suitable equivalents for each POI visited, though this is challenging without varying the amount of walking and atmosphere offered by each location [12,28].

Benford describes a framework for considering mixed reality experiences in terms of a participant's *trajectory* through it, considering how the different spaces involved, use of time, roles and interfaces forming the experience must all be carefully balanced [6]. The designer will have imagined an ideal *canonical* trajectory through an experience, with different users deviating from this, and unknown locations providing greater opportunity for variation, through the cognitive load required to navigate them, as well as considering what behaviour might be appropriate in a particular location, tied to Goffman's concept of *frames* [11,40]. Acting outside of the appropriate frame might cause the user to temporarily disengage from an experience through feeling awkward and self conscious [25,50]. The *The StoryPlaces Project* (2017) outlined a series of aesthetic and pragmatic considerations for designing location-based experiences, including aspects related to walking, safety and how locations may change over time [33].

Murray suggested narrative experiences in any new medium must balance user immersion, agency and transformation [31]. This suggests a potential future direction for this research. Offering increased agency can be related to video game research where the designer offers a world for the user to explore, with the hope the immersion offered means they will not be too drawn to the systems limitations [45]. In the storytelling game *Façade* (2005), taking an active role was found to lead to higher satisfaction, presence and enjoyment, though this was also linked to the game's believable characters and story [38,49]. Jane McGonigal suggests rewards in immersive experiences come from being encouraged to act beyond normal habits and engage with a space and those within it [29]. This parallels research into immersive theatre, suggesting audience members enjoy the added opportunities for sensory interaction, whilst also connecting to a narcissistic desire that the events directly relate to them [3,26].

3   Map Story Design and Procedure

Map Story was made in Unity with the AR features implemented using the ARFoundation plugin, incorporating ARKit for iOS and ARCore for Android, with SLAM positioning to align virtual objects in the real world. This enabled the app to work on iPhones 6s and later and non-lite Android handsets, though SLAM is ineffective in low ambient light levels, so users were asked to only use the app during daylight hours. Map Story also incorporated a bespoke narrative, that directed the user to six sites around their local neighbourhood, whilst attempting to locate a missing fictional character. Each of the six sites chosen were selected as places that would have a strong possibility of existing in the user's real vicinity, such as a public house, school and a church. Users would be guided to the real location in cases where it existed (*real sites*), alternatively visiting a suitable location that could be overlaid with a 3D model of the site described when no real version existed close by (*AR sites*).

On first starting the app, it would connect to the Mapbox API having located the user via GPS, and search for the six real world story sites close to their position. An error screen was presented if Mapbox could not detect any of the six requested sites in an approximate half mile radius around their position, offering the suggestion to try loading the app elsewhere. In cases where some of the six sites could not be found in the designated play area, users would then visit a mixture of real and AR sites. The AR sites would involve the user being guided to a suitable location to overlay a virtual model of the relevant site on top of their real-world surroundings using their phone camera, with the combined AR scene then visible on their phone display. Appropriate real-world locations chosen to place the AR sites varied between empty green spaces, street corners, or on top of other buildings. Additionally some of the real sites were swapped with AR ones in order that the total number of real and AR sites visited was kept roughly equal across the study. After selecting the six sites, an algorithm calculated a route between them, and the user's starting position to minimise the total distance walked, this requirement adding a restriction on the story's design to allow the six sites to be visited in any order. A real-time walking route to the next site was displayed on the in-app map provided.

Additional story was delivered to the user whilst walking to the next site, with CereVoice's *Text To Speech* (TTS) software converting all in-game text to audio, such that the app could be used hands free whilst walking. These story sections encouraged the user to look around, aiming to encourage Reid's magic moments, when an aspect of the story closely resembled the real world. On arriving at a designated AR site, users would be instructed to hold up their phones to overlay a virtual model on their surroundings. Once placed, events would then proceed the same as at the real sites, where users would search for a lost diary page containing new story details and backstory, this virtual diary page appearing in relation to the phone's accelerometer movement, with a large AR marker appearing if users had not found the page after a short time. On picking up the diary page by touching it on the screen, additional story would be revealed before directing the user to the next site. These stages of gameplay at each story site are shown in Fig. 1.

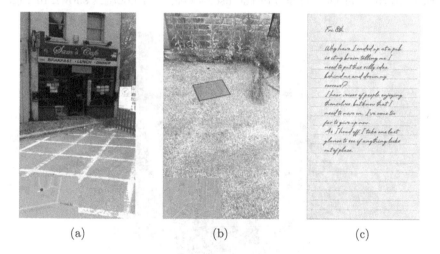

(a)   (b)   (c)

Fig. 1. Map Story gameplay. Users visit real world locations marked on a local map, some of which are augmented with a virtual model (a). At each location the user must locate a hidden diary page (b) to uncover new story details (c).

The app was refined after pilot testing, which included reducing the number of sites visited from nine to six, to reduce the length of the experience and amount of walking. An option to skip a story site was also introduced in case the user might not want to visit a suggested location, or it was inaccessible or too far away. Participants also raised concerns about the length of the questionnaires completed at each location, so the measures used were refined as described in Sect. 4.

3.1 Map Story Storyline

Map Story incorporates a new fictional narrative where a user is contacted to complete a questionnaire about themselves (actually the extroversion and openness sections of the Big-5 Personality Inventory) and then mysteriously receives a mobile phone in the post (in reality the user using their own phone). The phone received connects to the story of a local scientist who has gone missing, and the user is invited to visit the last six places the missing woman went, which are marked on a map displayed on the phone. The story places the user as a main character in the narrative alongside the missing scientist, and allows the six map locations to be visited in any order, based on minimising the walk between them. Clues to the overarching mystery are revealed through discarded diary pages discovered at each location, as well as through additional story presented as audio whilst walking. After visiting all six sites, the user is led to an open green area (such as a park), where they discover an AR portal they can walk through, to emerge in a fully virtual world visible on their phone screen. Here they finally catch up with the character they have been tracking, who had discovered a way to travel to this parallel version of the user's neighbourhood as shown in Fig. 2.

Fig. 2. Walking through the AR portal at the ending of Map Story.

4   Measures

After Map Story was built and refined through pilot testing, a short user study was conducted. Data was collected through the app by means of pre-questionnaire, a short series of questions repeated after visiting each real or AR story site, and a final post questionnaire. The pre-questionnaire asked users their age, gender, prior experience of AR technology and immersive experiences, as well as the extroversion and openness to new experience sections of the *NEO-FFI-3 Big-5 Personality Inventory* (BFI), these particular dimensions selected as particularly relevant to adopting a novel technology in public, where social play also poses a risk of embarrassment [11]. This formed a first investigation of their effectiveness in identifying different player types, given AR lacks a bespoke tool like the ITQ for VR, that identifies a relationship between a user's immersive tendency and their sense of presence in a VR world [51]. The post questionnaire adopted immersion measures from the *Augmented Reality Immersion* (ARI) questionnaire [15]. This questionnaire is based on Brown and Cairns immersion model incorporating three increasing levels of immersion as successive barriers to deeper immersion are removed. These three levels are further divided into two sub-categories as follows [7]:

1. **Engagement** - Interest and Usability.
2. **Engrossment** - Emotional Attachment and Focus of Attention.
3. **Total immersion** - Presence and Flow.

To provide a quantitative measure of the differences between the real and AR sites visited, participants were asked to rate six statements at each site visited before walking to the next location. The limited question set aimed to prevent a significant interruption in the story, and related to the following:

1. The match of the site visited relative to the one described.
2. The user's focus on the story whilst at the site.
3. Being able to imagine the story events playing out at the site.
4. The user's interest in continuing the story.
5. The usability issues experienced at the site.
6. The story being the user's primary intent (tied to being in a flow state).

Users could also provide their thoughts through the app about each real and AR site visited, as well as on completion of the story. Participants were also invited to take part in a structured interview about their experience which was transcripted and analysed alongside all open feedback. Map Story was also presented as part of a location-based experience workshop, to the Queen Mary, University of London English and Drama department, with this discussion also contributing additional feedback.

5 Results

5.1 Participants

Map Story was downloaded a total of 95 times for Android and 43 times for iOS. Data was only retained from those who successfully completed the experience and visited at least 4 out of 6 of their suggested story sites, given the in-app option to skip any locations that might not be easily accessible. This left 23 completed sets of user questionnaires (15 male, 6 female and 2 of unspecified gender). The participant demographics are shown in Table 1 along with the total number of real and AR sites visited across the study (58 real, 57 AR and 23 skipped), demonstrating the algorithm used was effective in equalling the number of real and AR sites visited, though still with a significant number of sites skipped. In addition twelve participants agreed to take part in a post interview providing more detail about their experience at both the real and AR sites visited, from their choice of location to use the app.

Table 1. Demographics of the 23 participants who took part in the Map Story user study (left) and a breakdown of all real and AR sites visited (right).

		Participant count		Site name	Site count	
					Real	AR
Gender	Male	15		School	12	7
	Female	6		Public house	12	8
	Other	2		Church	10	9
Age	18–29	9		Pond/Lake	6	15
	30–39	8		House	10	6
	40–49	5		Shop	8	12
	50+	1		Skipped sites	23	
Previous AR	Limited	17				
Experience	Appreciable	6				
Previous immersive	Limited	10				
Theatre experience	Appreciable	13				

The data collected was checked for internal consistency using Cronbach's alpha, with the results shown in Table 2, demonstrating good internal reliability in most cases, though with a slightly lower value in the emotional attachment dimension of the ARI questionnaire. The results for this dimension are still reported, though it is worthy of further discussion whether the questions may have generated confusion, or have been influenced by external distractions given

Table 2. Internal consistency of each of the study measures used.

Measure	Scale reliability	Mean score and sd
Big-5 extroversion (8 items)	$\alpha = 0.84$	M = 3.11, SD = 0.61
Big-5 openness (10 items)	$\alpha = 0.88$	M = 3.85, SD = 0.68
ARI interest (4 items)	$\alpha = 0.87$	M = 5.75, SD = 0.97
ARI usability (4 items)	$\alpha = 0.85$	M = 5.88, SD = 0.94
ARI emotional attachment (3 items)	$\alpha = 0.42$	M = 5.07, SD = 0.82
ARI focused attention (3 items)	$\alpha = 0.63$	M = 4.68, SD = 1.13
ARI presence (4 items)	$\alpha = 0.71$	M = 3.43, SD = 1.05
ARI flow (3 items)	$\alpha = 0.71$	M = 3.68, SD = 1.25

their completion in public. Additionally, a number of the measures showed a departure from a normal distribution after conducting a Shapiro-Wilk test. This influenced the choice of statistical analysis techniques used.

5.2 Immersion Relative to the Proportion of Different Sites Visited

The ARI immersion scores reported by each participant were correlated against the proportion of real and AR sites that each participant visited (each participant visiting a mixture of at least 4 real and/or AR sites). A Spearman rank correlation test was used due to the data deviating from a bivariate normal distribution, with a medium size positive correlation only suggested in terms of users' focus of attention and the proportion of AR sites visited (rho = 0.41, $p = 0.049$). An equivalent negative correlation for users' focus of attention score with the proportion of real sites visited was partially support by the correlation factor (rho = −0.38), though not significant at a 5% significance level ($p = 0.07$). However, with the limited sample size and resulting errors, this is suggested as a worthwhile area for further investigation.

Figure 3 displays the 6 ARI dimension scores across all participants, as well as the grouped scores according to Brown and Cairns 3 levels of increasing immersion. This provides evidence that the app was only effective in promoting the lowest level of immersion in terms of user engagement. A paired Wilcoxon signed rank test suggests each user's engrossment score was significantly lower than their engagement score ($r = 0.82$, $p < 0.001$), and similarly their total immersion score was less than their engrossment score ($r = 0.87$, $p < 0.001$). In this model the highest levels of immersion relate to a user experiencing both a sense of presence that they are part of the AR environment, alongside a sense of flow, related to an optimal experience.

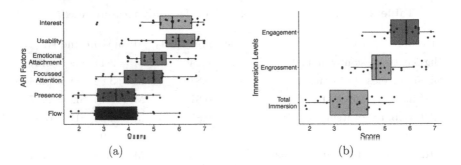

(a)   (b)

Fig. 3. The 6 ARI dimension scores for all participants (a), also summarised in terms of Brown and Cairns 3 increasing levels of immersion (b).

5.3   Ratings for Real and AR Sites

Six statements were rated to investigate differences between the two types of site, whether real or AR. Based on the null hypothesis that the responses were the same at each site, a Wilcoxon rank sum test was applied (the responses not being normally distributed) comparing the median scores for the sites visited. The scores for each of the six statements at the 58 real and 57 AR sites visited are shown in the box plots in Fig. 4 and suggest the null hypothesis is not valid for three of the statements at a 5% significance level ($p < 0.05$). The relevant statements are how well the site matched the one described in the story ($r = 0.51$, $p < 0.001$), how real the site felt in relation to the story events ($r = 0.27$, $p < 0.001$), both of which demonstrate a higher score in the case of the real sites,

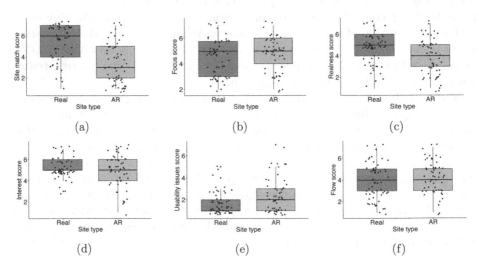

(a)   (b)   (c)

(d)   (e)   (f)

Fig. 4. Box plots showing the six statement ratings at the 58 real and 57 AR sites visited across the study. Each statement refers to the following aspects of the site (a) Site match, (b) User's focus, (c) Realness of events, (d) User interest, (e) Usability issues, (f) User's sense of flow.

though with only a medium effect size in terms of the site match. Additionally the score for usability difficulties was suggested as having a higher median value for the AR sites ($r = 0.21$ $p = 0.03$) though with a relatively small effect size. An equivalent result was obtained considering the mean responses to each of the six statements averaged across the real and AR sites visited by each participant. This comparison was calculated for verification purposes and the same three statements showed a significant difference comparing the real and AR sites.

A non-parametric Kruskal-Wallis rank sum test found no significant difference in user responses across the six different AR sites. This indicates no preference towards any 3D models used as AR overlays. However, the test is limited by the small number of data points for each AR site, and is reported for guidance only.

5.4   Varying Immersion for Different Users

A Spearman rank correlation test was used to look for evidence of a correlation between each ARI factor and each participant's reported extroversion and openness BFI scores, with a null hypothesis based on there being no relationship. This null hypothesis was supported by the results with no evidence of a correlation between any of the ARI dimensions and personality factors ($p > 0.05$ in all cases). The same result was confirmed in relation to each user's average scores across the AR and real sites they visited, with the six statements rated at each site showing no evidence of a correlation to their reported extroversion and openness scores. The six ARI dimension scores were further investigated for differences according to users gender or previous experience of AR and immersive theatre, by means of an unpaired Wilcoxon rank sum test. This test was limited by the number of users in each group, but again did not provide any evidence of a showing a significant difference in score at a 5% significance level.

5.5   Varying Immersion Based on Distance Walked Between Sites

The six statements completed at each site were also compared against the distance traversed to reach the site. Using a Spearman rank correlation test evidence for a small positive correlation (rho $= 0.29$, $p = 0.03$) was only detected in respect of how well the real sites matched the story, suggesting the possibility that a close match might offer a small reward for walking to the real site for some users. This is discussed further in the following section where the open feedback received offers an alternative picture based on the amount of walking involved.

6   Discussion

User feedback suggested Map Story was largely successful in its first aim to create a mobile AR story app that could be used almost anywhere, though identifying some areas for improvement, such as the limited number of available sites at certain map coordinates. This was primarily a result of the map API used, which also resulted in excess walking between some sites (>250 m), that led to some users not completing the experience citing, *"many locations were too far apart"*, and providing less data points for these longer walking distances as a result. Feedback also highlighted that users expect such an experience to finish back at their starting location unless notified otherwise in advance. The higher ARI focus of attention score for AR sites was supported by some user feedback, *"the AR elements definitely make it more engaging"*, tied to being offered something new in cases where users knew their neighbourhood well. This has been also been suggested as one contributing factor why Niantic's *Harry Potter:Wizards Unite* (2019) did not perform as well as their previous game Pokémon Go. Both games used the same POIs, with their familiarity potentially offering less incentive to play [24]. With Map Story one user commented, *"I felt knowing the local area well made to harder to think about it in terms of the new story"*, though they do not elaborate if the AR features made the task easier in this respect. The real sites scored higher in terms of matching the story, with most issues around them tied to the map data being out of date. Issues with the AR sites primarily related to the 3D model being overlaid awkwardly on top of the real world, providing a greater barrier to immersion. Users also reported the AR could have been used more effectively such as through offering greater interaction, *"I feel the AR could have fed way more into the story and given more chances to lose ourselves in the world"*. A couple of users also assumed they had been lead to the wrong location when they knew a real site equivalent existed nearby, causing confused at the request to place an AR scene. In this respect the AR markers used to let participants know they were searching in the right place for a diary page did not break immersion, but were cited as a comforting feature to let someone know they were looking in the correct place.

Feedback also suggested that the app was only successful in encouraging deeper immersion at particular moments, tied to Reid's magic moments where an aspect of the story temporarily paralleled something in the real world environment, *"a driver asked directions to the church which turned out to be the next location to visit"*. Passing by a real school provided an opportunity for magic moments, but several participants reported feeling uncomfortable using their phones near to where children were playing, raising an important ethical consideration for designing an app used in public spaces. Even when story events did not match the real world, some users demonstrated their desire for immersion in making the inconsistencies fit, *"not sure this pub operates anymore, it somehow matches the eeriness of the story"*. Encouraging deeper levels of immersion and engagement might come from offering increased agency and interaction with the virtual content. However, there are also questions around the suitability of quantifying experience using the standard models of presence and flow adapted to the ARI questionnaire's levels of immersion in Brown and Cairns model. The Pervasive GameFlow model devised for research into pervasive experiences, highlights the need to adjust the standard criteria for flow to occur in such cases, given players will inevitably report a greater awareness of their surroundings, which often also leads to greater focus on their personal intentions [19].

The story used in Map Story specifically allowed several real-world locations to be visited in any order, which by design led to it being experienced as mysterious and at times ambiguous. This was divisive, with some users enjoying the suspense and replaying audio tracks several times to listen for hidden clues, whilst others reported that it left them unsure of the main character's motivations. As a result whilst many reported enjoying the ending, others felt they were surprised when it did not match their interpretation of the events. This highlights the importance in developing a tool to identify user types in such AR experiences, which was not supported through the two dimensions of the Big-5 model adopted here. Additional suggestions for improving the app included a desire for improved visuals, as well as additional audio whilst walking, alongside audio cues to let users know they had arrived at the target location when using the app hands free. Additional audio narration would also benefit the chance of creating further magic moments by encouraging users to connect the story with their environment. The use of the TTS audio was generally well received, though a few participants found the voice distracting and slightly robotic, desiring a human narration. Several users also hoped that the personality questionnaire completed might have further personalised the experience. This is an ongoing research area with previous studies reporting its potential positive effect on user immersion [16,43,48].

7   Limitations and Future Work

The user study was carried out whilst there were ongoing Covid-19 pandemic restrictions regarding outside exercise. Despite the app offering a solo immersive story experience, this still had an effect on participant recruitment as demonstrated by the small sample size. This made some of the desired quantitative analysis impractical due to the limited number of participants of different age groups or with significant previous experience of using AR, and is why a more extensive qualitative analysis involving user post interviews was performed alongside the quantitative findings, to confirm the efficacy of the results. The restrictions also limited the ability to observe participants taking part, in order to see how different users reacted to using the AR app in public spaces.

Users took part using their own phones at their own choice of location. Whilst the app performed similarly on a range of handsets it was tested on, some variation in experience might be expected in relation to the screen size and the particular Android or iOS model used. The variety of locations poses the largest confounding variable given the variation in passers by, distractions, atmosphere and spacing of the story sites. There is an argument that the app is designed specifically for this purpose, and so should be tested *in the wild* as opposed to a lab environment, though the effect is evident in some users' scores and feedback, *"the area was very busy which made the experience less engaging"*. The choice of story poses another potential confounding variable given the range of users taking part. Collecting data primarily through the app added a challenge to confirm that all data retained was from those who completed the study appropriately.

To this end data was only kept from those who visited at least four out of six of the suggested story sites, the skip feature implemented after pilot testing given the risk of the map API referencing outdated map information. This limit on the data kept prevented users' data being retained who did not engage in a significant walk around their neighbourhood using the app. A further limitation was that users were only given a single opportunity to place the AR sites through their phones, which risked the virtual models being overlaid awkwardly on the real world. This is a key requirement for future iterations of the app, that users be given the opportunity to re-position any overlaid AR content before deciding its final location is appropriate. Salen and Zimmerman's *immersive fallacy* states that participants are aware their belief in the story world is voluntary, and will want to aid generating immersion, such as through helping to more seamlessly overlap the story world with the real world [29,46].

8 Conclusion

Map Story was largely successful in providing a real-world story that could be experienced anywhere through the addition of AR elements. Evidence for the benefits of such an approach are suggested through users' increased focus of attention on the story. It was suggested this offers a greater opportunity for a novel experience when the user is already familiar with their local area. Challenges arise around AR risking greater usability issues, as well as a user accepting the story events in relation to the virtual elements. The use of AR markers demonstrated benefits in comforting users, by letting them know that they were at the correct location, though more freedom to align virtual content relative to the real world is required for further iterations of the app, with evidence that the increased agency offered would help to enhance immersion rather than detract from it.

The BFI personality measures used did not show a relationship with users reported immersion levels, in spite of user feedback demonstrating several differences in opinion regarding the app. Personalising such an experience based on users' preferences is a worthwhile goal for AR experiences, though challenging due to the lack of specific tools for analysing AR experiences. As an example, excessive walking was found to be a deterrent to immersion for some users, though this could be controlled through a map API with a greater number of labelled map sites, or users might be encouraged to walk further through offering additional story content. A further improvement is that users desired to finish the app close to their starting point unless a different end location was notified in advance. The occurrence of magic moments did offer moments of high immersion, with the role AR might play in aiding the creation of such moments a further consideration for the next iteration of the app. AR needs to be used appropriately, as was deemed unnecessary or confusing when a similar real world equivalent existed nearby. However it was also shown to offer benefits in terms of a new experience in a possibly familiar location, as well as offering the potential for new opportunities for interaction in the story events, as proposed for a future revision of Map Story in the hope it can offer a more immersive user experience.

References

1. Abowd, G.D., Mynatt, E.D.: Charting past, present, and future research in ubiquitous computing. ACM Trans. Comput. Hum. Interact. **7**(1), 29–58 (2000)
2. Alha, K., Koskinen, E., Paavilainen, J., Hamari, J.: Why do people play location-based augmented reality games: a study on Pokémon GO. Comput. Hum. Behav. **93**, 114–122 (2019)
3. Alston, A.: Audience participation and neoliberal value: risk, agency and responsibility in immersive theatre AU - Alston. Adam. Perform. Res. **18**(2), 128–138 (2013)
4. Baker, C.: Virtual, artificial and mixed reality: new frontiers in performance. In: 2017 23rd International Conference on Virtual System and Multimedia (VSMM), Dublin, pp. 1–10. IEEE (October 2017)
5. Bartle, R., Philosophy Documentation Center: Presence and flow: ill-fitting clothes for virtual worlds. Techné: Res. Philos. Technol. **10**(3), 39–54 (2007)
6. Benford, S., Giannachi, G., Koleva, B., Rodden, T.: From interaction to trajectories: designing coherent journeys through user experiences. In: Proceedings of the SIGCHI Conference on Human Factors in Computing Systems, Boston, MA, USA, pp. 709–718 (April 2009)
7. Brown, E., Cairns, P.: A grounded investigation of game immersion. In: Extended Abstracts of the 2004 Conference on Human Factors and Computing Systems, CHI 2004, Vienna, Austria, pp. 1297–1300. ACM Press (2004)
8. Budvytyte, S., Bukauskas, L.: Location-based story telling for mobile tourist. In: 2006 7th International Baltic Conference on Databases and Information Systems, Vilnius, Lithuania, pp. 220–228. IEEE (2006)
9. Busselle, R., Bilandzic, H.: Measuring narrative engagement. Media Psychol. **12**(4), 321–347 (2009)
10. de Lima, E.S., Feijó, B., Furtado, A.L.: Player behavior and personality modeling for interactive storytelling in games. Entertain. Comput. **28**, 32–48 (2018)
11. Deterding, S.: Alibis for adult play: a Goffmanian account of escaping embarrassment in adult play. Games Cult. **13**(3), 260–279 (2018)
12. Ferreira, C., Maia, L.F., de Salles, C., Trinta, F., Viana, W.: Modelling and transposition of location-based games. Entertain. Comput. **30**, 100295 (2019)
13. Flanagan, M.: Locating play and politics: real world games & activism. Leonardo Electronic Almanac **16**(2–3), 1–13 (2007)
14. Flintham, M., et al.: Where on-line meets on the streets: experiences with mobile mixed reality games. In: Proceedings of the Conference on Human Factors in Computing Systems, Ft. Lauderdale, Florida, USA, pp. 569–576. ACM Press (April 2003)
15. Georgiou, Y., Kyza, E.A.: The development and validation of the ARI questionnaire: an instrument for measuring immersion in location-based augmented reality settings. Int. J. Hum Comput Stud. **98**, 24–37 (2017)
16. Gradinar, A., et al.: Perceptive media – adaptive storytelling for digital broadcast. In: Abascal, J., Barbosa, S., Fetter, M., Gross, T., Palanque, P., Winckler, M. (eds.) INTERACT 2015. LNCS, vol. 9299, pp. 586–589. Springer, Cham (2015). https://doi.org/10.1007/978-3-319-22723-8_67
17. Green, M.C., Brock, T.C.: The role of transportation in the persuasiveness of public narratives. J. Pers. Soc. Psychol. **79**(5), 701–721 (2000)
18. Innocent, T.: A framework for cloud aesthetics in mixed realities. In: Aceti, L., Thomas, P., Colless, E. (eds.) Leonardo Electronic Almanac, vol. 22. LEA/MIT Press, Cambridge, MA (2017)

19. Jegers, K.: Pervasive game flow: understanding player enjoyment in pervasive gaming. Comput. Entertain. **5**(1), 9-es (2007)

20. John, O., Srivastava, S.: The Big-Five trait Taxonomy: History, Measurement, and Theoretical Perspectives. Volume 2 of Handbook of Personality: Theory and Research. Guildford Press, New York (1999)

21. Kan, A., Gibbs, M., Ploderer, B.: Being chased by zombies!: understanding the experience of mixed reality quests. In: Proceedings of the 25th Australian Computer-Human Interaction Conference on Augmentation, Application, Innovation, Collaboration, Adelaide, Australia, pp. 207–216. ACM Press (November 2013)

22. Karapanos, E., Barreto, M., Nisi, V., Niforatos, E.: Does locality make a difference? Assessing the effectiveness of location-aware narratives. Interact. Comput. **24**(4), 273–279 (2012)

23. Ketchell, S., Chinthammit, W., Engelke, U.: Situated storytelling with SLAM enabled augmented reality. In: The 17th International Conference on Virtual-Reality Continuum and its Applications in Industry, Brisbane, QLD, Australia, pp. 1–9. ACM (November 2019)

24. Laato, S., Pietarinen, T., Rauti, S., Laine, T.H.: Analysis of the quality of points of interest in the most popular location-based games. In: Proceedings of the 20th International Conference on Computer Systems and Technologies, Ruse, Bulgaria, pp. 153–160. ACM (June 2019)

25. Licoppe, C., Inada, Y.: Emergent uses of a multiplayer location-aware mobile game: the interactional consequences of mediated encounters. Mobilities **1**(1), 39–61 (2006)

26. Machon, J.: Immersive Theatres: Intimacy and Immediacy in Contemporary Performance. Palgrave Macmillan, Basingstoke (2013)

27. MacIntyre, B., Bolter, J.D.: Single-narrative, multiple point-of-view dramatic experiences in augmented reality. Virtual Reality **7**(1), 10–16 (2003)

28. Macvean, A., et al.: WeQuest: scalable alternate reality games through end-user content authoring. In: Proceedings of the 8th International Conference on Advances in Computer Entertainment Technology, Lisbon, Portugal. ACM Press (November 2011) 1

29. McGonigal, J.: A real little game: the performance of belief in pervasive play. In: Proceedings of the 2003 DiGRA International Conference, Utrecht, The Netherlands (November 2003)

30. Mcmahan, A.: Immersion, engagement, and presence. In: Wolf, M.J.P., Perron, B. (eds.) The Video Game Reader. Routledge, New York, London (2003)

31. Murray, J.H.: Hamlet on the Holodeck: the Future of Narrative in Cyberspace. MIT Press, Cambridge, Mass (1998)

32. O'Neill, S.J., Benyon, D.R.: Extending the semiotics of embodied interaction to blended spaces. Hum. Technol. Interdisc. J. Hum. ICT Environ. **11**(1), 30–56 (2015)

33. Packer, H.S., Hargood, C., Howard, Y., Papadopoulos, P., Millard, D.E.: Developing a writer's toolkit for interactive locative storytelling. In: Nunes, N., Oakley, I., Nisi, V. (eds.) ICIDS 2017. LNCS, vol. 10690, pp. 63–74. Springer, Cham (2017). https://doi.org/10.1007/978-3-319-71027-3_6

34. Price, S., Jewitt, C., Sakr, M.: Embodied experiences of place: a study of history learning with mobile technologies: embodied experiences of place. J. Comput. Assist. Learn. **32**(4), 345–359 (2016)

35. Reid, J.: Design for coincidence: incorporating real world artifacts in location based games. In: Proceedings of the 3rd International Conference on Digital Interactive Media in Entertainment and Arts, Athens, Greece, pp. 18–25. ACM Press (2008)
36. Reid, J., Hull, R., Cater, K., Fleuriot, C.: Magic moments in situated mediascapes. In: Proceedings of the 2005 ACM SIGCHI International Conference on Advances in Computer Entertainment Technology, Valencia, Spain, pp. 290–293. ACM Press (2005)
37. Rodríguez, M.E.P.: Designing pervasive theatre: the chain reaction case, Volda, Norway, pp. 73–81 (2009)
38. Roth, C., Klimmt, C., Vermeulen, I.E., Vorderer, P.: The experience of interactive storytelling: comparing "fahrenheit" with "façade". In: Anacleto, J.C., Fels, S., Graham, N., Kapralos, B., Saif El-Nasr, M., Stanley, K. (eds.) ICEC 2011. LNCS, vol. 6972, pp. 13–21. Springer, Heidelberg (2011). https://doi.org/10.1007/978-3-642-24500-8_2
39. Scoresby, J., Shelton, B.E.: Visual perspectives within educational computer games: effects on presence and flow within virtual immersive learning environments. Instr. Sci. 39(3), 227–254 (2011)
40. Shin, J., Kim, H., Parker, C., Kim, H., Oh, S., Woo, W.: Is any room really ok? The effect of room size and furniture on presence, narrative engagement, and usability during a space-adaptive augmented reality game. In: 2019 IEEE International Symposium on Mixed and Augmented Reality, Beijing, China, pp. 135–144. IEEE (October 2019)
41. Sifonis, C.M.: Attributes of ingress gaming locations contributing to players' place attachment. In: Extended Abstracts Publication of the Annual Symposium on Computer-Human Interaction in Play, Amsterdam, The Netherlands, pp. 569–575. ACM Press (2017)
42. Spierling, U., Winzer, P., Massarczyk, E.: Experiencing the presence of historical stories with location-based augmented reality. In: Nunes, N., Oakley, I., Nisi, V. (eds.) ICIDS 2017. LNCS, vol. 10690, pp. 49–62. Springer, Cham (2017). https://doi.org/10.1007/978-3-319-71027-3_5
43. Stenton, S.P., et al.: Mediascapes: context-aware multimedia experiences. IEEE Multimedia 14(3), 98–105 (2007)
44. Suh, A., Prophet, J.: The state of immersive technology research: a literature analysis. Comput. Hum. Behav. 86, 77–90 (2018)
45. Tanenbaum, K., Tanenbaum, J.: Commitment to meaning: a reframing of agency in games. In: Digital Arts and Culture 2009. UC, Irvine (December 2009)
46. Tekinbaş, K.S., Zimmerman, E.: Rules of Play: Game Design Fundamentals. MIT Press, Cambridge, Mass (2003)
47. van Stegeren, J., Theune, M.: Towards generating textual game assets from real-world data. In: Proceedings of the 13th International Conference on the Foundations of Digital Games, Malmo, Sweden, pp. 1–4. ACM Press (2018)
48. Vayanou, M., Karvounis, M., Katifori, A., Kyriakidi, M., Roussou, M., Ioannidis, Y.: The CHESS project: adaptive personalized storytelling experiences in museums. In: Interactive Storytelling, vol. 4 (2014)
49. Vermeulen, I.E., Roth, C., Vorderer, P., Klimmt, C.: Measuring user responses to interactive stories: towards a standardized assessment tool. In: Aylett, R., Lim, M.Y., Louchart, S., Petta, P., Riedl, M. (eds.) ICIDS 2010. LNCS, vol. 6432, pp. 38–43. Springer, Heidelberg (2010). https://doi.org/10.1007/978-3-642-16638-9_7

50. Wiseman, S., van der Linden, J., Spiers, A., Oshodi, M.: Control and being controlled: exploring the use of technology in an immersive theatre performance. In: Proceedings of the 2017 Conference on Designing Interactive Systems, Edinburgh, United Kingdom, pp. 3–14. ACM Press (2017)
51. Witmer, B.G., Singer, M.J.: Measuring presence in virtual environments: a presence questionnaire. Presence Teleoperators Virtual Environ. **7**(3), 225–240 (1998)

Efficient Augmented Reality on Low-Power Embedded Systems

Alessandro Longobardi$^{(\boxtimes)}$ ⓘ, Franco Tecchia ⓘ, Marcello Carrozzino ⓘ,
and Massimo Bergamasco ⓘ

Scuola Superiore Sant'Anna, Mechanical Intelligence Institute, San Giuliano Terme PI,
56127 Pisa, Italy
alessandro.longobardi@santannapisa.it

Abstract. In this paper we propose a development technique for low-power devices with limited computing capacity to obtain efficient, high-performance and non-CPU-invasive Augmented Reality (AR) applications. The paper will discuss how to exploit both the available hardware and software resources. Many boards on the market are equipped with CPUs with low computing power together with GPUs for 2D/3D graphics and multimedia. The paper analyses the strengths of these architectures and how to exploit them. The Operating System (O.S.) also provides features that allow greater control over the system (e.g., avoid wasting resources) and its performance. The techniques proposed are then used, as an example, in the development of an AR application for remote assistance.

Keywords: Augmented reality · Low-power · GPU · Embedded system · Wearable system

1 Introduction

Nowadays, there are a multitude of low-power, small, wearable boards on the market.

These boards are often equipped with single-core processors with limited computing capacity, making it burdensome use the CPU inefficiently or to perform heavy computationally tasks. For this reason, it is necessary to exploit all the resources made available by the hardware: there are hardware chips in the processor's System on Chip (SoC) that can perform specific tasks very efficiently, both in terms of performance and power consumption. Concerning, for example, the various multimedia tasks: video compression, image processing or 2D/3D graphics. Performing these tasks in software (SW) adds a prohibitive load for this type of system.

1.1 Multimedia

Many SoCs have a GPU capable of multimedia functionality:

- Video encoding and decoding: supports many hardware compression standards like h264/h265/mjpeg.

L. T. De Paolis et al. (Eds.): AVR 2021, LNCS 12980, pp. 227–244, 2021.
https://doi.org/10.1007/978-3-030-87595-4_17

- Image encoding and decoding: support for jpg/png/bmp in hardware.
- Image processing: application of filters and effects.
- Image conversion: image format conversion (e.g., from YUYV to RGB and vice versa).
- Image resize: image downscaling and upscaling.

Exploiting the hardware (HW) features, from the developer's point of view, implies, use libraries/frameworks provided by the chip vendor that do not necessarily work on known standards. This adds constraints to the application design:

1. Availability only in certain languages.
2. Abstraction level.
3. Lack of documentation.

1.2 Bus and Memory

There are chips with special buses (e.g., mipi bus [11]) that allow certain peripherals, like a camera, to be connected directly to the GPU: avoiding unnecessary frame copy from GPU to CPU and vice versa, saving bandwidth.

In addition, many cards feature unified memory, which can be used to advantage by reducing memory bandwidth in graphics applications.

System memory that was previously owned only by the CPU is now shared between the CPU and GPU.

In a unified memory architecture with a unified addressing scheme, both devices share the same virtual address space. Therefore, instead of explicitly transferring data, the CPU can pass the pointer of input data to the GPU.

1.3 2d/3d Graphics

The graphics capabilities of these low-power cards are growing, with full support for vertex/fragment shaders, and higher fillrate.

However, care must be taken when updating textures or reading pixels, considering to take advantage of unified memory or other types of hardware acceleration to reduce memory bandwidth.

1.4 O.S. Feature

The O.S. of many embedded boards are based on the Linux kernel and therefore provide all the means for parallel and concurrent programming. In the design of AR applications, it is essential to exploit multi-threading. Design the software using periodic threads is a key factor for two reasons:

1. Logical: each thread has its own modular, limited and well-defined function.
2. Performance: periodicity is an excellent parameter to regulate the performance and system reactivity.

AR applications can be considered soft-real system, since if the operations are not executed within a deadline performance degrades. Many O.S. provide a series of tools that allow greater control over periodic threads in execution: in the Linux kernel, for example, there are a series of real-time schedulers. The objective of these schedulers is to reduce latencies and have a deterministic response time.

1.5 Applications

At the time of writing we are witnessing the COVID-19 pandemic which has changed the way of working in many sectors: remote assistance (, i.e. the possibility to supervise complex machines/systems remotely) has become increasingly essential.

Virtual reality applications for cultural heritage (e.g. remote museum tours) have proved to be a new way of disseminating culture.

Unfortunately, such applications require expensive and complex devices (e.g., htc vive, oculust rift, etc.).

The techniques described in this paper fit well with the applications described above and target low-cost devices, which are certainly more accessible to everyone.

In addition, with the spread of cloud computing, these techniques are even more fundamental, they concern the edge computing part (i.e. those tasks that must necessarily be performed on the edge device): many AR-cloud applications are based on streaming video to servers that will process the video and returning it with AR info, it is essential to adopt any mechanism that reduces the latency in processing the video on the end device.

2 Related Work

2.1 AR on Embedded GPU

The potential of GPUs in embedded systems has been discussed in recent times; Embedded devices can be used in various areas: AR, computer vision, IoT, etc..

Lopez et al. [3] identified the main HW. and SW. components required by AR systems. The processing architectures investigated are two:

- *Edge Systems*: all operations are performed on the device.
- *Cloud Systems*: operations are delegated to a server.

With the progress of Cloud technologies the second approach is interesting [6]. Unfortunately there are limitations due to latencies and bandwidth required [7] that make the Quality of Experience (QoE) [8] not satisfactory, making these technologies still not completely mature.

Therefore, it makes sense to continue investigating approaches based on edge computing.

Elteir et al. [4] investigated the potential of embedded GPUs in IoT boards as enablers for computationally intensive applications.

Due to the technological differences between the various embedded GPUs, it is difficult to develop high-level platform-independent frameworks. Such frameworks, for example, must take into account whether the GPU is discrete (dGPU) or integrate (iGPU), as dGPU has its own private memory space for the system and data, introducing overhead for copying data between the CPU and GPU. In contrast, iGPUs share the same memory space with the CPU without the need to copy data.

Interesting is the work of Cameanu et al. [5] in developing a Component-based development (CBD) approach that is independent of the CPU-GPU used. The limitation of their approach is for computationally oriented applications since the framework they developed is based on OpenCL.

2.2 Real-Time Support

Real-time operating systems are widely used in the embedded world. Since AR systems can be considered as soft-real time systems, limitations and benefits of using real-time techniques/approaches are being evaluated. Interesting is the analysis carried out by Elliott and Anderson [1] that highlights the limitations and constraints imposed by current GPUs:

- *Isolation:* most of the drivers are closed-source, then system isolation must be provided to protect from unknown behaviors. Since even soft real-time systems require provable analysis, the uncertain behaviors of the driver force integration solutions to treat it as a black box.
- *Throughput oriented:* The GPU sw. and hw. are designed to be used by only one process at a time. Low latency of operations and the sharing of GPU among processes are only supported to a limited degree.
- *GPU Interrupt handling:* interrupts are difficult to manage in a real-time system. Interrupts may occur periodically, sporadically, or at entirely unpredictable moments, depending upon the application. Interrupts often cause disruptions in a real-time system since the CPU must temporarily halt the execution of the currently scheduled task. The GPU driver must be designed to minimize the interrupt duration.

The authors found that GPU resources in soft real-time systems can be managed through a real-time CPU scheduler.

The Linux kernel offers several real-time schedulers [10] and also a patch to make the kernel real-time [9], which mitigates the limitations written earlier (e.g., interrupts are handled with threads (thus scheduled)).

3   System Model

In order to make the presented methodology clearer, let's evaluate a use case: developing a wearable device with an AR application for remote assistance.

The wearable device is equipped with a camera and head-mounted display (HMD), the device streams the camera (i.e., the point of view of the field operator) to one or more remote people (the expert operator) who provide information/indications in AR rendered on the head mounted display (HMD).

The wearable system is composed of:

- embedded board small in size, low-power and equipped with a SoC combining CPU /GPU sharing memory and Wi-Fi module.
- camera.
- audio module (sound card which can be integrated into the embedded board or external).
- HMD.

The proposed technique starts by identifying which tasks can be performed in HW. and which in SW.

Starting from the application requirements and cross-referencing the datasheet, identifying functions/services that can be implemented taking full advantage of the hardware acceleration. In this case we need to:

1. Acquire frames from the camera.
2. Rendering on HMD the camera frames along with the AR info received.
3. Rendering in a framebuffer the camera frame with some processing/filtering.
4. Encoding/decoding the framebuffer into a video stream.

Point 1 is obtained by exploiting dedicated camera interface: many embedded boards are equipped with a special bus, like the MIPI-CSI-2, that allows the GPU to be connected "directly" to the camera (we will deal with this aspect in the next Section).

Points 2 and 3 obviously require GPUs capable of handling graphical contexts. The HMD is used to show the camera frames along with the AR information coming from the expert operator, this type of information could be simple indications/text or complex 3D figures. In any case reduce the memory bandwidth between CPU and GPU is primary: if the camera frame is used as a texture, it must be saved in the same memory portion that the GPU will looking for.

Regarding point 4, targeting applications that require encoding/decoding of video streams: it is worth checking whether there is a dedicated HW. in the GPU for its processing. Many commercial cards are equipped with HW. acceleration for h264/h265 video encoding. In order to program them, low-level standards (e.g., OpenMax) up to higher-level frameworks (e.g., libav/openh264) can be used, allowing to create/manage/integrate video codecs inside applications with different abstraction levels.

In the proposed model the best solution is always to use low level standards, like OpenMax: they guarantee full control over configurable parameters, less overhead and moreover there is no risk of using SW. solutions without the developer *"awareness"*: this occurs very frequently in high level frameworks when an implementation is not available for a specfic HW., there is a fallback to SW. approaches which in embedded systems risk saturating the CPU.

4 Proposed Approach

4.1 Graphics Standard

The structure of the various standards for programming the GPU is often not clear: it is important to know the relationship between them and their interoperability.

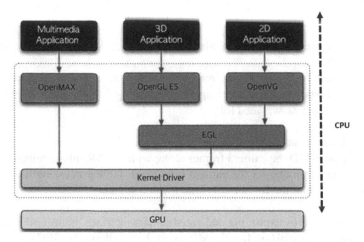

Fig. 1. GPU standards structure

The standards considered are:

- OpenMax: OpenMax is a unified abstraction layer that allows access to hardware that otherwise requires vendor specific APIs. OpenMax therefore allows a (sort of) portable implementation of software that utilizes such hardware. OpenMax provides an abstraction over hardware that is capable to perform operations with multi media (audio, images and video). Hardware can only be in one state at a time so it resembles a state machine. OpenMax maps to that state machine and provides an API to manipulate it.
- OpenGL ES: OpenGL ES is a cross-platform API for full-function 2D and 3D graphics on embedded systems, including consoles, phones, appliances, and vehicles. It consists of well-defined subsets of desktop OpenGL, creating a flexible and powerful low-level interface between software and graphic acceleration. OpenGL ES includes profiles for floating-point and fixed-point systems and the EGL specification for portably binding to native windowing systems. What distinguishes OpenGL ES from OpenGL is its emphasis on low-capability embedded systems. OpenGL ES is a simplified and tidied-up form of OpenGL but still has the same capabilities as OpenGL. The emphasis with this API is on 2D and 3D graphics, suitable for games programming and other high-demand graphics applications. It will work in cooperation with other windowing systems, such as the X Window System or Wayland, or where no other windowing system is running.

- OpenVG: OpenVG is a cross-platform API that provides a low-level hardware acceleration interface for vector graphics libraries such as Flash and SVG. OpenVG is targeted primarily at handheld devices that require portable acceleration of high-quality vector graphics for compelling user interfaces and text on small-screen devices, while enabling hardware acceleration to provide fluidly interactive performance at very low power levels. OpenVG is an alternative approach to graphics to OpenGL. While OpenGL renders onto textures, OpenVG is more concerned with drawing lines to form shapes and then rendering within those shapes.

- EGL: EGL is an interface between Khronos-rendering APIs such as OpenGL ES or OpenVG and the underlying native platform window system. It handles graphics context management, surface/buffer binding, and rendering synchronization and enables high-performance, accelerated, mixed-mode 2D and 3D rendering using other Khronos APIs. EGL is the "glue" layer between the higher-level APIs and the hardware. It isn't used extensively by the application programmer, just enough to give the higher level the hooks into the lower level. Both OpenGL ES and OpenVG sit above EGL.

Many manufacturers develop specific features for their hardware, which are accessible via so-called standards extensions:

- OpenGL extension: the OpenGL standard allows individual vendors to provide additional functionality through extensions as new technology is created. Extensions may introduce new functions and new constants, may relax or remove restrictions on existing OpenGL functions. Proprietary pixel format can be defined: how pixels are mapped in texture memory, many chip vendors create their own internal conventions, opaque to the programmer, that allow proprietary technologies to be used to the advantage of performance and power consumption.

- OpenMax tunneling: it is possible to exchange information between multimedia components (e.g., by directly passing camera frames to a video encoder) without involving the CPU.

- EGL extension: it is possible, to use a camera frame or decoded video frame directly as a texture. The solutions adopted by chip vendors use proprietary technologies (e.g., proprietary pixel format or special memory mapping exploiting unified memory architecture) that are available to the programmer as extensions to EGL. One of the most useful is the *EGL image*: this extension defines a new EGL resource type that is suitable for sharing 2D arrays of image data between client APIs., Although the intended purpose is sharing 2D image data, the underlying interface makes no assumptions about the format or purpose of the resource being shared, leaving those decisions to the application and associated client APIs.

4.2 Multithreading

Many embedded O.S. have support for multithreading, which is a powerful tool for structuring application tasks in a modular and logical way. In graphic/multimedia applications, the use of periodic threads is a versatile design choice: performance can be adjusted to dynamically scale according to the quality required or the CPU load.

The structure of periodic thread is similar the following:

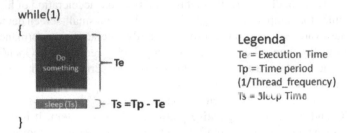

Fig. 2. Periodic thread structure

Threads along with the possibility of interconnecting them using the technologies/standards described in the previous paragraphs can be modeled as a series of high-level blocks that provide versatility in building applications on embedded devices (Fig. 3).

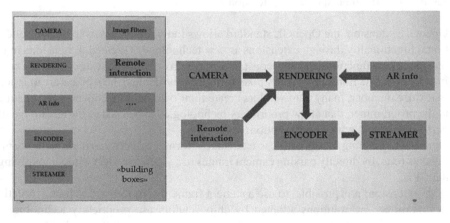

Fig. 3. The tasks implemented as threads can be modeled as high-level box.

4.3 Scheduling

Since AR systems can be considered soft real-time system (i.e., if the deadline is missed there is a performance degradation), it makes sense to investigate the real time schedulers made available by a multitude of O.S.

These allow greater control over the threads that are running.

Real-time systems require that tasks execution must follow a severe priority order. This requires that only the K highest-priority tasks be running at any given instant in time, where K is the number of CPUs. A variation to this requirement could be strict priority-ordered scheduling in a given subset of CPUs or scheduling domains. In both cases, when a task is runnable, the scheduler must ensure that it be put on a run-queue on which it can be run immediately—that is, the real-time scheduler has to ensure system-wide strict real-time priority scheduling. Unlike non-real-time systems where the scheduler needs to look only at its run-queue of tasks to make scheduling decisions, a real-time scheduler makes global scheduling decisions, considering all the tasks in the system at any given point. A real-time task scheduler would trade off throughput in favor of correctness, but at the same time, it must ensure minimal task ping-ponging.

Linux kernel offers the following schedulers type:

- SCHED_OTHER: each process is assigned a maximum time slice and a dynamic priority given by the sum of a base value and a value that decreases as the CPU time used increases. Dynamic priority update: when all the time of the ready processes is exhausted, the priorities of all processes are recalculated. It aims to ensure a fair distribution of CPU between all processes, and to provide good response times for interactive processes.
- REAL_TIME SCHEDULERS:

  - SCHED_FIFO: it implements a first-in, first-out scheduling algorithm. When a SCHED_FIFO task starts running, it continues to run until it voluntarily yields the processor, blocks or is preempted by a higher-priority real-time task. All other tasks of lower priority will not be scheduled until it leaves the CPU. Two equal-priority SCHED_FIFO tasks do not preempt each other.
  - SCHED_RR: is similar to SCHED_FIFO, except that such tasks are allocated time slices based on their priority and run until they finish their time slice. The default linux time slice is 100 ms.

Real-time schedulers allow to prioritize threads, thus having greater determinism.

Not all tasks are equal: there are some that are more important than others, so it is fair to give them higher priority. In a typical AR application, it may be preferable to prioritize the camera frame capture thread over the video-rendering thread. This can be useful in CPU overloading situations: sometimes a real-time application running on the target computer does not have enough time to complete processing before the next time step, an overload happens every time an execution step is triggered while the previous one is running. On low-power single-core device, this phenomenon can occur for a variety of reasons, whether related to the design of the applications themselves (optimistic system design, based on average rather than worst-case behavior) or to the kernel (interrupt bursts, kernel exceptions, etc.). Faced with this situation, establishing an order of what to maintain with stable performance and what to degrade is essential.

5 Experimental Results

The test setup of the techniques shown is a wearable system for remote assistance.

The application use case is show in Fig. 4.

The wearable device is equipped with a camera and viewers, this device streams what the operator in the field (called the field operator) sees to one or more remote

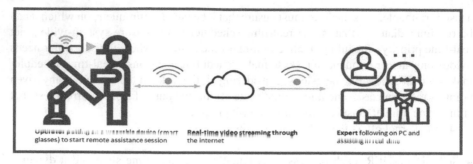

Operator putting on a wearable device (smart glasses) to start remote assistance session   Real-time video streaming through the internet   Expert following on PC and assisting in real time

Fig. 4. Remote assistance application example

persons (the expert operator) who provide information/indications in AR rendered on the viewers together with the video of the camera itself.

5.1 Hw. Architecture

The system is composed by:

- Embedded board: custom low power board is used, it features a Broadcom BCM2835 system on a chip, which includes a 700 MHz ARM1176JZF-S processor, VideoCore IV Graphics Processing Unit (GPU), and 1Gb of shared memory. It has 16 KB Level 1 cache and 128 KB Level 2 cache, that is used primarily by the GPU.
- Camera: the camera chosen uses 5MP Omnivision 5647 sensor, capable of 1080@30 fps, 720@60fps, 480p@90fps. The communication interface is based on a 15-pin MIPI Camera Serial Interface that directly communicates to the GPU.
- HMD: 1080p@60fps HMD is used.
- Audio: audio card featuring microphone and headphones
- Connectivity: 2.4 Ghz interface
- O.S.: Linux 4.9
- Battery

5.2 Sw. Architecture

The application has the following pipeline:
Regarding the application design, the following scheme is used:

- Camera and Video Splitter (OpenMax domain): connected through the tunnelling mechanism. The video splitter takes the camera signal as input and forwards it to two output ports as *egl image.*
- Video rendering (OpenGL domain): the camera frames along with AR info are rendered, the *egl image* is used directly as texture.
- Framebuffer rendering (OpenGL domain): this rendering stage is used to prepare the frame to transmit, effects and filters are applied to the frame (e.g., increase contrast, use edge detector shaders, etc.). Again, the *egl image* is used directly as a texture.

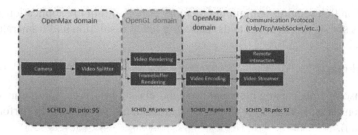

Fig. 5. Software pipeline

- Video encoding (OpenMax domain): the encoder takes the entire framebuffer object (as an *egl image*) as input and outputs an encoded video stream (e.g., h264/h265).
- Video streamer and the remote interaction: rely on classic communication protocols (e.g. udp/tcp/websocket, etc…).

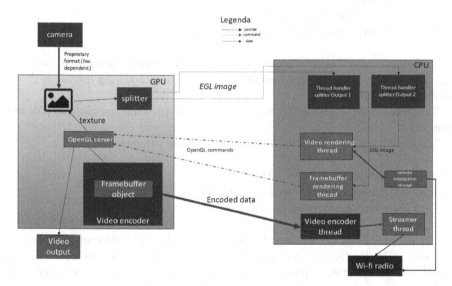

Fig. 6. CPU-GPU interaction

From an operational point of view, the CPU and GPU exchange the following information (Fig. 6):

4. GPU-> CPU: The *egl image* containing the camera frame. From developer's point of view is a simple pointer indicating the GPU memory area containing the camera frame.
5. CPU-> GPU: OpenGL commands are sent to the server that resides on the GPU.
6. GPU-> CPU: what is rendered in the framebuffer is encoded as a streaming video. The video encoder generates video packets transferred to the CPU. This is the only

operation that requires a minimum memory bandwidth in the application, the video packets size is proportional to the encoding level, resolution and framerate.

5.3 Benchmark

A comparison is made using both real-time and classic priorities, simulating overloading situations (i.e., load average above 1 by introducing threads which performs some computation)

Real-time priorities have been given to prevent blocking of camera frame acquisition and any form of deadlock in the block diagram pipeline (Fig, 5): output splitter threads that handle *egl image* must have the highest priority, we must assure their execution as soon as possible to render the newest frame.

The real-time scheduler used is SCHED_RR (with default time slice 100 ms), priority ranges from 1(low) to 99(high) is given according to the following scheme:

1. Splitter output threads: priority 95.
2. Rendering threads: priority 94.
3. Video encoder thread: priority 93.
4. Remote interaction & Video streamer: priority 92.

The threads period is given by the working frequency of the associated component (e.g., if the video rendering is at 60 fps, then the video rendering thread on CPU is running at 60 Hz).

The tests are performed setting high resolution and fps value, pushing the HW. to its limit.

The experiment number 1 (Table 1) has the flowing parameters:

- Camera: 1280x960 with target 30 fps.
- Video-Rendering: 1280x960 with target 60 fps.
- Video-Encoding: 1280x960 with target 30 fps.

The measured/real fps are lower because are near the GPU and camera limits.

Using SCHED_RR there is an increment on measured average fps, confirming the goodness of the proposed approach. The major benefit is notable under overloading conditions, since given the strict priority order the scheduling algorithm tries to reach the target fps.

Same considerations are valid for experiment 2 and 3.

Figure 7, 8 and 9 show for each component and experiment the measured FPS. SCHED_RR in overloading conditions has a huge improvement compared to overloading in SCHED_OTHER.

Table 1. Experiment 1: camera 1280x960@30fps, video rendering 1280x960@60fps, encoding 1280x960@30fps

Simulate overloading	Camera resolution	Camera fps (target/measured)	Rendering resolution	Rendering fps	Encoding resolution	Encoding fps	Scheduling
no	1280 × 960	30/23	1280 × 960	60/20	1280 × 960	30/13	SCHED_OTHER
no	1280 × 960	30/25	1280 × 960	60/25	1280 × 960	30/13	SCHED_RR
yes	1280 × 960	30/15	1280 × 960	60/12	1280 × 960	30/10	SCHED_OTHER
yes	1280 × 960	30/21	1280 × 960	60/21	1280 × 960	30/10	SCHED_RR

Table 2. Experiment 2: camera 640x480@60fps, video rendering 1280x960@60fps, encoding 640x480@30fps

Simulate overloading	Camera resolution	Camera fps (target/measured)	Rendering resolution	Rendering fps	Encoding resolution	Encoding fps	Scheduling
No	640 × 480	**60/47**	1280 × 960	**60/41**	640 × 480	**30/22**	SCHED_OTHER
No	640 × 480	**60/48**	1280 × 960	**60/42**	640 × 480	**30/22**	SCHED_RR
yes	640 × 480	**60/21**	1280 × 960	**60/15**	640 × 480	**30/10**	SCHED_OTHER
yes	640 × 480	**60/45**	1280 × 960	**60/40**	640 × 480	**30/21**	SCHED_RR

Table 3. Experiment 3: camera 1920x1080@30fps, video rendering 1920x1080@60fps, encoding 1280x720@30fps

Simulate overloading	Camera resolution	Camera fps (target/measured)	Rendering resolution	Rendering fps	Encoding resolution	Encoding fps	Scheduling
No	1920 × 1080	**30/15**	1920 × 1080	**60/15**	1280 × 720	**30/9**	SCHED_OTHER
No	1920 × 1080	**30/15**	1920 × 1080	**60/15**	1280 × 720	**30/12**	SCHED_RR
yes	1920 × 1080	**30/13**	1920 × 1080	**60/10**	1280 × 720	**30/8**	SCHED_OTHER
yes	1920 × 1080	**30/15**	× 1080	**60/15**	1280 × 720	**30/10**	SCHED_RR

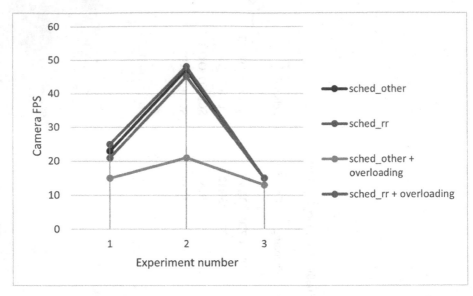

Fig. 7. Camera FPS variation considering experiment number and scheduling policy.

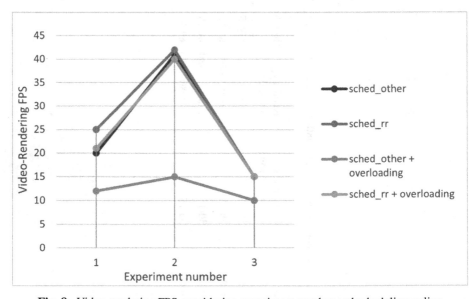

Fig. 8. Video-rendering FPS considering experiment number and scheduling policy.

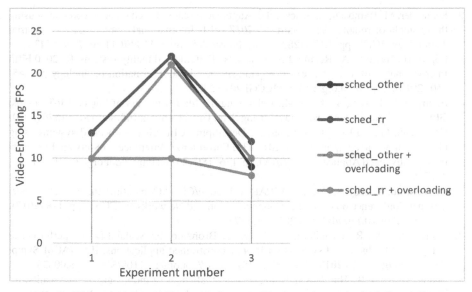

Fig. 9. Video-encoding FPS considering experiment number and scheduling policy.

6   Conclusions

The techniques shown provide generic guidelines on how to program embedded boards for augmented reality applications. It is shown how to take advantage of the unified memory and hardware acceleration available.

Structuring the application using periodic threads is a key-point, it allows to associate to each thread a specific and limited task, the periodicity is a good switch to adjust the performance.

Finally, it has been shown how the use of real-time scheduling policies allows a greater determinism of the application behavior, providing greater control in overloading situations.

As a use case an AR telemetry application for a low-power wearable system has been developed, validating the described approaches.

In the future it is interesting to evaluate the described approaches, especially related to the part of scheduling, on a full real-time O.S. as Linux PREEMPT-RT, which guarantee:

- Interrupts are handled with threads (thus scheduled).
- Spin locks replaced with mutexes.
- Priority inheritance is extended to the kernel.

References

1. Elliott, G.A., Anderson, J.H.: Real-world constraints of GPUs in real-time Systems. In: 2011 IEEE 17th International Conference on Embedded and Real-Time Computing Systems and Applications, pp. 48–54 (2011). https://doi.org/10.1109/RTCSA.2011.46

2. Schneider, M. Rambach, J., Stricker, D.: Augmented reality based on edge computing using the example of remote live support. In: *2017* IEEE International Conference on Industrial Technology (ICIT), pp. 1277-1282 (2017). https://doi.org/10.1109/ICIT.2017.7915547

3. López, H., Navarro, A., Relaño, J.: An analysis of augmented reality systems. In: 2010 Fifth International Multi-conference on Computing in the Global Information Technology, pp. 245-250 (2010). https://doi.org/10.1109/ICCGI.2010.24.

4. Elteir, M.K., Lazem, S., Azab, M.: Unleashing the hidden powers of low-cost IoT boards: GPU-based edutainment case study. J. King Saud Univ. Comput. Inf. Sci. 1319–1578 (2020)

5. Campeanu, G., Carlson, J., Sontilles, S.: Developing CPU-GPU embedded systems using platform-agnostic components. In: 2017 43rd Euromicro Conference on Software Engineering and Advanced Applications (SEAA), pp. 176–180 (2017). https://doi.org/10.1109/SEAA. 2017.20.

6. Hou, X., Lu, Y., Dey, S.:Wireless VR/AR with Edge/Cloud Computing. In: 2017 26th International Conference on Computer Communication and Networks (ICCCN) , pp. 1–8 (2017). https://doi.org/10.1109/ICCCN.2017.8038375

7. Maheshwari, S., Raychaudhuri, D., Seskar, I., Bronzino, F.: Scalability and performance evaluation of edge cloud systems for latency constrained applications. IEEE/ACM Symp. Edge Comput. (SEC) **2018**, 286–299 (2018). https://doi.org/10.1109/SEC.2018.00028

8. Zhang, W., Han, B., Hui, P.: On the networking challenges of mobile augmented reality. In: Proceedings of the Workshop on Virtual Reality and Augmented Reality Network (VR/AR Network 2017), pp. 24–29. Association for Computing Machinery, New York (2017).https:// doi.org/10.1145/3097895.3097900

9. Reghenzani, F., Massari, G., Fornaciari, W.: The real-time linux kernel: a survey on PREEMPT_RT. ACM Comput. Surv. **52**(1), 1–36 (2019). https://doi.org/10.1145/3297714

10. Scordino, C., Lipari, G.: Linux and real-time: current approaches and future opportunities (2006)

11. https://www.mipi.org/specifications/csi-2

Mixed Reality

Visualizing Building Energy Measurement Data in Mixed Reality Applying B.I.M.

Dietmar Siegele$^{(\boxtimes)}$ [iD], Paola Penna, and Michael Riedl

Fraunhofer Italia, Via A. Volta 13 A, 39100 Bolzano, Italy
`dietmar.siegele@fraunhofer.it`

Abstract. In modern Building Energy Management Systems (BEMS) visualizing measurement data is still a challenge. Intuitive approaches are rare, and the big data collected by more and more sensors in the Internet of Things (IoT) demands new concepts. We present in this paper an OpenXR application in a dollhouse style for off-site application. Further it allows to visualize on-site the data of specific sensors by scanning a QR-code. We use time-series based databases to enable fast queries and therefore a seamless integration within the application. Time-series based interactive diagrams integrated into geometrical holograms of buildings or parts of buildings (like floors), allows intuitive working also in multi-user scenarios by applying cloud anchors. The geometrical models are retrieved by applying BIM.

Keywords: Building energy management · Measurement data visualization · Building Information Modelling

1 Introduction

In modern Building Energy Management Systems (BEMS) visualizing measurement data is a main challenge [9]. Caused by the Internet of Things (IoT) initiatives the amount of collected data is increasing heavily. However, at the same time it is getting more and more difficult to interpret all that data and in particular to visualize them before interpretation can take place. Thus, combining geometrical data and measurement data into one interface is a main research topic in the area of BEMS. Mixed Reality (MR) can be a great part of that solution. We propose in this paper the concept of visualizing measurement data in a geometrical context, which is imported from Building Information Modelling (BIM). The novelty is to combine a dollhouse concept (third-person observer) with a real-world concept. This concept allows a very intuitive exploration of data and in a multi-user interface several users (at the same place or distributed) can explore data together on-site or off-site.

2 State of the Art

Mixed Reality (MR) was already applied in different areas of building construction. Most of the time the classical approach for visualization is used: Information is overlaid on real world geometry, like in [10] or [11]. However, when

© Springer Nature Switzerland AG 2021
L. T. De Paolis et al. (Eds.): AVR 2021, LNCS 12980, pp. 247–253, 2021.
https://doi.org/10.1007/978-3-030-87595-4_18

targeting to visualize time-series based data, as they occur in BEMS, these concepts are usually only slightly adapted. Such a concept was presented by [5], that used a time-series graph like on a screen. However, this does not allow to interact with the data. Moreover, in a multi-user scenarios this approach is non-intuitive, because it does not allow to customize the visualization of the data in the same view. Another concept was proposed by [1]. They overlaid shading areas or lines on the geometry (floors, walls) to visualize on-site in a room certain conditions. IoT-approaches of today focus on single-point measurement. Multi-point measurement (like thermal imaging) are rarely used and only these kind of measurements benefit from such an approach. This is likely also the reason, why [1] only presented a concept without results of a real use case. It is also very difficult from a technical point of view to reach the necessary accuracy of indoor positioning to achieve this with AR devices [7,12]. Other approaches, related to different possibilities of visualizing energy efficiency concepts by means of virtual reality, were proposed by [4]. They used interactive charts to visualize time-series based data. However, it was only presented in VR and the representation of the building structure was rudimentary. Applications for MR-devices (like HoloLens), are rare. An application for studying the improvement of HVAC systems in learning factories was proposed by [2]. However, no time-series data was visualized in that context. Third-person perspective on-site were presented by [6]. They used this concept to visualize data of a thermal imaging camera that measures the temperature of a façade (and thus the energy efficiency). However, this concept was not based on MR, but on AR by using a tablet. For connecting measurement data with BIM models, several approaches are available. In the literature they are mainly defined as Digital Twins, even if usually not full features of a Digital Twin are proposed. The process for integrating indoor comfort data collected by a monitoring system by applying a BIM-based model was described by [8].

This work proposes a digital multi-users interface realized by means of MR for visualizing measurement data in a geometrical context, realized through BIM. The approach shows a concept of exploring and analyzing monitoring data in a intuitive way and at the same time giving the possibility to several users to visualize off-site and on-site the data.

3   Methodology

Figure 1 shows the software architecture of our application. Data acquisition is carried out (applying LoRaWAN technology) and the data is saved in a time-series database (InfluxDB[1]). Unity is used to develop the XR application. We use the REST interface provided by InfluxDB to query the data from the database. For visualizing the timeseries data in Unity we use the Asset *Graph and Chart*[2].

We get the models for different environments from BIM models (here Autodesk Revit was used) by using FBX file format. Using another file format

---

[1] https://www.influxdata.com/.

[2] https://assetstore.unity.com/packages/tools/gui/graph-and-chart-78488.

than IFC[3] has in particular some advantages in keeping textures and details. Using different formats than the standardized IFC is at the moment state-of-the-art (like by Autodesk, compare the software tool Forge[4]). In the BIM model the unique identifiers (ID) of the sensors are stored as metadata. This allows us to get the specific data out of the database and to assign it to the corresponding geometry.

To catch specific data of a sensor in an on-site environment, QR-codes are used. The *OpenCV for Unity*[5] asset is used to realize this feature.

The application itself can run stand-online on a XR-device, like the HoloLens 2. However, for a better graphics (shading) and better performance we apply XR streaming. Multiple devices can be operated at the same time, while using the concept of cloud anchors to share the actual position of the dollhouse model.

The XR application is based on the Microsoft Mixed Reality Toolkit (MRTK 2.7) and is designed as an XR application and can therefore also be used on other XR-compatible devices.

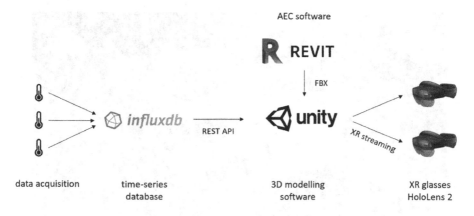

Fig. 1. Software architecture.

The XR application has several features:

- Dollhouse view of BIM-imported model with display of real-time data and time-series based interactive diagram as part of the hologram. In the model values like temperature are shown as numbers, occupancy can be displayed with avatars.
- Scanning of QR codes in an on-site environment for reading data of a specific sensor (real-time and time-series based diagram).
- Multi-user session for the dollhouse view.

---

[3] https://www.buildingsmart.org/.
[4] https://forge.autodesk.com/.
[5] https://assetstore.unity.com/packages/tools/integration/opencv-for-unity-21088.

4   Results and Discussion

In Fig. 2 a screenshot of the XR application is shown. We run the application on a Microsoft HoloLens 2. This is the dollhouse mode a flat within a building is visualized. In each room indoor air quality (IAQ) sensors are installed, which real-time values can be visualized as tooltips based on the MRTK. The tooltips change their orientation and size according to the position of the viewer and allow an intuitive and clear view of the data. Occupancy can be visualized with avatars in the corresponding rooms. Not only IAQ data can be visualized, but any kind of data measured in the according rooms. At the moment our concept concentrate all data measured from different sensors in one room to a single tooltip. A set of buttons allows the control of the model and the dollhouses are freely scalable and rotatable through the vertical axis. In the future also a concept of zones will be added to visualize bigger models without dedicated rooms, i.e. shopping centers.

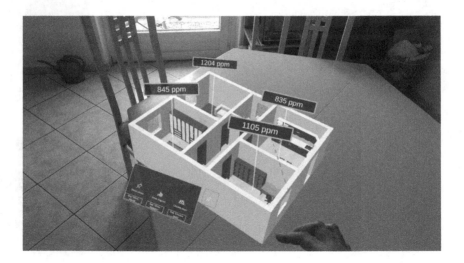

Fig. 2. Dollhouse view with real-time values.

In Fig. 3 we show a screenshot of the XR application with a time-series based diagram. It can be interactively controlled by using finger gestures. Sliding back-and forwards in time is enabled by this feature. A further development of the work will be to add features to these diagrams, such as shading colors, for intuitively visualizing information such as comfort measurements or safety areas. E.g., the CO_2 output can be assisted by using traffic light colors to quickly identify critical rooms or zones and time ranges.

When being on-site, the feature of Fig. 4 can be used. Scanning a QR-code assigned with the ID of the sensors allows to appear an additional hologram with the time-series based interactive diagram. In addition (here not visible) in the

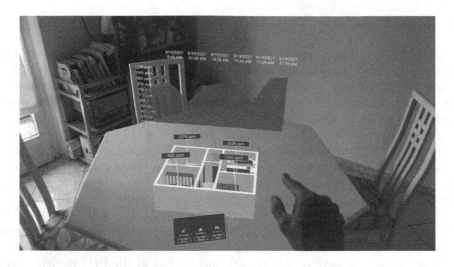

Fig. 3. Dollhouse view with time-series based diagrams.

geometrical model the position of the sensor is highlighted as a tooltip. On-site orientation for the user is significantly improved by using this feature. To allow free movements on-site, the hologram shown in Fig. 2 can also be detached and follows the user automatically. In addition an arrow shows always the position of the dollhouse, if it is not in the field-of-view of the user.

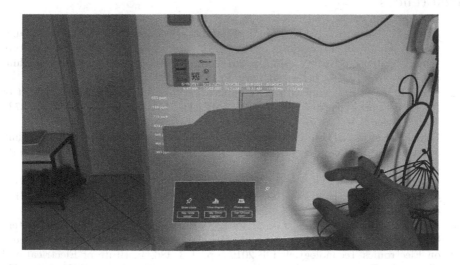

Fig. 4. Time-series based diagram assigned to a sensor.

5   Conclusion and Outlook

In this paper we presented a concept of an XR application for visualizing data in building energy management systems. Using time-series based interactive diagrams integrated into a geometrical hologram of a zone can help to improve the usability of such applications. Using time-series based databases allows fast querying if data and thus a seamless integration into the overall experience.

In the further development we want to get rid of the QR-codes on the sensors. We want to implement a BIM-based navigation algorithm for pre-positioning in combination with cloud anchors (based on landscapes) for an accurate positioning within a room (compare the same approach we use for a robotic applications [3]). This will allow an even better immersion and usability. In addition to the time-series based diagrams we will add additional diagram types. We want to add additional features for visualization, like a better visibility of sensors with sprites and surface shading for multi-point data or simulation data. On a long term we want to achieve a close to real-time import of the BIM model, where we target a server-based solution as an own application (automatic conversion from Revit-files or IFC to FBX or similar).

Acknowledgements. The research leading to these results has received funding from the European Regional Development Fund (Fondo Europeo di Sviluppo Regionale FESR Alto Adige 2014–2020) under the Grant Agreement n. FESR1141 CUP B54E20002030001.

References

1. Aftab, M., Chau, S.C.K., Khonji, M.: Enabling self-aware smart buildings by augmented reality. In: Proceedings of the Ninth International Conference on Future Energy Systems, e-Energy 2018, pp. 261–265. Association for Computing Machinery, New York (2018). https://doi.org/10.1145/3208903.3208943
2. Czarski, M., et al.: A mixed reality application for studying the improvement of HVAC systems in learning factories. In: Procedia Manufacturing, vol. 45, pp. 373–378. Elsevier B.V. (2020). https://doi.org/10.1016/j.promfg.2020.04.039
3. Follini, C., et al.: BIM-integrated collaborative robotics for application in building construction and maintenance. Robotics **10**(1), 1–19 (2021). https://doi.org/10.3390/robotics10010002
4. Häfner, P., Seeßle, J., Dücker, J., Zienthek, M., Szeliga, F.: Interactive visualization of energy efficiency concepts using virtual Reality (2014). https://doi.org/10.2312/eurovr.20141346
5. Jang, H., Choi, M.I., Lee, S., Lee, J., Park, S.: Building energy management system based on mixed reality for intuitive interface. In: 2019 2nd International Conference on Electronics Technology, ICET 2019, pp. 483–486. Institute of Electrical and Electronics Engineers Inc. (2019). https://doi.org/10.1109/ELTECH.2019.8839595
6. Liu, F., Jonsson, T., Seipel, S.: Evaluation of augmented reality-based building diagnostics using third person perspective. ISPRS Int. J. Geo-Inf. **9**(1) (2020). https://doi.org/10.3390/ijgi9010053

7. Minneci, G., Schweigkofler, A., Marcher, C., Monizza, G.P., Tillo, T., Matt, D.T.: Computer vision approach for indoor location recognition within an augmented reality mobile application. In: Luo, Y. (ed.) CDVE 2019. LNCS, vol. 11792, pp. 45–53. Springer, Cham (2019). https://doi.org/10.1007/978-3-030-30949-7_6

8. Penna, P., Regis, G.L., Schweigkofler, A., Marcher, C., Matt, D.: From sensors to BIM: monitoring comfort conditions of social housing with the klimakit model. In: Luo, Y. (ed.) CDVE 2019. LNCS, vol. 11792, pp. 108–115. Springer, Cham (2019). https://doi.org/10.1007/978-3-030-30949-7_12

9. Ramelan, A., Adriyanto, F., Hermanu, B., Ibrahim, M.H., Saputro, J.S., Setiawan, O.: IoT based building energy monitoring and controlling system using LoRa modulation and MQTT protocol. IOP Conf. Ser. Mater. Sci. Eng. **1096**(1), 012069 (2021). https://doi.org/10.1088/1757-899x/1096/1/012069

10. Riexinger, G., Kluth, A., Olbrich, M., Braun, J.D., Bauernhansl, T.: Mixed Reality for on-site self-instruction and self-inspection with building information models. In: Procedia CIRP, vol. 72, pp. 1124–1129. Elsevier B.V. (2018). https://doi.org/10.1016/j.procir.2018.03.160

11. Schweigkofler, A., et al.: Development of a digital platform based on the integration of augmented reality and BIM for the management of information in construction processes. In: Chiabert, P., Bouras, A., Noël, F., Ríos, J. (eds.) PLM 2018. IAICT, vol. 540, pp. 46–55. Springer, Cham (2018). https://doi.org/10.1007/978-3-030-01614-2_5

12. Siegele, D., Di Staso, U., Piovano, M., Marcher, C., Matt, D.T.: State of the art of non-vision-based localization technologies for AR in facility management. In: De Paolis, L.T., Bourdot, P. (eds.) AVR 2020. LNCS, vol. 12242, pp. 255–272. Springer, Cham (2020). https://doi.org/10.1007/978-3-030-58465-8_20

VIAProMa: An Agile Project Management Framework for Mixed Reality

Benedikt Hensen[(⊠)] and Ralf Klamma

Advanced Community Information Systems Group (ACIS) Chair of Computer Science 5, RWTH Aachen University, Aachen, Germany
{hensen,klamma}@dbis.rwth-aachen.de

Abstract. With the COVID-19 pandemic, distributed and remote working became a necessity but in agile project management, social interactions like daily standup meetings in Scrum are vital for the project success. Mixed reality can provide a new way of combining remote collaboration with innovative 3D visualizations to analyze the project status. In this paper, we present a visual immersive analytics framework for project management (VIAProMa). It imports data from project management tools like the GitHub issue tracker for open-source projects. With these task data as the basis, it can generate three-dimensional visualizations, e.g. about the overall progress or the competences of individual developers. Developers, stakeholders and end users can meet in the collaborative virtual environment as avatars and establish a spatial structure with the task cards and visualizations. Therefore, VIAProMa with its adapted and customized mixed reality project management features supports both the shared meetings and the information flow in the project. The shared environment makes it a suitable tool for DevOpsUseXR, an extension to the DevOps workflow, where end users are able to participate in the development process in mixed reality. The resulting implementation is available as an open-source project with cross-platform capabilities targeting the Microsoft HoloLens, HTC VIVE and Android smartphones, as well as tablets. The framework is applied in university teaching classes to convey agile methodology in mixed reality programming practices.

Keywords: Mixed reality · Project management · Agile methodology

1 Introduction

Agile project management practices like Scrum are commonly used for software development but also non-software projects, e.g. in industry [8]. An important factor for the success of an agile project is social interaction [4]. Even for open-source projects where contributors remain largely anonymous and do not know each other personally, establishing a community is important for the success

© Springer Nature Switzerland AG 2021
L. T. De Paolis et al. (Eds.): AVR 2021, LNCS 12980, pp. 254–272, 2021.
https://doi.org/10.1007/978-3-030-87595-4_19

of the project [4]. Due to the meeting restrictions of the COVID-19 pandemic, these remote settings are not only relevant for the open-source community but for every team. To support the community-building process in such remote settings, a persistent room is required where developers can meet virtually. Within such a virtual room, users should not only be able to steer and control the project milestones and tasks but they should also be able to monitor the progress, as well as the community using immersive analytics [9].

An intuitive solution for such a virtual meeting room is mixed reality. If it is not possible to meet in a real room because of pandemic constrictions but also resource limitations, the virtual room should be as immersive as possible. Here, remote collaborators can be represented by customizable avatars. This enhances the social presence and embodiment by mimicking real world meeting experiences in mixed reality [14]. They can interact with each other and the same content without technological borders [2]. For instance, a discussion can take place in a meeting and participants can generate visualizations in the same environment on the fly in order to strengthen their argumentation. Moreover, mixed reality provides a third dimension which can be utilized by the visualizations to improve the understanding of the viewed data. Another important aspect of successful software projects is the involvement of end users [19] or even the co-design of the application with them [11]. The mixed reality environment provides an ideal platform for this as the end users can join the same developer meetings in order to contribute their opinions and feedback.

Our goal is to investigate whether mixed reality is suitable to support and enhance project management workflows. Furthermore, we aim to identify the challenges and design solutions that are necessary to realize a mixed reality project management framework. In this paper, we present our approach to combine immersive visual analytics with project management. To evaluate the merging of these two concepts, we implemented a visual immersive analytics framework for project management (VIAProMa). This collaborative mixed reality platform allows developers, stakeholders and users to collaborate and administer open-source projects. With the subsequent evaluation of the software artifact, this paper contributes to the understanding of the DevOpsUseXR model [12].

The remainder of the paper is structured as follows. In Sect. 2, we present related approaches in the research. Section 3 describes the data visualizations that we envisioned and realized to support the project management process. After that, Sect. 5 describes further features and steps in the realization of VIAProMa like the collaborative environment. In Sect. 6, we present how we conducted the technical and user evaluations with its results. Section 7 contains a discussion how the realized framework can support project management workflows and which challenges remain for the future. The paper closes with a conclusion and outlook on future work on VIAProMa in Sect. 8.

2 Related Work

The research project lies at the intersection of the fields of mixed reality, immersive analytics and project management. In its original definition, mixed reality describes a spectrum between the real world and a completely computer generated environment [13]. Between these two extreme points, two intermediate forms can be distinguished. Augmented reality (AR) describes a mixture where one can predominately see the real world but there are some virtual elements integrated into the view. Augmented virtuality (AV) is the opposite of this as the user perceives a virtual environment into which elements of the real world are integrated. Since this definition, the term mixed reality has also been applied in slightly different contexts [18]. For instance, mixed reality can also be seen as a form of advanced augmented reality. Whereas AR is only able to overlay virtual content over the real world, mixed reality applications have an understanding of the real 3D space [18]. Therefore, they can integrate 3D objects seamlessly into the real world, e.g. by placing a virtual cup on a real table.

In the field of DevOps, different extensions to the original concept have been formulated. DevOps aims at closing the gap between developers and system maintainers and their conflicting interests [1]. Developers advance the software and would like to deploy updates with new features and bug fixes frequently to clients. In contrast to this, system maintainers try to avoid downtime of the system. Hence, once the software infrastructure is functioning, they aim at altering it as seldom as possible. To resolve this conflict, DevOps introduces a seamless interaction cycle between developers and system maintainers. It contains the phases of development, testing, deployment, monitoring and feedback. Automated pipelines like continuous integration and continuous deployment can support the DevOps cycle. They automatically test the code base and compile the code regularly, thereby catching potential errors in the code early on.

With DevOpsUse, as an extension to DevOps, the participation of the end user in the process was suggested [10]. In each phase, the end user can also interact with developers and maintainers. For instance, during development, a co-design process can happen. The end users can test prototypes and they can give feedback in-between cycles by stating new ideas and requirements. A possible Web tool for social requirements engineering is the Requirements Baazar [16]. Here, communities consisting of developers, stakeholders and end users can gather to formulate, discuss and vote on requirements of projects.

DevOpsUseXR is another expansion of this concept where all these activities can happen in a collaborative mixed reality environment [12]. End users, developers and maintainers can meet in mixed reality to collect ideas and discuss requirements. Users can directly provide feedback about their experience in the mixed reality environment without switching the device. Hence, DevOpsUseXR reduces technological barriers that are imposed on workflows where users would e.g. have to switch between desktop PCs and head-mounted displays.

In our implementation we also make use of gamification. In this concept, game elements are integrated into non-game scenarios to increase the motivation [5]. For instance, it has a positive effect to recognize and visualize the own progress in an otherwise large and complex project. Moreover, story and meaning can be added to activities to increase the perceived importance of the given task and to continuously work on it [17].

Previous research for combining agile development with mixed reality has mainly been concerned with teaching purposes. Applications can be used to simulate projects where Scrum can be applied and to give students practical experiences in an artificial and controlled environment. For instance, Caserman and Göbel created a serious game for teaching Scrum where students get to know Scrum roles, artifacts and the different meetings [3]. Here, other team members and roles are simulated by non-player characters. Radhakrishnan and Koumaditis present a similar approach where an immersive virtual reality environment enables students to learn about agile methodology [15]. Here, users collaborate in the virtual space and have a virtual Kanban board. The team gets a fixed project goal to furnish the interior of a miniature space using agile project management.

Our approach is to use real project data and fetch them from existing project management tools like the GitHub issue tracker. This way, users can inspect real-life data and they can continue working with their favorite productivity tools. Mixed reality becomes another available option to streamline meetings and support the community-building. Within the environment, users can monitor and steer the project.

3   Project Management Data Visualizations

In order to explore the characteristics of DevOpsUseXR, we developed a Visual Analytics framework for Project Management (VIAProMa). It offers a persistent mixed reality environment where developers, end users and stakeholders can collaborate to organize projects in an agile way. VIAProMa is a mixed reality framework for project management. It is based on the Unity 3D engine and the Mixed Reality Toolkit by Microsoft. The resulting application provides cross-platform access as it targets both AR and VR head-mounted displays like the Microsoft HoloLens and HTC VIVE. Moreover, it supports an AR mode for smartphones and tablets based on ARCore. VIAProMa integrates the Photon engine to create a shared experience. With its help, users can collaborate remotely in a shared 3D environment. Its code is available as an open-source repository on GitHub[1].

3.1   Task Cards

In order to provide insights about projects, VIAProMa imports data from the Requirements Bazaar and GitHub. The foundational data object are task cards. They are filled either with requirement items from Requirements Bazaar or issues from GitHub. Users can import new cards using a shelf where they are stored as virtual cards on its boards as depicted in Fig. 1. This shelf offers the possibility to list and filter the content of a selected project. A text input field at the top allows searching for specific cards within the project. Then, the user can drag out individual task cards and place them freely in the 3D scene. This gives a

---

[1] https://github.com/rwth-acis/VIAProMa.

team manifold opportunities to structure information in the three-dimensional space so that they can be accessed and viewed by everyone and at any time. The space is persistent and therefore, users can access the shared environment independently or synchronously. Since everyone is working in the same environment, updates are immediately propagated to all users and so newest information about the project is broadcast to all.

Fig. 1. Shelf with task cards

3.2   Kanban Boards

Apart from the free-space alignments, users can also construct Kanban boards and add the task cards to them. This tool provides single columns of the board so that users can build individual variations of Kanban boards as depicted in Fig. 2. For instance, instead of the default three categories "to do" "in progress" and "done", other categories can be chosen or additional ones added like "in review". Each column is renamable and its color can be altered in the configurations of the application. Moreover, the column provides scaling handles at its edges so that the area of the column can be scaled. The displayed list of cards in one column will adapt accordingly to the available space by switching into a pagination mode if there are too many task cards to show them all at once. There are no restrictions regarding the alignment of Kanban board columns. Therefore, users can also build three-dimensional variants that e.g. are curved. The "time travel Kanban board" is one variant that utilizes the three dimensional space and can be created with the tool. Here, the team can duplicate the Kanban board each week and only work on the newest copy. Individual copies are placed behind each other. This way, a stack of time slices is formed and the team members can walk past the boards and inspect how they changed over the course of the project.

Fig. 2. Immersive 3D Kanban board

3.3   Contribution and Competence Overview

Another 3D visualization for projects is the contribution overview. The visualization starts out as an empty wireframe box that can be pulled into the scene. After that, users can select task cards from the scene or directly inside of the shelf and mark them as relevant data for the visualization. Internally, the visualization analyzes the given task cards and assigns scores to contributors. For instance, five points are awarded for realizing a task, four points for opening a new one and one point for commenting or voting for a task. The resulting scores are normalized and shown to the user by displaying the name of the contributor and profile pictures with an according scale. Hence, the user will see a circle of arranged profile pictures and names where team members who contributed most to the selected set of tasks are the biggest item of the visualization. The third dimension is utilized by displaying a bar that starts at the back of the profile picture. Its length again signifies the weighted amount of contributions. However, it is also divided into more detailed sections that break up how the score was calculated as shown in Fig. 3.

By looking at these bars, the viewer can identify why somebody is considered a major contributor for the given set of tasks and whether they contributed by implementing code or by engaging in the community around the project. Apart from the contribution overview, the same visualization can also be used for a slightly different purpose. In its settings menu, there is a filter option where the user can type in keywords that must appear on the task cards, e.g. in the title or description. By adding a large amount of cards and filtering for specific topics, the visualization can help identify competences. For instance, if a developer is working on the existing login module of an application, it is possible to add all task cards of the project to the visualization and to search for keywords like "OAuth" or "OpenID Connect" in order to find an expert in this field. The resulting visualization will only show team members who contributed something to task cards that are related to the given keywords. This is a useful tool for the assignment of tasks in large, anonymous open-source projects as developers do not need to know each other but can still make educated decisions regarding the assignment of tasks within the community. Moreover, it can help new developers to get to grips with individual features of the existing application as they can search for the main contributors who previously worked on this feature and can ask them for advice.

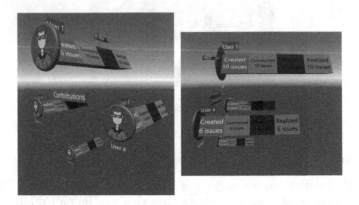

Fig. 3. Competence overview visualization

3.4   Gamified and Non-gamified Progress Bars

In long-term projects it is necessary to monitor the overall progress. VIAProMa supports this with progress bars that can be placed freely in the 3D space. Similar to all previous visualizations, users can instantiate a progress bar in the scene and fill it with task cards. The progress bar will then visualize the ratio of open tasks to tasks that are in progress and tasks that are closed. The progress bar is filled with a green bar for closed tasks and a yellow bar for tasks that are currently in development. The open tasks are represented by an empty section in the glass tube of the progress bar as visualized in Fig. 4. The status of a card is determined implicitly. A task card is open if it is not closed and no developer was assigned to it. The "in progress" label is added if an open task has an assigned developer. The system considers a task as achieved if the corresponding task item is closed. One can add all task cards to track the entire project progress or a sub-set of cards to monitor a single sprint.

In addition to these progress bars, VIAProMa also contains a gamified variant to indicate progress. This separate visualization makes use of a construction metaphor to represent work in the project. Instead of a progress bar, the visualization consists of a skyscraper. The construction of the skyscraper only commences if more assigned task items are realized. Here, finished tasks are represented by revealing the building from the bottom upwards. Tasks that are currently in progress are indicated with a scaffolding as shown in Fig. 5. Open tasks are symbolized by the air above the construction site. Similar to the bars in the progress bar, the height of each of these three sections is determined by

Fig. 4. Progress bar

the percentages of tasks for each category. If one of the buildings contains a lot of tasks that are currently in progress, a small animated crane is also instantiated at the top of the scaffolding. It can act as an indicator for parts of the project that are currently heavily under development. The motivational effect of this progress bar as a gamification element is supported in multiple ways. The application selects the visual style of the building at random from a pool of pre-modelled skyscrapers. Team members can only find out which building is hiding in the visualization by finishing the associated tasks. Moreover, in a project with multiple milestones or sprints, different building progress bars can be created. Over time this forms a city, giving team members the opportunity to visually reflect on the accomplished work and giving them the motivation to further grow the city.

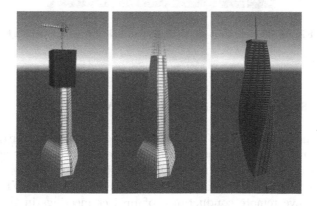

Fig. 5. Different examples of a gamified progress bar

3.5 Commit Statistics

VIAProMa also contains a visualization that does not work with the task data but instead reads information that is provided by the source services of GitHub. In a three-dimensional bar chart, the commit characteristics regarding the aggregated amount of commits per day and hour can be visualized. This 3D diagram helps users to understand the behavior of the developers and to identify peak productivity hours. This is a measure that can help in scheduling meetings. Moreover, the diagram also contains important indication points for stakeholders if the workload is too high or deadlines are set too tight. In this case, the diagram can indicate if more work happened after hours and on weekends. Based on these findings, stakeholders can take according measures by prioritizing and reevaluating the task backlog (Fig. 6).

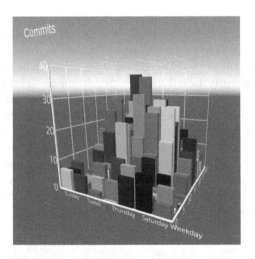

Fig. 6. The commit statistics visualization as a bar chart

4 Use Case Scenarios for VIAProMa

VIAProMa's main intended use case is to analyze and visualize project management data in mixed reality. This functionality can be applied for agile development and it acts as a tool for the DevOpsUseXR concept.

With its synchronous, remote collaboration environment, VIAProMa can especially improve remote conductance of project meetings in the agile workflow. For instance, VIAProMa offers support for the sprint kickoff meeting that is practiced in Scrum. Here, participants can meet in the virtual shared environment, both with AR and VR devices. Since they can see the avatars of others and they can walk around in the virtual space, the experience in VIAProMa imitates a physical meeting. The Scrum master can pull task cards from the shelf in order to discuss them with the developer team and the end users. During this discussion, participants have a three-dimensional space available in order to sort the open task tickets and categorize them spatially. For instance, they can assign meanings to positions in the room, e.g. by collecting tasks that should be tackled in the next sprint in one corner of the room. In contrast to existing 2D desktop-based applications, this also allows for distinguished categorizations. Since they have a 3D space available, teams can establish their own visual language and a sorting scheme that fits their project best. As an example, developers can group cards for the next sprint by clustering them. In the spatial alignment of the card, developers can express the priority of a card by its height in the room. This way, it immediately becomes evident if the next sprint will e.g. focus on new features, designs or bug fixing and the central tasks can immediately be identified. New features can efficiently be assigned to experienced and suitable developers using the competence overview.

Apart from the sprint planning, VIAProMa also offers support for the daily standup meeting that is conducted in Scrum. Within the collaborative environment, VIAProMa breaks up the static spatial nature of a meeting and replaces it with a visual poster session. Similar to a three-minute-madness on conferences, developers can prepare their report in a designated part of the room space by preparing issue cards and visualizations. The daily standup meeting is then conducted by walking through the space and listening to the brief presentations of each developer. Progress bars can be placed persistently in the room and allow stakeholders and developers to continuously track the sprint content. The visualization allows them to notice early on if the progress in a sprint is slower than expected, so that according measures can be taken.

A retrospective meeting of a sprint in Scrum can also be conducted using the virtual space of VIAProMa. Here, developers can instantiate suitable visualizations that show the process in the past sprint. Progress visualizations give an overview whether the sprint has been fulfilled or unclosed tasks need to be moved to a new sprint. A more detailed overview of this can also be set up on the Kanban board. Moreover, the team can identify the major contributors for the sprint or for individual aspects of the sprint using the competence overview.

5   Selected Implementation Details of VIAProMa

Apart from the visualization, we implemented specific features to realize the collaborative mixed reality environment.

5.1   Main Menu

The design of the UI is based on our previous mixed reality project GaMR from which we adapted individual UI elements like the created buttons [11]. One identified challenge based on our experiences with mixed reality development is the placement of the main menu. It must always be reachable but at the same time it should neither clutter the space nor obstruct the field of view. Therefore, we came up with a collapsible main menu. In its collapsed state, it is a small cube. If the user presses the button on the cube, it can unfold and presents its contents. Once a user has selected an option in the main menu, it automatically closes again. This way, the menu is only expanded if the user's attention is actually on the menu and an item is requested in the menu (Fig. 7).

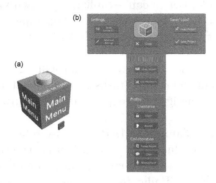

Fig. 7. Main menu in its compact form and the expanded form

5.2 Avatar-Based Collaborative Environment

Since VIAProMa supports remote collaboration, it visualizes the participants in a shared virtual environment as avatars. The avatar consists of a head and a torso. The position and orientation of the user's headset drive the avatar's pose. It is set up in a way that the head will always mimic the real head rotation of the user. The rest of the avatar will follow along with the given movements. Users are able to customize the appearance of the avatar in a dedicated UI menu as illustrated in Fig. 8. Here, a base face, the hair style, hair color, eye color, skin color, glasses and clothes can be chosen. Each avatar wears an ID card which displays the name and their role in the project for improved recognizability.

The collaborative environment is realized using the Photon PUN2 engine. Multiple sessions can be held in parallel as they are separated into virtual rooms. When a user starts the application, the networking module places them in a lobby. Here, they can join existing rooms or create new ones. Once participants are in a room, the collaborative features are enabled. They can see each other's avatars, objects are synchronized, a text chat becomes available and users can set up a voice chat.

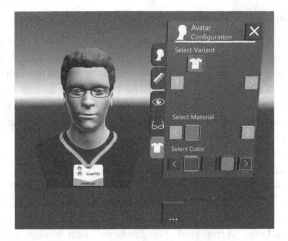

Fig. 8. UI for configuring the avatar

5.3   Login System

To identify the user and grant access rights, e.g. on GitHub, we implemented an OpenID Connect login system. The implementation is based on our previous solution deployed in the GaMR project [7]. However, it had to be adapted because Unity's compilation method for UWP switched from a C# project to IL2CPP which first converts the project to C++ source code. During the update process, we also expanded the login compatibility and functionality. Now, the login works both for installed apps on the HoloLens, on Android, for the standalone executable and in the Unity editor. A login button in the application opens the system's default Web browser with the login page of the OpenID Connect provider. We support both GitHub and Learning Layers login as the two login options for the GitHub issue system and the Requirements Bazaar. Once the user has logged in, a redirect takes place that brings the user back into the app and allows the system to read an authorization code. The authorization code is subsequently traded for an access token.

Depending on the platform two different solutions for capturing the redirection are deployed: For native applications on the HoloLens and Android, a custom URL scheme is registered as a deep link for the app, e.g. "viaproma:/". After the successful login, the redirection will lead to this custom URL scheme. Since the application is registered to handle the scheme, it is brought back into focus and an event is triggered which contains all parameters of the redirection. For the platform versions on the PC for the HTC VIVE and the debugging version for the Unity editor, the application opens a temporary server on the loopback address with a free port, e.g. "http://127.0.0.1:12345". The redirection is set up to lead to this given address and therefore, the server notices the request and can extract the necessary parameters of the redirection. The resulting access token is used to get user information like their name to show it on their avatar ID card and to gain write access on project management tools.

5.4   Integration into Existing Productive Processes

A major consideration in the development process of VIAProMa is the maintenance of high levels of efficiency and productivity. Hence, VIAProMa is designed
so that it does not disrupt collaborative workflows with accustomed tools like
GitHub. Instead, VIAProMa is compatible to GitHub issues and requirements
on Requirements Bazaar. Developers can continue using their established workflows by e.g. organizing issues on the Web interface but VIAProMa offers them
additional options for remote meetings and analytics insights. It is designed as an
additional tool which can be used to streamline synchronous and asynchronous
remote collaboration and to gain insights about the project.

VIAProMa imports requirements from Requirements Bazaar and issues from
GitHub and abstracts them to general tasks. This is done by a separated
frontend-backend architecture. The frontend asks for the task data at the REST-
ful API of the backend. After that, the backend then fetches the data from the
corresponding online API. Before returning them to the frontend, the service-
specific data structures are mapped to a generalized task object. This uses the
mapping schema shown in Fig. 9. The task object is constructed by considering
common properties of tasks, e.g. a title, a description, an assigned developer
and a flag whether the task is fulfilled. Hence, the frontend can work with the
abstracted tasks and does not need to introduce a new data structure for each
data source. For instance, the visualizations on the frontend all work with the
general task object and are therefore independent of the data source. Adding
a new data source like Gitlab to the system only requires the implementation
of the API client on the backend and the mapping of the data structure to the
general task object. On the frontend side only the UI needs to be adapted so
that the additional data can be requested by the user.

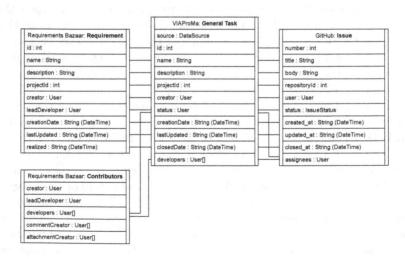

Fig. 9. Mapping of data structures to a general task object

5.5 Persistency

Created 3D rooms are saved by the system so that users can continue working in a scene at a later point. The application automatically saves the scene every five minutes and gives users the option to manually save it. Once a save process is initiated, the scene is converted to a JSON representation. This is executed by a central save-load manager. It keeps track of all savable objects which have a serializer component attached to it. The save call is propagated to the serializer component which is attached to a Unity GameObject. It is composed of multiple serializable classes that determine how the object is saved. This architecture is visualized in Fig. 10. Each serializable component implements an interface to execute the save and load calls. This way, reusable serializable modules emerge. For instance, there can be a module for saving the position, rotation and scale of an object. This component can then be reused on all objects for which this property should be stored. With a save call, the serializable components construct a key-value dictionary for each object. The serializer collects these dictionaries and merges them together into one key-value store for the object. This key-value store is also assigned an ID so that the object can be recognized later on. Every serializer returns its constructed key-value store to the save-load manager which converts it to a JSON string. The JSON string is then sent to the backend where it is stored.

For loading, this process is reversed. The JSON string of the given session is retrieved from the backend server and parsed into the key-value stores. After that, the save-load manager compares if an object with the given ID already exists in the current session. If this is the case, its values are overwritten and otherwise, a new object is created. The values are applied again by the serializable components which define how to read the keys and values from the dictionary.

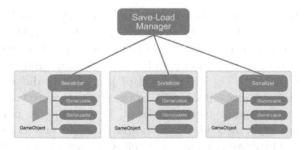

Fig. 10. Architecture of the save load system

6 Evaluation

We conducted a user evaluation and a technical evaluation to gain insights about the usability of the framework and its usefulness for agile project management in mixed reality.

6.1   Evaluation Setup

A user evaluation was conducted with the goal to assess the usefulness of the 3D visualizations, the usability of the application and the utility of the collaborative environment. Thus, fifteen computer science students worked with VIAProMa at our lab. Its setup follows the insights and experiences described by Dünser and Billinghurst [6]. As the first step, participants were asked to fill out a pre-questionnaire which collects data about their demographics and asks about previous experiences with mixed reality, as well as agile development practices. After filling out the form, they were assigned a Microsoft HoloLens or an HTC VIVE Pro and started the application. The participants worked with data from real open-source projects on Requirements Bazaar and GitHub. We provided milestones for these open-source projects and asked the participants to find a suitable spatial ordering to represent the milestone. Additionally, the participants should make use of the visualizations and Kanban boards in order to express the progress of the milestone and to gain insights on the project status. They were also asked to identify a suitable developer for a given task based on the competence visualization. While the participants were interacting with the application, we observed their behavior using the device portal of the Microsoft HoloLens and the casted preview feed of the HTC VIVE Pro. Once participants established a spatial structure, we joined the collaborative virtual environment so that the user could present the gained insights about the project. Finally, participants filled out a post-evaluation questionnaire. This form mainly contained qualitative questions on a Likert scale to answer the initial research questions, followed by a free-text section where participants could give more general comments and feedback.

6.2   Evaluation Results

In the pre-questionnaire, it became evident that nobody has had previous experiences with the Microsoft HoloLens. However, with the HTC VIVE, it was different as 47% reported that they had already used it. Here, five participants had used it one to three times prior and two participants indicated more than eight sessions with the HTC VIVE. 93% of participants did not develop 3D applications with the Unity engine. 87% of the students were familiar with concepts of agile project management. In detail, 11 participants named Scrum as their most known agile methodology, whereas Kanban and extreme programming were reported by two participants each. One person mentioned the scaled agile framework (SAFe).

The results of the final questionnaire show that the participants thought that the application gives an insight about the status of a project. Here they answered in the range from three to five on the Likert scale where 5 indicates strong agreement. The median was located at five and the lower quartile at 4.5. Regarding the assignment of a task to a competent developer, participants agreed with a median scale of four and a deviation between three and five that the framework helped them. For the visualizations, the issue cards were deemed the most useful as shown in Fig. 11. All other visualizations go a median score of four with a minimum score of three and a maximum score of five. Concerning the arrangement of the menus, the users stated at a median of four and an upper quartile of five that the menus are tangible and well-structured. The possibility to customize the Kanban board was well-received a median of four and a lower quartile of four, as well as an upper quartile of 4.5. All participants agreed with a score between four and five that the charts helped them understanding the status of the project. Regarding the usability of the application, users on median assessed the intuitiveness with a score of five and also with an upper and lower quartile of five. Even though the participants had little prior experience with mixed reality technologies, they considered the positioning of the 3D models in the space with a median of four. Here, the lower quartile resulted in a score of four and an upper quartile of five. We also asked them whether the application improves remote collaboration. The answers lied between a score of three and five with a median of five and a lower quartile of 4.5. The participants regarded the customization process of their avatar as fun with a median score of 5. Finally, 73% of the participants made use of the whole 3D space when arranging the imported objects like the task cards and visualizations to structure the project.

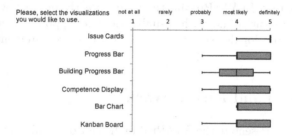

Fig. 11. Results regarding the usefulness of the visualizations

6.3 Technical Evaluation

We monitored the application's performance using the mixed reality toolkit's profiler window, the device portal of the Microsoft HoloLens and Unity's profiler. The framerate and memory consumption were evaluated separately for each supported platform. On the Microsoft HoloLens, a stable 60 frames per second are reached. This is the recommended value by Microsoft[2]. On a PC with a NVIDIA GTX 1070ti graphics card and an Intel i7 processor, we reached 90 frames per second for the VR device. On Android, ARCore caps the framerate at 30 frames per second to reduce the battery drainage. With this value, movement is still perceived as smooth and the framerate requirements are not as high as the screens are not directly in front of the eyes of the user.

---

[2] https://docs.microsoft.com/en-us/windows/mixed-reality/develop/platform-capabilities-and-apis/hologram-stability#frame-rate.

7   Discussion

The main challenge in the design of VIAProMa was to offer compatibility and efficiency for the usage in the day-to-day business of the users. We are aware that mixed reality cannot replace existing agile project management tools around which established workflows have already been constructed. Nevertheless, it can add an additional layer of interaction and insights. It has the potential to improve meetings and give an overview of the project status. The evaluation results show that its value lies in the fact that remote meetings get streamlined and that the teams can immerse in a three dimensional space which can be shaped to their liking. Moreover, it adds additional information that is not directly incorporated in existing project management tools, e.g. the competence overview. We plan to conduct an extended evaluation on a larger scale to gain meaningful results with newly added features.

The developed framework VIAProMa supports the feedback phase of the DevOpsUse cycle. It provides a shared mixed reality environment for remote collaboration where the different stakeholders, developers and end users can meet in a persistent environment. Users evaluated the 3D interface as intuitive. It allows end users without development knowledge to participate and understand the project progress. In VIAProMa, they can directly interact with tasks that are represented as cards and with visualizations as opposed to more technical tools that are fitted for developers. It supports both requirements engineering and sprint planning.

8   Conclusion and Future Work

In this paper we presented the VIAProMa framework which combines mixed reality with agile project management. We created and implemented a series of visualizations that allow users to gain insights about a given open-source project. The visualizations are based on task data by the Requirements Bazaar and GitHub. Accordingly, we adapted the UI to the mixed reality environment to ensure a good usability. Since VIAProMa should support meetings in the agile workflow and provide a persistent environment for this, collaboration features were added. Objects and visualizations can be shared with participants in real-time and remote contribution is made possible by representing users as customizable avatars. We evaluated the resulting implementation in a technical and a user evaluation. The results show that VIAProMa provides a series of use cases to support agile development. The visualizations were well-received by participants and the majority utilized the entire space to organize their project visually. In particular, the issue cards and bar charts with the commit statistics were found interesting by users. VIAProMa supports DevOpsUseXR by enabling end users to participate in developer meetings and to co-design the final product.

A series of solutions emerged from VIAProMa which fulfill common requirements for mixed reality projects. For instance, mixed reality applications in the realm of learning need to identify the current user with a login system to attribute learning success. Here, our cross-platform capable OpenID login solution can fulfill this requirement. Hence, we are currently extracting and modularizing the realized solutions. Like the VIAProMa framework itself, the resulting software artifacts will be made available publicly under an open-source license. This way, developers can directly import configurable modules to use them in their own mixed reality projects. Future work will also focus on extending the DevOpsUseXR support. For instance, VIAProMa could be extended by co-design tools that allow users to create mockups for UI elements. Another possible extension would be the integration of usage analytics in the VIAProMa environment. This way, collaborators could not just analyze the development process but also the way how users interact with their final application. Because of the data abstraction layer, VIAProMa can be extended with new data sources like Gitlab or Trello. This way, the platform can be compatible to a wider range of management tools. This will allow projects to integrate VIAProMa into their workflow while retaining their preferred development tools. The existing visualizations could also be used to inspect learning analytics data of individual students but also of entire courses. So, VIAProMa could also be transformed into a personalized student-mentor environment as a scalable solution for individual feedback.

After the completion of this start phase, the collaborative platform was operational, the connection to the project management tools functioned and their data could be visualized in mixed reality. An item of future work that is already in progress concerns using VIAProMa in teaching. We will continue to use VIAProMa as the foundation for software projects in our mixed reality labs that teach agile mixed reality development. An instance of the lab consists of short-term projects of different student teams who implement additional features in VIAProMa to create useful collaborative tools.

All in all, VIAProMa proves to be a suitable framework for agile project management and DevOpsUseXR. In its creation, a stable shared open-source platform emerged that can function as the basis of further collaborative mixed reality projects for cross-platform interactions.

References

1. Bass, L., Weber, I., Zhu, L.: DevOps: A Software Architect's Perspective. Addison-Wesley Professional (2015)
2. Billinghurst, M., Kato, H.: Collaborative augmented reality. Commun. ACM **45**(7) (2002). https://doi.org/10.1145/514236.514265
3. Caserman, P., Göbel, S.: Become a scrum master: immersive virtual reality training to learn scrum framework. In: Ma, M., Fletcher, B., Göbel, S., Baalsrud Hauge, J., Marsh, T. (eds.) JCSG 2020. LNCS, vol. 12434, pp. 34–48. Springer, Cham (2020). https://doi.org/10.1007/978-3-030-61814-8_3
4. Dabbish, L., Stuart, C., Tsay, J., Herbsleb, J.: Social coding in GitHub: transparency and collaboration in an open software repository. In: Poltrock, S. (ed.) Proceedings of the ACM 2012 Conference on Computer Supported Cooperative Work, p. 1277. ACM, New York (2012). https://doi.org/10.1145/2145204.2145396

5. Deterding, S., Dixon, D., Khaled, R., Nacke, L.: From game design elements to gamefulness: defining "Gamification". In: Lugmayr, A., Franssila, H., Safran, C., Hammouda, I. (eds.) The 15th International Academic MindTrek Conference, p. 9 (2011). https://doi.org/10.1145/2181037.2181040
6. Dünser, A., Billinghurst, M.: Evaluating augmented reality systems. In: Furht (Hg.) 2011 - Handbook of Augmented Reality, vol. 47, pp. 289–307. https://doi.org/10.1007/978-1-4614-0064-6_13
7. Hensen, B., Koren, I., Klamma, R., Herrler, A.: An augmented reality framework for gamified learning. In: Hancke, G., Spaniol, M., Osathanunkul, K., Unankard, S., Klamma, R. (eds.) ICWL 2018. LNCS, vol. 11007, pp. 67–76. Springer, Cham (2018). https://doi.org/10.1007/978-3-319-96565-9_7
8. Hoda, R., Salleh, N., Grundy, J.: The rise and evolution of agile software development. IEEE Software **35**(5), 58–63 (2018). https://doi.org/10.1109/MS.2018.290111318
9. Klamma, R., Ali, R., Koren, I.: Immersive community analytics for wearable enhanced learning. In: Zaphiris, P., Ioannou, A. (eds.) HCII 2019. LNCS, vol. 11591, pp. 162–174. Springer, Cham (2019). https://doi.org/10.1007/978-3-030-21817-1_13
10. Klamma, R., et al.: DevOpsUse - Scaling Continuous Innovation: D6.3: Learning Layers Project Deliverable (2018)
11. Koren, I., Hensen, B., Klamma, R.: Co-design of gamified mixed reality applications. In: Proceedings of the IEEE ISMAR 2018 Workshop on Creativity in Design with & for Mixed Reality, pp. 315–317 (2018). https://doi.org/10.1109/ISMAR-Adjunct.2018.00094
12. Lefrere, P., et al.: Roadmap and Sustainability: WP 8 — D8.4. http://wekit.eu/wp-content/uploads/2019/04/WEKIT_D8.4.pdf
13. Milgram, P., Kishino, F.: A taxonomy of mixed reality visual displays. IEICE Trans. Inf. Syst. **E77-D**(12), 1321–1329 (1994)
14. Piumsomboon, T., et al.: Mini-Me. In: Mandryk, R., Hancock, M. (eds.) Engage with CHI, pp. 1–13. The Association for Computing Machinery, New York (2018). https://doi.org/10.1145/3173574.3173620
15. Radhakrishnan, U., Koumaditis, K.: Teaching scrum with a virtual sprint simulation: initial design and considerations. In: Teather, R.J., et al. (eds.) 26th ACM Symposium on Virtual Reality Software and Technology, pp. 1–2. ACM, New York (2020). https://doi.org/10.1145/3385956.3422107
16. Renzel, D., Behrendt, M., Klamma, R., Jarke, M.: Requirements Bazaar: Social Requirements Engineering for Community-Driven Innovation. In: 21st IEEE International Requirements Engineering Conference: RE 2013, Piscataway, NJ, pp. 326–327. IEEE (2013). https://doi.org/10.1109/RE.2013.6636738
17. Sailer, M., Hense, J.U., Mayr, S.K., Mandl, H.: How gamification motivates: an experimental study of the effects of specific game design elements on psychological need satisfaction. Comput. Hum. Behav. **69**, 371–380 (2017). https://doi.org/10.1016/j.chb.2016.12.033
18. Speicher, M., Hall, B.D., Nebeling, M.: What is mixed reality? In: Proceedings of the 2019 CHI Conference on Human Factors in Computing Systems. CHI 2019, pp. 1–15. ACM, New York (2019). https://doi.org/10.1145/3290605.3300767
19. Tam, C., Da Moura, E.J.C., Oliveira, T., Varajão, J.: The factors influencing the success of on-going agile software development projects. Int. J. Project Manage. **38**(3), 165–176 (2020). https://doi.org/10.1016/j.ijproman.2020.02.001

Applications of VR/AR/MR in Cultural Heritage

The Experience "Mondrian from Inside". An Immersive and Interactive Virtual Reality Experience in Art

Juan Jesús Ruiz Toscano , Irene Fondón[ID], and Auxiliadora Sarmiento[(✉)][ID]

Departamento de Teoría de la Señal y Comunicaciones, Universidad de Sevilla, Avda. Descubrimientos S/N, 41092 Seville, Spain
{irenef,sarmiento}@us.es

Abstract. Technology and art can come together to create exciting experiences that bring the general public closer to different types of artworks. Virtual reality experiences are transforming the way cultural heritage institutions exhibit their works of art and the contextual information in which they were conceived. In this manuscript we present a virtual reality experience that combines the world of the sensory and the world of divulgation. The work carried out involved an in-depth analysis of the painting "Composition A" by Piet Mondrian and the design from scratch of a virtual environment based on it that highlights and deepens the nuances of the original painting. The developed experience allows to bring the painting to the public in an original, surprising and interactive way. The user is introduced into a virtual space where the painting takes on a special role, acting as the main element that allows the user to advance in a storytelling made up of ten scenes. When the user interacts with the painting, the virtual space in which they are immersed is modified, allowing them to advance from one scene to the next. Each scene delves into a relevant aspect of the painter's work and life, presenting the intended information in an attractive way using interactivity as the main tool. The experience is therefore immersive but also interactive, the latter characteristic being the main difference with respect to other virtual experiences related to the world of art that are purely immersive.

Keywords: Virtual reality experience · Virtual museum · Interactivity · Immersion

1 Introduction

Visual arts are not always easily understood by the majority of the population. In particular, abstract painting is one of the most fascinating forms of art when it is understood that art is more than just an isolated, timeless creation without a context. Sometimes, in order to understand a work of art, it is not enough to

Supported by Escuela Técnica Superior de Ingeniería, Universidad de Sevilla.

L. T. De Paolis et al. (Eds.): AVR 2021, LNCS 12980, pp. 275–289, 2021.
https://doi.org/10.1007/978-3-030-87595-4_20

focus all our attention on the painting and try to find meaning in it; we must also gain a deeper understanding of what the artist wanted to convey.

Virtual reality experiences (VRE) in art is a field with a wide range of opportunities. On the one hand, they recreate real or imaginary spaces and landscapes that allow art pieces and their exhibition discourse to be contextualised. On the other hand, they help to fix concepts through playful dynamics so that users can easily understand and remember them. Virtual Reality (VR) is a resource that is already being used in museums and art foundations to provide dynamism and interactivity, improve the experience of their visitors and attract new ones who see these exhibition spaces as something boring, static and old-fashioned [1–4]. Among the different VR applications we can highlight the virtual experiences that help to protect and display historical and ancient buildings [5] as well as VRE to better show cultural connotations of certain museum artefacts [6–8].

VRE can be classified according to three factors: immersion in a recreated real or imagined virtual world, interaction with objects and other agents present in the virtual space, and narration or the ability to choose between different possibilities, paths or even narrative outcomes. In immersive VR experiences one can experience an expanded universe in the first person, acting as visitors who walk through and explore the virtual space in real time. Nevertheless, immersive experiences can be enriched by adding interaction with the virtual environment, which provides a greater engagement for the audience and, at the same time, a deeper understanding of the work, reinterpreting the way people approach the art world.

In this manuscript, we present a storytelling type VRE that allows a user to approach abstract painting as a game or an adventure. VRE conceived with an aesthetic-interactive purpose can be considered playful experiences in themselves, even if they lack the characteristics of video games such as the completion of missions, the advancement of levels or the achievement of certain objectives. The experience developed, named "Mondrian from inside", has two of the three characteristics above: immersion and interactivity. In it, the user is immersed in the painting "Composition A" by Piet Mondrian and the cultural-historical context in which it was conceived.

The Dutch painter Piet Mondrian (1872–1944) is one of the greatest exponents of abstraction. Mondrian composed "Composition A" in 1923 in a Neoplasticism style. A digital representation of the painting is showed in Fig. 1. The painting consists of rectangular shapes in red, yellow, blue, grey, white and black separated by very thick black lines. Horizontality and verticality represent the opposite poles of existence: spiritual and material, feminine and masculine, positive and negative. According to Mondrian, "their union is happiness" [9]. Although the chosen work is of a purely two-dimensional nature where traditional perspective disappears, the simplicity of the forms allows for a three-dimensional representation suitable for bringing interactivity to the experience. In particular, the painting has been three-dimensionally modelled by adding different depths to the rectangles that make up the work. In the designed experience, the user is invited to interact with each of the resulting prisms to obtain information about different aspects of the author's life, artistic references or to design new scenes that allow the user to play while learning. This experience does not therefore seek immersion in a virtual space that recreates a three-dimensional place represented in a painting, but rather a playful and pedagogical experience for a better understanding of abstract art.

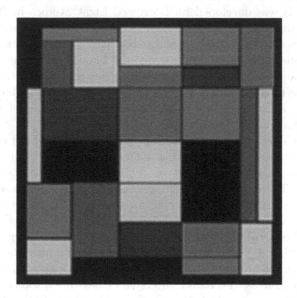

Fig. 1. Digital representation of "Composition A" by Piet Mondrian.

The developed VRE combines a number of mixed reality elements, including virtual hands interaction, dynamic environment configuration, audio and room-scale locomotion. In the experience, the user is neither restricted in gaze nor in movement, but can move relatively freely and fluidly through the virtual space. This prototype employs room-scale head-mounted displays (HMDs) Oculus Rift S which is equipped with two Touch controllers allowing to interact naturally with the virtual world and a workstation with a graphics processing unit (GPU).

The organisation of this article is as follows: Sect. 2 presents three immersive works that have served as inspiration for the development of the tool; Sect. 3 details the VR experience, showing the materials and the implemented storytelling through different scenes; and Sect. 4 presents the conclusions.

2   Related-Work

Among the different experiences offered by virtual reality, immersive experiences continue to be one of the most popular options for museums and art foundations for displaying and interpreting paintings because of the impressive sensation of being inside a painting. In this section we describe three immersive virtual reality experiences that have served as inspiration for the development of the application presented in this paper. These three experiences are entitled: "The Night Café: A VR Tribute to Vincent Van Gogh", "Enter the painting" and "Mona Lisa: Beyond the Glass".

The experience "The Night Café: A VR Tribute to Vincent Van Gogh" is a virtual environment that recreates and reconstructs the famous painting "Le Café de nuit". It was developed bu Borrowed Light Studios in 2015. Far from being a mere augmented reproduction of the painting, the product simulates the space covered by the painting and expands it to include areas of the cafe that do not appear in the original canvas, all while evoking the technique and aesthetics of the painting. It also incorporates elements from other paintings by the painter: the famous sunflowers, the chair, an NPC (Non-Player Character) that emulates the figure of Van Gogh and a fragment of his "La nuit étoilée" painting if we look out of the window.

In 2018, the Thyssen-Bornemisza Museum launched a project entitled "Enter the painting" [10] which proposed a visit to paintings from the museum's collection approached through virtual reality, so that the viewer can move through them. Three paintings were selected from its permanent collection: "Les Vessenots en Auvers" by Vincent van Gogh; "New York City, 3" by Piet Mondrian and "Chinese Glass with Flowers, Shells and Insects" by Balthasar van der Ast. The project visited several Spanish cities throughout 2018 and 2019. The experience, which lasts approximately five minutes, begins inside the Thyssen-Bornemisza Museum in the room where Van Gogh's painting hangs. On approaching the canvas, the visitor enters the wheat field, walks through it and approaches the houses in which Van Gogh was inspired, feeling the air moving the grain. Suddenly it turns dark and as the light breaks, the floor at the visitor's feet becomes transparent and he or she enter Piet Mondrian's painting with the sensation of rising up through a Manhattan made of lines and coloured cubes. The visitor can advance and move through this landscape, which is also a sound approach to the metropolis. Finally, when the visitor is facing the exit, he or she begins to receive the impact of petals, seeds and leaves that fly and even cross his face to compose, at the opposite end, the still life of Balthasar van der Ast.

Another high-quality immersive experience is "Mona Lisa: Beyond the Glass", which the Louvre Museum is offering in 2019 to commemorate the 500th anniversary of the artist's death [11]. The seven minute experience immerses us in the actual room where the painting is exhibited, revealing details invisible to the naked eye. The experience recreates the environment painted in the background of the painting and ends by inviting the user to climb into an imagined version of Leonardo's visionary flying machine and fly through the recreated landscape. It also shows the history behind the painting, information about the techniques used by da Vinci, the identity of the model and other works by the artist.

All of these immersive experiences lack user interaction in the sense that the experience is limited to a walk through the space without the possibility of manipulating objects (which appear merely visual), or interacting with characters.

3   The VRE "Mondrian from Inside"

The virtual reality experience presented in this paper is designed as a sequential narrative consisting of ten different scenes. Among the different conceptual elements that make up each scene are: interaction with elements of the environment recreated for that scene; the viewing of audiovisual content on virtual screens or the appearance of different three-dimensional models that can move around the virtual world. All of this without forgetting the pedagogical nature of the experience.

3.1   Materials

The proposed VRE has virtual objects and a 3D environment to interact with. We have used the professional 3D computer graphics software 3DS Max from Autodesk to obtain a three-dimensional model of the painting, showed in Fig. 2, and to model and render various three-dimensional objects with which the user can interact. The Unity 3D game engine have been employe to add interactivity to the experience. As mentioned above, Oculus Rift S headset has been selected for the VR immersion. This device has six degrees of freedom which track the rotation and position of itself and its Touch controllers in 3D space using a system known as Oculus Insight.

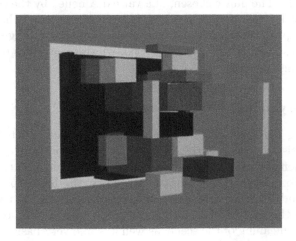

Fig. 2. 3D model of "Composition A" by Piet Mondrian. Each colour block has been modelled as a rectangular prism of a specific size so that no two blocks have the same dimensions. (Color figure online)

The virtual hands that float in space and are used to interact with the environment have been completed with arms formed by small confetti made up of the four main colours that make up the experience: red, yellow, blue and white. This is depicted in Fig. 3.

Fig. 3. Virtual hands and arms. (Color figure online)

Background music has also been inserted throughout the experience to make it more enjoyable. The music chosen, "La valse d'Amélie" by the composer Yann Tiersen [12], evokes the years when Mondrian lived in Paris, where the painter began to develop neo-plasticism. For the creation of the audio guide, the application "Text to speech robot" has been used, which transcribes text to audio in the specified language [13].

3.2 The Storytelling of "Mondrian from Inside"

The storytelling is composed of ten scenes, each of them related to a specific historical or artistic context of the author. The transition from one scene to the next occurs when the user presses one green prisms or block in the 3D model of the painting. To guide the user through the story, the block to be pressed can glow, vibrate and/or change colour. In this way it captures the user's attention. In some scenes the user listens to an audio guide that gives information about the context and meaning of the scene, as well as some very basic instructions for performing some kind of interaction. For the development of the audio guide we have followed some of the recommendations shown in [14].

We will now describe each of these scenes, relating them to various contextual aspects of the artist. The virtual reality experience developed has an approximate duration of 15 min.

The experience initially presents the 3D version of the artwork "Composition A" hanging from a brick wall surrounded by a dark environment with a sky full of stars. From the starting point of view of the user the painting appears to be a bidimensional entity. Nevertheless, as the user gets a little closer or changes its position, he or she can see that it is a three-dimensional model, as shown in Fig. 4a. After a few seconds, the audio guide begins explaining the application use and how the experience will be guided. This initial audio guide makes the user feel comfortable with the environment prior to the experience. When the explanation finishes, one block starts glowing in green. When the user press it, as shown in Fig. 4b, the Touch controls vibrate and the story advances to the next scene.

 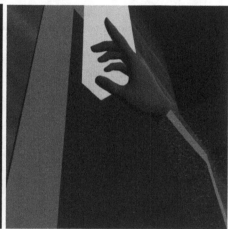

(a) The user's point of view when approaching the 3D model of the painting.

(b) User pressing the green block.

Fig. 4. Illustration of two selected moments of the scene 1. (Color figure online)

In the second scene the audio guide explains Mondrian's beginnings, highlighting his birthplace, profession prior to painting and artistic influences from his family, while a Dutch flag appears on the brick wall and a photograph of the artist appears in a spotlight near the painting [15], as depicted in Fig. 5a. When the user touches the photograph, a video begins to play on a large curved screen that appears behind the photograph, as shown in Fig. 5b. The video shows images of Amsterdam, the painter's birthplace on the dates of his birth [16]. At the end of the video, one of the cubes turns green and starts to glow, meaning that it is time to move on to the next scene.

In the third scene the audio guide explains Mondrian's beginnings as a painter. His early works, like those of a large number of artists, are naturalistic

(a) Mondrian's portrait.   (b) Video projection on a curved screen.

Fig. 5. Illustration of two selected moments of the scene 2. (Color figure online)

(a) Blue butterflies emerging from the pain-   (b) 3D model of the butterflies.
ting.

Fig. 6. Illustration of the butterflies of the scene 3. (Color figure online)

in style, based mainly on landscapes. To connect the experience with nature, the user is invited to press one of the blue cubes, which lights up intensely. When pressed, twelve butterflies emerge from different points in the space, following realistic trajectories, as seen in Fig. 6. The butterflies can change their trajectory if the user touches them with their virtual hands or if they collide with any other object in space. Again, one block starts glowing in green to move on to the next scene.

During the fourth scene, the audio guide explains the importance of two journeys, one to Paris and the other to New York, which had a significant influence on the painter's career. Mondrian moved to Paris in 1911, where he lived for two years, interested in the new artistic trends. During this period Pablo Picasso's Cubism encouraged him to seek out new artistic trends that led to the style that made him famous, Neo-Plasticism. In 1940 he moved to New York, where he established himself as a great artist and spent the last years of his life. By then his style was more lively and free. Several objects appear in the scene to commemorate these two journeys: a three-dimensional model of the Eiffel Tower [17], the painting "Les Demoiselles d'Avignon" by Picasso [18] which, when touched, activates a video of the streets of New York on dates similar to Mondrian's journey [19], a USA flag near the painting, and a plane flying through the sky from the Eiffel Tower to the USA flag [20]. To make the experience even more impressive, the aircraft material has been covered with a Mondrian painting in the same style as the "Composition A" painting. All these objects are shown in Fig. 7. Once the audio is finished, another block in the painting turns green and begins to glow and the next scene begins to play when the user presses it.

(a) Video projection on a curved screen behind the painting.   (b) 3D model of the Eiffel Tower, USA flag and plane.

Fig. 7. Illustration of some objects in scene 4 (Color figure online)

Mondrian also drew on music in composing his paintings during his last period in New York, where he discovered the vibrant rhythms of jazz. In the fifth scene, the eight white blocks of the 3D model of the painting become keys of a piano where each block corresponds to one of the fundamental notes of the C major scale. The user can create his own melody by pressing these blocks, as shown in Fig. 8a. To move on to the next scene, the user simply presses the green cube.

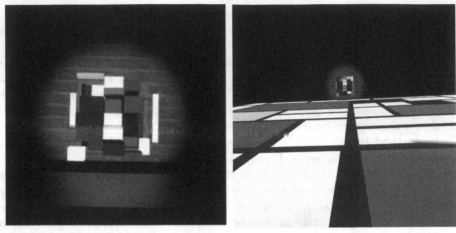

(a) White blocks associated to musical notes   (b) Floor and yellow blocks in scene 6.
in scene 5.

Fig. 8. Illustration of some objects in scenes 5 and 6. (Color figure online)

For Neo-Plasticism, light is fundamental at the conceptual level, it is the spiritual enlightenment that yearns for absolute (or universal) truth. In the sixth scene, the user is invited to play with the light in the room and can modify it clicking on the yellow blocks in the painting. To make the experience more visual, the floor is transformed into a large neo-plastic Mondrian's painting [15], through which the user can walk freely as depicted in Fig. 8b. At the beginning of the scene, the picture on the floor is not visible, so the surprise of its appearance when the user first clicks on the yellow block is striking.

The seventh scene deals with the influence of theosophy on Mondrian's painting which led to the simplification of the pictorial elements in his paintings to lines and rectangular planes of colour and non-colour. In this scene the floor remains the same as in the previous scene and the blocks with which the user interacts are the three red blocks in the painting. Each red block acts as a switch for the three primary colours. The first time the user presses one of the red blocks, a spotlight of one primary colour lights up on each floor block of the same primary colour. If the user presses the same red block again, the light of the spotlights changes from the primary colour to white light. When desired, the user can advance to the next scene by pressing the green cube.

In the eighth scene, the user can view other relevant Mondrian paintings such as "Composition C", "Lookalike", "The grey tree" and "Broadway Boogie-Woogie" [15]. The paintings appear around the subject suspended in the air at an appropriate distance for proper viewing. Each painting is illuminated by its own light in contrast with the darkness of the environment as shown in Fig. 10. The user can rotate to see all the pictures, but the most striking thing about this scene is that the paintings maintain this distance if the subject moves. In this way the art literally accompanies the user (Fig. 9).

(a) Yellow rectangles on the floor illumi-(b) Blue rectangles on the floor illuminated.
nated.

Fig. 9. Illustration of some illuminations in scene 7. (Color figure online)

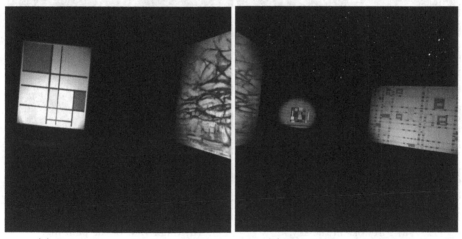

(a) Paintings around the user.   (b) Paintings around the user.

Fig. 10. Illustration of some objects in scene 8. (Color figure online)

The ninth scene is perhaps the most complete scene of the experience. Inspired by the successful Tilt Brush application by Google [21] the user is invited to paint in the air with his virtual hands. The Touch controls are then used to draw straight lines and dots with the colours of Mondrian's paintings. To paint dots on the positions where the virtual hands are located, the user must press one of the front triggers on the Touch controllers. As there are four triggers in total, two on each virtual hand, each trigger corresponds to a certain colour:

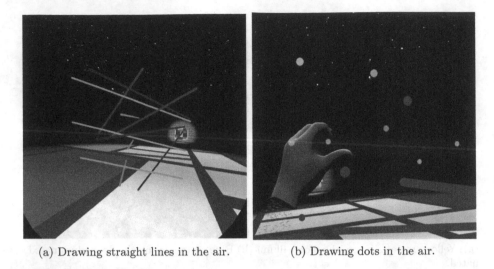

(a) Drawing straight lines in the air.   (b) Drawing dots in the air.

Fig. 11. Illustration of some lines and dots painted in scene 9. (Color figure online)

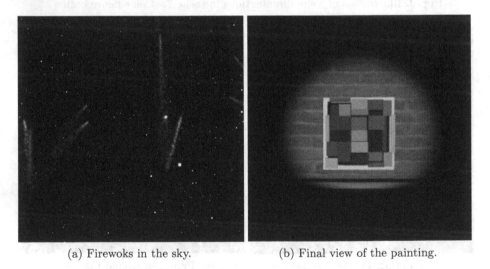

(a) Firewoks in the sky.   (b) Final view of the painting.

Fig. 12. Illustration of the end of the storytelling. (Color figure online)

red, blue, yellow and white. To create straight lines from one virtual hand to the other, the user must simultaneously press two triggers, one from each hand. The colour of the line is selected with the four top buttons on the Touch controllers, two on each controller. Finally, the side triggers on the Touch controllers are used to erase any paint in the air. It is interesting to note that this experience, besides being a lot of fun, can increase interest in art by being able to understand what an artist might feel in the process of creating his or her work (Fig. 11).

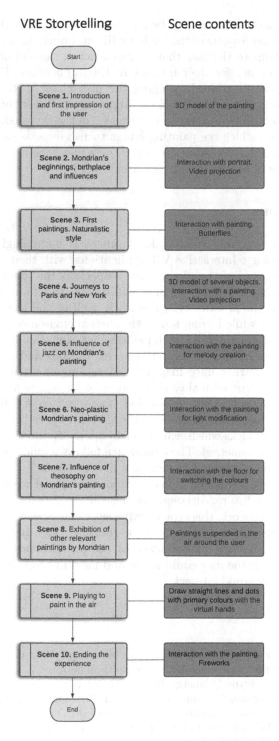

Fig. 13. Storytelling of the developed VRE.

At this point in the storytelling, the user has received interactive and auditory information on many aspects of the author's life and work. In the final scene, the audio guide explains to the user that he has reached the end of the experience and thanks him or her for their interest in the application. Textual words of the painter are also mentioned, bringing the user closer to the artist. To end the experience, one of the blue blocks is highlighted. When the user presses it several red, blue and yellow fireworks can be seen in the sky, as shown in Fig. 12a. Finally, the wall on which the painting hangs turns green, as shown in Fig. 12b, and the user can reset the scene to begin the experience again pressing it. A sequential scheme of the VRE is depicted in Fig. 13.

4   Conclusions

Art is continually evolving and its development is increasingly linked to the advance of technology. Interactive VR applications, with their immersive capabilities, can bring art closer to all audiences, especially the youngest. The person experiencing a painting in virtual reality will be able to retain more information about the author, the artistic style, the work itself or the historical context in which it was made, while having fun in the virtual environment.

The famous paintings of the Dutch painter Piet Mondrian featuring his iconic coloured rectangles are one of the ultimate expressions and representations of modern abstract art that have inspired generations of artists. In this paper, we have proposed a virtual reality experience for the study and understanding of one of these paintings, which is entitled "Composition A". In the developed VRE the painting takes on a three-dimensional form where the coloured squares become interactive blocks which, when touched, modify the virtual environment in which the user is immersed. The experience follows a guide designed to relate the action to certain aspects of Mondrian's life and work.

The tool we have developed is just a small example of what technology can offer to the art of the future. Although the designed experience has been based on a two-dimensional artwork, this type of experience can be developed for artworks containing any type of perspective or three-dimensionality. In this case, it would be necessary to recreate a virtual space of the place represented in the work of art through which the user could move and model objects and/or characters with which the user could interact.

References

1. Bekele, M.K., Pierdicca, R., Frontoni, E., Malinverni, E.S., Gain, J.: A survey of augmented, virtual, and mixed reality for cultural heritage. J. Comput. Cult. Herit. **2**(11), 36 (2018). https://doi.org/10.1145/3145534
2. Raptis, G.E., Katsini, C., Chrysikos, T.: CHISTA: cultural heritage information storage and reTrieval application. In: Ioannides, M., et al. (eds.) EuroMed 2018. LNCS, vol. 11197, pp. 163–170. Springer, Cham (2018). https://doi.org/10.1007/978-3-030-01765-1_19

3. Shehade, M., Stylianou-Lambert, T.: Virtual reality in museums: exploring the experiences of museums professionals. Appl. Sci. **10**, 20 (2020). https://doi.org/ 10.3390/app10114031
4. Kang, Y.; Yang, K.: Employing digital reality technologies in art exhibitions and museums: a global survey of best practices and implications. In: Guazzaroni, G., Pillai, A. (eds.) Virtual and Augmented Reality in Education, Art, and Museums, pp. 139–161. IGI Global, Hershey (2020)
5. Walmsley, A.P., Kersten, T.P.: The imperial cathedral in Königslutter (Germany) as an immersive experience in virtual reality with integrated 360° panoramic photography. Appl. Sci. **10**(4), 1517 (2020). https://doi.org/10.3390/app10041517
6. Schofield, G., et al.: Viking VR: designing a virtual reality experience for a museum. In: Proceedings of the Designing Interactive Systems Conference, ACM DIS Conference on Designing Interactive Systems 2018, Hong Kong, China, pp. 805–816. Association for Computing Machinery (ACM), New York (2018)
7. Fassi, F., Mandelli, A., Teruggi, S., Rechichi, F., Fiorillo, F., Achille, C.: VR for cultural heritage. In: De Paolis, L.T., Mongelli, A. (eds.) AVR 2016. LNCS, vol. 9769, pp. 139–157. Springer, Cham (2016). https://doi.org/10.1007/978-3-319-40651-0_12
8. See, Z.S., Santano, D., Sansom, M., Fong, C. H., Thwaites, H.: Tomb of a Sultan: a VR digital heritage approach. In 3rd Digital Heritage International Congress (DigitalHERITAGE) Held Jointly with 2018 24th International Conference on Virtual Systems & Multimedia (VSMM 2018), pp. 1–4 (2018). https://doi.org/10.1109/ DigitalHeritage.2018.8810083
9. Sylvester, D.: About Modern Art: Critical Essay, 1948–1996. Henry Holt and Company (1997)
10. Enter the painting Homepage. https://www.museothyssen.org/thyssenmultimedia/ entrar-cuadro. Accessed 1 Jun 2021
11. Mona Lisa: Beyond the Glass Homepage. https://arts.vive.com/us/articles/ projects/art-photography/mona_lisa_beyond_the_glass/. Accessed 1 Jun 2021
12. Yann Tiersen, R: La vals d'Amélie.Piano Cover (2019). https://www.youtube.com/ watch?v=uj9BihmugmI. Accessed 1 Jun 2021
13. Text to Speech Robot App. http://texttospeechrobot.com/tts/es/texto-a-voz/
14. Carrozzino, M., Colombo, M., Tecchia, F., Evangelista, C., Bergamasco, M.: Comparing different storytelling approaches for virtual guides in digital immersive museums. In: De Paolis, L.T., Bourdot, P. (eds.) AVR 2018. LNCS, vol. 10851, pp. 292–302. Springer, Cham (2018). https://doi.org/10.1007/978-3-319-95282-6_22
15. Piet Mondrian; Wikimedia Commons, the free media repository Homepage (1899). https://commons.wikimedia.org/wiki/Piet_Mondrian. Accessed 1 Jun 2021
16. Shiryaev, D.: [60 fps] A Trip Through the Streets of Amsterdam, Poland (1922). https://www.youtube.com/watch?v=6tykGHGhC00. Accessed 1 Jun 2021
17. Printable_models: Eiffel Tower V1. Free3D Homepage (2018). https://free3d.com/ 3d-model/-eiffel-tower-v1-470573.html. Accessed 1 Jun 2021
18. Picasso, P.: "Les Demoiselles d'Avignon". HA! Homepage (1907). https://historia-arte.com/obras/las-senoritas-de-avignon. Accessed 1 Jun 2021
19. Shiryaev, D.: [4k, 60 fps] A Trip Through New York City in 1911, Poland. https:// www.youtube.com/watch?v=hZ1OgQL9_Cw
20. Printable_models: Airplane V1. Free3D Homepage (2018). https://free3d.com/3d-model/airplane-v1-79106.html. Accessed 1 Jun 2021
21. Tilt Brush Homepage. https://www.tiltbrush.com/. Accessed 1 Jun 2021

Initial Evaluation of an Intelligent Virtual Museum Prototype Powered by AI, XR and Robots

Louis Nisiotis[1]([✉]) and Lyuba Alboul[2]

[1] University of Central Lancashire, Cyprus Campus, Pyla, Cyprus
LNisiotis@uclan.ac.uk
[2] Sheffield Hallam University, Sheffield, UK
L.Alboul@shu.ac.uk

Abstract. This paper presents the design, development and initial evaluation of an intelligent virtual museum prototype based on a new type of Cyber-Physical-Social Eco-System (CPSeS) framework aiming to merge the real with virtual worlds interchangeably using AI, XR and Robots. Whereas virtual environments have become prominent tools in many domains, offering shared and interactive virtual worlds, the proposed prototype incorporates multi-user and interactive functionalities together with a new agent, namely, a physical robot and its digital twin. The physical robot is located and acts in a real environment whilst its avatar (further referred to as its digital twin) lives in the virtual world. The users are able to see and explore both worlds simultaneously through the 'eyes' of the robot. Together with multi-user infrastructure and communication capabilities, the environment also involves additional agents guiding the user in the virtual world, and an educational game, aiming at developing a CPSeS capable of blending the real with digital worlds, and to be influenced by its users, real and artificial agents and elements. The user-based qualitative evaluation of the proposed system was favourable but also constructive providing the research team with valuable observations on its performance.

Keywords: XR · Robots · AI · Cyber-physical-social systems · Virtual museums

1 Introduction

The concept of Intelligent Digital Realities (IDR) has been recently introduced in scholar, industrial, and research and innovation development communities over the past few years, as a disruptive technological innovation domain focusing on implementing intelligent solutions to support and enhance a plethora of domains. The significant recent advancements in computing, networking, hardware, and software technologies have provided the opportunity for intelligent applications development, by exploiting these advancements in creative and innovative ways. One of the key technologies fostering the development of IDR is the implementation of Artificial Intelligence (AI) in convergence with other emerging disruptive technologies such as Internet of Things (IoT), Robotics,

© Springer Nature Switzerland AG 2021
L. T. De Paolis et al. (Eds.): AVR 2021, LNCS 12980, pp. 290–305, 2021.
https://doi.org/10.1007/978-3-030-87595-4_21

XR (eXtended Reality – a placeholder encapsulating Augmented (AR), Virtual (VR) and Mixed Reality (MR) technologies) and others. AI is referring to the collection of technologies enabling machines to perform advance operations such as sensing, comprehending, acting, and learning [1]. This advanced application of technology allows machines to demonstrate human-like cognitive functions such as learning, analysis and problem solving [2], and is one of the most significant computing achievements of recent times.

AI has been implemented in multiple technological application domains and it drew the attention of many scholars and scientific communities. One of the application domains recently utilized is in virtual environments, especially with the significant advancement of hardware and software in XR technologies over the years. For instance, the applications of AI in virtual environments and in robotic technologies are topics that have been investigated thoroughly by the scientific community over the past 20 years (i.e. [3]). The trend of using XR to support Human-Robot interaction has been recently came to light [4] as well as applications for combining XR and Robots for visualisation, simulation, teleoperation and remote attendance, bridging the gap between the technologies [5]. However, going beyond these recent trends, the convergence of AI with emerging disruptive technologies, for instance XR, Robotics, Digital Twins, Wearables, 5G and other as a fusion, provide the opportunity to create a new type of a Cyber-Physical-Social Eco-Society (CPSeS) of intelligent systems [5]. Such systems aim at blending the real with digital environments in such ways where the difference between real and digital worlds would become less distinct.

This paper describes the development and initial evaluation of an intelligent virtual museum working progress prototype based on the CPSeS framework using AI, Robotics and XR technologies as a fusion.

2   Background

2.1   Artificial Intelligence

"AI is most effective when it is conjoined with human intelligence, rather than replacing it. It highlights the idea that computers and humans have different strengths in the vast field of excellence: computers are much more efficient at doing arithmetic jobs and counting, while humans show a remarkable performance in logic and reasoning. These differing forms of intelligence are complimentary, not diametrically opposites" [6]. It is commonly explained in the form of 'weak' and 'strong' AI. Weak AI refers to the development and implementation of algorithms capable of supplementing or reproducing human intelligence. Strong AI attempts at creating machine intelligence capable of mimicking or surpassing human intelligence [7]. A range of AI methods exist such as Machine Learning (ML), Neural Networks, Deep Learning (DL), Natural Language Processing (NLP) and others. ML enables a system to learn through its own generated data [7]. Neural Networks and DL are also popular techniques in complex systems development. Neural Networks are networks of interconnected processing nodes that process information and perform actions [8], and DL is using structures and functionalities that resemble human brain operation [9]. Furthermore, NLP approaches allow machines to interpret and understand the meaning of spoken or written language [10, 11].

ML enables a system to learn through its own generated data. Neural Networks and DL are also popular techniques in complex systems development. Neural Networks are networks of interconnected processing nodes that process information and perform actions, and DL is using structures and functionalities that resemble human brain operation. Furthermore, NLP approaches allow machines to interpret and understand the meaning of spoken or written language [11]. The advancements in AI, in particular, in tandem with digital realities, offer opportunities to create systems capable to interact with real world, understand complexity of these interactions, and make the informed decisions about possible behavioural strategies.

2.2 Immersive Technologies

Immersive technologies refer to intuitive and interactive hardware technologies that blur the line between real and virtual worlds through digital means and enable users to experience the sense of immersion by offering them high quality or quantity of sensory information [12]. The term 'Immersive Technologies' is mostly associated with the XR technologies of VR, AR and MR [13]. VR refers to computer generated simulation of synthetic three-dimensional environments that can be experienced and interacted using specific hardware such as Head Mounted Displays (HMD), sensor equipped gloves and other equipment [14]. AR connects the real with digital worlds by creating enhanced and augmented realities [15]. Unlike VR where users fully immerse and interact with a completely artificial environment, AR aims at creating illusions that computer generated artificial elements exist in the real world in real time [16]. MR is a reality spectrum that utilises technology to blend real with virtual content, enabling the symbiosis of the real and virtual environments and their ability to interact with each other [17]. The different levels of reality in VR, AR and MR can be seen and comprehended in the Reality-Virtuality (RV) continuum proposed by Milgram et al. [17] depicted in Fig. 1 below.

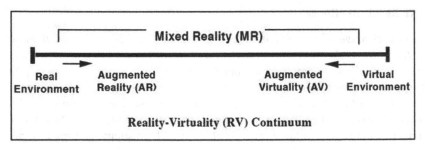

Fig. 1. Milgram and kishino's mixed reality on the reality-virtuality continuum [17]

In the RV continuum, AR mainly involves the real environment (RE) and focusses on the projection of virtual information on top of the real environment. On the contrary, Augmented Virtuality (AV) involves virtual elements more than the real environment.

The XR umbrella term encapsulating VR, AR and MR, refers to all real and virtual environments and human computer interactions generated through hardware technology, and its landscape is rapidly changing due to the significant cost reduction and increase in portability and comfortability [18]. The affordances of XR are being increasingly leveraged to support the efforts of evolution and digital transformation by governments, organisations, industrial stakeholders, scholars and individuals [19]. Especially the domain of XR and its convergence with other smart and intelligent technologies such as AI and Robots, as discussed in the following sections, can provide opportunities to develop innovative products and new types of intelligent realities.

2.3 AI in Virtual Environments

The implementation of AI in virtual environments is a concept that has drawn a lot of research interest recently. AI tools and techniques such as neural networks, machine learning, smart agents, heuristics and others, incorporated within virtual environment in synergy, enable to create new characteristics and functionalities [20]. For instance, the concept of adaptive virtual environments capable of taking into consideration the profile of each user and providing them with a different view have been under development for the past 20 years [21]. Such intelligent virtual environments are capable responding and managing the actions and changes that are occurring in the virtual environments to understand the users behaviour, by identifying their needs and requirements and suggest modifications to support, improve and enhance their interaction with the environment [22].

Similarly, many attempts to merge intelligent agents with virtual environments resulting in the development of the intelligent virtual environments field have also been drawing the attention of researchers [23]. These are environments comprised by interactive and intelligent entities (agents, objects etc.) [24]. Agents are entities that perceive and act on environments [25]. The implementation of intelligent virtual agents, guides and personal assistants in virtual environments capable of providing meaningful interactions with users and the environments by employing AI technologies and techniques have been developed over the past decade and are widely accepted [26, 27]. Voice recognition, synthesis and language understanding capabilities using AI modules and services has been used to develop intelligent social agents and integrate them to virtual environments to support agent-human interactions [26]. The ability to simulate human intelligence, behaviour, and cognition, and implement such capabilities in virtual environments provides unlimited opportunities in the development of immersive and intelligent digital worlds. Social simulations, autonomy, decision making, path planning and finding, and other AI techniques are available in the developer's toolkit, and in conjunction with the significant advancements in processing power and computer graphics provide the opportunity to deploy high fidelity virtual environments controlled or/and influenced by AI core mechanisms.

2.4 Cyber-Physical-Social Eco Systems (CPSeS)

Cyber-Physical Systems (CPS) are complex computing systems that drew the attention of many scholars in academia and in the industry. CPS employ their computational and physical capabilities (e.g. sensing, actuating, communicating) and integrate physical with information systems [28]. Common application of CPS can be found in many industrial domains such as aviation, manufacturing, waste management, smart structures and others

[29]. However, CPS are focusing on the integration of the physical with the computational world and are missing the important element of human interaction with the system [30]. Hence, a further extension of CPS is the introduction of the social element in the system architecture to cater for the human factor and social input influencing the system, and refer to as Cyber-Physical-Social Systems (CPSS) [31, 32]. A CPS connects the physical to the cyber space, while a CPSS introduces the social world into the interconnected system [33]. A further extension that has recently been proposed [5] and this paper further investigates, is the concept of a Cyber-Physical-Social Eco-Systems (CPSeS).

A CPSeS is different to the traditional CPS and CPSS approaches. The concept of a CPSeS [5] focuses on intelligent systems that seamlessly blends the real with digital spaces and the interplay of real and virtual agents involved in both worlds, engendered by humans and their social interactions, behaviour and intentions to make the difference between real and virtual worlds less noticeable. In a CPSeS, the real and virtual worlds are amalgamated using real and artificial agents that interact with humans and their avatars through both worlds in real time. The framework depicted below (Fig. 2) demonstrates the basic architecture of a CPSeS. In a CPSeS, remote users exist in the virtual world, which uses an integration layer that connects them to the physical layer using robotic agents that are physically placed in the real world, while the digital twin that represents them exists and interacts with remote users in the cyber space. Multiple robots and physical spaces can be interconnected and virtually represented in virtual spaces, where remote users can interact with them using the robots as actuators. Physical users in the real world also interact with the robots, where through their sensing functionalities are feeding information into the virtual space and establishing the communication between real and remote users in an Eco-System of multidirectional data stream. To date, initial prototypes of such system have been developed to support cultural heritage [5, 34–36] and education [37, 38].

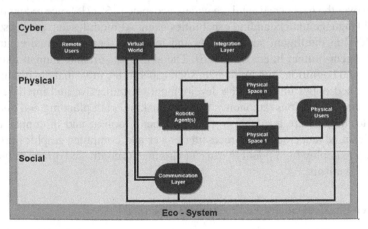

Fig. 2. The cyber-physical social eco-system framework [5]

2.5 Robotics

Due to the huge progress in robotics and automation in the last several decades, robots are now becoming part of our everyday life. Nowadays, robots can be found in various domains such as care and assistance [39], education and training [37, 38, 40, 41], security and rescue operations [42], entertainment [43], industrial operations, where in addition to the industrial robot manipulators, the robots also become a part of the work chain as collaborative robots, or co-workers [44], and many others. Robots have clear implementation missions in the proposed CPSeS and similar systems, facilitating presence of the remote users in the physical environment; provide opportunities for communication and cooperation with humans, enable actuation, teleoperation, and visual projection of the real world among other functions. Such a system enables users to see the real world through the eyes of robots, use the robots as guides and to interact with the real environment, and even communicate with other visitors in the real physical space. These capabilities are moving the robots outside research labs to integrate them in the society with purpose and intent. The combination of robots, immersive technologies, computer graphics, wearables, and other smart technologies as a fusion, can help to foster the ongoing digital transformation of our lives. The proposed CPSeS approach is used to bring life into the robots, which are not lifeless combination of hardware responding to programmable activities but are embodying remote humans and carry them through the experience, being their remote actuation mechanisms and the means of establishing communication with people in the real world. The 'humans within the robots', can experience this combination of tele-presence and tele-actuation through the immersive virtual environment, and take part in blended situations that can contribute into solving several issues pertaining accessibility, interaction, comprehensiveness and quality of experience.

3   System Description

To investigate the potentials of this framework, the development of a prototype system that demonstrates some of the attributes of the proposed CPSeS is underway. The Virtual Museum of Robotics (Fig. 3) is a multi-user virtual environment where users/visitors can connect and synchronously coexist and interact with each other, the environment, and with artificial agents and elements in the virtual world. The purpose of this Virtual Museum is to allow users to learn about the history of robotics and specific information about particular robots. To experience the environment, users connect using VR ready Android smartphone devices and cardboard based HMD's. In this environment, users can navigate and interact with several robotic exhibits, find out more about their purpose, history, and operation, and see simulation examples of how they are performing in action (Fig. 4). Users can find out more about several robotic projects by reading educational materials or watching videos placed in the virtual world. AI guide agents also exist in the environment that can be interacted through dialogue-based system to share information and guide users in the environment (Fig. 4). Users can also participate in a scavenger hunt/quiz type of educational game, where they need to locate the parts and rebuild a robot by correctly answering questions related to the history of robots (Fig. 5).

Fig. 3. The virtual museum of robotics

Fig. 4. Examples of robot simulation (left) and of a dialogue based AI guide agent (right)

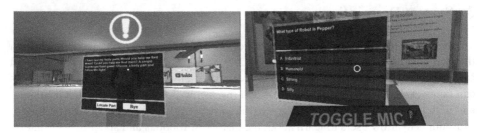

Fig. 5. Examples of scavenger hunt game

While navigating in the virtual world and interacting with its objects and with each other, users can also see and interact with the digital twin of a real robot which is physically placed at an exhibition space at Sheffield Hallam University (UK). This robot (Fetch) is an intelligent agent that connects the real with the virtual world where its real-world movement, actions, sensing, and data collection are fed and synchronously shadowed by its digital twin in the virtual space (Fig. 6). Robot Fetch is a mobile manipulator robot designed by Fetch Robotics [45] providing high resolution camera, laser scanning, environment scanning and mapping, autonomous and manual navigation, advanced sensors for object detection and recognition, collision and obstacle avoidance, and manipulation in dynamic environments among other capabilities. It also features a mechanical arm designed to reach, grab, and manipulate objects. The environment scanning and mapping capabilities of Fetch have been used to scan the exhibition environment, and a series of C + + operations have been deployed to enable the robot to autonomously navigate between points of interest, through instructions issued by users in the virtual world. The movement of fetch together with a live feed of the real world through the robot's camera are synchronously fed into the virtual world and projected in a screen in front of the digital twin.

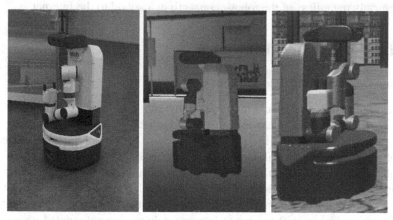

Fig. 6. The real (left) and digital twin (middle and right) of the robot fetch

3.1 Implementation Technology

To design the virtual environment, Unity 3D game engine was used together with C# scripting language [46]. To support the VR mode, Google VR [47] and Android SDK [48] libraries for Unity3D were implemented to build the smartphone application. To experience the VR environment, the Mr. Cardboard [49] HMD has been used. This particular HMD is featuring a thumb hole on the bottom of the device allowing users to touch the screen of the smartphone and perform several gestures, i.e., touch, swiping, double touches, and dragging. To support the multi-user component of the system, the free version of the Photon Engine networking infrastructure has been used, enabling 20 concurrent users to connect and synchronously coexist in the virtual environment [50]. The Photon Voice component to support Voice over IP [51], and custom text chat functionalities were implemented to support the social component of the system.

To connect the robot to the virtual world and develop its functionalities, the Robotic Operating System (ROS) was used in conjunction with specialized plugins. ROS is an open-source framework that provides a set of tools and libraries based on a publish/subscribe architecture that allows to distribute data between different nodes [52]. To connect the robot to its digital twin and establish bi-directional data transmission from the real world to the virtual space through the robot and vice-versa, RosBridge library [53] and ROS# [54] plugins have been implemented.

To enable users to establish connections to the robot from remote locations and see the robot's digital twin in the virtual world, 4G and Wi-Fi technologies were utilised. When attempting to develop this functionality however, the issue of dynamic IP allocation on 4G Wi-Fi devices managed by commercial ISP's was hindering the configuration and implementation of remote connections. This is a known networking issue, related to the limitations of port forwarding on ISP network level [55]. To address this, the research team has implemented a networking configuration using reverse SSH connection through a proxy server to allow connecting to the robot, enabling users to connect directly to the robot remotely regardless of the robot's connectivity method to the Internet.

4   Initial Environment Evaluation

4.1   Data Collection and the Impact of Covid-19

To collect initial data that would help evaluating and guiding the development of the system and the framework, plans for an extended evaluation study were initially made, aiming to collect information about user's perception of technology acceptance, their sense of presence in the virtual world and general usability of the virtual environment using quantitative and qualitative data collection instruments. However, the Covid-19 pandemic has posed challenges that have significantly hindered the development of the system and the plans for evaluation. The decision of the Universities participating in this research project to shift to remote learning delivery have disrupted access to the robotic equipment for the research team. Furthermore, the pandemic also hindered the efforts of recruiting people to participate in the experiments. Therefore, the research team has concentrated in implementing additional functionalities to the virtual environment aspect of the system and prepared an alternative initial evaluation study to investigate technical aspects and general usability of the system, which its results are discussed in the following sections.

To conduct this study, 4 male users aged between 21–26 have volunteered to participate. An open-ended questionnaire was designed and administered online at the end of the experience (Table 1). During the experiment, the research team was observing the users and robot's behaviour in the real and virtual world, as well as the general environment response to actions and events occurring in the virtual world.

Table 1. Questions used to initially evaluate the system.

Q1. What are your thoughts about the ability to see the real world through the eyes of the robot and interact with it in Virtual Reality?
Q2. What is your opinion about navigating in the virtual world and interacting with elements in the environment through the reticle (the white dot that expands) including the text chat?
Q3. What issues did you had during the experience?
Q4. How effective was the museum experience and which elements did you appreciate the most?

4.2 Experimental Procedure

To run this evaluation study, participants have been granted permissions to access the premises of the University of Central Lancashire, Cyprus Campus, where one of the principal researchers and co-author of this paper is affiliated with. Researchers have also been granted special permission to access the robotics lab at the Centre for Automation and Robotics Research at Sheffield Hallam University (UK) where the other principal researcher and co-author of this paper is affiliated with, to set up the robot. Users have participated in pairs of two, in two different sessions. Participants have followed a series of standardised experimental procedures during this experiment. Initially, users had to download and install the specific app on their Android smartphone. The cardboard HMD was provided to them in advance. Users had to calibrate the app with their HMD by following instructions on the app. Users were then asked to insert their smartphone into the HMD and follow on-screen instructions.

As soon as users connect to the environment, they land in a virtual orientation area, providing them information on how to use the environment, how to interact with objects and agents in the environment, and communicate with each through the textual chat. Users then teleported to the Virtual Museum area where they were instructed to navigate and read educational materials, interact with the robotic exhibits, and play an educational scavenger hunt quiz game. Users also interacted with the digital twin of the robot, which was synchronously navigating in the virtual space as it was navigating in the real world, providing a real time video feed of the real to the virtual world.

At the end of the virtual experience, a weblink to the questionnaire was provided to participants. To adhere with government Covid-19 protection guidelines, the HMD's were disinfected prior usage and were then gifted to the participants at the end of the session.

4.3 Results

The collected data was reviewed and analysed to initially identify technical problems, and usability issues, and the results are presented below.

Technical
One of the most significant technical issues that some of the participants have experienced in the virtual world was noticeable and sometimes significant frame drop on their devices

when they were navigated in graphic intensive areas of the environment. This was also found to have an impact on the battery life of their smartphone devices. In addition to this, their smart phones were also overheating due to prolonged usage.

Participant 2: *"Computationally expensive for smartphones (requires strong hardware). For instance, when I started the application the battery level was at 85% and after 20 min of use (application) the battery level falls to 20%. In addition to that, during the use of this application, the phone temperature increased."*

Internet connectivity and speed were also important technical determinants of the experience. Initially participants tried to connect to the system through the University Wi-Fi, however network restrictions were blocking the connection requests. When participants were connected through an open Wi-Fi connection which was relatively slow, they were experiencing delays in streaming the video feed of the real world, and delay issues in the synchronous response of the real robot and its digital twin.

Participant 1: *"Internet connection was the main issue... movement on the robot took a serious amount of time to be shown on the smartphone screen."*

It was identified that 4G connectivity was much better and users were getting consistent and better experience. However, the researchers have identified that there was still a delay in the live feed, which was nevertheless unnoticeable to the users. It was also identified that the delay in the digital twin's and the live video feed synchronization was different among devices, highlighting inconsistency in the experience.

Participants have indicated that the video feed was very good and have commented on the ability to view the world through the eyes of the robot very positively.

Participant 2. *"The live video feed from the robot was the most exciting part. It was a very fascinating and unique experience... The quality of the video was very good even when viewed from distance."*

Particularly, when participants were queried about the effectiveness of the museum experience and which elements they have appreciated the most, they all commented very positively, highlighting the ability to see the physical world and the digital twin of the robot.

Participant 1. *"Very effective! Generally, the whole concept and idea worth the same amount of appreciation. But the feature that makes the most difference is the video live feed through the eyes of the robot."*

Usability
The evaluation study also brought forward some usability issues that needs to be considered to improve the user experience. The use of a reticle pointer as the method to provide user interactivity with the elements in the virtual world was mainly perceived positively by users. Users indicated that it was easy to use, however they had to familiarise with its usage initially prior to being able to effectively interact. Especially when having to use the virtual keyboard to send messages, they have indicated difficulties on its effective use.

Participant 3: *"Texting was a little bit confusing but needed time to familiarise... It was easy to understand but very slow to communicate, it was not very easy".*

While interactable objects were found easy to identify and use, a particular user also identified an issue regarding the interactable distance of the objects, indicating that while the reticle pointer was easy to use, *"sometimes the interactable distance was too long that I accidentally opened dialogues I wasn't intending to"* (participant 4). Another user revealed that he found difficulties while interacting with the dialogue-based system of the AI guide agent, indicating that *"sometimes the dialogues where missing some information and were not navigating to where it was supposed to navigate me to"*. The research team have then identified bugs in the system that were then resolved.

While navigation in the virtual world was perceived easy, a particular user (Participant 4) indicated that more fluent movement mechanisms could be implemented: *"Navigating was easy without any dizziness, but the movement was awkward sometimes when you had to move left or right (e.g. rotate right, move forward then rotate left). A suggestion would be to add a way to move in sideways as well or fluently in all directions".*

5 Discussion

The CPSeS framework aims at guiding the development of a multi-user networked complex computing system capable of merging the real with digital worlds interactively to support a plethora of domains. This paper described a virtual reality museum based on the CPSeS framework using VR, Robots and Social Networking technologies. To investigate its potential and research impact, it is necessary to conduct a series of experimental studies to investigate the functionalities and user perceptions of the system implementation. Taking the initial results of the study described in this paper into consideration, it can be argued that the prototype, whilst hindered by some technical and usability limitations, is a working proof of concept demonstrating the implementation of a CPSeS capable of merging the real with virtual worlds and is influenced by its users and their behaviour, real and artificial elements. Users could access the virtual world and connect to the robot from remote location, interact with its digital twin and with agents and elements in the virtual environment concurrently. While the study has involved a small sample, several important issues have been identified for the research team to consider. This study serves as a necessary initial testbed that enabled the research team to gather some initial important insights to improve the system.

6 Conclusions and Future Work

This paper focuses on the initial evaluation of a Virtual Museum prototype based on the Cyber-Physical-Social Eco System framework. The results of this study provide important initial insights on technical and usability issues hindering the prototype system and enables the research team to understand them and act upon improving the system.

Overall perceptions regarding the content, interface design, look and feel of the environment were very positive. Users have indicated that the environment was quite immersive and mainly easy to use. Users appreciated and found the ability to see the digital twin and the real world through the eyes of the robot as very compelling but have identified a series of technical and usability issues, enabling the research team to act upon to improve the system. However, the opinion of additional participants needs to be collected and evaluated to be able to make more concrete inferences regarding the system, as the low number of participants is a significant limitation of this study. Nevertheless, it enabled the research team to collect some initial user reactions of the system, to better prepare for a complete evaluation study once the Covid-19 restrictions are loosened, and access to the labs and the University premises are re-established.

Future work is underway to implement additional robots into the system and to further develop the functionalities of Fetch robot. Functionalities such as image recognition, pick and place, and sorting are under development, leveraging the machine vision and artificial intelligence capabilities of the robot. The research team also works on implementing additional virtual agents using AI techniques to support the user during the experience in the virtual world.

Taking into consideration the potentials of the proposed CPSeS framework, the affordances of XR in convergence with Robots and other emerging disruptive technologies, intelligent and complex computing systems can be developed to address the needs of a plethora of domains and to contribute and support the ongoing efforts of the digital transformation of industry, education, the economy, the society, and our everyday lives in general.

Acknowledgements. The authors would like to thank the Centre for Automation and Robotics Research (CARR), Industry and Innovation Research Institute at Sheffield Hallam University (UK), and the School of Sciences at the University of Central Lancashire, Cyprus Campus, for providing the equipment and the working environment. Also, special thanks to the students: Robin Ghys, Jean-Alexis Hermel, Léo Dedeine, Grzegorz Szargot who have contributed to the development of the system, and to Dr Martin Beer for useful discussions. This paper is in memory of our dear friend, colleague and collaborator Professor Jacques Penders.

References

1. Daugherty, P., Carrel-Billiard, M.M.B.: Accenture Technology Vision (2018). https://www.accenture.com/t00010101T000000Z__w__/nz-en/_acnmedia/Accenture/next-gen-7/tech-vision-2018/pdf/Accenture-TechVision-2018-Tech-Trends-Report.pdf
2. Valin, J.: Humans still needed: an analysis of skills and tools in public relations. Chartered Ins. Public Relat. **23**, 1–12 (2018)
3. Luck, M., Aylett, R.: Applying artificial intelligence to virtual reality: intelligent virtual environments. Appl. Artif. Intell. **14**(1), 3–32 (2000)
4. Williams, T., Szafir, D., Chakraborti, T., Amor, H.B.: Virtual, augmented, and mixed reality for human-robot interaction. In: Companion of the 2018 ACM/IEEE International Conference on Human-Robot Interaction, Chicago, IL, USA pp 403–404. Association for Computing Machinery (2018)
5. Nisiotis, L., Alboul, L., Beer, M.: A prototype that fuses virtual reality, robots, and social networks to create a new cyber–physical–social eco-society system for cultural heritage. Sustainability **12**(2), 645 (2020)
6. Ghosh, A., Chakraborty, D., Law, A.: Artificial intelligence in internet of things. CAAI Trans. Intell. Technol. **3**(4), 208–218 (2018)

7. de Saint Laurent, C.: In defence of machine learning: debunking the myths of artificial intelligence. Eur. J. Psychol. **14**(4), 734–747 (2018)
8. Nielsen, M.A.: Neural Networks and Deep Learning, Vol. 25. Determination press, San Francisco (2015)
9. Contreras, S., Rosa, F.D.L.: Using deep learning for exploration and recognition of objects based on images. In: 2016 XIII Latin American Robotics Symposium and IV Brazilian Robotics Symposium (LARS/SBR), pp 1–6 (2016)
10. Jain, A., Kulkarni, G., Shah, V.: Natural language processing. Int. J. Comput. Sci. Eng. **6**(1), 161–167 (2018)
11. Remian, D.: Augmenting education: ethical considerations for incorporating artificial intelligence in education. Instr. Des. Capstones Collect. **52**, 1–54 (2019)
12. Slater, M.: Place illusion and plausibility can lead to realistic behaviour in immersive virtual environments. Philos. Trans. R. Soc B: Biol. Sci. **364**(1535), 3549–3557 (2009)
13. Handa, M., Aul, G., Bajaj, S.: Immersive technology–uses, challenges and opportunities. Int. J. Comput. Bus. Res. **6**(2), 1–11 (2012)
14. OxfordDictionary: Virtual Reality. https://www.lexico.com/definition/virtual_reality.
15. Klopfer, E., Squire, K.: Environmental detectives—the development of an augmented reality platform for environmental simulations. Educ. Tech. Res. Dev. **56**(2), 203–228 (2008)
16. Cawood, S., Fiala, M.: Augmented reality: a practical guide (2008)
17. Milgram, P., Colquhoun, H.: A taxonomy of real and virtual world display integration. Mixed reality: Merg. real virtual worlds **1**(1999), 1–26 (1999)
18. Alizadehsalehi, S., Hadavi, A., Huang, J.C.: From BIM to extended reality in AEC industry. Autom. Constr. **116**, 103254 (2020)
19. IEEE Digital Reality Initiative: Digital Transformation. https://digitalreality.ieee.org/images/files/pdf/DRI_White_Paper_-_Digital_Transformation_-_Final_25March21.pdf.
20. Garcia, T.J.L., Rodriguez-Aguilar, R.M., Alvarez-Cedillo, J.A., Alvarez-Sanchez, T.: Development of software architecture for a 3d virtual environment with the incorporation of a reactive intelligent agent. J. Theor. Appl. Inf. Technol. **97**(17), 4589–4599 (2019)
21. Lepouras, G., Vassilakis, C.: Adaptive virtual reality museums on the web in adaptable and adaptive hypermedia systems. In: Sherry, Y.C., George, D.M. (Eds.) IGI Global, Hershey (2005)
22. de Aquino, M.S., de Souza, F.d.F.: Adaptive virtual environments: the role of intelligent agents In: Practical Applications of Agent-Based Technology, pp. 87–110. INTECH Open Science (2012)
23. Kiourt, C., Pavlidis, G., Koutsoudis, A., Kalles, D.: Multi-agents based virtual environments for cultural heritage. In: 2017 XXVI International Conference on Information, Communication and Automation Technologies (ICAT), pp 1–6 (2017)
24. Osório, F.S., Musse, S.R., Santos, C.D., Heinen, F., Braun, A., Silva, A.D.: Intelligent virtual reality environments (IVRE): Principles, implementation, interaction, examples and practical applications. Virtual Concept (Proceedings-Tutorials) **1**, 1–64 (2005)
25. Russell, S., Norvig, P.: Artificial intelligence: a modern approach (2002)
26. Duguleană, M., Briciu, V.-A., Duduman, I.-A., Machidon, O.M.: A virtual assistant for natural interactions in museums. Sustainability **12**(17), 6958 (2020)
27. Petrović, V.M.: Artificial intelligence and virtual worlds–toward human-level AI agents. IEEE Access **6**, 39976–39988 (2018)
28. Lee, J., Bagheri, B., Kao, H.-A.: Recent advances and trends of cyber-physical systems and big data analytics in industrial informatics. In: International Proceeding of International Conference on Industrial Informatics (INDIN). pp 1–6 (2014)
29. Krogh, B.H.: Cyber physical systems: the need for new models and design paradigms. Presentation Report (2008)

30. Monostori, L.: Cyber-physical production systems: roots, expectations and R&D challenges. Procedia CIRP **17**, 9–13 (2014)
31. Xiong, G., et al.: Cyber-physical-social system in intelligent transportation. IEEE/CAA J. Automatica Sinica **2**(3), 320–333 (2015)
32. Naudet, Y., Yilma, B.A., Panetto, H.: Personalisation in cyber physical and social systems: the case of recommendations in cultural heritage spaces. In: 2018 13th International Workshop on Semantic and Social Media Adaptation and Personalization (SMAP), pp. 75–79 (2018)
33. Murakami, K.J.: CPSS (cyber-physical-social system) initiative-beyond CPS (cyber-physical system) for a better future. In: Keynote Speech, the First Japan-Egypt Conference on Electronics Communication and Computers JEC-ECC (2012)
34. Nisiotis, L., Alboul, L., Beer, M.: Virtual museums as a new type of cyber-physical-social system. In: De Paolis, L.T., Bourdot, P. (eds.) AVR 2019. LNCS, vol. 11614, pp. 256–263. Springer, Cham (2019). https://doi.org/10.1007/978-3-030-25999-0_22
35. Alboul, L., Beer, M., Nisiotis, L.: Robotics and virtual reality gaming for cultural heritage preservation. In: Resilience and Sustainability of Cities in Hazardous Environments, Napoli, pp. 335-345 (2019)
36. Alboul, L., Beer, M., Nisiotis, L.: Merging realities in space and time: towards a new cyber-physical eco-society. In: Dimitrova, M., Wagatsuma, H. (Eds.) Cyber-Physical Systems for Social Applications, IGI Global, Pennsylvania (2019). https://doi.org/10.4018/978-1-5225-7879-6
37. Nisiotis, L., Alboul, L.: Work-in-progress—converging virtual reality, robots, and social networks to support immersive learning. In: 2020 6th International Conference of the Immersive Learning Research Network (iLRN), pp. 308–311 (2020)
38. Nisiotis, L., Alboul, L.: Work-in-progress—an intelligent immersive learning system using AI, XR and robots. In: 7th International Conference of the Immersive Learning Research Network (iLRN), (2021)
39. Valchkova, N.F., Zahariev, R.Z.: Optimization of model operator for service robot, intended to service persons with disability. IFAC-PapersOnLine **52**(25), 174–179 (2019)
40. Papakostas, G., Sidiropoulos, G., Bella, M., Kaburlasos, V.: Social robots in special education: current status and future challenges. The Proceedings of JSME annual Conference on Robotics and Mechatronics (Robomec) **2018**, 1P1-A15. The Japan Society of Mechanical Engineers (2018)
41. Belpaeme, T., Kennedy, J., Ramachandran, A., Scassellati, B., Tanaka, F.: Social robots for education: a review. Sci. Rob. **3**(21), eaat5954 (2018)
42. Marques, M.M., et al.: Use of multi-domain robots in search and rescue operations—contributions of the ICARUS team to the euRathlon 2015 challenge. In: OCEANS 2016-Shanghai, pp 1–7 (2016)
43. Goswami, A., Vadakkepat, P.: Humanoid Robotics: A Reference. Springer, Dordrecht (2019)
44. Robla-Gómez, S., Becerra, V.M., Llata, J.R., González-Sarabia, E., Torre-Ferrero, C., Pérez-Oria, J.: Working together: a review on safe human-robot collaboration in industrial environments. IEEE Access **5**, 26754–26773 (2017)
45. FetchRobotics: Fetch Robotics. https://fetchrobotics.com/.
46. Unity3D: Unity 3D Game Engine Software. https://unity3d.com/.
47. GoogleVR: Google AR/VR. https://arvr.google.com/.
48. AndroidSDK: Android Studio SDK. https://developer.android.com/studio.
49. MrCardboard: Mr Cardboard HMD. https://mrcardboard.eu/.
50. PhotonEngine: Photon Engine. https://www.photonengine.com/pun.
51. PhotonEngine: Photon Engine Voice. https://www.photonengine.com/en/voice.
52. ROS: Robotic Operating System http://wiki.ros.org/.
53. RosBridge: Rosbridge Library. http://wiki.ros.org/rosbridge_library.

54. Ros#: ROS#. https://github.com/siemens/ros-sharp.
55. Hajjaj, S.S.H., Sahari, K.S.M.: Establishing remote networks for ROS applications via port forwarding: a detailed tutorial. Int. J. Adv. Rob. Syst. **14**(3), 1–13 (2017)

Virtual Reality in Italian Museums:
A Brief Discussion

Carola Gatto[1], Giovanni D'Errico[2], Giovanna Ilenia Paladini[3],
and Lucio Tommaso De Paolis[3(✉)]

[1] Department of Cultural Heritage, University of Salento, Lecce, Italy
carola.gatto@unisalento.it
[2] Department of Electrical Engineering and Information Technology, University of Naples,
Federico II, Naples, Italy
giovanni.derrico@unisalento.it
[3] Department of Engineering for Innovation, University of Salento, Lecce, Italy
{ilenia.paladini,lucio.depaolis}@unisalento.it

Abstract. This paper discusses the current use of Virtual Reality technology within the Italian museum field. It intends to provide a brief list of the main cases of VR applications developed for Italian museums, by focusing the discussion above the last year scenario. Indeed, during the lockdown period, due to the covid-19 pandemic, the use of technology in museums have been greater than in the previous years. The aim is to provide a brief description of this changed scenario in relation to the use of VR technology, attesting to best practices on the one hand and raising critical issues on the other.

Keywords: Virtual Reality · Virtual cultural heritage · Enhancement of museum

1 Introduction

The concept of Virtual Reality (VR) has been much debated. In general, we can assume that VR is a computer-generated environment, isolated from the real one, in which the user is immersed, and, in some cases, he can interact with some virtual objects [1]. This technology should be distinguished from Augmented Reality, which is the result of the integration of virtual computer-generated objects, within the real world, thus creating a new way of seeing and perceiving, halfway between real and virtual.

Rather than considering the two concepts simply as antithetical, however, it is more convenient to see them as situated at two contiguous points on a continuum, which we refer to as the Reality-Virtuality continuum [2]. According to this model, the extremity on the left of the continuum defines any environment that consists exclusively of real objects, includes everything that could be observed when viewing a real-world scene directly through eyes. The extremity on the right defines environments that consist only of virtual objects, such as conventional computer graphics simulations, either on a monitor or in an immersive environment.

Within this framework, it is useful to define a generic Mixed Reality (MR) environment as that portion of the continuum in which the real world and the virtual objects

L. T. De Paolis et al. (Eds.): AVR 2021, LNCS 12980, pp. 306–314, 2021.
https://doi.org/10.1007/978-3-030-87595-4_22

coexist in the same place. Some studies consider MR as an "alignment" of environments. This means a synchronization between a physical and a virtual environment or the alignment of a virtual representation with the real world, respectively [3].

Technological tools used by people in everyday life, for working as well as for their leisure time, are the result of a constant evolution, aimed not only at satisfying the needs of the individual, but also at recognizing and sometimes preventing them. This process has become increasingly rapid, arriving in the twentieth century to be exponential regarding the Information and Communication Technologies (ICT): VR technology also belongs to this category, and it is becoming ever more sophisticated and accessible.

2 A Brief History of Technology

The history of AR and VR technologies begins in the 1950s, when Morton Heilig, a film director and philosopher, wanted to conduct an experiment to involve the viewer within the activities of the cinema screen, through an, let's say today, "immersive" experience. In 1962, Heilig developed a model of his idea, which he described as "the cinema of the future", known as Sensorama [4]. This prototype was equipped with a 3D image projection system, vibrations, stereophonic sound, wind, and the reproduction of olfactory and tactile stimuli. Due to its excessive cost, the project remained unfinished and never reached the market.

Another breakthrough came in 1966, when Sutherland created the first prototype of a user-mounted augmented reality display, the so-called Head-Mounted Display (HMD). It was designed to display images from a computer and allow interactions, albeit primitive, with the user's movements.

In 1975, Myron Krueger set up an artificial reality laboratory called Videoplace. His idea was to create an artificial reality that surrounded users and responded to their movements and actions, in an interaction free of supports or mechanisms.

At the beginning of the 1990s, AR became a real field of study, and it is in fact from this period that the fundamental study conducted by Paul Milgram, professor at the University of Toronto, and Fumio Kishino, at the University of Osaka, dates back.

The first widely accepted definition of AR dates to 1997, when Ronald Azuma in his work "A survey of augmented reality" defined it as the combination of the following three factors: input of virtual objects into real environments, real-time interaction with these objects and integration into the user's visual field [5].

Starting from this period AR and VR experience a continuous evolution that brings these technologies to be widely experimented in different fields: from medicine to the industry, from education to entertainment, from mobile applications for tourism to platforms for archaeology and heritage in general.

The development of the libraries and software opens the door to a growing offer of contents and applications, corresponding to a growing demand from the market: in fact, in several sectors, companies and organizations have decided to invest in a new type of communication that, exploiting VR and AR, allows the user a dynamic and engaging experience.

VR is based on the concepts of immersion and presence, which also distinguish it from other forms of media [6]. Immersion is an objective construct that explains the physical configuration, while presence is a subjective construct [7]. Immersion can be seen as a measurable aspect of viewing technology [8], and presence as a product of the mind that is not tied to any specific technology and describes the feeling of "being there" [9].

Research shows that the more sophisticated the VR technology, the greater the degree of immersion and level of presence [10]. It can be summarized that the intensity of immersion and the level of engagement and interactivity in it are crucial for the realization of presence.

The degree of immersion changes depending on the experience and the hardware choices that are made upstream, in the experience design phase: applications in VR can be defined as either those based on wearable head-mounted systems, i.e., virtual reality viewers, composed of a stereoscopic display providing separate images for each eye and head movement tracking sensors, or some applications usable on monitors, or finally the so-called immersive quarries.

The academic discussion on the level of immersivity remains an open topic where different experiments lead to different arguments: for instance, in [11] automated virtual cave environments (CAVEs) are considered more immersive than head-mounted displays (HMDs).

HMDs can also be used in the case of AR technology: ideally these represent the most ergonomic and reliable solution to support complex manual tasks, as they preserve the natural point of view of the user. In AR they combine computer-generated content with the real-world view. The virtual content is rendered on a two-dimensional micro display and the lenses are placed so that the virtual object appears at a predefined and comfortable viewing distance on a plane [12].

Several such devices have recently been developed, particularly after the success of Microsoft HoloLens. Despite a surge in consumer access, the successful use of these devices in practical applications is still limited by the complexity of the calibration procedures required to ensure accurate spatial alignment between the real-world view and computer-generated elements.

In a recent classification it has been asserted that there are six types of interfaces for augmented, virtual and mixed reality systems: tangible, collaborative, device-based, sensor-based, hybrid, and multimodal interfaces, each one deserving a specific study [13].

3   Virtual Reality Experimentations in Italian Museums

In this section the first fundamental experiments in the museum sector with digital communication technologies are discussed, with a specific focus on the use of VR.

When people associate VR to the world of museums, they often speak of a virtual museum. At the time of its introduction in the early 1980s, a virtual (or digital) museum was the digital representation of the collections of a physically existing museum. This kind of realization met a twofold need. First, it offered curators an excellent solution both for archiving and consulting documentation on the collections and for managing administrative procedures (restoration, loans, etc.). The first configuration of the virtual museum coincided with the digitalization of the traditional index and inventory. At the same time, this technology could also be used to enhance the effectiveness of communication strategies, by encouraging a more conscious use of the museum's contents [14].

Fairly shared by the professions is the definition provided by V-MUST (Virtual Museum Transnational Network), a network of excellence funded by the European Union, which aims to provide the heritage sector with the tools and support to develop virtual museums that are educational, entertaining, enduring, and sustainable. According to this definition, a virtual museum is a digital entity that draws on the characteristics of a museum with the aim of complementing, enhancing, or augmenting the museum experience through personalization, interactivity, and richness of content. Virtual museums can act as a virtual footprint of a physical museum, or they can act independently, maintaining the status of authority conferred by ICOM in its definition of a museum [15].

Therefore, the definition of virtual museum differs from that of virtual tour, as they do not have the prerogatives of the museum itself. On a national level, several projects have been implemented over the years on the initiative of the Ministry of Cultural Heritage and Activities, with a view to creating a multimodal and connected cultural heritage system, such as the collaboration signed in 2011 between MIBAC and Google, which has provided the public with the possibility of taking virtual tours of some of the country's main archaeological sites. Street View allows users to explore world-famous wonders such as the excavations of Pompeii and Herculaneum, the Imperial Forum, the Colosseum and the Appia Antica Archaeological Park in Rome, the Villa D'Este in Tivoli, and the Reggia di Capodimonte in Naples.

Looking to the specific national museum contexts, the first multi-user virtual archaeological museum in Europe has been realized in 2008 and it was called Virtual Museum of Ancient Flaminia, available on-line or on-site inside the Roman National Museum of Dioclethian Thermal Baths, in Rome. It consists of four interactive stations, which allow users to enter this virtual reality environment at the same time. On the screen set up in the room, the exploration/visit is modified and updated in real time according to what the four users do in a dual perspective, individual and collective, with effects of general involvement. Four stops are planned in the "virtual journey": Ponte Milvio, the archaeological area of Grottarossa, the Villa of Livia and Malborghetto, a fortified farmhouse from the Middle Ages.

The Leonardo da Vinci National Museum of Science and Technology in Milan is one of the first institutions to equip itself, as early as 2014, with virtual reality visors and to provide visitors with immersive experiences for educational purposes, by means of an Oculus rift for immersive VR experience on board a submarine.

The project dedicated to the tomb of Nefertari, carried out in 2015 by ITLab IBAM CNR, has restored the tomb of Nefertari in three-dimensional form. The original environment was reconstructed in a room, through the projection of the virtual model, to be observed with special visors. The visitor was able to move around the room, making it possible to enjoy more than a traditional visit, enriched with information based on the study and analysis of the tomb and the description of the frescoes inside, the basic elements of the narrative.

Another of the first projects is the one realized by Zetema in 2016 for the visit of the Ara Pacis, entitled "l'Ara com'era", dedicated to the enhancement of the altar built by Augustus in Rome. The project is designed to give visitors an enriched experience, allowing them to see the colors that originally decorated the monument. This is done through a Samsung Gear VR visor which, in combination with a smartphone, allows access to certain Points of Interest, usable in AR or VR [16].

Another experimentation was conducted in 2017 at the MACRO in Rome, where it was possible to relive the experience of visiting the exhibition "From today to tomorrow. 24 h in contemporary art", which ended the previous year. Using Oculus Rift visors, one could move through the rooms, walk around the works, and rediscover a display that no longer exists. In this case VR becomes a means of preserving the memory of past exhibition, for a future audience.

Finally, another experience that combines VR with Spatial Augmented Reality (SAR), although not using head mounted displays, is that of "Invisible Archaeology", a temporary exhibition in 2019, conducted and promoted by the Egyptian Museum of Turin. The aim was to create an immersive exhibition, like a cave, in which video projections were the means to illustrate the results of the meticulous work of reassembling information, data and notions from the study and analysis of the finds. Focusing on the themes of research and interdisciplinarity as the tools with which to explore the biography of the Egyptological finds, and thanks to a strong emphasis on dissemination, the exhibition was able to actively involve the public by revealing, in ways and languages that are accessible to the younger generations in particular, the fascinating activity of investigation.

A further novelty of this exhibition is the possibility of taking a virtual tour. Developed in collaboration with Turin Polytechnic and the Robin studio, this project was produced using cameras capable of taking 360° photographs and generating a reconstruction of the tour. The possibility of using the virtual tour is an additional element that enriches the combination of real and digital content.

4 Lockdown: The Role of Virtual Reality

According to Istat in 2018, Italy boasts 4,908 museums, archaeological areas, monuments and eco-museums open to the public. So much so that in one Italian municipality out of three there is at least one museum structure [17].

The aim is now to provide a synthetic picture of how the world of museums has been modified by the impact of the Covid-19 epidemic, in relation to the adoption of digital technologies and the strategies of remote fruition implemented, with reference to the adoption of virtual reality solutions. For this reason, the most important statistical studies and data collections on a mainly national level are highlighted. This step is to be considered fundamental in the perspective of the search for a definition of the role of Virtual Reality in the museum context: what museums have experienced in the last year is and will remain a revolution of which, now, we must collect data to record the changes, and then analyze the results.

The Osservatorio per l'Innovazione Digitale nei Beni e Attività Culturali (Observatory for Digital Innovation in Cultural Heritage and Activities) of the School of Management of the Politecnico di Milano, in a study published by Il Sole 24 Ore in May 2020, recorded how during the months of travel restrictions the level of interest of Italians in online cultural activities increased. Moreover, in the last two years 83% of Italian museums, monuments and archaeological sites have invested in digital innovation, focusing mainly on services to support on-site visits (48%) and cataloguing and digitization of the collection (46%), both activities preparatory to rethinking the value proposition both online and onsite [18].

The International Council of Museums Italy (ICOM), from its first survey on the effects of the pandemic on museums, pointed out that the temporary forced closure of museums around the world has brought digital communication with the public to the fore. To name but a few, there is evidence of an increase in digital services on offer, including virtual tours.

The first results of the survey of museum audiences, published in July 2020, show that 71.5% of respondents visited the institutions' websites or social profiles during the period of closure due to the pandemic. Most females (75,8%), people aged between 55 and 64 (74,7%), and residents of central regions (74,5%) decided to access the digital content. 90% of the visitors of the museums' websites were satisfied (from quite to very) with the experience and the quality of the digital offers. Virtual visits and tours as well as cultural insights (e.g., presentation of works by experts) were the most popular. Computers and mobile phones are the two most frequently used devices, even in combination [19].

The surveys on digital communication in museums at the time of Covid-19, carried out by Icom Italia through direct observation, a survey with 5 macro-questions addressed to 353 museums in the first phase of the pandemic and a follow up on 130 museums following the DPCM of 3 November 2020, also explored the evolution of communication since the first lockdown, revealing that about half of the sample of museums analyzed revised their internal organization during the period of forced closure, dedicating more resources to digital communication and improving their performance even after reopening to the public.

The results were presented in an online conference in December 2020, entitled "Digital Communication of Museums: Challenges and Opportunities at the Time of Covid-19", show that most museums produced a very high percentage of ad-hoc content during this lockdown period, compared to the content usually published on their digital channels.

Moreover, it emerges that the museums' digital offer has significantly increased, mainly through an intensification of social media activities and the creation of new content (especially in the form of virtual tours, pre-recorded videos, live webinars, podcasts), which in many cases have given prominence to the collections held in storage, generating a reflection on the need to deal with their digitization [20].

The XII Civita Report Next Generation Culture, titled "Digital technologies and immersive languages for new cultural audiences" is an important opportunity to reflect on a wide range of digital transformation processes underway in the cultural sector, marked by the crisis of the pandemic period and more than ever affected by new developments.

In this analysis, technologies, which are already so essential in the processes of heritage conservation, are assumed to become increasingly part of the tools of production, use and dissemination of culture, as well as the primary means of communication. Wide margins of growth will concern museum gamification as well as interaction, thanks to innovative solutions of applying Virtual Reality and Augmented Reality [21]. Another survey aimed at the audience is the one commissioned by Impresa Cultura Italia-Confcommercio to analyze "cultural consumption" during the lockdown and carried out through interviews conducted between 18 and 21 May 2020 on a sample of

1,001 Italians aged between 18 and 74. This study examines the Italian digital cultural offer, comparing it with the data on "live consumption" for each sector. One figure that gives us pause for thought, however, is that relating to virtual visits to museums and archaeological sites: only 4% had made a complete virtual visit, compared with 17% who had looked at something but without paying much attention. 28% said they were not aware of the existence of online virtual visits and 51% knew about them but did not use them. However, the study does not discourage investment in this area, on the contrary, It reveals a very interesting fact. In fact, it reveals a very interesting fact. The data revealed that a crucial factor during lockdown is, and continues to be, stress. People's psycho-emotional state has suffered a slump which, according to this study, has greatly affected expectations of culture: basically, the number of those who want to enjoy cultural activities has grown (+15%) compared to December 2019, while there is a + 14% for those who want to "relax", a + 8% for those who want to "do something different". On the other hand, the percentages of all those who want to find a means of personal growth in culture dropped: −15% of those who want to expand their knowledge, −11% of those who want to learn new things [22].

A less explicit datum is the fact that the most recent projects, even those that arose because of the lockdown, make prevalent use of the desktop medium, since immersive Virtual Reality fruition, that is through a visor, is in any case understood as on-site fruition. This appears as a contradiction since VR should be able to guarantee an immersive remote fruition. However, although there are now low-cost VR viewers, these tools are not so widespread and therefore, in most cases, it is the cultural institution that sets up the tool on its premises, rather than adopting them as tools for remote fruition. Examples are the virtual tours of the Ancona Networked Museums (MIRA), the Uffizi Gallery in Florence and the Vatican Museums.

5   Conclusion

Based on these considerations, this is a phase of great change, in which museums are not only called upon to take on a new role in the social context, but must also remodel their traditional assets, creating new possible scenarios of experimentation with experience and assessing their impact also from a social and wellbeing point of view.

The museum is in fact a perceptive space, where perception is the process by which we receive information from the environment which the human brain processes and organizes to give it meaning.

In the museum environment, the infinite possibilities of creating semantic relationships between space, objects, medium and observer develop effects that can achieve different goals. Therefore, one cannot limit the concept of "space" to the "physical" one, or the concept of audience to the set of people "accessing" the museum space. Considering the impact museums have shown in this debate, it is necessary to experiment with new solutions to reach audiences in an effective way, even outside the physical space of the museum itself, without however breaking the strong connection of belonging to that space.

To bridge this gap, technologies can come into play. The idea is that the real and the virtual constitute a continuum, the result of a joint planning, and not an *aut-aut,* in the museum offer. Reproducibility" in Benjamin's sense [23] is therefore not a distortion of the "real" world or an annihilation of the aura of the work of art but opens new scenarios in which terms such as reality and aura take on new meanings, closer to the needs of today's public [24].

The pandemic also made it more urgent to adopt models of governance capable of combating inequalities and promoting inclusive welfare. Thanks to technology, the museum can be broken down and reassembled according to its specific purpose, without losing its identity as a structure capable of contextualizing meanings and generating a sense of belonging and identity, both individual and social.

In conclusion, most of the main Italian museums have a virtual tour available on the Internet, and, especially in response to the lockdown, more and more institutions have felt the need to publish their own virtual museum as a new way to make their collection accessible. There are new studies comparing virtual tours: in "Evaluating Museum Virtual Tours: The Case Study" [25], the virtual tour of sixteen Italian museums is closely analyzed. All the studies analyzed so far only partially meet the new requirements, as they often aim at replicating the experience of a live visit, through a screen or a cardboard.

VR, if accompanied by a solid storytelling that starts from the study of the museum collection, allows the creation of immersive, interactive, and collaborative virtual environments, it can represent a decisive paradigm of innovation both in a period of emergency and in normal life, able to cope with the most diverse storytelling needs. The physical presence of the visitor in the museum is certainly encouraged as much as possible, when this can be done in total safety, but it is necessary to prepare other tools of fruition, able to extend the museum space and intercept new targets.

VR can provide people with disabilities with alternative forms of access [26]. For instance, a visitor with a disability does not have the ability to visit the second floor of Shakespeare's birthplace in Stratford-upon-Avon: thus, site managers installed a VR exhibit on the second floor that offers a virtual tour of the upper floor [27].

In this way the museum can reach those people who, due to personal limitations, cannot go to the museum: reaching these audiences should be at the basis of the mission of an institution acting in the perspective of social welfare.

References

1. Cisternino, D., et al.: Virtual portals for a smart fruition of historical and archaeological contexts. In: Sixth International Conference Augmented and Virtual Reality, and Computer Graphics (AVR 2019), Santa Maria al Bagno (Lecce), Italy (2019)
2. Milgram, P., Takemura, H., Utsumi, A., Kishino F.: Augmented reality: a class of displays on the reality-virtuality continuum. In: Proceedings of SPIE 2351, Telemanipulator and Telepresence Technologies (1995)
3. Speicher, M., Hall, B., Nebeling, M.: What is Mixed Reality? (2019)
4. Carmigniani, J., Furht, B., Anisetti, M., Ceravolo, P., Damiani, E., Ivkovic, M.: Augmented reality technologies, systems and applications. Multimedia Tools Appl. **51**, 341–377 (2010)
5. Azuma, R.T.: A survey of augmented reality. Presence Teleoperators Virtual Environ. **6**(4), 355–385 (1997)
6. Slater, M., Sanchez-Vives, M.V.: Enhancing our lives with immersive virtual reality. Front. Robot. AI **3**, 74 (2016)

7. Gutiérrez, M.A.A., Vexo, F., Thalmann, D.: Stepping into Virtual Reality. Springer , London (2008). https://doi.org/10.1007/978-1-84800-117-6
8. Slater, M., Wilbur, S.: A framework for immersive virtual environments (FIVE): speculations on the role of presence in virtual environments. Presence Teleoperators Virtual Environ. **6**(6), 603–616 (1997)
9. Ijsselsteijn, W., Riva, G.: Being there: the experience of presence in mediated environments. In: Emerging Communication, vol. 5, p. 3 (2003)
10. Diemer, J., Alpers, G., Peperkorn, H., Youssef, S., Mühlberger, A.: The impact of perception and presence on emotional reactions: a review of research in virtual reality Front. Psychol. **6**, 26 (2015)
11. Carrozzino, M., Bergamasco, M.: Beyond virtual museums: experiencing immersive virtual reality in real museums. J. Cult. Herit. **11**–4, 452–458 (2010)
12. Cakmakci, O., Rolland, J.: Head-worn displays: a review. Disp. Technol. J. **2**, 199–216 (2006)
13. Bekele, M., Pierdicca, R., Frontoni, E., Malinverni, E., Gain, J.: A survey of augmented, virtual, and mixed reality for cultural heritage. J. Comput. Cult. Heritage **11**, 1–36 (2018)
14. Valentino, P.A.: I formati della memoria. Beni culturali e nuove tecnologie alle soglie del terzo millennio, a cura di P. Galluzzi, Firenze (1997)
15. Cordis Europa. https://cordis.europa.eu/project/id/270404/it. Accessed 1 June 2021
16. Mandarano, N.: Musei e media digitali, Carocci editore, Roma (2019)
17. Istat. https://www.istat.it/it/files/2019/12/LItalia-dei-musei_2018.pdf. Accessed 1 June 2021
18. Il Sole 24 Ore. https://www.ilsole24ore.com/art/nel-lockdown-musei-piu-social-ma-solo-su-quattro-ha-piano-digitale-ADYWzPT?refresh_ce=1. Accessed 1 June 2021
19. Icom Italia. http://www.icom-italia.org/musei-e-covid-19-questionario-di-icom-italia/. Accessed 1 June 2021
20. Icom Italia. http://www.icom-italia.org/wp-content/uploads/2020/12/ICOMItalia.ICOM_RL.Comunicazione.17dicembre.2020_Landi.pdf. Accessed 1 June 2021
21. Civita. https://www.civita.it/News/Presentazione-del-nuovo-Rapporto-Civita-Next-Genera tion-Culture.-Tecnologie-digitali-e-linguaggi-immersivi-per-nuovi-pubblici-della-cultura. Accessed 1 June 2021
22. Confcommercio. https://www.confcommercio.it/-/cultura-digitale-covid. Accessed 1 June 2021
23. Benjamin, W.: L'opera d'arte nell'epoca della sua riproducibilità tecnica, Einaudi, Torino, (1936), ed. italiana (1966)
24. Gatto, C., D'Errico, G., Nuccetelli, F., De Luca, V., Paladini, G.I., De Paolis, L.T.: XR-based mindfulness and art therapy: facing the psychological impact of Covid-19 emergency. In: De Paolis, L.T., Bourdot, P. (eds.) AVR 2020. LNCS, vol. 12243, pp. 147–155. Springer, Cham (2020). https://doi.org/10.1007/978-3-030-58468-9_11
25. Kabassi, K., Amelio, A., Komianos, V., Oikonomou, K.: Evaluating museum virtual tours: the case study of Italy. Information **10**(11), 351 (2019)
26. Eusebio, C., Teixeira, L., Carneiro, M. J.: Tools and Applications for Accessible Tourism. Business Science Reference (2021)
27. Goodall, B., Pottinger, G., Dixon, T., Russell, H.: Heritage property, tourism and the UK disability discrimination act. Property Manage. **22**(5), 345–357 (2004)

Uncovering the Potential of Digital Technologies to Promote Railways Landscape: Rail to Land Project

Ramonaa Quattrini[1], Roberto Pierdicca[1(✉)], Ana Belen Berrocal[2], Clara Zamorano[2], José Rocha[3], and Isabel Varajão[3]

[1] Department of Civil Engineering, Building and Architecture,
Via Brecce Bianche 12, 60131 Ancona, Italy
{r.quattrini,r.pierdicca}@staff.univpm.it
[2] ETSI Caminos, Polytechnic University of Madrid, Madrid, Spain
{anabelen.berrocal,clara.zamorano}@upm.es
[3] Center for Computer Graphics (CCG), University of Minho, Campus de Azurém,
Edifício 14, 4800-058 Guimarães, Portugal
isabel.varajao@ccg.pt

Abstract. This paper describes the preliminary results of Railtoland, an European project funded by the Erasmus + KA 203 call. The aim of the project is to explore the social and educational value of the European railways landscape as a common heritage and as a catalyst for processes of consolidation of European identity, social cohesion and shaping of local cultures, also for the well-being of individuals. To achieve such result, Digital Technologies such as Augmented and Virtual reality will be extensively used, in order to understand if the landscape surrounding the railways can be valorised to the broader public. A mobile application, featured with multiple functions enables the user to discover the landscape and the cultural heritage at different scales of representation, exploiting 3D modeling optimisation and geo-location. We expect to reach the broader public, collecting useful insight about the potential of Digital Technologies for the promotion of landscape.

Keywords: Augmented and Virtual reality · Mobile app · Landscape · Cultural heritage · Railways

1 Introduction

Intangible Cultural Heritage (CH), landscape and built heritage require to be more and more tied in order to boost the definition and the perceiving of common roots and identity in Europe. Since 2005, Faro's Convention [4] encourages to recognise that objects and places are not only important in themselves, but also in relationship to what is important about CH. They are important because of the meanings and uses that people attach to them and the values they represent. A very representative heritage, in this light, is undoubtedly the railways

L. T. De Paolis et al. (Eds.): AVR 2021, LNCS 12980, pp. 315–325, 2021.
https://doi.org/10.1007/978-3-030-87595-4_23

heritage, so far recognised as a technical heritage while recently it is highlighted as a crucial heritage in the building of the European history and distinctiveness. The Railtoland project[1] aims to explore the social and educational value of the European railways landscape as a common heritage and as a catalyst for processes of consolidation of European identity, social cohesion and shaping of local cultures, also for the well-being of individuals. The idea on the basis of project, financed in 2019 and currently on going, received reinforcement considering that the 2021 has been declared the European Year of Rail[2], aiming at supporting sustainable and green transition. The research presented in this paper tries to consolidate new paradigms and methods to become a stimulus to communities' engagement, heritage recognizability and territorial development. In this light, digitisation strategies are constituting an emerging field of research, boosting the availability of useful tools for heritage democratisation and landscape sense of belonging, beside the only tourist purpose. Yet, the potentials connected to the use of Digital Cultural Heritage (DCH) are underestimated [12]. Therefore, this paper presents a collaborative and inter sector research approach in which digitisation practices are applied to a peculiar railways line: the Oporto - Vigo Line. The research also moves from the lack of assessed protocols for the use of 3D and complex digital cultural assets and aims to fill a gap in educational activities for engineers and architects, easily transferable in professional skills.

2   The RAILtoLAND Project

RAILtoLAND is an European project funded by the Erasmus + KA 203 call for the internationalisation of higher education institutions. It involves six institutions from four different European countries and runs from 2019 to 2022. The RAILtoLAND project aims to explore the social and educational value of the European cultural landscape as a common heritage and as a catalyst for processes of consolidation of European identity, social cohesion, formation of local cultures and human well-being. To this end, RAILtoLAND draws on two essential resources of European cultural heritage: the railways network and the European cultural landscapes. Indeed, the railroad has played a key role in the physical construction of Europe, especially after the Second World War. Moreover, its structuring and cohesive function was essential in the consolidation of European identity. In addition, Europe has a great diversity of cultural landscapes of great aesthetic, symbolic and heritage value. A common heritage that reinforces the sense of community and improves the overall quality of life of its inhabitants. RAILtoLAND therefore seeks to train both higher education students from partner institutions and the general public in the recognition of the values and diversity of European railroad landscapes. To this end, the project tests innovative practices of open education supported by digital technologies. Among others, the design of a pilot project for a mobile application on the Oporto - Vigo

---

[1] https://railtoland.eu/.

[2] https://europa.eu/year-of-rail/index_en.

railway line, by which the landscape units along the line are explained and interpreted, as well as the singular points of natural or cultural interest. The design of the structure and contents of this application derives from a collaborative process of horizontal work between students and teachers and researchers involved in the project. This method facilitates the direct involvement and motivation of the student, who acquires an active role in the conceptualisation of a digital product of generalised use. Innovative learning techniques are used, such as learning by doing, which tries to break the gap between the theoretical world offered to the student and the practical experience essential to fix concepts, or Design Thinking, aimed at improving communication skills, creativity and critical thinking. It also aims to reinforce communication skills through collaborative work dynamics.

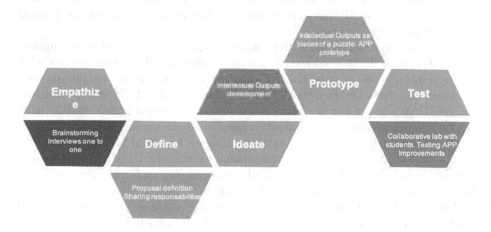

Fig. 1. The design thinking method applied to RailtoLand project

3 Digitization Strategies for Railways Landscape Heritage

Digital technologies for the creation of 3D models are nowadays the essential tools to undertake strategic actions at landscape level. Arguably, the 3D model can be the essential component in the synergy of mapping data, fieldwork and notation, perspectives and digital fabrication. The development of 3D modelling software by and large emerged from graphical software, architecture programs and computer gaming [7].

To support a development of identity generating landscapes, systematic measurements and documentation of how the public feels when running through the landscape are necessary. Realistic-looking landscape visualisations from a pedestrian perspective, are known to be suitable for experiencing landscape from different scales of representation [13]. The challenge, however, remains how landscape can be visualised as effectively and efficiently as possible. Specifically, the visualisation of multifaceted scenarios require additional amounts of stimuli development work, in which Augmented and Virtual Reality could play a pivotal role [2,3]. A key challenge for realistic-looking 3D visualisation is to simulate landscape at high fidelity. This is often difficult, due to time-intensive and costly workflows for geometry updates, and the adequate 3D model creation of landscape features, including buildings and/or vegetation.

In such scenario, the project activities consisted in the definition of two levels of representation, and to study the more suitable approach to warrant the right balance between details and accuracy. In other words, we focused on satellite imagery to produce the Digital Elevation Models and field surveys to focus on specific Points of interests.

The remotely sensed digitization activity was performed exploiting both Shuttle Radar Topography Mission (SRTM) and Landsat-8 datasets. We have produced a script in R that can be used for the reconstruction of the Digital Elevation Model [14].

The resolution of the model was not so high, but it's possible to improve the resolution to the desired level just downloading satellite imagery data with higher resolution or coupling them with other data acquisition techniques. It's important to stress the fact that ground surveying using GNSS system or airborne LIDAR surveys are, of course, more accurate than data from satellite. But the use of such acquisition techniques is also time-consuming and more expensive, so in many cases the use of satellite imagery for DEM reconstruction can be a good compromise. It can be convenient to consider DEM, created in this way, as a geographical basic map, in which is possible to further localise other data obtained with other acquisition techniques.

The on-field digitisation activity was designed starting from the list of 50 Points of Interest (POIs) along the railways line, defined by the partnership according to geography, territorial planning, cultural heritage and design experts. According to the didactic guide, that is one of the project outputs, they are clustered in a) Built Heritage (Constructed sets related to the railway line, Industrial clusters of a certain size); b) Natural Heritage (Fluvial, Fluvio-marine, Coastal, Wetlands, Landscape); c) Cultural Heritage (Military architecture, Traditional architecture, Ecclesiastical architecture, Urban architecture, Agricultural). Among all the POIs, the instrumental digital activities are planned to involve: Sao Bento Station and don Luis Bridge, in Oporto; Railway Museum of Lousado, Balneario do Casterjo, Viaducto de Durraes, 5 Fortresses on the seaside (namely: Forte da Vinha, Forte de Paçô, Forte do Cão, Forte da Lagarteira, Forte da Ínsua), the Fortaleza and a railway steel bridge in Valenca.

Thanks to remote sensing techniques and digital survey activities on field the following data will be able to populate the application and then to design the digital travel experience: texts, images, videos, sounds, 360° pictures, point clouds and 3D models.

Fig. 2. The final result from the computation of remotely sensed data

4   Designing a Traveller Digital Experience: The RailToLand App

Complying with the project's goals for developing a handheld railway navigation system, capable of providing didactic and interactive features to promote certain culturally and historically relevant Points of Interest (POI) along Oporto - Vigo track, a cross-platform mobile application was proposed. Its graphical layout and interactivity were specified based on a design process [9], which allowed a better understanding of the project scope, stakeholders requirements, as well as a more proper problem definition. Such design activities aimed to support and orient the development of an innovative solution that seeks to offer a satisfactory and

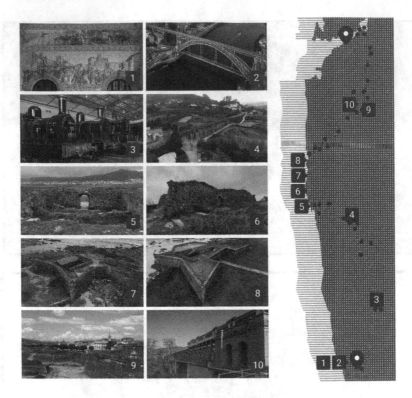

Fig. 3. The planned survey campaign regarding several POIs

meaningful experience to users. The involved creative stages are presented as follows.

The first stage of the design process (Research/Insigth) consisted in understanding the goals of the project and its underlying problem, throughout activities that involved research, meetings with the stakeholders, workshops, benchmarking, brainstorming sessions, and a live experience of the trip Oporto – Vigo.

In the second stage (Defining), the information gathered during the previous one was considered, along with the following macro-requirement: to improve train passengers experience, using railway Oporto - Vigo track as a case-study, by presenting entertaining digital contents while disseminating knowledge regarding the available cultural heritage sites and natural landscapes, accessible in the palm of the hand. After that, the definition of the problem in a user-centred view was pursued, which resulted in the specification of the 'How Might We' (HMW) questions.

To answer the HMW questions previously established, in the third stage (Ideation), a brainstorm session was performed among stakeholders, using Milanote online platform [11], where shared ideas were organised into groups that were afterwards filtered by priority, resulting in a list of features considered mandatory to be implemented. Following the Ideation, the Prototyping stage using

Fig. 4. Live experience pictures of the Porto - Vigo railways trip

Figma digital design online platform [5] was carried out. In this sense, firstly, some medium-fidelity wireframes were created. Then, an internal remote workshop with stakeholders took place, where an extensive checklist questionnaire allowed to evaluate, not only the design techniques implemented, but also the technological challenges associated with the integration of huge and computationally burdensome contents into mobile devices, which have limited processing power and storage. After gathering the feedback of the stakeholders, some refinements and internal pilot tests were made, which enabled to dive deeper into the development of the interactive prototype, considering the Usability Heuristics [10].

RailToLand mobile solution experience design should meet mobile users' unique requirements and restrictions, considering the following aspects, proposed by [8]: mobile user experience (UX) design focused on accessibility, discoverability and efficiency to optimise on-the-go interactive experiences.

Designing for mobile devices becomes more challenging than for laptop/desktop, not only because of the difference of screen sizes, but also due to the required balance between available computational resources and the amount and complexity of the content that can be integrated in a given application, with a corresponding impact on usability experience.

With this in mind, a cross platform app was developed, targeting both Android [6] and iOS Operative Systems [1], following the design principles of both platforms.

Regarding the logical organisation, we've clustered the app into 3 major tabs: 'Discover' tab, which provides pre-journey functionalities (Fig. 5 on the left); 'Experience' tab, to manage the ongoing experience (Fig. 5 on the right); and, finally, the 'Viewed' tab that handles post-journey experience features (Fig. 6 on the left). These tabs are described on the app onboarding screen, in the form of instructions to users.

More specifically, the discover tab is composed of a scrollable list of culturally and historically relevant POIs that can be found along Porto - Vigo railway track,

Fig. 5. RailToLand APP prototype: in the left side, the 'Discover' tab is presented; the right side depicts the 'Experience' tab in action

sorted according to the sequence of train stations, which allows users to preview the information about these POIs, in the form of text and images.

The core of the application is the 'Experience' tab that makes available a Porto - Vigo railway track digital map with overlaid POIs properly placed, based on real GPS coordinates. The proximity to POIs triggers notifications that indicate their relative position - providing visual tips that allow to grasp which is the window row (right or left) in line of sight with them -, as well as their distance. Moreover, the user can explore the different types of multimedia contents associated to POIs, including photos, videos, 3D Objects, Street View and, also, interact with the Augmented Reality mode. Bookmarking favourite POIS and sharing them on social media are available options, too. The map is delimited by Landscape Units, each one having an associated audible description media content that is timely delivered to the user when the train switches from one to another. It is also possible to view a location-based synchronised video recording of the train driver perspective, as well as to take pictures along the trip, which are stored in relation to the current Landscape Unit.

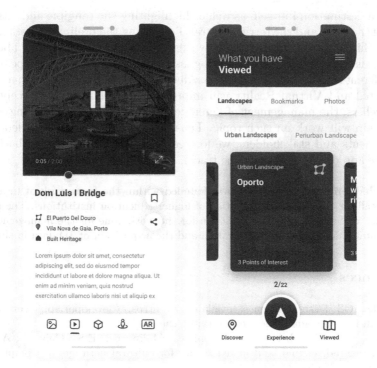

Fig. 6. RailToLand APP prototype: in the left side, the POIs contents interactions is presented; the right side depicts the 'Viewed' tab for post-experience utilisation purposes

Finally, the 'Viewed' tab regards to the post-trip moment and is composed by a scrollable list containing details of the previously traversed Landscape Units, bookmarked POIs and taken photos, which the user can easily revisit.

5   Conclusion and Future Steps

Railways allow the observation of landscapes in a unique way compared to other modes of transport because, on the one hand, their layout must be very faithful to the original topography of the terrain, at least in conventional trains, and on the other hand, because the traveller can surrender himself to contemplation. New technologies offer the unprecedented possibility of widening the passenger's viewing window by providing new perspectives or images from different periods, for example. This digital experience of the traveller also allows access to elements of interest beyond the traveller's visual reach. It is therefore an amplification of the scenic options of the journey, and an opportunity to make the journey attractive, not just a necessary way between two points of interest, origin and destination. Indeed, digital technologies applied to railway landscapes make the journey a destination in itself, as well as highlighting the tangible and intangible values of the train and the territories travelled. Being the preliminary stage of the project, this paper attempts to acknowledge the research community about the approach used to tackle the challenging issue of representing landscape and CH with different scales of representations. Albeit digital technologies such as mobile Augmented and Virtual Reality can improve railway landscape perception by the travellers, the management of heterogeneous 3D data is compelling and the partnership will work on such topic. Thus, beside transferring knowledge with both students and stakeholders, we foresee to collect the users' feedback when using the app directly in along the track.

Acknowledgement. The project was founded within the framework of Erasmus + KA 203 call for the internationalisation of higher education institutions. The authors would like to thank all the partners team for the work done for the management, the implementation of the mobile application and the acquisition of 3D data in situ.

References

1. Apple: iOS Design Themes, available at https://developer.apple.com/design/human-interface-guidelines/ios/overview/themes/
2. Bekele, M.K., Pierdicca, R., Frontoni, E., Malinverni, E.S., Gain, J.: A survey of augmented, virtual, and mixed reality for cultural heritage. J. Comput. Cult. Heritage (JOCCH) **11**(2), 1–36 (2018)
3. Cureton, P.: Strategies for landscape representation: digital and analogue techniques. Taylor & Francis (2016)
4. Fairclough, G., Dragićević-Šešić, M., Rogač-Mijatović, L., Auclair, E., Soini, K.: The faro convention, a new paradigm for socially-and culturally-sustainable heritage action? Culture **8**, 9–19 (2014)
5. Figma: Available at https://www.figma.com/
6. Google: Design for Android, available at https://developer.android.com/design/
7. Hochschild, V., Braun, A., Sommer, C., Warth, G., Omran, A.: Visualizing landscapes by geospatial techniques. In: Edler, D., Jenal, C., Kühne, O. (eds.) Modern Approaches to the Visualization of Landscapes. RSRL, pp. 47–78. Springer, Wiesbaden (2020). https://doi.org/10.1007/978-3-658-30956-5_4
8. Interaction Design Foundation: Mobile User Experience (UX) Design, available at https://www.interaction-design.org/literature/topics/mobile-ux-design/
9. Interaction Design Foundation: Design Thinking (2009). Available at https://www.interaction-design.org/literature/topics/design-thinking/
10. Nielsen, J.: 10 Usability Heuristics for User Interface Design (Apr 24, 1994; Updated Nov 15, 2020). Available at https://www.nngroup.com/articles/ten-usability-heuristics/
11. Milanote: Available at https://milanote.com/
12. Pierdicca, R.: Mapping Chimu's settlements for conservation purposes using UAV and close range photogrammetry. The virtual reconstruction of Palacio Tschudi, Chan Chan, Peru. Digital Appl. Archaeol. Cult. Heritage **8**, 27–34 (2018)

13. Quattrini, R., Pierdicca, R., Paolanti, M., Clini, P., Nespeca, R., Frontoni, E.: Digital interaction with 3d archaeological artefacts: evaluating user's behaviours at different representation scales. Digital Appl. Archaeol. Cult. Heritage **18**, e00148 (2020)

14. Salekin, S., Burgess, J.H., Morgenroth, J., Mason, E.G., Meason, D.F.: A comparative study of three non-geostatistical methods for optimising digital elevation model interpolation. ISPRS international journal of geo-information **7**(8), 300 (2018)

Mobile Extended Reality for the Enhancement of an Underground Oil Mill: A Preliminary Discussion

Lucio Tommaso De Paolis[1]($\boxtimes$), Sofia Chiarello[2], Giovanni D'Errico[3], Carola Gatto[2], Benito Luigi Nuzzo[2], and Giada Sumerano[2]

[1] Department of Engineering for Innovation, University of Salento, Lecce, Italy
lucio.depaolis@unisalento.it
[2] Department of Cultural Heritage, University of Salento, Lecce, Italy
[3] Department of Electrical Engineering and Information Technology,
University of Naples, Federico II, Naples, Italy

Abstract. The enhancement of the cultural heritage and the promotion of the territory, with a peculiar attention to alternative routes and decentralized places of interest, is receiving more and more attention from the ICT world. In particular, Extended Reality (XR) technology (Virtual, Augmented and Mixed Reality) is becoming quite pivotal in this process. In this context, two main critical issues are experienced: (a) places accessibility, in particular for sites that are often difficult to visit and (b) valorisation of itineraries and rural heritage, for those points-of-interest that are particularly important for the narration of the territory, even though outside the mainstream circuit. This is a perspective paper to preliminarily discuss the feasibility of two different widely used mobile applications, aimed at exploiting virtual and mixed reality technologies to promote an underground oil mill in Salento. The underlying problems and the steps that the authors intend to follow to develop the system will be briefly treated.

Keywords: Extended reality · Virtual cultural heritage · Mixed reality · Place accessibility · Rural heritage · Itineraries

1 Introduction

In the Salento area there are the so called "Green Gold Mines". This is a series of underground oil mills that, using the olives of the area, were used to produce the oil.

These environments were originally created for the preservation of wheat, but after the contact with the Byzantine culture occurred in the IX century, it was decided to change and devote themselves to the more complex and profitable oil trade.

Only a small part of this oil was used by farmers for alimentary purposes, in fact it was mainly exported from the port of Gallipoli to the big cities of Europe

© Springer Nature Switzerland AG 2021
L. T. De Paolis et al. (Eds.): AVR 2021, LNCS 12980, pp. 326–335, 2021.
https://doi.org/10.1007/978-3-030-87595-4_24

as a fuel capable of generating light or as a fundamental ingredient to produce soap. Only with the passing of centuries and the advent of electric energy, oil became one of the basic ingredients of Apulian and Salento cooking.

The oil mills were built underground between 2 and 5 m below street level, dug into the rock by enlarging karst cavities already present, for security reasons in order to hide to the sight of possible enemies the stages of processing but also for optimal production; the temperature of the underground mills remains at a constant 18 degrees Celsius year-round, and this keeps the oil flowing freely even during the chilly winter months of production [1]. The oil mills were accessed by a staircase (often covered with a barrel vault) that generally led into a large room where workers put the olives on a stone press, which consisted of a horizontal slab sitting under a vertical wheel. A mule attached to the milestone's wooden axel walked around the press, turning the wheel and crushing the olives into a paste. The olive paste was taken from the tanks and deposited on a stone where it was spread on discs in the shape of a rush crown (called "fiscoli") for pressing. At the foot of the press there was a well of circular or square shape, in which was inserted the wooden vat in which it collected the oil pressed from the presses [2].

Adjacent to the large room were set up the presses and several tanks dug into the rock. Other rooms were used as stables, kitchen, and dormitory of the workers. Without direct light, the "trappeto" (this is the ancient name of the underground oil mill) was illuminated by various lamps. The only source of light and air exchange came from one or two holes drilled in the center of the vault of the main compartment.

The working procedure took place with the "entry" of the olives from a funnel-shaped hole through which they were conveyed, by gravimetric fall, in the deposits (called "sciave") placed along the two side corridors.

Due to their construction characteristics and to the increasing industrialization, the underground oil mills have undergone an inexorable decline to the point of being completely abandoned. These environments play an important part in the context of the peasant culture and landscape of Salento and constitute significant evidence of the past and an important heritage of the present, which, although no longer suitable for current living conditions, contributes to the amazingness of these surviving places of a precious vanished world.

At the beginning of the XVI century, because of the growing danger of Turkish attacks, in the Kingdom of Naples and, in particular, in the Salento area, the Spanish viceroys ordered the improvement of coastal defense systems. In the hinterland the pre-existing watchtowers were readapted and new ones were built. They were, moreover, fortified castles, farms and strengthened the city walls. Torcito Farm, located near the current city of Cannole (Lecce, Italy), resting on a slight plateau, a few kilometers from the sea, was strongly exposed to the danger of Turkish attacks, but at the same time was a good point of sighting. For this reason, Torcito Farm was transformed from a simple house of farmers into a fortified farm. The antiquity of the village of Torcito is also attested by the existence of a crypt and some tombs dug into the rock related to a settlement of monks of greek - italic rite (sec. VIII–IX). Torcito Farm is shown in Figs. 1.

Fig. 1. Torcito farm

At Torcito Farm there is an extensive underground oil mill of considerable historical importance. Unfortunately, the oil mill is not preserved in good conditions and would need an important restoration. Figures 2 shows the underground oil mill of the Torcito Farm.

In this scenario technologies will allow the user to visit the underground oil mill of Masseria Torcito (which is currently closed to the public) not only by encountering it along the route of the Via Francigena, but also by installing the application in any other geographical context. The final objective will be to allow greater accessibility and to enhance, through the use of augmented and virtual reality, a place that, although not part of the usual tourist routes, is of great historical interest. In order to obtain the model of the hypogeum space, the photogrammetric acquisition of the site will be carried out and, at the same time, 360° spherical images will be acquired for the development of the VR application [3]. Similar acquisition technologies have been adopted in the case study of the Palmieri Hypogeum in Lecce, where the photogrammetric model is accessible via web, through portable devices and a stereoscopic workstation installed at the MUST in Lecce [4].

An application has also been developed for the chamber tombs of Taranto, using photomodelling and digital photogrammetry techniques that have made the model fully usable through the RealTime3D platform [5,6].

The use of AR and VR technologies for the enhancement of cultural heritage in rural settings often presents technological limitations due to the possible absence of an Internet signal in those areas. To overcome this problem, alternative solutions are often applied, such as the use of markers with the hybrid

Fig. 2. The underground oil mill of the Torcito farm

technique [7]. Currently, the technique of virtual portals is very interesting in the field of Mixed Reality applied to cultural heritage.

2   The Importance of Virtual Cultural Heritage

It is widely believed that cultural heritage is steadily declining. As new treasures emerge from previously unexplored or ignored places, more buildings and sites are being compromised by natural or human action. This process leads to the disappearance of important historical documents and artistic assets.

Modern technologies are getting involved in most spheres of human activities, they play an important role also in cultural heritage care. There is worldwide interest in Virtual Reality (VR) technology in Cultural Heritage to recreate historical sites and events for educational purposes. The importance and strength of VR lies in the ability to open places and see things not normally accessible to people.

Virtual Cultural Heritage (VCH) is the use of electronic media to recreate or interpret culture and cultural artifacts as they are today or as they may have been in the past. By recreating an environment or simulating something about an ancient culture, virtual heritage applications provide a bridge between the people of ancient culture and contemporary users [7,8].

One of the most important VR applications is the reconstruction of 3D environments aimed at the study of cultural heritage; Virtual Reality allows to examine high-resolution three-dimensional environments reconstructed using information retrieved from archaeological and historical studies and to navigate these environments to test new teaching methodologies or to evaluate learning [9,10].

The entertainment in educational applications is very important to create a motivating and successful environment for learning. Another important factor is immersion, a measure of absorption and engagement with the virtual environment, important to both entertainment and education. This introduces a new combined factor: edutainment, a neologism created by combining the words education and entertainment, refers to any form of entertainment aimed at an educational role. By combining the educational journey with entertainment components, edutainment makes the learning environment much more engaging and fun and the learning process less tedious [11].

Virtual reality (VR) technology allows the creation of edutainment applications for the public as well.

The development of video games for the promotion of cultural heritage has proven to be one of the best strategies, returning excellent results in terms of learning. Creating virtual environments in which to immerse students provides an easier way to learn about ancient cultures and places that no longer exist or may be too dangerous or too expensive to visit [12]. For an enjoyable and informative experience, it is crucial to allow the user to interact with the content, so that they can learn the targeted information in a stimulating way. Natural and easy ways to navigate the virtual environment and the availability of a shared virtual space also create new possibilities for collaboration and interaction [10]. Several VR/AR applications in cultural heritage have been developed with an aim to improve the knowledge of monuments and archaeological contexts in Salento.

For example, the MediaEvo project aimed to develop a multichannel and multisensory platform in cultural heritage and to experiment the realization of an educational game oriented to the knowledge of medieval history and society. Players can explore the city of Otranto (Lecce), reconstructed using available historical sources as it was in the Middle Ages, and learn about the medieval world through virtual experience [13,14]. Within an archaeological context the "absent" is often what needs to be told, what can be reconstructed through some traces, but not fully visible. Therefore, the main difficulty is the lack of tangible elements and the need is to "augment" reality. The best answer to this need comes from Augmented Reality technology that allows to convey accurate information to stimulate the user's interest and foster knowledge.

For example, an interesting mobile AR application has been developed to fully understand the history of two archaeological contexts in Salento: Museo Diffuso Castello di Alceste, located in San Vito dei Normanni (Brindisi), and Fondo Giuliano located in Vaste (Lecce). The result is an interactive learning scenario that allows visitors to become an active actor of their own fruition journey [15].

By jointly using Unmanned Aerial Vehicles and augmented reality in archaeology, it is possible to explore sites that are often not directly accessible by the user. In [16] is presented a feasibility study for the development of a location-based AR application to support the fruition of the ancient port of Lecce, called "Adriano Pier", in San Cataldo. An evolution of AR applications are the virtual portals that are the medium that allows the transition from reality (present) to virtuality (past) and vice versa Portals are virtual objects that are properly registered in the real scenario framed by the device camera. Their alignment with the surrounding environment should give the illusion of being physically in front of a door. The portal is located outdoor at some point of interest, so that user has the perception of passing through different space-temporal dimensions [17].

In [18] the authors present a study developed with the aim to promote and raise awareness of the Basilica of Saint Catherina of Alexandria in Galatina. Two technologies were used: Spatial Augmented Reality, better known as videomapping, to valorize the monument and narrate its story through images and sounds and Augmented Reality to facilitate the reading and interpretation of the most important frescoes located along all the internal walls of the Basilica. The goal is to create a unique path starting from the Basilica facade and continuing and winding through the interior spaces. The purpose of this research is to demonstrate how the combined use of these technologies can be considered a valid aid to support the enhancement, fruition, and understanding of a monument that is very important for the cultural heritage sector.

3   Fruition of the Underground Oil Mill of the Torcito Farm

For supporting the fruition and knowledge of the underground oil mill of the Torcito Farm, two different mobile applications are under development. These apps can allow the complementary fruition of this place, not easily accessible and inaccessible for some time. In particular, the VR app, usable through a cardboard, will allow the visit of the site in a context that does not require large spaces of movement favoring, at the same time, the total immersion of the user in the virtual environment. The virtual portals (MRTorcito), on the other hand, will allow an experience similar to the real exploration of the site; using your smartphone, you will be able to move in the virtual environment that you can access through the virtual portal and use a range of information as if you were moving within the real environment.

3.1   MRTorcito: Virtual Portals to Access the Underground Oil Mill

The fruition of the underground oil mills of the Torcito Farm through MRTorcito app is based on Virtual Portals solution, a Mixed Reality expedient able to offer a virtual transfer, useful for visiting often inaccessible places. Virtual portals are basically virtual objects properly overimposed on the real scenario where the user is located, which give to the user the illusion to stay in front of a virtual gate. Once properly registered the portals in the real scenario, users can access the virtual space by simply crossing them. It is not only a way to access not directly accessible portions of the site, but also to navigate through a virtual riconstruction of some historical parts of it. In this specific case, the virtual environment will be the result of a photogrammetrical reconstruction of the site.

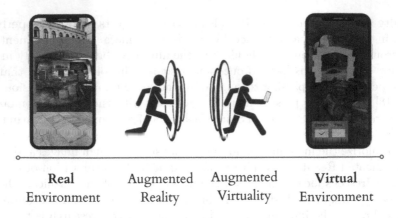

Real   Augmented   Augmented   Virtual
Environment   Reality   Virtuality   Environment

Fig. 3. Virtual portals in the virtual continuum.

The virtual space beyond the portal will represent an augmented virtuality space and the portal is the point to come back to the starting real point (see Fig. 3).

The application development is going to follow the following steps:

- Building of the virtual model of the underground oil mills;
- Modelling of additional elements that are not present in the current underground oil mills as they were destroyed;
- Overlapping of these additional elements in the 3D model of the underground oil mills;
- Porting in Unity of the obtained final model;
- Design and implementation of the virtual portal;
- Definition of specific animations;
- Design and development of the user interface.

More in detail, the three-dimensional model of the oil mill will be realized using photogrammetry processing the photographic sequences acquired on site using the software Agisoft Metashape. Once the obtained model will be imported on Blender, it will be implemented on eventual imperfections generated in the mesh. In additions, other three-dimensional elements that are not present in the current real environment and are typical tools of the underground oil mills (such as the millstone and the press) will be modeled. The obtained final model will be imported on Unity 3D, the platform used for creating and operating interactive, real-time 3D content [19].

3.2 VRTorcito: Navigation by Means of a Cardboard

The visit of the mill through VR technology will be allowed thanks to the shooting of 360° photos and the creation of an application usable through a cardboard.

Access to the application will be using a navigation menu operated by means of a gaze control, to allow the user to interact with the application without the use of any physical button. From the menu it will be possible to pass to the first spherical photo and using indicators it will be possible to visit the whole oil mill; the visit will be enriched by pop-ups with informative and popular background (see Fig. 4). The transition to the next scene will be extremely simple and intuitive using appropriate arrows superimposed on the scene.

From the technical point of view the navigation between the spherical photos will be done thanks to a script that will allow the physical change of the spheres, to which will be applied a material (with custom shader) having as texture the 360° image of the mill.

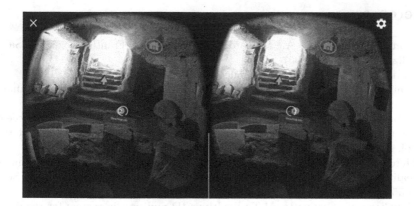

Fig. 4. VRTorcito app.

4   Conclusions and Future Work

Starting from this preliminary discussion, the project will be developed, in order to provide different technological tools for exploring the underground oil mill of Torcito Farm. For supporting the fruition, two different mobile applications will be developed. In particular, the VR app, usable through a cardboard, will allow the visit of the site in a context that does not require large spaces of movement favoring, at the same time, the total immersion of the user in the virtual environment. The virtual portals (MRTorcito), on the other hand, will allow an experience similar to the real exploration of the site. A point of discussion will regards this last MR application, since it needs more steps of implementation, that sometimes can rise some technical issues.

For this, the project foresees two phases:

– phase 1: realization of the virtual portal through the insertion of a plane endowed with a particular material that will allow to see us through, hiding the rest of the model that surrounds the portal. A material will be applied to the model of the underground oil mill so that it is not displayed until the portal is passed.

– phase 2: the application will be subsequently implemented with the addition of animations to the virtual models of the press and the mill, adjusting the on and off by two buttons. This temporal switch will allow to see the mill as it appears today and as it would have been in the past, with the presence of the machinery in operation.

After the step of implementation, some tests will be conduct in order to measure the accuracy and the effectiveness of the applications. The results collected will be topic of another paper.

References

1. Monte, A., Cappello, A., Mainardi, M., Palma, P.: Frantoi ipogei del Salento. Edizioni del Grifo (1995)
2. Fasano, L.M.: Il trappeto sotterraneo in Terra d'Otranto. Capone (1991)
3. Fanini, B., d'Annibale, E.: A framework for compact and improved panoramic VR dissemination. In: GCH, pp. 33–42 (2016)
4. Gabellone, F., Ferrari, I., Giuri, F., Chiffi, M.: The palmieri hypogeum in lecce from the integrated survey to the dissemination of contents. In: 2015 Digital Heritage, vol. 1, pp. 247–254. IEEE (2015)
5. Merchán, M., Merchán, P., Pérez, E.: Good practices in the use of augmented reality for the dissemination of architectural heritage of rural areas. Appl. Sci. **11**, 2055 (2021)
6. Gabellone, F., Giannotta, M.T.: Realtime 3D multimedia system for the distance visiting of cultural heritage. A case study on the chamber tombs in via Crispi, Taranto. In: XX CIPA International Symposium, International Cooperation to save Cultural Heritage, Torino (2005)
7. Bekele, M.K., Pierdicca, R., Frontoni, E., Malinverni, E.S., Gain, J.: A survey of augmented, virtual, and mixed reality for cultural heritage. J. Comput. Cult. Heritage (JOCCH) **11**, 1–36 (2018)
8. Checa, D., Bustillo, A.: Advantages and limits of virtual reality in learning processes: Briviesca in the fifteenth century. Virtual Reality **24**(1), 151–161 (2019). https://doi.org/10.1007/s10055-019-00389-7
9. Bustillo, A., Alaguero, M., Miguel, I., Saiz, J.M., Iglesias, L.S.: A flexible platform for the creation of 3D semi-immersive environments to teach cultural heritage. Digital Appl. Archaeol. Cult. Heritage **2**, 248–259 (2015)
10. Checa, D., Gatto, C., Cisternino, D., De Paolis, L.T., Bustillo, A.: A framework for educational and training immersive virtual reality experiences. In: De Paolis, L.T., Bourdot, P. (eds.) AVR 2020. LNCS, vol. 12243, pp. 220–228. Springer, Cham (2020). https://doi.org/10.1007/978-3-030-58468-9_17
11. De Paolis, L.T., Aloisio, G., Celentano, M.G., Oliva, L., Vecchio, P.: Experiencing a town of the middle ages: an application for the edutainment in cultural heritage. In: 2011 IEEE 3rd International Conference on Communication Software and Networks, pp. 169–174. IEEE (2011)
12. De Paolis, L.T., Aloisio, G., Celentano, M.G., Oliva, L., Vecchio, P.: A game-based 3D simulation of Otranto in the middle ages. In: 2010 Third International Conference on Advances in Computer-Human Interactions, pp. 130–133. IEEE (2010)

13. Paolis, L.T.: Walking in a virtual town to understand and learning about the life in the middle ages. In: Murgante, B., et al. (eds.) ICCSA 2013. LNCS, vol. 7971, pp. 632–645. Springer, Heidelberg (2013). https://doi.org/10.1007/978-3-642-39637-3_50

14. De Paolis, L.T., Aloisio, G., Celentano, M.G., Oliva, L., Vecchio, P.: Mediaevo project: a serious game for the edutainment. In: 2011 3rd International Conference on Computer Research and Development, vol. 4, pp. 524–529. IEEE (2011)

15. Cisternino, D., Gatto, C., De Paolis, L.T.: Augmented reality for the enhancement of Apulian archaeological areas. In: De Paolis, L.T., Bourdot, P. (eds.) AVR 2018. LNCS, vol. 10851, pp. 370–382. Springer, Cham (2018). https://doi.org/10.1007/978-3-319-95282-6_27

16. Botrugno, M.C., D'Errico, G., De Paolis, L.T.: Augmented reality and UAVs in archaeology: development of a location-based AR application. In: De Paolis, L.T., Bourdot, P., Mongelli, A. (eds.) AVR 2017. LNCS, vol. 10325, pp. 261–270. Springer, Cham (2017). https://doi.org/10.1007/978-3-319-60928-7_23

17. Cisternino, D., et al.: Virtual portals for a smart fruition of historical and archaeological contexts. In: De Paolis, L.T., Bourdot, P. (eds.) AVR 2019. LNCS, vol. 11614, pp. 264–273. Springer, Cham (2019). https://doi.org/10.1007/978-3-030-25999-0_23

18. Cisternino, D., et al.: Augmented reality applications to support the promotion of cultural heritage: the case of the Basilica of saint Catherine of Alexandria in Galatina. J. Comput. Cult. Heritage (JOCCH) **14**, 1–30 (2021)

19. Haas, J.K.: A history of the unity game engine (2014)

Applications of VR/AR/MR in Medicine

Design of a Serious Game for Enhancing Money Use in Teens with Autism Spectrum Disorder

Ersilia Vallefuoco[1]($\boxtimes$) (iD), Carmela Bravaccio[2] (iD), Giovanna Gison[3],
and Alessandro Pepino[4] (iD)

[1] SInAPSi Centre, University of Naples Federico II, Naples, Italy
`ersilia.vallefuoco@unina.it`
[2] Department of Translational Medical Sciences, University of Naples Federico II,
Naples, Italy
`carmela.bravaccio@unina.it`
[3] Department of Mental, Physical Health and Preventive Medicine,
University of Campania Luigi Vanvitelli, Naples, Italy
`giovanna.gison@unicampania.it`
[4] Department of Electrical Engineering and Information Technology,
University of Naples Federico II, Naples, Italy
`pepino@unina.it`

Abstract. People with Autism Spectrum Disorder (ASD) show often substantial difficulties to understand the concept of money and how to manage it. The majority of them are not independent, even for the most basic financial activities. In this paper, we illustrated the design of a serious game (SG), *€UReka*, for teens with ASD to train skills useful to recognize and discriminate Euro coins and banknotes and to use them in real-life situations. We followed SGs frameworks for people with ASD and we adopted a participatory design, involving a multidisciplinary team. We included a short version of our game design document to explain how serious contents, game elements, and needs of the players with ASD were balanced in our SG. *€UReka* consists of two 3D mini-games set in real-life environments, with a simple storyline and user-friendly graphics. The player can individualize their gaming experience, customizing some game options based on their preferences and needs. We developed a first game prototype that will be evaluated through a usability test. In future works, a specific study will be planned to assess possible benefits from training with *€UReka*.

Keywords: ASD · Neurodevelopmental disorder · Serious game ·
Game design · Daily living skills

1 Introduction

Autism Spectrum Disorder (ASD) is defined as a complex neurodevelopmental disorder characterized by deficits in social communication and social interaction,

© Springer Nature Switzerland AG 2021
L. T. De Paolis et al. (Eds.): AVR 2021, LNCS 12980, pp. 339–347, 2021.
https://doi.org/10.1007/978-3-030-87595-4_25

and by limited patterns of interests, activities, and behaviors [1]. It is often linked to intellectual disability, psychiatric impairments, and other kinds of comorbidities [17]. Several studies [6,10,12] reported that only a small percentage of people with ASD become independent in adult age. Hence, most adults with ASD require different levels of support, mainly provided by families that consequently are often under a great deal of stress [9,15]. On the other hand, the lack of self-sufficiency and employability among adults with ASD has an economic impact on society [2].

Money management is an important daily living skill, promoting and improving an independent life for people with disabilities within the different contexts of life [13,20,21]. In a qualitative study [5], 27 interviewed youth with ASD (16–25 years old) expressed concern regarding their lack of familiarity with money use and they reported problems even in basic skills, such as counting money or paying. While money usage may appear easy to learn and practice, it is actually quite complex and composite for people with ASD because money is an abstract concept and its use involves different abilities and knowledge simultaneously [3,8]. This can be briefly illustrated by considering a classic example of money usage: payments. In this activity, besides discriminating and recognizing money, mathematical skills (e.g., being acquainted with concept of quantity, counting, and doing arithmetic calculations) are necessary. Moreover, these skills have to be generalized and then applied to money usage in different life contexts. In addition, payments also require skills not related to money usage at all, such as attention, communication, and social skills [13].

Studies over the past two decades have provided good evidence to support using serious games (SGs) for teaching specific skills to children and youth with ASD [7,19]. Similar to other technological approaches, SGs respond to different needs of people with ASD: providing structure and predictable environments, giving priority to the visual channel, decomposing multiple steps into single levels, offering the possibility to repeat actions, providing feedback in different forms and regulating sensor inputs [4,11,18,22]. However, unlike other approaches, SGs display the structure of a traditional digital game, including game elements that can support the learning process and can be more attractive for children and youth with ASD [22]: in fact, as reported by Mazurek et al. [16], they spend more than two hours per day playing videogames, and they generally play more than people with other disabilities.

In this paper, we described the design of a 3D serious game €ureka, for teens with ASD aimed at understanding and handling money, specifically Euros. We also included a shorter version of our game design document to describe and illustrate game flow and structure.

2   Methods

Our SG design required a multidisciplinary expert team to determine the needs of our target audience, to identify the game elements that could be attractive for them, as well as to guarantee a balance between game and serious content. Specifically, we adopted a participatory design [14], involving a child neuropsychiatrist, a psychologist, therapists, young adults with ASD, and biomedical engineers who are experts of technologies for people with ASD. Periodic team meetings were scheduled during the design and development phases to review each step, solve problems, and make decisions for each stage in an iterative process.

Several frameworks currently exist for SGs design for people with ASD, including both general frameworks providing universal recommendations [18, 22] and more specific ones providing effective indications to design SGs for particular application contexts [4, 11, 20]. We mainly followed the design guidelines proposed by Tsikinas et al. [20], focused on SGs aimed at improving independent living skills in people ASD. This approach stresses the importance to provide an individualized gaming experience in order both to enhance immersion of players with ASD and consider their heterogeneous needs. Individualization should include customization of certain game elements, especially sensor inputs, features of game avatars, and game difficulty. Another crucial game element that should be considered is the challenge factor: the game has to be stimulating, introducing progressively new tasks and goals based on the player's capabilities and their previous performance. Moreover, the authors suggested that SGs should be set in real-life contexts and reproduce real-life situations to facilitate the generalization process of trained skills and to respond to the difficulties of people with ASD in comprehending fictional narratives. In addition, SGs should provide the possibility to repeat game actions and levels to foster predictability and to facilitate the mastering of trained skills. A feedback system involving both visual and audio clues should be planned and provided to inform the player on the validity of their actions. Visually, simple and clear graphics should be used to avoid distracting players.

Furthermore, our research team added other key components to our SG design to motivate players and to provide a positive gaming experience. SGs should offer instructions and tutorials to guide players with ASD and to facilitate the gameplay [4]. In order to improve player engagement, a storyline, fun game elements, and a reward system should all be included while considering the interests of the target audience [18]. Based on these considerations, we elaborated a game design document to detail our designing process and to facilitate SG development.

2.1 Game Design Document

Description. Our SG, *€UReka*, consists of two different mini-games: *Shooting a basketball* and *Shopping in a coffee shop*. They are 3D games providing training for Italian teens with ASD to help them discriminate, understand, and handle money (€). When launching the application, the player has to create their avatar, choosing a character and providing a nickname. Subsequently, in the *€UReka*'s title screen, the player can select one of the two proposed mini-games and set up specific options (music and audio volumes, character customization, and game input controls). After choosing the mini-game, the player can select a level. More advanced levels are initially locked, so that the player can only select a new level if they have completed the previous one; otherwise, they will have to repeat the level until they succeed. Each mini-game starts by introducing a main mission through a supporting character. A menu can be accessed to exit, save, return to the title screen, and edit settings. Upon completion of a level, the player receives an award depending on their game score.

Shooting a basketball: this mini-game focuses on recognizing and discriminating Euro coins and banknotes. The player has to associate the required money to the right image, number, and textual name before shooting a basketball in the basket featuring the correct option. The player has to shoot three times for each level (see Fig. 1): (1) first, they have to shoot the ball in the basket matching the image of the required money; (2) then they have to shoot the ball in the basket matching the number of the required money; (3) finally, they have to shoot the ball in the basket matching the textual name of the required money. Therefore, the game trains image to image, image to number, and image to text associations.

Shopping in a coffee shop: this mini-game aims to support money handling in a real-life setting. The player has to help a supporting character to buy products in the gym's coffee shop. The supporting character indicates the products to buy and gives the player a wallet with specific money at the beginning of a level. Then the player has to find the several products in the coffee shop, go to the cashier, select the right money from the wallet based on the amount due, and finally pay.

Goals. Our *€UReka*'s main purpose is to improve money-related skills. In particular, it aims to train and improve: coins and banknotes recognition; discrimination between coins and banknotes; association of image, number, and text to the corresponding money; money-related maths skills; money handling; understanding of payment dynamics; change management; understanding of the concept of the price.

Target Audience. Following Tsikinas et al. [20], we identified teens with ASD (aged 13–19 years) needing to learn and train their management skills as our main target audience.

Storyline. As suggested by Tang et al. [18], we provided a simple storyline with straightforward dialogues. In *Shooting a basketball*, the story revolves around a challenge: "Whoever shoots the ball in the right basket will earn an award!" The supporting character is a basketball coach providing information on the required money that the player has to identify each time. On the other hand, *Shopping in a coffee shop* focuses on helping the basketball coach to buy products in a coffee shop. Overall, the characters are: the player character (a boy or a girl) that can be selected at the game start; the basketball coach, a supporting character, who illustrates the game and its missions and helps the player by providing instructions when necessary (NPCs); coffee shop staff interacting with the player when required based on the game missions (NPCs); people spending their time in the coffee shop.

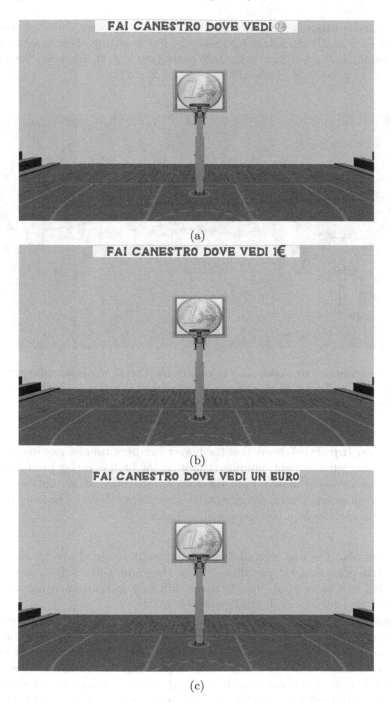

Fig. 1. Screenshots of the *Shooting a basketball* mini-game. The figure shows screenshots of the *Shooting a basketball* prototype. For each game level, the player has to shoot a basketball in the basket matching the required money. Image to image (a), image to number (b), and image to text (c) associations are required.

Game Environment. Different pictures and images were collected from the web and used as 3D guidelines to design the game setting. The *Shooting a basketball* mini-game is set in a basketball court (see Fig. 1), whereas *Shopping in a coffee shop* is set in a gym's coffee shop (see Fig. 2).

Fig. 2. Screenshot of the coffee shop environment. The figure depicts the game environment developed for the *Shopping in a coffee shop* prototype, which is set in the coffee shop of a gym and reproduces a real-life setting.

Player and Inputs. Actions that the player can perform are: moving back and forth; moving left and right; jumping; shooting the ball; selecting products in the coffee shop; selecting money from their wallet; selecting menu options. Before starting to play, the player can customize their input device, choosing between a joystick controller or a keyboard with a mouse.

Game Levels. The first level of each mini-game is designed as a special session with instructions that are useful to explain the game and its dynamics, as recommended by Carlier et al. [4]. The game difficulty increases progressively with each level. Specifics for each mini-game are as follows:

Shooting a basketball comprises 15 levels, one for each type of coin and banknote, starting from €0.01 and progressively reaching €500. For each game level, the player has to identify and choose a basket among two options, the correct choice being the one with an image of the required money. In the first few levels, the possible coins to choose from have clearly distinct colors and designs (e.g., €0.10 vs. €0.05); after the €0.50 level, the choice is between similar coins (e.g., €1 vs. €2) and between banknotes and coins sharing a few numbers (e.g., €10 vs. €1, €200 vs. €20).

Shopping in a coffee shop consists of 10 levels with increasing difficulty. More specifically, the game difficulty encompasses different elements: finding products in the coffee shop, the number of products to buy, money available in the wallet, and math calculations. For instance, in the tutorial level, the basketball coach asks the player to buy only one water bottle and the wallet contains only two coins (€0.50 and €1). In subsequent levels, with an added variety of products to buy and money to choose from, simple math calculations are required to understand the amount due and to calculate the change.

User Interface. As recommended by different frameworks [4,11,18], the user interface has a simple design that shows written messages for each game mission, including instructions, dialogues, and feedback. The written messages appear in a separate panel on top of the screen for game missions/instructions, at the bottom for dialogues, and in the middle for the feedback. The game messages and instructions are in Italian and are written in a simple and clear language.

Reward and Feedback System. For both mini-games, the game score is calculated based on the accuracy percentage of game activities performed. At the end of each level, the player can receive a reward depending on the game score they achieved, specifically three stars (80 < game score ≤ 100), two stars (60 < game score ≤ 80) or one star (40 < game score ≤ 60). At the end of each mini-game, if all levels have been unlocked with the maximum score, the player will receive a special bonus: the title of best player. Additionally, during the game, the player will receive audio and textual feedback, both positive and negative, when they complete each task in order to reinforce their correct game actions or help them understand their possible mistakes.

Sound and Music. The goal of music within a game is to set the mood of the world, as well as to provide a feedback to the player. Our game features a basic music loop that is not too fast and can be heard in all game. Two different sounds are included for negative and positive feedback respectively. Sounds and music can be adjusted by the player in the settings; the audio can be turned off completely if it creates problems to the player.

Technical Specifications. Unity (version: Unity 2019.4.4 Personal (64) bit) was chosen as a game engine and the game should be executed as a Windows PC application.

3   Discussion

The current study presented an Italian SG, *€UReka*, that was designed to support teens with ASD in developing and training essential skills, specifically, understanding money and its management. The game was designed as a set of two mini-games: *Shooting a basketball* aimed to train money recognition and discrimination, while *Shopping in a coffee shop* aimed to improve money management in real-life settings. Both mini-games were engineered as 3D games with multiple game levels at increasing difficulty. We designed a clear user interface, an intuitive storyline, a system of feedback and rewards, and the possibility to customize certain game elements, such as the player character, adjusting the audio settings and choosing the game levels.

In accordance with a previous study [3], the *Shooting a basketball* mini-game provides game dynamics conceptually based on the technique of association; namely, the player has to associate a coin or a banknote to the right image, number, and text. However, in contrast with this previous study, the association here is not carried out through a drag and drop mechanism, but it was implemented through a specific dynamic – shooting a basketball – in order to motivate and engage the player towards the goals. With *Shopping in a coffee shop*, we designed a life simulation game where the player has to follow real-life steps of the shopping experience. From a design point of view, this is in line with SGs proposed by other similar studies [3,8] and SGs developed to improve daily living skills [20]. In fact, reproducing a real-life experience can increase the immersion level of players with ASD while also facilitating the transfer of trained skills from the virtual world to real life [18,22].

A first SG prototype was developed following the design document. We scheduled a usability test with a target group to evaluate possible changes, supplementing and restyling the prototype. Currently, €UReka was tested on a PC running Microsoft Windows 10 (provided with 16 GB RAM and Intel Core i5 7th Generation) by young adults with ASD who are members of our design team. They described the game as pleasant, user-friendly, and motivating. However, based on the results of a future usability test, we plan to introduce common difficulty progression modes – easy, medium, hard – in order to individualize the game experience and to respond to all the needs of people with ASD. In future works, we will plan and organize a clinical trial to evaluate the efficacy and effectiveness of the SG-based training.

References

1. American Psychiatric Association: Diagnostic and Statistical Manual of Mental Disorders (DSM-5®). American Psychiatric Association, Washington (2013)
2. Cakir, J., Frye, R.E., Walker, S.J.: The lifetime social cost of autism: 1990–2029. Res. Autism Spectrum Disord. **72**, 101502 (2020)
3. Caria, S., Paternò, F., Santoro, C., Semucci, V.: The design of web games for helping young high-functioning autistics in learning how to manage money. Mob. Netw. Appl. **23**(6), 1735–1748 (2018). https://doi.org/10.1007/s11036-018-1069-0
4. Carlier, S., Van Der Paelt, S., Ongenae, F., De Backere, F., De Turck, F.: Empowering children with ASD and their parents: design of a serious game for anxiety and stress reduction. Sensors **20**(4), 966 (2020)
5. Cheak-Zamora, N.C., Teti, M., Peters, C., Maurer-Batjer, A.: Financial capabilities among youth with autism spectrum disorder. J. Child Fam. Stud. **26**(5), 1310–1317 (2017)

6. Eaves, L.C., Ho, H.H.: Young adult outcome of autism spectrum disorders. J. Autism Aev. Disord. **38**(4), 739–747 (2008)
7. Grossard, C., Grynspan, O., Serret, S., Jouen, A.L., Bailly, K., Cohen, D.: Serious games to teach social interactions and emotions to individuals with autism spectrum disorders (ASD). Comput. Educ. **113**, 195–211 (2017)
8. Hassan, A.Z., et al.: Developing the concept of money by interactive computer games for autistic children. In: 2011 IEEE International Symposium on Multimedia, pp. 559–564. IEEE (2011)
9. Hoffman, C.D., Sweeney, D.P., Hodge, D., Lopez-Wagner, M.C., Looney, L.: Parenting stress and closeness: mothers of typically developing children and mothers of children with autism. Focus Autism Other Dev. Disabil. **24**(3), 178–187 (2009)
10. Howlin, P., Goode, S., Hutton, J., Rutter, M.: Adult outcome for children with autism. J. Child Psychol. Psychiatry **45**(2), 212–229 (2004)
11. Khowaja, K., Salim, S.S.: A framework to design vocabulary-based serious games for children with autism spectrum disorder (ASD). Univ. Access Inf. Soc. **19**, 1–43 (2019). https://doi.org/10.1007/s10209-019-00689-4
12. Magiati, I., Tay, X.W., Howlin, P.: Cognitive, language, social and behavioural outcomes in adults with autism spectrum disorders: a systematic review of longitudinal follow-up studies in adulthood. Clin. Psychol. Rev. **34**(1), 73–86 (2014)
13. Malagoli, M.: Laboratorio Euro. Programma per l'insegnamento dell'uso dell'euro ad alunni con difficoltà, Erickson (2001)
14. Malinverni, L., Mora-Guiard, J., Padillo, V., Valero, L., Hervás, A., Pares, N.: An inclusive design approach for developing video games for children with autism spectrum disorder. Comput. Hum. Behav. **71**, 535–549 (2017)
15. Marsack-Topolewski, C.N., Samuel, P.S., Tarraf, W.: Empirical evaluation of the association between daily living skills of adults with autism and parental caregiver burden. Plos one **16**(1), e0244844 (2021)
16. Mazurek, M.O., Engelhardt, C.R.: Video game use in boys with autism spectrum disorder, ADHD, or typical development. Pediatrics **132**(2), 260–266 (2013)
17. Scottish Intercollegiate Guidelines Network (SIGN): Assessment, diagnosis and interventions for autism spectrum disorders. SIGN, Edinburgh (2016)
18. Tang, J.S.Y., Falkmer, M., Chen, N.T.M., Bölte, S., Girdler, S.: Designing a serious game for youth with ASD: perspectives from end-users and professionals. J. Autism Dev. Disord. **49**(3), 978–995 (2018). https://doi.org/10.1007/s10803-018-3801-9
19. Tang, J.S., Chen, N.T., Falkmer, M., Bölte, S., Girdler, S.: A systematic review and meta-analysis of social emotional computer based interventions for autistic individuals using the serious game framework. Res. Autism Spectr. Disord. **66**, 101412 (2019)
20. Tsikinas, S., Xinogalos, S., Satratzemi, M., Kartasidou, L.: Designing a serious game for independent living skills in special education. In: European Conference on Games Based Learning, pp. 748-XXIII. Academic Conferences International Limited (2019)
21. Westling, D.L., Fox, L., Carter, E.W.: Teaching students with severe disabilities. Merrill Upper Saddle River, NJ (2000)
22. Whyte, E.M., Smyth, J.M., Scherf, K.S.: Designing serious game interventions for individuals with autism. J. Autism Dev. Disord. **45**(12), 3820–3831 (2014). https://doi.org/10.1007/s10803-014-2333-1

Proposed System for Orofacial Physiotherapy Based on a Computational Interpretation of Face Gestures to Interact with a 3D Virtual Interface

Ivón Escobar, Edwin Pruna[✉], Silvia Alpúsig, Paola Calvopiña, and Gabriel Corrales

Universidad de Las Fuerzas Armadas ESPE, Sangolquí, Ecuador
{ipescobar,eppruna,sealpusig,jpcalvopina1}@espe.edu.ec

Abstract. This work presents the development of a game-based in system that interprets facial gestures to interact with a 3D virtual interface, aimed at strengthening the facial muscles of children suffering from diseases that produce alterations in speech, chewing, breathing and others related to movements of the facial muscles. The system is mainly based on algorithms that recognize the user's facial gestures captured through Microsoft Kinect 2.0. In addition, the experimental results obtained from the application of a test based on the SUS usability scale are presented and discussed to measure the usability of the system.

Keywords: Virtual interface · Face tracking · Microsoft Kinect 2.0 · Gestural interaction · Unity 3D

1 Introduction

In this days and age, in early childhood centers and in inquiry pediatrics is frequent to find boys with several problems in orofacial region, it is due to childhood neurological pathologies such us: cerebral palsy (CP), syndromes or simply because the infant was born premature [1]. On the one hand, in the different pathologies, voluntary movements are carried out through extensor and hypertonic expressive reactions, that slow or prevent the free movement of the joints, causing permanent atrophies in certain muscle groups of the face. On the other hand, the main characteristic of these syndromes is its muscular hypotonia that affect the following areas: labial, lingual, pharyngeal and the whole of the orofacial muscles; in both cases, therapy is recommended to regulate the proper functioning of the orofacial area [2, 3].

First of all, among the affectations that can occur in children by not having a good functioning of the orofacial area, are: disorders in breathing, chewing, swallowing, poor diet and language [4, 5]. Feeding is essential for the growth of an infant, but in most cases due to the affectation they have at the neurological level, they can present poor nutrition. For instance, within the comorbidities that accompany CP, eating disorders. and swallowing (SWT) are prominent as a source of morbidity and mortality [6, 7]. Researches carried out show high percentages of prevalence of dysphagia in this condition: 43% [8], and 99% [9]. Diet allows child to consume food adequately, achieving

L. T. De Paolis et al. (Eds.): AVR 2021, LNCS 12980, pp. 348–362, 2021.
https://doi.org/10.1007/978-3-030-87595-4_26

progress in weight and height or in turn maintaining them [10], If there is a change in feeding, it may be due to any difficulty in sucking, biting, chewing, handling food in the oral cavity, controlling spittle, and swallowing [11].

In addition, Development of oral language in the early childhood education stage is very important, since it is the instrument that will allow children to carry out a satisfactory school learning, on which all subsequent knowledge will be based [12]. Moreover, orofacial exercises are part of a speech therapy and seek to stimulate vibration, and stretch of muscles, to strengthen the weak functions of language and facilitate feeding as it works on sucking, swallowing and chewing [13]. Orofacial exercises include gesticulation, vocalization, breath exercises, absorption, lip and tongue. Therapists devise a series of games for children to improve their orofacial motor skills, like: use of the dice to imitate facial gestures of an image, blowing bubbles, inflating the cheeks are the most common exercises in orofacial therapy [14–16].

Nowadays, state-of-the-art technologies have been gaining ground in terms of virtual rehabilitation focused mainly on the upper and lower limbs [17–20], orofacial therapies have few studies [21–23] and some research are focus specifically on tongue training [24]. The use of devices such as the Kinect has given good results in oral rehabilitation and in tongue training specially for patients suffering from dysphagia and dysarthria [25, 26], as it is a non-invasive device, it allows to the systems developed for virtual rehabilitation may be used by any patient with different pathologies or syndromes [25–27].

In this context, the present work presents the development of a virtual system that uses the Microsoft Kinect 2.0 as a single and main input device which digitally captures the movements of the user's face in real time. Furthermore, digital data of the user's face movements is processed by the algorithms implemented so that the virtual interface recognizes defined facial gestures and run subroutines of graphical animations. The implementation of the virtual interface is based on the use of computer-aided design, CAD, and graphics engines as a complement to Unity software for high-quality graphics and animations in 3D virtual games controlled by facial gestures. These features allow the reproduction of attractive and intuitive games that catch the patient's attention so that the orofacial physiotherapy process is not monotonous. Besides, the system consists of software routines that allow the selection of levels of complexity and the storage of the data of the results of the rehabilitation session, as a function that facilitates, to the expert professional, the future analysis of the patient's evolution.

This work is organized in IV Sections including the Introduction. Section 2 presents the development of the algorithms used in the system based on the use of Microsoft Kinect 2.0 SDK for face tracking and Unity functions. Section 3, presented the experimental results and discussion that validate the implementation, functionality and the achieves of the proposed system, and finally in Sect. 4, are the conclusions.

2   Development of the Virtual Orofacial Physiotherapy System

2.1   Virtual System Operation

The main element of the system is the face of an avatar, which has been designed to interact with the user. The Kinect 2.0 device captures the movements of the user's face while mimicking the avatar, the general scheme of the proposed virtual system is shown

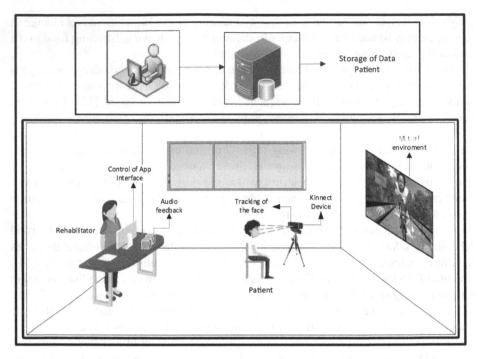

Fig. 1. General scheme of the proposed virtual system.

in Fig. 1. The data corresponding to the movements of the face are used in an algorithm that recognizes when a facial gesture has been made correctly. Facial gesture recognition is used to execute 3D graphic movement animations in a virtual interface developed and programmed in the Unity software. The virtual applications created allow monitor and stimulate the user to exercise the muscles of his face by performing different gestures, meanwhile at the same time capturing their attention in the fulfilment of goals and positive feedback.

The routines programmed in the Unity software based in C # language is the main structure of the system. The virtual interface developed allows the system to interact with users. The rehabilitation user is involved, who defines the parameters governing the difficulty and objectives of the virtual game, and the patient user, who carries out his rehabilitation session through the challenges required by the virtual game.

With the help of the Microsoft Kinect 2.0 device, data from strategic points on the user's face is acquired. The subroutine implemented for the operation of the system allows the recognition of the human face. The variations of the facial expressions made by the user are compared with the data of the movement of the face of a virtual avatar. Animations, menus, user data log, game options, 3D object collision detectors, and others, are found in the rest of the subroutines.

In the software Unity, the so-called Play Objects are created, which is nothing more than using a programming based on classes and objects, they are also associated with C

scripts that define and control the operation of the game. The data and some objects of the game depend on the operation of another game, similar to a parallel execution.

2.2 Recognition of Face Gestures Through Microsoft Kinect 2.0

The application is designed to promote the movement of a person's facial muscles in an entertaining way; Microsoft Kinect 2.0 device is used to capture the movement of strategic points on the human face in real time which are associated with the movements of a virtual avatar's face. The person will exercise the muscles of their face by making different gestures (smile, sadness, surprise, open your mouth, raise your eyebrows, among others) to overcome the series of challenges contained in virtual games.

A mesh of 1347 points or vertices, which forms the face of the avatar, to associate them with the points that Microsoft Kinect 2.0 is capable of reading. Figure 2 illustrates the associated points.

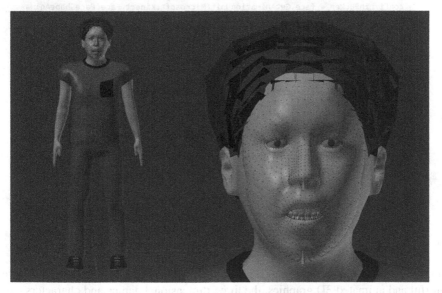

Fig. 2. Points or vertices, which form the face of the avatar

Algorithms are implemented to associate the data provided with the Kinect of human face points with the movements of the avatar's face area; algorithms that recognize that the person is making a certain (smile, sadness, surprise, open your mouth, raise your eyebrows, among others), algorithms that count hits and misses.

```
if (face != null){

        function_associate_kinect_face_points_with_3DModel(faceModel, face);

        confi_JawOpen=face.GetAnimationUnit(Microsoft.Kinect.Face.FaceShapeAnima-
        tions.JawOpen);
        confi_JawSlideRight = face.GetAnimationUnit(Microsoft.Kinect.Face.FaceShapeAni-
        mations.JawSlideRight);
        confi_LeftcheekPuff = face.GetAnimationUnit(Microsoft.Kinect.Face.FaceShapeAni-
        mations.LeftcheekPuff);
        confi_LefteyebrowLowerer = face.GetAnimationUnit(Microsoft.Ki-
        nect.Face.FaceShapeAnimations.LefteyebrowLowerer);
        confi_LefteyeClosed = face.GetAnimationUnit(Microsoft.Kinect.Face.FaceShapeAni-
        mations.LefteyeClosed);
        confi_LipCornerDepressorLeft = face.GetAnimationUnit(Microsoft.Ki-
        nect.Face.FaceShapeAnimations.LipCornerDepressorLeft);
        confi_LipCornerDepressorRight = face.GetAnimationUnit(Microsoft.Ki-
        nect.Face.FaceShapeAnimations.LipCornerDepressorRight);
        confi_LipCornerPullerLeft = face.GetAnimationUnit(Microsoft.Ki-
        nect.Face.FaceShapeAnimations.LipCornerPullerLeft);
        confi_LipCornerPullerRight = face.GetAnimationUnit(Microsoft.Ki-
        nect.Face.FaceShapeAnimations.LipCornerPullerRight);
        confi_LipPucker = face.GetAnimationUnit(Microsoft.Kinect.Face.FaceShapeAnima-
        tions.LipPucker);
        confi_LipStretcherLeft = face.GetAnimationUnit(Microsoft.Ki-
        nect.Face.FaceShapeAnimations.LipStretcherLeft);
        confi_LipStretcherRight = face.GetAnimationUnit(Microsoft.Ki-
        nect.Face.FaceShapeAnimations.LipStretcherRight);
        confi_LowerlipDepressorLeft = face.GetAnimationUnit(Microsoft.Ki-
        nect.Face.FaceShapeAnimations.LowerlipDepressorLeft);
        confi_LowerlipDepressorRight = face.GetAnimationUnit(Microsoft.Ki-
        nect.Face.FaceShapeAnimations.LowerlipDepressorRight);
        confi_RightcheekPuff = face.GetAnimationUnit(Microsoft.Kinect.Face.FaceShapeAni-
        mations.RightcheekPuff);
        confi_RighteyebrowLowerer = face.GetAnimationUnit(Microsoft.Ki-
        nect.Face.FaceShapeAnimations.RighteyebrowLowerer);
        confi_RighteyeClosed = face.GetAnimationUnit(Microsoft.Kinect.Face.FaceShapeAni-
        mations.RighteyeClosed);

}
```

2.3 Virtual Interface Functionalities

The virtual environment has been designed based on content for children, it has very colorful and animated 3D graphics, the three-dimensional games and characters easily capture the child's attention, this causes their experience with the system to be lively and entertaining and also motivates them to children perform facial exercises from a traditional therapy. In each virtual game there are different challenges and objectives to be met, the animations, score or error time indicators depend on each game environment, as well as positive feedback, informative and stimulating messages are shown. Sounds are generated in each environment, which is feedback controlled by application algorithms.

Figure 3 Shows the main menu that the application has, it is divided into 3 sections: the registration of user data, the indication of date and time and finally the selection of games; each game in turn has intuitive menus where you can define parameters such as the desired level and certain game actions.

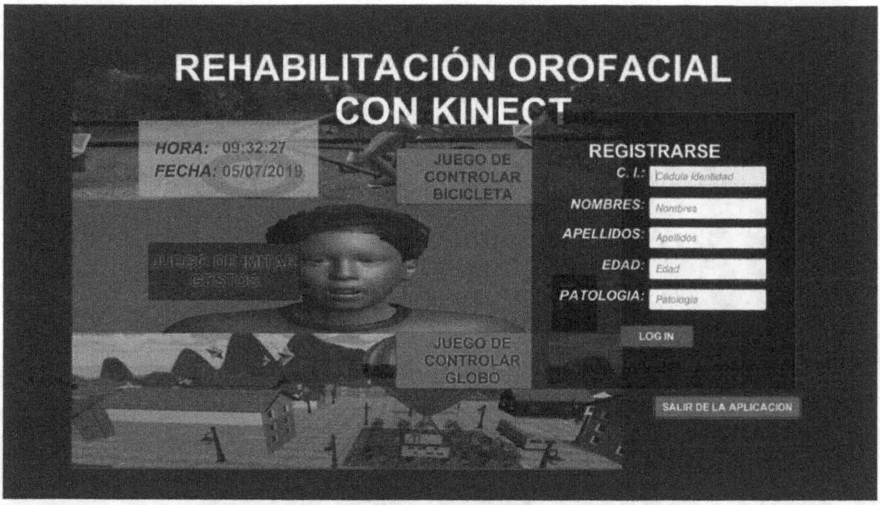

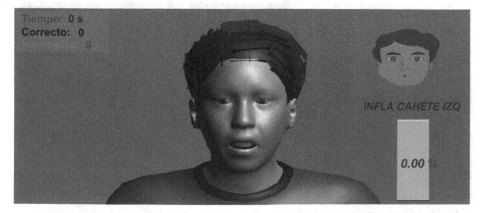

Fig. 3. Virtual system main menu

Figure 4 shows the game (i) related to mimic facial gestures, it is designed to capture the user's attention so that they relate their presence to a child's avatar as if it were a virtual mirror, so that they forget that you are in a therapy session and concentrate only on imitating the gestures requested by the game. The aim of the game is to pay attention to the gesture requested and to carry it out. All requested gestures must be completed in the shortest possible time. The game counts the number of gestures completed correctly (mark as correct), as well as the life of the game which decreases and decreases faster if the requested gesture is not made (marked as incorrect). The patient (game user) must stand in front of the Kinect device for the game to start automatically. Randomly requested facial gesture indicators will appear and the person should imitate them until a green bar is one hundred percent full.

Fig. 4. Virtual environment of the game of imitating facial gestures

The set (ii) shown in Fig. 5, it is designed so that the user controls the movements of the bicycle (front, left and right) by making certain facial gestures, so that they collect as many prizes as possible, avoid obstacles and reach the goal in the shortest possible time.

Fig. 5. Virtual environment of the game to control a bicycle by facial gestures

The game (iii) that controls a hot-air balloon, is designed so that the user controls the movements of the hot-air balloon (lifting, front, back, left and right) by doing certain facial gestures, so that they should collect the requested number of prizes in the shortest possible time.

The patient (game user) must stand in front of the Kinect device for the game to start automatically. They must perform the gestures configured to control the direction of movement of the hot-air balloon and meet the objective of the game. Also, when they are touching the prize, they must make the gesture configured to collect it.

Fig. 6. Virtual environment of the game of controlling a hot-air balloon by facial gestures

The gambling will validate if the exercise has been completed and is being done correctly and counts this as a success as well as the time it takes for the hot-air balloon to reach the finish line. Game environment is shown in Fig. 6.

The movement control of the main objects (avatar, bicycle and balloon) of each game is associated with the data provided with the Kinect of points of the human face and with the movements of the avatar's face area, whose recognize that the person is making a certain gesture (smile, sadness, surprise, opening the mouth, raising the eyebrows, among others).

3 Results and Discussion

Currently, virtual reality has been gaining ground as a complement to traditional rehabilitation therapies [21–23]. This section shows the initial results of the work divided into three aspects: the first shows the operation of each game and the related facial movements. In the second section, the results obtained from the application of the SUS usability test to six children are analyzed. Finally, it is analyzed whether the application is entertaining and motivates users to perform the exercises correctly, generating benefits for the rehabilitation process.

3.1 Experimentation of the Virtual Rehabilitation System

A computer with the following characteristics is used to run the proposed system: Intel core i7-7500 2.9 GHz seventh generation, 16 GB RAM, an Intel HD 620 graphics card, 64-bit Windows 10 Home operating system. The implemented algorithms and animations of the application are executed satisfactorily, however, the response of the execution can be improved with a computer of advanced characteristics, especially related to the graphic card [17].

Once the user is positioned in front of Microsoft Kinect 2.0 to perform the exercise, it may be necessary to wait for some time until the Kinect device recognizes the user's facial gestures and a follow-up is performed. The game will start automatically, activity carried out by the patient will be guided by the therapist at all times and will define the repetitions, challenges and/or levels of the play through the interactive and intuitive menu that is part of the application. The menu also allows you to select one of the three virtual games and their corresponding levels. Facial gestures made by the user must be well defined otherwise it will count as a mistake.

The first game is like a virtual mirror, they can see how the avatar imitates the user's gestures automatically, while a picture and the message of the gesture to be made appear on the right side of the screen. The images sequence of the operation of the first virtual game is shown in Fig. 7.

The second virtual game consists of driving a bicycle. The virtual environment represents a path through a forest; movement of the bicycle occurs when the user makes the predetermined facial gestures that will control the bicycle, as shown in Fig. 8. The application identifies and records the time spent and the number of prizes collected during the trajectory.

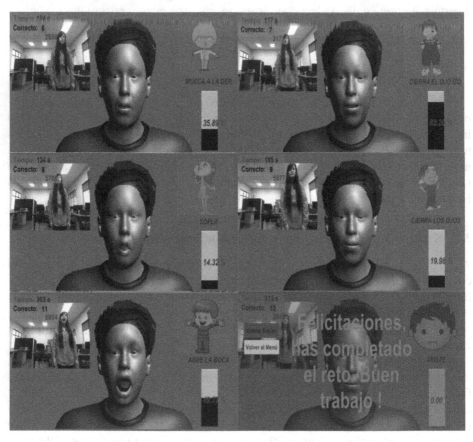

Fig. 7. Images sequence of the game 1 functioning.

Fig. 8. Game 2 image sequence working.

The third virtual game is based on a hot-air balloon, whose movements will be controlled by the gestures set in the menu. The virtual environment represents a city and you can feel the sensation of the hot-air balloon rising. When they perform the facial gestures correctly, the animation is produced that allows you to advance the balloon, as shown in the image sequences in the Fig. 9. Application identifies and records the time elapsed, the number of awards achieved and the crashes produced during the journey.

Fig. 9. Image sequence of game 3 working.

3.2   Usability of the Virtual Rehabilitation System

The system was initially validated by a speech therapist. The traditional therapy special-ist uses graphic cards to mimic gestures to strengthen the facial muscles of his patients. The use of the system by the specialist is acceptable. Interaction, environments, ani-mations, 3D graphics, sounds, menus and feedback through indicator messages are the factors that the specialist highlights as interesting in the system, because they achieve the stimulation of children. The specialist's experience concludes that the use of technology in traditional therapies provokes more interest in children and therefore better benefits for their recovery.

The System Usability Scale (SUS) was applied to six children between the ages of eight and ten to obtain the weighting of the system's usability. The questions asked focused on aspects such as animation, interaction and functionality of the games (Table 1).

Table 1. Evaluation of the usability of the system.

Questions	Number of the answers				
	Strongly disagree	Disagree	Almost agreed	Agreed	Full agreed
Q1. Did you like the 3D graphics and environment of the game?	–	–	–	2	4
Q2. Are the game directions extremely difficult?	5	1	–	–	–
Q3. Did you find the games easy?	–	–	–	–	6
Q4. Did you find the games boring and tiring?	6	–	–	–	–
Q5. Do you feel that the application motivates you to do the exercises correctly?	–	–	–	1	5
Q6. Do you consider that the game does not have a good level of concentration?	5	1	–	–	–

(*continued*)

Table 1. (*continued*)

Questions	Number of the answers				
	Strongly disagree	Disagree	Almost agreed	Agreed	Full agreed
Q7. Do you think the interface makes you feel like you are inside the game?	–	–	–	1	5
Q8. Did you feel any discomfort in your eyes during the game?	5	1	–	–	–
Q9. Would you like to do speech therapy using these games?	–	–	–	–	6
Q10. Did you need a lot of explanation to use the game?	5	1	–	–	–

Ten questions were asked, where each question can be scored from 1 to 5, where 1 indicates total disagreement and 5 total agreements. To obtain the results of the six surveys carried out, the average results obtained were added together and then the SUS scale was applied to obtain the final number 38.67, which multiplied by 2.5 gives a SUS score value of 96.7. Given that the theoretical maximum is 100 points, this result indicates that the proposed system reflects a high acceptance by the users who participated in the experiment. In addition, the survey showed that the participants are motivated to play; the environments, messages, sound and the challenge proposed in each game are interesting for each of them.

Both the specialist and the participants consider that the proposed system can stimulate to interactively perform a traditional speech therapy as well as a correct performance in rehabilitation activities.

From the observations made by the specialist, it is necessary to consider the duration of each game, in order to match the rehabilitation time of a traditional therapy.

Finally, it can be stated that the objective of the present work has been achieved, as the user can perform rehabilitation therapies in an entertaining and enriching way and not in a boring and monotonous way as traditional therapies usually are.

3.3 Discussion of the Rehabilitation Benefits Achieved

The positive feedback generated by the proposed system from users is one of the most important aspects to highlight. The use of virtual reality as part of traditional rehabilitation therapy especially for children, it causes interest in the use of these systems and that the movements and activities planned for therapy are carried out in an integrated manner.

From the results obtained, it can be determined that the proposed games activate the concentration of the children and motivate them to carry out a series of orofacial exercises based on the fulfilment of challenges. These activities that in traditional therapy were monotonous and boring become entertaining.

In the experiment carried out it could be observed that children feel pressure in the area of the face but in spite of this they continue to carry out the activity with the aim of achieving the desired score. Furthermore, this indicates that the muscle tone of the face is being strengthened.

4 Conclusions

This paper presents the implementation of a non-invasive system based on a virtual application, which is programmed to assist and stimulate the patient in orofacial physiotherapy. In the testing it has been possible to promote the performance of exercises such as swell cheeks, blowing, kissing, smiling, etc. They favor the good functioning of the orofacial area. Virtual environments developed in Unity software contain high-quality animated graphics and 3D environments. The games created present challenges that cause the user to feel motivated and interested in performing rehabilitation activities. The SUS Usability test yielded a weighting of 96.7, which reflects that the proposed system has a high acceptability by the users who participated in the experiment. The use of the Microsoft Kinect 2.0 device allows the tracking of the movement of the user's face while allowing the same movement to be associated with a 3D facial model, and makes it possible to implement algorithms based on readings of confidence values of movements of a set of specific points of the face positioned over the eyes, mouth and cheeks. These characteristics of the device can be used in future work, for the construction of other facial gestures to be recognized according to the requirement and indications of the physiotherapist, enhancing the effectiveness of recognition with machine learning algorithms.

Acknowledgment. The authors thank to Universidad de las Fuerzas Armadas ESPE for financing the research project VR-CHILD.

References

1. Salinas, L., et al.: Clinical characterisation and evolution after therapeutic intervention of de-glution disorders in hospitalised paediatric patients. Neurol Mag. **50**(3), 139–144 (2010)
2. Oliva, L.: Neurorehabilitation. Panamericana, Madrid (2012)
3. Métayer, L.M.: Cerebral-motor re-education of the young child. Masson, Barcelona (2001)
4. Mendoza, P.: Effectiveness of an orofacial stimulation programme in children with Down syndrome with swallowing disorders. Case studies (2014)
5. Bacco, R., et al.: Eating and swallowing disorders in children and young people with cerebral palsy: a multidisciplinary approach. Las Condes Med. J. **25**(2), 330–342 (2014)
6. Salghetti, A., Martinuzzi, A.: Dysphagia in cerebral palsy. Eastern J. Med. **17**(4), 188 (2012)

7. Otapowicz, D., Sobaniec, W., Okurowska-Zawada, B., et al.: Dysphagia in children with infantile cerebral palsy. Adv Med Sci. **55**(2), 222–227 (2010)
8. Parkes, J., Hill, N.A.N., Platt, M.J., Donnelly, C.: Oromotor dysfunction and communication impairments in children with cerebral palsy: a register study. Dev. Med. Child Neurol. **52**(12), 1113–1119 (2010)
9. Calis, E.A., Veugelers, R., Sheppard, J.J., Tibboel, D., Evenhuis, H.M., Penning, C.: Dysphagia in children with severe generalized cerebral palsy and intellectual disability. Dev. Med. Child Neurol. **50**(8), 625–630 (2008)
10. Arvedson, J.C.: Swallowing and feeding in infants and young children. GI Motility online (2006)
11. Arvedson, J.C.: Assessment of pediatric dysphagia and feeding disorders: clinical and instrumental approaches. Dev Disabil Res Rev. **14**(2), 118–127 (2008)
12. Salvador, M.B.: The importance of oral language in early childhood education. Classroom magazine on Educational Innovation, p. 46 (1996)
13. Barrón, F., Robles, A., Elizondo, J., Riquelme, M., Riquelme, H.: Oromotor therapy and dietary supplementation, improved feeding skills and nutrition for patients with cerebral palsy. Rev. Esp. Nutr. Comunitaria **23**(4) (2017)
14. Mercado, K..: Orofacial exercises and their relationship to oral language development. Early childhood perspec. **4**(4) (2017)
15. Arvedson, J., Clark, H., Lazarus, C., Schoolling, T., Frymark, T.: The effects of oral-motor exercises on swallowing in children: an evidence-based systematic review. Dev. Med. Child. Neurol. **52**(11), 1000–1013 (2010)
16. Camilo, J.: Oromotor alterations presented by children with high neurological risk in the western telethon children's rehabilitation centre, Guadalajara, Jalisco (2013)
17. Pruna, E., Corrales, G., Gálvez, C., Escobar, I., Mena, L.: Proposal for muscle rehabilitation of lower limbs using an interactive virtual system controlled through gestures. In: De Paolis, L.T., Bourdot, P. (eds.) AVR 2018. LNCS, vol. 10851, pp. 60–77. Springer, Cham (2018). https://doi.org/10.1007/978-3-319-95282-6_5
18. Pruna, E., Acurio, A., Tigse, J., Escobar, I., Pilatásig, M., Pilatásig, P.: Virtual system for upper limbs rehabilitation in children. In: De Paolis, L.T., Bourdot, P., Mongelli, A. (eds.) AVR 2017. LNCS, vol. 10325, pp. 107–118. Springer, Cham (2017). https://doi.org/10.1007/978-3-319-60928-7_9
19. Albiol-Pérez, S., et al.: A novel approach in virtual rehabilitation for children with cerebral palsy: evaluation of an emotion detection system. In: Rocha, Á., Adeli, H., Reis, L.P., Costanzo, S. (eds.) WorldCIST'18 2018. AISC, vol. 746, pp. 1240–1250. Springer, Cham (2018). https://doi.org/10.1007/978-3-319-77712-2_119
20. Sajan, J.E., John, J.A., Grace, P., Sabu, S.S., Tharion, G.: Wii-based interactive video games as a supplement to conventional therapy for rehabilitation of children with cerebral palsy: a pilot, randomized controlled trial. Dev. Neurorehabil. **20**(6), 361–367 (2017)
21. Carrapiço, R., Guimarães, I., Grilo, M., Cavaco, S., Magalhães, J.: 3D facial video retrieval and management for decision support in speech and language therapy. In: Proceedings of the 2017 ACM on International Conference on Multimedia Retrieval. ACM (2017)
22. Máximo-Bocanegra, N., Martín-Ruiz, M.L.: An innovative serious game for the detection and rehabilitation of oral-facial malfunction in children: a pilot study. J. Sens. (2017)
23. Ochoa-Guaraca, M., Pulla-Sánchez, D., Robles-Bykbaev, V., López-Nores, M., Carpio-Moreta, M., García-Duque, J.: A hybrid system based on robotic assistants and mobile applications to support speech therapy for children with disabilities and communication disorders. Virtual Campuses **6**(1), 77–87 (2017)
24. Kothari, M., Svensson, P., Jensen, J., Holm, T.D., Nielsen, M.S., Mosegaard, T., ... & Baad-Hansen, L.: Tongue-controlled computer game: a new approach for rehabilitation of tongue motor function. Arch. Phys. Med. Rehabil. **95**(3), 524–530 (2014)

25. Pan, T.Y., Wong, Y.X., Lee, T.C., Hu, M.C.: A Kinect-based oral rehabilitation system. In Orange Technologies (ICOT), In: 2015 International Conference, pp. 71–74, IEEE (2015)
26. Wang, Y.X., Lo, L.Y., Hu, M.C.: Eat as much as you can: a kinect-based facial rehabilitation game based on mouth and tongue movements. In: Proceedings of the 22nd ACM international conference on Multimedia, pp. 743–744. ACM (2014)
27. Wang, Y.X., Lo, L.Y., Hu, M.C.: Eat as much as you can: a kinect-based facial rehabilitation game based on mouth and tongue movements. In: Proceedings of the 22nd ACM international conference on Multimedia, ACM (2014)

A Virtual Reality Based Application for Children with ADHD: Design and Usability Evaluation

Giuseppina Bernardelli[1], Valeria Flori[1,2], Luca Greci[3], Arianna Scaglione[1],
and Andrea Zangiacomi[3(✉)]

[1] Università degli Studi di Milano, Milano, Italy
{g.bernardelli,valeria.flori}@unimi.it,
arianna.scaglione@studenti.unimi.it
[2] Scientific Institute IRCCS Eugenio Medea, Bosisio Parini, Italy
[3] Institute of Intelligent Industrial Technologies and Systems for Advanced Manufacturing,
National Research Council, Milan, Italy
{luca.greci,andrea.zangiacomi}@itia.cnr.it

Abstract. This work presents a VR based serious game for children with ADHD
and aims at providing an evaluation of the acceptability and the usability of an
application developed to create a meaningful and motivating environment for the
child, capable of supporting the development of the various attentional components. Due to the Covid-19 pandemic the evaluation was performed online offering
also the opportunity to test the feasibility of a validation remotely performed. The
expert involved in the study expressed a positive judgment on the application,
considering it understandable and easy to use. Moreover, they confirmed that the
actions performed by the operator, during the remote sessions, were clear and
made it possible to understand the tasks required within by the serious game, thus
enabling to provide evidence on such kind of remote validation.

Keywords: Virtual reality · Attention Deficit Hyperactivity Disorder · Cognitive
rehabilitation · Serious game

1 Introduction

Numerous studies show how virtual reality (VR) can be applied to different areas of
medicine, in particular to neuro-motor and cognitive rehabilitation, through a learning
process in a digital simulation context of the real world [1]. From an analysis of the
literature it emerges that VR has started being used for the rehabilitation treatment of
children with Attention Deficit/Hyperactivity Disorder (ADHD), a behavioral syndrome
characterized by a difficulty in maintaining attention and controlling the impulsivity
accompanied by an excessive level of motor activity, and several works have demonstrated the related benefits [2, 3]. These symptoms can manifest themselves differently
depending on the specific case: in fact, there will be children in whom inattention will
be greater or children in whom we will have greater hyperactivity and impulsiveness.
This heterogeneity of the disorder, in turn, can cause further associated disorders as

© Springer Nature Switzerland AG 2021
L. T. De Paolis et al. (Eds.): AVR 2021, LNCS 12980, pp. 363–375, 2021.
https://doi.org/10.1007/978-3-030-87595-4_27

the inattention connected to excessive levels of motor activity can cause poor academic performance. Due to the impulsiveness, the child may have difficulty in relating to his peers and, due to the constant disapproval from teachers and parents, this could cause in him a low self-esteem and a demotivation. For this reason, it is very important to diagnose ADHD in time as the symptoms will continue to persist even in adulthood, negatively impacting different contexts of daily life, both from a work point of view, with difficulty in completing tasks, and relational, with a difficulty in maintaining ties. The symptoms of the disorder present an onset already from 3 years of age, however the diagnosis is made only from 8–10 years of age, a period in which the child attends primary school and in the school environment the difficulties begin to become evident. Treatment varies according to the specific case and the severity of the disorder. In severe cases the rehabilitation program is also associated to a pharmacological intervention in order to mitigate the impulsive and hyperactive aspects typical of the symptoms, so that the child can be more involved in the execution of a task.

Basing on such considerations, this work proposes a VR based serious game for children with ADHD and aims at providing an evaluation of the acceptability and the usability of the developed application in order to create a meaningful and motivating environment for the child capable of supporting the development of the various attentional components and offer an engaging experience. According to literature on rehabilitation of children suffering from ADHD, the treatment adopted through the proposed solution can be personalized basing on personal and specific needs of the single child. Moreover, in comparison to previous works, it focuses on everyday living activities with the goal to promote different kind of outcomes as better explained in Sect. 3.

2   VR and ADHD

First studies for the application of VR for the treatment of ADHD were focused on the development of the Virtual Classroom (VC) [4] that revealed to provide a valuable support not only for the evaluation of the ADHD but also as a promising rehabilitation tool of attentional processes. The VC, also called AULA, can be assessed according to some parameters, recorded during the sessions and which include [5–8]: commission and omission errors, average response time, motor activity (through sensors positioned on the user it is possible to check superfluous movements), quality of attention.

The studies taken into consideration on the evaluative use of VR show that subjects with ADHD, compared to healthy children, have a greater number of errors of omission and commission, an excess of motor activity, a slower response time and a lower score in processing speed and working memory. All studies agree on the effectiveness of VR because: it has a greater ecological validity; it is possible to quantify measures that would not be possible to consider through traditional tests; it allows to perform a behavioral monitoring that is recorded in the VR system; the environment created can be customized basing on the characteristics of the patient. Moreover, it can be designed to provide fun ad engagement, motivating the patient to use this new technology.

VR has been used extensively over the past 20 years to assess attention, cognitive and behavioral aspects, proving to be a valuable resource for improving diagnostic accuracy and eliminating possible subjective biases which, in the worst case, could produce an error of evaluation with serious consequences [9].

With regard to the therapeutic and rehabilitative aspect, literature is numerically lower than the use of VR as an evaluation tool and the existing studies are mostly recent.

Among these, Parsons et al. [9], support the thesis that VR can support rehabilitation in children with ADHD as it allows to: provide stable and controlled stimuli over time; adjust to the specific needs of the patient; motivate the patient through pleasant and easy-to-use environments; create safe learning environments to minimize time, costs and errors; favor the development of cognitive abilities and improve behavioral aspects. Shema-Shiratzky et al. [10] demonstrated how VR has good efficacy in training children with ADHD by creating a combined motor-cognitive activity in which the child, while walking on a treadmill, must avoid obstacles and listen to a short story about which some questions will be asked.

If we consider aspects such as inattention, hyperactivity and impulsiveness, the virtual environment allows an increase in attentional performance with a consequent decrease in distractions and impulsive character. This is what Bioulac et al. [11] observed in their study carried out considering three groups of children, aged between 7 and 11, randomly assigned to treatment with the drug methylphenidate, psychotherapy or VR. The results showed that the group subjected to treatment with drugs and that subjected to VC present almost similar effects but impulsivity significantly decreases for the second group, thus allowing to have a number of correct responses similar to the group treated with the drug.

The study by Ou et al. [12] highlighted how performing balance and coordination exercises can improve attention in children with ADHD. This innovative exercise modality was created with the aim of enhancing the rehabilitation of children with ADHD which, at times, can be repetitive and easily attributable to indolence. Although there are still few studies concerning the treatment of ADHD in developmental age, the results obtained so far are promising: in fact, thanks to the virtual environment, it is possible to train attention and memory by creating an environment similar to reality, but which offers the possibility of being controlled through precise and systematic measurements [1]. What emerges from the literature regarding the rehabilitation of ADHD is that the treatment is personalized according to the case, based on age, secondary disorders and the severity of symptoms. In fact, this disorder is very heterogeneous and with different characteristics depending on the child; for this reason, it is important to start with an accurate and personalized therapeutic intervention for the individual patient, including in the approach all the key persons and roles involved in the child's growth process.

According to the literature, the advantages of its use as a rehabilitation tool concern the ecological validity of the proposal and the possibility of customizing the environment for each patient with important consequences in terms of motivation and adherence to treatment [1–3, 10–13].

3 The ADAD Application

The application proposed in this work refers to a prototype of serious game aimed at providing children suffering from ADHD with a meaningful and motivating environment able to support the development of the various attention components. The aim was to realize a solution characterized by a simple game dynamic, able to be understood by school-age children.

Accordingly, it has been decided to focus on features allowing the reproducibility of everyday living environments and activities that can be carried out in them enabling to:

- promote the orientation of attention and organized visual search;
- inhibit impulsiveness through waiting times and specific pre-established elements in the game;
- support attentional skills by promoting more sustained attention spans;
- strengthen memory and learning;
- motivate the child and strengthen his self-esteem also in terms of self-efficacy.

3.1 HW and SW

The game was developed using Unity, a cross-platform game engine developed by Unity Technologies. The VR system chosen to visualize and interact with the VR environment is the Oculus Quest by Facebook, an all-in-one gaming headset that works without being plugged into a PC or another device. The kit is composed of an immersive headset and two touch controllers enabling to interact with the virtual environment. Oculus Quest offers a high-quality image, it mounts two OLED screens with a resolution of 1600×1440 pixels, one for each eye, and reduces the onset of cyber-sickness thanks to a 72 Hz refresh. Moreover, the system reduces the risk of falling as the headset isn't tethered to external devices. Oculus Quest has an integrated audio speaker to play sounds (Fig. 1).

Fig. 1. The virtual environment of the ADAD game.

The Touch controllers are handheld units, each featuring an analog stick, three buttons, and two triggers allowing to perform several actions in the virtual reality environment (grab, pinch, point and click, etc.). Each controller is equipped with a set of infrared LEDs that allows the controllers to be fully tracked in 3D space by the headset's tracking cameras and to be represented in the virtual environment. Moreover, by using the controllers and the cameras mounted on the headset, the user can draw a guideline around the play area. The area drawn is considered as a safe space where the user can move safely, whenever the user is too close to the borders, the Oculus Quest draws a virtual rid warning the user of the danger of collision.

3.2 The Serious Game Dynamics

The aim of the serious game (SG), called ADAD, is to find a target object and put it in a basket. ADAD is set inside a room furnished with few elements: a carpet, a sofa, a table, a lamp, a blackboard, a bookcase, a small table, and a basket. The flow consists in observing a target object, showed in front of the blackboard for a certain time, according to the difficulty level; finding the object inside the room, grabbing and placing it inside the basket as shown in Fig. 2.

The SG starts with a warm-up stage to let the player become familiar with the equipment: the headset and the controllers. At the beginning of the warm-up, a digital voice tells the user to touch a cube appearing in front of him/her to start playing (see Fig. 3). The request is repeated until the user accomplish this task. If the voice intervenes three times because no action is performed, the intervention of the operator is requested. Once the player touches the cube, it vanishes, and a book appears in a random position inside the room while the digital voice tells the user to grab it and put it in the basket. Each time the book is placed inside the basket a positive acoustic feedback is provided. After three successful attempts, a voice warns the user that the first level of the game is about to begin.

Fig. 2. The object to grab showed in the blackboard (left) and then in the VE (on the right)

The SG is divided into six levels of increasing difficulty, and each of them consists of 3 rounds; once the three rounds have been completed, the game move on to the next level (see Fig. 4). The parameters used to implement the increasing difficulty are shown in Table 1: target objects, target object viewing time, time to complete the task, and distractors.). While playing the user can make two potential kinds of mistakes in terms of elapsed time and wrong target object.

The former occurs when the time fixed to put the item in the basket ends, the latter if a wrong object is placed in the basket. Both the errors return negative audio feedback and activate specific facilitators to sustain attention, visual research, and working memory:

a voice remember the user to get the target object after the first error and a visual aid is provided (the target object is highlighted) reinforced by a voice prompt ("take the highlighted object") after the second wrong attempt.

Fig. 3. The digital voice tells the user to touch a cube in front of him/her to start playing

If the user needs the visual aid to complete a round, he/she must repeat it. If more visual aids are used in the same game level, the level must be repeated too.

The dynamics in the game phase are the same of the warm-up: touch the cube, look at the target object, find it, and place it into the basket. Each target object displayed in the room during the game will remain, as distractors, in the next rounds and levels, increasing the complexity of the scene. At the start, once the user has touched the cube appearing in front of him/her, a countdown is shown on the blackboard to advice that something is about to happen: the target object will thus shortly appear. According to the difficulty level, different kind of tasks and related cognitive efforts in terms of attention are requested. For example, the warning acts on the phasic alert (attention orientation) and on the tonic alert (ability to maintain an adequate level of performance for a certain time). In the first three levels, a pre-attention activity is carried out to train the child for the task and gain confidence in how to perform the activity. While playing levels from 1 to 3, the "top-down" attention is mainly stimulated: the user must actively search, in the virtual environment, for something he/she has just seen (visual research, attention orienting, and selective attention).

The higher complexity of level 3 mainly relies on the fact that the target objects to be searched are similar to the previous ones already placed in the room in level 1 and 2 but they present different colors, thus requiring the child to be fairly involved in selective attention (difference between objects). Furthermore, in addition to exercising memory, the child must also be able to not respond impulsively (thus stimulating inhibition and concentration). In levels 4 and 5, acoustic and visual distractors are added with the intent to exercise and stimulate more the user attention on the task to be performed:

the "bottom-up" attention is therefore stimulated (concentration, selective attention, inhibition, control of interference, divided attention). Accordingly, in each round of level 4 and in round 3 of level 5, the ticking of a clock is played while the object target is shown on the blackboard, in level 5, round 1, a horn sound is also played. In level 5, round 2, conversely, no sounds are played but a visual distractor is shown: a butterfly flying around the room.

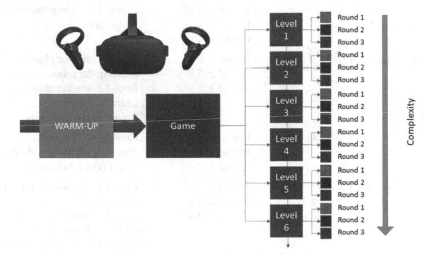

Fig. 4. The flowchart representing levels of the ADAD game

Level 6 presents a different kind of task compared to the previous ones to stimulate the supervisory attentional system (SAS): the object shown on the blackboard is not the target, but it is similar to the one to find in the room. The competence stimulated by level 6 are thus: inhibition, interference control, distributed attention and working memory. The parameters used to implement the increasing difficulty are shown in Table 1.

For each session of the ADAD game, the current level of difficulty, the total time used to complete the task, the target object and eventual errors or hesitations can be stored on a XML file, downloadable from the VR device (Fig. 5).

4 Validation with Experts

4.1 Participants and Methods

The aim of this first validation was to assess the acceptability and usability of the proposed environment as a tool for supporting children suffering from ADHD. The involvement of such kind of experts enabled thus to further test the functionalities and design of the application, providing also suggestions for possible improvements. Moreover, a secondary scope was to evaluate the feasibility of a validation remotely performed.

This observational study was conducted in January 2021, involving a panel of four experts with a specialization in bioengineering. Median age of the experts was 34,

Table 1. Parameters to set the difficulty of the ADAD game task for each level

Level No	Time to complete the task	Target viewing time	Distractors
1	Round 1 to 3: 30 s	Round 1: 8 s Round 2: 6 s Round 3: 4 s	Round 1: no distractors Round 2: objects added in the room Round 3: no distractors
2	Round 1 to 3: 30 s	Round 1: 4 s Round 2: 4 s Round 3: 4 s	Round 1 to 3: objects added in the room
3	Round 1 to 3: 20 s	Round 1: 6 s Round 2: 6 s Round 3: 6 s	Round 1: similar objects added in the room Round 2: similar objects added in the room Round 3: no distractors
4	Round 1 to 3: 20 s	Round 1: 4 s Round 2: 4 s Round 3: 4 s	Round 1 to 3: acoustic distractor while viewing the object (clock ticketing)
5	Round 1 to 3: 20 s	Round 1: 4 s Round 2: 4 s Round 3: 4 s	Round 1: acoustic distractor (horn sound) Round 2: visual distractor (butterfly flying around) Round 3: acoustic distractor (clock ticketing)
6	Round 1 to 3: 20 s	Round 1: 4 s Round 2: 4 s Round 3: 4 s	Round 1 to 3: no distractors

25 years and they were all females. Due to their research background with VR they all hold a direct and profound experience with the technology.

For this study, two different tools have been applied. The first one is the Technology Acceptance Model (TAM) questionnaire [14], which represents a predictive statistical model of the acceptance for a technology and for its future application [15] that has been widely used in literature to: analyse acceptance and use of information technologies in working context; assess user acceptance towards VR [16–19] and evaluate acceptance of a disposal by patients in rehabilitation contexts.

In this case the validation process adopted the TAM-3 [20] in order to analyse usability of the digital environment by technical experts. In particular, three out of the 16 constituent constructs of TAM-3 have been considered, with a total of 10 items:

- perceived ease of use, 4 item (PEOU);
- perceived enjoyment, 3 item (ENJ);
- output quality, 3 item (OUT).

Fig. 5. An example of the visual hints: the highlighted pen on the floor

As anticipated, beside the TAM questionnaire, a semi-structured interview was also self-administrated to participants in order to investigate some more specific aspect of the serious game as, for example, the realism of the VE, the length of the game, difficulty levels and their progression, hints and guides, strengths and weaknesses and possible suggestions for improvements. Due to the COVID-19 pandemic, that dramatically restricted face-to-face activities, the evaluation has been remotely performed through Skype platform. Participants have been thus asked to attend a session of the VR based serious game and to answer then the questionnaires. The session lasted approximately 30 min and, after an initial introduction illustrating the dynamics of the game and the sequence of related levels, was focused on the vision of a game session performed on line by a researcher of the team. Possible questions were answered at the end of the demo and evaluation materials were also distributed.

4.2 Results

The phase of data analysis took place after the collection of questionnaires from experts and consisted in two stages. For what concerns TAM, items have been grouped according to the reference constructs in order to calculate the mean of scores for each specific category and analyse the level of agreement or disagreement of participants with respect to the 7-point Likert scale applied in the questionnaire. Referring to the open questions of the semi-structured interview, answers have been coded according to a qualitative analysis by two separate researchers.

TAM. Data analysis highlights that the answers from experts for each considered construct have scores higher than 5, that means from "somewhat agree" to rise (see Fig. 6.1).

In details, focussing of specific answers, it emerges that the evaluation of the OUT construct (output quality) all experts judged feedbacks from the application easily understandable. Moreover, three experts consider the proposed VR solution enjoyable and all of them evaluate the interaction (PEOU) clear and easy to use (see Fig. 6.2).

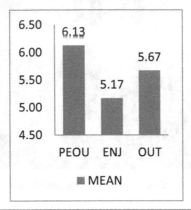

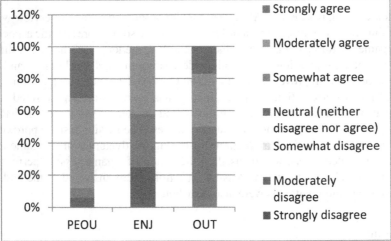

Fig. 6. TAM results from expert evaluation

Semi-structured Interview. According to collected answers, most of respondent were satisfied about the realism of the environment: one expert rated it as realistic and three experts as quite realistic. The same percentage (3) judged the length of the game as adequate to the increasing complexity of levels while one of expert define the pace as really pressing. All participants consider the guiding voice, although understandable, artificial. This may represent a critical aspect of the digital environment due to the lack of vocal inflections that could affect the understanding of some messages.

Concerning the hints, one participant considers them useful, half of them quite useful and only one neutral. In particular, the experts think that the yellow halo used to highlight the target can enable its identification.

For what concerns object recognition, the experts expressed a neutral opinion towards the difficulty progression in the different levels (not easy, nor difficult). This progression is considered by all the participants to be quite adequate, with a gradual increase in the complexity of the targets. This aspect represents a strength of the VE.

Moreover, when asked about the age range in which the tool could be proposed, half of the experts argue that the VR environment is adequate for 10 years old children while one of them considers it suitable from 8 years old users on but only in case of children with good cognitive abilities. The remaining one suggest to start from 9 years old users, but with adequate attention, as the guidelines recommend the use of VR devices only from 12–13 years of age. All participants finally argue they were able to complete autonomously the requested tasks, thank you to the warm-up phase enabling to learn the game dynamics and flow and to the guiding voice providing clear instruction on how to perform tasks. Despite this, some complexities arose due to the remote modalities in one of respondents probably due to the suboptimal internet connection.

5   Conclusions and Future Work

This work aims at studying the acceptability ad usability of a VR-based application developed to support clinicians in the treatment of children with ADHD. According to literature on rehabilitation of children suffering from ADHD, the treatment proposed through the developed solution can be personalized on the basis of the single child and its personal and specific needs. Though it has to be acknowledged that the sample was small, the active participation in the training sessions and the unanimous positive judgement of the participants had led to the conclusion that the application was well accepted and user friendly for the experts. Moreover, experts confirmed that the actions performed by the operator, during the remote sessions, were clear and made it possible to understand the tasks required within by the serious game, enabling to provide evidence on the feasibility of a validation remotely performed.

This first validation phase offered indeed the opportunity not only to test the system with experts, but also to highlight what are the critical aspects not emerged in the preliminary test phase performed within the research team. Starting from the analysis of these issues, possible improvement to the system have being identified from the technological point of view. First, the software will be made able to handle automatically the level selection, excluding the intervention and the potential errors committed by the operator.

Further development of this work will include, as a conclusion of this first step, a validation also with clinical experts for what concerns the usability and acceptability of the solution. According to necessary improvements emerged from the validation with experts, a secondary validation phase will then involve healthy children and, following, children with ADHD.

References

1. Weiss, P.L., Kizony, R., Feintuch, U., Katz, N.: Virtual reality in neurorehabilitation. In: Selzer, M., Clarke, S., Cohen, L., Kwakkel, G., Miller, R. (eds.). Textbook of Neural Repair and Rehabilitation. Cambridge University Press (2006). https://doi.org/10.1017/CBO978051 1995590
2. Shiri, S., Tenenbaum, A., Sapir-Budnero, O., Wexler, I.D.: Elevating hope among children with attention deficit and hyperactivity disorder through virtual reality. Front. Hum. Neurosci. **8**, 198 (2014)
3. Bashiri, A., Ghazisaeedi, M., Shahmoradi, L.: The opportunities of virtual reality in the rehabilitation of children with attention deficit hyperactivity disorder: a literature review. Korean J. Pediatr **60**(11), 337 (2017)
4. Rizzo, A.A., et al.: The virtual classroom: a virtual reality environment for the assessment and rehabilitation of attention deficits. CyberPsychology Behav. **3**(3), 483–499 (2000)
5. Díaz-Orueta, U., Garcia-López, C., Crespo-Eguílaz, N., Sánchez-Carpintero, R., Climent, G., Narbona, J.: AULA virtual reality test as an attention measure: convergent validity with Conners' continuous performance test. Child Neuropsychol. **20**(3), 328–342 (2014)
6. Adams, R., Finn, P., Moes, E., Flannery, K., Rizzo, A.S.: Distractibility in attention/deficit/hyperactivity disorder (ADHD): the virtual reality classroom. Child Neuropsychol. **15**(2), 120–135 (2009)
7. Bioulac, S., Lallemand, S., Rizzo, A., Philip, P., Fabrigoule, C., Bouvard, M.P.: Impact of time on task on ADHD patient's performances in a virtual classroom. Eur. J. Paediatr. Neurol. **16**(5), 514–521 (2012)
8. Parsons, T.D., Bowerly, T., Buckwalter, J.G., Rizzo, A.A.: A controlled clinical comparison of attention performance in children with ADHD in a virtual reality classroom compared to standard neuropsychological methods. Child Neuropsychol. **13**(4), 363–381 (2007)
9. Yeh, S.C., Tsai, C.F., Fan, Y.C., Liu, P.C., Rizzo, A.: An innovative ADHD assessment system using virtual reality. In: 2012 IEEE-EMBS Conference on Biomedical Engineering and Sciences. IEEE, pp. 78–83, December 2012
10. Shema-Shiratzky, S., et al.: Virtual reality training to enhance behavior and cognitive function among children with attention-deficit/hyperactivity disorder: brief report. Dev. Neurorehabil. **22**(6), 431–436 (2019)
11. Bioulac, S., et al.: Virtual remediation versus methylphenidate to improve distractibility in children with ADHD: a controlled randomized clinical trial study. J. Attention disord., 1087054718759751 (2018)
12. Ou, Y.-K., Wang, Y.-L., Chang, H.-C., Yen, S.-Y., Zheng, Y.-H., Lee, B.-O.: Development of virtual reality rehabilitation games for children with attention-deficit hyperactivity disorder. J. Ambient. Intell. Humaniz. Comput. **11**(11), 5713–5720 (2020). https://doi.org/10.1007/s12 652-020-01945-9
13. Barba, M.C., et al.: BRAVO: a gaming environment for the treatment of ADHD. In: De Paolis, L.T., Bourdot, P. (eds.) AVR 2019. LNCS, vol. 11613, pp. 394–407. Springer, Cham (2019). https://doi.org/10.1007/978-3-030-25965-5_30
14. Davis, F.: Perceived usefulness, perceived ease of use, and user acceptance of information technology. MIS Q. **13**(3), 319–340 (1989). https://doi.org/10.2307/249008
15. Morelli, S., D'Avenio, G., Rossi, M., Grigioni, M.: Utilizzo delle tecnologie sanitarie: uno strumento per la valutazione dell'accettazione da parte degli utenti. Istituto Superiore di Sanità (Rapporti ISTISAN 20/27), Roma (2020)
16. Bertrand, M., Bouchard, S.: Applying the technology acceptance model to VR with people who are favorable to its use. J. Cyber. Ther. Rehabil. **1**(2), 200–210 (2008)

17. Lee, J., Kim, J., Choi, J.Y.: The adoption of virtual reality devices: the technology acceptance model integrating enjoyment, social interaction, and strength of the social ties. Telemat. Inform. **39**, 37–48 (2019)
18. Manis, K.T., Choi, D.: The virtual reality hardware acceptance model (VR-HAM): extending and individuating the technology acceptance model (TAM) for virtual reality hardware. J. Bus. Res. **100**, 503–513 (2019)
19. Mahalil, I., Yusof, A.M., Ibrahim, N.: A literature review on the usage of Technology Acceptance Model for analysing a virtual reality's cycling sport applications with enhanced realism fidelity. In: 2020 8th International Conference on Information Technology and Multimedia (ICIMU) IEEE, pp. 237–24. (2020, August)
20. Venkatesh, V., Bala, H.: Technology acceptance model 3 and a research agenda on interventions. Decis. Sci. **39**(2), 273–315 (2008)

A New Technique of the Virtual Reality Visualization of Complex Volume Images from the Computer Tomography and Magnetic Resonance Imaging

Iva Vasic[1]([✉]), Roberto Pierdicca[1]([✉]), Emanuele Frontoni[1]([✉]), and Bata Vasic[2]([✉])

[1] Università Politecnica delle Marche, Ancona, Italy
vasic@iva.silicon-studio.com, {r.pierdicca,
e.frontoni}@staff.univpm.it
[2] Faculty of Electronic Engineering, University of Nis, Nis, Serbia
bata.vasic@ppf.edu.rs

Abstract. This paper presents a new technique for the virtual reality (VR) visualization of complex volume images obtained from computer tomography (CT) and Magnetic Resonance Imaging (MRI) by combining three-dimensional (3D) mesh processing and software coding within the gaming engine. The method operates on real representations of human organs avoiding any structural approximations of the real physiological shape. In order to obtain realistic representation of the mesh model, geometrical and topological corrections are performed on the mesh surface with preserving real shape and geometric structure. Using mathematical intervention on the 3D model and mesh triangulation the second part of our algorithm ensures an automatic construction of new two-dimensional (2D) shapes that represent vector slices along any user chosen direction. The final result of our algorithm is developed software application that allows to user complete visual experience and perceptual exploration of real human organs through spatial manipulation of their 3D models. Thus our proposed method achieves a threefold effect: i) high definition VR representation of real models of human organs, ii) the real time generated slices of such a model along any directions, and iii) almost unlimited amount of training data for machine learning that is very useful in process of diagnosis. In addition, our developed application also offers significant benefits to educational process by ensuring interactive features and quality perceptual user experience.

Keywords: Virtual reality · Computer tomography · Magnetic Resonance Imaging · Mesh processing · Artificial intelligence

1 Introduction

The past decade has witnessed a steady increase in multi-dimensional representations of medical models and processes utilizing advanced concepts in Artificial Intelligence (AI) to enhance capabilities of the existing VR and AR software tools [1, 2] in variety

© Springer Nature Switzerland AG 2021
L. T. De Paolis et al. (Eds.): AVR 2021, LNCS 12980, pp. 376–391, 2021.
https://doi.org/10.1007/978-3-030-87595-4_28

of applications such as diagnosis, pre-operation planning, various simulations, and also in educational and clinical trainings [3–5].

Increasing the efficiency of in-vivo diagnostics and consequently on adequate educational techniques relies on equipment/hardware that uses the knowledge of the anatomy of human bodies giving the both semantic and visual information [6]. As a representative example CT and MRI systems with developed image processing software are continuously refined to provide very exact visual information of even tiny parts of the human body [7]. However, due to technological limitations even the superiority of above mentioned expensive hardware is not sufficient to provide completely accurate information. Imperfections are mostly related to relatively small resolution of scanned images as well as in the insufficient number of scanning steps (number of the obtained image slices). This problem is solved by employing software algorithms based on image processing that interpolate intermediate steps and uneven attenuation of different tissue types [8]. The State-of-the-art hardware equipment and software improvements still do not meet all the requirements of medical doctors with even extensive experience in traditional diagnostic. This is exactly the where new VR and AR techniques provide significant benefits.

In response to new requirements, the automatic 3D model generation has been implemented in standard CT and MRI scanner software packages based on mathematical Radon transformations [9]. Although these improvements have shown measurable diagnostic results, the automatically generated 3D models have contained significant geometric and topological irregularities to be completely usable in its source form. In order to meet the visual criteria for displaying 3D models, lot of visualization techniques have been proposed. However, such methods are mainly based on Computer Aided Design (CAD) and manual construction models and computer animations using existing software [10]. This approach enables impeccably high-quality representation of the model, where the model usually does not correspond to the real geometric details of the CT and MRI models.

Our approach combines 3D mesh processing process and software coding within the gaming VR engine using complex volumetric images obtained from CT and MRI. Algorithm operates on real representations of human organs without any structural approximations of the real physiological shape. In order to obtain realistic representation of the mesh model geometrical and topological corrections are performed in the term of smoothing and materialization of the mesh surface with preserving real shape and geometric structure. Using simple mathematical intervention on the 3D model and mesh triangulation the second part of our algorithm ensures an automatic construction of new 2D shapes that represent vector slices along any user chosen direction. The final result of our algorithm is developed software application that allows to user complete visual experience and perceptual exploration of real human organs through spatial manipulation of their 3D models Thus our proposed method achieved threefold effect: i) high definition VR representation of real models of human organs, ii) the real time generated slices of such a model along any directions, and iii) practically unlimited source of training data for the AI learning. In addition, our developed application also offers significant benefits to educational process by ensuring interactive features and quality perceptual user experience.

The paper is organized as follows. The Sect. 2 describes the general notations and defines main group of problems in the VR visualization of real models of human organs as a consequence of errors in segmentation of the volumetric images from CT and MRI devices. In this section we also briefly describe achievements of several known methods that give solutions in overcoming particular visualization issues. Our algorithm is described in detail within the Sect. 3. This section also contains theoretical background of used technique with mathematical and geometrical notations. All steps of proposed algorithm are explored with developed software codes used for 3D mesh model manipulation and transformation. Experimental results with visual illustration of our method contribution are shown in the Sect. 4. The brief conclusion and the further work directions are given in Sect. 5.

2 General Notations and Problem Definition

All modalities of medical imaging techniques are widely used and very effective in diagnosis, treatment planning, and evaluation especially in qualitative and semi-quantitative inspections performed by experienced medical doctors. However, the complex features of particular medical images can complicate the analysis and also slow down a successful diagnosis. In order to make the complex characteristics of the medical picture acceptable and perceptually understandable, defining anatomy using 3D geometric modeling and visualization becomes necessary in clinical practice, but also in the fields of education.

Modern technologies in the field of medical imaging have reached a multitude of general requirements in diagnosis until the emergence of new visual criteria in almost all areas of clinical model analysis [11]. In order to recognize the overall problem of the concept of visualization 3D geometric structures obtained from CT and MRI scanners we defined the schematic structure of the visualization process (Fig. 1).

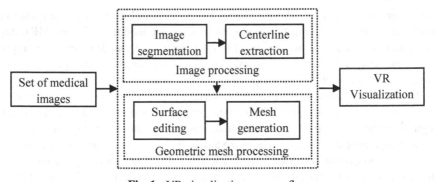

Fig. 1. VR visualization process flow

The abundant number of images obtained from CT or MRI scanners ensures the visualization by segmentation particular tissue types and modeling of the 3D geometric structures. Regardless to usability of scanned images itself, in this paper we concentrate to prove that generated 3D structures with some geometric interventions are fully useful for visualization and educational concepts, and also spur ideas for scientific or clinical predictions.

2.1 Image Processing Problems

The first group of problems is related to CT and MRI hardware and quality of process-ing software tools. All images from the set are distinguished from each other by the attenuation value of scanned tissue (X-ray absorption and scattering in CT scanning and static X-ray imaging), dimension, type of motion, and timescale and periodicity of the motion (in the case of CT and MRI scans of the non-static anatomic structures). The balance of signal-to-noise ratio and spatial resolution affect the quality of the image and consequently the amount of image editing and segmentation before the visualization. Good visualization depends also on the choice and affordability of appropriate image modality, but this group of issues is actually the radiologists' field of research and we will not dig deeply into this area. Since our point of interest is the visualization, we will consider that the whole image processing and segmentation part of processes are performed satisfactory precise.

At the beginning of the whole process shown in Fig. 1 is the set of slice images along the main axes in 3D space. The standard CT and MRI format of the scanned image set is DICOM (Digital Imaging and Communications in Medicine). The example of arbitrary selected slice of the CT scanned heart structure is shown on Fig. 2 using ITK-SNAP software [12].

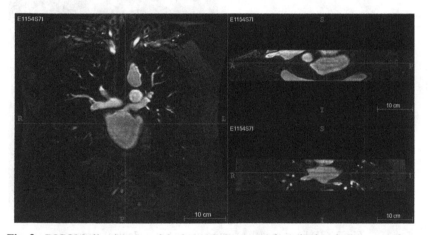

Fig. 2. DICOM slice images of the heart across coronal, sagittal and transverse planes

Segmentation and centerline extraction within the image processing step are covered by the common standalone software engines for the medical 2D images visualization: ITK-SNAP [12], MITK [13], and 3D Slicer [14]. However, the quality of the obtained 2D volume images is often insufficient for the construction of satisfactory precise 3D structures, which are actually a demand of challenging medical diagnosis.

2.2 Mesh Generation Problems

Previously mentioned problems require more profound involvement of notable mathe-matical functions such as Radon transform for the generation of 2D vector shapes and

3D structures. The Radon transformation R_f is a function defined on the space of straight lines $L \in \mathbb{R}^2$ by the line integral along each line [9]:

$$R_f(L) = \int_L f(x)|dx| \tag{1}$$

The function $f(x) = f(x, y)$ is a continuous function, which the double integral $\iint \left(|f(x)|/\sqrt{x^2 + y^2} \right) dx dy$ extending over the whole plane converges, and it holds that:

$$\lim_{r \to \infty} \int_0^{2\pi} f(x + r\cos\phi, y + r\sin\phi)d\phi = 0 \tag{2}$$

Visualization plugins of CT and MRI supporting software packages already relays on some similar functions. However, post-processing techniques are unable to completely solve the issue of irregular meshes that CT and MRI provide. The next Fig. 3 illustrates the real 3D STL (stereo-lithography) model of the heart, and detail of its mesh area with topological and geometrical errors.

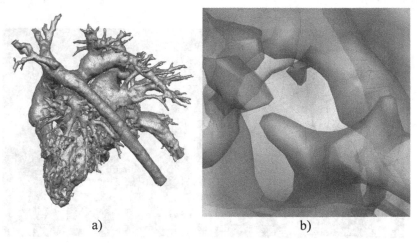

a)   b)

Fig. 3. 3D heart model: a) entire mesh, b) topological errors.

Such errors have strong influence on the further operations of visualization in general, and particularly on the materialization process. This negative influence decreases an overall perceptual visibility of the structures of interest. In order to find an appropriate solution in solving structural geometrical issues, we can define two crucial types of topological errors: i) isolated vertices and structures, and ii) shared geometric primitives (vertices and faces) that belong to multiple anatomic structures. Both types of mesh errors we may consider as a result of imperfection of image processing algorithms and methods. In other hand we have to observe such results from the medical point of view. In this context, some of isolated and/or shared structures may be part of real anatomic structure "invisible" to artificial eyes that hardware equipment represent.

In contrary to problems described in previous subsection where image processing algorithms tries to improve accuracy and increase scanning resolution, according, according to our knowledge there is no automatic methods that can successfully solve geometrical problems of already generated meshes. However, some of the existing approach can be very useful in the process of refining the mesh geometry and removing topological errors [15]. Corrections of the second type of errors require medical consultation and semi-automatic and even manual intervention on the mesh geometry. The combination of existing techniques and the improvement of appropriate algorithms can lead to the successful overcoming of problems and geometric structures that meet the criteria of visualization.

2.3 Training Set for Machine Learning

Achievements of AI achievements are mostly inspired from the nontrivial problems in medical sector and human biology. The strength of powerful neural networks (NN) always relies on rich training data. Although some of the medical areas have abilities to ensure lot of information, the lack of information in other medicine fields is evident. Insufficient data availability can be often a reflection of a complex and expensive technological process of diagnosis, but also of inefficient, unsafe, and uncertain invasive diagnostic techniques.

CT and MRI imaging technologies are classified as very expensive diagnostic methods, so the amount of available scanned data is very limited, especially when the order of magnitude of the data required for machine learning is taken into account. The power of AI was mainly used in the processes of image generation and segmentation [16], while the results were insufficiently used in the 3D geometry analysis and education. In these segments our approach offers possibilities in collecting almost unlimited amount of data for the machine learning and thus significant improvement of the both, diagnostic and education fields.

3 Our Algorithm

Our method is focused on the three research targets: i) high definition VR representation of CT and MRI generated volumetric models, ii) the slices generation along any direction, and iii) obtaining the training data for the machine learning in medical diagnosis purpose. According to these emphases, our algorithm proposes the complete framework of mesh processing and visualization steps presented in Fig. 1.

All including processes with relevant operations and techniques are presented in the flowchart (Fig. 4) with introduced general notations of all used variables, features and functions.

The input of proposed method is the CT or MRI generated mesh of a given 3D surface $M(V,F) \in \mathbb{R}^3$, where $V(v_x, v_y, v_z)$ and $F(i)$ are respectively matrices of all Cartesian vertex coordinates and faces constructed by indexes $i = 1, \cdots , n$ of n belonging vertexes.

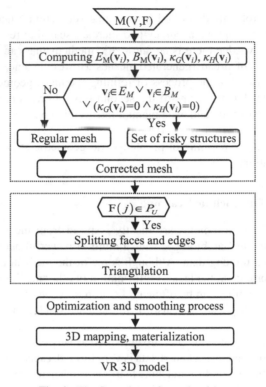

Fig. 4. The flow chart of our algorithm

3.1 Mesh Correction

In order to locate mesh errors and undefined isolated structures, the first step includes the main computations of geometrical and topological features. Within this step algorithm extracts the matrix of the topological error vertices E_M, and the matrix of boundary vertices B_M [1] for each vertex $\mathbf{v}_i(v_{xi}, v_{yi}, v_{zi})$. Using these matrices as well as the sign and a threshold value[2] of $\kappa_G(\mathbf{v}_i)$ and $\kappa_H(\mathbf{v}_i)$ we first extract all risky vertices and structures. The matrix of risky vertices is actually an union of matrices EM, BM and a set of vertices which satisfy the condition: $\kappa_G(\mathbf{v}_i) = 0 \wedge \kappa_H(\mathbf{v}_i) = 0$. The result of this step is the set of isolated geometric structures of irregular topological properties and shapes, but the recognition and classification of specific anatomical structures are excluded from an automatic processing. Their importance for the further process is estimated by medical doctors.

---

[1] Boundary vertices are often important for shape creation, and algorithm leaves to user a choice of their removing from the mesh.

[2] Threshold values of all elimination criteria, including Gaussian and mean curvature values, are adjustable.

3.2   Slicing the Mesh Along User Direction

This part of algorithm is strongly related to the geometric operations and computations over the mesh surface and their primitives. Quality of CT or MRI generated geometric structure is crucial for all further computations and results. The internal structures of scanned organs are especially important because the accuracy of our representation depends on their definition. In order to theoretically describe the details of our idea, we assume that the scanned model contains all internal structures and that they are topologically regular.

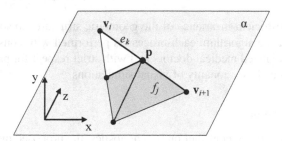

Fig. 5. Mesh face f_j intersected by the plane α

For the given regular mesh $M \in \mathbb{R}^3$ we define set of triangular faces $F(f_1, \cdots, f_m)$ constructed by the three vertex indices associated to their Euclidean coordinates. Consequently, each triangle face f_j of the mesh surface is defined by the coordinates of corresponding vertices. Each of the two corresponding vertices virtually forms an edge between them (Fig. 5). The intersection point $\mathbf{p}(x, y, z)$ of the edge of interest $e_k(\mathbf{v}_i, \mathbf{v}_{i+1})$ and the desired plane $\alpha : ax + by + cz = 0$ is calculated by solving the pair of simple plane and edge equations. In our case the intersection plane is fixed along an axis defined by the user, whereas the whole mesh is aligned and rotated according to this axis. Intersection plane thus have a simple form: $\alpha' : y = s$, where s is a numeric value acquired in real time from the user mouse roll position. Coordinates of intersection point of the plane α' and edge between vertices $\mathbf{v}_i(v_i^x, v_i^y, v_i^z)$ and $\mathbf{v}_{i+1}(v_{i+1}^x, v_{i+1}^y, v_{i+1}^z)$ are calculated as follows:

$$\frac{x - v_i^x}{v_{i+1}^x - v_i^x} = \frac{y - v_i^y}{v_{i+1}^y - v_i^y} = \frac{z - v_i^z}{v_{i+1}^z - v_i^z} = s \qquad (3)$$

Each face of the mesh which correspondent edges intersect with given plane needs to be divided to new three triangular faces[3] according to intersection points. The new edge between two intersection points defines the segment of the whole intersection spline, which is actually defined segment of our new slice.

If we take into account that the user can arbitrarily rotate the mesh model and manage the positions of the intersection planes in 3D space, the number of cross sections of the model is practically unlimited. Collecting all of resulting slices with the corresponding diagnosis data we can form huge training set for machine learning.

---

[3] The face is not divided if the one of vertex belongs to the intersection plane.

3.3 Optimizing Mesh for Visualization

Although CT and MRI techniques produce volumetric images that can be used in monochromatic 2D and 3D visualization, in the VR applications, such a solid models are not perceptually attractive and cannot be used in their original form [17]. In addition, geometry and topology are often defined by sharp faces and shapes, which do not correspond to real shapes of organs. Within the final step our algorithm applies optimization [18] and simplification operations to prepare complex geometric structures for real-time manipulation. On the other hand, we use a semi-automatic mapping and materialization method to achieve a smooth and perceptually acceptable final result of the mesh model.

Due to the insufficient invariance of the geometric structures to some of the methods in this part of the algorithm, each process is performed with constant control and evaluation by specialized medical doctors and with strict respect for preserving natural forms of anatomy and functionality of visual simulations.

3.4 VR for Education

In addition to a significant contribution to diagnostics, the proposed method introduces innovations in the educational approach. The perceptually refined model is imported into a developed gaming VR application, which raised the visual experience to a new level. This approach provides measurable knowledge acquisition through interaction between students and our smart VR application, on the one hand, and enrichment of application content using artificial intelligence on the other.

4   Experimental Results

In the experimental phase of our work, we used geometric structures, obtained from some of well-known segmentation software, which we mentioned in the Sect. 2.1. The result of such semi-automatic process is very commonly a generated 3D mesh in the STL file format that is actually native to the stereo-lithography 3D printing technique. As an experimental geometrical structure, the real heart model is loaded in Matlab software where we performed mesh inspection using our developed software functions [15].

Calculating the main features noted in Fig. 4, all risky primitives are located and selected over the whole mesh, which finalized the process of forming both matrices: matrix of the topological error vertices E_M, and the matrix of boundary vertices B_M. Geometrical and topological errors in forms of isolated vertices, edges and faces are immediately removed from the mesh, whereas other risky types of geometrical structures, such as elongated faces, boundary edges and isolated sub-structures, are located and corrected/removed according to the heart anatomy literature [19] in strict consultation with skilled medical doctors - cardiologists or/and cardio surgeons.

4.1   Geometrical and Topological Modification of 3D Mesh Model

Mesh simplification and optimization procedure is performed in next task in order to avoid post-scanning computations within different applications and tools that we use for mapping and materializing processes. The main criterion in choosing a level of simplification is preserving the shape of the mesh model that is actually a key demand of the visualization and diagnostic globally. In this task whole mesh area paved by rough triangle faces is additionally relaxed with the mesh smoothing algorithm. In order to meet the perceptual requirement of visualization and achieve satisfactory user experience, realistic textures are produced and assigned to the virtual model. Left (a) and right (b) images in the following Fig. 6 show the 3D model of the heart before and after refinement respectively.

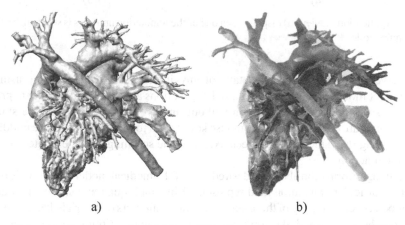

a)   b)

Fig. 6. 3D heart model: a) source model from CT scanner, b) refined and texturized VR model.

Unlike the mixed photogrammetry and video technologies, which is a conceptual base of the majority of conventional 3D scanners, the nature of CT and MRI imaging technologies cannot ensure photographic recordings of scanned surfaces. Moreover, these technologies are not constructed to provide any colour information of the scanned tissues. This fact indicates all technologies: optimization; correction; refinement; smoothing; mapping; and materialization as mandatory tasks within any algorithm for visualization of CT and MRI scanned models.

4.2 3D Visualization Using Gaming Software Engine

Using all previous tasks our algorithm produced 3D mesh model that is suitable for the high quality visualization. The next action in proposed method goes toward to ensure the interactive features that are useable for both educational purposes: teaching and learning. In order to provide the quality user experience these features in our application [20] are written in C# programming language and developed within Unity engine [21].

Although the all gaming engines have been mostly used for interactive design and development in the gaming industry, we proved in this paper their successful employment in scientific medical and education fields. We have communicated all their results and ideas visually. Our developed application offers of the following interaction possibilities:

a)   b)

Fig. 7. Application preview: a) display when one of the annotation numbers is selected, b) display of the quiz mode.

- Observation of all perceptual details of any inserted medical model by using the computer mouse functions. All required user actions are simplified in order to provide easy way to perform manipulation without any previous experience. The standard commands are developed: the left mouse key is used for object rotation, the middle one for moving the camera along screen axis, and the scrolling action executed zooming in or out action.
- Obtaining information about the desired part of the medical model. Each part is related to the particular annotation field represented by small quadratic shape and a unique number. By clicking any of these very noticeable numbers on the right hand side of the screen, the textbox with the corresponding anatomic description appears (Fig. 7.a).
- Testing and evaluating knowledge of students from all previous observations using the quiz mode. This application mode contains interactive fields with questions and several offered answers per each question. Testing software code compares selected choice with the right answer and shows the test result in the form of visual information (Fig. 7.b).

4.3 Comparative Results of Mesh Slicing Methods

In most of cases diagnostic process can be successfully performed using the standard method for observing CT and MRI volumetric models by scrolling in depth along transverse, sagittal and vertical axes [12, 14]. However, in remarking anomalies and analysing certain parts of cardiac anatomy such as aorta, more convenient viewing angle is required. Our method provides slicing along any direction, and thus meets the requirements for the shape assessment and measurements.

In order to demonstrate measurable comparison between visualizing methods, 3D heart model is used as an example. Imperfections or distortions of certain slice views are easily observed on relatively regular shapes, so we separated the aortic area from the rest of the model to emphasize all differences. The correct shape of the aortic section and the advantage of our approach in relation to standard software diagnostic tools are clearly perceptible in the following Fig. 8.

The elliptic shape (Fig. 8a) of the model intersection corresponds to the output of the existing slicing methods [12, 14], whereas our algorithm provides the closely circular

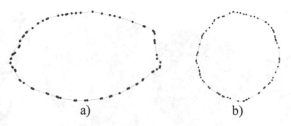

Fig. 8. 2D shapes of the aorta 3D model obtained from: a) the standard transverse slicing plane; b) Our method - 30^0 rotated transverse slicing plane.

section (Fig. 8b) of the aorta. Therefore, it is obvious that our approach ensures greater accuracy of assessment and analysis, and thus consequently correct diagnosis. Additionally to the picturesque evidence of the accuracy and suitability of aortic dissection obtained from our algorithm, Table 1 gives a comparison of numeric values of the aortic features that are important in remarking anomalies and diseases.

Table 1. The aorta mean diameter values (in mm)

Case 1	Case 2	Standard tools	Our method
24.8	24.3	26.75	24.5

The first column value (Case 1) represents mean diameter of the normal ascending aorta commonly used in the medical literature [22]. The value in second column (Case 2) is the mean value of the MRI examinations of the normal thoracic aorta of 66 subjects aged in range 19.1–82.4 years [23]. The result for each person is obtained from four measurement made in the axial plane (supravalvular, at the mid-part of the ascending aorta, at the level of the arch on the ascending and descending aorta), and one in a sagittal plane (at the top of the arch).

Our approach superiorly provides calculation of all important features, including diameter, along the entire aorta with just one measurement. The value in the fourth column we obtained by calibrating the slicing plane in order to be always perpendicular to the aortic flow axis. Assuming the 3D model is calibrated to measure the mean aortic diameter in the value range given from the literature, we clearly notice a considerable deviation of the values in one measurement of standard slice tools (Column N°3).

4.4   Experimental Test of Our Algorithm

Our algorithm is experimentally tested on various arbitrary 3D models[4] with completely different geometrical and topological structures, shapes and complexity.

The visual results and precision of the method are shown in the previous figure (Fig. 9), which also illustrates equally successful operation on compact meshes and

---

[4] 3D models are downloaded from the website Embodi3D [24].

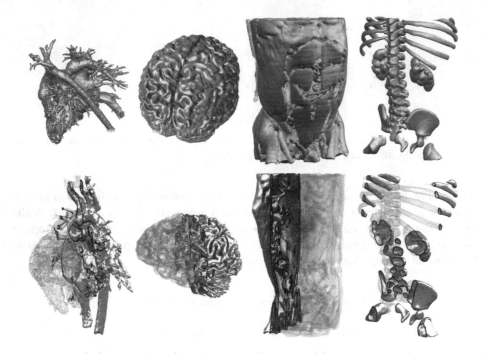

Fig. 9. Our algorithm in action: renderings and slicing results (red lines)

complex 3D geometric structures. In addition, we give in Table 2 numerical features of original and optimized 3D models; and numerical values obtained before and after slicing, as well as slicing speed for each model. It can be noticed that our algorithm is pretty fast and operates on a complex model of kidney and spine in 14 s.

Table 2. Comparative results of the mesh slicing procces over different 3D models: DC – Coordinate of a slicing plane, T– The slicing computation time

3D model	Complexity	DC (x, y, z)	# Vertices	#Faces	T (sec)
Heart	Original	0, 80, 0	122,408	245,962	4
	50% Optimized		61,204	123,530	2
Brain	Original	0, 50, 0	332,152	664,988	7
	50% Optimized		166,076	334,120	4
Torso	Original	0, 30, 0	497,751	996,198	10
	50% Optimized		248,875	498,446	6
Kidney and spine	Original	0, -220, 0	534,394	1,068,777	14
	50% Optimized		267,197	534,383	7

4.5 Theoretical Model of Machine Learning Using 3D Model Slicing

This paper introduced a new idea of use a virtual application in the AI learning process and presented the new theoretic method of the training set forming. Although the construction of NN has significant influence on its efficiency, in this paper we focused on the training data quantity and quality. In addition to numerous effects of our VR application to medical diagnosis and education, it has also strong potential in the machine learning, particularly in training set forming.

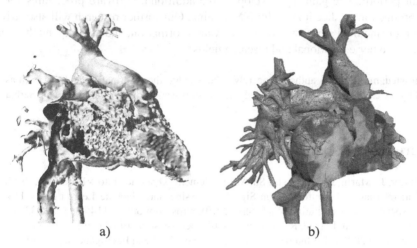

a)   b)

Fig. 10. Slices of the 3D model along Y axis: a) Matlab isosurface, b) Unity application slicer

According to simple mathematical equations given in Sect. 3.2 we preliminary developed an example procedures for 3D mesh slicing using Matlab isosurface and C# functions. The result of both techniques respectively is shown in the previous figure (Fig. 10).

Both slice images are associated to the same 3D model and to same medical case or diagnose. Thus, all different camera views in combination with slices along all direction are potential source of almost unlimited number of training data.

5 Conclusion and Future Works

In this paper, we presented a novel technique that offers a systematic method for the VR visualization complex volume images from the CT and MRI imaging devices. We combined 3D mesh processing and software coding within the gaming engine. Experimental practical results showed real VR representation of human organs without any structural approximations of the real physiological shape. The second part of algorithm ensured an automatic construction of new 2D shapes using mathematical intervention on the 3D model and mesh triangulation. Constructed shapes represent vector slices along any user chosen direction. As the final result we developed software application that allows to user complete visual experience and perceptual exploration of real human organs through spatial manipulation of their 3D models.

We also introduced the new theoretical method of use a virtual application in the machine learning process. Experimental simulation proved significant potential of our algorithm and almost unlimited amount of training data for machine learning that is very useful in process of diagnosis and education. The limitations of the proposed technology are only reflected in the small number of processed CT and MRI models. However, our future works will include using a bigger set of different 3D models and improving overall performance gain, by developing the additional software procedures for real time production of slice images for NN training. Our further research will also strive to cover more medical areas and provide relevant information, and also expand the area of interest to other educational and research fields.

Acknowledgments. The authors sincerely acknowledge the information and suggestions provided by the cardiologist Miomir Randjelovic, Cardiovascular diseases clinic in Nis, Serbia.

References

1. Suttor, J., Marin, J., Verbus, E., Su, M.: Implement AI service into VR training, SPML. In: 2nd International Conference on Signal Processing and Machine Learning, pp. 114–121. Association for Computing Machinery (2019). https://doi.org/10.1145/3372806.3374909
2. Gluck, A., Chen, J., Paul, R.: Artificial intelligence assisted virtual reality warfighter training system. In: 2020 IEEE International Conference on Artificial Intelligence and Virtual Reality (AIVR). Utrecht, Netherlands, vol. 1, pp. 386–389. IEEE Computer Society (2020). https://doi.org/10.1109/AIVR50618.2020.00080
3. Klein, J., et al.: Technical section: visual computing for medical diagnosis and treatment. Comput. Graph. **33**(4), 554–565 (2009). https://doi.org/10.1016/j.cag.2009.04.006
4. Xia, J., et al.: Three-dimensional virtual-reality surgical planning and soft-tissue prediction for orthognathic surgery. IEEE Trans. Inf. Technol. Biomed. **5**(2), 97–107. IEEE (2001). https://doi.org/10.1109/4233.924800
5. Ullrich, S., Kuhlen, T.: Haptic palpation for medical simulation in virtual environments. IEEE Trans. Vis. Comput. Graph. **18**(4), 617–625. IEEE (2012). https://doi.org/10.1109/TVCG.2012.46
6. Chang, G., Morreale, P., Medicherla, P.: Applications of augmented reality systems in education. In: Gibson, D., Dodge, B. (eds.) Proceedings of SITE 2010--Society for Information Technology & Teacher Education International Conference, pp. 1380–1385. Association for the Advancement of Computing in Education (AACE), Waynesville, NC USA (2010)
7. Jeena, R.S., Kumar, S.: A comparative analysis of MRI and CT brain images for stroke diagnosis. In: 2013 Annual International Conference on Emerging Research Areas and 2013 International Conference on Microelectronics, Communications and Renewable Energy, pp. 1–5. IEEE, Kanjirapally, India (2013). https://doi.org/10.1109/AICERA-ICMiCR.2013.6575935
8. Karani, N., Zhang, L., Tanner, C., Konukoglu, E.: An image interpolation approach for acquisition time reduction in navigator-based 4D MRI. Med. Image Anal. **54**, 20–29 (2019). https://doi.org/10.1016/j.media.2019.02.008
9. Toft, P.A.: The Radon Transform - Theory and Implementation. Technical University of Denmark, Kgs. Lyngby, Denmark (1996)

10. Fradi, A., Louhichi, B., Mahjoub, M.A, Eynard, B.: 3D Object retrieval based on similarity calculation in 3D computer aided design systems. In: 2017 IEEE/ACS 14th International Conference on Computer Systems and Applications (AICCSA), pp. 160–165. IEEE, Hammamet, Tunisia (2017). https://doi.org/10.1109/AICCSA.2017.101

11. Cheng, P.C: Handbook of Vascular Motion. Stanford University, CA, United States, Academic Press (2019)

12. ITK-SNAP: Imaging ToolKit-SNAP, University of Pennsylvania, Philadelphia, Pennsylvania, University of Utah, Salt Lake City, Utah. http://www.itksnap.org

13. MITK: Medical Imaging Interaction ToolKit, German Cancer Research Center Division of Medical Image Computing, Heidelberg, Germany

14. 3D Slicer, Harvard University, Cambridge, Massachusetts. https://www.slicer.org

15. Vasic, B.: Ordered Statistics Vertex Extraction and Tracing Algorithm (OSVETA). Adv. Electr. Comput. Eng. 12(4), 25–32 (2012). https://doi.org/10.4316/AECE.2012.04004

16. Marks, P.: Deep Learning Speeds MRI Scans. Commun. ACM 64(4), 12–14 (2021). https://doi.org/10.1145/3449060

17. Kerr, J., Ratiu, P., Sellberg, M.: Volume rendering of visible human data for an anatomical virtual environment. Stud. Health Technol. Inf. 29, 352–370 (1996). https://doi.org/10.3233/978-1-60750-873-1-352

18. Kauffman, M.: Optimizing Your Autodesk® 3ds Max® Design Models for Project Newport. Autodesk University 2009 (2019). http://au.autodesk.com/?nd=material&session_material_id=6296

19. Faletra, F., Pandian, N., Yen Ho, S.: Anatomy of the Heart by Multislice Computed Tomography. Wiley-Blackwell (2008)

20. Vasic, I.: Virtual heart application. http://iva.silicon-studio.com/Heartapp.zip

21. Unity: Multiplatform, Unity Technologies. https://unity.com

22. Aronberg, D.J., Glazer, H.S., Madsen, K., Sagel, S.S.: Normal thoracic aortic diameters by computed tomography. J. Comput. Assist. Tomogr. 8(2), 247 (1984). PMID: 6707274

23. Garcier, J.M., Petitcolin, V., Filaire, M., et al.: Normal diameter of the thoracic aorta in adults: a magnetic resonance imaging study. Surg. Radiol. Anat. 25, 322–329 (2003). https://doi.org/10.1007/s00276-003-0140-z

24. https://www.embodi3d.com/files/

Active and Passive Brain-Computer Interfaces Integrated with Extended Reality for Applications in Health 4.0

Pasquale Arpaia[1,2]($\boxtimes$), Antonio Esposito[3], Francesca Mancino[1], Nicola Moccaldi[1], and Angela Natalizio[1]

[1] Department of Electrical Engineering and Information Technology (DIETI), Università degli Studi di Napoli Federico II, Via Claudio 21, 80138 Naples, Italy
pasquale.arpaia@unina.it
[2] Interdepartmental Center for Research on Management and Innovation in Healthcare (CIRMIS), University of Naples Federico II, Naples, Italy
[3] Department of Electronics and Telecommunications (DET),Politecnico di Torino, Corso Castelfidardo 39, 10129 Turin, Italy

Abstract. This paper presents the integration of extended reality (XR) with brain-computer interfaces (BCI) to open up new possibilities in the health 4.0 framework. Such integrated systems are here investigated with respect to an active and a passive BCI paradigm. Regarding the active BCI, the XR part consists of providing visual and vibrotactile feedbacks to help the user during motor imagery tasks. Therefore, XR aims to enhance the neurofeedback by enhancing the user engagement. Meanwhile, in the passive BCI, user engagement monitoring allows the adaptivity of a XR-based rehabilitation game for children

Preliminary results suggest that the XR neurofeedback helps the BCI users to carry on motor imagery tasks with up to 84% classification accuracy, and that the level of emotional and cognitive engagement can be detected with an accuracy greater than 75%.

Keywords: Brain-computer interface · Extended reality · Health 4.0 · Motor imagery · Attention monitoring

1 Introduction

The term "extended reality" (XR) has been recently introduced to enclose possible combination of real and virtual environments [1]. Although literature proposes a continuous scale ranging from reality to virtuality [2], XR is usually declined into three possibilities: virtual reality, mixed reality, and augmented reality. On the whole, these technologies might enhance the human-machine interaction by exploiting computer-generated perceptual information, which may or may not be overlapped with the real world [3]. In healthcare, the great potential of XR has been addressed to many applications, such as surgery [4,5], rehabilitation [6,7], and clinicians training [8,9]. This applies particularly to the

L. T. De Paolis et al. (Eds.): AVR 2021, LNCS 12980, pp. 392–405, 2021.
https://doi.org/10.1007/978-3-030-87595-4_29

health 4.0 framework, which introduces customization and real-time adaptation in patient care [10]. The exploitation of XR technologies enhances health-related services such as prevention, diagnosis, and treatment from either the patients' and caregivers' point of view. In such a scenario, a decentralization of the health system is highly desirable since moving from the hospital to the patient's home leads to cost saving and optimization of therapeutic outcome [11]. To this aim, novel mobile devices are boosting this evolution primarily due to their wearability and portability [12], as well as their increasing availability on the market.

As a further development, integrating XR with a brain-computer interface (BCI) guarantees unprecedented interactions between a human and the external world. Indeed, a BCI is a novel mean of interaction relying on direct measurement of brain activity and it is receiving itself much investment from the scientific and technical communities [13,14]. Through a BCI, both control and monitoring are possible: a user can communicate his/her intentions to a machine by voluntarily modulating brain waves, or the machine can acquire information about the mental state of the user [15]. Intuitively, such an interface has found many applications in healthcare [16], but it has been also investigated for other fields. For instance, BCI systems have been proposed in conjunction with virtual reality for controlling an avatar or navigating a virtual environment [17]. Their application address either able-bodied people and paralyzed patients that may restore basic communication. Moreover, a survey has highlighted that BCI enables hands-free interaction for extended reality [18] for applications in medicine, robotics, and domotics. In that work, head mounted devices were mostly considered as feasible for real life applications. Nonetheless, it was also shown that the development of XR-BCI system still deserves more efforts.

In addressing wearability and portability, the brain activity is acquired by means of electroencephalography (EEG), which is also non-invasive and relatively low-cost [19]. On the other side, optimizing user-friendliness could lead to performance loss. Therefore, investigating different approaches has been crucial in the implementation of daily-life applications. Different paradigms can be taken into account in developing a BCI. A useful distinction is between reactive, active, and passive [20]. In a *reactive BCI*, the user voluntarily exposes to sensory stimulation, and the brain potentials evoked by that are exploited for communication and control. As an example, a recent work reports the implementation and validation of an XR-BCI monitoring system for health 4.0 relying on visually evoked potentials [21]. In there, smart glasses are simultaneously used for stimulating the user and for data visualization. Meanwhile, stimulation is not required in *active and passive BCIs* because their operation relies upon voluntary modulation of spontaneous brainwaves or detection of involuntary activity, respectively. This basic difference makes them more user-friendly, and hence suitable for daily-life applications. Given that, the present work focuses on active and passive paradigms implemented in conjunction with XR. In the active XR-BCI, the system is based on the detection of motor imagery, while the passive XR-BCI system is based on engagement monitoring. Both systems find wide application in health 4.0 because they can be used for enhancing human-machine interaction for able-bodied users, or they can be exploited in customized rehabilitation.

The remainder of the paper is organized as follows. Section 2 discussed the implementation and the preliminary results of a motor imagery-based (active) BCI exploiting a neurofeedback in virtual reality. Then, Sect. 3 reports the validation of an EEG-based component for engagement detection in an adaptive XR rehabilitation system. Conclusions and implications are addressed in Sect. 4.

2   Active BCI

2.1   Background

An active BCI derives its outputs from brain activity directly and consciously controlled by the user, independently from external events [22]. The most typical paradigm employed for an active BCI is undoubtedly the motor imagery. In there, the user imagines a specific movement for a control application, for instance controlling a wheelchair or navigating a virtual environment. Remarkably, the user must train before being capable of performing a mental task properly. Moreover, the system performance also depend on the user ability to focus on the imagery task. In this regard, neurofeedback (NF) helps the users to self-regulate brain rhythms and it increases both the user's motivation and attention span. NF is accomplished by providing sensory information related to the ongoing neural activity for the BCI user. In particular, the creation of a dedicated virtual environment allows to engage the user. This is especially true in the field of rehabilitation, where XR-BCI systems have been helping patients to avoid "feeling like a patient", though remaining in a clinical surrounding [23].

Currently, visual feedback is a widely employed modality in the field of BCI/NF. However, in recent years, other modalities have been also exploited, such as auditory and haptic. Some studies tested the impact of unimodal feedback modalities on system performance and user comfort, and they resulted quite equivalent [24]. Therefore, recent studies are exploring the possibility of using multiple feedback modalities simultaneously because that may be more effective than simple unimodal feedbacks [25]. Hereafter, the combination of visual and vibrotactile feedback is investigated by relying on XR technologies.

2.2   System Implementation

An XR-BCI prototype was implemented to investigate the effects of a multimodal feedback during motor imagery. Virtual reality was taken into account in this first prototype. The task consisted of controlling both intensity and direction of a moving virtual object. Multimodal feedback was obtained by merging visual and vibrotactile modalities. In details, the visual feedback was provided by the movement of a virtual ball on a PC screen, while the vibrotactile one was given by a wearable suit with vibrating motors. Intensity and direction of the feedbacks were determined by means of the user's brain activity, measured

(a) PC monitor for visual feedback.

(b) Wearable and wireless suit for vibrotactile feedback.

Fig. 1. Hardware components of the XR-BCI system for multimodal (visual plus vibro-tactile) feedback.

through EEG. The feedback actuator of the XR-BCI system are shown in Fig. 1, while the EEG acquisition hardware is shown in Fig. 2.

In this prototype, a generic PC monitor was used to provide the visual feedback. However, this will be replaced by smart glasses to provide a more immersive experience and hence furtherly increase user engagement. A Unity application was purposely developed to have a virtual environment with a rolling ball, as well as to control the haptic suit. Gravity was applied to the ball to attach it to the virtual floor, while an EEG-modulated force is applied to the ball during the experiments. Note that the applications also indicated the task to carry out (Fig. 1a). Vibration was modulated according to the ball position in aiming to augment immersiveness by a simple multi-sensory stimulation. The hardware for vibrotactile feedback consisted of a wireless suit from bHaptics Inc. This has a 5×4 matrix of vibration motors both on front and back of the torso. The intensity of the vibration can be varied for each motors, thus allowing the creation of customized patterns. The suit is shown in Fig. 1b. Finally, the employed EEG acquisition system consisted of the Olimex EEG-SMT acquisition board and two bipolar channels. The EEG signals were collected by four active dry electrodes by means of a differential measurement between each pair of them. The measurement electrodes were placed at C3 and C4, while the reference electrodes for the differential measurement were placed at Fp1 and Fp2, respectively. A ground electrode was also placed on the left ear lobe. Electrodes were hold by a soft headband.

During each trials, the virtual ball could roll to the left or to the right of the display according to the detected brain activity. Vibration was simultaneously provided by the haptic suit on the left or on the right part of the torso. The target task was decided by a cue-based paradigm. In particular, with reference to Fig. 3, the user was relaxed until an indication appeared at time $t_{CUE} = 2$ s;

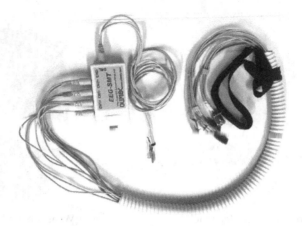

Fig. 2. Low-cost wearable EEG acquisition system.

then, motor imagery started at $t_{MI} = 3$ s and it was stopped 5 s later. In this time interval, feedback was provided to the user depending on the detected brain activity. Notably, while the direction was chosen according to the detected motor imagery class, the class score modulated ball velocity and vibration intensity, respectively.

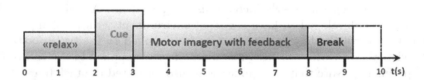

Fig. 3. Timing diagram of a single trial in the BCI experiment with neurofeedback.

The algorithm for EEG processing was the *filter bank common spatial pattern* (FBCSP), a widely adopted approach in MI-BCI [26,27]. Of course, the algorithm was adjusted to provide feedback in real-time. Its main blocks were (i) an array of bandpass filters, (ii) the "common spatial pattern" (CSP) for extracting spatial features from the filtered EEG signal, (iii) a selector of features that discards the less informative ones, and (iv) a naive Bayesian Parzen window (NBPW) classifier. Notably, the classifier exploits signal features to assign a class probability to each trial. Therefore, the most probably class was assigned to the incoming EEG data for each trial, while the class probability was exploited as a score. These two pieces of information were exploited to modulate the intensity and direction of the feedback, respectively. It should be noted that the algorithm had to be trained by means of labeled EEG data. Since the users were completely new to the system, there were no available data for them, and the algorithm had to be trained from already available datasets. Furthermore, in adapting the algorithm for real-time processing, the trained model had to classify 1.0 s-long time windows starting from t_{MI} and progressively shifting of 0.5 s. This implies that, in the 5 s-long motor imagery window, the signal was classified to provide feedback 9 times.

2.3   Preliminary Results

First experiments with the multimodal feedback were conducted by considering two motor imagery tasks, namely left versus right imagery. Each user was instructed to mentally visualize the left part of the upper body or the right one by particularly focusing on the respective arm. During each trial, the XR-based feedback aimed to help the user in the motor imagery task. In particular, a positive feedback should have strengthen the correct imagination of the indicated direction, while a negative feedback would have indicated the need to improve the mental task execution. Unfortunately, a wrong feedback could also be misleading for the user, thus implying that the brain activity classification had to be as accurate as possible.

The classification algorithm was trained on the data of the best subject from the BCI competition III dataset 3a (subject "k3b"). This public dataset contains data from 60 EEG channels related to four motor imagery tasks and visual feedback was provided during their acquisition. Hence, the algorithm training relied upon the left hand and the right hand imagery tasks, and two-channels data were extracted to match the EEG channels of the proposed system. The algorithm was implemented in Matlab, which communicated with the Unity application to match the timing protocol and provide feedbacks.

Four subjects (one female) participated to the preliminary experiments. Among them, two subjects had already experience with a reactive XR-BCI systems, but only one already had experience with motor imagery. The experiment was design for executing 80 trials per each subject, divided into 2 runs of 40 trials each. However, due to technical problems, two subjects carried out less trials (down to 30). Note that during the preliminary experiments, the user was wearing the suit and the EEG cap while seated on a comfortable chair in front of the PC monitor and he/she was asked to limit unnecessary movements during the EEG acquisition. Indeed, movements affect the EEG electrodes stability. Instead, it was evaluated that vibrations associated with the haptic feedback did not influence the EEG acquisition.

After the experiments with feedback in real time, an offline accuracy assessment was conducted to evaluate the XR feedback efficacy. Firstly, the cross-validation was considered. In this procedure, acquired EEG data are split several times in training and evaluation data, so that the accuracy can be calculated for each split. The cross-validation accuracy is then obtained as the mean of these accuracies, and the associated standard deviation can be obtained as well. In the present case, a 4-folds cross-validation with 5 repetitions was considered, meaning that data was split 5×4 times in 75% for training the algorithm and 25% for using the algorithm in classifying data (evaluation phase). The accuracy in the evaluation phase can be obtained by knowing the true labels of evaluation data.

Clearly, this would not be possible in real applications, but labels are indeed known for all data during these experiments. After the cross-validation, another accuracy assessment was conducted by dividing in half the available data, so that the first half could be used for training and the second half for evaluation. Note that in both procedures, data were considered subject-by-subject.

The results are reported in Table 1. Apart from subject S3, the accuracies are above the chance level (50% for two classes). Cross-validation accuracy goes up to 84% for subject S2, which is relatively high for the motor imagery field. However, this performance is not confirmed by evaluation accuracy, which is only 65%. Instead, cross-validation accuracy and evaluation accuracy are compatible for S4, and the resulting 70% is still an acceptable result.

Table 1. Classification results for the preliminary experiments with four subjects.

Subject	Cross-validation accuracy	Standard deviation	Evaluation accuracy
S1	63%	14%	68%
S2	84%	6%	65%
S3	40%	19%	50%
S4	69%	8%	70%

In synthesis, the relatively good classification accuracies obtained in the preliminary experiments suggest that the multimodal XR neurofeedback might help the user during the mental tasks. However, experiments with further subjects are necessary to better validate the system design. Furthermore, feedback modalities should be better investigated in order to optimize the XR environment for utmost engagement. Portability of the visual feedback will be enhanced by replacing the PC monitor with a virtual reality visor, but augmented and mixed reality could be investigated as well. Then, the motor vibration should be better modulated to offer a more realistic haptic sensation.

3   Passive BCI

3.1   Background

The notion of passive BCI was officially defined at the 4th Graz BCI Conference [28].

In passive BCI field, a promising application is the engagement detection. The engagement detection can be applied in several field such as rehabilitation, academy, or work According to Lamborn, engagement stands for active participation and concentrated attention in opposition to superficial participation or apathy [29]. Many researchers, defined three types of engagement: emotional engagement, behavioural engagement and cognitive engagement [30]. High emotional engagement level is related to the positive emotional reply to a task.

Cognitive engagement represents the mental effort required to perform activities.

Finally, behavioral engagement is evaluable by the direct observation of the individual physical effort produced during the activities.

Moreover, the concept of engagement must be associated to motivation. For example, according to Maehr and Meyer motivation, conceptualized in terms of direction, intensity, and quality of individual energies, answers to the question of why for a given behavior. In addition, Maier and Seligman argue that lack of motivation can lead to individual negative cognitive and emotional states (disengagement) [31].

3.2 Adaptive VR Based Rehabilitation

An adaptive rehabilitation game platform is proposed for rehabilitation of children with neuro-psychomotor deficits. The rehabilitation tasks change accordingly to the engagement of the user. The cognitive and emotional engagement were assessed by means the EEG signals. By combining the different levels of cognitive and emotional engagement, four different states can be identified: (i) *participation* (high level of both emotional and cognitive engagement), (ii) *boredom* (low cognitive engagement and low emotional engagement), (iii) *stress* (high cognitive engagement and low emotional engagement), and (iv) *distraction* (low cognitive engagement and high emotional engagement).

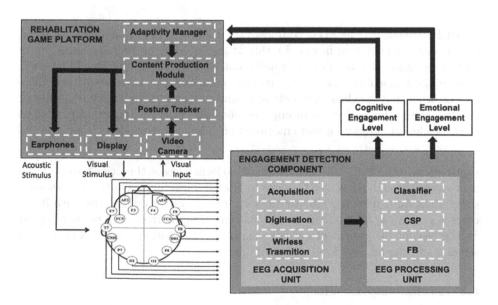

Fig. 4. Architecture of the adaptive rehabilitation game platform

Architecture. The system architecture is shown in Fig. 4 and it is composed by a *Rehabilitation Game Platform* and an *Engagement Detection Component.* The main hardware of the Rehabilitation Platform is the GE73 Raider RGB 8RF-212IT Gaming Notebook (Intel i7-8750H, 16 GB of RAM, 256 GB NVMe SSD and 1 TB HDD, nVidia GTX 1070 Graphics Card, Windows 10 Home) The Platform proposes the rehabilitative task to the patient through the *Monitor* and the *Earphones.* The Monitor used is a Philips's Monitor (223V5LHSB2 LCD-TFT Monitor for Desktop PC 21.5 Inch" LED, Full HD, 1920 × 1080).

The visual stimulus is an avatar chosen by the patient (bee, ladybug, girl, or fish). The auditory stimulus is a background music. The *Content Production Module* updates the audio-visual stimuli as a function of two inputs.

The first input is an information about the user's posture. It comes from the *Posture Tracker* on the base of the images acquired by the *Video Camera.* The second input contains the patient status information. It is elaborated by the *Adaptivity Manager* on the base of the emotional and the cognitive engagement levels detected by the *Engagement Detection Component.*

The latter is organized into two blocks: the *EEG Acquisition unit* and the the *EEG Processing Unit.* The EEG Acquisition unit acquires and digitizes the patient EEG signal and subsequently sent it to the *EEG Processing unit* by wireless transmission. In the EEG Processing unit, a custom *Filter Bank* (FB) filters the EEG signal by 12 pass-band filter. Then the *Common Spatial Pattern* (CSP) realizes the feature extraction and selection. Finally, the *Classifier* identifies the engagement levels of the patient.

Data Processing. The FB decomposes the EEG into 12 frequency bands using fourth order Chebyshev filters. In this study, a total of 12 band-pass filters with 4 Hz bandwidth were used, equally spaced from 0.5 to 48.5 Hz. Then CSP, a supervised machine learning algorithm, polarized the variance of the EEG signals according the class they belong to and maximized the discriminability of the two classes for each type of engagement. The FB-CSP outputs are sent to the Classifier the cognitive and emotional engagement levels detection.

Operation. The Rehabilitation Game Platform asseses the orientation of the user visage through the Video Camera to launch the activity. During the activity, the patient must fix the avatar to move it. The avatar completes the path if the correct posture is maintained by the patient. The activity content is adapted on the base of the patient state. For example, if the patient was experiencing a stress state, the activity level was simplified.

3.3   Preliminary Results

An experimental campaign was carried out to validate the Engagement Detection Component of the adaptive rehabilitation game platform.

The participants included in the experimental activity were children aged between five and eight years (three males and one female) suffering from disturbances in motor-visual coordination. The children were affected by double hemiplegia, motor skills deficit with dyspraxia, neuropsychomotricity delay (NPM), and severe NPM delay in spastic expression from perinatal suffering, respectively. The experimental campaign took place during the hours already scheduled for rehabilitation activities. The wearability of EEG based component was guaranteed by the use of the Emotive Epoc + [32] for the EEG signal acquisition.

The experimental protocol was authorized by the University Federico II ethical commission. Families signed the informed consent before the experiment. The procedures were implemented in accordance with the appropriate directive and guidelines. EEG signals were acquired during the rehabilitation sessions for a total of thirty minutes per week. The acquisition was conducted in a room illuminated by solar light and provided with air swap. Each child was asked to sit in front of the display wearing the EEG cap and the adhesion of the electrodes on the scalp were checked. Then, the audio-visual stimuli were produced to launch the activity. During the activity, the child had to fix the avatar to move it, maintaining eye contact and a correct posture.

Each session were video recorded. A multidisciplinary equipe realized the video classifications, (and, therefore, the EEG tracks classification), identifying all the transitions between two consecutive states (i.e. from *participation* to *stress*) crossed by the subjects. The children completed all the sessions without expressing discomfort during the use of the proposed devices. Moreover, the measurements of emotional engagement exhibited a strong prevalence of high level. Therefore, elements emerged confirming that the system does not represent an element of discomfort for the users.

As preliminary analysis, the Median Absolute Deviation (MAD) algorithm, was implemented [33] to identify and eliminate anomalous trials from the EEG dataset.

Subsequently, the EEG signal was divided into epochs. Two types of epoch divisions were simultaneously performed: 3 s epoch and 9 s epoch. The Independent Component Analysis (ICA) was implemented to remove artifacts from the signals. Thend the signals were filtered with Filter Bank and the Common Spatial Pattern was applied for feature extraction and selection.

Finally, different classifiers were compared in addressing a two-class (high-low) classification problem both for cognitive and emotional engagement.

Moreover, both intra-subjective and inter-subjective classifications were implemented.

As concern inter-subjective classification, under-sampling was realised to balance the dataset by reducing the size of the abundant class. Subsequently, the data classification was implemented with three different classifiers: Support Vector Machine (SVM), Linear Discriminant Analysis(LDA) and K-Nearest Neighbors(KNN). The EEG features were input to above mentioned classifiers whose hyperparameters were optimized with a grid-search cross-validation procedure.

The results are shown in Table 2 and Table 3.

Table 2. Best subject-independent accuracy (and relative classifier) obtained for the cognitive engagement detection

Classifier	3 s Epoch	9 s Epoch
SVM	74.7% ± 3.1%	73.3% ± 4.7%

Table 3. Best subject-independent accuracy (and relative classifier) obtained for the emotional engagement detection

Classifier	3 s Epoch	9 s Epoch
kNN	69.0% ± 2.5%	72.3% ± 3.2%

About the intra-subjective classification, data balancing wasn't realized before the classification. In this case, Support Vector Machine (SVM), Artificial Neural Network (ANN) and Graph based Neural Network(GNN) were used. The EEG features were input to above mentioned classifiers whose hyperparameters were optimized with a 3-fold cross-validation procedure. The results are shown in Table 4 and Table 5.

Table 4. Best subject-independent accuracy (and relative classifier) obtained for the cognitive engagement detection

Classifier	Subject	3 s Epoch	9 s Epoch
ANN	1	70.0% ± 19.6%	70.2% ± 19.9%
	2	65.1% ± 6.0%	65.1% ± 3.2%
	3	68.08% ± 1.8%	69.2% ± 1.4%
	4	71.4% ± 7.9%	74.6% ± 6.1%

Table 5. Best subject-dependent accuracies (and relative classifier) obtained for the emotional engagement detection

Classifier	Subject	3 s Epoch	9 s Epoch
GCNN	1	60.0% ± 2.9%	61.6% ± 3.4%
	2	73.9% ± 8.6%	75.1% ± 7.1%
	3	77.7% ± 5.7%	79.5% ± 5.3%
	4	85.1% ± 5.1%	87.2% ± 4.6%

4 Conclusion

The present manuscript has discussed possible integration of XR and BCI addressed to health 4.0 applications. Indeed, XR technologies are extensively proposed nowadays to enhance prevention, diagnosis, and treatments in health-care. Therefore a BCI, furnishes a novel mean for control and monitoring, so that the user can communicate with a machine by modulating his/her brain activity, or the machine can be adapted to the detected mental state of the user.

In these regards, motor imagery was investigated as an active BCI paradigm in which the spontaneous brain activity is measured during the mental visualization of a movement. The XR feedback, provided either visually and with haptic stimulation, aims to enhance the user's engagement to help movements imagination. Classification accuracies were assessed to test the XR neurofeedback efficacy. It resulted that up to 84% classification accuracy was obtained in cross-validation, while evaluation accuracy is up to 70%. Compared to typical results in motor imagery classification, these values are encouraging and suggest that further experiments may be required to better assess the system efficacy. Foreseen applications for this XR-BCI system concern motor rehabilitation or the control of robotic prostheses.

Emotional and cognitive engagement were detected in the framework of passive BCI. A wearable EEG based component of an adaptive rehabilitation game platform was prototyped and validated on 4 children. Experimental results, reported a subject independent accuracy of 73.3 % and 72.3 % for the emotional and cognitive engagement, respectively when an epoch of 9 s was adopted. The subject-dependent accuracy increased up to 87.2% in the case of cognitive engagement detection for the fourth subject. Considering the lack of studies on the engagement detection by a passive BCI, the results lead to consider this line of research as very promising.

References

1. Marr, B.: What is extended reality technology? A simple explanation for anyone. https://www.forbes.com/sites/bernardmarr/2019/08/12/what-is-extended-reality-technology-a-simple-explanation-for-anyone/ (2019)
2. Schnabel, M.A., Wang, X., Seichter, H., Kvan, T.: From virtuality to reality and back (2007)
3. Interrante, V., Höllerer, T., Lécuyer, A.: Virtual and augmented reality. IEEE Comput. Graph. Appl. **38**(2), 28–30 (2018)
4. Pelargos, P.E., et al.: Utilizing virtual and augmented reality for educational and clinical enhancements in neurosurgery. J. Clin. Neurosci. **35**, 1–4 (2017)
5. Kim, Y., Kim, H., Kim, Y.O.: Virtual reality and augmented reality in plastic surgery: a review. Archi. Plast. Surg. **44**(3), 179 (2017)
6. Dunn, J., Yeo, E., Moghaddampour, P., Chau, B., Humbert, S.: Virtual and augmented reality in the treatment of phantom limb pain: a literature review. NeuroRehabilitation **40**(4), 595–601 (2017)
7. Mubin, O., Alnajjar, F., Jishtu, N., Alsinglawi, B., Al Mahmud, A.: Exoskeletons with virtual reality, augmented reality, and gamification for stroke patients' rehabilitation: systematic review. JMIR Rehabil. Assistive Technol. **6**(2), e12010 (2019)
8. Lee, C., Wong, G.K.C.: Virtual reality and augmented reality in the management of intracranial tumors: a review. J. Clin. Neurosci. **62**, 14–20 (2019)

9. Sutherland, J., et al.: Applying modern virtual and augmented reality technologies to medical images and models. J. Digital Imaging **32**(1), 38–53 (2019)

10. Tortorella, G.L., Fogliatto, F.S., Mac Cawley Vergara, A., Vassolo, R., Sawhney, R.: Healthcare 4.0: trends, challenges and research directions. Prod. Plann. Control **31**(15), 1245–1260 (2020)

11. Dorsey, E.R., Topol, E.J.: State of telehealth. N. Engl. J. Med. **375**(2), 154–161 (2016)

12. Chatsopoulos, D., Bermejo, C., Huang, Z., Hui, P.: Mobile augmented reality survey: from where we are to where we go. IEEE Access **5**, 6917–6950 (2017)

13. Hu, K., Chen, C., Meng, Q., Williams, Z., Xu, W.: Scientific profile of brain-computer interfaces: bibliometric analysis in a 10-year period. Neurosci. Lett. **635**, 61–66 (2016)

14. Saha, S., et al.: Progress in brain computer interface: challenges and potentials. Front. Syst. Neurosci. **15**, 4 (2021)

15. Wolpaw, J.R., Birbaumer, N., McFarland, D.J., Pfurtscheller, G., Vaughan, T.M.: Brain-computer interfaces for communication and control. Clin. Neurophysiol. **113**(6), 767–791 (2002)

16. Soekadar, S.R., Birbaumer, N., Slutzky, M.W., Cohen, L.G.: Brain-machine interfaces in neurorehabilitation of stroke. Neurobiol. Dis. **83**, 172–179 (2015)

17. Friedman, D.: Brain-computer interfacing and virtual reality. Handbook of Digital Games and Entertainment Technologies, pp. 1–22 (2015). https://doi.org/10.1007/978-981-4560-52-8_2-1

18. Si-Mohammed, H., Sanz, F.A., Casiez, G., Roussel, N., Lécuyer, A.: Brain-computer interfaces and augmented reality: a state of the art. In: Graz Brain-Computer Interface Conference (2017)

19. Tan D., Nijholt, A.: Brain-computer interfaces and human-computer interaction. In: Tan D., Nijholt A. (eds.) Brain-Computer Interfaces. Human-Computer Interaction Series. Springer, London (2010). https://doi.org/10.1007/978-1-84996-272-8_1

20. Zander, T.O., Kothe, C., Jatzev, S., Gaertner, M.: Enhancing human-computer interaction with input from active and passive brain-computer interfaces. In: Tan D., Nijholt A. (eds.) Brain-Computer Interfaces. Human-Computer Interaction Series. Springer, London (2010). https://doi.org/10.1007/978-1-84996-272-8_11

21. Arpaia, P., De Benedetto, E., Duraccio, L.: Design, implementation, and metrological characterization of a wearable, integrated AR-BCI hands-free system for health 4.0 monitoring. Measurement **177**, 109280 (2021)

22. Thurlings, M.E., van Erp, J.B., Brouwer, A.-M., Werkhoven, P.J.: EEG-based navigation from a human factors perspective. In: Brain-Computer Interfaces, pp. 71–86. Springer, London (2010). https://doi.org/10.1007/978-1-84996-272-8_5

23. Khan, M.A., Das, R., Iversen, H.K., Puthusserypady, S.: Review on motor imagery based bci systems for upper limb post-stroke neurorehabilitation: from designing to application. Comput. Biol. Med. **123**, 103843 (2020)

24. Fleury, M., Lioi, G., Barillot, C., Lécuyer, A.: A survey on the use of haptic feedback for brain-computer interfaces and neurofeedback. Front. Neurosci. **14**, 528 (2020)

25. Sollfrank, T., et al.: The effect of multimodal and enriched feedback on SMR-BCI performance. Clin. Neurophysiol. **127**(1), 490–498 (2016)

26. Ang, K.K., Chin, Z.Y., Wang, C., Guan, C., Zhang, H.: Filter bank common spatial pattern algorithm on BCI competition IV datasets 2a and 2b. Front. Neurosci. **6**, 39 (2012)

27. Arpaia, P., Donnarumma, F., Esposito, A., Parvis, M.: Channel selection for optimal eeg measurement in motor imagery-based brain-computer interfaces. Int. J. Neural Syst. **31**(3), 2150003 (2020)

28. Zander, T.O.: Enhancing human-machine systems with secondary input from passive brain-computer interfaces. In: Proceeding of 4th International BCI Workshop, 2008, pp. 44–49 (2008)

29. Lamborn, S., Newmann, F., Wehlage, G.: The significance and sources of student engagement. Student Engagement Achievement Amercian Secondary Schools, pp. 11–39 (1992)

30. Appleton, J.J., Christenson, S.L., Kim, D., Reschly, A.L.: Measuring cognitive and psychological engagement: validation of the student engagement instrument. J. School Psychol. **44**(5), 427–445 (2006)

31. Grawcmeyer, B., Mavrikis, M., Holmes, W., Gutiérrez-Santos, S., Wiedmann, M., Rummel, N.: Affective learning: improving engagement and enhancing learning with affect-aware feedback. User Model. User-Adap. Inter. **27**(1), 119–158 (2017). https://doi.org/10.1007/s11257-017-9188-z

32. Emotiv Epoc+ technical specifications. https://emotiv.gitbook.io/epoc-user-manual/introduction-1/technical_specifications

33. Leys, C., Ley, C., Klein, O., Bernard, P., Licata, L.: Detecting outliers: do not use standard deviation around the mean, use absolute deviation around the median. J. Exp. Soc. Psychol. **49**(4), 764–766 (2013)

An Augmented Reality-Based Solution for Monitoring Patients Vitals in Surgical Procedures

Pasquale Arpaia[1], Federica Crauso[2], Egidio De Benedetto[3(✉)],
Luigi Duraccio[4], and Giovanni Improta[2]

[1] Interdepartmental Research Center in Health, University of Naples Federico II,
80125 Naples, Italy
pasquale.arpaia@unina.it
[2] Department of Public Health, University of Naples Federico II, 80131 Naples, Italy
{federica.crauso,giovanni.improta}@unina.it
[3] Department of Electrical Engineering and Information Technology,
University of Naples Federico II, 80125 Naples, Italy
egidio.debenedetto@unina.it
[4] Department of Electronics and Telecommunications, Politecnico di Torino,
10129 Turin, Italy
luigi.duraccio@polito.it

Abstract. In this work, an augmented reality (AR) system is proposed
to monitor in real time the patient's vital parameters during surgical procedures. This system is characterised metrologically in terms of transmission error rates and latency. These specifications are relevant for ensuring real-time response. The proposed system automatically collects data
from the equipment in the operating room (OR), and displays them
in AR. The system was designed, implemented and validated through
experimental tests carried out using a set of Epson Moverio BT-350 AR
glasses to monitor the output of a respiratory ventilator and a patient
monitor in the OR.

Keywords: Augmented reality · Health 4.0 · Latency · Measurement
system · Monitoring system · Operating room · Patient's vitals ·
Real-time monitoring · Smart glasses · Ventilator · Wearable

1 Introduction

The 4th industrial revolution in healthcare is reflected in an ever-increasing
impact of digital in order to improve the service in addition to saving both economic resources and time. It starts from the most advanced technical instrumentation such as the application of robotics to surgery up to the implementation
of digital interfaces for the relationship with the patient. The use of different
technologies such as the internet of things (IoT) [5,14,27]; artificial intelligence

© Springer Nature Switzerland AG 2021
L. T. De Paolis et al. (Eds.): AVR 2021, LNCS 12980, pp. 406–415, 2021.
https://doi.org/10.1007/978-3-030-87595-4_30

[3]; machine and deep learning [2,10,33]; cloud computing [24]; additive manu-facturing [9]; wearable sensors [15,28,29,31]; and augmented and virtual reality (AR and VR) [6,13,16,21,30,32]. All these technologies contribute to the devel-opment of cyber-physical systems with intrinsic monitoring features [4,17,18]. In surgery, an important use of AR consists in the superimposition of medical images on patients during the execution of the surgical procedure [19]. Another important advantage is the ability to monitor in real time the patient's vital parameters with the ability to access additional information from the electronic medical record. All this information is made available on AR glasses worn by nurses. In order to improve the efficiency of procedures, put in place in the operating room (OR) you could equip the surgical team with smart glasses AR allowing real-time monitoring of the state of health of the patient even at a distance from the electromedical equipment. In this way the surgical team can focus its attention on the patient and the task to be performed. In this way the surgical team can focus its attention on the patient and the task to be per-formed. Previous work addressed the possibility of using AR to visualize the patient's vital parameters [11,12,20,23,26]. In [23], the authors focused on the number of times the anesthesiologist had to shift attention from the patient to the equipment, achieving a significant reduction of more than a third through a head-mounted AR display (HMD). The use of AR HMD has also been studied in [26], along with auditory visualization to avoid distractions to the anesthesiolo-gist in the operating room. More recently, in [11], a bio-monitoring platform has been developed for the supervision of personnel operating in critical infrastruc-tures. The platform collects a series of signals in order to determine the optimal physiological profile of the staff. In [20] was also implemented a mixed reality system for real-time measurement and visualization, hands-free, of blood flow and vital signs.

In the above-mentioned works, attention is focused on the usability of the sys-tem without measuring its performance. On the other hand, for remote surgical procedures it is important to ensure that information is transmitted correctly, virtually and without latency. For example, in work on health monitoring sys-tems [1,22] the main challenges and requirements regarding real-time wireless data transmission were explored. In other words, various parameters such as the transmission bandwidth, the number of interruptions per time unit, the average duration of stops, the monitoring delay, energy efficiency and reliability have been analysed. It is clear from these studies that any video/audio delay of more than 300 ms should be avoided in order to ensure correct interaction between the user and the system. On the basis of these considerations, a metrological design of an automatic system based on AR is presented to support the medi-cal team during surgical procedures. The system captures vital parameters from electromedical instruments in the operating room and visualizes them in real time on a set of glasses AR [8]. The proposed system has been implemented and validated experimentally with the aim (i) of verifying the correct functionality of the system, and (ii) of assessing its reliability in the transmission of data, in terms of real-time communication. The latter was done by assessing the accu-

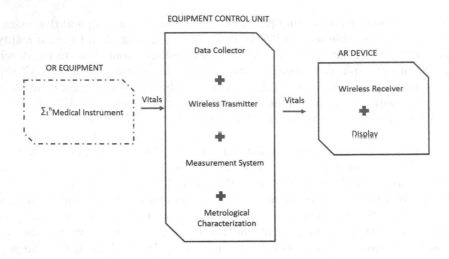

Fig. 1. Architecture of the proposed monitoring system.

racy and latency of the system and verifying their compatibility with the strict requirements of the operating theatre.

This paper is organized as follows: Sect. 2 presents the system describing its architecture and software operation. In Sect. 3, a case of use in comparison with the experimental tests of metrological characterization is reported. Finally, in Sect. 4, conclusions are drawn.

2   Design

This section deals with the design of a real-time monitoring system based on AR, with focus on (i) architecture and (ii) metrological characterization module, in terms of requirements for real-time wearable healthcare applications [1,22]. Overall, the design choices comply with the strict requirements of the health sector. The system was designed to be used by those responsible for monitoring vital signs in the operating room, such as nurses or anaesthetists. The system would allow the medical staff to view the useful information without turning to the monitoring equipment allowing them to act promptly in case of emergency situations. Finally, based on the suggestions of surgeons of the Federico II hospital, the maximum acceptable latency during surgical procedures should be lower than 2 s. Thanks to these preliminary considerations, the design of an AR-based monitoring system was adapted to the basic requirements of the scope considered.

2.1   Architecture

The architecture was designed to maximise wearability and ease of use. In fact, the user will only have to wear the AR viewer and start the application. Another strength lies in the modularity and flexibility, as the number and type of medical instruments can be modified according to the specific context. It can be seen that a *Wireless Transmitter*, integrated with the *ECU*, transmits in real time the data to the *AR Device*: this captures the vital parameters and displays them in AR, superimposed on the view of the physical world [25]. *ECU* is also equipped with a *Measurement System*, to analyze *accuracy, data-update delay* and *communication latency*. *Precision* (expressed as a percentage), is defined as the number of packets correctly decoded, divided by the total number of packets received.

The *data-update delay* is the time needed by the system to update the acquired vital parameter values, while the *communication latency* is the delay in wireless transmission. In addition, at the request of the user, the *ECU* processes the results of the *Measurement system*, to perform a *Metrological characterization* of the monitoring system as a whole. As a result, a *Metrological Certificate* is generated which summarizes the performance of the system.

The architecture has also been developed to make appreciable the ease of selecting the different parameters using the viewer. In fact the presence of the *ECU* provides two main advantages. First of all, it allows to generalize the application; the system, in fact, can be interfaced with different AR devices or with different operating room equipment. In addition, the *ECU* allows to include possible processing strategies, such as displaying alarms if vital parameters exceed pre-established thresholds, or displaying the results of the predictive algorithm that predicts possible aggravating patient trends.

2.2   Metrological Characterization

The AR-based system includes an off-line feature of self-metrological characterization. On user demand, the *Metrological Characterization* shown in Fig. 1 computes (i) the transmission accuracy (related to both the equipment and the communication protocol); (ii) the data-update delay (related to the equipment); and (iii) the communication latency (related to the communication protocol). To this aim, when the user wants to assess the metrological performance, different experimental sessions, each consisting of several runs, are carried out automatically [7]. For each run, the transmission accuracy, A (%), is assessed as:

$$A = \frac{N_{packets} - E}{N_{packets}} \cdot 100 \tag{1}$$

where $N_{packets}$ is the number of packets sent; and E is the error count when a packets is not correctly decoded.

Then, for each session, the accuracy mean value μ_A and the standard deviation σ_A are assessed. Hence, the 3-sigma uncertainty is computed by taking into account the total number of runs, according to:

$$u_A = \frac{k \cdot \sigma_A}{\sqrt{N}} \tag{2}$$

where $k = 3$ is the coverage factor, corresponding to 99.7% confidence interval, and N is the total number of runs.

Finally, the time interval necessary to refresh the data coming from the devices is measured. In particular, for each packet within a run, the time related to data-update and to wireless communication is assessed. At the end of each run, the mean value and the standard deviation of these quantities are evaluated. When the test session is completed, the pooled mean and the pooled uncertainty are assessed, taking into account the different number of packets sent for each run. The pooled mean of the update time μ_t is evaluated through the following equation:

$$\mu_t = \frac{\sum_{i=1}^{N} \mu_{ti} \cdot l_i}{\sum_{i=1}^{N} l_i} \tag{3}$$

where μ_{ti} is the mean of the update time evaluated for each run; and l_i is the number of packets for each run.

The pooled uncertainty (u_t) is assessed as follows:

$$u_{tpo} = \sqrt{\frac{\sum_{i=1}^{N} u_{ti}^2 \cdot (l_i - 1) + \sum_{i=1}^{N} l_i \cdot (\mu_{ti} - \mu_t)^2}{\sum_{i=1}^{N} l_i - 1}} \tag{4}$$

where u_{tpo} is the pooled uncertainty of the update time; u_{ti} is the 3-sigma uncertainty (assessed through (2)) of the update time evaluated for each run; μ_t is the pooled mean of the update time: μ_{ti} is the mean of the update time evaluated for each run; and l_i is the number of packets for each run (according to (3)). A further evaluation of the uncertainty is carried out, taking into account the law of propagation of uncertainty. Assuming μ_t as the weighted mean among the runs, as expressed by (3), the 3-sigma uncertainty is also evaluated through the following equation:

$$u_{tpr} = \sqrt{\sum_{i=1}^{N} \left(\frac{\partial \mu_t}{\partial \mu_{ti}} \cdot u_{ti} \right)^2} \tag{5}$$

where u_{tpr} is the uncertainty of the update time evaluated with the law of propagation of uncertainty, assuming the independence between each run.

When the metrological self-characterization of the system is completed, a metrological report summarizing the (i) transmission accuracy; (ii) data-update delay; and (iii) communication latency, is produced for the user.

3   Case Study

The monitoring system based on AR was validated and characterized metrologically through experimental tests carried out at the University Hospital Federico II. Figure 2 shows a photo taken during the experiments.

The OST headset is the Moverio BT-350 AR smart glasses. The perceived screen size of the glasses is 2 m at 5 m projected distance, with a refresh rate

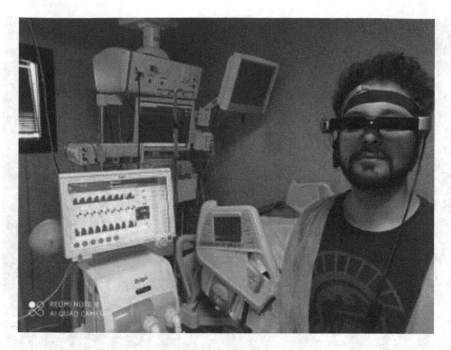

Fig. 2. Picture of the experimental validation (Reprinted from [7] Copyright (2021), with permission from Elsevier).

30 Hz. The cost of these glasses is relatively low (in the order of 500 Euros); hence, it anticipates the possibility of a large-scale use. A dedicated Android application (running on the Moverio BT-350) was specifically developed by the Authors, aiming to receive the vital parameters from the instrumentation via TCP/IP protocol.

The used ventilator is the Drager Infinity V500, while the patient monitor is the Drager Infinity V500. Both these pieces of equipment are generally available in the operating room; hence, they represent an interesting case study.

In order to emulate the patient's lung, a non self-inflatable bag was connected to the ventilator. Figure 3 shows what the user sees through the AR glasses.

The main parameters from the ventilator are shown and in addition to this information is also reported the real-time variation of oxygen saturation.

Moreover, it is possible to alternate between the different waveforms coming from the Monitor. The advantage in using the AR is the overlapping of the parameters to the user's vision, avoiding distractions of the same allowing a prompt response in emergency situations. Thanks to the modularity of the system architecture, each subsystem can be adapted to the specific context. After establishing the connection between the glasses and the laptop (to which the monitor and ventilator are connected) the data from the instrumentation are collected and displayed. Every block of the system was implemented to ensure a data transmission without degradation. Another fundamental aspect was to make the user

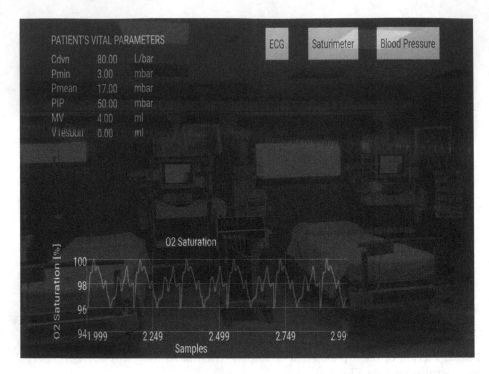

Fig. 3. Image of the user's view through the AR glasses (Reprinted from [7] Copyright (2021), with permission from Elsevier).

comfortable throughout the test avoiding problems such as motion sickness. For each session the performance was evaluated in terms of average value of accuracy and the dev std. Thus, the 3-sigma uncertainty was evaluated taking into account the total number of executions, according to (2). Last parameter evaluated is the latency of the system seen as three contributions: (i) ventilator update, (ii) monitor update and (iii) TCP communication/IP. At the end of each analysis, the average value and the standard deviation of these quantities were evaluated. At the end of the session the evaluation of the aggregate average was carried out μ_t and uncertainty 3-sigma σ_{tpo}, taking into account the different number of packets sent each run, according to (3) and (4). Uncertainty was also been assessed through the law of propagation of uncertainty. Assuming μ_t as a weighted average between series, as explained in (3), the uncertainty 3-sigma u_{tpr} can be evaluated by (5). Overall, the two approaches to assessing measurement uncertainty led to compatible results.

4   Conclusion

A system for real-time acquisition and visualization of vital signals using augmented reality was described. The implementation was based on both metrological performance and the users of this application or the medical team. The surgeon's assistant and/or the anesthesiologist wears the AR glasses, which visualize in real time the vital parameters acquired by the operating room equipment without having to constantly look at the medical device.

In addition, at the request of the user, the system automatically evaluates its metrological performance in terms of transmission accuracy, delay in updating data and communication latency. The system was designed, implemented and validated experimentally through measurements using equipment available in the operating room. The design of an AR-based monitoring system was adapted to the requirements of the scope considered, thus paving the way for the future practical implementation of the system. After the preliminary functional validation of the system, metrological characterization was carried out with focus on the rate of transmission error, the display refresh time, and the latency induced by the communication, to demonstrate the effectiveness of the proposed system. It was observed that the measured accuracy is over 97%, and the latency introduced by the Android application to receive the parameters varies in the order of milliseconds, which fully meets the aforementioned health requirements. This is an important step that aims to improve through AR the effectiveness of medical procedures in the Health 4.0 framework, while preserving the real-time requirements of the application context.

Acknowledgment. This work was carried out as part of the "ICT for Health" project, which was financially supported by the Italian Ministry of Education, University and Research (MIUR), under the initiative 'Departments of Excellence' (Italian Law no. 232/2016), through an excellence grant awarded to the Department of Information Technology and Electrical Engineering of the University of Naples Federico II, Naples, Italy.

References

1. Alesanco, A., García, J.: Clinical assessment of wireless ECG transmission in real-time cardiac telemonitoring. IEEE Trans. Inf Technol. Biomed. **14**(5), 1144–1152 (2010)
2. Alharthi, A.S., Yunas, S.U., Ozanyan, K.B.: Deep learning for monitoring of human gait: a review. IEEE Sens. J. **19**(21), 9575–9591 (2019). https://doi.org/10.1109/JSEN.2019.2928777
3. Alotaibi, B.: Utilizing blockchain to overcome cyber security concerns in the internet of things: a review. IEEE Sens. J. **19**(23), 10953–10971 (2019)
4. Angrisani, L., Grazioso, S., Di Gironimo, G., Panariello, D., Tedesco, A.: On the use of soft continuum robots for remote measurement tasks in constrained environments: a brief overview of applications. In: 2019 IEEE International Symposium on Measurements and Networking, M&N 2019 (2019). https://doi.org/10.1109/IWMN.2019.8805050
5. Angrisani, L., Arpaia, P., Esposito, A., Moccaldi, N.: A wearable brain-computer interface instrument for augmented reality-based inspection in industry 4.0. IEEE Trans. Instrum. Meas. **69**, 1530–1539 (2019)

6. Arpaia, P., Dallet, D., Erra, E., Tedesco, A.: Reliability measurements of an augmented reality-based 4.0 system for supporting workmen in handmade assembly. In: 24th IMEKO TC4 International Symposium and 22nd International Workshop on ADC and DAC Modelling and Testing, pp. 190–195 (2020)
7. Arpaia, P., De Benedetto, E., Duraccio, L.: Design, implementation, and metrological characterization of a wearable, integrated AR-BCI hands-free system for health 4.0 monitoring. Measurement **177**, 109280 (2021). https://doi.org/10.1016/J.measurement.2021.109280
8. Arpaia, P., De Benedetto, E., Dodaro, C.A., Duraccio, L., Servillo, G.: Metrology-based design of a wearable augmented reality system for monitoring patient's vitals in real time. IEEE Sens. J. **21**(9), 11176–11183 (2021). https://doi.org/10.1109/JSEN.2021.3059636
9. Bernasconi, R., Meroni, D., Aliverti, A., Magagnin, L.: Fabrication of a bioimpedance sensor via inkjet printing and selective metallization. IEEE Sens. J. **20**(23), 14024–14031 (2020)
10. Bloomfield, R.A., Teeter, M.G., McIsaac, K.A.: A convolutional neural network approach to classifying activities using knee instrumented wearable sensors. IEEE Sens. J. **20**, 14975–14983 (2020)
11. Cepisca, C., Adochiei, F.C., Potlog, S., Banica, C.K., Seritan, G.C.: Platform for bio-monitoring of vital parameters in critical infrastructures operation. In: 2015 7th International Conference on Electronics, Computers and Artificial Intelligence (ECAI), pp. E-7. IEEE (2015)
12. Chang, J.Y.C., Tsui, L.Y., Yeung, K.S.K., Yip, S.W.Y., Leung, G.K.K.: Surgical vision: Google glass and surgery. Surg. Innov. **23**(4), 422–426 (2016)
13. Condino, S., et al.: Hybrid simulation and planning platform for cryosurgery with Microsoft Hololens. Sensors **21**(13) (2021). https://doi.org/10.3390/s21134450
14. Corchia, L., et al.: Fully-textile, wearable chipless tags for identification and tracking applications. Sensors **20**(2) (2020). https://doi.org/10.3390/s20020429
15. Corchia, L., Monti, G., De Benedetto, E., Tarricone, L.: Low-cost chipless sensor tags for wearable user interfaces. IEEE Sens. J. **19**(21), 10046–10053 (2019). https://doi.org/10.1109/JSEN.2019.2927823
16. Cutolo, F., Fida, B., Cattari, N., Ferrari, V.: Software framework for customized augmented reality headsets in medicine. IEEE Access **8**, 706–720 (2020). https://doi.org/10.1109/ACCESS.2019.2962122
17. Grazioso, S., Tedesco, A., Selvaggio, M., Debei, S., Chiodini, S.: Towards the development of a cyber-physical measurement system (CPMS): case study of a bioinspired soft growing robot for remote measurement and monitoring applications. ACTA IMEKO **10**(2), 103–109 (2021). http://dx.doi.org/10.21014/acta.imeko.v10i2.1123
18. Grazioso, S., et al.: Design of a soft growing robot as a practical example of cyber-physical measurement systems. In: IEEE Metrology for Industry 4.0 and IoT Proceedings. IEEE (2021). https://doi.org/10.1109/MetroInd4.0IoT51437.2021.9488477
19. He, C., Liu, Y., Wang, Y.: Sensor-fusion based augmented-reality surgical navigation system. In: 2016 IEEE International Instrumentation and Measurement Technology Conference Proceedings, pp. 1–5 (May 2016)
20. McDuff, D., Hurter, C., Gonzalez-Franco, M.: Pulse and vital sign measurement in mixed reality using a Hololens. In: Proceedings of the 23rd ACM Symposium on Virtual Reality Software and Technology, pp. 1–9 (2017)

21. Meyer, J., Schlebusch, T., Fuhl, W., Kasneci, E.: A novel camera-free eye tracking sensor for augmented reality based on laser scanning. IEEE Sens. J. **20**, 15204–15212 (2020)
22. Muhammed, T., Mehmood, R., Albeshri, A., Katib, I.: UbeHealth: a personalized ubiquitous cloud and edge-enabled networked healthcare system for smart cities. IEEE Access **6**, 32258–32285 (2018)
23. Ormerod, D., Ross, B., Naluai-Cecchini, A.: Use of an augmented reality display of patient monitoring data to enhance anesthesiologists' response to abnormal clinical events. Stud. Health Technol. Inform. **94**, 248–250 (2003). https://doi.org/10.3233/978-1-60750-938-7-248
24. Pace, P., Aloi, G., Gravina, R., Caliciuri, G., Fortino, G., Liotta, A.: An edge-based architecture to support efficient applications for healthcare industry 4.0. IEEE Trans. Ind. Inform. **15**(1), 481–489 (2019)
25. Rauschnabel, P.A., Ro, Y.K.: Augmented reality smart glasses: an investigation of technology acceptance drivers. Int. J. Technol. Mark. **11**(2), 123–148 (2016)
26. Sanderson, P.M., et al.: Advanced auditory displays and head-mounted displays: advantages and disadvantages for monitoring by the distracted anesthesiologist. Anesth. Analg. **106**(6), 1787–1797 (2008)
27. Schiavoni, R., et al.: Feasibility of a wearable reflectometric system for sensing skin hydration. Sensors **20**(10), 2833 (2020). https://doi.org/10.3390/s20102833
28. Spanò, E., Di Pascoli, S., Iannaccone, G.: Low-power wearable ECG monitoring system for multiple-patient remote monitoring. IEEE Sens. J. **16**(13), 5452–5462 (2016)
29. Teague, C.N., et al.: A wearable, multimodal sensing system to monitor knee joint health. IEEE Sens. J. **20**(18), 10323–10334 (2020). https://doi.org/10.1109/JSEN.2020.2994552
30. Viglialoro, R., Condino, S., Turini, G., Carbone, M., Ferrari, V., Gesi, M.: Augmented reality, mixed reality, and hybrid approach in healthcare simulation: a systematic review. Appl. Sci. (Switz.) **11**(5), 1–20 (2021). https://doi.org/10.3390/app11052338
31. Wannenburg, J., Malekian, R., Hancke, G.P.: Wireless capacitive-based ECG sensing for feature extraction and mobile health monitoring. IEEE Sens. J. **18**(14), 6023–6032 (2018)
32. Wehde, M.: Healthcare 4.0. IEEE Eng. Manage. Rev. **47**(3), 24–28 (2019). https://doi.org/10.1109/EMR.2019.2930702
33. Zhang, B., Hong, X., Liu, Y.: Multi-task deep transfer learning method for guided wave-based integrated health monitoring using piezoelectric transducers. IEEE Sens. J. **20**(23), 14391–14400 (2020)

Applications of VR/AR/MR in Education

Development of Virtual Laboratory Work on the Base of Unity Game Engine for the Study of Radio Engineering Disciplines

Ye. A. Daineko[1]([⊠]), B. A. Kozhakhmetova[1], A. E. Kulakayeva[1], D. D. Tsoy[1], A. Z. Aitmagambetov[1], D. S. Gubsky[2], M. T. Ipalakova[1], and A. M. Seitnur[1]

[1] International Information Technology University, Almaty, Kazakhstan
y.daineko@iitu.edu.kz
[2] Southern Federal University, Rostov-on-Don, Russia

Abstract. Radio engineering courses are complex for comprehension from the visual point of view. Therefore, this aspect decreases the level of understanding among students that study them. But the problem can be solved by explicit demonstration of inner hidden processes.

The paper covers the development of virtual laboratory work based on the Unity game engine allowing investigation and discovery of the experience of radio engineers. The article's structure gradually goes through all the stages of the development process. Beginning with a literature review and observation of existing software, it continues with a physical and mathematical basis that lies in the core of the application. Then goes the describing part, which indicates programming tools. Particularly the Unity game engine features are shown.

After that, the work sheds light on the development process, where each stage and every part of the application is indicated.

Keywords: Unity game engine · Radio frequency spectrum · Radio emission source · Small spaceCraft · Radio monitoring · Virtual laboratory work · Radio engineering disciplines · 3D modeling · C# (CSharp)

1 Introduction

Currently, with the introduction of information and communication technologies into the educational process, the use of multimedia teaching tools has become more and more relevant not only in lectures, but also in laboratory classes. This factor is particularly important in the context of the current situation of the coronavirus pandemic. On the basis of the order of the Minister of Education and Science of the Republic of Kazakhstan [1], training with the use of distance learning technology has been introduced in educational institutions. Distance learning technology implies the organization of the educational process at a distance, in which a student and a teacher are separated from each other, and the interaction between them is carried out using information and communication technologies.

L. T. De Paolis et al. (Eds.): AVR 2021, LNCS 12980, pp. 419–427, 2021.
https://doi.org/10.1007/978-3-030-87595-4_31

A laboratory work, being one of the teaching methods, is designed to consolidate the theoretical material of the student in practice. To perform the laboratory work, you must have specialized equipment and tools. In the course of performing laboratory tasks, students acquire skills in working with equipment, conducting various measurements and experiments. For more effective executing of laboratory classes, with the use of interactive and multimedia processes, in many higher educational institutions virtual laboratory works are increasingly being used. This article discusses the creation of a virtual laboratory work for distance learning on the study of radio systems of SHF and EHF ranges. The main tasks of the virtual laboratory work for students are to master the general theory of building radio communication systems of SHF and EHF ranges, to learn the principles of operation of devices for generating, transmitting, receiving and processing radio signals, to be able to measure the main characteristics of the radio signal, and also to acquire skills in working with the receiving and transmitting equipment of various radio communication systems.

To date, there are a large number of specialized programs for modeling and calculation of radio communication channels. Consider some of them: ANSYS HFSS, CST Microwave Studio, MATLAB/Simulink, Wireless InSite, ZETLAB.

ANSYS HFSS is a software for three-dimensional electrodynamic modeling, created for the design and simulation of high-frequency devices (HF) and antennas [2]. This program is the most popular and finds application in the design of antennas, antenna arrays and complex elements of HF and SHF circuits.

CST Microwave Studio is designed for fast and accurate numerical simulation of RF devices, such as antennas, filters, power couplers. The program is also used to analyze problems of signal integrity and electromagnetic compatibility in the time and frequency domains using rectangular or tetrahedral partitioning grids [3].

MATLAB/Simulink is a dynamic modeling environment for complex technical systems and devices. Simulink, being a MATLAB subsystem, performs system simulation. A large number of components (blocks) in the Simulink library allows you to create complex models of radio communication channels, to study the structure of the radio signal, the antenna part of the radio system.

The Wireless InSite program is a specialized program that allows calculating the radio path for various types of buildings (large cities, villages, etc.). The program allows you to design wireless communication lines, optimize the antenna coverage of communication systems, and analyze the key characteristics of the communication channel for the HF and SHF frequency ranges. Also, the Wireless InSite program can simulate future 5G mobile communication networks operating in the millimeter frequency range [4].

The ZETLAB virtual laboratory is a specialized program that provides the capabilities of spectral analysis of signals, measurement of electrical parameters, generation, recording and reproduction of signals [5].

All the considered simulation programs have their own advantages and allow you to reproduce the processes occurring in the real operating conditions of the system. It is also worth noting that virtual laboratory works give students the opportunity to expand their scientific potential, as well as increase their knowledge in the practical part of the works.

This article is devoted to the development of a software application for measuring the main parameters of a satellite earth station.

2 Physical and Mathematical Support

The purpose of the virtual laboratory work being developed is to measure the main parameters of the earth station of satellite communications, as well as to study the features of the propagation of radio waves in the SHF and EHF ranges and to estimate the energy budget of the satellite radio channel.

Figure 1 shows a simplified block diagram of a typical earth station (ES). The station contains a receiving antenna, a receiving path including a low-noise amplifier, frequency converters "down" and the receiving part of the modem (demodulator), a transmission path consisting of a modulator, a frequency converter "up", and a power amplifier. In addition, the ES includes guidance, monitoring and control systems and additional equipment.

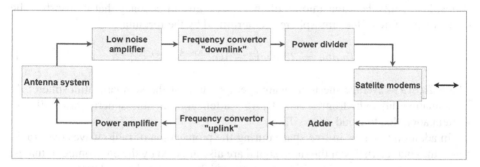

Fig. 1. Simplified block diagram of a typical earth station.

The propagation of radio waves is most significantly influenced by the electrophysical parameters of the Earth, the ionosphere, the troposphere, the terrain, etc. Taking all these factors into account at the same time is a very difficult task, but depending on the frequency range, the role of each of them varies. Therefore, when studying issues related to the propagation of radio waves in a particular range, it is advisable to build a model that, on the one hand, will reflect all the most significant properties of the Earth and its atmosphere for a given range of waves, and on the other – would be easy to study.

When designing a satellite system, it is necessary to consider such parameters as: power quality factor G/T, cross-polarization decoupling of the antenna for receiving and transmitting, equivalent isotropically radiated power (EIRP), the level of intermodulation products transmitter, the level of spurious emissions; out-of-band emissions, an estimate of the energy budget radio line «Ground-based transmitter – On-board receiver», etc.

The calculation of the energy budget of the radio line should begin with the determination of the value of the EIRP, which is determined by the formula [6]:

$$P_{EIRP} = P_t + G_t - L_t, \text{ (dBW)} \tag{1}$$

where P_t – is the power of the transmitter, dBW; G_t – is the transmitter antenna gain, dB; L_t – is the loss in the feeder path of the transmitter, dB.

The signal strength at the input of the receiving device is calculated as:

$$P_{in} = EIRP - \sum L + G_r - L_r, \text{(dBW)} \qquad (2)$$

where L_r – receiver input loss, dB; L – total loss, dB; G_r – receiving antenna gain, dBi.

It is also necessary to take into account the total power of the noise generated at the receiver input by different sources (equivalent noise temperature). The equivalent noise temperature of the system is calculated as follows [7]:

$$T_{eq} = T_A \cdot L_r + 290 \cdot (1 - L_r) + (F - 1) \cdot 290, \text{(K)} \qquad (3)$$

where T_A – is the noise temperature of the antenna, K; F – is the noise coefficient of the receiver; L_r – loss in the receiver, dB.

The radio emission of the earth's atmosphere is thermal in nature and is fully due to the absorption of signals in the atmosphere. Due to thermodynamic equilibrium, the atmosphere emits the same amount of energy at a given frequency that it absorbs. The noise temperature of the atmosphere is determined by the formula:

$$Tn.atm = Ta.ave\left(1 - 10^{(-Ar-Ac-Ag)/10}\right) \qquad (4)$$

where $Ta.ave$ – average thermodynamic temperature of the standard atmosphere; Ar – attenuation due to hydrometeors, dB; Ag – attenuation in atmospheric gases, dB; Ac – attenuation due to cloud cover, dB.

In addition to losses in free space during the propagation of radio waves over radio bands the characteristics of the radio signal are also affected by the environment, that is, the radio wave experiences additional losses, which are defined as follows:

$$\sum L = L_r + At + L_{pol} + L_{p.t} + L_{p.r} + L_{int}, \text{(dB)}, \qquad (5)$$

where At – total attenuation of radio signals in the atmosphere; L_{pol} – polarization losses; $L_{p.t}, L_{p.r}$ – losses caused by pointing errors of transmitting and receiving antennas, dB; L_{int} – other losses associated with inter-symbol interference, interference of neighboring channel, dB.

The gain of the earth station antenna for reception and transmission can be estimated by the well-known formula:

$$G = 20, 4 + 20lgD + 20lgF + 10lg\eta, \text{(dB)}, \qquad (6)$$

where D – antenna mirror diameter, m; F – operating frequency, GHz; η – antenna surface utilization factor (typical value is $0,4 \div 0,6$).

Calculation of the power quality factor G/T at the working angle of the antenna is done by the formula:

$$G/T = L + L_{ATM} + RBW + k - EIRP_{SC/ES} + (P_S - P_N), \text{[dB/K]}, \qquad (7)$$

where L is the free space loss in the direction of the ES, dB.

$$L = 92,45 + 20 * lgS + 20 * lgF$$

where S – is the slant range, km.

$$S = 6378 * ((43,705 - \mathrm{Cos}^2\beta)^{1/2} - \mathrm{Sin}\,\beta)$$

where b – angle of ES location, deg.; F – reception frequency, GHz; L_{ATM} – atmospheric losses; k – -228,6 dBW/Hz – Boltzmann constant; $EIRP_{SC/ES}$ – EIRP SC in the direction of satellite ES, dBW: P_N – P_{Nm} + δ, dBW. Typical total correction δ = + 1,7 dB.

$$PS - 10 * lg(10^{0,1*(\mathrm{Ps\,m})} - 10^{0,1*(\mathrm{PN})}),\ \mathrm{dBW}.$$

Also, when designing the radio line «Ground radio transmitter – On-board receiver», additional losses should be determined, which can include:

The losses caused by the guidance error are calculated using the formula:

$$L_{qui} = 12 * \left(\frac{\mathrm{APE}}{BW}\right)^2,\ (\mathrm{dB}) \tag{8}$$

where BW – width of the antenna pattern, deg; APE – pointing angle error, deg.

Polarization losses are calculated as [6]:

$$L_{pol} = -10log_{10}\left(\frac{1}{2}\left[1 + \frac{4e_{t*e_r}}{(1+e_t^2)(1+e_r^2)} + \frac{(1-e_t^2)(1-e_r^2)\cos(2*pol)}{(1+e_t^2)(1+e_r^2)}\right]\right),\ (\mathrm{dB}) \tag{9}$$

where e_t, e_r – coefficient of ellipticity of polarization of transmitting and receiving antennas; pol – type of polarization, rad.

The total attenuation of radio signals in the atmosphere is calculated by the formula [8]:

$$\mathrm{At} = A_g + \sqrt{(A_r + A_c)^2 + A_s^2},\ (\mathrm{dB}) \tag{10}$$

where Ag – attenuation in atmospheric gases, dB; Ar – attenuation due to hydrometeors, dB; Ac – attenuation due to cloudiness, dB; As – fading depth, dB.

This virtual laboratory work can be used to study the basic principles of construction of satellite communication systems, Earth remote sensing satellites, etc.

Development of virtual laboratory works for studying radio engineering disciplines is based on such publications of the International Telecommunication Union (ITU) as «Radio Regulations», handbooks on radio control, ITU-R recommendations, reports on regulation of radio frequency spectrum use and satellite orbits.

3 Technological Basis

In the heart of the virtual laboratory work development, there is Unity Game Engine. [9]. It is a cross-platform game development environment from Unity Technologies. It works with multiple sets of devices and platforms and makes cross-platform development easier. For example, Unity allows building applications for personal computers, smartphones, mixed reality devices, web browsers, virtual reality devices, game consoles, etc. It is used for development of apps for a wide range of fields such as cinema, entertainment, industry and others.

Another advantage of the engine is multiple plugins that improve the development process. Plugins allow to easily embed different features into projects. One more feature of Unity is the rich physics that stands behind it. It helps to create realistic procedures that are very close to the real ones. The physics calculations are done by the PhysX physics engine from NVIDIA.

Apart from that Unity has many inner tools and allows users to set up every single detail in the project. Clear and simple user Drag&Drop interface, which is easy to customize makes software development fast and understandable. In general, Unity is a set of different tabs: Scene, Game, Inspector, Project. Each of the tabs contains a specific set of objects or characteristics that can be changed. Thus, every user can debug the game directly in the editor. The game engine supports C# programming language. It provides the user with an opportunity of controlling every game object in the scene. Also, Unity has a rich toolset for visual features setup.

4 Development of a Virtual Laboratory Work

To develop the laboratory work, the most important points were identified, which allow to understand the principle of operation of radio monitoring system on the basis of small spacecraft (SSC). In addition to the computational part, the visualization turned out to be an important component, as it is a demonstration of the process of radio monitoring that allows determining radio emission sources (RES) (Fig. 2 and 3).

As a result, the scene template was created (Fig. 4), consistent with the order of the work.

Thus, the work consists of two elements that are important for the user and understanding of the system: observing ground-based RES and SSC and performing calculations. The first one was realized with the help of 3D models of the SSC and the Earth, corresponding to the reality. And the second one was realized thanks to the algorithm of calculations inside the virtual laboratory work. It was divided into three stages:

1) power calculation;
2) calculation of latitude;
3) calculation of longitude.

Performance of these calculations is sequential and corresponds to the order of the laboratory work. Such an approach allows focusing the user's attention, because the transition to each subsequent step implies the performance of the previous one: the

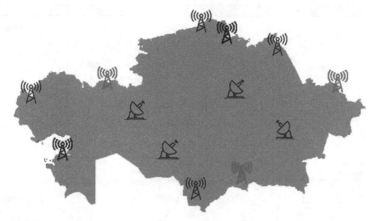

Fig. 2. Ground-based RES of various ranges

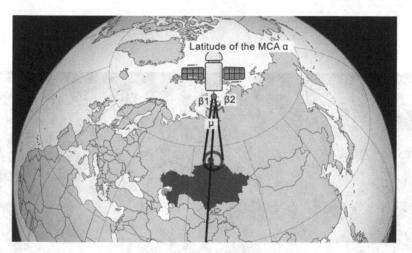

Fig. 3. RES coordinate definitions

calculation of longitude is impossible without calculating power and latitude at the software level (Fig. 5).

The application logic was written in C#. There are three main classes inside the scene: UIController, SceneLogicController and CalculationsController. The first script – UIController is responsible for UI control, the second – CalculationsController implements the calculations necessary for work; the third one – SceneLogicController controls the behavior of elements of the scene itself: the Earth, SSC, RES system, as well as the interaction between them and UI.

Thus, the laboratory work was performed, allowing to study the principles of radio monitoring system operation.

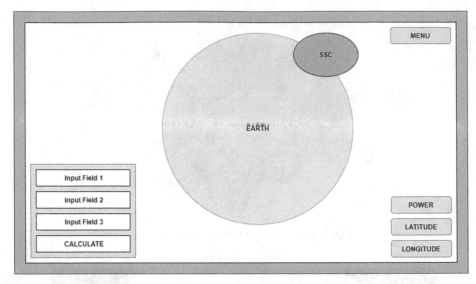

Fig. 4. Scene template

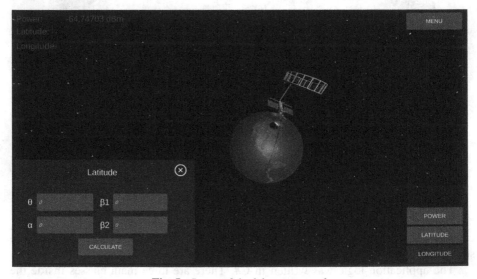

Fig. 5. Scene of the laboratory work

5   Conclusion

The article examined how new technical tools are changing the usual learning process. The world experience of education is also studied and presented, together with innovations caused by the pandemic.

The process of developing a virtual work for studying the operation of a radio monitoring system is presented. In the future, it is planned to increase the number of topics for which new laboratory works will be performed. The functionality of the laboratory work described in the article will also be expanded to provide users with a deeper understanding of radio engineering processes. The authors believe that the created virtual laboratory for the radio engineering disciplines meets the requirements of modernity and is effective in the study of this subject. Currently, we are constantly working on the development of new practical tasks and laboratory works for their integration into the laboratory.

This research has been funded by the Science Committee of the Ministry of Education and Science of the Republic of Kazakhstan (Grant No. AP08857146).

References

1. Order of the Minister of Education and Science of the Republic of Kazakhstan, №123. On strengthening measures to prevent the spread of COVID-19 coronavirus infection in educational institutions, for the period of the pandemic, 01 April 2020
2. Ansys HFSS. https://www.ansys.com/products/electronics/ansys-hfss. Accessed 09 February 2021
3. CST Microwave Studio. http://www.eurointech.ru/eda/microwave_design/cst/CST-MICROW AVE-STUDIO.phtml. Accessed 13 February 2021
4. Remcom Homepage. https://www.remcom.com/wireless-insite-em-propagation-software. Accessed 15 February 2021
5. Zetlab Homepage. https://zetlab.com/programmnoe-obespechenie/. Accessed 21 February 2021
6. Kantor, L.Ya.: Satellite communication and broadcasting. Radio and Communications, Moscow (1988)
7. Recommendation ITU-R P. 453–12.: Radio wave refraction index: its formula and refraction data. Series P. Radio wave propagation, 09 2016
8. Recommendation ITU-R P. 618–12.: Data on the propagation of radio waves and forecasting methods necessary for the design of Earth – space communication systems, 07 2015
9. Unity3d Homepage. https://unity3d.com/company. Accessed 24 February 2021

Mobile Augmented Reality Apps in Education: Exploring the User Experience Through Large-Scale Public Reviews

Jessica Lizeth Domínguez Alfaro[(✉)] [ID] and Peter Van Puyvelde[ID]

Department of Chemical Engineering, KU Leuven, 3001 Heverlee, Belgium
jessicalizeth.dominguezalfaro@kuleuven.be

Abstract. Augmented reality (AR) is considered one of the top technologies that will revolutionize the future of education. Real-time interaction, different formats of visualization, and the merge of the real and digital world may open up new opportunities for teaching and learning. Although AR is easily accessible via mobile phones, the extent to which this technology will be adopted greatly depends on the user experience. The user reviews of mobile applications or so-called "apps" are a potential source of information for designers, software developers, and scholars interested in understanding the user experience. This study investigates the current state of the user experience of augmented reality apps by extracting and classifying the information from reviews published in the Google Play Store. A set of 116 educational mobile AR apps were mined from the Google Play Store, and a total of 1,752 user reviews were retrieved and classified. Results suggest developers of educational mobile AR apps need to solve technical problems, improve certain features, and provide more explicit instructions to users. Regardless of these needs, users recognize that these apps have great potential as educational tools. Future developments should focus on tackling these shortcomings, expanding the use of AR apps to more fields of education, and targeting specific audiences to extend the technology adoption.

Keywords: Augmented Reality · App reviews · Data mining · Mobile learning · User experience

1 Introduction

With the advances in mobile computing, Augmented Reality (AR) capabilities have been combined with wireless devices such as smartphones and tablets [31], this implementation is called Mobile Augmented Reality (MAR) [27]. As a result, the use of AR has spread over many sectors such as entertainment, industry, games, tourism, and education [34]. In education, AR is considered

Electronic supplementary material The online version of this chapter (https://doi.org/10.1007/978-3-030-87595-4_32) contains supplementary material, which is available to authorized users.

L. T. De Paolis et al. (Eds.): AVR 2021, LNCS 12980, pp. 428–450, 2021.
https://doi.org/10.1007/978-3-030-87595-4_32

one of the technologies that are revolutionizing teaching and learning. Unlike other technologies, it often only requires a handheld device [13]. Several studies have documented via systematic reviews the different uses, advantages, and disadvantages of AR in educational settings [6,11,21,26,46]. However, the state of this technology for educational purposes in the public market has not been analyzed.

Current examples of user experience research of AR public apps have shown that 1) users like AR applications, 2) technical features strongly influence user satisfaction, and 3) the risk-benefit ratio of using a certain AR app influence the rate of adoption. Nonetheless, none of these researchers focused on public educational apps [19,27,32,38].

This study analyzes educational MAR applications from the Google Play Store and synthesizes user reviews into insights for improvement. Due to the number of applications and user reviews, the analysis is a challenging task. This study takes advantage of an automatic tool derived from data mining techniques to aid in qualitative and quantitative analysis.

In addition, to user reviews, this study analyses some of the indicators that users consider before downloading an app, such as ratings, number of installs, release dates, app sizes, and AR-type. Since the user experience starts from the moment the user selects and downloads an application [9], the study of such metrics can provide valuable insights.

Additionally, the levels and fields of education are analyzed using the International Standard Classification of Education (ISCED) [48] used by other researchers [11,20]. This serves to identify the educational sector that an AR application targets.

Overall, this study aims to answer the following research questions:

- RQ1: What are the main problems, feature demands, and opinions expressed by the users of educational MAR apps published in the Google Play Store?
- RQ2: What are the main characteristics in terms of price, size, rating score, installs, release dates, and AR types of educational MAR apps?
- RQ3: Which are the levels and fields of education that educational MAR apps published in the Google Play Store target?

2   Background and Related Work

2.1   MAR and Education

Mobile Technology has opened up opportunities for learners to access ubiquitously to learning content. Today, this access has been enriched by blending other technologies such as Augmented Reality (AR). Initially developed for the aerospace industry [14], AR is described as a system that "supplements the real world with virtual (computer-generated) objects that appear to coexist in the same space as the real world", and its main features are its capability to combine the real and virtual environments, the real-time interaction, and the alignment of digital content with the real world [10].

In general, AR systems can be divided into three types: marker-based, marker-less, and location-based. Marker-based AR uses artificial markers (e.g., QR codes, fiducial markers, or images) placed in the real environment to detect the position and display the virtual objects. Marker-less AR tracks the natural features of physical objects in the environment. Whereas location-based AR employs the position data of the devices, determined by Global Positioning System (GPS) or Wi-Fi to deploy the virtual content [16, 43, 51].

MAR is getting more attention in education as recent evidence suggests that AR has several affordances that allow supporting meaningful learning. For example, AR can enrich learning experiences with 3D objects, which can help visualize abstract or unobservable phenomena. It can annotate spaces with overlaid information or combine digital and physical objects, creating hybrid learning environments [6, 11, 21, 52]. These affordances have been linked to several learning effects which has proven some of the main advantages of implementing this technology as a new educational tool. Some of these effects are related to the improvement of spatial abilities and memory retention, the decrease in cognitive overload, and the increase in motivation [6, 11, 21, 52] .

Despite the evident evolution of AR, there exist some limitations regarding its use in educational settings. These limitations are related to both pedagogical and technical aspects. Pedagogically, previous research has established that AR can be unwieldy, distracting, and cognitively demanding for students [6, 11, 21, 52]. Concerning technological aspects, most reported limitations are related to the usability and design of AR apps. For instance, AR systems can have difficulties maintaining the virtual content, detecting the user's location, and can be technically challenging to implement by teachers as the virtual content is not easy to create.

Given these challenges, some authors have argued that for AR to be successfully integrated into educational settings, well-designed user experiences are needed [16, 20]. This paper attempts to explore the user experience in more detail by examining the technological challenges that users of public educational MAR apps are experiencing directly from the user reviews, which may serve to inform instructional designers on how to improve the user experience of their systems.

2.2   User Experience of MAR Applications

According to the ISO 9241-210, user experience (UX) is defined as the "person's perceptions and responses resulting from the use and anticipated use of a product, system or service" [28].

Previous studies on UX of MAR applications have found that users value the practical application or usefulness, the relevant content, the ease of use, and the absence of technical difficulties [19, 38]. Furthermore, the emotional perception of users can influence the experience as observed by Dirin and Laine [19] where users have positive emotions such as encouragement, excitement, and interest. Similarly, Li et al. [32] found that the satisfaction of users can be a motivation to continue or stop using a MAR application.

Although not prescriptive, this work aims to add to the efforts of other researchers by analyzing the user experience of mobile AR users within the context of educational apps.

2.3 User Reviews and App Data as a Source of Information

Application distribution platforms or apps stores contain rich information that can help software engineers and designers during the design process [24, 39]. They contain public reviews reflecting users' experience and app metadata such as price, number of installs, release dates, rating, app size, etc., which provides an overview of the app characteristics.

User review analysis can be used to quantitatively summarize the topics contained in the reviews and to gain insights from a qualitative examination of the content [49].

Nicholas et al. [35] used the user reviews of 48 apps for bipolar disorder to analyze the user perspectives of these apps qualitatively. Similarly, Alqahtani and Orji [7] analyzed reviews of mental health apps to reveal what users of such apps like and dislike.

However, using app reviews as sources of information comes with some challenges. App reviews can be short, unstructured, grammatically incorrect, and depending on the app; they can be abundant, which can make it a complex and time-consuming process to extract information from them [24, 41].

Regardless of these challenges, when compared to other resources such as focus groups or surveys, the reviews provide direct, and numerous feedback for the stakeholders involved in the app development [25]. Moreover, the topics included in such reviews contain relevant information from the user experience such as the ideas, the needs, and the experience with a certain app that may potentially inform scholars who are interested in understanding the context of a particular app [39].

In this study, user reviews are used as a source of information (e.g., identify problems of existing apps, requested features from the users, etc.), and unlike other scholars, we used an automatic and public tool developed by Panichella et al. [41] to classify the content of the reviews into relevant categories that allow the detailed analysis of the requests and information in a procedural way with low processing time.

3 Methodology

The general methodology of data processing consists of three main phases: app extraction, review extraction, and review classification (Fig. 1). The Google Play Store was chosen as the data source. This decision was made due to a relatively larger amount o f apps in Google' s app store when compared to the Apple Store [17].

3.1 App Extraction

The first step was to extract a list of apps from Google Play using an open-source scraping tool, called google-play-scraper (version 7.1.2) [37]. The "search" function provided by this library allows the extraction of the app identifiers corresponding to the results from a search in the Google Play store using any term. The search terms used are: "augmented reality education", "augmented reality education apps", "augmented reality educational apps", "ar education", "ar education app" and "ar application for education". These were chosen by using a keyword tool [3].

For each search term, a maximum of 250 apps was retrieved, which gave 1500 apps from all search terms. Out of these 1500 apps, only 440 were unique, i.e. not repeated in the list. The metadata from each app were retrieved using the "app" function from the scraping tool mentioned earlier from the unique list.

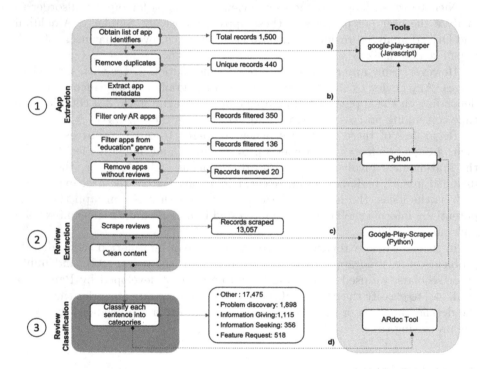

Fig. 1. The General methodology for data processing. The main phases are 1) app extraction, 2) review extraction, and 3) review classification. This figure summarizes the specific steps followed in each phase, the results, and the tools used. a) "search" function [37]; b) "app" function [37]; c) "reviews" function [30]; d) automatic data mining tool [41]

Finally, an additional cleaning step to remove non-AR apps was performed by assuming that AR apps must contain in their title or description the keywords "ar" or "augmented reality". Applications that did not contain any of these non-case-sensitive keywords in the title or the description were removed from the database. As a result, the data-set was reduced to 350 apps.

3.2 Review Extraction

From the previously cleaned app's database, a subset was created from apps that fall under the app store "Education" class; only 136 apps satisfied this criterion. The user reviews were mined using a different open source scraping tool called Google-Play-Scraper (version 0.0.2.2) [30] coded in Python. The reviews from each app were extracted using the function "reviews". In total, 13,057 single reviews were obtained from 116 apps. It is important to mention that even though 136 apps were mined, only 116 apps contained reviews.

3.3 Review Classification

To automatically classify the content of the reviews, the App Reviews Development Oriented Classifier (ARdoc) developed by Panichella et al. [41] was used. This tool combines three feature extraction techniques: Natural Language Processing (NLP), Text Analysis (TA), and Sentiment Analysis (SA). Using a machine learning (ML) algorithm, ARdoc automatically classifies the sentences of the reviews into a predefined taxonomy. The taxonomy includes five categories: information giving, information seeking, feature request, problem discovery, and other. The taxonomy emerged from previous research, which combined common topics from user reviews and comments given by developers [40, 41]. In this study, the Java API version of the ARdoc tool was used. The feature combination of text structures and sentiment analysis ("NLP+SA") was employed since, according to Panichella et al. [41], this combination of features allows a higher classification precision, recall, and F-measure (all ranging between 84–89%).

In total 21,362 sentences from 13,057 reviews of 116 apps were classified. It is important to note that most of the reviews contained more than one sentence; therefore, the number of reviews is smaller than the number of sentences.

The extraction of informative reviews was performed to analyze the content of each sentence and derive conclusions. For this purpose, it was assumed that informative reviews are those which contain sentences classified into "problem discovery", "information giving", "information seeking", and "feature request". As a result, the filtering step consisted of the removal of reviews with sentences that had all been classified as "other" by the ARdoc tool; the total informative reviews were 3,065. It is important to note that not all the apps contained informative reviews; therefore, the reviews used for further analysis only come from 86 apps. The complete data-set and classification can be found in the Supplementary Information.

A manual inspection of the informative reviews was performed to derive more specific and detailed conclusions. The application "Sky View Lite" was excluded due to the high number of reviews (1,313). In total, 1,752 reviews were further analyzed (Table 1). It is important to mention that all reviews were divided

manually into mutually exclusive groups corresponding to the app categories
from ARdoc. Most of the reviews contained more than one sentence that could
belong to different categories. If a review had sentences classified into different
classes, the priority was given based on the review context. In addition, another
class, denominated "Irrelevant", was added to reviews with vague or unclear
statements.

Finally, each of the informative reviews was manually analyzed and assigned
to a broad topic. These topics were derived from those defined by Pagano and
Maalej [39] and subsequently used by Panichella et al. [40] to define the taxonomy
of ARdoc [41]. If the content of the review was not related to any of these topics,
a new broad topic was created.

3.4   App Characteristics Extraction

All the metadata of each application obtained in Sect. 3.1 was formatted in a
table for further analysis (see Supplementary Material).

3.5   Classification Under Fields and Levels of Education

To classify the apps according to the levels of education, the International Standard Classification of Education (ISCED) [48] was used in its aggregated level.
The app developers' description was manually examined to identify the level and
field of education targeted by the app. Each app can be classified into several
levels. If the target level was not explicitly expressed, the app was assigned considering other features such as images, videos, and educational content reported
in the app description. If this information did not provide clear indications,
the apps were labeled as "Not Classified". On the other hand, if the fields of
education were not explicitly expressed, the apps were classified as "N/A" (see
Supplementary Material).

4   Results and Discussion

This section summarizes the findings related to the user reviews and their classification using the ARdoc tool, the characteristics of the AR apps obtained from
the metadata of each application and the survey of the educational levels and
fields.

4.1   What Are the Main Problems, Feature Demands, and Opinions
Expressed by the Users of Educational MAR Apps Published
in the Google Play Store?

As described in Sect. 3.3, the reviews extracted from 116 educational apps were
classified by the ARdoc tool. As a result, 1,752 reviews were analyzed.

From Table 1, it can be seen that the largest number of reviews correspond to
problem discovery (1,142/1,752). These reviews come from 70 apps, meaning that

Table 1. Classification of informative reviews as described in Sect. 3.3. This classification contains the number of reviews per category, the percentage in relation to the total of reviews, the average app score rating per category, and the number of apps on each category

Category	Number of reviews	Percentage of total reviews ($N = 1,752$)	Average score per category	Number of apps
Problem discovery	1,142	65%	1.6	70
Information giving	317	18%	3.8	56
Feature request	135	8%	3.9	29
Information seeking	125	7%	3.0	38
Irrelevant	33	2%	2.9	17

from the total of apps with informative reviews, 81% (70/86) of apps have reviews that report problems. Additionally, according to these reviews, the average score rating of the app is 1.6 out of 5 stars, which is the lowest between the categories.

Problem Discovery. Among the category of "problem discovery", six broad topics were identified. Specifically, it was identified that users have problems with functionality of the app, specific features, general service, hardware, software, and content.

In this category, most problems with AR apps were found to be related to the functionality of the apps. Although some reviews were not descriptive, for example, some users provide reviews that indicate a problem such as "app is not working" or "app did not work", the high number of reviews related to this topic suggests that some users are not able to use the AR apps, install them or even use basic functionality. Commenting on AR functionality, one of the users said, "only concern is that ar does not work it is just freezes or shows a black screen" (from the Physics Lab app).

Hardware-related problems were found on 14 apps. The most common problems related to hardware are camera autofocus, battery consumption, and phone overheat. Users from different apps expressed these observations. Commenting on phone overheat, one user said: "it's pretty good and awesome for children even for adult it's fun! but it makes my phone overheat and shutdown always. . ." (from the Animal 4D+ app). Regarding battery consumption, one user commented: "expeditions is dramatically draining my phones battery. I am wondering why my phone is dead. looked at history and found that expeditions was responsible for using up 40% of my battery even though I have not used it in several days..." (from the Expeditions app).

Software-related problems were classified as those reviews in which users explicitly express the appearance of an error message, issues with the mobile data, or software compatibility. For example, one user stated: "tried in 3 devices. failed to initialize Vuforia" (from Human Anatomy AR app).

Another recurrent problem expressed by users was content-related. Either the AR content was not available, it was not working, or the access to it was absent. A user said: "this is not a good app the animations are really too short, and, in some topics, the audio is not available..." (from Cambridge Explore app).

Thus, from the analysis of the "problem discovery" category, users of educational MAR apps experience issues of diverse nature which can be related to several factors. However, the technical hurdles related to the AR technology such as power consumption, AR functionality, and real-time interaction or unavailability of content must be a high priority to developers as these problems will cause users to stop using the applications [32,38]. For example, power consumption can be solved through energy-saving techniques, reduce power consumption from GPU, and the use of active cooling methods to control the temperature of handheld devices [15]. To improve AR functionality, developers can leverage improved tracking methods. For instance, hybrid tracking technology tackles the computational inefficiency of handheld devices and network performance [44]. Finally, Web services, together with the implementation of emerging 5G networks, can help to reduce the issues related to the content and real-time interaction by improving the data transmission rate. As mobile device computational efficiency tends to be limited, especially in low-end devices, apps that rely on web services may be able to provide a better experience.

Information Giving. The reviews in this category account for 18% (317/1,752, see Table 1) of the total informative reviews coming from 45 apps, and the corresponding average score rating according to these reviews is 3.8 out of 5 stars.

Five broad topics were identified from the content analysis of this group of reviews. Some of these topics were also identified by [39,40]. The most common issues are praise, dispraise, helpfulness, shortcoming, and other feedback.

The following reviews illustrate some examples of praises found in the dataset. One user of the AR mondly app stated: "unique ar experience! mondly ar proves augmented reality can be the future of language learning!". Another user from the Expeditions app commented: "I love using this app with my students. I used a google expeditions kit from @aquilaeducation and my students absolutely loved traveling all over the world!".

On the other hand, users also expressed their discontent. It is important to note that most of the criticisms made by users mostly come together with a "problem discovery". Therefore it was not usual to find dispraise sentences alone but combined with a specific issue or a dissuasion statement. For example, one user expressed: "I didn't even liked to give one star it is not a good app don't download it I hate it" (from Space 4D+ app). Another example of reviews is "the worst app ever. Waste of time. Do not download this app" (from Physics Lab app).

Another common topic among the "information giving" category was the "helpfulness" topic. In general, these reviews where a particular application was practical or helpful. Among the total of apps, 29 apps have reviews related to this topic. Commenting on the learning experience, one of the users said: "a great app to learn and practice chemistry for grade 10 students! you should try using it" (from Dat Thin Pone app). And another user stated: "thanks a lot for the app its awesome and very helpful for the students who cannot afford physical lab" (from Physics Lab app).

Some users provide information about concrete aspects of apps they are not satisfied with. These types of reviews were classified under the "shortcoming" topic. It is important to mention that even though shortcomings seemed to be similar to problems classified under the "problem discovery category", they differ on the intention expressed by the user. While a problem is a fact that the user experience, the shortcoming derives from subjective opinion. For example, users unsatisfied with markers expressed, "maybe works but need to print markers. no thanks! only free trial" (from the Predators AR app). This review not necessarily implies that the marker does not work but only that the user is not happy with printing it. In the same fashion, another user said, "please provide instructions. ok, I downloaded the file and yes it works and works well. but having to have the target image is not practical" (from the Augmented Reality Solar System app).

The most common shortcomings include payment options, privacy concerns, and instructions provided by developers. For example, a user of the Quiver 3D coloring app shared: "I really like your app, but I wish you did not have to buy everything separately and you could buy a membership or whatever. I understand that you have to make money, but I would also like if there were more free pages. thanks!" . Regarding privacy concerns, a user said: "it requests to spy on you", and another expressed: "the app wants to access my contacts and to make and manage phone calls. This is a coloring app. I do not see why it needs the ability to make calls. . ." (from the Quiver 3D coloring app). Finally, related to the app instructions, a user from the Physics lab app expressed "it is alright if you understand physics but for people for do not understand it needs more instructions for people who don't understand. The instructions that you currently have a very hard to understand..." .

Overall, the results indicate that most users tend to write reviews when they are extremely satisfied or highly dissatisfied (praise or dispraise), but they do not provide specific insights unless the user gives specific details. In addition, users share the helpfulness of certain apps and some shortcomings that they experienced, such as lack of instructions, dislike towards markers, payment issues, and privacy concerns.

Taking into account these observations, developers can improve the user experience by providing clear explanations about why the AR systems require certain permissions. This information can be provided before and during the use of each application, and although not all users may understand the justification of the system requirements, providing the data will allow them to choose with an informed view [23].

Users also provide information about the real-life scenarios in which MAR educational apps were found helpful. According to these findings, MAR apps can be useful when students cannot be in a particular place e.g., classroom, laboratory, or historical place. Therefore, developers and practitioners can concentrate efforts on developing experiences for users that cannot be physically present in the same learning environment of their interest. Nowadays, this will not be hard to realize after the recent pandemic where these scenarios are more "normal" [22].

Feature Request. The "feature request" category accounts only for 8% (135/1,752) of the reviews analyzed coming from 29 apps (Table 1). Interestingly, the users providing those reviews gave a higher rating score (3.9 stars) when compared to users sharing other types of reviews. In general, three types of requests were identified among this group of reviews: 1) content, 2) feature, and 3) general improvements.

The content request was one of the main demands of users. A user stated: "could you please add more information in the app when you peel off the layers? students will learn even more about it. nicely done!" (from the Human eye-Augmented Reality app). Commenting on the addition of features, one user said "fun app. for kids and adults alike their comments are: would be good if we could draw our own pictures! maybe for a future update?..." (from the Quiver 3D coloring app). Finally, concerning the request for improvements, one user stated: "the first app to use ar core and does it in a brilliant way. Would be great if you could expand the app to include placement options (placing on a surface) and have the atoms react to light". (from the Atom Visualizer for ARCore app).

The current request of users of AR apps may be partly explained by the fact that the developers are exploring the technology; thus, they might be showing only some examples showcasing how the technology/app can be used but not necessarily offering a "complete" experience. Therefore, future developments may dive into further educational content integration while maintaining good design, which can be achieved through a multidisciplinary collaboration of scholars. For instance, app developers can leverage multimedia instructional design techniques to enhance learning, and practitioners can validate content and learning outcomes of students through evaluation studies.

Information Seeking. The "information seeking" category is defined by sentences expressed by users attempting to obtain information [41]. One hundred twenty-five reviews from 38 apps were classified under this category which accounts for 7% of the sum of informative reviews. The average rating score provided by users in this category was 3.0 out of 5 stars (Table 1).

Among the reviews in this group, two main topics were identified. Users asking about "how to use" and "how or where to get content/marker" were the most popular questions. Regarding the question of "how to use?" a user expressed: "do not understand how to use it the screen say scan the flat surface. what flat surface? do I need one of those printed qr cards or what someone help me" (from the Apollo's Moon Shoot AR app). Content-related, one user asked, "from where I can get the image?" (from the AR Dino Roar app).

Other questions were related to AR elements. For example, a user asked, "what is an AR marker" (from the iBugs AR app). Another one said "i do not have an ar maker why is it that you need a AR maker. Improvement I want for my child that you do not need a AR maker." (from the Predators AR app).

Although less common, privacy concerns were also found under this category. This topic was identified under "information giving", however, some users express this concern as questions rather than as statements. For example, one user said: "why do I need to give permissions to make calls?" (from the AR animals app) and another stated: "a great way to make your pictures come alive and an underused technology. my kids (and me) love it. but why is there a permission to know my precise location?" (from the Quiver 3D coloring app).

In summary, these results show the common queries that users of MAR apps have. Interestingly, the most popular questions correspond to the function and the use of AR. It is not clear for some users how to use certain apps, what a marker is, or where to get the content. A possible explanation for this might be that there is a lack of information provided by developers, which confuses users, or they are still unfamiliar with the concept of AR. Thus, clear explanations, more intuitive interactions, or familiar cues can be integrated into the systems to familiarize users with the technology.

4.2 What Are the Main Characteristics in Terms of Price, Size, Rating Score, Installs, Release Dates, and AR-types of Educational MAR Apps?

To answer this question, we used the metadata extracted in Sect. 3.1. The data includes price, app size, ratings, number of installs, and release dates.

Price. In terms of price, most apps were reported as "free" except for the app called "Quiver Education". This result suggests that most users can access AR apps for free. However, from the data extracted, it was not possible to determine whether extra paid content was available to the user after download.

For educational purposes, this is a positive result as students would have access to the AR content. Even if the "in-app purchases" are present, the students may have a higher chance to access the content if the practitioners or institutions are able to assess the content for free and provide students with the resources.

App Size. Regarding the app size, which is the amount of memory in megabytes (MB) that each app occupies in the phone, only 105 apps declared this data. The other 11 apps contained the legend "varies with device". This information, as noted by D'Heureuse et al. [18], does not include the "in-app downloads", which refers to additional data (e.g., music, videos, 3D models).

The estimated average app size is 51.6 MB with a variance of 25.6 MB. This result is larger than the app size of "all apps" inside the Google Play Store, which was reported to be 15 MB in 2017 [12]. A possible explanation for this result may be due to multimedia content such as video, images, and 3D models. These common resources, in regular apps, account for most of their size, which may suggest that for AR apps, this also applies. Generally, when apps are optimized by developers, the size is reduced. However, in the case of MAR educational apps, the optimization process may not be a priority due to the novelty of the technology.

The app size is a factor that developers consider since it can be related to how often an app is installed [5] or as Mahmood [33] suggested, it may impact how the app is rated by users. For users, this information is vital to assess how much memory does their device needs to run AR apps. Furthermore, app size can also be relevant for scholars and practitioners looking for the successful use of AR apps among their audience. This issue may be overcome by the use of cloud services and Web-based AR applications. These approaches can be suitable since users will not have to download any application to their phones, and the digital content can be display in the cloud. However, these applications are still scarce, and experience other challenges related to mobile networks [45].

Rating Score. With respect to the ratings, Google Play Store uses a five-star scale ranging from low (1 star) to high (5 stars). The average rating of all apps ($N = 116$) is 3.2 stars with a standard deviation of 1.5 stars. According to the stats reported in AppBrain [8], the average rating for all apps in the Google Play store is 4.1 stars. Therefore, the educational MAR apps from the data-set are on average rated lower than other apps. It is difficult to explain this result since the rating can be associated with multiple factors. According to Tian et al. [50] the rating of an app is mainly influenced by the size of the app, the number of promotional images on the app store, and the target software version. In general, this finding reflects that the user experience of educational MAR apps is not optimal when compared to conventional apps.

Number of Installs In the case of the number of installs in the Google Play Store, they are expressed in terms of ranges rather than exact numbers. The ranges are expressed as follows: (0–5), (5–10), (10–50), (50–100), (100–500), (500–1000), etc. To explore if the rating score is correlated with how much an app is downloaded, the install range was compared with the weighted average score rating. Figure 2 shows the relationship between the weighted average score versus the number of installs or download ranges.

As shown in Fig. 2, apps with a small number of installs (e.g., 50–100) have a high rating score, then the score of the apps starts to drop with respect to the number of installs until the range (10,000–50,000), from that install range, the app score appears to increase in value again. As noted by other authors [18], this behavior can be possibly explained by the following hypothesis. Apps with few downloads have a rating score which is likely influenced by a small number of users (probably from people known by the developer) whereas, apps in larger install ranges receive feedback from more users. For apps that go beyond 10,000 downloads, the rating starts increasing respectively with more downloads as a result of user satisfaction and popularity.

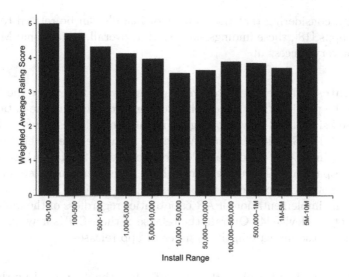

Fig. 2. Weighted average score per install range

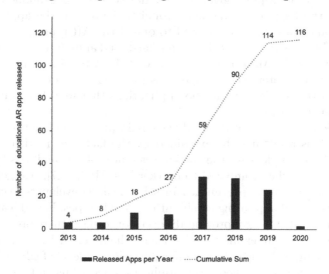

Fig. 3. Total educational MAR apps released per year since 2013 and its cumulative sum

For educational MAR apps, the number of apps in the large install range (1M–5M and 5M–10M) is very low. Just four apps in the 1M–5M range were found (Animal 4D, Expeditions, Devar, and Quiver), and only one app (Skyview) in the 5M–10M range. A possible explanation for this might be that the novelty of AR among users and developers is still present. Likewise, the use of the technology as an educational tool has not reached its maturity, thus leading to limited use, disinterest in installing the apps, or dissatisfaction of the users.

Additionally, considering that the number of installs can be related to the success of the apps [18], these findings suggest that overall, educational MAR apps are still not very successful.

Release Dates. The release dates were also analyzed to explore the evolution of MAR in the public market. According to Fig. 3, the apps in the data-set have been released since 2013, having a higher number of releases between 2017 and 2019. Since 2017, Google LLC and Apple Inc. have released their application programming interfaces or software development kits (SDKs): ARCore [2] and ARKit [1] respectively. These platforms allow developers and users of iOS and Android to create AR apps for mobile devices [36]. Other SDKs such as Vuforia have eased the implementation of AR capabilities regardless of the main operating system of the device [4]. Overall, the release of these SDKs may be a possible explanation for the increase in the number of app releases.

AR-Types. Finally, to explore the type of AR technology used by the mobile applications, the description given by the developers was examined manually. In case that the technology was not explicitly expressed, the application was downloaded and subsequently assigned to one of the AR types.

As it can be observed from Table 2, marker-based apps account for the majority of the apps (66%). Marker-less apps account for 23% of the apps and hybrid types only for 11%. Interestingly, nine apps were found to mix marker-less technology and virtual reality. Finally, no applications that used location-based AR were found in the data-set.

As mentioned, the majority of educational apps were classified as marker-based apps. This result may be explained by the fact that marker-based technology is easier to implement, the tracking is more robust, and it is less computational expensive when compared to marker-less AR [11,47]. Altogether, these results suggest there are opportunities for scholars and developers to create more marker-less apps and apps using combinations of AR-types. For educational purposes, each type of AR may provide different outcomes; therefore, it would be interesting to have more explicit guidelines on the different learning affordances that each tracking technology has to offer per field and level of education so that user and practitioners can choose the application according to their needs.

Table 2. The number of apps per type of AR technology

AR-type	Number of apps	Percentage of total ($N = 116$)
Marker	76	66%
Marker-less	27	23%
Marker-less and VR	9	8%
Marker and marker-less	4	3%
Irrelevant	33	2%

4.3 Which Are the Levels and Fields of Education that Educational MAR Apps Published in the Google Play Store Target?

To understand the educational target (levels and fields of education) of the MAR apps in the Google Play Store, each application was assigned to a field and level of education of the corresponding ISCED classification according to the information identified in the developer's description.

Table 3. The number of apps on each aggregated level of education according to the ISCED [48]

Aggregated level of education	Number of apps	Percentage of total ($N = 116$)
Levels 0–2	78	67.2%
Levels 3–4	4	3.4%
Levels 3–4 & or 5–6	22	19%
Not classified	12	10.3%
Irrelevant	33	2%

Table 3 shows that most apps target the aggregated levels 0–2 (67.2%). This observation is in line with previous studies of educational apps, which have found that most developers target preschool and primary school-age children [42]. Interestingly, this finding is contrary to that of Bacca et al. [11] who found that most AR studies target higher levels of education. One possible explanation for this is that the app market locates the "kids app market" into several industries, and developers use the term "educational" or tag words like "kindergarten", "middle school" , etc. to sell apps for the children audience, but they do not necessarily develop the apps with an educational purpose, or this specific audience [29].

It is important to note that for some apps (10%), the target level was not explicitly expressed. This outcome may be relevant for future developers who aim to get students interested in their apps. Adding this information may also allow practitioners to get more confidence in using a certain app in a formal setting.

Table 4 shows that most of the apps were classified in the broad fields of "Generic programs and qualifications" and "Natural Sciences, Mathematics and Statistics". Overall, these results reflect those of Bacca et al. [11], who also found that science was the most popular field for AR studies suggesting that this is due to the advantages that AR provides when teaching abstract concepts. However, further studies and app development in different fields of education are recommended to expand and leverage the advantages that AR may bring in various educational areas. For example, the public market of educational MAR apps can exploit more apps in the context of science and engineering but for higher levels of education with validated educational content. Also, new apps can target adult learners who may not be considered under the International

Table 4. Classification of the apps according to the aggregated level of ISCED of broad fields of education [48] in descending order and the corresponding general topics

ISCED broad fields	General topics	Number of apps	Percentage of total ($N = 116$)
00 Generic programs and qualifications		79	68%
	Natural science, animals	16	14%
	Multiple areas	15	13%
	Natural science, space	14	12%
	Literacy	12	10%
	Art	7	6%
	Natural sciences	6	5%
	History	3	3%
	Natural science, biology	2	2%
	Foreign language	1	1%
	Geography	1	1%
	Mathematics	1	1%
	Social skills	1	1%
05 Natural sciences, maths & statistics		13	11%
	Chemistry	7	6%
	Physics	4	3%
	Mathematics	2	2%
N/A		12	10%
	Visualization platform	6	5%
	Museum	4	3%
	Game	1	1%
	Marketing	1	1%
09 Health and welfare		9	8%
	Anatomy	9	8%
07 Engineering, Manufacturing & Construction		3	3%
	Engineering	3	3%
01 Education 02 Arts and humanities 03 Social sciences, journalism & information 04 Business, administration & law 06 Information & Communication technologies (ICTs) 08 Agriculture, forestry, fisheries & veterinary		0	0%

Standard Classification of Education (ISCED). Developers even can venture into new fields such as social sciences and business or administration, which may have new interesting affordances. Moreover, public institutions can collaborate with developers in making free, content-validated, and relevant for particular curricula educational MAR apps for a wide range of students.

5   Limitations of the Study

The design of the current research is subject to limitations. First, the search of the apps through Google Play Store is subjected to a limit of 250 apps per search term. Although the method ensures that the considered apps are the ones the user can find by using the same words, the data-set can be extended if other forms of search are used, for instance doing searches from different locations and different languages or adding results from websites. Second, the use of only six search terms can be a source of bias when creating the data-set; a more exhaustive list of terms might improve the broadness of the apps found. Even though the criteria for choosing the terms relies on the popular terms searched by users, there might be words that can also lead to AR apps and were excluded in this study. Third, the selection of mobile apps only from the Google Play Store limits the spectrum of apps. This opens the possibility for future research regarding an extension of MAR educational apps from the iOS store and the possible comparison with Google Play Store apps. Another limitation comes from using ARdoc to classify the reviews. The tool has its own "accuracy" and intrinsic biases derived from its assumptions and characteristics. In addition, even though the taxonomy used by [41] is in line with the objective of this study, the exclusion of reviews with the "Other" tag may have excluded sentences with relevant data. Finally, the extracted reviews may not be representative of the total amount of users of the MAR apps. In general, only users more inclined to share their thoughts are represented in the data-set. However, the group can still be considered diverse as the apps are used by different target audiences, and the reviews show diverse perspectives.

6   Conclusions and Future Work

The present research aimed to extract general information about educational MAR apps published in the Google Play Store and to examine the user experience through the classification and analysis of user reviews.

This study found that most users of educational MAR apps encountered various problems that hamper their experience (65% of reviews classified as problem discovery). Only a few apps appeared in the "high install" range, suggesting that the adoption of educational MAR apps is still in its infancy. More AR apps have appeared since 2017 due to the availability of Google and Apple SDKs, which may suggest that the adoption of the technology can reach maturity in the near future if the new apps are more liked by the users and developers leverage the recent advances of AR.

Although marker-based AR was the most popular technology used in the apps, its practical shortcomings may block AR adoption, as expressed by some users. Improving upon these shortcomings and focusing on future developments of AR, such as marker-less technologies, may improve the user experience and increase the adoption of the technology.

Among the problems experienced by users of the current MAR apps, the application's functionality was the most popular one. Therefore, exploring in more detail what are the causes of these problems may provide a better chance to enhance the adoption of the technology. However, since users often do not provide detailed information, these results need to be interpreted with caution. Regarding the "helpfulness" of AR apps for users, this study has found that some users, regardless of the limitations of the apps, can recognize specific scenarios where AR apps are helpful. These observations align with what several AR studies in educational settings have acknowledged regarding the advantages of education. However, unlike these controlled studies, the reviews showed some real-life examples from a subjective perspective of the user.

The most popular demands among users were content-related. Users generally request additional content as most apps only provide a few models for visualization, target images, or limited free content. Future app developments can be concentrated on creating apps with a more comprehensive experience other than merely displaying a limited amount of multimedia.

Finally, this study has found that most apps in the data-set target childhood education and the most popular field of exercise is science. These findings may offer opportunities for developers and scholars interested in expanding the use of AR in education. Still, continuous efforts are needed to make AR more accessible to a more diverse audience. This study did not assess the "educational" value of the apps, and therefore further research with a stronger focus on educational purpose is suggested. Future studies can include, for example, the assessment of multimedia learning principles inside the public MAR apps. On the other hand, developers could focus on providing detailed explanations about each application, its use, and certainly validated content to improve the user experience of educational MAR apps users.

Undoubtedly, future research towards addressing technical issues must be a priority for researchers to ensure that AR can be well-integrated with society, regardless of its use. More significant multidisciplinary efforts are needed to ensure that well-develop MAR apps with relevant educational content are available for more people no matter their level of education, country, or current device.

To aim for increased AR adoption as an educational tool, developers, educators, designers, and scholars may understand and address user concerns while boosting learners' educational value and experience. Altogether, academic research and public sources, such as user reviews explored in this study may provide the relevant information needed to achieve this goal.

Acknowledgements. This project has received funding from the European Union's EU Framework Program for Research and Innovation Horizon 2020 under Grant Agreement 812716.

References

1. Apple Developer (2021). https://developer.apple.com/augmented-reality/
2. Google Developers (2021). https://developers.google.com/ar
3. Keyword Tool (2021). https://keywordtool.io/app-store
4. Vuforia Engine (2021). https://library.vuforia.com/getting-started/overview.html
5. Ahasanuzzaman, M., Hassan, S., Bezemer, C.P., Hassan, A.E.: A longitudinal study of popular AD libraries in the Google Play Store. Empir. Softw. Eng. **25**(1), 824–858 (2020). https://link.springer.com/article/10.1007/s10664-019-09766-x
6. Akçayir, M., Akçayir, G.: Advantages and challenges associated with augmented reality for education: a systematic review of the literature. Educ. Res. Rev. **20**, 1–11 (2017). https://doi.org/10.1016/j.edurev.2016.11.002
7. Alqahtani, F., Orji, R.: Insights from user reviews to improve mental health apps. Health Inform. J. **26**(3), 2042–2066 (2020). https://doi.org/10.1177/1460458219896492
8. AppBrain: Android and Google Play statistics, development resources and intelligence (2020). https://www.appbrain.com/stats
9. Arifin, Y., Sastria, T.G., Barlian, E.: User experience metric for augmented reality application: a review. Procedia Comput. Sci. **135**, 648–656 (2018). https://doi.org/10.1016/j.procs.2018.08.221
10. Azuma, R., Baillot, Y., Behringer, R., Feiner, S., Julier, S., MacIntyre, B.: Recent advances in augmented reality. IEEE Comput. Graph. Appl. **21**(6), 34–47 (2001). https://doi.org/10.1109/38.963459
11. Bacca, J., Baldiris, S., Fabregat, R., Graf, S., Kinshuk: Augmented Reality Trends in Education: a systematic review of research and applications. J. Educ. Technol. Soc. **17**(4), 133–149 (2014). http://www.jstor.org/stable/jeductechsoci.17.4.133
12. Boshell, B.: Average App File Size: Data for Android and iOS Mobile Apps (2017). https://sweetpricing.com/blog/2017/02/average-app-file-size/
13. Brown, M., et al.: 2020 educause horizon report teaching and learning edition. Tech. rep., EDUCAUSE, Louisville, CO (2020). https://www.learntechlib.org/p/215670
14. Caudell, T., Mizell, D.: Augmented reality: an application of heads-up display technology to manual manufacturing processes. In: Proceedings Twenty-Fifth Hawaii International Conference System Science, no. 2, pp. 659–669. IEEE (1992). https://doi.org/10.1109/HICSS.1992.183317
15. Chen, H., Dai, Y., Meng, H., Chen, Y., Li, T.: Understanding the characteristics of mobile augmented reality applications. In: 2018 IEEE International Symposium Performance Analysis of Systems and Software, pp. 128–138. IEEE (2018). https://doi.org/10.1109/ISPASS.2018.00026
16. Cheng, K.H., Tsai, C.C.: Affordances of augmented reality in science learning: suggestions for future research. J. Sci. Educ. Technol. **22**(4), 449–462 (2013). https://doi.org/10.1007/s10956-012-9405-9
17. Clement, J.: Statista (2020). https://www.statista.com/statistics/276623/number-of-apps-available-in-leading-app-stores/
18. D'Heureuse, N., Huici, F., Arumaithurai, M., Ahmed, M., Papagiannaki, K., Niccolini, S.: What's app?: A wide-scale measurement study of smart phone markets. ACM SIGMOBILE Mob. Comput. Commun. Rev. **16**(2), 16–27 (2012). https://doi.org/10.1145/2396756.2396759
19. Dirin, A., Laine, T.: User experience in mobile augmented reality: emotions, challenges, opportunities and best practices. Computers **7**(2), 33 (2018). https://doi.org/10.3390/computers7020033

20. Garzón, J., Acevedo, J.: Meta-analysis of the impact of augmented reality on students' learning gains. Educ. Res. Rev. **27**, 244–260 (2019). https://doi.org/10. 1016/j.edurev.2019.04.001
21. Garzón, J., Pavón, J., Baldiris, S.: Systematic review and meta-analysis of augmented reality in educational settings. Virtual Real. **23**(4), 447–459 (2019). https://link.springer.com/10.1007/s10055-019-00379-9
22. Glassey, J., Magalhães, F.D.: Virtual labs - love them or hate them, they are likely to be used more in the future. Educ. Chem. Eng. **33**, 76–77 (2020). https://doi. org/10.1016/j.ece.2020.07.005
23. Harborth, D., Pape, S.: Investigating privacy concerns related to mobile augmented reality apps - a vignette based online experiment. Comput. Human Behav. **122**, 106833 (2021). https://linkinghub.elsevier.com/retrieve/pii/S0747563221001564
24. Iacob, C., Harrison, R.: Retrieving and analyzing mobile apps feature requests from online reviews. In: 2013 10th Working Conference on Mining Software Repositories, San Francisco, CA, USA, pp. 41–44. IEEE (2013). https://doi.org/10.1109/MSR. 2013.6624001
25. Iacob, C., Harrison, R., Faily, S.: Online reviews as first class artifacts in mobile app development. In: Memmi, G., Blanke, U. (eds.) MobiCASE 2013. LNICST, vol. 130, pp. 47–53. Springer, Cham (2014). https://doi.org/10.1007/978-3-319-05452-0_4
26. Ibáñez, M.B., Delgado-Kloos, C.: Augmented reality for STEM learning: a systematic review. Comput. Educ. **123**, 109–123 (2018). https://doi.org/10.1016/j. compedu.2018.05.002
27. Irshad, S., Rohaya Bt Awang Rambli, D.: User experience of mobile augmented reality: a review of studies. In: 2014 3rd International Conference on User Science and Engineering, pp. 125–130. IEEE (2014). https://doi.org/10.1109/IUSER.2014. 7002689
28. ISO: ISO 9241–210: Ergonomics of human-system interaction Part 210: Human-centred design for interactive systems (2019)
29. Jeffery, B.: The Kids App Market (2019). https://www.bjornjeffery.com/2019/05/ 31/the-kids-app-market-a-strategic-overview/
30. Jo, M.: google-play-scraper (2020). https://github.com/JoMingyu/google-play-scraper
31. Kourouthanassis, P.E., Boletsis, C., Lekakos, G.: Demystifying the design of mobile augmented reality applications. Multimed. Tools Appl. **74**(3), 1045–1066 (2015). https://doi.org/10.1007/s11042-013-1710-7
32. Li, H., Gupta, A., Zhang, J., Flor, N.: Who will use augmented reality? An integrated approach based on text analytics and field survey. Eur. J. Oper. Res. **281**(3), 502–516 (2020). https://doi.org/10.1016/j.ejor.2018.10.019
33. Mahmood, A.: Identifying the influence of various factor of apps on google play apps ratings. J. Data Inf. Manage. **2**(1), 15–23 (2020). https://doi.org/10.1007/ s42488-019-00015-w
34. Mekni, M., Lemieux, A.: Augmented reality: applications, challenges and future trends. In: 13th International Conference Applied Computer Computational Science, pp. 205–214. WSEAS Press (2014). http://www.wseas.us/e-library/ conferences/2014/Malaysia/ACACOS/ACACOS-29.pdf
35. Nicholas, J., Fogarty, A.S., Boydell, K., Christensen, H.: The reviews are in a qualitative content analysis of consumer perspectives on apps for bipolar disorder. J. Med. Internet Res. **19**(4), e105 (2017)

36. Nowacki, P., Woda, M.: Capabilities of ARCore and ARKit platforms for AR/VR applications. In: Zamojski, W., Mazurkiewicz, J., Sugier, J., Walkowiak, T., Kacprzyk, J. (eds.) DepCoS-RELCOMEX 2019. AISC, vol. 987, pp. 358–370. Springer, Cham (2020). https://doi.org/10.1007/978-3-030-19501-4_36

37. Olano, F.: Google-Play Scraper (2020). https://github.com/facundoolano/google-play-scraper#search

38. Olsson, T., Salo, M.: Online user survey on current mobile augmented reality applications. In: 2011 10th IEEE International Symposium Mixed and Augmented Reality, pp. 75–84. IEEE (2011)

39. Pagano, D., Maalej, W.: User feedback in the appstore: an empirical study. In: 2013 21st IEEE International Requirements Engineering Conference, pp. 125–134. IEEE (2013). https://doi.org/10.1109/RE.2013.6636712

40. Panichella, S., Di Sorbo, A., Guzman, E., Visaggio, C.A., Canfora, G., Gall, H.C.: How can i improve my app? Classifying user reviews for software maintenance and evolution. In: 2015 IEEE International Conference on Software Engineering, Bremen, Germany, no. 2, pp. 281–290. IEEE (2015). https://doi.org/10.1109/ICSM.2015.7332474

41. Panichella, S., Di Sorbo, A., Guzman, E., Visaggio, C.A., Canfora, G., Gall, H.C.: ARdoc: app reviews development oriented classifier. In: Proceedings 2016 24th ACM SIGSOFT International Symposium Foundations of Software Engineering - FSE 2016, vol. 13–18-Nove, pp. 1023–1027. ACM Press, New York (2016). https://doi.org/10.1145/2950290.2983938

42. Papadakis, S., Kalogiannakis, M.: Mobile educational applications for children: what educators and parents need to know. Int. J. Mob. Learn. Organ. **11**(3), 256 (2017). https://doi.org/10.1504/IJMLO.2017.085338

43. Pence, H.E.: Smartphones, smart objects, and augmented reality. Ref. Libr. **52**(1–2), 136–145 (2010). https://doi.org/10.1080/02763877.2011.528281

44. Qiao, X., Ren, P., Dustdar, S., Liu, L., Ma, H., Chen, J.: Web AR: a promising future for mobile augmented reality - state of the art, challenges, and insights. Proc. IEEE **107**(4), 651–666 (2019). https://doi.org/10.1109/JPROC.2019.2895105

45. Qiao, X., Ren, P., Nan, G., Liu, L., Dustdar, S., Chen, J.: Mobile web augmented reality in 5G and beyond: challenges, opportunities, and future directions. China Commun. **16**(9), 141–154 (2019). https://doi.org/10.23919/JCC.2019.09.010

46. Radu, I.: Augmented reality in education: a meta-review and cross-media analysis. Pers. Ubiquitous Comput. **18**(6), 1533–1543 (2014). https://doi.org/10.1007/s00779-013-0747-y

47. Roberto, P., Emanuele, F., Primo, Z., Adriano, M., Jelena, L., Marina, P.: Design, large-scale usage testing, and important metrics for augmented reality gaming applications. ACM Trans. Multimed. Comput. Commun. Appl. **15**(2), 1–18 (2019). https://doi.org/10.1145/3311748

48. Schneider, S.L.: The international standard classification of education 2011. In: Birkelund, G.E. (ed.) Cl. Stratif. Anal., Comparative Social Research, vol. 30, pp. 365–379. Emerald Group Publishing Limited (2013). https://doi.org/10.1108/S0195-6310(2013)0000030017

49. Thach, K.S.: User's perception on mental health applications: a qualitative analysis of user reviews. In: 2018 5th NAFOSTED Conference Information Computer Science, pp. 47–52. IEEE (2018). https://doi.org/10.1109/NICS.2018.8606901

50. Tian, Y., Nagappan, M., Lo, D., Hassan, A.E.: What are the characteristics of high-rated apps? A case study on free android applications. In: 2015 IEEE International Conference on Software Maintenance and Evolution, pp. 301–310. IEEE (2015). https://doi.org/10.1109/ICSM.2015.7332476

51. Wojciechowski, R., Cellary, W.: Evaluation of learners' attitude toward learning in ARIES augmented reality environments. Comput. Educ. **68**, 570–585 (2013). https://doi.org/10.1016/j.compedu.2013.02.014
52. Wu, H.K., Lee, S.W.Y., Chang, H.Y., Liang, J.C.: Current status, opportunities and challenges of augmented reality in education. Comput. Educ. **62**, 41–49 (2013). https://doi.org/10.1016/j.compedu.2012.10.024

Development of an Augmented Reality System to Support the Teaching-Learning Process in Automotive Mechatronics

E. Fabián Rivera[1], Edison E. Morales[1], Carla Cristina Florez[2] (ID),
and Renato M. Toasa[2(✉)] (ID)

[1] Instituto Superior Tecnológico, Universitario Oriente, La Joya de los Sachas EC-220101,
Ecuador
{frivera,emorales}@itsoriente.edu.ec
[2] Universidad Tecnológica Israel, Quito, Ecuador
{cflorez,rtoasa}@uisrael.edu.ec

Abstract. This article details the development of an augmented reality system to support the teaching-learning process, focused on the area of automotive mechatronics for gasoline vehicles. The application facilitates the user the interaction with the parts of the internal combustion engine in order to locate them in the assembly and disassembly process; in addition, the user can visualize the simulation of the thermodynamic cycle of the engine in improvements of the learning process. The geometric model of the elements of the Otto cycle internal combustion engine is made in CAD software, the development of the application and incorporation of the models and animations is done in Unity 3D. The execution of the Augmented Reality application during the pandemic originated by COVID-19 was essential to give continuity to the professional training process in the Automotive Mechatronics career, since the development of the teaching process was carried out solely online.

Keywords: Augmented reality · Automotive mechatronics · Teaching and learning processes · Unity

1 Introduction

At present, the world is going through a digital era, which has allowed the development of new technologies, such as virtual reality (VR), augmented reality (AR) and mixed reality (MR) [1], this has allowed the development of a combination of virtual space with a realistic environment to perform everyday activities, and the teaching-learning process is no exception, virtual models have been developed to support the education process, the work [2] affirms that: "The more realistic the simulation experience, the more intense the interactivity and perceptibility that can be provided", these 3D models are used to simulate real elements and students can visualize the objects, the closest as possible to reality.

L. T. De Paolis et al. (Eds.): AVR 2021, LNCS 12980, pp. 451–461, 2021.
https://doi.org/10.1007/978-3-030-87595-4_33

Since the beginning of 2020, the COVID-19 pandemic has impacted the entire world and forced schools of all backgrounds to close their doors and opt for virtual education. At the peak of the COVID-19 pandemic, which occurred in early April 2020, more than 1,484,715,875 students were affected worldwide [3], this caused some students to lose their learning, others to abandon their studies, in addition to the evident inequality due to the digital divide. In this sense, educational centers changed their teaching methods, where virtual and augmented reality of physical objects was less affected, since the virtual model allows simulating all the interaction between the student and the object under study.

In the educational field, 3D digital models facilitate the teaching of contents related to real objects such as buildings, vehicles, medical phenomena, etc., which can occasionally be complex and/or abstract for students [4]. In the industrial field, and even more so in the vehicle assembly area, 3D models are a fundamental tool for manipulating the different elements that make up the vehicle.

Several authors highlight the use of this type of technology in education and vehicle assembly. Initially Rivera et al. [5], presented the development of a training system in augmented reality; oriented to the teaching and learning process in the area of Automotive Mechanics for hybrid vehicles, the initial results show that there is a great acceptance by the users, improving the learning of work environments. On the other hand, in the work [6], a virtual training system for the recognition and assembly of automotive mechanics components is described, where the experimental results show the efficiency of the system generated by the human-machine interaction oriented to develop skills in the automotive mechanics area. In the automotive industry, several AR applications have been developed and analyzed to improve processes such as shortening production time, improving efficiency and saving production costs [7].

In reference to the learning process, the paper entitled "Augmented Reality and Virtual Reality in Education Myth or Reality?" [8], explains the reasons behind the new boom of AR and VR and why their actual adoption in education will be a reality in the near future, they mention that these radical changes and new models of teaching and learning must meet the needs of the 21st century learner, as their skills focus on cognitive, autonomous, collaboration and flexibility, and innovation aspects [9]. Finally, in 2021, a paper is published that develops an AR application to improve the teaching and learning process in Engineering Sciences [10], This application is validated with surveys to teachers, who detail the improvements obtained. Due to the COVID 19 pandemic, it cannot be fully implemented, but it is expected to be done in the coming months.

In this context, the present work proposes the development of an augmented reality system to support the teaching of automotive mechatronics. In this context, the animation and simulation of the thermodynamic cycle of the engine was carried out, in addition to emulating the process of assembly and disassembly of the gasoline engine in a three-piston Zotye vehicle.

The rest of the document is organized as follows Sect. 2 describes the formulation of the problem based on the needs of students who interact with vehicles in their teaching process, Sect. 3 presents the virtual environment and animation where the AR system, its architecture and the development process are detailed, Sect. 4 shows the analysis of the experimental results and finally the conclusions are shown in Sect. 5.

2 Problem Definition and Conceptualization

The COVID-19 pandemic poses a challenge to the socio-economic and educational system worldwide. Therefore, it is necessary to innovate with new tools for learning, and that is what technology should move towards, a new concept of education with virtual models that allow the user an almost real interaction of the different objects modeled, these specific aspects that affect the teaching process must be considered [11–13]:

Level of student and teacher satisfaction.

Experience in virtual models.

Types of tools.

Resource consumption by the system.

In this order of ideas, it is necessary to develop virtual AR or VR models to support the educational process, where both teachers and students have experienced a significant change in the academic process with these technologies.

As an initial case study, an AR system for the assembly of a vehicle will be developed for learning the subject of automotive mechanics and electronic injection.

Based on the above, it is necessary to determine the objects involved and that will be modeled for this article, it is important to first expose certain basic concepts of automotive mechanics.

2.1 Model Conceptualization

Use of three-dimensional geometric models (3D models) [14] made in software applying the fundamental principles of technical drawing, to obtain models close to reality is very useful for the development of auto parts, manufacturing industry in general. The use of this type of technology in the teaching-learning process has a positive impact because it helps the student to know and identify the elements that make up an internal combustion engine, in addition to recognizing the thermodynamic cycles involved in its operation, without the need for physical components. Among the advantages that can be mentioned, there is access to the teaching material without the need to be in a laboratory or workshop.

CAD software (Computer Aided Design) [15] is a computational tool for modeling three-dimensional elements through the use of operations and parameters.

The Geometric model proposed in this work requires four stages: (i) Selection of the working plane; (ii) Sketching of the two-dimensional geometry of the object. (iii) Dimensioning and insertion of geometric relationships. Creation of the three-dimensional operation. The first three stages correspond to the definition of the 2D sketch. The final stage is part of the three-dimensional definition, once the model of each of the components has been made; the assembly is carried out, which consists of joining each of the pieces to make a whole, see Fig. 1

For the purposes of this research, a model of an internal combustion engine is developed, which is a thermal machine that transforms the chemical energy of the fuel (gasoline) into mechanical energy (movement). It is called an internal combustion engine because the whole process takes place inside a cylinder.

Fig. 1. Geometric model of Zotye Z100 engine elements.

Engine model developed consists of the following elements [16]: *i) Engine block*: It is the most important part of the engine, it is anchored to the body of the vehicle by means of an elastic joint, which is responsible for absorbing vibrations so that they are not transmitted to the body; *ii) Cylinder head*: It is the element that creates a seal with the upper part of the engine block, it is joined by its flat surfaces, between these there is a gasket, they are joined by people to ensure tightness; *iii) Piston*: The piston is the engine element that moves inside the cylinder with reciprocating linear motion, serving the cylinder as a guide; *iv) Connecting rods:* Its function is to transmit the movement of the piston towards the crankshaft, it transforms the linear motion into rotary motion; *v) Crankshaft:* It is the driving shaft that receives the force produced during combustion, through the connecting rods, this force is transformed into torque that is responsible for turning the crankshaft; *vi) Camshaft:* Its main function is to control the opening and closing time of the intake and exhaust valves; *vii) Valves:* These components are located in the cylinder head or cylinder head of the engine, their function is to open and close the air inlet and exhaust gas outlet orifices. The intake valve always has a larger diameter to give priority to cylinder filling.

An internal combustion engine produces work by performing cycles, which are detailed below, see Fig. 2. a) *Intake*: The piston has a downward movement from the PMS (Upper Dead Point) towards the PMI (Lower Dead Point), the intake valve opens and the air-fuel mixture enters; b) *Compression*, the intake valves close and the piston starts its upward movement, from the PMI towards the PMS the air-fuel mixture is compressed; c) *Explosion*: The combustion starts through the spark jump of the spark plug, product of the force produced by the explosion the piston has a downward movement from the PMS towards the PMI. The intake and exhaust valves are closed; d) *Exhaust*: The intake valve opens, the piston starts its upward movement from the PMI to the PMS, the gases produced in the combustion are expelled to the outside.

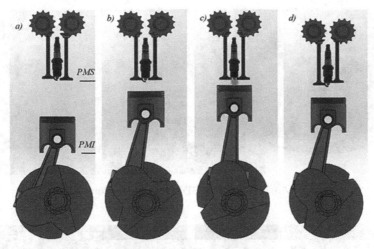

Fig. 2. Duty cycle Zotye Z100 motor.

3   Virtual Environment and Animation

This section describes the development of the augmented reality application, which consists of the following stages: *i) 3D Design Visualization; ii) Importing the 3D object into Unity; and finally, iii) Development of the training environment.*

3.1   3D Design Visualization

Vuforia Engine is used to facilitate the construction of AR-based applications which consists of an augmented reality-oriented development kit (SDK) for the Unity 3D video game engine. It allows the localization of virtual elements on real environments or objects. The visualization of 3D digital content in real environments is done using Ground Plane, since it allows placing digital models on horizontal surfaces and even locating content in the air by means of anchor points. To emulate the Ground Plane with the playback mode, the positional device tracker is used, the Ground Plane template must be used and positioned on a flat surface or even on the Zotye engine head as shown on Fig. 3.

3.2   Importing 3D Model into Unity

3D models of the Zotye vehicle engine components are structured in CAD-SolidWorks software. To import the engine and its elements developed in SolidWorks it is required to save the file in the extension (.IGIS), then using the 3ds Max program the model is imported considering the proportion, scale and use of materials for texturing as shown in Fig. 4, finally the model is exported using the extension (.FBX); since it has the characteristics of GameObject in order to place the object in the training scenes of the Unity virtual environment.

Fig. 3. Visualization of the 3D design on the Zotye head.

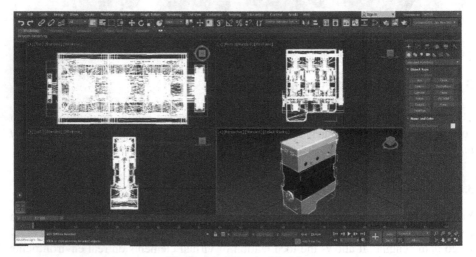

Fig. 4. Modeling in 3Ds Max

3.3 Development of Training Environment

The augmented reality system allows user interaction through virtual environments; in order to optimize training times in processes that require high costs for the assembly of large machines such as internal combustion engines; therefore, the training environment contains two scenes: i) Thermodynamic Cycle of the Engine, the development of the animations and the design of the frames is done in the animation panel of Unity; they are based on the operation of the engine of the Zotye vehicle. Additionally, to improve the control in the training scene, a script is designed to animate the change of states based on the thermodynamic cycles separately.

In Fig. 5. It is possible to appreciate the scene corresponding to the fuel intake, the simulation of the engine cycle driven by the virtual buttons. i) Explosion and Implosion, to perform the simulation of the assembly and recognition of the system parts, the Animator Controller is used (see Fig. 6), the animation clips are linked according to the parameters designed in the script, additionally the scene presents animations of position

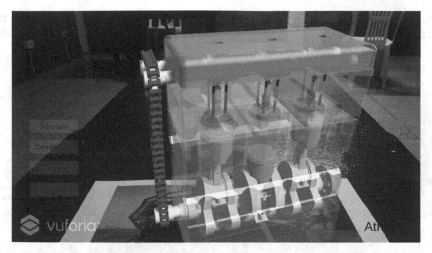

Fig. 5. Engine thermodynamic cycle scene

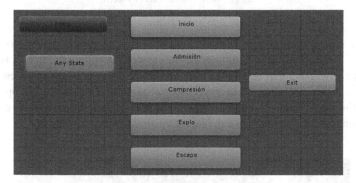

Fig. 6. Animator controller

and scale that allow identifying the parts and applications of the system separately, thus enhancing the interaction between the user and the system.

4 Experimental Results

This section is focused on the experimental results and operation of the augmented reality application, focused on the teaching-learning process with training in Automotive Mechatronics. Through the 3D simulation of the engine thermodynamic cycle, identification of its components and assembly of the system, resources are optimized, since the usual practical development demands time and cost of preparation of the system and its components.

For initial testing the application must be installed on an Android mobile device. At the beginning of the execution, the main menu corresponding to the training of the thermodynamic cycle of the engine and the explosion and implosion of the system is displayed as shown in Fig. 7, the access to the training scenes is done by pressing the virtual buttons.

Fig. 7. Main menu – RA system

The operation of the thermodynamic cycles is guided by animations to allow the user an intuitive and didactic handling of the system. In the simulation it is possible to appreciate processes that are not visible inside the internal combustion engine such as the fuel inlet through the intake manifold to the engine injectors, the opening and closing of the intake and exhaust valves, the thermodynamic cycles of the engine and the expulsion of CO_2 through the exhaust manifold as shown in Fig. 8.

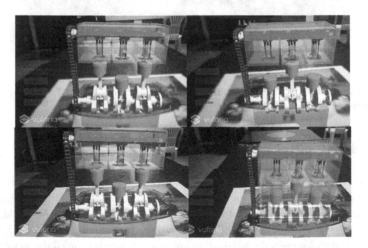

Fig. 8. Simulation of the engine thermodynamic cycle

In Fig. 9, the process of disassembly and assembly of the system can be observed. The purpose of the animation is to guide the user in the identification of the elements involved in the thermodynamic cycles of the engine, proceeding to identify each essential part of both the system and the engine, for example, the injectors, the intake manifold, the intake and exhaust valves, the engine block, the pistons, crankshafts, among others.

Fig. 9. Implosion system

To ensure that users (Students and Teachers) can use the AR system not restricted by a difficult user interaction, we conducted usability tests to evaluate whether:

The system is easy to use by the students.

The system is easy to learn, and the students are satisfied with the functionalities of the application.

To ensure the success of the application, the author should think like end users and anticipate the needs that exist.

To determine the usability of the system, a questionnaire of 10 pre-questions was applied, where the answers have a range of 1 to 5, 1 = completely disagree and 5 = completely agree. The method for evaluating the answers consists of subtracting 1 from the results of the odd numbered questions. The results of the even numbered questions are subtracted from the result of 5. The final result must be multiplied by 2.5 to obtain a value of 100%, see Table 1.

Table 1. Validation survey

N°	Questions	Score	Operation
1	Do I need the guidance and support of an instructor to start the training?	2	$5 - 2 = 3$
2	Does the system help me understand the thermodynamic cycle of the engine?	4	$4 - 1 = 2$
3	Is the system applicable in homes considering virtual education?	5	$5 - 1 = 4$

(continued)

Table 1. (*continued*)

N°	Questions	Score	Operation
4	Would you use the system to support the teaching-learning process?	4	$4 - 1 = 2$
5	Does the system provide the user with adequate physical security?	5	$5 - 1 = 4$
6	Do I consider the training system to be inconsistent or incomplete?	2	$5 - 2 = 3$
7	Does the system provide support to the development of practices considering the confinement by COVID-19?	4	$4 - 1 = 2$
8	Would you use the system frequently?	4	$4 - 1 = 3$
9	Do you consider that those processes that demand time in assembling and disassembling elements should be carried out in AR?	3	$5 - 3 = 2$
10	Is the system easy and intuitive to use?	5	$5 - 1 = 4$
			29

Table 1 shows the questionnaire applied to determine the usability percentage for the augmented reality system of the thermodynamic cycle of the Zotye vehicle engine, based on the analysis it was determined that the usability percentage is 72.5%.

The initial results are based on the teachers' comments, since due to the pandemic it has not been possible to validate it with students. In general, and according to the teachers' experience, they affirm that this AR system will allow a better understanding by the student in the area of automotive mechanics.

5   Conclusions

The use of the Augmented Reality application provides continuity to the teaching process in the area of Automotive Mechatronics, allowing them to improve the technical and practical training of users by immersing them in the analysis and simulation of the Otto cycle, as well as in the assembly and disassembly process of the gasoline engine.

The learning environment through the application minimizes the use of resources and preparation time, guaranteeing the learner a reliable and safe learning environment. The application is accessible to any user with a mobile device and Android operating system higher than 4.2.

As future planned work we establish the development of an electronic injection system of a vehicle by implementing the power supply system in conjunction with the sensors that govern the correct injection of fuel into the engine.

References

1. Williams, T., Tran, N., Rands, J., Dantam, N.T.: Augmented, mixed, and virtual reality enabling of robot deixis. In: Chen, J.Y.C., Fragomeni, G. (eds.) VAMR 2018. LNCS, vol. 10909, pp. 257–275. Springer, Cham (2018). https://doi.org/10.1007/978-3-319-91581-4_19
2. Zhang, Y.: Development of WebGL-based virtual teaching platform for mold design. Int. J. Emerg. Technol. Learn. **13**(06), 16–28 (2018). https://doi.org/10.3991/ijet.v13i06.8581

3. UNESCO: Perturbación y respuesta de la educación de cara al COVID-19 (2021). https://es.unesco.org/covid19/educationresponse. Accessed 02 Mar 2021
4. Izquierdo Pardo, J.M., Pardo Gómez, M.E., Manuel, I.L.J.: Modelos digitales 3D en el proceso de enseñanza-aprendizaje de las ciencias médicas. In: Medisan, vol. 24, no. 5, pp. 1035–1048 (2020)
5. Rivera, E.F., Pilco, M.V., Espinoza, P.S., Morales, E.E., Ortiz, J.S.: Training system for hybrid vehicles through augmented reality. In: Iberian Conference on Information Systems and Technologies, CISTI, vol. 2020, June 2020. https://doi.org/10.23919/CISTI49556.2020.9141020.
6. Quevedo, W.X., et al.: Virtual reality system for training in automotive mechanics. In: De Paolis, L.T., Bourdot, P., Mongelli, A. (eds.) AVR 2017. LNCS, vol. 10324, pp. 185–198. Springer, Cham (2017). https://doi.org/10.1007/978-3-319-60922-5_14
7. Halim, A.Z.A.: Applications of augmented reality for inspection and maintenance process in automotive industry. J. Fundam. Appl. Sci. 10(3S), 412–421 (2018). https://doi.org/10.4314/jfas.v10i3s.35
8. Elmqaddem, N.: Augmented reality and virtual reality in education. Myth or reality? Int. J. Emerg. Technol. Learn. 14(03), 234 (2019). https://doi.org/10.3991/ijet.v14i03.9289
9. Göksün, D.O., Kurt, A.A.: The relationship between pre-service teachers' use of 21st century learner skills and 21st century teacher skills. In: Education & Science ve Bilim, vol. 42, no. 190 (2017)
10. Nur Idawati, M., Enzai, N.A., Ab, M.A.H., Ghani, S.S., Rais, S.M.: Development of augmented reality (AR) for innovative teaching and learning in engineering education. Asian J. Univ. Educ. 16(4), 99 (2021). https://doi.org/10.24191/ajue.v16i4.11954
11. Khanna, D., Prasad, A.: Problems faced by students and teachers during online education due to COVID-19 and how to resolve them. In: Proceedings of 2020 6th International Conference Education Technology ICET 2020, pp. 32–35 (2020). https://doi.org/10.1109/ICET51153.2020.9276625
12. Baek-Young, C., Sejun, S., Rafida, Z.: Smart education: opportunities and challenges induced by COVID-2019 pandemic. In: 2020 IEEE International Smart Cities Conference (2020)
13. Toasa, R.M., Baldeón Egas, P.F., Gaibor Saltos, M.A., Perreño, M.A., Quevedo, W.X.: Performance evaluation of WebGL and WebVR apps in VR environments. In: Bebis, G., et al. (eds.) ISVC 2019. LNCS, vol. 11845, pp. 564–575. Springer, Cham (2019). https://doi.org/10.1007/978-3-030-33723-0_46
14. Jamali, A., Abdul Rahman, A., Boguslawski, P., Kumar, P., Gold, C.M.: An automated 3D modeling of topological indoor navigation network. GeoJournal 82(1), 157–170 (2015). https://doi.org/10.1007/s10708-015-9675-x
15. "CAD Software|2D And 3D Computer-Aided Design|Autodesk. https://www.autodesk.com/solutions/cad-software. Accessed 14 May 2021
16. Escudero Fernández, S., Gonzalez Gonzalez, J., Rivas Cuadrado, J.L., Suarez Linares, A.: Motores Pk 2016. Macmillan (2016)

Evaluation of Proprietary Social VR Platforms for Use in Distance Learning

Fabio Genz[1]([✉])[ID], Niklas Fuchs[1][ID], Daniel Kolb[2][ID], Simone Müller[2][ID],
and Dieter Kranzlmüller[1,2][ID]

[1] Ludwig-Maximilians-Universität München, Munich, Germany
fabio.genz@nm.ifi.lmu.de
[2] Leibniz Supercomputing Centre, Garching near Munich, Germany

Abstract. Distance learning in form of video chats or the streaming of recorded lectures are common ways for schools and universities to maintain teaching under the restrictions of the global SARS-CoV-2 pandemic. One possibility to improve distance learning can be the use of virtual reality (VR). To this day there are no common guidelines for educators for using VR, and therefore no recommendations to decide which platform to use and what specific requirements they entail. This paper presents an evaluation of currently available proprietary social VR platforms for the use in distance learning. Based on results of expert interviews ($n = 4$) with educators and an online survey ($n = 92$) of students, we identified ten relevant criteria for teaching in VR. We compiled a list of 155 currently available proprietary social VR platforms, which we filtered and evaluated. The results indicate that current social VR platforms can provide an easy and affordable way for educators to access the usage of VR in education, although we could not determine a single best social VR platform. Our recommendations rather provide different most suitable platforms for particular learning applications depending to respective educational requirements. Our research provides a guideline for interested educators in order to find an affordable entry into the usage of VR in education. Building on this, future research can shed light on questions of didactic effects, user-friendliness, or data protection.

Keywords: Virtual reality · Education · Distance learning · Social VR Platforms

1 Introduction

The global SARS-CoV-2 pandemic poses a major challenge for schools and universities to deliver adequate education to their students [12]. Learning in video chats and watching recorded lectures has become the daily routine for many students [5] when universities and schools had to stop their in-classroom teaching. Students and teachers have mixed opinions about this new form of learning, but this switch to digital learning can in turn open the doors for other technologies to improve learning outcomes. One of the technologies that has seen a

© Springer Nature Switzerland AG 2021
L. T. De Paolis et al. (Eds.): AVR 2021, LNCS 12980, pp. 462–480, 2021.
https://doi.org/10.1007/978-3-030-87595-4_34

strong increase in popularity in the past decade is VR: a 3D, multi-sensorial, immersive, real time, and interactive simulation of a space [19] that can provide students with exclusive first-person experiences that were previously impossible to obtain in formal education [45]. While the technology and early devices have already been known since the 1960s, more affordable VR devices have only recently started to appear. Today, users can experience immersive VR experiences with high-quality head-mounted displays (HMD) for under $300 [8,42]. There are also stand-alone HMDs, which do not require a powerful and expensive computer to operate. In addition to the availability of suitable hardware, teachers also need to have the proper software to execute their lessons and provide learning material. Custom made and specialised software is often expensive or requires a lot of time to be created. As part of the recent rise in popularity for VR, numerous social VR platforms, which provide virtual environments (VE) for people to meet and interact in VR, have been developed in the past years. These platforms are already available and likely to be more affordable than custom designed software. Building on the thesis and survey results of Fuchs [9], this work will therefore elaborate a methodology in order to evaluate the potential use of social VR platforms for distance learning. The focus is clearly on the technical consideration and evaluation, which is why pedagogical factors have been deliberately neglected.

2   Related Work

Since the creation of the first virtual reality device in the 1960s [39], a lot of research on VR and its applications has already been done. The following sections provide a short overview of topics related to VR and its benefits and challenges.

2.1   Presence and Immersion

Presence and immersion are two of the key aspects when talking about VR. But there is no consensus about the specific meaning among researchers yet. Both terms have at times been used synonymously, while being strictly separated in other cases. One explanation of their correlation was provided by Slater et al. [32]: "Presence is a human reaction to immersion". Following this explanation, presence describes how present the user feels inside VR, while immersion is how the user's senses are stimulated by external devices. Measuring the level of immersion is done by examining how the user's senses are targeted by the devices used. Presence on the other hand is much harder to evaluate from an objective point of view, as there are lots of different aspects that affect it. Pan et al. [27] found that errors in the visual representation, such as lagging graphics and flickering images, can have a negative impact on the user's perception of presence. In 2009, Jin [15] discovered that the individual representation of users inside the VE affects their perception of presence as well. Even the personal traits of users were found to have a major influence on how present the user feels in a study by Janssen et al. [14].

2.2   VR in Education

Over the past few decades, the potential of using VR in education has frequently been discussed. Winn [45] elaborated how immersive VR can enable students to have unique experiences that are otherwise impossible to achieve in formal education. Other studies showed more applications, in which using VR outperformed other teaching methods: Duff, Miller, and Bruce [6] compared virtual patients to actors playing patients in a medical study and found that users perceived the virtual patients as more realistic. Legault et al. [21] compared traditional learning methods for learning Mandarin to an immersive VR experience, which resulted in the VR experience showing better learning outcomes for participants. Various other studies [23, 38, 47] compared immersive VR simulations to other teaching methods and concluded that the usage of immersive VR simulations can lead to students showing greater motivation and interest as well as better results in tests. Kyaw et al. [18] analysed 31 studies dealing with education of medical health professions in order to compare VR learning methods to other forms of digital learning. They found out that the usage of VR lead to better learning results for the students. A different approach on how to enhance teaching methods by using VR was presented by Dyer et al. [7], who let nursing care personnel experience age-related conditions, which proved to be an effective teaching method to teach students to develop empathy. Merchant et al. [25] performed a meta-analysis of over 60 studies in a more general approach to evaluate whether a VR environment has a positive effect on teaching. They concluded that a VR environment is indeed effective for teaching in higher education and further found that, among different kinds of VR scenarios, game scenarios showed the best learning outcomes for students. In a study about teaching truss mechanics to engineering students, Banow and Maw [2] found that students using VR showed significantly better learning outcomes compared to the students using traditional teaching methods.

Focusing on the aspects of social interaction in VEs, Williamson et al. [44] demonstrated that the social behaviours in VR workshops mirror the social behaviours of real-life workshops. However, they highlighted the need for VR platforms to provide the users with diverse means of expressing themselves, as otherwise several social cues present in real life get lost. On the other hand, a survey by Yarmand et al. [46] found that many students are unwilling to share their videos, which hinders social interaction within class and poses a significant challenge to teachers. Educators who are met with static or even no images of their students have difficulties reading the engagement of their class. This impedes encouraging student participation, e.g. by addressing individuals directly. Hence, teaching in VR needs to account for the students' preference of not showing their real faces or surroundings while still communicating emotions, expressions or reactions to teachers and classmates. Additionally, studies by Petersen, Mottelson, and Makransky [28] as well as Gao et al. [11] found that the visual representation of the teacher and students influences the knowledge gained by learners in VR settings. This further reinforces the need for customisation options for classroom avatars.

2.3   Cybersickness

One drawback of using VR is the medical condition called cybersickness. Users of VR devices can experience symptoms similar to those of motion sickness. Those symptoms can range from mild symptoms like sweating, fullness of stomach, and dryness of mouth to more severe ones, like headache, vertigo, and vomiting [20].

LaViola [20] found that technical parameters, such as lag, position tracking errors, and flicker, are possible triggers for the occurrence of cybersickness. He further states that a refresh rate of at 30 Hz is generally enough to remove the issue of flicker. He also found individual factors, such as gender, preexisting illnesses, and age, to affect the occurrence and severity of cybersickness. Higher visual realism was found to cause more symptoms of cybersickness than lower visual realism in a study by Tiiro [41].

A qualitative study by Wang and Suh [43] about how users adapt to cybersickness in VR revealed that a change in body posture, adjusting the position of the HMD, resting the eyes, and slower movement can reduce the user's discomfort. They also had users reporting that the repeated use of the same VR application has decreased their feeling of cybersickness.

2.4   Internet Connection

According to Mangiante et al. [22], the internet requirement for what they call early stage VR with a resolution of 1K × 1K px, equivalent to 240p TV resolution, is 25 Mbit/s and a latency of 40 ms. A video resolution of 4K × 4K px, comparable to high definition (HD) TV, already requires 400 Mbit/s and a latency of 20 ms. This shows how important the aspect of sufficient internet connection is for a successful implementation of VR for education purposes. As an example, in 2019, about 5% of households in Germany had no internet access and the average connection speed was at just 24.64 Mbit/s. This vastly increased in 2020, when an average mobile internet connection of 57 Mbit/s with a latency of 33 ms and a fixed broad band connection of 118 Mbit/s with a latency of 21 ms were measured [26]. There has yet to be conclusive research done to evaluate whether the currently available internet infrastructure is enough to provide all students suitable circumstances for the use of VR in education.

3   Concept

Since, to the best of our knowledge and previous research, there are no uniform guidelines for the use of VR in teaching to date, there are neither recommendations for educators which platform would be best suited for this, nor which technical requirements are involved.

In the following, we present a methodology for the evaluation of currently available VR platforms for the potential use in distance learning. Our approach essentially consists of four main steps, which can be seen in Fig. 1. We begin the process with qualitative and quantitative studies to identify the individual

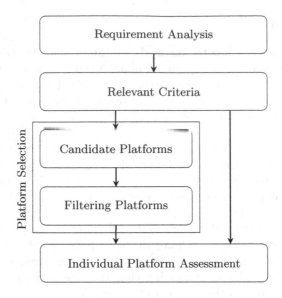

Fig. 1. This flowchart illustrates our concept to identify and evaluate the social VR platforms. First we conduct a requirement analysis, which allows us to formulate relevant criteria. We then use these criteria to select and filter the platforms. We finally analyse the remaining platforms individually.

requirements of educators and students (*Requirement Analysis*). Based on this data we define specific criteria which allow us to evaluate the suitability of the respective tested social VR platform (*Relevant Criteria*). In the next step (*Platform Selection Process*), currently available proprietary social VR platforms are firstly identified (*Candidate Platforms*) and subsequently reduced to a manageable selection (*Filtering Platforms*). Finally, the remaining platforms are individually subjected and compared to each other, regarding how well they meet the identified criteria, for final recommendations (*Individual Platform Assessment*).

4   Results and Discussion

To evaluate social VR platforms for the potential use in distance learning, we applied the methodology presented in Sect. 3. The observation period was between December 2020 and February 2021.

4.1   Requirement Analysis

For the identification or relevant criteria we chose a two-pronged approach: On the one hand we used expert interviews to gather qualitative data and thereby deeper insights from didactic experts. On the other hand we used an online survey to collect quantitative data on the needs of students.

Expert Interviews - Design. To carry out the qualitative analysis, we conducted four expert interviews and subsequently analysed them in detail. The use of expert interviews requires not only a general clarification of the definition of an expert itself, but also the examination of an appropriate interview format.

The expert status requires the completion of general training as well as training related to specialised knowledge. The corresponding qualification, in turn, is proven by the acquisition of a socially recognised and thus validated proof in form of a respective certificate [33].

Regarding the correct format of expert interviews, there is an ongoing discussion in the literature. Since it is neither clear how, nor whether it is possible at all to place expert interviews on a secure methodological basis, we recommend conducting the interviews in form of open questions without a rigid, restrictive, and thus possibly result-falsifying method until this debate has been clarified [3].

As our interviewees wished to remain anonymous, they will be referred to as I_1, I_2, I_3 and I_4.

- I_1 is a university professor for computer science at a German technical university.
- I_2 is a university professor of literature at a German non-technical university.
- I_3 is a teacher at a grammar school in Germany and is seconded part-time to a university.
- I_4 is a university professor at the department of computer science at a German technical university.

Furthermore, based on the given expert definition, the interviewed persons could doubtless be called experts from the fields of didactic and teaching.

In each of the four interviews, twelve questions were asked in the order presented in Table 1. The interviews were conducted in German, hence the questions were translated from German.

Expert Interviews - Results. All four experts showed a basic awareness for the use of VR in education. While I_1 plans to use VR for a project in the near future, I_2 and I_4 have already used VR in education. Due to their affiliation with a technical university, only I_1 and I_4 considered the technical requirements for the use of VR to be given. In addition to suitable hardware, for example in form of sufficiently powerful computers, slow internet connections at the workplaces were also identified as possible bottlenecks. With regard to a possible budget, the statements differed relatively widely. I_1 estimated the possible budget of their university for VR applications to be at least as high as for licences for other applications used in teaching, e.g. Zoom, and mentioned that up to 20 000 € should not be a problem. I_2 mentioned that a budget of up to 200 € is still an acceptable price for the use of a VR platform in a course. I_3 did not give an exact price, but stressed that with an annual budget of only 700 € for the school's IT department, costs should be kept as low as possible. Due to a complete lack of budget for courses, I_4 stated that the platforms would even have to be free of charge. Even if provided with funding, they mentioned that the budget would

Table 1. Structure of the expert interviews

ID	Question
E1	Have you tried using VR in education before?
E2	Do you have access to a computer powerful enough to run VR applications at your work place?
E3	Do you have access to a fast and stable enough internet connection at your work place?
E4	How much may a VR application cost for the use in your lectures?
E5	How do you evaluate the teaching setting of a classroom without media support and just a teacher presenting content in front of the class?
E6	How do you evaluate the teaching setting of a classroom with media support, e.g. sound, video, and text?
E7	How do you evaluate the teaching setting of an interactive and customisable environment?
E8	How important is easy usability for VR platforms?
E9	How detailed and realistic do you want a VR platform to be, to be suitable for teaching?
E10	Where do you see the biggest obstacles for using VR in education?
E11	What are essential qualities for a VR platform to be suitable for education?
E12	Would you like to see VR integrated into education?

probably be around 5 € per student. However, it must be mentioned that none of the interviewees have budget responsibility according to their own statements. In the context of the presentation of the different potential settings, all interviewees agreed that this mainly depends on the application case and the respective, associated requirements. Due to the assumed highest degree of immersion, all interviewees saw the greatest potential for teaching in an interactive and customisable environment (E7). However, they mentioned that the higher variety of possibilities and the possible distractions in such an environment do not necessarily lead to better teaching results. All four respondents agreed that the usability of a VR application should be as simple and natural as possible. The demand for level of detail and realism within the virtual world is again highly dependent on the use case. While the representation of certain objects, e.g. anatomically correct body parts in a medical course or the recreation of "real" social interaction, requires a high degree of detail and realism as possible, in some cases only simple representations or symbols are needed. However, I_4 noted that a higher level of detail and "cool look" could positively influence users' motivation and opinion of VR applications. Currently, the biggest obstacles are seen in technical limitations. I_1 mentioned that their university, even after a lot of work, were not able to organise proper online programming exams. Hence, they deem organising a VR course as too much of a challenge and expect it to ultimately fail due to hardware and software problems. In addition, the possible lack of acceptance and understanding of VR were also seen as potential limiting factors. However, the general consensus was that the technology offers many possibilities and should be used in education in the future.

We gather from the results of the interviews that the requirements for VR applications for the use in education depend strongly on the respective use case, which in turn affects the respective technical requirements. The interviewees saw the greatest advantages in the use of VR in education in the display and joint viewing of relevant objects. In addition to a high level of detail and possible interaction possibilities, the objects should also be easy to create or be able to be uploaded to the platform in common file formats. In addition, the realistic representation of social interaction between the participants was also considered as relevant. This is, for example, also reflected in the possibilities for self representation. Due to budget uncertainty, it appears that free VR applications have the greatest chance for acceptance and use in education.

Online Study - Design. For the quantitative research we applied a survey with prospective users, since the expectations of users of distance learning with VR are of great interest. The survey was mainly distributed in social media groups for students and lecturers. Over a six-week period, combined with active advertising, a total of 92 students participated in the survey. After a short introduction about how immersive VR can be used in education, the survey consists of five questions (see Table 2). Q1 through Q3 allow only single selection, Q4 allows the selection of multiple answers and Q5 asks participants to place a slider on a scale from 0 (low realism) to 100 (high realism). The online study was conducted in German, hence the questions were translated from German.

Online Study - Results. The majority of participants answered Q1 with agree or rather agree. While 18% were neutral, another quarter tended to disagree or completely disagreed with this statement. The results of Q2 show that the availability of fast internet is not given for all students. Almost a quarter of the participants have access to an internet connection of less than 50 Mbit/s and only about 14% have access to more than 100 Mbit/s. Nevertheless, more than 33% of the participants could not answer this question at all due to lack of knowledge, which could change the results again in case of a corresponding future works. The results of Q3 show a clear tendency towards a relatively low willingness to pay, with 50% of participants saying they would only use VR in education as part of free offerings. 32 % would accept up to 25 € per semester, 14% up to 50 €, and only about 3% would be willing to pay up to 100 € or more. The results of Q4 show that with 89%, high costs were seen as the biggest obstacle. This was followed by the considerable hardware requirements and a stable and fast internet connection. Complicated handling and lack of interest

Table 2. Online survey of students $(n = 92)$: Prompts Q1–Q5, response options and results

Q1: I would like to use VR in education.				
Agree	Rather agree	Neutral	Rather disagree	Disagree
17	35	17	20	3

Q2: What internet connection do you currently have at home?					
No internet	<20 Mbit/s	21–50 Mbit/s	51–100 Mbit/s	> 100 Mbit/s	I don't know
0	6	16	26	13	31

Q3: How much money would you be willing to spend on the use of VR in education per semester?			
Free of charge	Up to 25 €	Up to 50 €	More than 50 €
46	30	13	3

Q4: What are the biggest obstacles to the use of VR in education?				
High costs	Complicated handling	Internet connection	Technical equipment	Motivation and interest
82	43	53	57	39

Q5: On a scale of 0 to 100, how realistic do you want the virtual environment to be?				
0–19	20–39	40–59	60–79	80–100
3	16	26	35	12

were named as the fourth and fifth biggest obstacles. In addition to the obstacles already mentioned, in descending order, privacy, copyright, feasibility and the inconvenience of having to wear an HMD and, e.g. take it off in order to take notes, were mentioned in the free field. The results of Q5 basically show a wide range of user ratings, with the lowest user rating 6 and the highest 100. The average user rating was 58 and the median was 61.

4.2 Relevant Criteria

In total, we identified ten relevant criteria from the *Requirement Analysis*. The platforms considered are tested for suitability with regard to these identified criteria.

Preliminary Filtering. We assigned the five readily verifiable selection criteria to this category. Platforms that fail to fulfil at least one of these selection criteria are eliminated. We regard platforms that fulfil all these selection criteria as social VR platforms which are generally suitable for distance learning.

- *Availability*: The social VR platform must be available and accessible during the respective test period in order to be able to test it.
- *HMD Support*: HMDs are used in a majority of studies in the context of higher education and could be seen as a potential prerequisite for immersive learning experiences [30]. Therefore the social VR platform must support the usage of an HMD.

- *Costs*: Only cost-free platforms are considered against the background of uncertain budgets and low willingness to pay.
- *No Age Restrictions*: Adult content is avoided in view of the fact that potential users might include minors. Therefore only social VR platforms without age restrictions are considered.
- *Content Creation*: One decisive advantage of using VR in education is the possibility to present educational content in a creative, unique and interactive way in 3D. Since there is no complete 'out of the box' solution, only social VR platforms were considered that offer options to upload or directly create content in the VE. Simple VR experiences without customisable content are therefore not considered.

Popularity Check. The second category includes only one criterion. Here, popularity refers to the number of users. We use this metric as a simplified measure for the probability of continued support by developers. However, it must be emphasised that user numbers are not directly related to suitability in terms of distance learning. The potential risk here is rather seen in a possibly unsustainable recommendation. We obtained the number of users on the basis of publicly available information or through direct communication with the developers and operators of the respective platform.

- *Popularity*: The number of average daily users.

Aspects to Analyse. The third category includes all criteria that are considered relevant for conducting a comparative analysis of the remaining platforms. The platforms selected in this step all have the basic prerequisites for the use in distance learning. The comparison on the basis of the respective identified criteria of this category should provide a solid foundation for possible recommendations. For this purpose, the individual platforms are examined more closely. The criterion *Content Creation* already appeared as a criterion in the context of the knockout category. However, the criterion is applied slightly different in the respective category. In the knockout category it was only tested for basic feasibility on the basis of publicly available information. In this category, the criterion is applied in form of a detailed usage and functionality test for each platform individually.

- *Content Creation*: As described above.
- *Social Interaction*: Individual character representation and communication with other users within the VE.
- *Hardware and Software Requirements*: Requirements of the respective social VR platforms in terms of computation power.
- *Internet Connection*: Requirements regarding the internet connection.
- *Cross-Platform Support*: Ability of users to access the same VE from different devices.

4.3   Platform Selection Process

Within the platform selection process, we compiled a list of currently available social VR platforms. We then reduced the list by applying the identified *Relevant Criteria*. The identification of the currently available platforms as well as the filtering process are subsequently described.

Candidate Platforms. There is a large number of available social VR applications online. A detailed and potentially comprehensive compilation of currently available social VR platforms and virtual worlds is provided by the work of academic librarian Ryan Schultz [31]. This list was cross-checked with several other lists of currently available social VR platforms to verify completeness [10,13,16,17,29]. This, however, did not reveal any additional platforms.

Table 3. Average daily users of social VR platforms as of February 2021. The number for FRAME was provided via E-Mail by the developer in February 2021. The user number for Tivoli Cloud VR is an estimation based on the observed number of concurrent users in February 2021.

Platform name	Average daily users	Time of data
AltspaceVR	15 (on Steam) [34]	January 2021
Anyland	3 [35]	January 2021
FRAME	500	January 2021
Mozilla Hubs	No information found	n/a
Neos VR	110 [36]	January 2021
Roblox	31 000 000 [4]	January 2021
Sansar	14 [37]	January 2021
Sinespace	1700 [40]	March 2019
Tivoli Cloud VR	less than 10	February 2021

Filtering Platforms. In a first step, the formerly identified 155 available social VR platforms were selected by applying the identified *Preliminary Filtering* criteria. On the basis of publicly available information, only nine social VR platforms were able to meet the respective requirements for *Availability*, *HMD Support*, *Costs*, *No Age Restrictions* and *Content Creation* (see Table 3). If there was no information publicly available, the respective platform was also excluded. The nine remaining social VR platforms all meet the requirements for the potential use in distance learning.

In order to ensure a potential higher degree of long-term developer support, the *Popularity* criteria was applied for the remaining nine social VR platforms. Therefore, the average daily users per month were compared. In cases where no public information was available, the operators or developers of the respective platform were contacted directly.

Table 3 shows the average daily users of each selected social VR platform. We chose 100 average daily users as the lower population threshold. This leaves Roblox, Sinespace, FRAME and Neos VR are therefore part of the individual assessment in the next step. With regard to Mozilla Hubs, consistent and reliable user figures were not available and direct contact attempts were not answered or could barely provide any further information.

4.4 Individual Platform Assessment

Assessment Design. We used the HMD Oculus Quest for our tests. The Oculus Quest is a stand-alone HMD that can run VR applications independently. However, since the stand-alone configuration does not support all VR applications due to higher computing requirements, the Oculus Quest was connected to a computer via a USB 3.0 cable. This allows the computer to supplement the computing power of the Oculus Quest. The computer used for the test is equipped with an AMD Ryzen 5 3600 6-core processor, an NVIDIA RTX 2070 Super graphics card and 16 GB of DDR4 RAM. The recommended system requirements for the tested VR platforms were met or exceeded in all cases. All quality settings were set to the highest available options for the tests. Regarding the internet connection, the computer was connected via LAN to a DSL internet connection with 63.67 Mbit/s downstream and 12.73 Mbit/s upstream on average.

We then used this setup in the following step in the individual assessment to evaluate and analyse the respective platform.

As far as available, the *Hardware- and Software Requirements* are taken from the publisher. In the case of missing information, the respective developers were contacted and thus missing information was supplemented as best as possible. As a measure of visual fidelity, the frame rate during the internet connection test described below was documented. The display quality was set to the highest available setting for each of the evaluated platforms.

For the examination of *Social Interaction*, the possibilities for customising avatars as well as available functionalities for communicating with other users through text, speech, gestures and emotes were considered.

To evaluate *Content Creation*, we examined the options for uploading or creating content, as well as the respective possibilities for interacting with content in more detail.

Cross-Platform Support, as part of this analysis, describes the ability of users to access the same software from different devices, such as computers, mobile devices and HMDs. Many VR platforms offer such forms of cross-platform support. The different access options, required accounts and software needed were taken from the respective websites and listed for each platform.

Internet Connection refers to the performance of each VR platform in terms of latency and average bandwidth usage. We measured these attributes over a time windows of five minutes, during which we cycled through the provided functionalities of the different platforms. In order to monitor the internet traffic for each computer process individually, we recorded the used upstream and downstream bandwidth with NetBalancer. Information on latency was taken directly from the platform-own monitoring where possible and, in cases where it was not possible, from the resource manager of the operating system.

Assessment Results. After using the earlier mentioned assessment methodology, we found the following results:

For internet use and performance, the results of the 5-minute test are presented in Table 4.

For *Hardware- and Software Requirements*, FRAME, Neos VR and Sincespace state almost identical requirements, with a medium level CPU and graphics card from 2014 and 4 GB RAM. Because Roblox does not state specific requirements for the use of their platform in VR mode, the system requirements are for the desktop use and therefore much lower compared to the other platforms.

For *Social Interaction*, information about communication methods and body tracking is shown in Table 4. FRAME offers only basic avatar models with limited customisation options and no emotes or gestures. Roblox also also simple character designs, but additionally also a large shop for customisation options and more than 50 emotes and gestures is available. Sinespace uses realistic avatar designs with over 100 sliders to adjust certain details together with 13 available emotes and gestures. It also features a shop where users can publish their own assets to customise avatars. Neos VR supports 49 file formats for uploading 3D avatars. With various options to integrate and adjust features of avatar models, as well as the possibility of full body tracking, a realistic model of the user can be created. There are no default emotes or gestures available, but the support of full body tracking, including lip and eye tracking, enables users to use natural gestures and emotes in the VE.

For *Content Creation*, each platform has its own approach on how to create and present content. FRAME only offers the option to add elements to a variety of predesigned spaces. All customisation is done within the platform, either in desktop or in VR mode. Roblox and Sincespace have their own separate creation tools, where users can freely design VEs, assets and functionalities. In Neos VR, users perform all content creation in VR. Adding, modifying and creating assets can all be done with the tools available in VR. The number of supported data formats for images, 3D models, audio files and video files can be seen in Table 4.

For *Cross-Platform Support*, all platforms are accessible via desktop and VR. Mobile access is supported for FRAME, Roblox and Sinespace.

4.5   Discussion

The expert interviews and the online survey showed that an added value is to be expected through the use of VR in distance education. In addition to advantages in the area of social interaction, we see the possibilities of presenting interactive 3D content in VR as decisive advantages of VR in general.

Table 4. Individual analysis and test results of each platform

Criteria	FRAME	Neos VR	Roblox	Sinespace
Frame rate (fps)	101–140	26–48	54–60	36–60
Latency (ms)	110–116	127–180	52–78	109–144
Average bandwidth used (Mbit/s)	0.06	9.27	9.44	5.74
Full body tracking	✗	Up to 11 tracking points	✗	✗
Text/Voice chat	✓/✓	✓/✓	✓/✗	✓/✓
Supported image data formats	2	33	4	11
Supported 3D model data formats	4	49	2	4
Supported audio data formats	1	No data	2	4
Supported video data formats	4	No data	12	1

Since the requirements for VR applications are very diverse, e.g. due to different subjects in education, it is difficult to recommend a single best social VR platform for digital distance learning.

Rather, the most suitable platform for a particular application depends on a number of factors, such as the technical equipment, the content available for presentation, the number of students and lecturers, the nature of the training itself and certainly a degree of personal preference.

The system requirements for using social VR platforms are significant, which are reflected in the results. The system requirements for the Sinespace and Neos VR platforms and the requirements for the Oculus Link and SteamVR software are at a similarly high level. The Roblox and FRAME platforms do not specify explicit requirements for use in VR mode, but due to the significantly lower level of detail compared to the other platforms, it can be assumed that their requirements are also lower.

Framerate test results can be used to evaluate the visual performance of each platform. This is, however, highly dependent on the complexity of the currently displayed scene in the VE.

In terms of social interaction, the platforms studied differ greatly from each other. The Neos VR platform offers by far the most sophisticated and extensive features for communication and interaction possibilities. With the help of the multitude of supported input devices for full body tracking, lip tracking and eye tracking, interactions between users in VR become almost lifelike. The platforms Roblox and FRAME, offer only basic communication options, which, combined with the low level of realism of the avatars, does not help to improve social interaction possibilities. Sinespace offers a higher degree of visual realism, but the provided communication and interaction options are poor.

In terms of content creation and uploading, there were also significant differences. Neos VR offers by far the most comprehensive range of content creation options within VR. With advanced creation tools and scripts, as well as dozens of supported data formats, Neos VR wass able to replicate any of the trials and experiments we ran possible on the other platforms. However, the multitude of possibilities is very much at the expense of usability given the state of the user interface in VR. we question to what extent this can be seen as an advantage or even a disadvantage for the planned use in education.

FRAME, on the other hand, offers the simplest framework of all the platforms compared for creating a VE quickly and easily, sharing content with the available tools and communicating with other users. This may already be sufficient in the education sector for some applications of VR, thus enabling a quick and easy entry into the use of VR in education.

It should be noted that by limiting the results to free social VR platforms, platforms that might be more suitable in terms of functions were possibly excluded. Furthermore it must be mentioned that the qualitative and quantitative data were collected in a highly developed country, which is why the results are only of limited significance when viewed globally and may differ in a less developed country.

5   Conclusion

The aim of this work was to compile criteria relevant to the deployment of proprietary social VR platforms in distance learning. We then applied these criteria to a list of currently available social VR platforms to identify promising candidates for use in education. In order to gather and group individual requirements, we conducted fours interviews with experts from didactic fields and an online study among students with 92 participants.

In total, ten criteria could be classified as relevant with regard to distance learning in VR. *Availability* describes that the social VR platforms must be available during the test period. *HMD Support* is a potential prerequisite for immersive learning experiences. *Costs* ensures, that only free platforms are considered. *No Age Restrictions* describe that adult content is avoided, since we expect at least some of the users to be minors. *Content Creation* relates to the options for uploading or directly creating content in the VE, as well as the respective possibilities for interacting with this content. *Popularity* refers to the popularity in order to maintain the support of developers. *Social Interaction* refers to possibilities of individual character representation and communicating with other user within the VE. *Hardware and Software Requirements* considers the requirements of the respective social VR platforms in terms of computation power. *Internet Connection* considers the requirements regarding the internet connection. *Cross-Platform Support* relates to a cross-platform support in order to enable user a to access the same VE from different access devices.

We compiled a list of 155 currently available social VR platforms. By applying We were able to reduce this to a manageable selection of four platforms which in turn were subjected to a more detailed examination and furthermore compared with each other in an individual assessment.

Although the results of this analysis indicate that social VR platforms are certainly an option for expanding the existing possibilities of distance learning through the use of VR, no single best social VR platform for digital distance learning could be recommended. The recommendation of a certain platform is strongly linked to the respective requirements of the different potential applications of VR for education. Therefore recommendations head into the direction of a most suitable platform for a particular application.

Nevertheless, since there have been no uniform guidelines for the use of VR in teaching so far, the presented and directly applied methodology of this work provides value in many respects.

In light of the recent SARS-CoV-2 pandemic and associated, often time-critical decision-making concerning teaching in schools and universities, our criteria can support rapid and valid solutions.

6   Future Work

There are numerous research questions that should be examined more closely in future work and, if possible, also explored in less developed countries. Some suggestions, which in some cases might possibly build on the results presented here, will be made in the following.

To be able to shed more light on the general didactic effects of the use of social VR platforms in education, the evaluation of concrete use cases would be beneficial. Particularly, use cases in the context of simulating and analysing 3D content can further highlight the advantages of VR for educational purposes.

Another interesting research question with regard to user-friendliness might be, to what extent the platforms are considered as simple and comprehensible enough for educators to use them widely in their courses. For the evaluation, teaching objectives could be defined which are taught in the context of the use of selected social VR platforms and the creation of a VE. Based on a survey conducted on how easy or difficult it is to create the VE in the social VR platform, a further selection criterion might be developed for the respective social VR platform for an even finer selection of potentially suitable platforms to be used in education.

Another important topic is data protection. As users can use additional devices to increase the level of immersion, a lot of data could potentially be obtained on the respective used social VR platform. This raises questions such as what user data is stored, how it is processed and what it is or could be used for.

Finally, the options for representing oneself as well as expressing emotions or social cues during VR distance learning warrant closer inspection. Especially 'unconventional' avatars can offer advantages and, to date, little explored potential [24]. This research can likewise be expanded to cover education of adults and senior citizens [1].

Acknowledgements. We would like to thank Thomas Odaker, Elisabeth Mayer and Lea Weil, who supported this work with helpful discussions and feedback.

References

1. Baker, S., et al.: Avatar-mediated communication in social VR: an in-depth exploration of older adult interaction in an emerging communication platform. In: Proceedings of the 2021 CHI Conference on Human Factors in Computing Systems. CHI 2021, Association for Computing Machinery, New York, NY, USA (2021). https://doi.org/10.1145/3411764.3445752
2. Banow, R., Maw, S.: First results from a study on the efficacy of using virtual reality (VR) to teach truss mechanics. In: Proceedings of the Canadian Engineering Education Association (CEEA) (2019). https://doi.org/10.24908/pceea.vi0.13763
3. Bogner, A., Littig, B., Menz, W.: Interviewing Experts. Springer (2009). https://doi.org/10.1057/9780230244276
4. Craft.co: Roblox company profile (2021). https://craft.co/roblox. Accessed 31 May 2021
5. Dhawan, S.: Online learning: a panacea in the time of COVID-19 crisis. J. Educ. Technol. Syst. **49**(1), 5–22 (2020). https://doi.org/10.1177/0047239520934018
6. Duff, E., Miller, L., Bruce, J.: Online virtual simulation and diagnostic reasoning: a scoping review. Clin. Simul. Nurs. **12**(9), 377–384 (2016). https://doi.org/10.1016/j.ecns.2016.04.001
7. Dyer, E., Swartzlander, B.J., Gugliucci, M.R.: Using virtual reality in medical education to teach empathy. J. Med. Libr. Assoc. JMLA **106**(4), 498–500 (2018). https://doi.org/10.5195/jmla.2018.518
8. Facebook Technologies, LLC: Oculus quest 2: Our most advanced new all-in-one VR headset (2020). https://www.oculus.com/quest-2/. Accessed 31 May 2021
9. Fuchs, N.: Comparison of Virtual Reality Social Platforms under the Aspect of Digital Distance Teaching. Bachelor thesis, Ludwig-Maximilians-Universität München (2021)
10. G2.com Inc: Best VR collaboration in 2021 (2021). https://www.g2.com/categories/vr-collaboration. Accessed 31 May 2021
11. Gao, H., Bozkir, E., Hasenbein, L., Hahn, J.U., Göllner, R., Kasneci, E.: Digital transformations of classrooms in virtual reality. In: Proceedings of the 2021 CHI Conference on Human Factors in Computing Systems. CHI 202121, Association for Computing Machinery, New York, NY, USA (2021). https://doi.org/10.1145/3411764.3445596
12. Goetz, M.: Distance Learning in der COVID-19 Krise: Ein Praxischeck. Medienimpulse 58(2) (2020). https://doi.org/10.21243/mi-02-20-19
13. Hayden, S.: 10 free apps to hang out with friends in VR (2020). https://www.roadtovr.com/10-apps-hang-friends-vr/. Accessed 31 May 2021
14. Janßen, D., Tummel, C., Richert, A., Isenhardt, I.: Towards measuring user experience, activation and task performance in immersive virtual learning environments for students. In: International Conference on Immersive Learning, vol. 621, pp. 45–58. Springer International Publishing (2016). https://doi.org/10.1007/978-3-319-41769-1_4
15. Jin, S.A.A.: Avatars mirroring the actual self versus projecting the ideal self: The effects of self-priming on interactivity and immersion in an exergame, wii fit. Cyberpsychol. Behavior **12**(6), 761–765 (2009). https://doi.org/10.1089/cpb.2009.0130
16. Johansson, N.: Best apps for VR meetings 2021 (2021). https://immersive.ly/best-vr-apps-productive-remote-meetings/. Accessed 31 May 2021

17. Kim, S.J.: List of the most popular social VR platforms (2018), https://www.vrandfun.com/popular-social-vr-platform-list/. Accessed 31 May 2021
18. Kyaw, B.M., et al.: Virtual reality for health professions education: systematic review and meta-analysis by the digital health education collaboration. J. Med. Internet Res. **21**(1) (2019). https://doi.org/10.2196/12959
19. Latta, J.N., Oberg, D.J.: A conceptual virtual reality model. IEEE Comput. Graphics Appl. **14**(1), 23–29 (1994). https://doi.org/10.1109/38.250915
20. LaViola, J.J.: A discussion of cybersickness in virtual environments. ACM SIGCHI Bull. **32**(1), 47–56 (2000). https://doi.org/10.1145/333329.333344
21. Legault, J., Zhao, J., Chi, Y.A., Chen, W., Klippel, A., Li, P.: Immersive virtual reality as an effective tool for second language vocabulary learning. Languages **4**(1) (2019). https://doi.org/10.3390/languages4010013
22. Mangiante, S., Klas, G., Navon, A., Zhuang, G., Ran, J., Silva, M.: VR is on the edge: How to deliver 360° videos in mobile networks. In: Proceedings of the Workshop on Virtual Reality and Augmented Reality Network, pp. 30–35. Association for Computing Machinery, New York, NY, USA (2017). https://doi.org/10.1145/3097895.3097901
23. Maresky, H.S., Oikonomou, A., Ali, I., Ditkofsky, N., Pakkal, M., Ballyk, B.: Virtual reality and cardiac anatomy: exploring immersive three-dimensional cardiac imaging, a pilot study in undergraduate medical anatomy education. Clin. Anat. **32**(2), 238–243 (2019). https://doi.org/10.1002/ca.23292
24. McVeigh-Schultz, J., Isbister, K.: The case for "weird social" in VR/XR: a vision of social superpowers beyond meatspace. In: Extended Abstracts of the 2021 CHI Conference on Human Factors in Computing Systems. CHI EA 2021. Association for Computing Machinery, New York, NY, USA (2021). https://doi.org/10.1145/3411763.3450377
25. Merchant, Z., Goetz, E.T., Cifuentes, L., Keeney-Kennicutt, W., Davis, T.J.: Effectiveness of virtual reality-based instruction on students' learning outcomes in k-12 and higher education: a meta-analysis. Comput. Educ. **70**, 29–40 (2014). https://doi.org/10.1016/j.compedu.2013.07.033
26. Ookla, LLC.: Germany's mobile and broadband internet speeds (2020). https://www.speedtest.net/global-index/germany. Accessed 31 May 2021
27. Pan, X., et al.: The responses of medical general practitioners to unreasonable patient demand for antibiotics - a study of medical ethics using immersive virtual reality. PloS one **11**(2) (2016). https://doi.org/10.1371/journal.pone.0146837
28. Petersen, G.B., Mottelson, A., Makransky, G.: Pedagogical agents in educational VR: an in the wild study. In: Proceedings of the 2021 CHI Conference on Human Factors in Computing Systems. CHI 2021. Association for Computing Machinery, New York, NY, USA (2021). https://doi.org/10.1145/3411764.3445760
29. Pita, P.: List of social VR apps and projects (2017). https://virtualrealitytimes.com/2017/04/16/social-vr/. Accessed 31 Mar 2021
30. Radianti, J., Majchrzak, T.A., Fromm, J., Wohlgenannt, I.: A systematic review of immersive virtual reality applications for higher education: design elements, lessons learned, and research agenda. Comput. Educ. **147** (2020). https://doi.org/10.1016/j.compedu.2019.103778
31. Schultz, R.: Comprehensive list of social VR platforms and virtual worlds (2020). https://ryanschultz.com/list-of-social-vr-virtual-worlds/. Accessed 31 May 2021
32. Slater, M., Lotto, R., Arnold, M., Sanchez-Vives, M.: How we experience immersive virtual environments: the concept of presence and its measurement. Anuario de psicología **40**(2), 193–210 (2009)

33. Sprondel, W.M., Grathoff, R.: Alfred Schütz und die Idee des Alltags in den Sozial-wissenschaften. Ferdinand Enke Verlag (1979)
34. Steamcharts: Altspacevr (2021). https://steamcharts.com/app/407060. Accessed 31 May 2021
35. Steamcharts: Anyland (2021). https://steamcharts.com/app/505700. Accessed 31 May 2021
36. Steamcharts: Neos VR (2021). https://steamcharts.com/app/740250. Accessed 31 May 2021
37. Steamcharts: Sansar (2021). https://steamcharts.com/app/586110. Accessed 31 May 2021
38. Stepan, K., et al.: Immersive virtual reality as a teaching tool for neuroanatomy. Int. Forum Allergy Rhinol. **7**(10), 1006–1013 (2017). https://doi.org/10.1002/alr.21986
39. Sutherland, I.E.: A head-mounted three dimensional display. In: Proceedings of the 9–11 December 1968, Fall Joint Computer Conference, Part I, pp. 757–764. Association for Computing Machinery, New York, NY, USA (1968). https://doi.org/10.1145/1476589.1476686
40. Takahashi, D.: Sinespace teams up with unity to sell do-it-yourself virtual world SDK (2019). https://venturebeat.com/2019/03/19/sinespace-teams-up-with-unity-to-sell-do-it-yourself-vr-items-in-asset-store/. Accessed 31 May 2021
41. Tiiro, A.: Effect of Visual Realism on Cybersickness in Virtual Reality. Master's thesis, University of Oulu (2018)
42. Ung, G.M.: Razer's open-source headset aims to disrupt virtual reality (2015). https://www.pcworld.com/article/2865515/razers-open-source-headset-aims-to-disrupt-virtual-reality.html. Accessed 31 May 2021
43. Wang, G., Suh, A.: User adaptation to cybersickness in virtual reality: a qualitative study. In: 27th European Conference on Information Systems (ECIS 2019): Information Systems for a Sharing Society (2019)
44. Williamson, J., Li, J., Vinayagamoorthy, V., Shamma, D.A., Cesar, P.: Proxemics and social interactions in an instrumented virtual reality workshop. In: Proceedings of the 2021 CHI Conference on Human Factors in Computing Systems. CHI 2021. Association for Computing Machinery, New York, NY, USA (2021). https://doi.org/10.1145/3411764.3445729
45. Winn, W.: A Conceptual Basis for Educational Applications of Virtual Reality. Technical publication r-93-9, Washington Technology Center (1993). http://www.hitl.washington.edu/research/education/winn/winn-paper.html
46. Yarmand, M., Solyst, J., Klemmer, S., Weibel, N.: "it feels like i am talking into a void": Understanding interaction gaps in synchronous online classrooms. In: Proceedings of the 2021 CHI Conference on Human Factors in Computing Systems. CHI 2021. Association for Computing Machinery, New York, NY, USA (2021). https://doi.org/10.1145/3411764.3445240
47. Zhao, J., Xu, X., Jiang, H., Ding, Y.: The effectiveness of virtual reality-based technology on anatomy teaching: a meta-analysis of randomized controlled studies. BMC Med. Educ. **20**, 1–10 (2020)

Applications of VR/AR/MR in Industry

Regional Aircraft Interiors Evaluation in a Real Time Ray-Traced Immersive Virtual Environment

M. Guida$^{(\boxtimes)}$ and P. Leoncini

CIRA Centro Italiano Ricerche Aerospaziali, Via Maiorise snc., 81043 Capua (Caserta), Italy
{m.guida,p.leoncini}@cira.it

Abstract. This paper describes the Immersive VR Interiors Simulator developed by the VR Lab @ CIRA, the Italian Aerospace Research Centre, through which, leveraging the immersive approach and the first-person interaction, it was possible to carry out reachability, habitability and comfort tests of a new regional aircraft prototype.

More than one seats configuration was loaded in the app preparation phase in order to setup a switch logic among them. In the same way, by simply pressing the buttons on his/her handheld controller, users could change internal and external lights conditions.

The experimental activity was focused to the seating zone of the passengers' cabin. Overall cabin assessment, with the user standing in the cabin (including navigation, seat row ingress/egress and embarkment/disembarkment) and with the user in a seating position (PSU and try table reachability and usability tests) were carried out in order to improve and optimize the features of the aircraft interiors.

The protocol followed by CIRA for the human-in-the-loop subjective assessment of innovative design of regional aircraft interiors included two user questionnaires: the first one specific for the purposes of the core evaluation, the second one aiming at validating the user acceptance of VR, of the immersive approach, and of the specific VR application itself. In this paper, the results of a subjective test campaign made up of #24 testing subjects are presented.

Keywords: Subjective comfort assessment · Immersive VR · Unreal engine 4 · Aircraft interiors

1 Introduction

The immersive VR application described in this paper has been developed within the CASTLE project framework (CAbin Systems design Toward passenger welLbEing) [1] in order to carry out subjective tests of an innovative design concept for cabin interiors of a future regional aircraft. The workflow proposed consists of a user-centred evaluation process of design concepts to be performed when the interiors model is still at a digital design stage. In this way feedbacks on how comfortable the solutions have been perceived

© Springer Nature Switzerland AG 2021
L. T. De Paolis et al. (Eds.): AVR 2021, LNCS 12980, pp. 483–498, 2021.
https://doi.org/10.1007/978-3-030-87595-4_35

by sample passengers could be send to the designers at a very early stage of the project workflow and, over all, before to realize any physical mock-up of the aircraft [2].

In fact, even if the most relevant environment for such kind of comfort evaluation should be, of course, a physical mock-up of a real passenger cabin built up for the purpose, a virtual prototype can give designers a good feeling of future user acceptance before building up anything physical. Obviously as long as the virtual representation and the related experience are of a very good level of representativeness (the graphics representation has to be a credible virtual counterpart of the designed interiors in terms of 3D models and material rendering, and the sensory experience has not to be misleading for the testing people) [3].

User tests regarded various aspects of the comfort relevant to designers' interests: visual comfort (style, pleasantness), and ergonomic comfort (spaciousness, objects and command reachability and usability) [4].

2   The Immersive VR Application Used for Subjective Tests

The Virtual Interiors Immersive Simulator is based on the game engine software Unreal Engine 4 (UE4), developed by Epic Games [5], and allows to get a high-fidelity graphics experience achieved through the capabilities of setting all lighting parameters and materials characteristics.

The application employed CAD data supplied by the partners of CASTLE project. In particular, the models were sent to CIRA in STEP format for the 3D model part of the environment, while images were passed aside as material textures along with a comprehensive document describing the mapping of materials to interiors surfaces (Fig. 1).

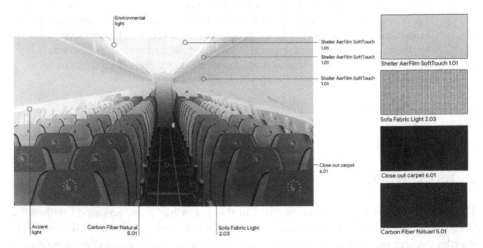

Fig. 1. Scheme definition of colours, materials and finishes for the VR model developed.

The head-mounted display (HMD) for the immersive visualization maximizes the sense of "being at the center of the virtual scene" [6] for the user thanks to the coverage of its field of view by the graphic scene visualized. Thanks to its touch system able to return vibration feedback, very important for reachability analysis, the Oculus Rift headset, developed and manufactured by Oculus VR [7], a division of Facebook Inc., has been the Virtual Reality HMD used for the aircraft interiors' standing and sitting evaluation session of ergonomics.

The user assessment of comfort aspects of the passenger cabin of a regional aircraft requires the best lifelike rendering quality possible at immersive VR rates. Interactivity requirements include freely moving within the whole cabin environment, switching among different interiors configuration (seats materials, curtain and panels), interacting with objects and movable parts of furniture in the cabin interiors in order to perform tests wrt. his/her own body size [8–11].

The VR runtime application, even if conceived for real-time rendering for keeping up with interactive frame rates (target frame rate for the Oculus Rift is 90 Hz), offers to the users a quite good rendering quality with a high number of complex lights and expensive rendering effects (Fig. 2).

Fig. 2. The immersive VR application developed in Unreal Engine 4.26.

An avatar for male and female people, sized at start-up with the user in standing position, allows the users to see their own body into the virtual environment. The movement of the head, in terms of position and orientation (six degrees of freedom, 6-DoF) is connected to the virtual camera; the movement of the hands controls their virtual counterparts in the 3D scene. Furthermore, by only using head and hands HMD tracking data and the blending of predefined full body avatar animations, whole body movements are reproduced resembling user's actual ones.

Furthermore, an aircraft noise audio track was added into the virtual environment in order to increase the testers' sense of presence and the identification with the passenger role. A seats row, kindly provided by the seat designer and manufacturer partner in the project (Fig. 9), allows users to carry out the tasks in sitting position on a real aircraft seat corresponding to its virtual counterpart.

The developed application allows the users to switch between two seat fabrics (in two different lining configuration), turn on/off the internal lights (and adapt the intensity), move across a day range the sun light, manually interact with the stowage bin, with the tray table and with the PSU (turning PSU light on/off) by means of the hand controllers, remove the front hulkhead curtain in order to access the service area, be teleported elsewhere in the cabin space.

Other commands are activated by an operator under tester request (all the user-activatable ones, teleport to specific zones, initial calibration of avatar mannequin size).

2.1 Global Illumination in Unreal

The application, thanks to Unreal Engine's dynamic lighting methods, offers a real-time Ray Traced Global Illumination (RTGI) solution to light the interiors scene with bounce lighting from dynamic light sources [12]. This solution enables the user to change lighting and automatically update to the objects within the scene, making it possible to simulate time of day transitions and turning on/off lights.

Through the Real-Time Ray Tracing (RTRT) it was possible to create an interactive experience with subtle lighting effects, more natural, producing soft shadowing for lights, accurate ambient occlusion (AO), interactive global illumination, reflections and more all happening in real-time [13, 14].

Ray Traced Shadows allowed to simulate soft area lighting effects for all the objects in the virtual cabin environment. This means that, based on the light's source size or source angle, an object's shadow has sharper shadows near the contact surface than farther away where it softens and widens (Fig. 3).

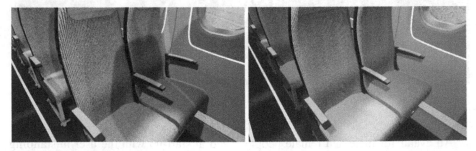

Fig. 3. Ray-traced shadows compared to (the less complex) non ray-traced ones.

Through the Ray Traced Reflections (RTR) it was possible to simulate accurate environment representation supporting multiple reflection bounces. Multiple bounces recreate real-time inter-reflection between reflective surfaces in the scene (Fig. 4).

Fig. 4. Ray-traced reflections on the back of the seats compared to non ray-traced ones.

Ray Traced Translucency (RTT) allowed to accurately represents glass materials with physically correct reflections, absorption, and refraction on transparent surfaces (Fig. 5).

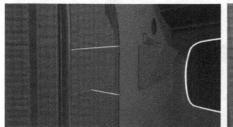

Fig. 5. Ray-traced glass translucency compared to non ray-traced one.

Due to the complexity of the scene, in order to give back some runtime performance, the ray tracing based global illumination method used was the final gather-based technique instead of the brute-force one that is more accurate but more expansive in terms of graphics performance. This technique introduces some limitations the main of which is that it's currently limited to a single bounce of indirect diffuse GI.

2.2 Physics-Based Manual Interaction

Physics simulations improves the immersion value of every virtual scene because it helps users believe that they are interacting with the simulation and that it is responding in a realistic way and thus empowers the virtual passenger to evaluate reachability and usability of the features of the virtual objects to be tested all around him/her [15, 16].

All the movable object in the application are subjected to physics and are joined to the scene with realistic hinge mechanisms. The stowage bin, the cup holder and the tray table to be tested all behave like their real counterparties. In particular, the stowage bin can be opened by a lock/unlock system connected to his handle (Fig. 6) as well as the tray table can be overturned by rotating the pawl locking (Fig. 7).

Furthermore, even if there isn't any haptic response when the objects subject to physics are touched, a first contact force feedback, provided by the hand controllers vibration, gives to the users the capability to understand when the collision between his/hers own hands and the virtual objects within the virtual world happen.

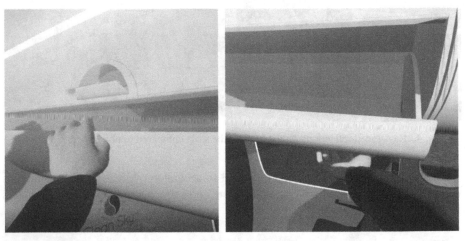

Fig. 6. Opening/closing the stowage bin.

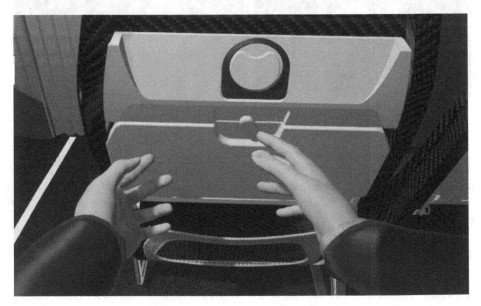

Fig. 7. User opening the tray table.

3   The Concept Design Under Evaluation

The VR test campaign on the Regional Aircraft Interiors involved 24 people aged between 35 and 66 years with an average age of 49.7 years. The gender of participants was distributed between males and females with a significant prevalence of men (83.3% vs. 16.7%). Flight experience, measured in number of flights performed, was higher than 10 times for the 75% of the users. The heights were distributed from 160 cm to 195 cm with an average height of about 175 cm (Fig. 8).

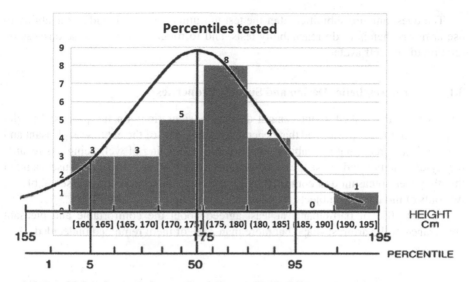

Fig. 8. Distribution of the height percentiles of the tested subjects.

Due to the COVID pandemic emergency, the subjective tests of the Regional Aircraft, held in the VR Lab @ CIRA, were conducted thanks to a sanitization device, the Cleanbox CX1 (see Fig. 9), which ensured to kill 99,8% of bacteria and viruses, including COVID-19, between one test and another.

Fig. 9. The immersive VR test setup @ CIRA VR Lab with the Cleanbox CX1 VR HMD sanitizing device and the physical seat row provided by the seat manufacturer partner in the project.

The questionnaire submitted after the test in immersive VR considers the ability to use arms and hands to do reachability tests, and to roughly measure spaciousness by relating to one-self avatar.

3.1 General Aesthetic: Design and Surface Properties

Testers were first asked about general design considerations on the proposed model (Fig. 10). All the people agreed that general style/aesthetic of the cabin was pleasant and at least 75% agreed that the cabin suggests a general feeling of well-being. As regards the style/aesthetics and the shape of the seat, between 80% and 90% of the users agreed that they were pleasant and comfortable. Of the two solutions proposed (see Table 1), two outs of three of the subjects tested preferred the first set of fabrics.

Almost 70% of participants at least agreed about the comfortable and pleasant appearance of the armrest shape but more than 33% of them remained undecided.

Fig. 10. General aesthetic of the cabin.

Table 1. The two sets of fabrics proposed for the cabin seats.

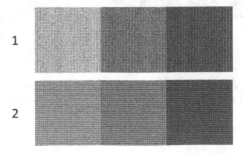

3.2 Tray Table

About the Tray Table (Fig. 11), more than 90% of the users agreed to consider it pleasant, easy to reach and to open/close. More than 75% at least agreed to consider the table adequate to eat/read/use the laptop even if more than 20% of them remained undecided.

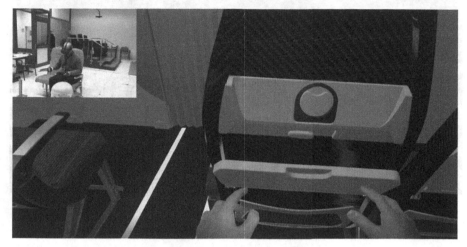

Fig. 11. Tray Table opening

3.3 General Posture, Accessibility and Living Space

The whole of the users agreed, strongly almost 40%, to be happy with the view from the seat and more than 80% had the feeling of being in a spacious environment. As concern the space around the seats, even if more than 80% agreed to consider sufficient the space for accessing the seat and the leg room, only 50% found the seat have enough space to stretch their own legs and almost 40% remained undecided on the availability of space (Fig. 12).

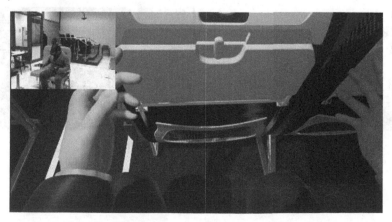

Fig. 12. Space for accessing the seats and the leg room

3.4 Cabin Lining

As concern the Cabin Lining, more than 95% of the participants agreed, strongly more than 40%, that the cabin ensures a good external view from the windows (Fig. 13).

Fig. 13. Evaluation of the view from the window

3.5 Stowage Bin and PSU

About the Stowage Bin, more than 90% of the users agreed to consider it easy to reach/use, almost 40% of them strongly and more than 95% of them agreed to consider the Stowage bin to be spacious enough for their luggage, almost 50% strongly. Concerning the PSU ease of use, almost 75% of them at least agreed but more than 20% disagreed. More than 85% at least agreed to consider the PSU easy to reach and less than 10% disagreed (Fig. 14).

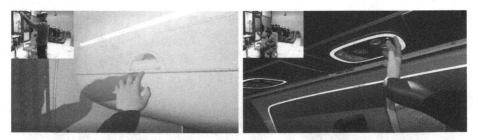

Fig. 14. Stowage Bin and PSU accessibility tests.

4   Rationale of the Immersive VR-Based Subjective Evaluation Process

Subjective tests – i.e. tests done by humans by their senses as their own personal unchallengeable judgment, strongly depend on how each single tester actually perceive the submitted stimuli. In the case of comfort tests in an immersive virtual environment, test results are mostly dependent on how "good" is the virtual environment built to represent the design to give a rate. Stimuli are constituted by the 3D graphics rendered of the cabin environment to the HMD at interactive rate, by the interactions allowed to users within the cabin environment, and by the feedbacks the application has set up to alert the user [17].

By these considerations, a strong pre-condition for taking in the right consideration the results of a user's subjective test campaign is that the simulating virtual environment can be considered a valid synthetic representation of the proposed design from several point of views: the correspondence (adherence) to the designer's intentions (the VE well represents the designer's project), the way to leverage user senses to convey the project. Simply put, a very good design could be possibly judged negatively due to the poor way for the representing virtual environment to "present" it to human testers.

When building up a VE application, several source of errors could lead to a "bad" virtual representation, either of technical/technological nature (poor interface devices such as the HMD, its tracking capabilities, hand controllers, bad computer performances hitting the application frame rate and rising latency, low graphics rendering quality too far from reality, etc.), or dealing with a possible mis-correspondence of the 3D virtual model of the environment with the one the designer has modelled (3D shapes, materials, lights, external lighting conditions, etc.). The latter problem can arise when the design software and the one used for the VR are not the same or a data/format conversion has been needed for interfacing them, a/o when data passed from design to VR are possibly not complete or just "described" rather than hardcoded in data files. Other than doing the same work twice, this possibly leads to doing the same thing in different ways – e.g. a material could be characterized in different ways in two different software, not to mention that insufficient input could leave the VE implementer an "interpretation" freedom error prone [18].

Yet, while the data-related source of badness of a VR representation of a design can be worked around by a verification of the final VE by the designers, the application-related ones must be checked by submitting the VR application to a larger audience in order to be somehow "certified" by a sufficient number of judgments.

Thus, side by side the comfort test of the new-generation interiors proposed for the business jet a subjective test of the immersive VR application itself must be done with the idea that it constitutes the transfer medium of the design to be evaluated to the testers, and that a bad VE application ends up to invalidate results of the subjective tests regarding the design.

The protocol followed by CIRA for the subjective testing of the Regional aircraft included two user questionnaires, based on Likert five-points scales [19]. The first one specific for the purposes of the core evaluation i.e. the comfort aspects, a second one aiming at validating the user acceptance of VR, of the immersive approach, and of the VR application just experience.

5 Results of the Subjective Tests Regarding the Immersive VR Approach and the VR Application

The whole of the users enjoyed the VR Experience. As anticipated, the same #24 people, that tested the design against aesthetics and accessibility aspects, were asked to evaluate the application used for the VR experience, and, in general, the immersive VR approach for the purposes of the tasks requested. In the following a synthesis of the user considerations and related rates.

The Virtual Reality experience has been fascinating (charming), fine, good, and nice for all the participants, warm, active, predictable and funny for a large part of the audience, and almost not frightening or sad at all for all the users.

Almost 90% of the testers was able to control events. The environment responded to the actions nearly 95% of the testers have undertaken. Experiences done in the virtual environment have seemed quite conforming with those of the real world at least partly to whole of the users and enough to almost 90% of them.

About 90% of the users felt at least quite able to explore and actively inspect the environment with sight, as well as they felt the feeling of moving within the virtual environment very convincing, partially about 10% of them. More than 85% of them was very or quite able to carefully examine the objects in the virtual environment.

Three out of four testers adapted to the virtual environment experience at least quickly. 75% of the testers felt almost enough competent in moving and interacting with the virtual environment at the end of the experience and the percentage rises to over 95% if we consider also people who felt mediumly competent.

The quality of the head-mounted display interfered or distracted little three out of four testers during the performance of the assigned tasks or the activities required. Almost the whole of the users answered that the quality of the graphics rendering affected positively the execution of the assigned tasks or the required activities. On the other and, the interface devices (HMD, the connecting cable, hand controllers) have interfered little or very little with the execution of the assigned tasks or the required activities for 70% of the testers but much or very much for more than 10% of them.

The small tracked area limited, in more of 50% of the cases little or not at all and in the other cases partially or much, the performance of the required activities.

Three out of four testers have been able to concentrate much on the tasks assigned or on the tasks required rather than on the mechanisms used to perform these tasks or activities.

The users rated the Virtual Reality experience as a whole positive or very positive. Their performance in the Virtual Reality environment was satisfactory for more than 95% of the participants.

Among the sensory aspects of Virtual Reality that could be improved, most rated were:

- the perception of oneself;
- the perception of touching objects;
- sound/noise as manipulation feedback;
- the congruence between the movement of objects and the sound associated with it.

Practical aspects of Virtual Reality tested that could be most improved by the testers' opinion:

- the HMD comfort;
- the hand controller comfort;
- the tracked area;
- the area where the VR experience has been held.

Most of them could actually reproduce in real the operations performed in Virtual Reality.

Almost all of the testers could explore the environment by moving with their head, while a total of almost 80% could actually explore the environment by moving with their whole body. The large majority of them felt comfortable in the virtual environment.

During the Virtual Reality experience, as well as at the end of the Virtual Reality experience they felt:

- very little disoriented;
- little or normally emotioned;
- little or very little troubled;
- very little indifferent;
- much or normally happy;
- very little embarrassed;
- normally or much satisfied;
- little or very little frustrated;
- very little or normally relieved;
- very little disappointed.

During and at the end of the Virtual Reality experience, they have experienced very little of all these sensations: nausea, disgust, stress, dizziness, tension, anxiety, boredom (being annoyed), while at the end they zeroed almost all these negative sensations.

As to users' opinion, performance that can be obtained in Virtual Reality mostly depends on the functionality of a Virtual Reality application and on technological capabilities of Virtual Reality rather on individual skills or person's mood.

About 90% of the interviewed think it is possible to make a visual quality assessment in Virtual Reality and that it is possible to carry out an assessment of the reachability of commands and accessibility of objects.

Thus, by concluding, the comprehensive additional questionnaire has pointed out that both immersive VR and the specific VR application have largely passed the acceptability threshold to be considered reliable for the task of the subjective tests proposed.

6 Concluding Remarks

For what concerns the visual comfort, the test campaign showed that most of the users found the proposed configurations pleasant and comfortable.

The interactions with the objects during the execution of the assigned tasks were considered adequately good. Notwithstanding the lack of a haptic feedback, the tray table, the PSU and the seats allowed the users to interact with them, for the proposed tests, in a sufficiently natural way.

The evaluations made by the analyzed group of users regarding living space comfort were quite satisfactory. Only the space for stretching legs was judged insufficient or difficult to assess especially by taller people.

User answers collected for the second questionnaire have, in turn, validated in a very positive way the VR application used, and the immersive VR approach for subjective comfort tests. This gives more confidence in the results of the subjective tests of the design concept that was under primary assessment.

Definitely, the interviewed think it is possible to make a visual quality assessment in Virtual Reality and that it is possible to carry out an assessment of the reachability of commands and accessibility of objects.

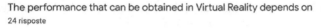

The performance that can be obtained in Virtual Reality depends on
24 risposte

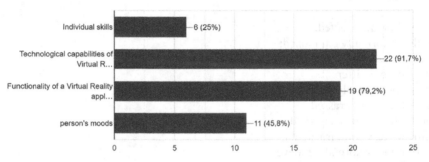

7 Conclusions and Future Works

For our VR research lab the presented application has been the first opportunity to test the use of ray tracing in a pre-production industrial application leveraging the newest NVIDIA GeForce GTX 3090 graphics card. The support of hardware-accelerated ray tracing in Unreal 4.26 has been implemented timely and quite in continuity with the rendering parameters ruling the non-GI rendering infrastructure, thus being able to enable ray traced scene rendering by few switches and parameters adjusting in the IDE. By not pushing output quality uselessly too far, graphics performances – our main concern – was never an issue, and the GPU performance graph shows there's still a margin for further rendering quality improvement.

We look forward to evolve future projects of this kind to a multisensory VE, in which the testing passenger feels more and more immersed in a lifelike cabin environment. Additional sensory feedback to feed a user in order to contribute to identify oneself with the impersonating role may include temperature, humidity, and air flows, airline brand smells, more audio feedbacks for whatever happened in the cabin, tactile and grasping force feedback for ergonomics evaluations, rumble feedbacks to key parts of the user body bumping to environment (e.g. knees bumping into the front seat when seated and getting up), and populating the cabin with realistically moving autonomous virtual passengers.

Finally, whilst subjective, confronting their own sensations with the one of others in a collaborative virtual environment, thus actually helping each other in forming one's own opinion may surely improve the robustness of the process quality of the assessments, aside from definitely making the joint testing experience fun.

The feedback obtained from the virtual simulation analysis of comfort will be verified and eventually validated through physic tests in the cabin full scale demonstrator as part of the activities of Leonardo - Aircraft Division for REG-IADP WP 3.2.

Acknowledgements. The work has been done within the AIRFRAME ITD. Grant Agreement n° CS2-AIR-GAM-2014-2015-01, aiming at delivering cabin interiors design of future regional aircraft that maximize the wellbeing of passengers, including PRM and crew, considering the travelling needs and requirements that are foreseen in the future of air transportation. The cabin configuration requirements, target and constraints have been provided by Leonardo - Aircraft Division in accordance with cabin layout of passenger accommodation (Leonardo proprietary) of the Clean Sky 2 Regional Aircraft Conventional Demonstration Platform.

References

1. https://www.cleansky.eu/
2. ISO DIS 9241–210: Ergonomics of human system interaction - part 210: human-centred design for interactive systems. Technical report. International Organization for Standardization (2010)
3. Aromaa, S., Väänänen, K.: Suitability of virtual prototypes to support human factors/ergonomics evaluation during the design. Appl. Ergon. **56**, 11–18 (2016)
4. Vink, P., Bazley, C., Kamp, I., Blok, M.: Possibilities to improve the aircraft interior comfort experience. Appl. Ergon. **43**, 354–359 (2012)
5. https://www.unrealengine.com/en-US
6. Riva, G., et al.: Affective interactions using virtual reality: the link between presence and emotions. Cyberpsychol. Behav. **10**, 45–56 (2007)
7. https://www.oculus.com
8. Di Gironimo, G., Leoncini, P., Patalano, S.: Realizzazione di un "Walk Through" all'interno della cabina passeggeri del Piaggio P180 Avanti: confronto tra due ambienti di visualizzazione e sviluppo. In: Proceeding of Convegno Nazionale XIV ADM e XXXIII AIAS Innovazione nella Progettazione Industriale, Bari, Italy (2004)
9. Mudliyar, P., Ingale, Y., Bhalerao, S., Jagtap, O.: Virtual reality for interior design. Int. J. Res. Advent Technol. **2**, 260–263 (2014)
10. More, S., Wagh, T., Suryawanshi, Y.: Virtual reality of interior architecture. Int. J. Adv. Res. Ideas Innov. Technol. **5**, 1443–1445 (2019)
11. Heydarian, A., Pantazis, E., Carneiro, J.P., Gerber, D., Becerik-Gerber, B.: Towards understanding end-user lighting preferences in office spaces by using immersive virtual environments. Autom. Construct. **81**, 56–66 (2017)
12. Wald, I., Purcell, T.J., Schmittler, J., Benthin, C., Slusallek, P.: Realtime ray tracing and its use for interactive global illumination. In: EUROGRAPHICS 2003, Granada, Spain (2003)
13. Wald, I., et al.: Applying ray tracing for virtual reality and industrial design. In: IEEE Symposium on Interactive Ray Tracing, Salt Lake City, UT, USA (2006)
14. Dietrich, A., Wald, I., Schmidt, H., Sons, K., Slusallek, P.: Realtime ray tracing for advanced visualization in the aerospace industry. In: Proceedings of the 5th Paderborner Workshop Augmented & Virtual Reality in der Produktentstehung, Paderborn, Germany (2006)

15. Stone, R., Panfilov, P.B., Shukshunov, V.E.: Evolution of aerospace simulation: from immersive virtual reality to serious games. In: Proceedings of 5th International Conference on Recent Advances in Space Technologies - RAST2011, Istanbal, Turkey (2011)
16. Prittiporn, L., Jinuntuya, P.: Interactive 3D simulation system in game engine based collaborative virtual environment for architectural design communication. In: Proceedings of 14th International Conference on Computer Aided Architectural Design Research in Asia, Yunlin, Taiwan (2009)
17. Jimenez-Mixco, V., et al.: Application of virtual reality technologies in rapid development and assessment of ambient assisted living environments. In: Proceedings of 1st ACM SIGMM International Workshop on Media Studies and Implementations that Help Improving Access to Disabled Users, Beijing, China (2009)
18. Kaleja, P., Kozlovská, M.: Virtual reality as innovative approach to the interior designing. J. Civ. Eng. **12**, 109–116 (2017)
19. Joshi, A., Saket, K., Chandel, S., Pal, D.K.: Likert scale: explored and explained. Curr. J. Appl. Sci. Technol. **7**, 396–403 (2015)

An Immersive Training Approach for Induction Motor Fault Detection and Troubleshooting

Gustavo Caiza[1], Marco Riofrio-Morales[2], Angel Robalino-Lopez[3],
Orlando R. Toscano[4], Marcelo V. Garcia[2,5(✉)], and Jose E. Naranjo[2]

[1] Universidad Politecnica Salesiana, UPS, 170146 Quito, Ecuador
gcaiza@ups.edu.ec
[2] Universidad Tecnica de Ambato, UTA, 180103 Ambato, Ecuador
{mriofrio3650,mv.garcia,jnaranjo0463}@uta.edu.ec
[3] Instituto Superior Tecnológico Victoria Vásconez Cuvi, ISTVVC,
050103 Latacunga, Ecuador
arobalino@institutovvc.edu.ec
[4] Instituto Superior Tecnológico España, ISTE, 180103 Ambato, Ecuador
orlandor.toscanor@iste.edu.ec
[5] University of Basque Country, UPV/EHU, 48013 Bilbao, Spain
mgarcia294@ehu.eus

Abstract. Industry 4.0 has gained drive in the last few years since most companies at the industrial level need to update and optimize their production chain. Restructuring their processes and improving their human resources skills is imperative if they want to remain competitive. This research presents the development of a virtual reality system for induction motor troubleshooting training. Two sample groups were taken as references. The first one was trained with the VR system, while the second group worked with a conventional methodology. With the use of the proposed system, there was a time reduction of 57.73%. In terms of knowledge acquisition, it was possible to confirm, with a p-value lower than 0.05, that the VR system is more efficient than the conventional methodology. Finally, the system's usability was evaluated utilizing the System Usability Scale (SUS), obtaining an average value of 73.33.

Keywords: Optimization · Industrial training · Virtual reality · Induction motors

1 Introduction

The development of personnel knowledge should progress along with innovation. It is fundamental to improve the productive chain of an organization. As of now, it is new to join preparing with virtual instruments; this implies diminishing expenses and ensuring the learning of the data bestowed to the staff. The focal responsibility of virtual preparing is to produce quick and simple to utilize solutions for human resources [3,6].

© Springer Nature Switzerland AG 2021
L. T. De Paolis et al. (Eds.): AVR 2021, LNCS 12980, pp. 499–510, 2021.
https://doi.org/10.1007/978-3-030-87595-4_36

The 4.0 revolution allows this sort of innovation, consequently permitting an efficient management. Most businesses have been compelled to enter this new time to get more effective creation strategies. The main tools inside this era are VR, augmented reality (AR) and extended reality (XR), utilized for staff preparing.

The main recipients of this innovation are the raw materials' industry, which allows for automatic control of the process. These technologies are said to have a wide range of uses, from educational, military, medical to industrial machinery maintenance [1].

The health crisis and the monetary emergency that the world is encountering make innovation a definitive factor in addressing these challenges. On an industrial level, employers also have a serious impact, trying to ensure employee health, avoid physical contact and seek new ways to implement robotized work. Create products for the industrial sector using virtual platforms and applications is a means to neutralize the damage caused by the pandemic [13].

It is clear that with the application of virtual techniques, the frequency of work and interpersonal relationships will change [11]. The current and future alternative is virtual reality. This is to avoid the industrial environment and to maintain human integrity. It is an option available in all industrial manufacturing processes [14].

Likewise, technological advancements make it possible for us to apply virtual fields to all industries and surprisingly to people's everyday lives. Similarly, this is a major factor as many companies have adopted this model to train all processes in the industrial sector. The main benefit by adopting virtual reality is improved performance in industrial projects. In addition, it is an element that seeks continuous improvement over other organizations and an industrial competitive advantage. [4,14].

In this article, we will explain the development of VR system for fault detection training of three-phase motors and its comparison with conventional training systems. This system was developed using the Unity 3D graphics engine and Blender.

This article is divided into six sections, including the introduction. In Sect. 2, the objectives of the study are detailed. In Sect. 3, the developed interfaces are explained, while in Sect. 4, the usability evaluation is deployed. In Sect. 5, the results are discussed; and, in Sect. 6, the conclusions and future works are studied.

2   Case of Study

This study compares two types of training in fault detection and repair of three-phase electric motors. The first is based on lessons that apply as usual in the health crisis we are boldly facing. A virtual classroom with videos, slides and video calling software. The second uses an immersive VR app. The app uses interactive content and sensors to provide users with a fully immersive experience. See Fig. 1.

Due to the high probability of failure with this type of engine, the failures in this study are the most common and easy to detect and are described below.

- **Broken Bars:** It reduces the smooth operation efficiency of the induction motor. The problem starts with a broken bar and if not fixed in time will cause more rotor bars to break. Therefore, these machines require regular maintenance [8].
- **Inter-turn short circuits:** They are caused by damage to the insulating coating of the windings. This can also affect the entire coil and adjacent coils. Mechanical stress, high current or thermal shock are some causes of insulation. When this damage occurs, it will cause vibration problems in the machine and cause serious magnetic field damage [5].

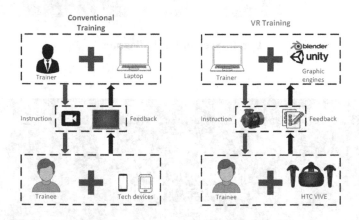

Fig. 1. Conventional and VR training

3   Interactive System Design

The graphic environment limits the space in which the user develops and learns to identify possible faults in the electric motors. Here the Unity 3D graphics engine and Blender design software were used. An interactive interface was also created with the HMD and HTC VIVE command.

In Fig. 2, it can be identified that the VR system consists of three modules. i) Overview: Learn the technical concepts of three-phase asynchronous motors in a general presentation. This was done through the video. ii) Engine failures: Allows the user to recognize the failures caused by bar breakage or short circuit and learn how to fix them. iii) Test: Required to evaluate the knowledge acquired by the apprentice.

When the system is started, users will be immersed in a mechanical workshop, perfecting their presence and feeling themselves in an environment useful for industrial learning. Here they will be presented with a menu of options where they can choose to start the workout or exit the system. See Fig. 3. When the user agrees to start training, a video will be displayed explaining the basics of the induction motor, its parts, and the application. When finish the video, the button to move on to the next scene is activated. This can be appreciated in Fig. 4.

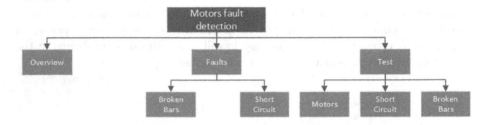

Fig. 2. System block diagram

Fig. 3. Options menu

In Fig. 5, the rated data of the motor is running and the phase signal of the oscilloscope is displayed. The first mistake users have to learn is broken bars. We also simulated the characteristic sound of this engine to help users get used to a real environment. With this interface, the learner can use buttons to view on a map the signal difference between a non-faulty motor and a faulted motor.

There is auditory feedback in this scene, which explains that the amplitude in the frequency range of 75 to 110 Hz decreases to lower values of −40 dBV compared to a standard signal. On the other hand, it is also taught that there is an increase in amplitude in the frequency range from 100 to 110 Hz. Finally, it is established that another characteristic of this type of failure is the creation of lateral peaks near 70, 40 and 50 Hz with oscillating amplitudes around −10 dbV. See Fig. 6.

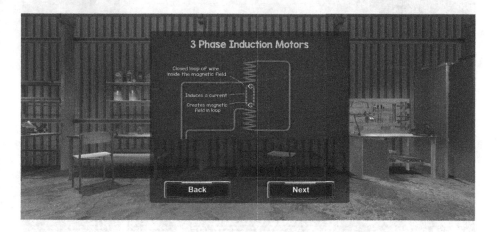

Fig. 4. Tutorial

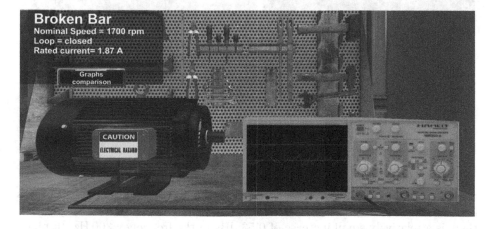

Fig. 5. Broken bars fault

When the user understands this information, the disassembled motor will be displayed. That is, the case and stator are not visible. A rotating red arrow identifies visible physical damage and draw students' attention. The above described can be seen in Fig. 7. The user is then trained on how to repair it. We chose to braze here because it is the most common way to repair minor damage in small rotor bars. When the repair is complete, the damage is gone and the apprentice can move on to the next fault. See Fig. 8.

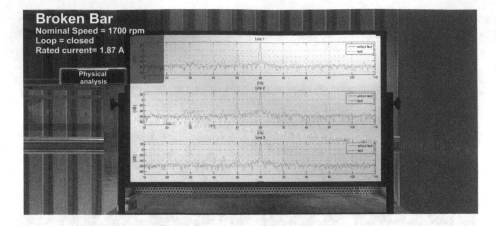

Fig. 6. Broken bars: graphs comparison

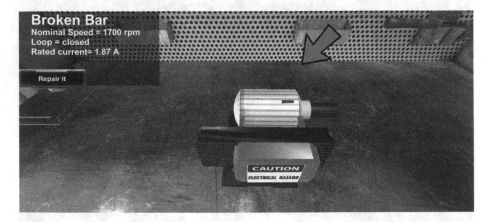

Fig. 7. Broken bars fault: physical damage

The scenes developed for the inter-turn short circuits failure are similar. The rated motor data displayed on the screen is different, so the actual status of this fault can be created. In Fig. 9, the user will be able to learn that, in phase 3, there is a relatively small increase of 0.53 dBv in the frequency 300 Hz. In phase 1, the spectral signal moves 11 dBv above the signal without failures. Finally, in the three phases, it can be seen that 180 Hz, the signal spectrum increases 23 dBv above the noise level [2].

Finally, a questionnaire of 10 multiple-choice questions was set up to evaluate the knowledge acquired by each user. Four are for understanding bars breakage failures, four are for short circuits between turns, and two are for a general understanding of three-phase electric motors. Each question has three options, only one of which is appropriate. To ensure the reliability of the response, it is recorded and cannot be changed. In Fig. 10, it is shown that after finishing the

Fig. 8. Broken bars fault: brazing process

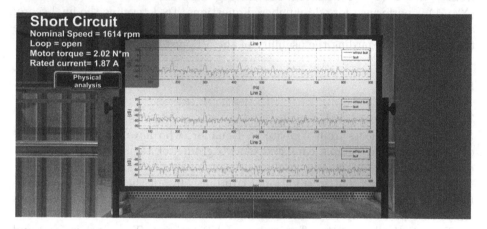

Fig. 9. Short circuit: graphs comparison

test a scene with all the test information will be generated, i.e., username, time and score.

4 System Usability Scale

Scores from 0 to 100 determine the efficiency of the developed system. Products with more than 80 are excellent and are rated A. Systems rated from 70 to 80 are considered acceptable and rated B. A score from 50 to 70 indicates a poor system and are rated C. Finally, systems with a score below 50 rated D [9].

FINAL SCORE: Marco R. 8

FINAL TIME: 47 seg

EXIT   Highscore: Marco Riomu 9

Fig. 10. Test feedback

Each of the even-numbered questions is scored by subtracting the user's score from 5, that is $(5 - Y)$. Instead, subtracting one from the user-generated score $(Y - 1)$ is performed for odd-numbered questions. To determine the final score, add the number of positive and negative questions and multiply by 2.5 to produce the final result regarding the usability of the VR system [12].

5   Results

To achieve the goals of this study, the experiment was designed with the participation of students from Ambato in Ecuador, who have a basic knowledge of electronics. The sample consisted of two groups of 15 participants each. A control group and an experimental group were created.

Figure 11 shows that in traditional training, 50% of the points are concentrated on 6 or higher, except for a score of 3. The virtual reality-based method states that 50% of the scores are 8 or higher.

To statistically test the effectiveness of VR training, T student is used and is based on two assumptions: i) H_0 There isn't a significant difference between traditional training and VR training; and ii) H_1 There is a significant difference between traditional training and VR training. The confidence level was $\alpha = 5\%$.

The ShapiroWilk test determines the normality of observations for samples containing less than 30 data. The significance values for regular training and VR were 0.908 and 0.934. This verifies that there is a normal distribution. A Levene test with a significance value of 0.36 was performed to determine the equivalence of the variances.

With these parameters calculated, the significance value was obtained (0.000003). Below 0.05, this value is more likely to reject H0 and accept H1, VR training is more effective than traditional training, with solid knowledge, information retention and proper understanding of the procedures presented.

Meanwhile, each of the two induction motor maintenance training courses have been timed to determine if there is resource optimization. Traditional instruction was given to the control group for a fixed period of 60 min. During this phase, the professional's presentation, proposed modules, and the test were

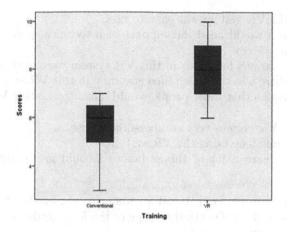

Fig. 11. Conventional and VR scores

considered. In contrast, the virtual reality training was conducted at different times. The total experience time lasted an average of 25 min 36 s.

In Fig. 12 it can be seen that learning in VR can save a lot of time. We found that the optimized time was 57.73% compared to regular training. This analysis shows that learning through Industry 4.0 help to gain better understanding. In conclusion, induction motor maintenance operators can gain more experience and learn through this technology. On the other hand, the optimization of resources is essential to reduce costs and improve industry efficiency.

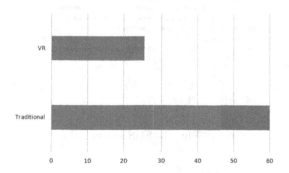

Fig. 12. VR vs conventional training time

As with other studies, acceptance assessment was performed through a survey that followed the guidelines presented by SUS [7,10]. The following items were included in the survey:

1. I think that I would like to use this VR system frequently.
2. I found the VR system unnecessarily complex.

3. I thought the VR system was easy to use.
4. I think that I would need the support of a technical person to be able to use this VR system.
5. I found the various functions in this VR system were well integrated.
6. I thought there was too much inconsistency in this VR system.
7. I would imagine that most people would learn to use this VR system very quickly,
8. I found the VR system very cumbersome to use.
9. I felt very confident using the VR system.
10. I needed to learn a lot of things before I could get going with this VR system.

The second group answered 10 statements using the Likert scale. The average value obtained was 73.33. Due to the range of the final grade, it can be said that it is a friendly and intuitive system.

In Fig. 13, the participants' grades are deployed. Users find every module of the system appropriate. According to the SUS, induction motor troubleshooting training is accepted by 12 people. On the other hand, the other three people scored below 70 points, so they claim that the VR system was not easy to use.

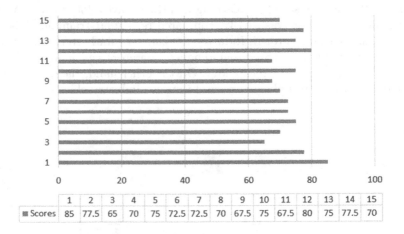

	1	2	3	4	5	6	7	8	9	10	11	12	13	14	15
■ Scores	85	77.5	65	70	75	72.5	72.5	70	67.5	75	67.5	80	75	77.5	70

Fig. 13. SUS scores

6 Conclusions and Future Work

A VR system has been developed for the training in terms of induction motor troubleshooting. The SUS methodology has shown that users consider the system suitable. However, since this is the first version of the model, there are still factors to consider, such as system interaction, responsiveness, and robustness. It is also recommended to use other methodologies to evaluate the usability of the system, as well as to follow specific guidelines to create the scenarios efficiently.

Acknowledgements. The authors recognize the supported bringing by Universidad Tecnica de Ambato (UTA) and their Research and Development Department (DIDE) under project CONIN-P-256-2019.

References

1. Baygin, M., Karakose, M., Akin, E.: ITHET 2016: 2016 15th International Conference on Information Technology Based Higher Education and Training (ITHET): 8–10 September 2016, Istanbul, Turkey. Institut of Electrical and Electronics Engineering (2016)
2. Caiza, G., Garcia, C.A., Naranjo, J.E., Garcia, M.V.: Assessment of engineering techniques for failures simulation in induction motors using numerical tool, pp. 307–319 (2021)
3. Cervera, M., Grandon, N., Rivera, M., Besoain, F.: Improving the selection of IQF raspberries in processing lines: A Virtual Reality approach for training and selecting personnel. In: 2018 IEEE Biennial Congress of Argentina, ARGENCON 2018, pp. 1–7 (2019)
4. Davila Delgado, J.M., Oyedele, L., Beach, T., Demian, P.: Augmented and virtual reality in construction: drivers and limitations for industry adoption. J. Constr. Eng. Manage. **146**(7), 04020079 (2020)
5. Fireteanu, V., Constantin, A.I., Leconte, V., Lombard, P.: Analysis of the evolution of stator short-circuit and rotor bar breakage faults in a squirrel-cage induction motor. In: SPEEDAM 2018 - Proceedings: International Symposium on Power Electronics, Electrical Drives, Automation and Motion, pp. 190–195 (2018)
6. He, Q., Cheng, X., Cheng, Z.: A VR-based complex equipment maintenance training system. In: Proceedings - 2019 Chinese Automation Congress, CAC 2019, pp. 1741–1746 (2019)
7. Kim, S.U., Lee, K., Cho, J.H., Koo, K.C., Kim, S.B.: Toward an evaluation model of user experiences on virtual reality indoor bikes. Eur. Sci. J. **7881**(June), 1857–7881 (2017)
8. Maloma, E., Muteba, M., Nicolae, D.V.: Effect of rotor bar shape on the performance of three phase induction motors with broken rotor bars. In: Proceedings - 2017 International Conference on Optimization of Electrical and Electronic Equipment, OPTIM 2017 and 2017 International Aegean Conference on Electrical Machines and Power Electronics, ACEMP 2017, pp. 364–369 (2017)
9. Meldrum, D., Glennon, A., Herdman, S., Murray, D., McConn-Walsh, R.: Virtual reality rehabilitation of balance: assessment of the usability of the Nintendo Wii & #x00AE; fit plus. Disabil. Rehabil. Assistive Technol. **7**(3), 205–210 (2012)
10. Naranjo, J., Urrutia Urrutia, F., Garcia, M., Gallardo-Cardenas, F., Franklin, T., Lozada-Martinez, E.: User experience evaluation of an interactive virtual reality-based system for upper limb rehabilitation. In: 2019 6th International Conference on eDemocracy and eGovernment, ICEDEG 2019 (2019)
11. Rozo-García, F.: Revisión de las tecnologías presentes en la industria 4.0. Revista UIS Ingenierías **19**(2), 177–191 (2020)
12. Sharfina, Z., Santoso, H.B.: An Indonesian adaptation of the system usability scale (SUS). 2016 International Conference on Advanced Computer Science and Information Systems, ICACSIS 2016, pp. 145–148 (2017)

13. Urbina Pérez, M.G., Mecalco Reyes, J., Muñoz Herrera, C.A., Cruz Silva, S.P.: Las fortalezas y debilidades de los ambientes virtuales/digitales en crisis sanitarias; caso de estudio Covid-19 en México (November), pp. 1–7 (2021)
14. Wang, C.: Research on panoramic image processing technology based on virtual reality technology. In: Proceedings - 2019 International Conference on Virtual Reality and Intelligent Systems, ICVRIS 2019, pp. 55–58 (2019)

Saliency Detection in a Virtual Driving Environment for Autonomous Vehicle Behavior Improvement

Csaba Antonya(iD), Florin Gîrbacia(✉)(iD), Cristian Postelnicu, Daniel Voinea(iD), and Silviu Butnariu(iD)

Transilvania University of Brasov, 29 Eroilor, 500036 Brasov, Romania

{antonya,garbacia,cristian-cezar.postelnicu,daniel.voinea,
butnariu}@unitbv.ro

Abstract. To make the best decisions in real-world situations, autonomous vehicles require learning algorithms that process a large number of labeled images. This paper aims to compare the automatically generated saliency maps with attention maps obtained with an eye-tracking device in order to provide automated labeling of images for the learning algorithm. To simulate traffic scenarios, we are using a virtual driving environment with a motion platform and an eye-tracking device for identifying the driver's attention. The saliency maps are generated by post-processing the driver's view provided by the front camera.

Keywords: Driving simulator · Autonomous vehicle · Saliency map

1 Introduction

Autonomous vehicle development in the last decade has increased substantially. All major car manufacturers have launched their own semi o fully autonomous vehicles and they continuously work on extending the range, reducing energy consumption, reducing the time to market and also developing new simulation techniques. Software and hardware-in-the-loop simulations of autonomous vehicles are often overlooking the human factor [1]. A driver is expected to react based on his experience to different tracks and environmental conditions (variations in weather, tire degradation, fuel consumption). The testing of virtual cars in a multi-modal virtual environment is an important step in the validation process of new concepts and technologies. Virtual driving environments (VDE) are providing the user realistic feedback regarding the required visual, auditory, haptic, and kinesthetic information. The most common way of imposing the motion of the driving simulator is by the 6 degrees of freedom Stewart hexapod platform. A driving simulator with realistic interaction, operating environment and feedback eliminates the difficulties of the road test but allows the understanding of driving behavior, testing driver assistant systems, and traffic research.

Driving and especially safe driving is a collection of competencies that are acquired, refined, automated and maintained. Driving behavior can also be influenced by the

© Springer Nature Switzerland AG 2021
L. T. De Paolis et al. (Eds.): AVR 2021, LNCS 12980, pp. 511–518, 2021.
https://doi.org/10.1007/978-3-030-87595-4_37

driver's desire for smooth driving [2]. The main parameters proposed in the literature to assess driver behavior are the longitudinal and the lateral accelerations [3], which can be reproduced accurately with the VDE. Driver behavior can be modeled as a dynamic system in a phase transition framework as changes in the physiological system [4] and is also correlated with age, gender and sensation seeking [5]. The evaluation of driving scenarios is complex because it is subject on many closely interconnected variables depending not only on the different types of drivers but also on the road environment, the traffic characteristics and the categories of road infrastructure.

Machine learning and artificial intelligence are the cornerstones of autonomous vehicle development. The data for the construction of the model of the environment is provided by sensors like cameras, radar, and lidar. Complex driving maneuvers require a detailed model of the environment, and deep-learning algorithms based on image processing are of great importance. For training the neural networks, labeled images are required, which can be obtained manually or automatically from a driving simulator. Attention allocation analysis and prediction of the user on the driving scene can help the image labeling process [6].

In this paper, we are proposing a verification metric for the automated labeling of images using the saliency map comparing it with the attention map obtained with an eye-tracking device. For this, we are proposing a VDE with a motion platform and an eye-tracking device. The front-camera image (the driver's view) is post-processed for obtaining the saliency map and this is compared with the attention map. We are interested in the accuracy of the automated salient region detection in case the decision made by the human driver in a specific traffic situation.

2   The Virtual Driving Environment

The proposed virtual driving environment is composed by a motion platform, a driving seat with pedals, a steering wheel and a Tobii eye tracking device [7]. The Stewart platform is the MOOG 6 DOF 2000E, which is a six degree of freedom motion platform (Fig. 1). The dynamic model of the platform was developed, analyzed and a co-simulation environment was proposed in [8]. The performance of a driving simulator is defined by the Motion Cueing Algorithm, which is a system of filters that takes into account the limits of the simulator as well as the threshold of the driver's motion perception to reproduce simulated vehicle acceleration.

In the VDE, the dynamic model of the vehicle and the visual feedback is provided by the CARLA simulator. CARLA is an open-source software platform, which is intended to be a system that includes individual projects developed to smooth the process of development, training and validation of autonomous management systems. The CARLA simulator consists of a scalable client-server architecture in which the server manages the simulation itself: sensor playback, physics calculation, updates on the state of the world and its actors and connects to client modules that control the logic of the actors on stage and set the conditions of the world, using as programming environments Python or C++ [9]. The basic structure of the CARLA simulator is composed of traffic management subsystem, sensors, recording subsystem, simulator integration subsystem in other learning environments, various libraries with maps, weather conditions and sets of actors, as well as a series of predefined routes and scenarios [9].

To highlight the simulation capabilities of the CARLA platform, in [10] three types of autonomous leadership are analyzed: a classic modular pipeline, an end-to-end model trained by imitation learning and an end-to-end model. to-end trained through hardened learning. Driving software was tested, testing various sensors (camera and LiDAR), using a real-time hardware-in-the-loop simulation system without constraints based on the CARLA platform [11]. The paper [12] proposes a complex method, which can achieve a self-driving scale-ball, which can manage massive car traffic scenarios (over 7,000 km traveled) using a high-fidelity driving simulator, respecting traffic rules and in a wide variety of environments (urban, rural, highway, narrow roads, roundabouts and pedestrian crossings).

In [13] it is proposed to study the quality of the results obtained artificially compared to the results obtained with the help of real sensors, in the field of object detection with LiDAR. Vehicle control activities were analyzed by precise decoding of motion intention using the BMI-VCS method - Integration of brain-machine interface (BMI) neurotechnology with vehicle control systems (VCS). [14] is studying the possibility that defective autonomous vehicles can be driven, in the event of a breakdown, with the help of tele-driving. This system is an extension of the CARLA open-source simulator, responsible for rendering the driving environment and ensuring an evaluation of the reproducible scenario.

Fig. 1. The proposed virtual driving environment

3   Visual Saliency Detection and Gaze Tracking

For the driver's visual system, certain parts of the driving scene present crucial information. These are the perceptually salient regions that contain semantically meaningful information.

Saliency detection is a process of location of important objects or regions in an image. The quality of the salient region labeling is very important since it will control the accuracy and the capability of the autonomous vehicle to find the right path in its surroundings. Image labeling and semantic segmentation can be completed manually or can be automatized. Manual image segmentation and labeling is a time-consuming process, because of the high volume of images in different driving scenarios. Automatic salient region detection can be bottom-up and top-down modes [15]. The bottom-up approach is fast, data-driven, and task-independent, while the top-down is based on supervised learning and are task-oriented.

Salient region retrieval is used in various filed like automotive or robotics. It is used in vehicle headlights detection with the region-of-interest segmentation method together with the pyramid histogram of oriented gradients features detection in a support vector machine classifier [16]. In [17] the saliency map is used in the prediction for making braking decisions. This application is using a deep neural network to predict salient features, then relate these with driving decisions. Dang et al. is proposing a visual saliency–aware receding horizon exploration for path planning of aerial robots with a two-step optimization paradigm [18].

Eye-tracking in the VDE is used to obtain the point of gaze, the spot on which the user is focusing. Eye-tracking devices were successfully used in drivers' testing in perceiving objects in the visual field [19] and to determine fatigue driving state [20].

Studies in eye movement during driving are showing that there are different salient regions on which the users are focusing their attention. In a survey on 40 subjects, Deng et al analyzed the eye-tracking data when viewing traffic images [21]. They concluded that the driver's attention was mostly concentrated on the end of the road in front of the vehicle.

Fig. 2. The virtual driving scenario implemented using Carla simulator

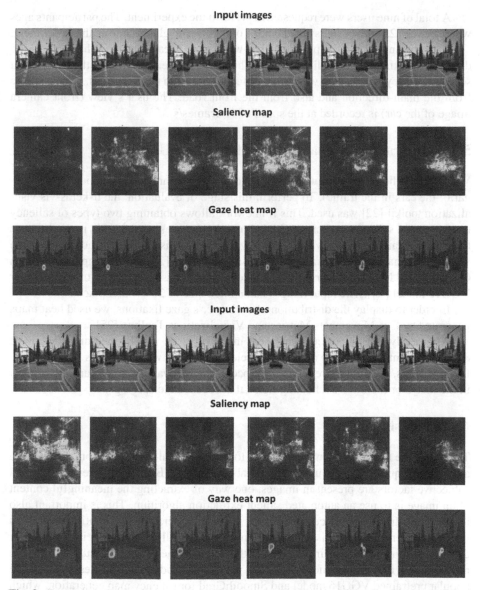

Fig. 3. Examples of saliency maps obtained using SmoothGrad and gaze heat maps generated from the input images recorded from virtual driving scenario

4 Experimental Setup for the Saliency Detection in Driving Scenario

In the Carla simulator we implemented the following scenario: the user is driving the ego-car along a secondary road, then the ego-car is reaching an intersection where the user is waiting for the possibility to turn right on the main road (Fig. 2).

A total of nine users were requested to perform the experiment. The participants ages were between 25 and 41 years old and none of them wore glasses during the experiment.

At the beginning of the experiment, they were asked to calibrate the Tobii eye tracking device by looking at 5 predefined points. Then each of them performed the experiment scenario. The eye movement was recorded for 10–20 s. On the main road, there is traffic from the main direction and also from the front road. The user's view (front camera image of the car) is recorded at the speed of 10 frames/s.

5   Comparative Evaluation of Saliency and User's Gaze

Visualizing saliency maps is used in order to detect relevant image regions (in our scenario: the cars in the traffic). To perform this stage of evaluation, the tf-keras-vis visualization toolkit [22] was used. This framework allows obtaining two types of saliency maps: vanilla saliency or SmoothGrad. SmoothGrad was used in this paper because the results obtained with the vanilla saliency map were noisy. SmoothGrad improves the visibility by sharpening the gradient-based saliency maps [23]. For the implementation a Convolutional Neural Network (CNN) model was used based on the pre-trained popular VGG16 model [24]. The input images had a fixed size of 224×224 pixels.

In order to display the distribution of each user's gaze fixations, we used heat maps generated by Eye Movements Metrics and Visualizations Toolbox [25].

After analyzing the saliency and heat maps (Fig. 3), we obtained an accuracy of 83.3% regarding the overlap of predicted relevant regions with the user's gaze fixation. In some cases, where the overlap did not occur, the car was absent or partially present in the image or there were reflecting lights that focused the user's gaze.

6   Conclusions

To prepare the future autonomous vehicles to deal with real-word situation, the learning algorithms require tremendous number of labeled images. Because different objects and subjective factors are present in images, one way of extracting the meaningful content of an image is to use an automated salient extraction algorithm. This is important also in advanced driver assistance systems for warning generation by situation awareness models. Drivers are using visual perception and are usually focusing their attention for decision-making on the main features of the scenery ahead, like the curvature of the road ahead, neighboring vehicles, bicycles, pedestrians and other obstacles. We used the popular pretrained VGG16 model and SmoothGrad for saliency map generation, which accomplished 83.3% accuracy. The interpretation of scene from an event-reasoning point of view using automated salient region detection is an important step in image labeling for autonomous vehicle's behavior training and improvement. In the future, we will apply the discussed method to create datasets for driving decisions based on saliency maps.

Acknowledgement. This work was supported by a grant of the Ministry of Research, Innovation and Digitization, CNCS/CCCDI – UEFISCDI, project number PN-III-P2-2.1-PED-2019-4366 within PNCDI III (431PED).

References

1. Riener, A., Jeon, M., Alvarez, I., Frison, A.K.: Driver in the loop: Best practices in automotive sensing and feedback mechanisms. In: Meixner, G., Müller, C. (eds.) Automotive user interfaces. HIS, pp. 295–323. Springer, Cham (2017). https://doi.org/10.1007/978-3-319-49448-7_11

2. Wang, J., Sun, F., Ge, H.: Effect of the driver's desire for smooth driving on the car-following model. Physica A: Stat. Mech. Appl. **512**, 96–108 (2018)

3. Vaiana, R., et al.: Driving behavior and traffic safety: an acceleration-based safety evaluation procedure for smartphones. Mod. Appl. Sci. **8**(1), 88 (2014)

4. Mirman, J.H.: A dynamical systems perspective on driver behavior. Transp. Res. F: Traffic Psychol. Behav. **63**, 193–203 (2019)

5. Witt, M., Kompaß, K., Wang, L., Kates, R., Mai, M., Prokop, G.: Driver profiling–data-based identification of driver behavior dimensions and affecting driver characteristics for multi-agent traffic simulation. Transp. Res. F: Traffic Psychol. Behav. **64**, 361–376 (2019)

6. Deng, T., Yan, H., Qin, L., Ngo, T., Manjunath, B.S.: How do drivers allocate their potential attention? Driving fixation prediction via convolutional neural networks. IEEE Trans. Intell. Transp. Syst. **21**(5), 2146–2154 (2019)

7. Tobii homepage. https://www.tobii.com/. Accessed 20 Feb 2021

8. Antonya, Cs., Irimia, C., Grovu, M., Husar, C., Ruba, M.: Co-simulation environment for the analysis of the driving simulator's actuation. In: 7th International Conference on Control, Mechatronics and Automation (ICCMA), Delft, Netherlands, pp. 315–321 (2019)

9. CARLA - Open-source simulator for autonomous driving research, homepage. https://carla.org/. Accessed 5 May 2021

10. Dosovitskiy, A., Ros, G., Codevilla, F., Lopez, A., Koltun, V.: CARLA: an open urban driving simulator. In: Conference on Robot Learning PMLR, pp. 1–16 (2017)

11. Brogle, C., Zhang, C., Lim, K.L., Bräun, T.: Hardware-in-the-loop autonomous driving simulation without real-time constraints. IEEE Trans. Intell. Veh. **4**(3), 375–384 (2019)

12. Cai, P., Wang, H., Sun, Y., Liu, M.: Learning scalable self-driving policies for generic traffic scenarios. arXiv preprint arXiv:2011.06775 (2020)

13. Dworak, D., Ciepiela, F., Derbisz, J., Izzat, I., Komorkiewicz, M., Wójcik, M.: Performance of LiDAR object detection deep learning architectures based on artificially generated point cloud data from CARLA simulator. In: 24th International Conference on Methods and Models in Automation and Robotics (MMAR), pp. 600–605 (2019).

14. Hofbauer, M., Kuhn, C.B., Petrovic, G. Steinbach, E.: TELECARLA: an open source extension of the CARLA Simulator for tele-operated driving research using off-the-shelf components. In: IEEE Intelligent Vehicles Symposium (IV), Las Vegas, USA (2020)

15. Xue, J.R., Fang, J.W., Zhang, P.: A survey of scene understanding by event reasoning in autonomous driving. Int. J. Autom. Comput. **15**(3), 249–266 (2018)

16. Shang, J., Guan, H.P., Liu, Y., Bi, H., Yang, L., Wang, M.: A novel method for vehicle headlights detection using salient region segmentation and PHOG feature. Multimedia Tools Appl. 1–21 (2021)

17. Aksoy, E., Yazıcı, A., Kasap, M.: See, attend and brake: an attention-based saliency map prediction model for end-to-end driving. arXiv preprint arXiv:2002.11020 (2020)

18. Dang, T., Papachristos, C., Alexis, K.: Visual saliency-aware receding horizon autonomous exploration with application to aerial robotics. In: 2018 IEEE International Conference on Robotics and Automation (ICRA), pp. 2526–2533 (2018)

19. Xu, J., Min, J., Hu, J.: Real-time eye tracking for the assessment of driver fatigue. Healthc. Technol. Lett. **5**(2), 54–58 (2018)

20. Kapitaniak, B., Walczak, M., Kosobudzki, M., Jozwiak, Z., Bortkiewicz, A.: Application of eye-tracking in drivers testing: a review of research. Int. J. Occup. Med. Environ. Health **28**(6), 941 (2015)
21. Deng, T., Yang, K., Li, Y., Yan, H.: Where does the driver look? Top-down-based saliency detection in a traffic driving environment. IEEE Trans. Intell. Transp. Syst. **17**(7), 2051–2062 (2016)
22. tf-keras-vis toolkit. https://github.com/keisen/tf-keras-vis. Accessed 11 Apr 2021
23. Smilkov, D., Thorat, N., Kim, D., Viégas, F., Wattenberg M.: Smoothgrad: removing noise by adding noise. arXiv preprint arXiv:1706.03825 (2017)
24. Simonyan, K., Zisserman, A.: Very deep convolutional networks for large-scale image recognition. arXiv preprint arXiv:1409.1556 (2014)
25. Krassanakis, V., Filippakopoulou, V., Nakos, B.: EyeMMV toolbox: an eye movement post-analysis tool based on a two-step spatial dispersion threshold for fixation identification. J. Eye Mov. Res. **7**(1) (2014)

Authoring-By-Doing: An Event-Based Interaction Module for Virtual Reality Scenario Authoring Framework

Killian Richard[1,2,3]([✉]), Vincent Havard[1], and David Baudry[1]

[1] LINEACT, CESI, 76800 Saint-Étienne-du-Rouvray, France
{krichard,vhavard,dbaudry}@cesi.fr
[2] ENSAM, Université Art Et Métiers ParisTech, 75013 Paris, France
[3] Oreka Ingénierie, 50100 Cherbourg, France

Abstract. Virtual reality (VR) and augmented reality (AR) have already shown their advantages in industrial use during these last years. Nevertheless, the authoring and editing process of virtual and augmented contents are still time-consuming and even more for complex industrial scenarios. Therefore, it is important to simplify the authoring process. For this purpose, we are working on a framework called INTERVALES. This model aims to ease virtual and augmented environments and complex operation orchestration. We present here an evolution of our framework and an interaction module using events allowing us to build scenarios using authoring by doing and making it more interoperable with others frameworks.

Keywords: Virtual reality · Augmented reality · Authoring · UML modeling · Virtual reality training system · Events manager

1 Introduction

Virtual reality effectiveness in terms of learning, training and positive impact on performance has been proved already and validated through time [1–4]. Moreover, augmented reality has also shown its efficiency in terms of support and guidance performance [5–7]. In the industrial context, given the complexity of manufacturing systems and their rapid evolution, virtual environments are increasingly used to train operators on industrial operations such as assembly or maintenance tasks [8]. The concept of learning factories based on physical industrial system equipment associated with virtual environments for training is developing to allow for various training scenarios and situations [9].

However, it greatly depends on the way it was designed to share knowledge. By this fact, an important focus has to be done on virtual and augmented environments authoring to define the feasible actions and scenarios within it. Nevertheless, this important part is still time-consuming during development time. As explained by [10], there is "a lack of tools to quickly and easily prototype and test new AR/VR user experience". Indeed, there is an observable offset between proposed solutions in literature and reality within development companies. This is mainly due to virtual environments or AR authoring

© Springer Nature Switzerland AG 2021
L. T. De Paolis et al. (Eds.): AVR 2021, LNCS 12980, pp. 519–527, 2021.
https://doi.org/10.1007/978-3-030-87595-4_38

processes which are different following developers' experiences and companies' policies or the allotted time. Moreover, companies use different developers-oriented libraries and assets to speed up developing time.

Several model approaches exist and one is based on UML language for virtual and augmented content authorings like MASCARET [11], #FIVE [12], or [13]. UML modeling allows a structured formalism representing the environment, the possible interactions, and scenarios. Even if it requires the expert to comply with it, industrial companies or in the IT field, UML type of representation or close to UML are commonly used, which facilitates its integration. Therefore, UML models can easily be adapted, within an industrial context, to implement XR tools, which allows simple concepts to author augmented and virtual environments.

In this context, we are currently working on a framework called **INTERVALES** for **INTER**active **V**irtual and **A**ugmented framework for industria**L** **E**nvironments and **S**cenarios. This model aims to ease virtual and augmented environments and complex operation orchestration. This framework has been used for the design of a VR training environment of a learning factory [14] and several limitations have been observed regarding the necessary skills for the tasks and scenarios definitions in the model.

To acquire and formalize knowledge about the tasks to be performed, methods based on learning from demonstration are used in robotics to teach assembly operations [15]. In the field of intelligent tutorial systems, the creation of content based on demonstration has been explored. For virtual environments, recent works have studied the approaches of authoring by doing [16]. It allows to record actions performed by an expert and to play these actions for learning purposes.

In a similar approach, this paper proposes an authoring-by-doing model for virtual reality scenario authoring. It is based on an event-based interaction module integrated into the INTERVALES framework and applied to an industry 4.0 use case. By adding, this new module, we improved the scenario authoring using INTERVALES but also make the event interoperable with others frameworks.

2   Prototype of Framework and VR Training Environment

The case study used for the design of our framework is an Industry 4.0 learning factory [14]. The use case is composed of manual and cobotic workstations for an assembly process. The need to train an operator on the assembly of an industrial system on a manual workstation. The physical industrial workshop is composed of 6 workstations for the assembly and quality control of products (Fig. 1). Each workstation has its own instructions sheet.

As an example, one of the operations is used. In this operation, the operator needs to:

- Take a 360 mm profile "P360" (Fig. 2- 1),
- Slide a fixture key "LARD" to exactly 160 mm (Fig. 2- 2),
- Place a corner fixing "FIXA1" on the fixture key (Fig. 2- 3),
- Place a screw "B820" in "LARD" and "FIXA1" (Fig. 2- 4),
- Screw "B820" in the "LARD"

Fig. 1. VR environment of the learning factory.

Model	Workstation	Process	Operation
BOOSTER	1	Subset 1	10

N° Step	Part	Description	Quantity
1	P360	Profil – 360 mm	1
2	LARD	Fixture key	1
3	FIXA1	Corner fixing 1	1
4	B820	Bolt M8 x 20	1

Fig. 2. A workstation's instructions sheet

To train the operator, a virtual environment is set up and the required parts and the feasible interactions need to be defined as well as the expert need to define each scenario's task within the virtual environment. The development of this VR training environment is based on INTERVALES framework. Its architecture (Fig. 3) aims to satisfy content (parts, interactions) and scenarios authoring by IT people, but also by job experts or trainers. Thus, they will be able to deliver training in VR or guidance in AR to end-users. It is composed of modules defining the different concepts. Firstly, the **INTERVALES Entity-Feature module** brings the concepts of **Entity** and **Feature** closed to "Object-Relation" oriented models [12, 17] and allows defining each asset characteristics. The **Entity** represents the 3D object and it is composed of **Feature** to define how it should behave.

From the 3D CAD model, a library of 150 entities corresponding to different parts of the system (product assembly, tools, mobile robot and cobot, storages, …), has been implemented. When features and relationships are created, they can be used in the VR environment to freely assemble each of these parts. As an example, in the case study, the

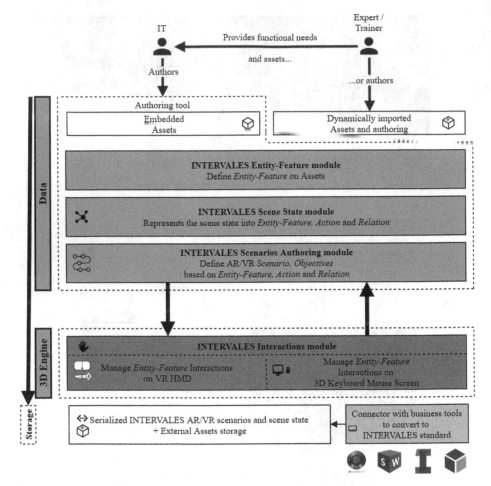

Fig. 3. INTERVALES architecture: the authoring part.

360 mm is an Entity and it contains 2 features to snap other profiles to it and 4 features allowing to slide the fixture key on each side (Fig. 4).

Thank to that it is possible to define **Actions** (performed on one Entity or Feature), or **Relation** (performed between two Features) inside the **INTERVALES Scene state module** and create possible interactions. This module is in charge of gathering all Relations done between Features placed on each Entity. Based on the status of the scene, the **INTERVALES Scenarios Authoring module** allows IT or the expert/trainer to define scenarios thanks to **Tasks** and **Objectives** based on the actions the end-user must perform. Thus, the **INTERVALES interaction module** is in charge of managing all interactions made by the user on Entity and Feature and thus, edit the scene state. This module can take into account the devices used (VR controller or mouse, keyboard) to adapt interactions made by the content and scenario authors. When interacting with the Entity, and based on the Feature it has, each object can create Relation with others.

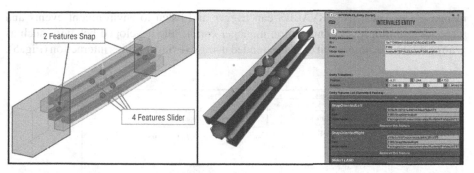

Fig. 4. (Left) Defining features of the P360 part as a concept; (Right) Defining features in unity 3D

All this data (scenarios and scene state) can be serialized/deserialized in a standard file (.JSON) based on the model.

Therefore, the authoring process of virtual or augmented environments involves these modules. However, as presented in the introduction, following a first implementation in a use case [14], limitations were observed. Concerning interaction notifications, the framework appears to be too closed, making interoperability difficult since other frameworks can hardly communicate with it. Also, the developed concepts were locked with the 3D engine used (Unity). Indeed, although an interaction module is integrated, interaction libraries are already existing and used by IT experts in their development processes. It is therefore important that the framework can adapt itself and interpret the interactions generated by commonly used libraries (For example, VRTK [18] for virtual reality or MRTK [19] for mixed reality). Even if the authoring process of scenarios has been simplified, it still needs to be done by defining each task and objectives one by one in the model. To allow the job expert to author the scenario, we explore in this paper an authoring-by-doing. Consequently, there is a need to decorrelate the scenario data from the rendering engine/application to ease the authorizing of training scenarios, especially in VR.

Following these observations, the proposed solution needs to; Ease its integration in companies' VR/AR application development processes; Ease the authoring process using the authoring-by-doing method; Ease collaboration with other existing frameworks and assets used by IT; Allow triggering or/and catching interaction events from different assets.

3 Event-Based Interaction Manager and Authoring-By-Doing Process

The main objective of this evolution is to open the event data inside the interaction manager to reuse it for scenario authoring. Also, this will make the interaction module interoperable with external libraries' interaction events or other existing frameworks like [20].

The two main components of this proposition are the event manager and the interaction manager. First, the event manager's purpose is to centralized the event management in one place. Thus, INTERVALES can trigger and listen to environment events and respond accordingly. The interaction manager can handle developed behavior such as grab or drop for example or it can be extended using existing libraries interaction (Fig. 5).

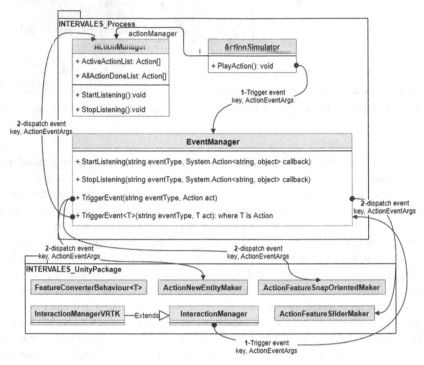

Fig. 5. Proposed workflow event.

The proposed workflow has been integrated into the INTERVALES Model (See Fig. 3). As explained in Sect. 2, the framework describes the environment and possible interactions within using the concept of **Action** and **Relation**. Each defined action has a corresponding **Maker** inside the 3D Engine. The maker is in charge of visually represent the action consequence. Let's take the case of an assembly scenario where an operator needs to screw a screw in a nut. Using VRTK, developers can use available assets, allowing them to detect collision between them then through a connector notify the INTERVALES InteractionManager. It will notify the EventManager. The framework processes the event data, here if the two parts can match their following feature properties and define a resulted action (ActionManager). In this case, a relation "Screw" has been done. Then, the EventManager is notified of this action and dispatch the event through the corresponding Maker. If the application is in record mode, the corresponding task is added in a way to author a scenario. To finish, the Maker will move and snap the screw inside the nut to represent the screw action.

To illustrate the authoring by doing process we use the assembly task presented in Fig. 2 as an example. The expert runs the virtual environment in record mode and performs the assembly following the instruction sheet to author the scenario. He takes a

360 mm profile, slides a fixture key, and snaps a corner fixing on it (Fig. 6 – A). Thus, on each action the job expert has done in the VR environment, an event is triggered and action is registered as an action done (Fig. 6 – B) in the same order (Take = ActionNewEntity; Slide = RelationSlider; Snap = RelationSnapOriented) with the concerned entities and features references. Then, the corresponding action can be converted as a new task in a scenario using the event-based manager. In the end, a JSON file containing the tasks can be exported (Fig. 6 – C).

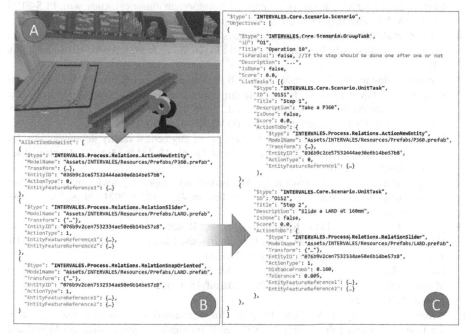

Fig. 6. (A) Actions done in VR by IT/expert; (B) actions done registered; (C) action converted as tasks to do inside the scenario authored-by-doing

4   Conclusion and Perspectives

In this paper, we presented a VR training environment of a learning factory based on INTERVALES framework. We proposed an implementation of an event-based interaction module for our framework allowing us to trigger and dispatch events through the internal modules and external libraries. Thereby, it is possible to register action events during runtime and allow authoring-by-doing by converting them into tasks to do. Also, it is thus possible to follow scenario interactions using existing development libraries by developing connectors to catch and trigger needed events which are now accessible.

The next step is to finish the development of the INTERVALES framework as part of a more advanced proof of concept including this new event system.

References

1. Borsci, S., Lawson, G., Broome, S.: Empirical evidence, evaluation criteria and challenges for the effectiveness of virtual and mixed reality tools for training operators of car service maintenance. Comput. Ind. **67**, 17–26 (2015)
2. Merchant, Z., Goetz, E.T., Cifuentes, L., Keeney-Kennicutt, W., Davis, T.J.: Effectiveness of virtual reality-based instruction on students' learning outcomes in K-12 and higher education: a meta-analysis. (2014). https://doi.org/10.1016/j.compedu.2013.07.033
3. Su, C.-H., Cheng, T.-W., Su, C.-H., Cheng, T.-W.: A Sustainability innovation experiential learning model for virtual reality chemistry laboratory: an empirical study with PLS-SEM and IPMA. Sustainability **11**, 1027 (2019). https://doi.org/10.3390/su11041027
4. Feng, Z., et al.: Towards a customizable immersive virtual reality serious game for earthquake emergency training. Adv. Eng. Inform. **46**, 101134 (2020). https://doi.org/10.1016/j.aei.2020.101134
5. Havard, V., Baudry, D., Savatier, X., Jeanne, B., Louis, A., Mazari, B.: Augmented industrial maintenance (AIM): a case study for evaluating and comparing with paper and video media supports. In: De Paolis, L.T., Mongelli, A. (eds.) AVR 2016. LNCS, vol. 9768, pp. 302–320. Springer, Cham (2016). https://doi.org/10.1007/978-3-319-40621-3_22
6. Henderson, S., Feiner, S.: Exploring the benefits of augmented reality documentation for maintenance and repair. IEEE Trans. Vis. Comput. Graph. **17**, 1355–1368 (2011). https://doi.org/10.1109/TVCG.2010.245
7. Wang, Z., et al.: The role of user-centered AR instruction in improving novice spatial cognition in a high-precision procedural task. Adv. Eng. Inform. **47**, 101250 (2021). https://doi.org/10.1016/j.aei.2021.101250
8. Naranjo, J.E., Sanchez, D.G., Robalino-Lopez, A., Robalino-Lopez, P., Alarcon-Ortiz, A., Garcia, M.V.: A scoping review on virtual reality-based industrial training. Appl. Sci. **10**, 1–31 (2020). https://doi.org/10.3390/app10228224
9. Riemann, T., Kreß, A., Roth, L., Klipfel, S., Metternich, J., Grell, P.: Agile implementation of virtual reality in learning factories. Proc. Manuf **45**, 1–6 (2020). https://doi.org/10.1016/j.promfg.2020.04.029
10. Nebeling, M., Speicher, M.: The Trouble with augmented reality/virtual reality authoring tools. In: Adjunct Proceedings - 2018 IEEE International Symposium on Mixed and Augmented Reality, ISMAR-Adjunct 2018. pp. 333–337 (2018)
11. Buche, C., Querrec, R., De Loor, P., Chevaillier, P.: MASCARET: pedagogical multi-agents system for virtual environment for training. J. Distance Educ. Technol. **2**, 41–61 (2004). https://doi.org/10.1109/CYBER.2003.1253485
12. Bouville, R., Gouranton, V., Boggini, T., Nouviale, F., Arnaldi, B.: #FIVE : High-level components for developing collaborative and interactive virtual environments. In: 2015 IEEE 8th Workshop on Software Engineering and Architectures for Realtime Interactive Systems, SEARIS 2015, pp. 33–40 (2017)
13. Martínez, H., Laukkanen, S., Mattila, J.: A new flexible augmented reality platform for development of maintenance and educational applications. Int. J. Virtual Worlds Hum. Comput. Interact. (2014) https://doi.org/10.11159/vwhci.2014.003
14. Badets, A., Havard, V., Richard, K., Baudry, D.: Using collaborative VR technology for lean manufacturing training: a case study. Presented at the VRIC ConVRgence 2020: 22nd Virtual Reality International Conference, Laval Virtual, Laval, France (2020)
15. Myers, K., Gervasio, M.: Solution authoring via demonstration and annotation: an empirical study. In: Proceedings of IEEE 16th International Conference on Advance Learning Technology ICALT 2016, pp. 212–216 (2016). https://doi.org/10.1109/ICALT.2016.114

16. Wolfartsberger, J., Niedermayr, D.: Authoring-by-doing: animating work instructions for industrial virtual reality learning environments. In: Proceedings - 2020 IEEE Conference on Virtual Reality and 3D User Interfaces, VRW 2020. Institute of Electrical and Electronics Engineers Inc., pp. 173–176 (2020)
17. Mollet, N., Gerbaud, S., Arnaldi, B.: STORM: a generic interaction and behavioral model for 3D objects and humanoids in a virtual environment. In: IPT-EGVE 13th Eurographics Symposium on Virtual Environment, pp. 95–100 (2007)
18. VRTK: Virtual Reality ToolKit. https://vrtoolkit.readme.io/
19. MRTK: Mixed Reality ToolKit. https://github.com/microsoft/MixedRealityToolkit-Unity
20. Lanquepin, V., Lourdeaux, D., Barot, C., Carpentier, K., Lhommet, M., Amokrane, K.: HUMANS: a HUman models based artificial environments software platform. ACM Int. Conf. Proc. Ser. (2013). https://doi.org/10.1145/2466816.2466826

Development of a Virtual Reality Environment Based on the CoAP Protocol for Teaching Pneumatic Systems

William Montalvo Lopez[1], Pablo Catota[1], Carlos A. Garcia[2],
and Marcelo V. Garcia[2,3]

[1] Universidad Politecnica Salesiana, UPS, 170146 Quito, Ecuador
wmontalvo@ups.edu.ec, pcatota@est.ups.edu.ec
[2] Universidad Tecnica de Ambato, UTA, 180103 Ambato, Ecuador
{ca.garcia,mv.garcia}@uta.edu.ec
[3] University of Basque Country, UPV/EHU, 48013 Bilbao, Spain
mgarcia294@ehu.eus

Abstract. The use of virtual environments in education and research has increased due to the covid pandemia, because students need to develop skills that are acquired in physical laboratories. For this reason, this research presents the design of a virtual reality (VR) didactic module of electro-pneumatics FESTO™ cylinders developed in Unity 3D™ software, which allows the manipulation of pneumatic systems within the simulation. The virtual environment works synchronously with the real module, transmitting instructions using the Constrained Application Protocol (CoaP) to a Raspberry PI card that controls the real pneumatic system. This type of application allows students to perform practices with greater freedom and without restrictions, and without the need to be in a laboratory to use the required equipment and resources.

Keywords: Constrained Application Protocol (CoaP) · Virtual environment · Virtual reality systems · Pneumatic systems

1 Introduction

Nowadays, the constant technological advancement has made virtual reality gain momentum not only in the entertainment space, but has also let these advances relate to new technology such as: medicine, building modeling, design of automation systems, education, among others. Virtual reality environments let students experience experiential learning, where they can interact and even manipulate equipment and make physical connections. These environments can be engineered in software such as: Unity 3D, Blender, SolidWorks, LabVIEW, Flash 3D, among others [6]. Research in the industrial field related to virtual reality lets the user iterate and manipulate the prototype within the simulation, allowing a better understanding of the design and make corrections if the project does not meet the functionality parameters [9].

© Springer Nature Switzerland AG 2021
L. T. De Paolis et al. (Eds.): AVR 2021, LNCS 12980, pp. 528–543, 2021.
https://doi.org/10.1007/978-3-030-87595-4_39

Currently virtual laboratory applications have been designed for teaching in areas such as: automation and control, pneumatic systems, electrical engineering, control system [2]. In education, it is relevant to have virtual laboratories in different areas of engineering due to the fact that in some universities or institutes of higher education, there are no laboratories with the necessary equipment for student learning or because of the large number of students studying they do not have access to a laboratory. For this reason, this work seeks to contribute to research on the development of virtual reality applications where users can perform their practices related to pneumatic systems that helps to understand the operation of the elements used in an actual laboratory.

This article is structured as follows: Sect. 2 presents a series of related studies that encouraged the development of this work. Section 3 presents the case study used for the research method. In Sects. 5 shows the architecture of the platform based on UML diagrams. Section 6 presents the implementation of the VR platform based on low-cost boards are showed. The implementation of the communication based on the protocol CoAP is discussed in Sect. 4. The discussion of results is presented in Sect. 7. Finally, the conclusions and future work are presented in Sect. 8.

2   Literature Review

Recent technological advances and consumer-level prices for virtual reality hardware and related peripherals have become affordable due to technological improvements; for this reason, there is interest in their use for education and training [5]. The goal of integrating virtual and remote labs is to assess students' knowledge not only at lower levels but also in intermediate and higher-level students. In the labs, they can reinforce and feedback on what they have learned in the classroom [11].

The project developed by J. Xie et al. [12] proposes a virtual monitoring method for hydraulic supports based on the digital twin theory. This method simulates hydraulic supports that combines the digital model with the actual or physical part, being of great help for monitoring all the management and connection processes of hydraulic supports during their entire life cycle. To determine its correct operation, despite the 1% error presented in the height measurements of the hydraulic supports between the virtual interface and the actual part.

At Bulacan State University, a virtual laboratory for pneumatic systems practices was developed due to the high demand of users in the physical laboratory. The pieces were created in Blender and Unity for the development of the 360-degree virtual environment ad the researchers created a simple experiment consisting of the movement of a simple cylinder operated by a pneumatic switch. The project employs HTC Vive equipment to place students in a fully immersive 3D virtual reality environment. The software was executed through Steam which allowed students to interact via controllers to simulate the actual environment. The researchers selected groups of students from the University of Electronic Engineering to use the application so that the level of acceptability of the application in terms of reliability, cost, maintainability, safety, usability, efficiency could be evaluated using a Likert scale. The results obtained show the overall mean is 4.188 being this a satisfactory rating in the students' practice [1].

At the Technical University of Ambato was developed a virtual environment of a FESTO electro-pneumatic system in Unity Pro 3D which works synchronously with the actual module. To transfer the instructions to the existent part, a Raspberry PI card is used, which through MQTT protocol sends data to the card to visualize the movement of the cylinders in the real electro-pneumatic system. The practice begins with an example proposed by the teacher where the student, using the Oculus Rift device, has to make the connections in the virtual environment. In the end, from Unity, the instructions are sent to the Raspberry PI to start with the circuit test. The research indicates that is very important to design applications of this type that help the student to practice in the virtual environment to become familiar with the elements that are used in practice, through results it was observed that the application help them to better understand its operation according to the tests performed [3].

Based on the literature reviewed in the different research articles can be indicated that this degree work will have good support and will contribute to the creation of VR applications for education, use of IoT protocol (CoaP) for communication between equipment and, due to the pandemic will serve for the student to perform their practices on pneumatic systems [3].

3   Case Study

Nowadays, VR is common used in entertainment and research applications. In the latter area, several projects are being carried out for training in industry and education. Through its use, it has been proven that users obtain significant learning by interacting with the virtual environment as in an actual laboratory [4,10].

In the industry, it is crucial to have this type of tools that allow constant training of personnel and lower costs in this field that is very important, even more so due to the introduction of new technology of industry 4.0, which forces industries to be at the forefront of technological progress to satisfy the customer with quality products and be more competitive.

In education, it is crucial to encourage research related to VR because these applications would help students to use virtual laboratories to perform their practices without prior authorization and, in that way, they would gain experience in the manipulation of the elements that in the future would make up the work environment. Therefore, when they have to use a tangible laboratory, the percentage of accidents and material damage during the manipulation of objects to develop the practice proposed by the teacher would be reduced [7].

The aim of this research is to create a VR application that shows a pneumatic systems laboratory in order for the student can assemble pneumatic sequences and see the working routines. This is useful because a lot of laboratories are closed due to the health emergency caused by coronavirus; this application will help the theory taught in class by the teacher through computer packages that allow video calls, are very useful for the user through the immersive VR experience, can train and reinforce their knowledge.

4   CoAP Protocol Implementation in VR Platform

The CoAP protocol architecture is showed in Fig. 1. The architecture has a client programmed into the Unity 3D software and a CoAP server implemented using the software Node-Red include on the laptop where the VR system runs. To manage and send the sequence to the real FESTO pneumatic module a Raspberry PI board with a CoAP client is used.

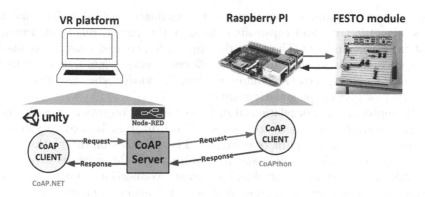

Fig. 1. Coap architecture

The CoAP protocol is implemented in Unity 3D for communication between the virtual laboratory and the actual FESTO electro-pneumatics module [8]. To achieve this objective, we used the CoAP.NET library, which lets send a CoAP request of type confirmable (CON) or ACK that serves to confirm or receipt messages, with one of the GET, POST, PUT, or DELETE methods. This request is sent through an endpoint (IEndPoint) to its destination, which is bound to a particular IP address and port. After sending a request, the VR platform can expect a response with a synchronous or asynchronous call in Fig. 2.

To use this protocol in Unity 3D, the DLL files must be generated from the CoAP.NET project, and then the generated files must be exported to the folder containing the Project scripts. To communicate with the Raspberry PI card a CoAP client, the button (Virtual Environment Button) is created for each of the different sequences; from the Menu script that contains the code of all the controllers implemented in the application, to send a request to the server hosted on Node-Red on the computer.

```
public void BotonFinalizarPractica(string EscenarioPrueba)
{
    SceneManager.LoadScene("EscenarioPrueba");
    CoapClient client = new CoapClient();
    Request request = new Request(Method.GET);
    //request.URI = new Uri("coap://[::1]/hello-world");
    request.URI = new Uri("coap://192.168.1.110:5683/conexioncoapF1");
    request.Send();
    // wait for una response
    //Response response = request.WaitForResponse();
}
```

Fig. 2. Code that lets the communication between client and server.

5   Software Architecture Design

The architecture design is a relevant point to evaluate because it allows meeting the study objectives and constraints through the virtual reality environment construction for training. Therefore, the application created must be oriented to the user's demands so that through the different scenes created, they can have a clear technical perspective and obtain evident knowledge when using the virtual laboratory of FESTO pneumatic systems.

The representation of relationships, processes, and objects is complicated in a single diagram, for this reason, a User Case diagram is used to shows the general flow of the platform (see Fig. 3). The modules of the platform were defined: i) Recognition module and ii) Training module, which is divided into two: training of electrical, control and pneumatic connections, training of control scheme design; and, iii) Evaluation module of the acquired knowledge.

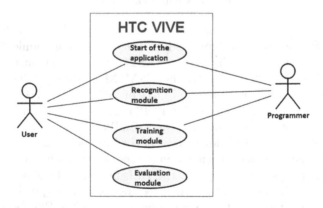

Fig. 3. User's scenario diagram

The virtual reality application created is conformed of several components related to the modules of the user case, which allows solving the proposed activities. These components are linked through dependency relationships shown in

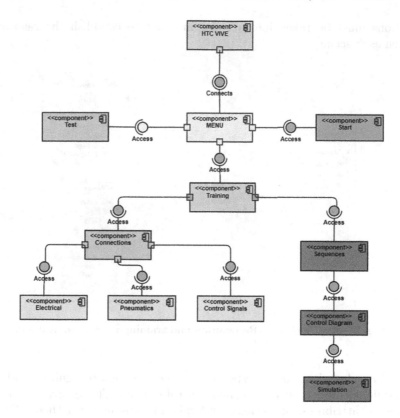

Fig. 4. Component diagrams.

Fig. 4. This diagram displays that the recognition and training modules are directly related because it is in this part where the user will be able to identify all the components of the virtual FESTO module used for the practice. Through the training module, the user will be able to interact with the components, observe the electrical and pneumatic connections, in addition, to elaborate the design of the control circuit to perform the selected sequence. In the end, there is an evaluation module that allows calculating the knowledge acquired by the user during the practice.

To show how the software is developed we used the Unified Modelling Language (UML) Class Diagrams. This kind of diagrams determine the set distribution existent in the system because in these diagrams the classes, attributes, operations, and relationships between objects are traced. For the construction of these diagrams we should take into account the app creation in Unity 3D. This tool uses scenes and scripts programmed in C# to assign functionalities using code to each site, for this reason, the classes, attributes and operations must be taken into account to then establish the relationship that exists between each area. This tool uses scenes and scripts programmed in C# to assign functionalities through a code to each place; for this reason, the classes, attributes, and operations must be taken into account in order to establish the relationship between each scene.

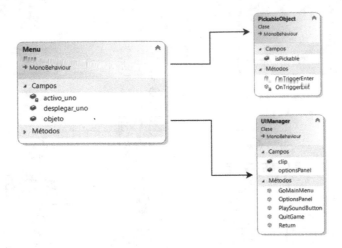

Fig. 5. Class diagram - Recognition and training module connection.

The first class diagram corresponds to the connection recognition and training module (electrical, pneumatic, and control signals). This diagram establishes the classes, attributes, operations, and relationships between them. The first class diagram of the system shown in Fig. 5 shows its structure in Table 1 shows the description of each of the classes that make up the module

Table 1. Description of the recognition and training module connections.

Class	Description
Menu	Set that corresponds to the scene that allows the students to select the start of the application through buttons with programming use
PickableObject	Set corresponding to the scene created for interaction with 3D modeled objects
UIManager	Set corresponding to the scene that allows the students to select the menu options or start one sequence

Figure 6 shows the implementation of the class structure diagram for the HTC VIVE glasses that allow the user to live the virtual reality experience, diagram shows the classification that composes it, the methods, attributes, and relationships that exist between them. On the one hand, it is relevant to mention that in this recognition module, the user can observe the 3D modeled objects animations through the glasses, where he/she will be able to move items employing the controls and perform the activities proposed in the developed application. Table 2 shows the description of each classification that constitutes this training module.

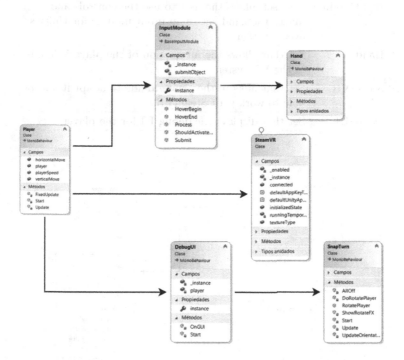

Fig. 6. Training module - Implementation of HTC VIVE glasses

Figure 7 shows the class diagram structure for the training module that corresponds to the control diagram; in this diagram, you can see all the sets that compose it, the methods, attributes and relationships between them. On the one hand, in this diagram, it can be seen that there are association relationships. Table 3 shows the description of each of the classes that constitutes this training module.

Figure 8 shows the structure of the class diagram for the simulation of the training module; in this diagram, you can observe the set that composes it, the methods, attributes, and relationships that exist between them. On the one hand, it is relevant to mention that in this training module the user can observe the objects modeled in 3D animations, which simulate the sequence selected at the beginning. Table 4 shows the description of each set that constitutes this training module.

Table 2. Description of the recognition module – Glasses implementation HTC VIVE.

Class	Description
Player	A set that allows the user to see the Player position and the virtual reality camera
InputModule	This set allows the user to use the controls and makes the hand act as an input module for Unity's event system
Hand	Set that allows the interaction of the player's hands in the VR system
SteamVR	Set that links to the CameraFade to adapt it and be able to work with SteamVR
DebugUI	Set that displays the debug UI for the player

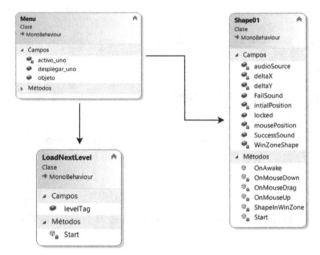

Fig. 7. Diagram of classes - Training module control diagram

Table 3. Description of training module control diagram

Class	Description
Menu	Set that corresponds to the scene that allows you to select one of the proposed sequences to carry out the practice through buttons
LoadNextLevel	Set corresponding to the scene that allows us to visualize the download of the control diagram to the Raspberry PI at the end of the puzzle
Shape01	Set that contains the software used to drag and drop the sequence graphs into the correct box

Table 4. Description of the simulation training module

Class	Description
Menu	This set lets you change the simulation scene through some buttons for visualizing the selected sequence operation
PickableObject	Set corresponding to the scene created for the attachment of the 3d modeled objects in the FESTO module

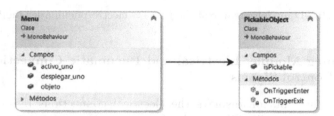

Fig. 8. Diagram of classes - Simulation training module

6 Interface Design

The virtual environment defines the space where the user interacts with the virtual module of Electroneumática FESTO through the different components in 2D and 3D. Through HTC VIVE glasses, immersion and fluid interaction are achieved between the user and the graphic interface designed in Unity 3D, where the user carries out the proposed activities in each of the scenes. To achieve this purpose, we integrated the assets of the HTC VIVE glasses downloaded from the unity store, whose function is to link the graphical interface of Unity with the virtual reality glasses. The following shows each of the interfaces that make up the developed application.

6.1 Designing 3D Models

For the design of the virtual environment the 3D models of the FESTO Electropneumatics module must be available. These models are created in Autodesk Inventor and exported in an Obj file type for being used in Unity 3D; in some cases Blender is used for correcting model the 3D parts. The models created that constitute the virtual environment are (1) 2/3 double solenoid valves, (2) double-acting pneumatic cylinder, (3) Festo pneumatic module structure, (4) limit switches, (5) connection elements (electrical and pneumatic), (6) air distributor, (7) 24 V power supply module, (8) Rpi input and output module; as shown in Fig. 9. In addition, textures, meshes, rendering, and color were added to each of these 3D elements so that the user feels a greater realism during practice.

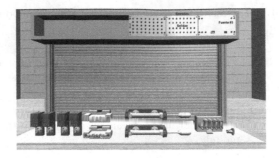

Fig. 9. 3D models creator of the FESTO electro-pneumatics module

6.2 Training Module: Electrical and Pneumatic Connections and Control Signals

Pressing the first button displays the electrical connections between the 3D objects placed in the FESTO module of the virtual environment. Pressing the second button displays the pneumatic wiring between the double-acting cylinders, solenoid valves, and air distributors. Finally, by pressing the third button, you can see the connections of the inputs and outputs of the control signals (see Fig. 10) to be sent to the Raspberry PI data acquisition card.

When finalizing, the user will be able to observe all the existing connections between the 3D objects in this interface the user must select in the options menu the following graphic interface: the first option lets you go to the interface where the user can select the sequences of the practice, the second button lets you return to the visualization of the connections and the third button lets you return to the start menu.

6.3 Training Module: Selection of the Sequence and Design of the Control Scheme

In this interface, the user will choose the practice sequence to develop. Once the user selects the simulation, he/she must solve the design of the control scheme (ladder). Then, they can assemble in parts as in a puzzle in the following interface. On completing the jigsaw, the user will see an option that indicates that the control diagram has been assembled correctly.

In this interface, the user can download the control scheme to the Raspberry Pi board via CoAP protocol, as shown in Fig. 11. At the end of the download, the user can close the tab and then press the virtual return button that lets you start the operation of the selected sequence, both in the virtual environment and in the actual FESTO module and to achieve this purpose, CoAP protocol uses the transmission of instructions to the Raspberry PI, where the inputs and outputs of the sensors and solenoid valves are connected.

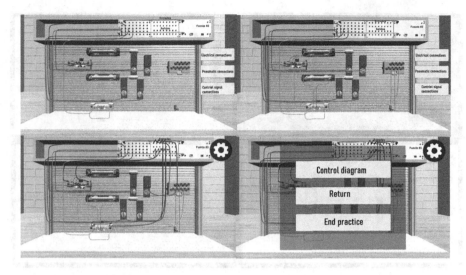

Fig. 10. Training of electrical, pneumatic connections and control signals.

6.4   Training Module: Visualisation of the Operation of the Selected Sequence

Once the user has finished assembling the control diagram (Ladder), the user can visualize the interface of the virtual FESTO module with the electrical and pneumatic connections and control signals where the user can observe the operation of the selected sequence with the help of the HTC VIVE VR glasses. In this interface, the user can visualize the movement of the double-acting cylinders, the actuation of the limit switches when they are retracted, and the operation of the solenoid valves, as shown in Fig. 12.

In this scene, sounds are integrated into the 3D objects that generate movement and lights to the solenoid valves; a power button on the module in which one the user will feel a greater realism when observing the operation through the glasses. From this interface, the end practice button sends the stop instruction via CoAP protocol to the Raspberry card to stop the operation of the equipment of the actual module. The user can use this button to return to the interface where the start menu is located; there, the user should press the test button to start the evaluation.

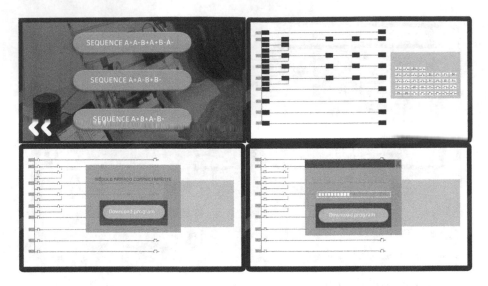

Fig. 11. Sequence selection and design of the control scheme

7   Latency Tests on Data Transmission via CoAP Protocol

Once the VR application has been developed, functional tests have been carried out between the virtual environment and the real FESTO module, to verify if the communication by CoAP protocol meets the requirements of functionality and, therefore, the objectives of the degree work. For data storage and processing, the tool called Wareshark is used, which is an open-Source protocol analyzer, in this program data is taken when performing the communication using CoAP protocol from Unity 3d, Node-Red, and Raspberry PI, introducing traffic on the network. By performing this test it can be seen that during the data exchange

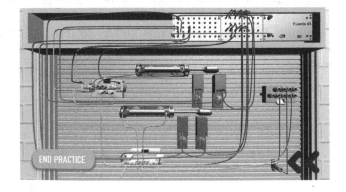

Fig. 12. Visualization of the pneumatic system function.

when connecting via wifi there is no data loss between the server located in Node-Red and clients located in Unity 3D and Raspberry PI.

Figure 13 shows the data exchange, where the server and the client use the GET method for data exchange, these data are sent through the URI - Path: "UnityRpi". In the red circle, you can see the response sent to the client hosted on the Raspberry PI from the server. This figure also shows the communication port (5683) and the bits corresponding to the message size (63 bytes). In this part of the communication, it is important to indicate that there was no data loss when exchanging messages because the protocol is easy to implement and does not need many resources for data transmission.

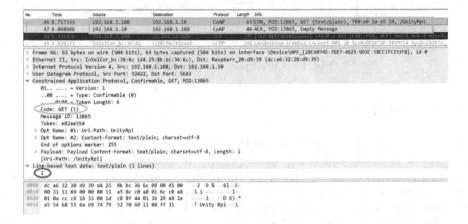

Fig. 13. Communication between the CoAP server and client using the GET method.

The data transmission was performed several times, so that the Wireshark tool captures as many packets as possible, thereby analyzing the existing performance of lost packets between the communication between the virtual reality application and the Raspberry. For this work it is proved that this protocol is low cost, does not consume more resources and above all the bandwidth it uses is minimal compared to MQTT. The Fig. 14 shows the number of CoAP packets exchanged in 1 min. The approximate time it takes to exchange packets after CoAP communication has started is 8 milliseconds. It is also observed that there are no lost packets during data transmission

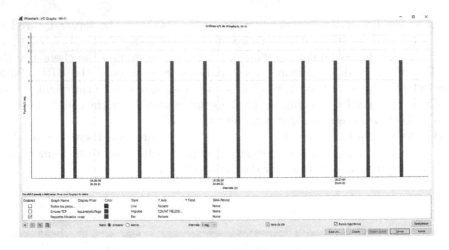

Fig. 14. CoAP packets transmitted.

8   Conclusions

The design of a virtual environment that allows the realization of practices on pneumatic systems, that is to say, allows the interaction with the objects and allows the design of the control diagram and the visualization of the operation of the sequence selected by the user, was satisfactorily carried out. In addition, it allows demonstrating the operation in the real FESTO module.

The integration of the CoAP protocol to the project through the CoAP.NET libraries for Unity 3D and CoAPthon for Python in low-cost hardware, allowed to establish communication using IoT protocols between the virtual environment and the physical FESTO module, so that they work synchronously when selecting one of the sequences established in the project by the user.

It is important to create virtual reality applications for education, since it allows users to have access to a virtual laboratory with greater freedom, in which they can be trained and understand how the practice is developed, in order to reduce accidents and material damage when performing the practice in a real laboratory.

Acknowledgements. The authors recognize the supported bringing by Universidad Tecnica de Ambato (UTA) and their Research and Development Department (DIDE) under project CONIN-P-256-2019.

References

1. dela Cruz, D.R., Mendoza, D.M.M.: Design and development of virtual laboratory: a solution to the problem of laboratory setup and management of pneumatic courses in bulacan state university college of engineering. In: 2018 IEEE Games, Entertainment, Media Conference (GEM), pp. 1–23. IEEE (2018)

2. Evstatiev, B., Evstatieva, N., Trifonov, D.: Development of a virtual laboratory in logic design. In: 2019 16th Conference on Electrical Machines, Drives and Power Systems (ELMA), pp. 1–4. IEEE (2019)
3. Garcia, C.A., Caiza, G., Naranjo, J.E., Ortiz, A., Garcia, M.V.: An approach of training virtual environment for teaching electro-pneumatic systems. IFAC-PapersOnLine **52**(9), 278–284 (2019)
4. Keßler, D., Arntz, A., Friedhoff, J., Eimler, S.C.: Mill instructor: teaching industrial cnc procedures using virtual reality. In: 2020 IEEE International Conference on Artificial Intelligence and Virtual Reality (AIVR), pp. 231–234. IEEE (2020)
5. Kučera, F., Haffner, O., Kozák, Š.: Connection between 3d engine unity and microcontroller arduino: a virtual smart house. In: 2018 Cybernetics & Informatics (K&I), pp. 1–8. IEEE (2018)
6. Li, C., Li, J.: Development and design of virtual experiment system based on 3dsmax and virtools technology. In: 2018 Chinese Control And Decision Conference (CCDC), pp. 4275–4280. IEEE (2018)
7. Matthes, C., et al.: The collaborative virtual reality neurorobotics lab. In: 2019 IEEE Conference on Virtual Reality and 3D User Interfaces (VR), pp. 1671–1674. IEEE (2019)
8. SmeshLink®: Coap.net. http://open.smeshlink.com/CoAP.NET/ (2016), accedido en diciembre del 2020
9. Soriano, A., Ponce, P., Molina, A.: A novel design of virtual laboratory. In: 2019 20th International Conference on Research and Education in Mechatronics (REM), pp. 1–6. IEEE (2019)
10. Tovar, L.N., Castañeda, E., Leyva, V.R., Leal, D.: Work-in-progress—a proposal to design of virtual reality tool for learning mechatronics as a smart industry trainer education. In: 2020 6th International Conference of the Immersive Learning Research Network (iLRN), pp. 381–384. IEEE (2020)
11. Wuttke, H.D., Hamann, M., Henke, K.: Integration of remote and virtual laboratories in the educational process. In: Proceedings of 2015 12th International Conference on Remote Engineering and Virtual Instrumentation (REV), pp. 157–162. IEEE (2015)
12. Xie, J., Wang, X., Yang, Z., Hao, S.: Virtual monitoring method for hydraulic supports based on digital twin theory. Min. Technol. **128**(2), 77–87 (2019)

Optimizing Collaborative Robotic Workspaces in Industry by Applying Mixed Reality

Dietmar Siegele[1]([77]) (ID), Dieter Steiner[1] (ID), Andrea Giusti[1] (ID), Michael Riedl[1], and Dominik T. Matt[1,2] (ID)

[1] Fraunhofer Italia, Via A. Volta 13 A, 39100 Bolzano, Italy
dietmar.siegele@fraunhofer.it
[2] Free University of Bozen-Bolzano, Piazza Universitá 5, 39100 Bolzano, Italy

Abstract. Collaborative robots (cobots) find increased use in industrial workspaces. The aspects of safety and ergonomics are important challenges when designing such workspaces. In this work Mixed Reality (MR) and Virtual Reality (VR) are used for the design of cobot workspaces in industrial environments. ROS (Robotic Operating System) together with Unity is used to simulate and visualize cobot applications. Simulated and real robotics are merged into one tool developed for Extended Reality (XR). To allow early planning in VR, existing industrial environments are reconstructed digitally using state-of-the-art 3-D laser scanners. VR and MR are then applied to test the developed scenarios in various environments, like variation of workspace or robot. In addition, an external tracking system allows us to monitor a human operator and to visualize ergonomics and to mitigate potential safety risks.

Keywords: Cobot · Ergonomics · Industry 4.0 · ROS · Mixed reality

1 Introduction

One target of Industry 4.0 is a high level of collaboration between human workers and industrial robots, with the aim of improving overall efficiency and productivity [24]. Modern industrial automation enjoys an increasing presence of collaborative robots (cobots), which reduce the necessity to enclose robots in safety cages and enabling new modes of man-machine interaction. In such configurations humans and machines are allowed and even encouraged to come in close contact. Thus it is of highest importance to ensure well-defined task sharing and to establish reliable safety protocols protecting the human worker from physical harm [22].

Thus, the application of cobots manifests the following main challenges:

– Safe working environment for the human co-worker,
– Design of efficient workspaces, in terms of time and costs, and
– Ergonomically optimized workplaces.

© Springer Nature Switzerland AG 2021
L. T. De Paolis et al. (Eds.): AVR 2021, LNCS 12980, pp. 544–559, 2021.
https://doi.org/10.1007/978-3-030-87595-4_40

The use of Mixed Reality (MR) and Virtual Reality (VR) can help to overcome these challenges [7]. In an overarching goal we target to optimize the efficiency of such workspaces and how they can be designed in an ergonomic way, while at the same time creating a safe environment for the workers. In this work, we focus on how MR could assist the design of collaborative workspaces by using a workflow from an experimental setup to real setups. We combine this in a laboratory setup. Thus, we did a comprehensive literature review to highlight important aspects when designing the setup of such a laboratory. Subsequently, we present the setup of the laboratory and some preliminary results.

2   State of the Art

2.1   VR, AR and MR for Robotics and Industry 4.0

In the last years, impressive work has been carried out in the application of VR/AR/MR in an Industry 4.0 context, and many suitable applications have been identified. In this paper, we focus on results related to human–robot collaboration (HRC).

A quality review on AR and VR applications for Industry 4.0 was published by [3]. In that work, the authors state that these technologies enable new ways of interaction with the workers, the shop floor, and the whole enterprise. Workers strengthen their perception of the product and its processes becoming an active part of the manufacturing decision-making as they influence the design of the manufacturing network. They highlight several key advantages: the application to production plant control and diagnostics; safety and security of production systems; improvement of planning activities including resource matching; product design and reconfiguration; provision of the required information at operational and enterprise-level; improvement of cooperation between humans and machine; teaching workers complex tasks in a safer manner to increase their productivity.

A systematic review of Augmented Reality interfaces for collaborative industrial robots carried out by [4] aimed at identifying the main strengths and weaknesses of AR with industrial robots in HRC scenarios. The results suggest that AR technology shows its effectiveness also in this particular domain. With respect to traditional approaches, AR systems are faster and more appreciated by users.

A similar literature review on using AR with HRC was done by [8]. They state that future space exploration will demand the cultivation of human-robotic systems, however, little attention has been paid to the development of human-robot teams. Current methods for autonomous plan creation are often complex and difficult to use. According to them, a system that enables humans and robotic systems to naturally and effectively collaborate is needed. Effective collaboration takes place when the participants are able to communicate in a natural and effective manner. Moreover, the common understanding between conversational participants, shared spatial referencing and situational awareness, are identified as crucial components of communication and collaboration.

An AR software suite for enabling human-robot interaction in flexible robotic assembly lines was proposed by [12]. Even if stated as Augmented Reality, they use more a kind of Mixed Reality for this application. Their goal is to support operators in production systems employing mobile robots. These robot workers may increase an assembly system's flexibility while supporting humans, given their ability to navigate to different workstations and change tools for performing various assembly tasks. Unfortunately, their software stack is not publicly available.

The human-robot contactless collaboration with mixed reality interface presented by [10] proposed a control system based on multiple sensors for the safe collaboration of a robot with a human. New constrained and contactless human-robot coordinated motion tasks are defined to control the robot end-effector so as to maintain a desired relative position to the human head while pointing at it. Simultaneously, the robot avoids any collision with the operator and with nearby static or dynamic obstacles, based on distance computations performed in the depth space of an RGB-D sensor. The various tasks are organized with priorities and executed under hard joint bounds using the Saturation in the Null Space (SNS) algorithm. Direct human-robot communication is integrated within a mixed reality interface using a stereo camera and an augmented reality system.

An application of Augmented Reality combined with cobotics to toolmaking, allowing the user of the system to interact with the robot (or a simulation thereof) and guide it to the task at hand was proposed by [7]. The authors used an environment based on ROS and Unity, communicating using ROS Sharp. A similar system is presented by [21], using MR for planning and manipulation of robotic trajectories, combining the HoloLens and ABB proprietary simulation software.

Improvements in human-robot handover by using MR were shown by [18]. They state that MR devices, such as the Microsoft HoloLens, allow the augmentation of real environments with visualized sensor data as well as simulation of robotic parts like virtual robot heads or arms attached to a physical robot. This enables HRI experiments that were difficult or impossible to conduct before.

A concept for a mixed-reality learning environment tackling challenges identified regarding HRC is shown in [29]. Existing technologies were examined and evaluated for usage in the context of HRC training.

The impact of MR on a hand guiding task with a holographic cobot was shown by [23]. They present an interface in which some tangible feedback is provided through ultrasound-based mid-air haptics actuation. In addition, they report about a case study evaluating the impact that this haptic feedback may have on a pick-and-place task of the wrist of a holographic robot arm.

A mixed-perception approach for safe human–robot collaboration in industrial automation was proposed by [1]. They addressed safety by designing a reliable safety monitoring system for cobots. The main idea here is to significantly enhance safety using a combination of recognition of human actions using visual perception and interpretation of physical human–robot contact by tactile perception. Two different deep learning networks are used for human action recognition and contact detection, which in combination, are expected to lead to the enhancement of human safety and an increase in the level of cobot perception about human intentions.

A work on communicating and controlling robot arm motion intent through mixed-reality head-mounted displays applying the framework *ROS Reality* was published by [26]. Their interface allows users to adjust the intended goal pose of the end effector using hand gestures.

2.2 Planning Cobot Workplaces

In [16] the design of a safety framework for the coexistence of an operator with a standard industrial robot is shown. The authors devised safety measures and requirements for the coexistence and implemented them on an actual prototype cell. They use gesture commands to interact with the robotic system.

An atlas of physical human-robot interaction is available in [5]. The authors give an overview of issues to consider when tackling safe and dependable HRI and propose some benchmarks to assess safety and dependability.

An extensive review on human–robot collaboration in an industrial environment is provided in [30]. The authors give a specific focus on issues related to physical and cognitive interaction, highlighting the importance of safety and intuitive programming. They also present commercial solutions and show industrial applications where cobotics are advantageous.

The development of a collaborative human-robot manufacturing cell in the automotive context is shown by [2]. They show that collaborative robotics can greatly reduce fatigue and strain on workers, and that gesture monitoring is a viable approach for interacting with a robotic system.

An extensive survey on safety during HRI is given in [13]. The authors give a broad overview of issues and risks and extensively discuss them and highlight possible strategies to tackle them.

The term *collision event pipeline* is introduced in [9]. The authors describe a single framework for detecting, isolating, and identifying collisions, highlighting the computational needs and general advantages and disadvantages of different methods.

In [19] and [20] the author highlights the ergonomic impact of cobotics and AR/VR respectively, noting that these technologies permit new ways of interaction between operator and machine. The author also emphasizes that these new tools need to be designed ergonomically, otherwise prolonged use may put an unnecessary physiological and physiological strain on the long-term user.

2.3 Coupling of ROS and Unity

Several different approaches for coupling ROS with Unity or another 3D-based software that can be utilized for AR/VR/MR can be found in the literature:

An implementation of an augmented teleoperation system based on (ROS) can be found in [14].

ROS Reality, a Virtual Reality framework using consumer-grade hardware for ROS-enabled robots is shown in [32]. It is an open-source, over-the-Internet tele-operation interface between any ROS-enabled robot and any Unity-compatible VR headset. They use ROS Bridge (a standard package provided by ROS to enable the integration of applications over Ethernet) and wrote custom Csh scripts for Unity. Since publishing the paper, no further work was carried out on this framework. It supports only subscribing and publishing joint states. Applied research based on this framework is presented in [26, 27] and [31], however, the improvements seem not to be publicly available.

An operator interface for multi-robot systems and VR was developed by [25]. The main goal was the development of immersive monitoring and commanding interfaces, able to improve the operator's situational awareness without increasing its workload. To achieve this, the available technologies and resources were analyzed and multiple ROS packages and Unity assets are applied, again also ROS Bridge. Some applications were also presented, however, this framework is not available to the public.

A Mixed Reality-based simulation for mobile delivery robots was proposed by [15]. They used the *ROS Bridge* and the Unity AR foundation to realize the interface. This work is not publicly available and is very focused on mobile robots.

A more open and general framework for coupling Unity with ROS is provided by Siemens. ROS Sharp is available on Github[1], but there are no known scientific publications available. ROS Sharp allows the connection of publishers, subscribers, and services to ROS. The main limitations are, that the library must be recompiled, which is the reason why, e.g. for the HoloLens, additional adoptions are necessary. Another drawback is the fact, that they are using a JSON-based communication protocol. JSON has the benefit of being a human-readable format, but encoding and decoding it costs precious processing time and bandwidth. As a result streaming images or point clouds is mostly infeasible.

At the end of the year 2020, Unity presented their own implementation of a ROS connector. It was made available on Github[2]. The implementation is based on ROS Sharp, but there is no need for recompilation after changes. Also, the creation of various data types necessary to e.g. work with ROS messages or services is significantly easier and more comprehensive. They also rely on compressed binary coding for transferred data, allowing for image streaming in nearly real-time.

Initially VISUAL was using ROS Sharp, but we encountered significant restrictions and low user-friendliness. After Unity published its own implementation, we changed the framework. It also benefits from the advanced simulation capabilities of Unity, which allow us to simulate the robot directly in Unity, without the need for Gazebo (which is part of ROS, but again, not very user-friendly).

---

[1] https://github.com/siemens/ros-sharp.
[2] https://github.com/Unity-Technologies/Unity-Robotics-Hub.

3 Methodology

3.1 Laboratory Setup

In this work we propose the setup of a laboratory, called VISUAL (Virtual SimUlator for Automation Laboratory) (compare Fig. 1). The laboratory setup allows one to:

- Acquire a three-dimensional capture of an existing working environment using a survey-grade LIDAR-scanner.
- Use the three-dimensional capture of the actual working environment for a design phase in 3D-software (Unity).
- Use Virtual Reality to test the designed workplace. The use of force feedback gloves (SenseGlove) allows for a highly immersive experience in this phase.
- Simulate the cobot using the articulation joint system based on Nvidia's PhysX 4.
- Use real-time coupling of ROS (Robot Operating System) with Unity allows integrating the real controller setup early on and facilitates future portability.
- Use Mixed Reality glasses (*Microsoft HoloLens 2*) to test the designed workspaces in the real environment. A compiled application permits this also remotely without the need for physical presence in the laboratory.
- Use a motion tracking system to assess the ergonomic impact on the operator while wearing MR glasses and carrying out his tasks.
- Combining virtual with real assets allows for safe trajectory planning. The operator can test the movement of the robot in a MR setup superimposed on the real robot. When the operator is satisfied with the simulated results, the operation of the real hardware can be directly started via the MR interface.
- Use for the training of operators in VR and MR. Operators need to be trained on the system, also to get comfortable with it (which increases acceptance and security). This can be done in an early stage in VR and then in MR in the real working environment, even if the robotic hardware is not yet available.

3.2 Hardware Architecture

The hardware architecture we used is shown in Fig. 2. It is built around two processing nodes. The first node (*ROS-Master*) running Ubuntu 20.04 is responsible for the high-level control of the robotic arm and the RGB-D-Sensor (*Intel RealSense D435i*). The other node (*Processing Node*), running Microsoft Windows 10, is used for processing motion tracking data. For motion tracking, a solution from Qualisys with eight tracking cameras is used. We use a time synchronization with the Linux PC running ROS. The node also interfaces with the tactile glove (*SenseGlove Developer Edition*). When using VR glasses, Unity is running on this node and streams the XR-app. The MR-Glasses (*Microsoft HoloLens 2*) are used to display the XR-app in the MR-mode. It is connected via WiFi. The robotic arm (here a *Universal Robots UR10e*) is also connected to the network. The robotic arm provides a high-level interface for ROS but has its own hardware controllers and safety control is carried out by the robot itself.

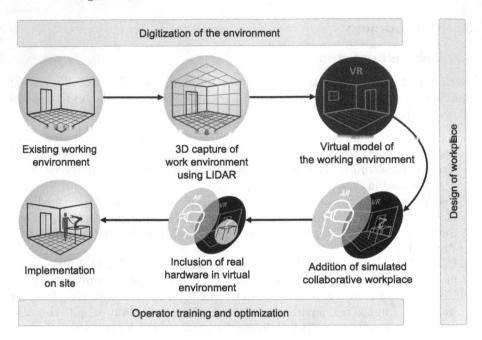

Fig. 1. Workflow in VISUAL.

3.3 Software Architecture

On the software side, we can distinguish three different software stacks (compare Fig. 3). Two of them are running on the processing nodes described in the previous section, and one on the HoloLens.

The robotics stack is built on *Ubuntu 20.04* and the Robotic Operating System (ROS) *Noetic Ninjemys*. On top of it we use the *Universal Robots driver*[3],

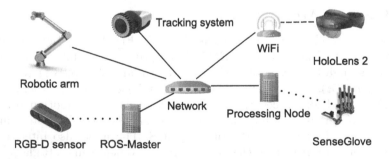

Fig. 2. Hardware architecture of VISUAL.

---

[3] https://github.com/UniversalRobots/Universal_Robots_ROS_Driver.

MoveIt[4] and the *ROS-TCP-Endpoint* by Unity[5]. The Universal Robot driver establishes the connection to the robotic arm interface. It allows sending trajectories and commands for the gripper. With MoveIt the planning of the trajectories is carried out. The *ROS-TCP-Endpoint* allows the connection to Unity. It is used to create an endpoint to accept ROS messages sent from a Unity scene. All types of messages and services can use this service, as the necessary code can be automatically created within C# for each functionality. The application logic of VISUAL is packaged into an application-specific module that uses the *ROS-TCP-Endpoint* and *MoveIt*.

The processing stack is built on *Microsoft Windows 10* and the *Unity Engine (2020.3f1)*. We employ the *ROS-TCP-Connector* to interface to the robotics system, and the *Microsoft Mixed Reality Toolkit* (MRTK 2.6.1) to create an XR-Application. The application-specific logic is implemented in Unity using C#. Moreover, this stack includes the *Qualisys Track Manager* (QTM) to process the motion tracking data, and the *SenseGlove SDK* to interface with the tactile glove.

The HoloLens stack is derived from the processing stack and build from the same Unity project. This allows for fast development on the main computer and rapid deployment to the HoloLens visor.

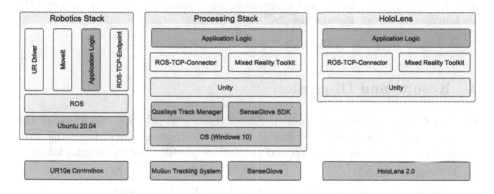

Fig. 3. Software architecture of VISUAL.

3.4 Ergonomics and Safety

For the tracking of the operator's body, we decided to use a commercially available motion tracking system. We use a system based on the *Qualisys Miqus M3* motion tracking cameras and an of-the-shelf motion capture suit. This system has various benefits, the most relevant to VISUAL being the provided integration modules for ROS and Unity. This allows us to have direct access to the operator's skeleton model in both processing systems.

---

[4] https://moveit.ros.org.
[5] https://github.com/Unity-Technologies/ROS-TCP-Endpoint.

Having the operator skeleton available in the robotics system allows us to implement an additional operator safety layer. Based on the work done in [6,28], the robot can slow down, respectively stop its motion when it comes close to the operator, before even having physical contact.

On the other hand, having a precise skeleton model of the operator allows to simultaneously also perform a basic assessment of operator ergonomics. Especially joint angles and overall posture can be evaluated in real-time and allow for a user-centric design of the overall workplace (compare [11]) (Fig. 4).

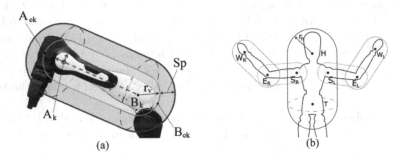

(a)   (b)

Fig. 4. Use of Sphere-Swept-Lines as dynamic safety zones (a) on robotic arm and (b) for human skeleton as described in [28].

4   Results and Discussion

In the following section, we want to demonstrate the principal workflow of the proposed methodology and the results that can be achieved. We want to highlight the main challenges in each step and the future potential of the methodology.

4.1   3D-capture of the Current Working Environment

In the first step, the existing working environment is scanned using LIDAR scanners. Modern laser scanners, as used in our environment, reach accuracies in the sub-millimeter range and have a working range of more than 50 m. By using stationary and mobile laser scanners, even complex industrial environments with machines (compare Fig. 5, where a laser cutter was scanned) can be digitized accurately. This high accuracy facilitates also the design of difficult scenarios where precise path planning of the robotic arm is necessary. 3D point clouds can look very impressive as first (like Fig. 5), but they have some significant drawbacks when used VR or MR. As they represent only a set of points, a surface - that can be rendered - must be attached to each point. This surface can be a circular or square area. To achieve a high level of immersion in VR, the size of this surfaces must be scaled depending on the distance to the viewer. Also, they do not represent closed surfaces, which creates artifacts when using shadows. Thus, the preferred solution is to first create a mesh out of the point cloud. For creating these meshes several commercial and open-source tools are available. They usually have in common, that the model needs to be split into sub-models to achieve good results when using automatic algorithms. Manual adaption of the meshes is time-intensive and in many real-work applications not target-oriented. We suggest to use horizontal sub-dividing of the model when applying this method to larger scenes.

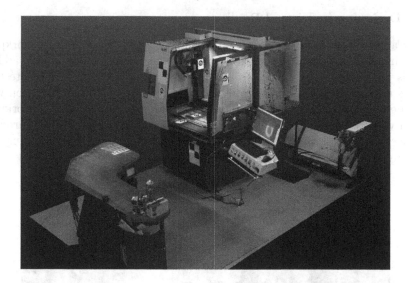

Fig. 5. Example of point cloud of working environment.

4.2 Coupling of ROS and Unity Robot Simulation

In our case study, we use the package *MoveIt* to carry out the trajectory planning of the arm. For the controller itself (a kind of task manager), we programmed a ROS service *pickandplace*. The ROS service can then be called from Unity in a C# script. When a button is touched in the virtual/mixed environment, this script is invoked and the associated task is executed. So far, the (exact) coordinates are given directly by Unity to ROS to simplify the process. For a real-world application, the Intel *RealSense* is applied to detect the shape of the object to be gripped and to determine the best gripping position.

The simulation of robots in ROS is usually carried out by applying a tool called *Gazebo*. However, additional modeling is needed to work with this tool and it is far away from being as user-friendly as Unity. Thus, we apply Unity and the new articulation joint system. The results obtained by that simulation are very fast and accurate. Compared to *Gazebo* (which we used for previous projects) Unity is much more user-friendly and results can be obtained faster. Applying the URDF-importer a model can be imported into the editor very quickly and joints are already pre-configured. Modeling surfaces with real physics is only possible in Unity and delivers very good results. As Unity can also simulate lighting via raytracing, this opens up interesting possibilities for using it together with machine learning algorithms. The only drawback so far (that also *Gazebo* shows) is the missing support of parallel manipulators like those are often used for grippers

4.3   Designing in Virtual Reality

Unity allows us to combine previously scanned assets from the real workplace with virtual ones (compare Fig. 6, a virtual table and robotic arm were added). In this phase, it is very simple to add objects based on CAD models, test the results using VR glasses and then move them or swap them out based on what the operator experiences in VR. This allows for rapid iteration of workplace design without costly (in terms of time and money) investments into hardware. Furthermore, the ability to include captured assets enables experimenting with rearrangement of existing environments, without disrupting production.

Fig. 6. Designing of working environment in VR.

4.4   Testing with Mixed Reality in Real Working Environment

In a further step, the proposed laboratory permits to bring the virtual assets into the real world using an MR visor (compare Fig. 7). In this phase, the previously designed workspace can be tested in a real working environment. This allows for optimizing the placement of components and on-site training of operators. It is also possible to place e.g. a virtual robot onto an existing, real work table, to further test and refine the workplace design. As distributed working is getting more and more important, this setup allows also to send a potential costumer only the access to the MR app, and he can test the developed setup in it's real environment while instructed by a person in a remote place.

One of the main remaining challenges in this field is to work with large holograms. Usually in industrial use-cases with cobots the holograms get quite huge (in the range of $2\,m^2$). Due to the restricted field-of-view it can be difficult to work with this holograms.

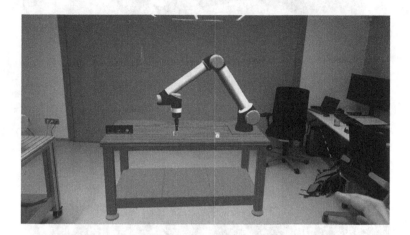

Fig. 7. Testing in MR. Virtual assets placed in real environment.

An other aspect enabled by the proposed setup is the overlay of virtual and real setup (compare Fig. 8). This allows an operator to test certain operations with the virtual robot. He is only executing them on the real hardware when he is satisfied with the results of the simulation. Especially when manipulating fragile and/or costly workpieces this could help avoiding damage to workpieces and workplace. Trajectory planning can be more efficient in terms of time required and accuracy.

An optional phase foreseen in the laboratory covers testing ergonomically and safety aspects. The operator is asked to wear a motion capture suit, permitting precise capture of his body movements. On one side, this permits assessment of ergonomics according to RULA [17] which assigns scores based on joint angles, on the other side, precise assessment of possible (near-) collisions is made possible (compare Fig. 9).

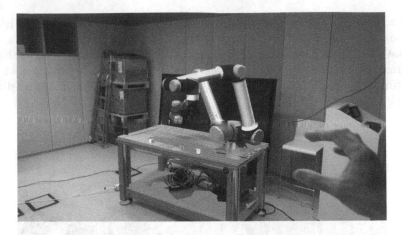

Fig. 8. Virtual and real robot in MR.

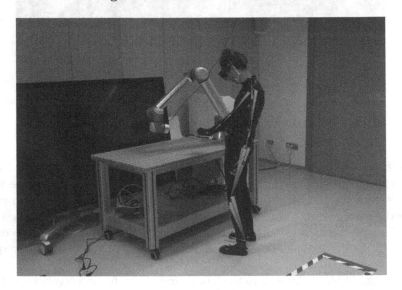

Fig. 9. Evaluation of ergonomically and safety aspects.

5   Conclusion and Outlook

In this paper we have described a laboratory setup, using state-of-the-art technology, for designing, planning and evaluating of collaborative robotic workspaces in MR. It allows for various degrees of virtualization, covering the whole spectrum, from purely virtual to purely real assets. The individual components used are industry proven, and each of them has an active user base, hopefully ensuring longevity and long-term compatibility.

Using ROS allows us to work with a widely applied framework for robotics. This enables a quick transition from design to application phase. Unity makes it possible to simulate the robots with highly-accurate physical solvers.

As an outlook we plan to extend this setup further, allowing e.g. for direct designing and modification of the workplace in VR/MR by being able to add objects directly from a library of virtual assets. Intelligent pre-placement of assets is also an interesting possible extension, as it would permit faster initial designs. Using advances in real-time tracing will also allow to develop control and vision algorithms based on machine learning in the same environment. The integration of force-feedback will be improved to enable a more realistic immersion, both, in VR and MR. This is essential to enable the setup for training purposes.

Acknowledgement. The research leading to these results has received funding from the European Regional Development Fund (Fondo Europeo di Sviluppo Regionale FESR Alto Adige 2014–2020) under the Grant Agreement n. EFRE1079 CUP B51G17000280001.

References

1. Amin, F.M., Rezayati, M., van de Venn, H.W., Karimpour, H.: A mixed-perception approach for safe human-robot collaboration in industrial automation. Sensors **20**(21), 1–20 (2020). https://doi.org/10.3390/s20216347, www.mdpi.com/journal/sensors
2. Cherubini, A., Passama, R., Crosnier, A., Lasnier, A., Fraisse, P.: Collaborative manufacturing with physical human-robot interaction. Rob. Comput. Integr. Manuf. **40**, 1–13 (2016). https://doi.org/10.1016/j.rcim.2015.12.007
3. Damiani, L., Demartini, M., Guizzi, G., Revetria, R., Tonelli, F.: Augmented and virtual reality applications in industrial systems: a qualitative review towards the industry 4.0 era. IFAC-PapersOnLine **51**(11), 624–630 (2018). https://doi.org/10.1016/j.ifacol.2018.08.388
4. De Pace, F., Manuri, F., Sanna, A., Fornaro, C.: A systematic review of augmented reality interfaces for collaborative industrial robots. Comput. Ind. Eng. **149**, 106806 (2020). https://doi.org/10.1016/j.cie.2020.106806
5. De Santis, A., Siciliano, B., De Luca, A., Bicchi, A.: An atlas of physical human-robot interaction (2008). https://doi.org/10.1016/j.mechmachtheory.2007.03.003
6. Di Cosmo, V., Giusti, A., Vidoni, R., Riedl, M., Matt, D.T.: Collaborative robotics safety control application using dynamic safety zones based on the ISO/TS 15066:2016. Adv. Intell. Syst. Comput. (2020). https://doi.org/10.1007/978-3-030-19648-6_49
7. Gajšek, B., Stradovnik, S., Hace, A.: Sustainable move towards flexible, robotic, human-involving workplace. Sustainability (2020). https://doi.org/10.3390/su12166590
8. Green, S.A., Chen, X.Q., Billinghurst, M., Chase, J.G.: Human robot collaboration: An augmented reality approach a literature review and analysis. In: 2007 Proceedings of the ASME International Design Engineering Technical Conferences and Computers and Information in Engineering Conference, DETC2007. vol. 4, pp. 117–126 (2008). https://doi.org/10.1115/DETC2007-34227

9. Haddadin, S., De Luca, A., Albu-Schäffer, A.: Robot collisions: a survey on detection, isolation, and identification. IEEE Trans. Robot. **33**(6), 1292–1312 (2017). https://doi.org/10.1109/TRO.2017.2723903

10. Khatib, M., Al Khudir, K., De Luca, A.: Human-robot contactless collaboration with mixed reality interface. Robot. Comput. Integr. Manuf. **67**, 102030 (2021). https://doi.org/10.1016/j.rcim.2020.102030

11. Kim, W., Huang, C., Yun, D., Saakes, D., Xiong, S.: Comparison of joint angle measurements from three types of motion capture systems for ergonomic postural assessment. Adv. Intell. Syst. Comput. (2020). https://doi.org/10.1007/978-3-030-51549-2_1

12. Kousi, N., Stoubos, C., Gkournelos, C., Michalos, G., Makris, S.: Enabling human robot interaction in flexible robotic assembly lines: an augmented reality based software suite. In: Procedia CIRP, vol. 81, pp. 1429–1434. Elsevier B.V. (January 2019). https://doi.org/10.1016/j.procir.2019.04.328

13. Lasota, P.A., Fong, T., Shah, J.A.: A Survey of Methods for Safe Human-Robot Interaction. now Publishers Inc (2017). https://doi.org/10.1561/9781680832792

14. Lee, D., Park, Y.S.: Implementation of augmented teleoperation system based on robot operating system (ROS). In: IEEE International Conference on Intelligent Robots and Systems, pp. 5497–5502. Institute of Electrical and Electronics Engineers Inc. (December 2018). https://doi.org/10.1109/IROS.2018.8594482

15. Liu, Y., Novotny, G., Smirnov, N., Morales-Alvarez, W., Olaverri-Monreal, C.: Mobile delivery robots: mixed reality-based simulation relying on ros and unity 3D. In: IEEE Intelligent Vehicles Symposium, Proceedings, pp. 15–20. Institute of Electrical and Electronics Engineers Inc. (2020). https://doi.org/10.1109/IV47402.2020.9304701

16. Magrini, E., Ferraguti, F., Ronga, A.J., Pini, F., De Luca, A., Leali, F.: Human-robot coexistence and interaction in open industrial cells. Robot. Comput. Integr. Manuf. **61**, (2020). https://doi.org/10.1016/j.rcim.2019.101846

17. McAtamney, L., Nigel Corlett, E.: RULA: a survey method for the investigation of work-related upper limb disorders. Appl. Ergon. **24**(2), 91–99 (1993). https://doi.org/10.1016/0003-6870(93)90080-S

18. Meyer Zu Borgsen, S., Renner, P., Lier, F., Pfeiffer, T., Wachsmuth, S.: Improving human-robot handover research by mixed reality techniques (2018)

19. Munoz, L.M.: Ergonomics in the Industry 4.0: Collaborative Robots. J. Ergonomics **07**(06), (2017). https://doi.org/10.4172/2165-7556.1000e173

20. Munoz, L.M.: Ergonomics in the industry 4.0: virtual and augmented reality. J. Ergonomics **08**(05), (2018). https://doi.org/10.4172/2165-7556.1000e181

21. Neves, J., Serrario, D., Pires, J.N.: Application of mixed reality in robot manipulator programming. Ind. Robot (2018). https://doi.org/10.1108/IR-06-2018-0120

22. Pacaux-Lemoine, M.P., Trentesaux, D.: Ethical risks of human-machine symbiosis in industry 4.0: insights from the human-machine cooperation approaCh. In: IFAC-PapersOnLine, vol. 52, pp. 19–24. Elsevier B.V. (January 2019). https://doi.org/10.1016/j.ifacol.2019.12.077

23. Pinto, A.R., Kildal, J., Lazkano, E.: Multimodal mixed reality impact on a hand guiding task with a holographic cobot. Multimodal Technol. Interact. **4**(4), 1–21 (2020). https://doi.org/10.3390/mti4040078

24. Rauch, E., Matt, D.T.: Status of the implementation of industry 4.0 in SMEs and framework for smart manufacturing. In: Matt, D.T., Modrák, V., Zsifkovits, H. (eds.) Implementing Industry 4.0 in SMEs, pp. 3–26. Springer, Cham (2021). https://doi.org/10.1007/978-3-030-70516-9_1

25. Koubaa, A. (ed.): Robot Operating System (ROS). SCI, vol. 778. Springer, Cham (2019). https://doi.org/10.1007/978-3-319-91590-6

26. Rosen, E., et al.: Communicating and controlling robot arm motion intent through mixed-reality head-mounted displays. Int. J. Robot. Res. **38**(12–13), 1513–1526 (2019). https://doi.org/10.1177/0278364919842925

27. Rosen, E., Whitney, D., Phillips, E.K., Ullman, D., Phillips, E., Tellex, S.: Testing Robot Teleoperation using a Virtual Reality Interface with ROS Reality. Technical Report (2018). https://www.researchgate.net/publication/325474628

28. Scalera, L., Giusti, A., Vidoni, R., Di Cosmo, V., Matt, D.T., Ricdl, M.: Application of dynamically scaled safety zones based on the ISO/TS 15066:2016 for collaborative robotics. Int. J. Mech. Control **21**, 41–49 (2020)

29. Sievers, T.S., Schmitt, B., Rückert, P., Petersen, M., Tracht, K.: Concept of a mixed-reality learning environment for collaborative robotics. In: Procedia Manufacturing, vol. 45, pp. 19–24. Elsevier B.V. (January 2020). https://doi.org/10.1016/j.promfg.2020.04.034

30. Villani, V., Pini, F., Leali, F., Secchi, C.: Survey on human-robot collaboration in industrial settings: safety, intuitive interfaces and applications. Mechatronics **55**, 248–266 (2018). https://doi.org/10.1016/j.mechatronics.2018.02.009

31. Amato, N.M., Hager, G., Thomas, S., Torres-Torriti, M. (eds.): Robotics Research. SPAR, vol. 10. Springer, Cham (2020). https://doi.org/10.1007/978-3-030-28619-4

32. Whitney, D., Rosen, E., Ullman, D., Phillips, E., Tellex, S.: ROS reality: a virtual reality framework using consumer-grade hardware for ROS-enabled robots. In: IEEE International Conference on Intelligent Robots and Systems, pp. 5018–5025. Institute of Electrical and Electronics Engineers Inc. (December 2018). https://doi.org/10.1109/IROS.2018.8593513

3D Virtual System for Control Valve Calibration

Pepe Ibáñez, Edwin Pruna(✉), Ivón Escobar, and Galo Ávila

Universidad de Las Fuerzas Armadas ESPE, Sangolqui, Ecuador
{pfibanez,eppruna,ipescobar,gravila}@espe.edu.ec

Abstract. A 3D virtual system for the calibration of control valves is presented, the design is made based on the P&ID diagram of the industrial level process, 3D modeling software is used for the design of the components; for the creation of the virtual environment, animations and interactions Unity 3D software is used, also a flowchart of the calibration of the control valve is created. The developed environment provides a simulation with a high level of realism due to the integration of HTC vive glasses, as well as efficiently allows training in control valve calibration.

Keywords: Valve calibration · Virtual environment · Level system · Unity

1 Introduction

With the beginning of automation, instrumentation has great importance because thanks to the measuring instruments and actuators it is possible to perform automatic control in a more efficient way than in manual control. In automatic process control, the most commonly used final control elements are the control valves are mechanical device that allow start, stop or regulate the flow of liquids or gases through a moving part (stem-plunger) that opens, closes or partially obstructs an orifice or conduit [1, 2].

Periodic calibration of control valves is of great importance in industrial plants, it ensures the increase of manufacturing yield thanks to the reduction of the number of rejections of the manufactured product [3]. The calibration procedure of control valves consists in obtaining the "signature" of the valve which is the graphical record of the state of the valve-actuator assembly (measurement of hysteresis, dead zone and linearity, graphs or signatures of the positioner, actuator, supply pressure in relation to the stem travel) [4, 5].

Professionals in the area of automation and control in their training should know the procedure of calibration of control valves, for this there are didactic training systems in calibration of control valves, one of the limitations to acquire these didactic systems is its high cost, which significantly affects the practical learning of professionals mentioned above.

Currently, virtual reality allows the creation of virtual environments with similarity to real processes, providing realistic environments with a high level of detail and low cost. Several scientific works are developed in the area of automation and control with virtual reality, in [6] they develop an interactive didactic system for learning the technique of

© Springer Nature Switzerland AG 2021
L. T. De Paolis et al. (Eds.): AVR 2021, LNCS 12980, pp. 560–572, 2021.
https://doi.org/10.1007/978-3-030-87595-4_41

cascade control of industrial processes, a virtual environment with immersion is used for the emulation of the behavior of a level industrial process that can be monitored and controlled through an HMI (Human-Machine Interface). The virtual environment has been created through Computer Aided Design software and a graphic engine; they obtain good experimental results that allow validating the system. In [7] they develop a virtual environment of a manufacturing cell. The virtual cell interacts with a Siemens S7–300 programmable logic controller (PLC) that allows the operator to build and validate a PLC code inside the virtual model, currently the work done is used to verify their control program instead of testing it in the real work cell, and provides information that helps to prevent errors. In [8–10] they develop virtual systems for the area of engineering education, they obtain good results in the applications.

In this work we present the development of a 3D virtual system for the calibration of control valves, for this purpose a virtual environment of an industrial level process is created, with industrial instruments and equipment developed in Unity 3D, a methodology of calibration of a control valve is created. The scheme of the project is shown in Fig. 1.

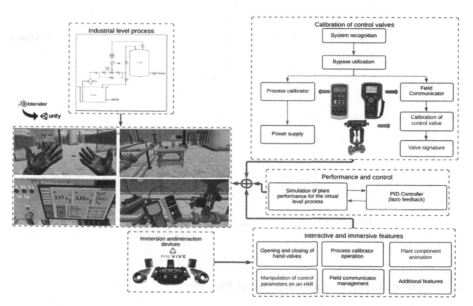

Fig. 1. Project scheme

The present work consists of four sections including the introduction, Sect. 2 presents the design of the 3D environment, the third section presents the results and the fourth section presents the conclusions.

2 Design of the 3D Virtual Environment

This section describes the steps carried out for the design of the virtual environment.

2.1 Design of the P&ID Diagram.

In the system two tanks are considered, the first one corresponds to the process tank and the second one is a reservoir tank that allows the recirculation of the liquid, the equipment and industrial instruments used are: a level transmitter, a level controller, a level control valve with its respective bypass for calibration. ISA 5.1 and ISA 5.3 standards are used in the design, Figure 2 shows the P&ID diagram of the industrial level process.

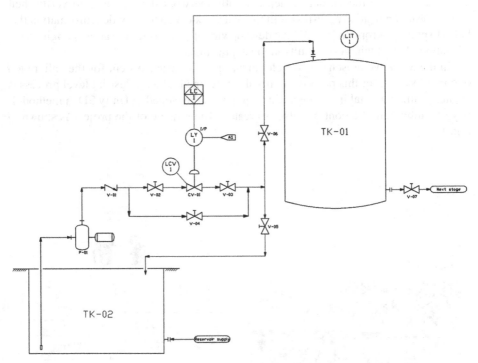

Fig. 2. P&ID diagram of a training station for the level control of a tank.

2.2 3D Modeling of the Industrial Level Process

The design of the industrial process is divided into two stages:

In the first stage, using AutoCAD Plant 3D software the industrial process is developed based on the P&ID diagram (Fig. 2), for this purpose the stages presented below are performed (Fig. 3) and (Fig. 4).

In the second stage, using Blender software, the modeling of the complementary objects, the correction of the models and the configuration of rotation points are carried out. At this stage the model acquires all the necessary characteristics to be used in the virtual environment (Fig. 5) and (Fig. 6).

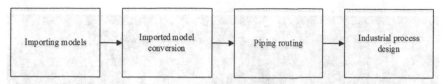

Fig. 3. Stages carried out in AutoCAD Plant 3D for the creation of the virtual environment

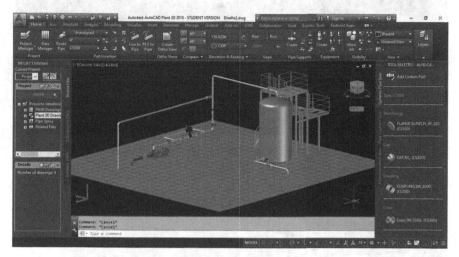

Fig. 4. Industrial level process designed in AutoCAD 3D.

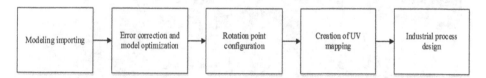

Fig. 5. Steps performed in Blender to enhance details of the virtual environment

2.3 Implementation of the Virtual Environment of the Industrial Process in Unity 3D

Unity 3D software is used for the implementation of the virtual environment, the stages are indicated below:

Design, assignment of materials, textures and lighting
The final design of the industrial level process in FBX. format is imported to Unity 3D, the model is placed in the scene to configure and assign the materials to each object, models are also added, the lighting of the environment is configured and effects that improve the graphic quality of the environment are implemented. The following figure shows the virtual environment developed in Unity 3D.Fig. 7. Industrial level process including lighting, details, effects and textures designed in Unity 3D.

Fig. 6. Final design of the industrial process of level control

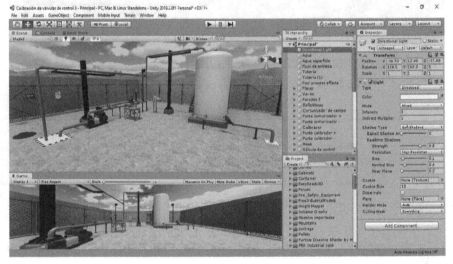

Fig. 7. Industrial level process including lighting, details, effects and textures designed in Unity 3D

Simulation of the behavior of the level plant

Industrial processes represent their operation by means of mathematical expressions, in this sense to simulate the behavior of the level plant in the Unity 3D environment, the Bernoulli principle is used which, for this case, is defined as follows:

$$\frac{dh}{dt} = \frac{q_{in} - q_{out}}{A} \tag{1}$$

$$q_{in} = k_1 a_1 \tag{2}$$

$$q_{out} = k_2 a_2 \sqrt{2gh} \tag{3}$$

Equations 1–3 are used to simulate the operation of the industrial level plant; these equations include the parameters presented below:

h : Tank level (0–6 m).

q_{in} : Inlet flow into tank (0–50 gpm).

q_{out} : Tank outlet flow rate.

A : Area of tank (1.5 m).

k_1 : Valve constant at tank inlet (0.05).

k_2 : Valve constant at the tank outlet (0.015).

a_1 : Valve opening at tank inlet (0–100%).

a_2 : Tank outlet valve opening (0–100%).

g : Gravity (9.8 m/s^2).

Implementation of the PID control algorithm

For the control of the level plant the PID control algorithm is used, since it is easy to implement, it is a robust controller and it is the most used in industrial processes, the equation implemented in Unity is presented below.

$$y(t) = K_p e(t) + ki \int_0^t e(\tau) d\tau + kd \frac{de}{dt} \tag{4}$$

For the tuning of the controller (Eq. 4), the trial and error method was used, obtaining the following values: kp $= 2.5$

$$ki = 0.05$$

$$kd = 2.7$$

Implementation of the human-machine interface (HMI)

For the development of the HMI, the visualization interface used in industrial process control and supervision systems was reviewed and considered. The implementation of the aforementioned visualization interface is done using the UI (User Interface) tools in Unity 3D. For the design a main screen is considered, which will have three access options, the following is a description of the visualization interfaces implemented: i) Process visualization interface, in this interface the design of the process tank is made as well as the design of the pipes and instruments of the industrial process level, also the variables are presented: set point, process value, control value and the type of control to be executed (manual or automatic). ii) Operation visualization interface, this interface implements the options for the user, set point change, change from manual to automatic control, controller tuning and alarm visualization. iii) Trend visualization interface, this interface implements two trends, the first one will allow the visualization of the set point, the process value, and the second trend will allow the visualization of the control value. The following figure shows the implemented interfaces (Fig. 8).

Fig. 8. Visualization interfaces implemented

Implementation of the Bypass

For the development of the Bypass, the operation of a bypass used in level control systems with a control valve as the final control element was reviewed and considered. The respective animations are programmed for the operation of the control valve, as well as the animations of the manual valves, the same ones that can be manipulated with the controls, which will allow the simulation of the maintenance of the control valve, next the implementation of the bypass is presented.

Fig. 9. Bypass implementation

Programming of animations and characteristics of the objects, to achieve an immersive virtual environment

All the necessary features and animations have been programmed and implemented to achieve a virtual environment that simulates the level control of a tank and provides the possibility for the user to observe inside the tank, including the animation of gloves controlled with the HTC vive controls, which allow the manipulation of the valves, as well as linking the HTC VIVE system (helmet, cameras, etc.) in order to emulate the calibration in an immersive way. Finally, the animation of the calibration equipment is included: Process calibrator (yellow equipment) and field configurator (blue equipment). The following figure shows the developed system (Fig. 10).

a)   industrial level process

b)   Control valve calibration system.

Fig. 10. Completed virtual environment

2.4   Creation of a Control Valve Calibration Process Flowchart

For the development of the flow chart of the calibration process of a control valve, an experimental calibration procedure performed in the laboratory level control station is taken as a reference, as well as the operation of the virtual system developed, the steps of the calibration process are presented below.

3   Results

Functional tests were performed to determine the system immersion, the operation in automatic-manual mode, the operation of its industrial instruments, the calibration procedure of the control valve was also performed. The results are presented below:

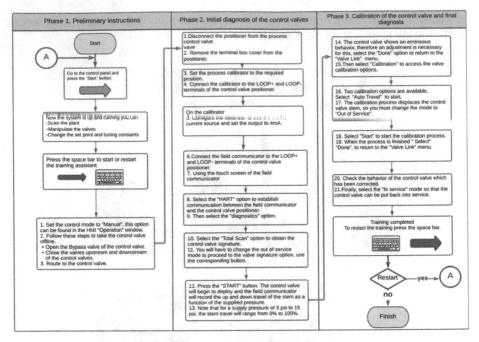

Fig. 11. Flow chart of the control valve calibration process

3.1 Creation of a Control Valve Calibration Process Flowchart. Results of the Immersive Virtual Environment

With the inclusion of the HTC VIVE virtual reality glasses and their respective sensors, a virtual environment with immersion is obtained, which includes the animation of hand movements (controlled with the HTC Vive controllers), so that the user can use the system in a friendly way. The following figure shows the images of the virtual environment with immersion in operation (Fig. 12).

Fig. 12. Images of the virtual gloves in motion for the manipulation of industrial instruments.

3.2 Results of the Operation of the Virtual Level System

The implemented control system is a closed loop, the 3D virtual environment contains a level transmitter, a PID controller with the method of tuning groping, as a final control element the control valve, to visualize the trends and variables of interest is implemented the human machine interface, in addition the animation of the level tank with water inside was performed. The following figure shows the virtual system in operation (Fig. 13).

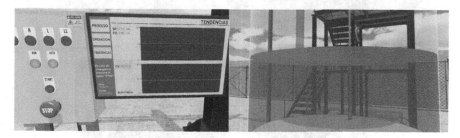

Fig. 13. Real-time operation of the virtual level system

3.3 Control Valve Calibration Results

Following the flow chart (Fig. 11) the control valve calibration procedure was performed, the results are presented below.

A training assistant included in the virtual environment is enabled, which indicates the steps to be performed for the calibration procedure of the control valve, the calibration sequence is presented in the next figures (Fig. 14), (Fig. 15), (Fig. 16), (Fig. 17) and (Fig. 18).

Fig. 14. Switching the level control system to manual mode

Calibration analysis. The signature obtained (Fig. 19) allows determining that the control valve is out of calibration since there is no linear relationship between the pressure control signal (3-15PSI) and displacement percentage (0–100%).

Fig. 15. Bypass valve enabling procedure (Out service control valve)

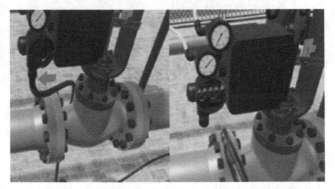

Fig. 16. Disconnecting the positioner from the control valve for connection of the calibrator

Fig. 17. Connection of the process calibrator (current generation 4mA)

It is necessary to adjust the control valve, for this the field configurator is programmed to perform a self-adjustment (adjustment procedure of the valve positioner), Fig. 20 shows that the signature obtained allows to verify that the control valve was adjusted and is calibrated, since there is a linear relationship between the control signal pressure (3-15PSI) and percentage of displacement (0–100%).

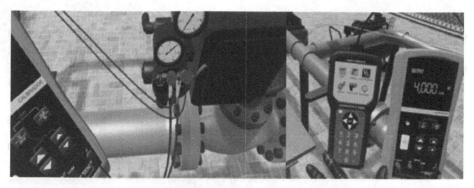

Fig. 18. Connection and parameterization of the field configurator

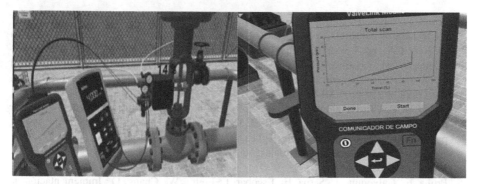

Fig. 19. Valve calibration process and obtaining the valve signature

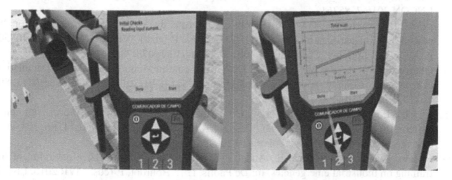

Fig. 20. Control valve adjustment procedure

4 Conclusions

The implemented virtual system has all the components of an industrial level process, for the calibration procedure the steps that are performed in a real calibration are considered.

The integration of HTC vive glasses provide a high level of immersion and by means of HTC controls the virtual gloves are manipulated, for the different tasks in the virtual environment (modification of the human machine interfaces, movement of the valves, etc.).

The virtual system is a low-cost solution, as well as an alternative for the training of instrumentation professionals in the calibration procedure of control valves.

The integration of all stages in the virtual 3D system allows real-time operation since it does not depend on other software for industrial process level control.

As future work will develop a multi-user system that allows the use of the calibration system to multiple users.

References

1. Pruna, E., Bayas, F., Cocha, H., Escobar, I., Gordon, A., Constante, P.: "Implementation of a simulator of industrial processes. In: 2016 IEEE International Conference on Automatica (ICA-ACCA), pp. 1–6 (2016). https://doi.org/10.1109/ICA-ACCA.2016.7778494
2. Chadeev, V.M., Aristova, N.I.: Control of industrial automation. In: 2017 Tenth International Conference Management of Large-Scale System Development (MLSD), pp. 1–5 (2017). https://doi.org/10.1109/MLSD.2017.8109604
3. Liqun, H., Pei, T.: Development of auto-on-line calibration and adjustment system for power plant spring safety valve. In: 2004 IEEE Region 10 Conference TENCON 2004, vol. 4, pp. 597–600 (2004). https://doi.org/10.1109/TENCON.2004.1415003
4. Antonio, C., Instrumentos industriales, su ajuste y calibración, 3a edn. Marcombo S.A., Barcelona-España (2009)
5. Pruna, E., Calvopiña, J., Serna, E., Escobar, I., Freire, W., Chang, O.: Implementación de una herramienta didáctica para el diagnóstico de válvulas de control. In: 2016 IEEE Biennial Congress of Argentina (ARGENCON), pp. 1–6 (2016). https://doi.org/10.1109/ARGENCON.2016.7585261
6. Pruna, E., Rosero, M., Pogo, R., Escobar, I., Acosta, J.: Virtual reality as a tool for the cascade control learning. In: De Paolis, L.T., Bourdot, P. (eds.) AVR 2018. LNCS, vol. 10850, pp. 243–251. Springer, Cham (2018). https://doi.org/10.1007/978-3-319-95270-3_20
7. Guerrero, L.V., López, V.V., Mejía, J.E.: Virtual commissioning with process simulation (Tecnomatix). Comput.-Aided Des. Appl. 11(sup1), S11–S19 (2014). https://doi.org/10.1080/16864360.2014.914400
8. Yugcha, E.P., Ubilluz, J.I., Andaluz, V.H.: Virtual training for industrial process: pumping system. In: De Paolis, L.T., Bourdot, P. (eds.) AVR 2019. LNCS, vol. 11614, pp. 393–409. Springer, Cham (2019). https://doi.org/10.1007/978-3-030-25999-0_33
9. Rosero, M., Pogo, R., Pruna, E., Andaluz, V.H., Escobar, I.: Immersive environment for training on industrial emergencies. In: De Paolis, L.T., Bourdot, P. (eds.) AVR 2018. LNCS, vol. 10851, pp. 451–466. Springer, Cham (2018). https://doi.org/10.1007/978-3-319-95282-6_33
10. Lei, Z., Hu, W., Zhou, H., Zhong, L., Gao, X.: DC motor control in a 3D real-time virtual laboratory environment. In: Proceedings of 2015 12th International Conference on Remote Engineering and Virtual Instrumentation (REV), pp. 18–23, (2015). https://doi.org/10.1109/REV.2015.7087257

3D Virtual System of a Liquid Filling and Packaging Process, Using the Hardware in the Loop Technique

Israel S. Aguilar, Jorge L. Correa, and Edwin P. Pruna$^{(\boxtimes)}$

Universidad de las Fuerzas Armadas ESPE, Sangolquí, Ecuador
{isaguilar,jlcorrea,eppruna}@espe.edu.ec

Abstract. This article presents a virtual automation system for the filling and packaging of liquids developed in the Unity3D graphics engine, complemented with the Hardware In The Loop simulation technique to integrate the sig-nals from simulated sensors and actuators with the use of the Arduino board and the S7-1200 programmable logic controller. The virtual system provides a three-dimensional environment with a high level of detail, the industrial instrumentation has the appearance and functionality similar to real instruments. In order to allow users to become familiar with the industrial elements of the process and complement learning in the field of automation in an interactive way.

Keywords: Unity 3D · Automation · Control · Virtualization · Industry

1 Introduction

The definition of industrial automation is the integration of technologies for the autonomous monitoring and control of industrial processes, in order to eliminate human intervention in production tasks, as well as to maximize resources and ensure operator safety [1].

The automation of batch processes is widely used today, since by means of a programmable logic controller (PLC) each stage of the process is controlled. The productive processes of filling and packaging of liquids are widely used in different industrial plants such as: beverage factory, canning factory, pharmaceutical industry, etc. These processes allow to obtain the final product through a set of stages such as: container dispensing, liquid dosing, sealing, transport and verification of the exact amount of product in each container, providing the user with a high-quality product at a fair price. [2].

In this sense, professionals in the automation area must have specialized and updated technical knowledge in this area. For this, there are didactic systems in the area of industrial automation, which contribute to the training of the professional, the cost of these systems in many cases is high, which makes their acquisition difficult.

Currently, virtual reality is an alternative that allows simulating industrial processes in different areas, used in industrial automation training, as a complement to virtual systems, the Hardware In The Loop (HIL) simulation technique is used, which reduces

© Springer Nature Switzerland AG 2021
L. T. De Paolis et al. (Eds.): AVR 2021, LNCS 12980, pp. 573–587, 2021.
https://doi.org/10.1007/978-3-030-87595-4_42

costs and time in terms of developing complex test systems. In the case of industrial processes where a high range of instrumentation is needed for their construction [3]; By means of a simulation system with HIL it is possible to carry out all kinds of functional tests with the necessary iterations before implementing a real system [4]. In addition, this technique can be used as a didactic resource that allows users to become familiar with all types of systems, without the need to resort to expensive and difficult-to-acquire plants or processes [5].

In this context, several scientific works were developed in virtual systems using the HIL technique, in [4] the HIL simulation technique is implemented in the field of industrial robotics, the simulation technique allows to verify and evaluate advanced control algorithms, the simulation of processes or systems in 3D environments are used in the educational field where it is required to perform constant testing of systems in real time. In addition, HIL technology is widely used in various simulation applications, such as research. In [6] they use the HIL concept to regulate the dynamics of a thermal plant with an embedded control system in an FPGA and a PID controller using LabView software, obtaining a system with many benefits that saves costs in prototype construction, detecting and diagnosing failures before a real implementation. Another advantage of implementing HIL with an FPGA embedded system is that the automation is done in real time, allowing complex designs with shorter response times.

The Virtual systems of industrial plants are used in recent years and more frequently nowadays by the health emergency (Covid-19), since online education requires the development of virtual laboratories as a possible learning alternative [7]. In industry the virtualization of environments acquires importance, since they allow the evaluation of complex processes in various areas through the use of specialized software [8]. Within industrial automation, 3D virtual environments have been developed where it is evident how people interact with virtual elements with characteristics similar to reality [9, 10].

This article consists of 5 sections including the introduction, Sect. 2 presents the structure of the system, Sect. 3 presents the development of the virtual environment, Sect. 4 presents the results and finally Sect. 5 presents the conclusions.

2   System Structure

The paper presents the design and implementation of a virtual 3D system for a liquid filling and packaging process. The movement control programming of a robotic arm with three degrees of freedom for object manipulation is carried out. Also in the Unity 3D software, the simulation of the operation of the equipment and instruments of the industrial plant is developed, the electrical inputs and outputs that simulate sensors and actuators (HIL) are integrated which allows the control of the process with industrial equipment (Siemens S7–1200 Programmable Logic Controller).

Figure 1 shows the general structure of the implemented system.

3   Virtual Environment

For the development of the virtual environment the objects are obtained from Unity 3D sources and for the specific objects a computer aided design software was used, these

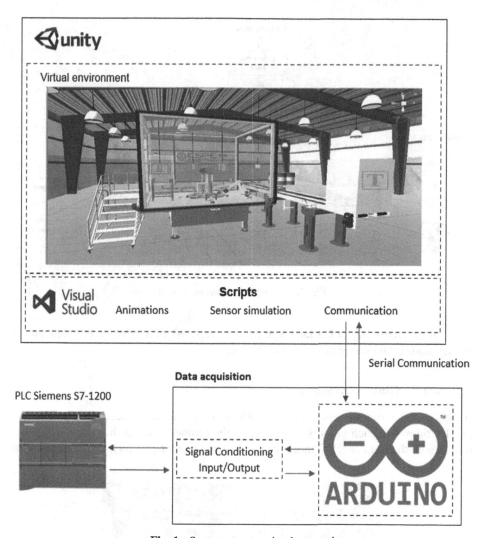

Fig. 1. System structure implemented

objects are exported to 3Ds Max software to convert them to .fbx format and use them in the virtual environment (Fig. 2); each stage of the process has objects in which the scripts are linked as components to animate the operation of sensors, actuators and elements that intervene in the automation process. In order to provide an environment similar to the real one, grass, trees, clouds, solar lighting, etc. were placed.

The virtual environment consists of 5 stages, the first one consists of dispensing glasses for the process, the second stage doses the liquid in each of the containers, the third stage seals the glasses or containers with a lid, the fourth stage is responsible for moving the sealed glasses to a container, through a robotic arm with 3 degrees of freedom and finally the fifth stage classifies the product by total weight and determines whether it is accepted or rejected. The animations of the 3D environment are made from object

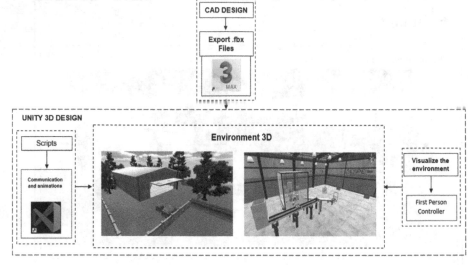

Fig. 2. Virtual environment design

oriented programming in C# language in the integrated development environment of Visual Studio. The stages are described below.

3.1 Step 1 - Glasses Dispenser

At this stage a structure was designed in which the glasses are placed and by means of an electric piston each glass is dispensed on the turntable, which has eight holes that moves with the help of a DC motor coupled to an encoder (sensor), there are also two

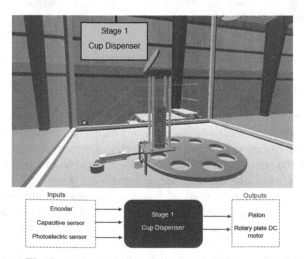

Fig. 3. Virtualization of the first stage of the process

presence sensors, a capacitive sensor to detect whether or not a glass is on the turntable and a photoelectric sensor that detects whether there are glasses in the container.

The animation of the discrete sensors is done using the tool provided by unity3D called "Collider". It allows to detect collisions produced when the meshes of the objects have some type of interaction. When the presence or absence of an object is detected, the properties of the sensor are modified and the color of the indicator LEDs is animated. Figure 3 sensors and actuators used in stage 1.

3.2 Stage 2 - Liquid Dosing

The second stage consists of a tank containing the liquid to be dosed, the amount of liquid will be measured through a level sensor located on the tank cover. By means of a photoelectric sensor, the correct position of the vessel is checked, and then the liquid is dosed; to control the amount of liquid in the vessel there is an On/Off control valve and for weight control there is a scale that shows the total weight in grams (Fig. 4).

For the variation of the level in the tank, the position on the Y-axis is considered, the scale of a cylinder is also modified according to a certain percentage (0–100%), a mapping of values is performed to determine the position and scaling of the cylinder according to the percentage of liquid in the tank; in addition, transparency and textures are added to the simulated object.

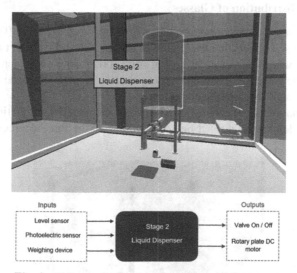

Fig. 4. Virtualization of the second stage of the process

3.3 Stage 3 - Lid Dispenser

In this stage, a photoelectric sensor is used to detect the correct position of the glasses and a capacitive sensor to detect the presence of caps on the container structure, a servomotor is included coupled to a suction cup that allows a rotation of 0 and 180 degrees, and by means of a linear actuator the glasses are sealed. Figure 5 shows the sensors and actuators involved in this stage.

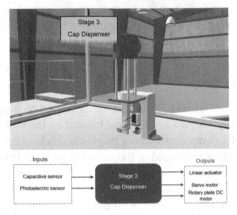

Fig. 5. Virtualization of the third stage of the process

3.4 Stage 4 - Distribution of Glasses

Three presence sensors, a robotic arm and a conveyor belt are used (Fig. 6). The first photoelectric sensor detects that the container has arrived at the correct position, so that the robotic arm with 3 degrees of freedom transports it to a container. The capacitive sensor detects the presence of containers placed in the dispenser and the last laser sensor detects the correct position of the container.

For the animation of the robotic arm, objects were added that function as pivots and contain all the elements that must move according to the three degrees of freedom of

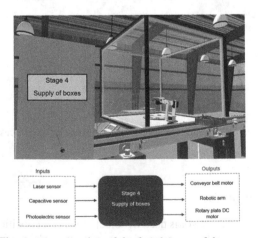

Fig. 6. Virtualization of the fourth stage of the process

the mobile manipulator, the range of movement of the degrees of freedom is between 0° and 360° according to the rotation in each axis (X, Y, Z).

3.5 Stage 5 - Product Classification

In the final stage the container is placed on the scale with the action of the conveyor belt to check that the weight of the containers is correct. A piston placed at the end of the conveyor belt rejects the product that does not comply with the established conditions, and if the product has the correct weight, the action of the conveyor belt sends it to the moving platform for transport (Fig. 7).

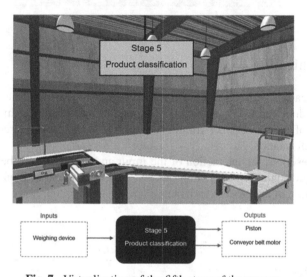

Fig. 7. Virtualization of the fifth stage of the process

3.6 Creation of the First-Person Controller (Character)

To observe the process and movement through the virtual environment, a first-person character is created. The character resource is included in the free Unity packages and must be downloaded from the Unity Assets Store.

The created character contains three essential elements, the main camera of the project with which the environment is visualized, a script with which parameters such as walking speed, jumping height, sensitivity, etc. are controlled and adjusted, and an audio source that generates the walking sounds (Fig. 8).

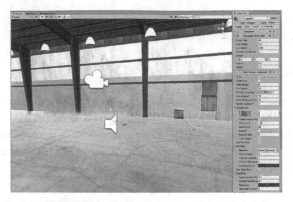

Fig. 8. First person object added to the 3D scene

4 Communication

The communication between the electronic board (Arduino) and the virtual system (Unity 3D) is done through the serial communication protocol, for this the baud rate and the name of the serial port (Arduino-Unity 3D) must be configured, ensuring the exchange of information.

Figure 9 describes the interaction of the input and output signals between the programmable logic controller, the Arduino board, and the communication with Unity 3D for the simulation of the process variables.

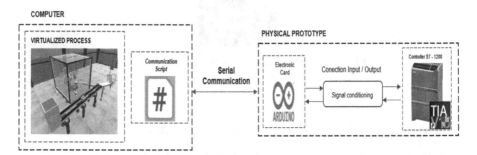

Fig. 9. Communication between virtual environment and industrial controller (PLC)

The industrial process is animated by means of scripts that contain the programming for the elements that make up the virtual environment, each script communicates with the main script, which guarantees a global access point without the need to instantiate several times the 3D object containing the programming. Through the script that establishes the communication, the data is added to a text variable to exchange the status information of the sensors and actuators in the established protocol.

5 Results

For the validation of the results, the automation of the process is carried out by means of the Siemens S7-1200 programmable logic controller and the operation of each of the virtual stages is checked according to the programming carried out in the PLC, through the exchange of sensor and actuator signals.

To automate the virtual process through the PLC it is necessary to know the process, determine the number of inputs and outputs corresponding to the system instrumentation and understand the functionality of each of the stages.

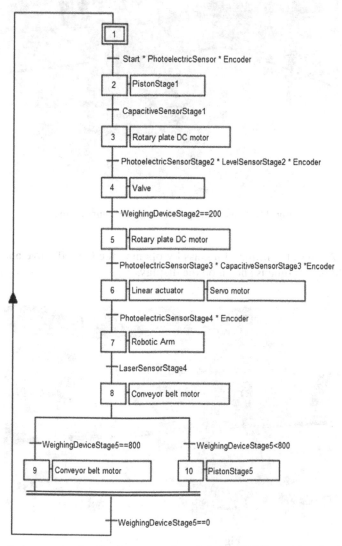

Fig. 10. Grafcet programming for the automation of the liquid filling and packaging process.

Once the signals from the simulated sensors were connected to the respective inputs of the PLC, each action of the actuators was programmed according to the sequential operation of each stage of the simulated process. The universal programming language for PLC Grafcet is used for the automation of the process as shown in Fig. 10.

Figure 11 shows the first stage implemented and the capacitive sensor indicator LEDs (Red and Green) are on because they detect the presence of glasses, and the piston and the DC motor that moves the rotary table are used as outputs.

Fig. 11. Stage 1 in operation (Color figure online)

Figure 12 shows the filling of a glass by opening the On/Off valve and the current liquid weight in real time is shown on the display.

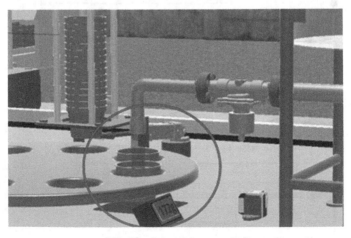

Fig. 12. Stage 2 in operation

Stage 3 verifies the operation of the capacitive sensor and the photoelectric sensor, and as outputs the linear actuator and the servo motor; Fig. 13 shows the action of the linear actuator and the suction cup sealing the lid of the vessel.

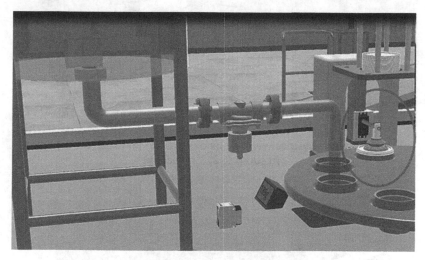

Fig. 13. Stage 3 in operation

In the fourth stage, the movement control of the robotic arm is observed according to the sequence programmed in the PLC, to manipulate the glass and place it in the respective positions of the container.

Figure 14 shows the programmed sequence of the robotic arm to place the first glass in the container.

In the last stage, the weight of the product lot is verified (accepted or rejected).

In Fig. 15(a) the balance measures the weight composed of four glasses of 200 g each, when measuring 800g the lot is accepted. Figure 15(b) shows that the balance measures 700 g, so the lot is considered rejected.

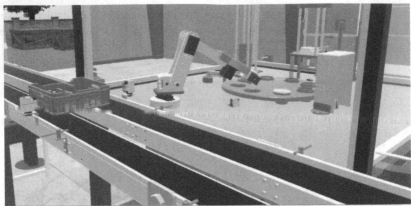

(a) First motion sequence with angles of 30°,123° and 103° for degrees of freedom 1, 2, 3 respectively.

(b) First motion sequence with angles of 183°,120° and 79° for degrees of freedom 1, 2, 3 respectively.

Fig. 14. Programmed sequence of the robotic arm to place the first glass in the container.

Finally, Fig. 16 shows the product classified according to total weight, two containers of product were considered as accepted and one rejected.

The implemented system is tested by users of the automation area, who express that the virtual environment is easy to understand and intuitive, the stages are well organized and with the necessary information for a correct operation, as well as a contribution to the training in industrial automation through the use of PLC and Grafcet programming.

The implementation of the HIL technique allows the generation of electrical signals from sensors and actuators (standard voltage signals), which will allow the virtual system to be automated with PLCs from different manufacturers.

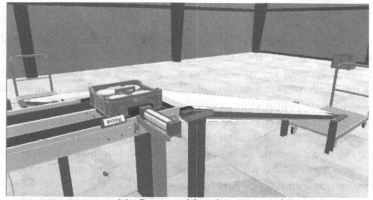

(a) Lot considered as accepted

(b) Lot rejected, weight < 800 grams

Fig. 15. Stage 5 in operation

Fig. 16. Classified final product

6 Conclusions

The virtual system implemented is a low-cost proposal for training in sequential process automation, the animations of the 5 stages are performed correctly (simulation of sensors, actuators, components of the virtual environment). Hardware in the Loop integration allows the use of physical industrial controllers (PLC S7-1200), providing users with more familiarity with industrial processes than a simple simulation. In addition, it was verified that there is synchrony in the execution times (controller-virtual environment).

The system implemented through the Hardware In The Loop simulation technique allowed the virtualization of the industrial process and its automation with the use of a real PLC. The research conducted will help training in the programming of logic controllers for industrial process automation and familiarization with the behavior of sensors and actuators in a virtual way. The instrumentation and all types of industrial elements used in the virtual environment were designed to be as close to reality as possible in terms of appearance and physical behavior.

The operation of the system was validated through the programming of the five stages that make up the process in the programmable logic controller Siemens S7-1200, and the automation sequence was fulfilled in real time through the correct operation of sensors and actuators simulated in each of the stages of the process.

Acknowledgements. The authors would like to thank the Universidad de las Fuerzas Armadas ESPE for the support for the development of this work, especially the project 2020-PIC-017-CTE "Simulación de proceso industriales, mediante la técnica Hardware in the Loop, para el desarrollo de prácticas en Automatización Industrial".

References

1. Páez Logreira, H., Zabala Campo, V., Zamora Musa, R.: Análisis y actualización del programa de la asignatura Automatización Industrial en la formación profesional de ingenieros electrónicos. Revista Educación En Ingeniería **11**(21), 39–44 (2016)
2. Panchi Olivo, S.F., Herrera Sinchiguano, W.P.: Diseño y construcción de un módulo didáctico de un sistema de automatización de llenado y envasado de sólidos, utilizando sensores fotoelécricos,capacitivos,encoders,galgas extensiométricas y brazos robóticos , para el laboratorio de redes industriales y control de procesos de la Universidad de las Fuerzas Armadas ESPE (2015)
3. Wältermann, P.: Hardware-in-the-loop: the technology for testing electronic controls in automotive engineering (2009)
4. Santo Guanoluisa, L., Tandalla Arequipa, R.: Collaborative Control of Mobile Manipulator Robots through the Hardware in the Loop Technique (2021)
5. Pruna, E., Jimenez, I., Escobar, I.: Hardware-in-the-loop of a flow plant embedded in FPGA, for process control. In: Reddy, A.N.R., Marla, D., Simic, M., Favorskaya, M.N., Satapathy, S.C. (eds.) Intelligent Manufacturing and Energy Sustainability. SIST, vol. 169, pp. 181–189. Springer, Singapore (2020). https://doi.org/10.1007/978-981-15-1616-0_17
6. Caldas Flautero, O., Jiménez Gómez, S., Mejía Ruda, E., Avilés Sánchez, O., Amaya Hurtado, D.: Control system of a plant embedded in FPGA using hardware in the loop. Dyna, **80**(179), 51–59 (2013). http://www.scielo.org.co/scielo.php?script=sci_arttext&pid=s0012-73532013000300006&lng=en&tlng=es. Accessed 11 June 2021

7. Ray, S., Srivastava, S.: Virtualization of science education: a lesson from the COVID-19 pandemic. J. Proteins Proteomics **11**(2), 77–80 (2020). https://doi.org/10.1007/s42485-020-00038-7
8. Kao, C.H.: Testing and evaluation framework for virtualization technologies. Computing **99**(7), 657–677 (2016). https://doi.org/10.1007/s00607-016-0517-6
9. Rosero, M., Pogo, R., Pruna, E., Andaluz, V.H., Escobar, I.: Immersive environment for training on industrial emergencies. In: De Paolis, L.T., Bourdot, P. (eds.) AVR 2018. LNCS, vol. 10851, pp. 451–466. Springer, Cham (2018). https://doi.org/10.1007/978-3-319-95282-6_33
10. Pruna, E., Rosero, M., Pogo, R., Escobar, I., Acosta, J.: Virtual reality as a tool for the cascade control learning. In: De Paolis, L.T., Bourdot, P. (eds.) AVR 2018. LNCS, vol. 10850, pp. 243–251. Springer, Cham (2018). https://doi.org/10.1007/978-3-319-95270-3_20

Virtual Environment for Control Strategies Testing: A Hardware-in-the-Loop Approach

Silvia Alpúsig[✉], Edwin Pruna, and Ivón Escobar

Universidad de las Fuerzas Armadas ESPE, Sangolquí, Ecuador
{sealpusig,eppruna,ipescobar}@espe.edu.ec

Abstract. This work presents the development of a system based on the Hardware-In-the-Loop (HIL) simulation to carry out tests of controllers within a virtual environment consisting of a fully characterized industrial plant to emulate its real behavior. The virtual environment has been implemented using Blender and the Unity3D graphics engine, achieving a high level of realism in the models and their characteristics. In addition, a data acquisition method has been implemented through the generation and reading of electrical signals that allows the communication between the virtual plant and the controller that needs to be tested.

Keywords: Virtual environment · Hardware-in-the-Loop · Unity3D · Processes control

1 Introduction

The control strategies used in the process industry, such as manufacturing plants, nuclear plants, etc., are decisive for the optimal performance of each stage that make up a system. The control algorithms, designed to execute tasks autonomously, require a preliminary validation before commissioning the controller, for which they must be thoroughly tested in order to debug errors and guarantee their permanent and reliable execution [1]. However, the constant growth of modern control systems, in terms of size and complexity, hinders the logistics for verification based on testing the controllers within a physical plant that requires sensors, actuators and mechanical systems, which results in higher time consumption, high implementation costs and risk of equipment damage [2, 3].

In this context, is essential an efficient environment for the creation and validation of prototypes that groups all the user's requirements, capable of providing relevant data so that the system verification is effective and truthful. Therefore, it is required a much more complete simulation than the traditional, which can represent the characteristics of the system in terms of production, components workflow and machine efficiency together with the control algorithm. This need can be solved through the Hardware-In-The-Loop (HIL) technique, which is a real-time simulation of all the subsystems that make up a complex engineering system, which are modeled and coupled through numerical models for a complete representation. This simulation can be carried out in an embedded system or in a computer [4–7]. Thus, a control algorithm can be validated in a realistic way using the simulated sensors and actuators to verify the response of the

© Springer Nature Switzerland AG 2021
L. T. De Paolis et al. (Eds.): AVR 2021, LNCS 12980, pp. 588–602, 2021.
https://doi.org/10.1007/978-3-030-87595-4_43

system once the controller acts on them, this through a communication interface between the simulated system and the actual controller involved in the HIL architecture [5].

Nowadays, HIL simulation is widely used because of its low cost, details level, high effectiveness and safety that offers in various fields like electronics, robotics, automotive industry, energy industry and, recently, in education of processes control and automatisms [5–13]. Generally, these applications use a graphical interface that, in many cases, does not allow a realistic perception of the system or even dispenses with it. This is a problem when considering and evaluating different critical scenarios within the operation of the plant and, therefore, the ability of the controller to compensate disturbances. In addition, if these applications are used for educational purposes, the absence of an adequate graphical interface difficults the understanding of the system and therefore the learning process.

The alternative that some developers have used recently is the implementation of virtual environments, which allow the relevant data of the simulated system to be monitored and analyzed. Mainly, applications have been developed for testing vehicles and robotic platforms [14–18]. Using virtual environments for educational purposes is a teaching-learning method that has been studied and applied successfully at various levels due to the benefits it offers by providing experiences that cause a great impact on students. This strategy can take users to scenarios that are not easily accessible, all in a safe way and with the possibility of remaining in them for a long time, carrying out specific tasks that are useful to acquire knowledge [19–22]. In the case of engineering education, so-called "digital twins" are frequently used, which are virtual replicas of products or processes, including their physical and functional characteristics, to be used for different purposes such as analysis, simulation, control, improvement of processes, among others [23, 24].

Based on the fundamentals described in previous paragraphs, this article describes the development of a system based on Hardware-In-The-Loop simulation to test controllers using an interactive virtual environment that emulates the behavior of an industrial plant. The system will allow the user to manipulate the components of the plant to evaluate the response of the controller to critical scenarios and in a random manner. Communication between the virtual plant and the controller is implemented through the generation of electrical signals that represent the data from sensors and actuators. The virtual environment has been designed in Blender and the simulation, which includes the characterization of the plant components, has been fully implemented in Unity3D graphics engine. This article is organized into V sections, including the Introduction. Section 2 describes the structure of the system. Section 3 details the development of the system. In Sect. 4 the results are presented, including the performance analysis of a control algorithm after its testing through the system. Finally, the conclusions are presented in Sect. 5.

2 System Structure

The developed system, based on HIL simulation, uses specialized hardware and software tools that allow an optimal implementation and effective coupling between each of the stages. Figure 1 presents a diagram that describes the interaction between the devices and the programs used.

Fig. 1. System structure

The first stage consists of the simulation of an industrial plant, which is implemented in a computer, specifically in the Unity3D graphics engine. This plant is characterized based on a mathematical model which allows a simulation of its response in real time. This simulation includes all the inherent peculiarities of the real system, in this way it is possible to evaluate different critical scenarios interactively. To achieve this, it was implemented the ability to go through the entire environment, opening and closing valves, manipulate the setpoint, monitor plant parameters, etc.

Then, the data acquisition stage is implemented based on Arduino MEGA 2560 board, which serves to transform the simulation data into electrical signals to be used by the external devices that need to be tested. Also, this card allows the reading of voltage signals, which are converted into useful numerical data for the simulation. In addition, a signal conditioning stage is used to make them usable by any controller for its validation.

Finally, given the characteristics and approach of the proposed system, the use of industrial controllers is proposed for the verification of control algorithms.

3 Application Development

3.1 Virtual Environment

The virtual environment is designed from a steam generation system that uses a boiler. In general, steam generation is carried out by means of a boiler that evaporates the water inside, which has been previously treated in a previous stage. The control objective is the regulation of the water level in the boiler drum, for which a pneumatic control valve, level and flow transmitters are used. This system has been chosen for all the instrumentation it requires, which is beneficial to be used in engineering education, in addition, the variables involved in the process allow to test different control techniques to evaluate its performance in a comparative form. For this, the P&ID diagram of the system is taken as a basis, which is shown in Fig. 2.

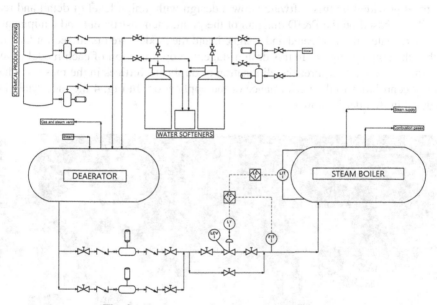

Fig. 2. Steam generation system P&ID diagram

The development of the virtual environment consists of several stages in which different specialized programs are used for the design of the plant and its subsequent characterization. The general workflow, used to create the environment, is described in Fig. 3.

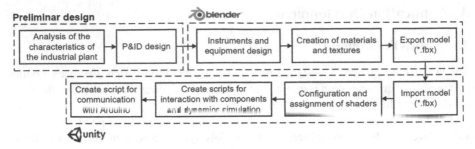

Fig. 3. Virtual environment design workflow

Design of the Industrial Plant

The 3D modeling of the industrial plant is completely implemented in Blender since the tools provided by this software allow a design with a high level of detail and realism. Then, based on the P&ID diagram of the plant, each instrument and equipment is designed, materials are created and assigned, and the models are optimized for later use within the graphic engine. In this design stage, the optimization of each model is very important, that is, it requires the elimination of duplicate vertices in the meshes, which greatly contributes to the performance of the application. In Fig. 4 the industrial plant modeled in Blender is shown.

Fig. 4. Industrial plant designed in Blender

The software used for 3D design allows modelling of objects with a high level of detail, which contributes to the realism of the application. In Fig. 5 the level and flow transmitters modeled in Blender are shown.

For each model, a pivot point was configured in a consistent location. This setting is important for creating animations and implementing user interaction with the objects.

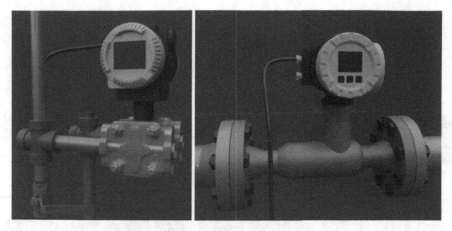

Fig. 5. Level transmitter (left) and flow transmitter (right) design

For example, in the actuator of a manual valve it is required that the pivot point be in the center of it to be able to execute its opening and closing in a correct and natural way, as shown in Fig. 6.

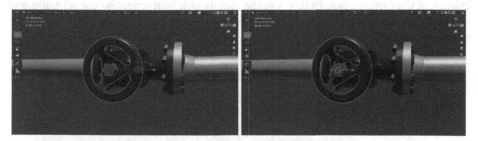

Fig. 6. Displaced pivot point (left) is corrected to rotate valve actuator on its axis (right)

The model of the industrial plant is exported in FBX format, which can be imported into Unity3D.

Characterization, Animation and Simulation
The plant model is imported in FBX format in Unity3D, where all the components are characterized. For this, materials or shaders are created and configured for each of the models since those created in Blender are not compatible with the graphics engine. Then, the lighting sources, shadows, etc. are configured. These details are necessary to achieve the desired realism, see Fig. 7.

Fig. 7. Virtual environment developed in Unity3D

An HMI (Human-Machine Interface) has been designed for the monitoring and control of the virtual plant. In this way the user is able to manipulate the set-point and monitor the response of the system. The windows that make up the HMI have been created using UI (User Interface) tools such as buttons, sliders and texts, see Fig. 8.

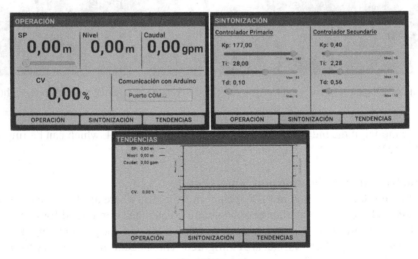

Fig. 8. HMI windows

The data of the flow and level transmitters are presented using UI tools as in the case of the HMI, see Fig. 9.

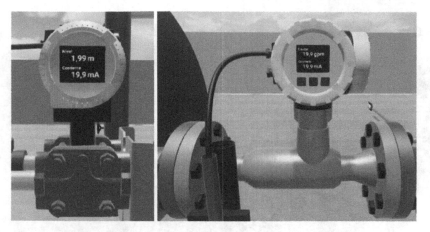

Fig. 9. Level transmitter (left) and flow transmitter (right) data

The control valve has been animated through a script that controls its stroke from an input data in a range from 0 to 100%. Thus, the movement of the actuator and the deflection of the pressure gauge that indicates the pressure supplied to the valve have been implemented, as shown in Fig. 10.

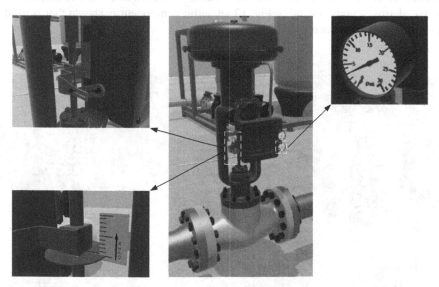

Fig. 10. Control valve animation

Manual valves are interactive, so they can be opened and closed proportionally as required by the user. To achieve this, a collider must be assigned to the valve actuator and the respective script that will allow interaction with the object, as shown in Fig. 11.

Characteristic sounds for industrial equipment are added to enhance user experience and application realism. These sounds are obtained from real equipment and are placed on

Fig. 11. Interactable manual valve

the corresponding models within the application. In this way, through the tools provided by Unity3D, it is possible that the audio clips are reproduced repetitively and propagate in a realistic way through the environment. Sounds have been added to buttons, switches, pumps, alarms, among others. In Fig. 12 an audio component is shown that is used to reproduce the sounds required for that area.

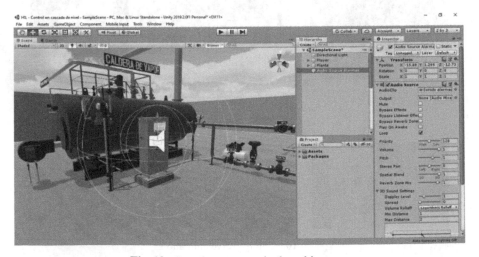

Fig. 12. Sound component in the cabinet area

Once the interactive characteristics of the environment have been defined, the script that allows the simulation of the dynamic response of the plant is implemented. For this, the behavior is modeled through an equation that involves the parameters of a real plant. In this way, the behavior of the plant is approximated through a mathematical model which allows a simulation in real time for the testing of controllers. The data produced by the simulation in each sampling period is reflected in the corresponding instruments and is used to reproduce the animations previously configured. In Fig. 13, it is possible to observe the output of the system (water level) before a step input and the data corresponding to each process variable in the respective instruments and in the HMI.

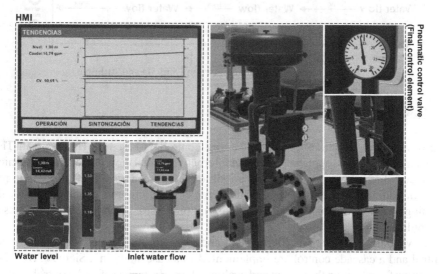

Fig. 13. Step response of the system

In this way, a suitable virtual industrial process is obtained to be used in tests with controllers of all kinds.

3.2   Data Reading and Writing

For testing purposes, a communication interface is required that allows data exchange between the physical controller and the implemented simulation. For this case, an Arduino MEGA 2560 board is used due to the features it offers and its availability in the market.

The simulation data is sent to the Arduino through serial communication, this data is transformed into DC electrical signals to be used by the controller. In the same way, Arduino is capable of reading DC signals to transform them into numerical data usable in the simulation. At this stage, it is necessary to implement signal conditioning since Arduino generates voltages as PWM and these are not suitable to be read by some controllers. In Fig. 14, a diagram is shown describing the data exchange between the simulation in Unity3D and the controller. These numerical data are transformed into character strings for transmission, in this way the sending is optimal and the resolution of the data is maintained.

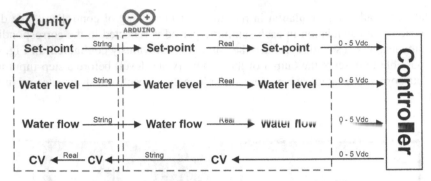

Fig. 14. Data management between Unity3D and Arduino

4   Results

The developed application focuses on testing controllers based on Hardware-In-The-Loop simulation. This application uses an interactive virtual environment as a graphical interface, which allows to recreate the possible critical scenarios of the process in real time. In addition, this system can be used for engineering education, mainly in the teaching of automation and control of industrial processes, given the characteristics of the application.

To validate the operation of the system and its performance, a classical single-loop control and a cascade control are implemented as a case study in a Siemens S7–1200 PLC to perform tests on the system and evaluate the performance of each control strategy in a comparative way. To carry out the analysis of each control method, the data of the variables of interest of the process have been obtained and graphs have been generated to comparing the results, in addition, a disturbance is applied to the process that consists of the closure of a manual valve in the steam boiler feed pipe, see Fig. 15.

Fig. 15. Application of a disturbance in the water inflow

It was used the PID algorithm for the implemented controllers in both control architectures. In Table 1, the controllers tunning constants are presented, it was used the Lambda tunning method for all cases. This method uses an intermediate parameter which allows the user to adjust the output until achieve the required performance.

Table 1. Tunning constants for each control architecture

Control architecture	Kp	Ti	Td
Single loop control	12.4326	15.4	1.0214
Cascade control			
Primary controller	6.4292	15.4	1.0214
Secondary controller	0.399	2.28	0.5614

In Fig. 16, the results of a test performed to evaluate the response of the system for the single loop control strategy and for the cascade control are presented. The tests were carried out under the same conditions and the data were exported to interpret them graphically and analytically. In addition, the reaction of the system to the applied disturbance can be observed, which complements the analysis.

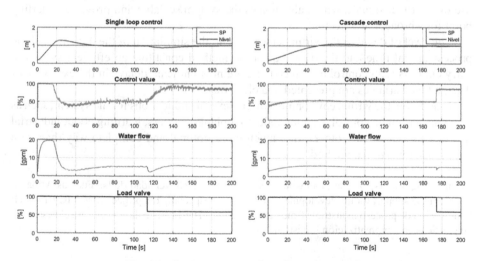

Fig. 16. Single loop control vs. Cascade control

From this test, performance parameters can be calculated that will allow choosing the ideal control algorithm for regulating the water level of the boiler drum. Table 2 shows the parameters that allow evaluating the performance of each control strategy, this values can be calculated through the previous graph or using a software to analize a data set.

Table 2. Performance parameters for each control strategy

Control strategy	Overshoot	Establishment time	IAE
Single loop control	30.61%	62.27 s	18.62
Cascade control	6.93%	102.1 s	24.56

As has been seen, the system allows the control algorithms to be tested to be widely evaluated since their performance can be observed in real time and it is also possible to export the data corresponding to the process variables for a detailed analysis.

5 Conclusion

The developed application allows to test controllers in a satisfactory way, through the simulation of the dynamic characteristics of a steam generation system using a boiler. This simulation, which uses the Hardware-In-The-Loop paradigm, use an interactive virtual environment as a graphical interface, which allows manipulating various elements of the plant to widely evaluate the performance of a control algorithm, as observed in previous sections. It should be noted that the system allows the testing of all types of controllers in a transparent way, without requiring additional programming thanks to the use of electrical signals, which also makes the system scalable and provides a starting point for a broader architecture.

The level of detail of the virtual environment, the simulation of the dynamics of the process in real time and the data acquisition method constitute an efficient system to carry out tests with controllers, since there are no significant delays in the exchange of data and the variables are presented in a clear way.

In addition, the virtual environment offers several applications for the system, such as teaching automatic control, training industrial plant operators, learning about industrial instrumentation, among others, in a much more optimal and complete way than with traditional educational methods.

Acknowledgements. The authors would like to thank the Universidad de las Fuerzas Armadas ESPE for the support for the development of this work, especially the project 2020-PIC-017-CTE "Simulación de proceso industriales, mediante la técnica Hardware in the Loop, para el desarrollo de prácticas en Automatización Industrial".

References

1. Fernández, B., Blanco, E., Merezhin, A.: Testing & verification of PLC code for process control. In: Proceedings of ICALEPCS (2013)
2. Jiang, W., Sun, L., Chen, Y., Ma, H., Hashimoto, S.: A hardware-in-the-loop-on-chip development system for teaching and development of dynamic systems. Electronics **10**(7), 801 (2021)

3. Zhao, L., Roh, M.I., Ham, S.H.: Performance analysis of an active heave compensation system on an offshore supply vessel using the hardware-in-the-loop simulation. J. Mar. Sci. Technol. **26**(5), 678–691 (2018)

4. Park, S.C., Park, C.M., Wang, G.N., Kwak, J., Yeo, S.: PLCStudio: simulation based PLC code verification. In: 2008 Winter Simulation Conference, pp. 222–228. IEEE, December 2008

5. Rad, C., Maties, V., Hancu, O., Lapusan, C.: Hardware-In-The-Loop (HIL) simulation used for testing actuation system of a 2-DOF parallel robot. In: Applied Mechanics and Materials, vol. 162, pp. 334–343. Trans Tech Publications Ltd. (2012)

6. Zamiri, E., Sanchez, A., Yushkova, M., Martínez-García, M.S., de Castro, A.: Comparison of different design alternatives for hardware-in-the-loop of power converters. Electronics **10**(8), 926 (2021)

7. Muraspahic, S., Gu, P., Farji, L., Iskandarani, Y., Shi, P., Karimi, H.: Hardware-in-the-loop implementation for an active heave compensated drawworks. Open Eng. **2**(2), 201–211 (2012)

8. Pătră, N., Tomus, A.M., Angela, E., Vali, S.: Creating hardware-in-the-loop system using virtual instrumentation. In: 2011 12th International Carpathian Control Conference (ICCC), pp. 286–291. IEEE, May 2011

9. Dosoftei, C.C., Popovici, A.T., Sacaleanu, P.R., Gherghel, P.M., Budaciu, C.: Hardware in the loop topology for an omnidirectional mobile robot using matlab in a robot operating system environment. Symmetry **13**(6), 969 (2021)

10. Sala, A., Bondia, J.: Teaching experience with hardware-in-the-loop simulation. IFAC Proceedings Volumes **39**(6), 123–128 (2006)

11. Osen, O.L.: On the use of hardware-in-the-loop for teaching automation engineering. In: 2019 IEEE Global Engineering Education Conference (EDUCON), pp. 1308–1315. IEEE, April 2019

12. Tang, X., Xi, Y.: Application of hardware-in-loop in teaching power electronic course based on a low-cost platform. Comput. Appl. Eng. Educ. **28**(4), 965–978 (2020)

13. Tejado, I., Serrano, J., Pérez, E., Torres, D., Vinagre, B.M.: Low-cost hardware-in-the-loop testbed of a mobile robot to support learning in automatic control and robotics. IFAC-PapersOnLine **49**(6), 242–247 (2016)

14. Zhang, Z., Zhang, M., Chang, Y., Aziz, E.S., Esche, S.K., Chassapis, C.: Collaborative virtual laboratory environments with hardware in the loop. In: Cyber-Physical Laboratories in Engineering and Science Education (pp. 363–402). Springer, Cham (2018). Doi: https://doi.org/10.1007/978-3-319-76935-6_15

15. Merkisz, J., Grzeszczyk, R.: Virtual reality and hardware in-the-loop testing methods in the ecall in-vehicle module research and verification. In: Advanced Microsystems for Automotive Applications 2010, pp. 347–356. Springer, Heidelberg (2010)

16. Bin Hasnan, K., Saesar, L.B., Herawan, T.: A hardware-in-the-loop simulation and test for unmanned ground vehicle on indoor environment. Procedia Eng. **29**, 3904–3908 (2012)

17. Lee, G., Ha, S., Jung, J.I.: Integrating driving hardware-in-the-loop simulator with large-scale VANET simulator for evaluation of cooperative ECO-driving system. Electronics **9**(10), 1645 (2020)

18. Wang, Z., Li, J., Yang, C., Yang, Y.: A hardware-in-the-loop simulation platform for distributed UAV swarms. In Journal of Physics: Conference Series, vol. 1678, No. 1, p. 012006). IOP Publishing, November 2020

19. Pruna, E., Rosero, M., Pogo, R., Escobar, I., Acosta, J.: Virtual Reality as a Tool for the Cascade Control Learning. In International Conference on Augmented Reality, Virtual Reality and Computer Graphics, pp. 243–251. Springer, Cham (2018). Doi: https://doi.org/10.1007/978-3-319-95270-3_20

20. Santos, I., Soares, L., Carvalho, F., Amaral, W., Raposo, A.: Virtual Reality Engineering Workflow

21. Philippe, S., et al.: Multimodal teaching, learning and training in virtual reality: a review and case study. Virtual Real. Intell. Hardware **2**(5), 421–442 (2020)
22. Holly, M., Pirker, J., Resch, S., Brettschuh, S., Gütl, C.: Designing VR experiences-expectations for teaching and learning in VR. Educ. Technol. Soc. **24**(2), 107–119 (2021)
23. Dozortsev, V., Agafonov, D., Slastenov, I., Baulin, E.: Digital twins in industrial process engineering
24. Lin, T., et al.: Dynamic design method of digital twin process model driven by knowledge-evolution machining features. International Journal of Production Research, 1–19 (2021)

Inspection and Verification Training System of Production Lines in Automated Processes, Through Virtual Environments

Brayan Pila, Efraín Alcoser, Edwin Pruna(⊠), and Ivón Escobar

Universidad de las Fuerzas Armadas ESPE, Sangolquí, Ecuador
{bdpila,realcoser,eppruna,ipescobar}@espe.edu.ec

Abstract. This work presents the development of a training system in an interactive virtual environment, for the inspection and verification of a bottled bottle, in the final production line of a bottling plant, through the use of an artificial vision camera applied in a plant. Virtual, which presents the emulation of the quality control process in an industry. In addition, the system allows training within an industrial plant for the detection of faults such as the amount of liquid, lid alignment and label placement, in commercially manufactured products, and mainly in the development of skills for the configuration of a machine vision camera.

The training system has been created using a CAD tool and the Unity3D graphics engine, which provide a high level of realism, offering immersion and interaction between the components of the environment and the user.

Keywords: Virtual environment · Unity 3D · Bottler

1 Introduction

Currently in the industries, significant improvements are being made for the automation of the production and operation areas of the companies with the aim of improving economic efficiency, using the integration of applications that replace manual processes, accelerating the execution time of the tasks and eliminating human mistakes that can be made [1].

Industrial automation is defined as a set of technologies that result in machine and industrial system operations without significant human intervention and achieve superior performance over manual operation [2]. Automation marks a new era worldwide, which will probably force industries to invest and innovate in new technologies that allow them to develop products in shorter times, without losing sight of the inspection and verification of the production line for control. quality of finished products.

In the context of automation, inspection and verification of finished products for quality control is of great importance in production processes, this process was carried out by people with prior knowledge to find such defects, where they spent a large amount of time, energy and money checking products manually. However, traditional inspection

© Springer Nature Switzerland AG 2021
L. T. De Paolis et al. (Eds.): AVR 2021, LNCS 12980, pp. 603–620, 2021.
https://doi.org/10.1007/978-3-030-87595-4_44

can be replaced, especially if it is done in an automated way in most manufacturing industries to ensure that poor quality or defective products do not reach the end consumer [3].

Increasing demands for product quality and efficiency make the introduction of automated inspection systems necessary. These systems employ image processing techniques and can quantitatively characterize complex sizes, shapes, color, and textural properties of products [4], in an industry it is essential to establish a safe and reliable work environment, to efficiently execute each of the stages of industrial processes, currently there are training systems for the inspection and verification stage for quality control, these systems provide user experience, gives them confidence and improves their skills for optimal performance [5], very few industries have these technological training systems due to the high economic cost required for the acquisition and implementation of these equipment in an industrial plant.

Virtual reality (VR) is a commonly computer-generated or assisted three-dimensional simulation of some aspect of the real or fictional world, in which the user has the sensation of belonging to or interacting with that synthetic environment. Currently in the scientific community there are investigations with virtual reality oriented to automation, these virtual environments generate learning environments that will allow the development of skills and competencies in the user's professional field [6–10].

Considering the high cost and difficult access to a physical training system, and the difficulty to carry out quality tests in plants in continuous operation, due to the economic loss that it would generate; The present work describes the development of a virtual environment of a beverage bottling plant developed in Unity 3D software, where the operator can interact and have an immersion with the different processes of the plant and in conjunction with an artificial vision camera (hardware) that allows to emulate the inspection and verification of the bottles packaged as a final product for the respective quality control. Next, in Fig. 1 the structure of the system is presented.

2   Development

The virtual environment of a beverage bottling plant is developed through CAD design techniques, and the Unity 3D software to digitize the terrain and develop the operating animations of the elements of the industrial process, for the creation of the industrial environment is considered the basic process of packaging water bottles, considering the stages of filling, sealing and labeling of bottles. For the design, an instrumentation piping diagram (PI&D) was generated, according to the verification of the operation of the industrial process in question, the following figure shows the P&ID diagram of the bottle packaging process.

For the creation of the virtual environment, the realism and interaction of all the elements that make up the system are important, where several design stages are considered, based mainly on the virtualization of its elements through specialized programs in the characterization of 3D objects and all the Data corresponding to the industrial variables of the virtual plant are managed through the Modbus TCP/IP protocol. Figure 4 shows the diagram that describes the implementation process of the virtual reality training system (Figs. 2 and 3).

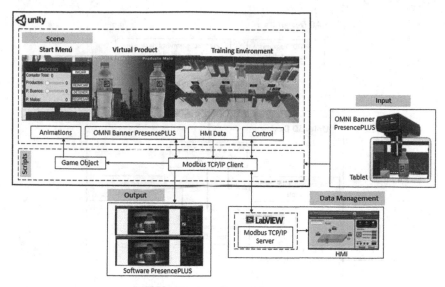

Fig. 1. The structure of the system.

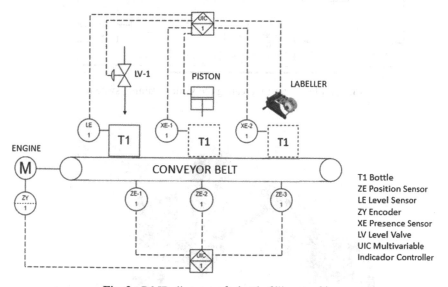

Fig. 2. P&ID diagram of a bottle filling machine.

2.1 CAD Design

At this stage, the SolidWorks Software develops the 3D CAD design that corresponds to each of the three stages: filling, sealing and labeling, creating individual elements that are incorporated into the virtual environment of the plant as shown in Fig. 4, and using the 3dsMax program, a file with the Flimbox format (*. fbx) is obtained that is compatible with the Unity graphics engine, as shown in Fig. 5.

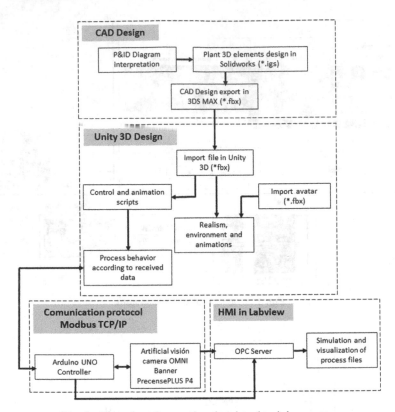

Fig. 3. Flow chart for creating the virtual training system.

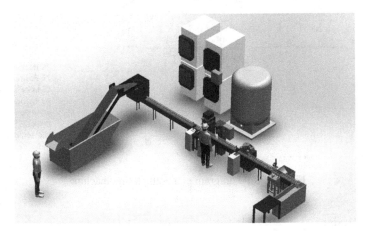

Fig. 4. CAD design made in SolidWorks.

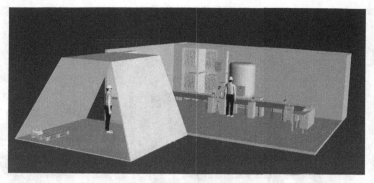

Fig. 5. CAD design exported to 3dsMax.

2.2 Unity 3D Environment

The file (*. Fbx) is imported to the Unity3D software where the assembly and assignment of materials of all the components is carried out to develop the virtual environment, an important aspect to generate a high level of realism, and therefore of interactive immersion with the user, adding their details, lighting, shadows, etc. to the environment. These details do not affect the functionality of the process, but provide greater user comfort and realism for the industrial environment, as show in Fig. 6 and Fig. 7.

Fig. 6. Virtual environment developed in Unity 3D.

2.3 Virtualized Bottled Bottle

In the packaged bottle is where the inspection and verification analysis of the quality in production is carried out, for this reason the 3D development of said final product obtained from the production line is essential, two specific elements are developed for each process, detailing among them an item in good condition that corresponds to a

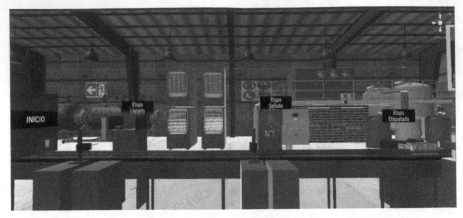

Fig. 7. Stages of filling, stamping and labeling virtualized in Unity 3D.

product accepted in the production batch without any failure and another item in poor condition that corresponds to a rejected product in the production batch with any failure respectively, where three characteristics were designed that were taken in counts as failures to classify the final product.

The production error 1 designed in Unity3D is the detection of the liquid fill level, in Fig. 8 (a) the state corresponding to a bottle without any failure is shown and in Fig. 8 (b) the bottle is shown with an excess liquid error.

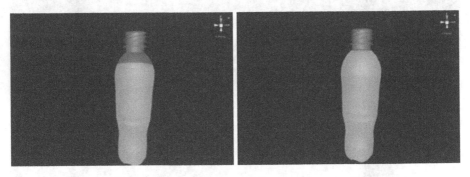

(a) Bottle without production error.   (b) Bottle with excess liquid error.

Fig. 8. Design of production error 1 in Unity3D.

Production error 2 designed in Unity3D is the misplacing of the bottle cap, in Fig. 9 (a) the state corresponding to a bottle without the production error is shown and in Fig. 9 (b) it is shown presents the bottle with a cap placement error.

Production error 3 designed in Unity3D is the erroneous printing of the QR code on the bottle label, in Fig. 10 (a) the status corresponding to a bottle without the production error is shown and in Fig. 10 (b) the bottle with the QR code printing failure is presented.

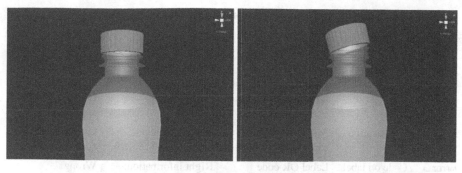

(a) Bottle without production error.   (b) Bottle with cap misplacement error.

Fig. 9. Design of production error 2 in Unity3D.

(a) Bottle without production error.   (b) Bottle with printing error in the QR code
Correct Code: Fresh   Incorrect code: <

Fig. 10. Design of production error 3 in Unity3D.

Table 1 shows the specifications of each production error, for this program-ming scripts are developed that allow the random generation of bottles with errors corresponding to their design.

2.4   Avatar Design

It is essential to be able to mobilize within the virtual environment to visualize the process in detail, for this a player or character is created which is the basis for user interaction with movement within the 3D environment, for the creation of this character all were designed the characteristics of the avatar and its animations in Adobe Fuse see Fig. 11, and thus to be able to integrate it to Unity3D, the avatar has an appearance according to the environment to carry out control and visualization tasks of the bottling plant.

Once the character and its animations have been imported into Unity, an animation controller called "Animator Controller" is created in the folder tree of our project, creating a movement diagram that allows the character to walk forward, walk backward, turn, jump, etc., in addition, a vision tool is added, which is available in Unity3D in the project

Table 1. Errors in the output of the final product - water bottle.

Error	Name	Specification	Factor of acceptance	Factor of rejection
Error 1	Liquid level	Failure in the existence of more or less amount of liquid	Correct Liquid Level: 600 ml approx	Greater than 600 ml Less than 600 ml approx
Error 2	Cap location	Failure to place the cap on the bottle	Correct location degrees: 180° approx	Greater than 180° approx
Error 3	Code on label	Label QR code printing failure	Right information: Fresh	Wrong information: <

Fig. 11. Avatar designed in Adobe Fuse.

manager as "Camera", the camera options were configured in the third person to be able to add it to the avatar through a programming script, it is observed in Fig. 12 the creation of the vision tool within Unity 3D.

The avatar allows the interaction of the menu with the virtual process, where the options are created to select the total batch of products that need to be generated, selecting among them how many good and bad products need to be generated for the respective process, a total counter is created of all the final products that come out in that production line, in addition to implementing the navigation buttons as shown in Fig. 13.

2.5 Animation of the 3D Virtual Environment

The virtual environment was integrated with programming scripts that are made in Visual Studio C++ language, which allowed simulations of the environment, each script developed was linked to an object in the environment to perform a certain function, for example, move the bottle by the conveyor belt to a certain position as shown in Fig. 14,

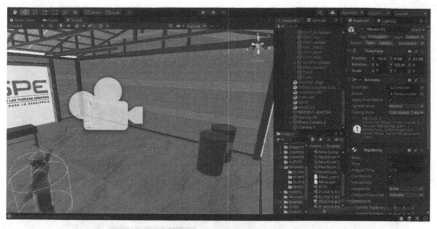

Fig. 12. 3D object from Unity3D's "Camera" vision tool.

Fig. 13. Interaction of the avatar with the main menu.

the bottle disappear, stop an object for a moment and then move it again, etc., in the same way the sensors and actuators are linked to their script of operation, in virtual presence sensors the action of determining the absence or presence of an object is determined by the Raycast tool, and for actuators a script is used whose function is determined by moving an object or activating an indicator.

2.6 MODBUS TCP/IP Communication Protocol

To establish bidirectional communication between the controller (Arduino UNO) and the Unity 3D development tool, the industrial communication protocol Modbus TCP/IP is used within an Ethernet network as shown in Fig. 15, for Modbus communication is They create programming scripts used in data management, both in the IDE of the controller and Visual Studio of Unity 3D, in addition the transfer areas are defined by registers for their identification, in Fig. 16 the data sent and received is shown Unity 3D platform using Modbus TCP/IP.

Fig. 14. Movement of the bottle on the conveyor belt.

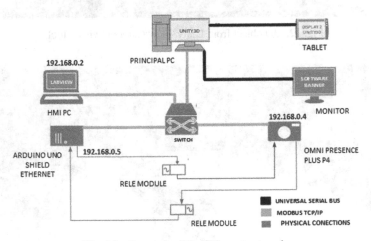

Fig. 15. Structure of the Ethernet network.

2.7 OMNI BANNER PRESENCE PLUS P4 Camera

For the inspection and verification analysis of the packaged bottle in the final production line, the OMNI BANNER PRESENCE PLUS P4 artificial vision camera was used, which by means of a standard image and with its respective training allows to approve or reject the packaged bottle. For this training it is necessary to carry out various configurations which will allow detecting objects, position, reading QR codes or barcodes, among other applications depending on the user's need, in Fig. 17, the use of the "detection" tool is observed. of objects".

Finally, by using a first-person camera within the simulation and the Wired XDisplay tool we can have the same Unity3D process on a Tablet as shown in Fig. 18, the final stage of the process will be read by the OMNI camera Banner PresencePLUS, since this stage is the one that corresponds to the inspection and verification of the products that the camera reads.

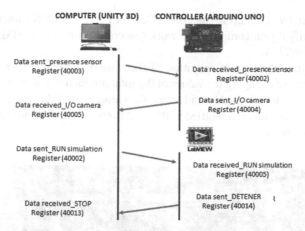

Fig. 16. Data transfer by Modbus TCP/IP.

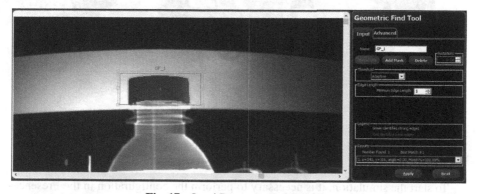

Fig. 17. Omni Banner camera settings.

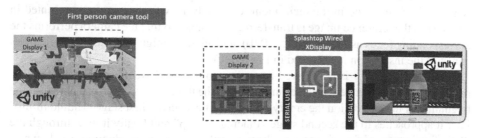

Fig. 18. Tablet as a display device for the finished product.

3   Results

The virtual training system developed focuses on the generation of a batch of bottles packed in perfect condition and another batch of bottles with random production errors, so that the user can carry out the automation of inspection and verification of the bottles in the environment, by configuring the OMNI Banner PresencePLUS camera. In addition, to be able to verify if your configuration work was correct through the HMI of the camera software and LabVIEW.

To demonstrate the correct operation of the training system, experiments are presented that consist of changing the values of the total production batch and the number of erroneous bottles that is desired in said batch, the values to start the process are presented in the Fig. 19 with a total of 20 bottled bottles, 12 bottles in good condition and 8 bottles with production errors.

Fig. 19. Process start menu.

To start the simulation, it is necessary to perform the configuration in the Presence-PLUS camera software, so that it can detect the correct level of liquid inside the bottle, the correct location of the cap and the correct labeling of it, this procedure is performed with a reference image in the main menu of "Analysis with the camera" presented in Fig. 20 (a), the reference image is transferred to a Tablet so that the camera performs the corresponding focus as shown in Fig. 20 (b), and all the configuration so that the camera can start the inspection is observed in Fig. 20 (c).

Once the chamber is configured according to the user's requirement, the bottling process begins, the process has the simulation of the three stages described above, at the beginning of the simulation the empty bottle goes through the first stage "Liquid filling" later it approaches to the second stage "Placing the cap" and finally it goes through the "Labeling" stage, giving rise to a packaged bottle finished in production, as shown in Fig. 21.

The production errors arise from the three random error events programmed according to the user has determined the number of bottles in bad condition that he needed in his batch of products, Fig. 22 shows a bottle generated with error 1 and 2 in the simulation of process.

Each bottled bottle, passing through the three production stages, enters the inspection process by the OMNI Banner PresencePLUS P4 camera, for this the camera captures

(a) Analysis menu for the camera.

(b) Reference image displayed on the Tablet.

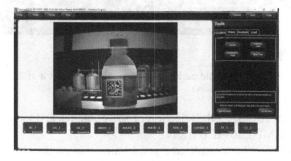

(c) Inspection tools for the bottle.

Fig. 20. Inspection and verification setup for the bottle.

the image shown by the Tablet to carry out the analysis, this process is triggered by a signal sent from the simulation to the camera by a virtualized presence sensor, obtaining the following results:

1.- For a bottle without production errors, the simulated industrial process (image of the bottle) is shown in Fig. 23 (a), in Fig. 23 (b) the correct inspection of the bottle is observed by of the chamber and Fig. 23 (c) shows the acceptance of the bottle packed by the training system displayed on the HMI (LabVIEW).

2.- For a bottle with production errors, the simulated industrial process (image of the bottle) is presented in Fig. 24 (a), in Fig. 24 (b) the inspection of the bottle error by the

Fig. 21. Stage of packaging the bottle in the virtual environment.

Fig. 22. Bottle packed with production error 1 and 2.

camera and Fig. 23 (c) shows the rejection of the bottle packed by the training system displayed on the HMI (LabVIEW).

To verify if the user has completed a good training in product inspection and verification, the values obtained in the visual interface of the camera and the values obtained in the HMI designed in LabVIEW are analyzed, making a comparison with the values entered at the beginning of the test. simulation, Fig. 25 shows the comparative results of the simulation, the inspection camera, and the LabVIEW HMI.

(a) Image capture by the camera of a bottle without errors.

(b) Accepted inspection result.

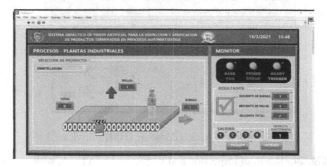

(c) Acceptance of the packaged bottle (HMI Labview).

Fig. 23. Result of the inspection and verification of a bottle without errors.

(a) Camera image capture of a buggy bottle.

(b) Inspection result rejected.

(c) Rejection of packaged bottle (HMI Labview).

Fig. 24. Result of inspection and verification of a bottle with errors.

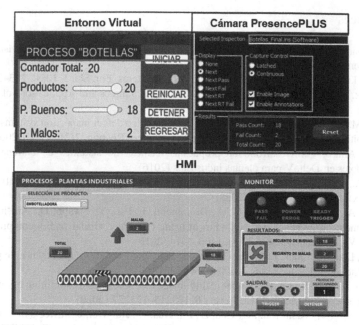

Fig. 25. Comparative results of simulation, the camera and the HMI of LabVIEW.

4 Conclusions

A training system of an immersive virtual environment was implemented, for the training of operators and students in the inspection and verification of the production line for the quality control of the finished products. The immersion that the system provides to users is achieved by the high level of detail in the design of the 3D objects implemented.

The virtual environment developed presents an adequate operation, and generates a high level of realism since the artificial vision camera detects all the designed details, and allows the analysis to be carried out as if it were a real process.

The operation of the training system was validated by subjecting it to several experimental tests and verifying that the final result of the advanced visual inspection camera and the main process menu respectively show the same amount of data from the virtualized processes.

Finally, the training system can help develop the skills of field operators and engineering students in quality control issues in automated production lines by providing useful and lasting knowledge over time.

Acknowledgements. The authors would like to thank the Universidad de las Fuerzas Armadas ESPE for the support for the development of this work, especially the project 2020-PIC-017-CTE "Simulación de proceso industriales, mediante la técnica Hardware in the Loop, para el desarrollo de prácticas en Automatización Industrial".

References

1. Vilaboa, J.: Gestión de la automatización de plantas industriales en Chile. Revista Facultad de Ingeniería, Chile **12**(01), 33–41 (2004)
2. Abdu, I.O.: Architecture of industrial automation systems. Eur. Sci. J. **10**(3), 273–283 (2014)
3. Alcock, R., Pham, D.: Smart Inspection Systems: Techniques and Applications of Intelligent Vision Academic Press, London (2002)
4. Park, M., Jin, J.S., Au, S.L., Luo, S., Cui, Y.: Automated defect inspection systems by pattern recognition. Int. J. Sig. Process. Image Process. Pattern Recogn. **2**(2), 31–42 (2009)
5. Rojas Alfaro, G.: Desarrollo de propuestas técnicas de sistemas de entrenamiento de operadores en DeltaV para plantas industrials (2016)
6. Ren, A., Chen, C., Luo, Y.: Simulation of emergency evacuation in virtual reality. Tsinghua Sci. Technol. **13**(5), 674–680 (2008)
7. Steed, A., Friston, S., Lopez, M.M., Drummond, J., Pan, Y., Swapp, D.: An 'in the wild' experiment on presence and embodiment using consumer virtual reality equipment. IEEE Trans. Vis. Comput. Graph. **22**(4), 1406–1414 (2016)
8. Si, W., Liao, X., Qian, Y., Wang, Q.: Mixed reality guided radiofrequency needle placement: a pilot study. IEEE Access **6**, 31493–31502 (2018)
9. Cao, H., Shang, X., Qi, H.: Virtual reality image technology assists training optimization of motion micro-time scale. IEEE Access **8**, 123215–123227 (2020)
10. Shih-Ching, Y., Yuan-Yuan, L., Chu, Z., Pin-Hua, C., Jun-Wei, C.: Effects of virtual reality and augmented reality on induced anxiety. IEEE Trans. Neural Syst. Rehabil. Eng. **26**(7), 1345–1352 (2018)
11. Criscione, J.: Realidad Virtual y su aplicacion como servicios de entrenamiento (2018)

3D Virtual System of a Distillation Tower, and Process Control Using the Hardware in the Loop Technique

Edwin Pruna[✉], Geovanna Balladares, and Hugo Teneda

Universidad de las Fuerzas Armadas ESPE, Sangolquí, Ecuador
{eppruna,vballadares,hateneda}@espe.edu.ec

Abstract. This work presents the development of a 3D virtual environment of a binary distillation tower, and by means of the Hardware in the Loop (HIL) technique allows the training of users in process control. The virtual environment has instruments, equipment, animations and sounds of a high degree of quality existing in a binary distillation plant, the design is done using CAD tools and the Unity 3D graphics engine. The proposed system is a low-cost alternative developed with a high level of detail for the automatic control of a binary distillation tower, it also allows to develop several tests without risk of accidents with the comfort that the user requires for learning.

Keywords: Virtual reality · Distillation tower · Hardware in the loop · Process control

1 Introduction

Nowadays the industry focuses on many production areas, one of them is the chemical industry where the binary distillation tower is an important part [1, 7], its operation is based on separating compounds from a mixture by applying different degrees of temperature and pressure, and depending on the volatility of each element the distillate and sediment are obtained [2, 8].

The demands in current industrial processes require that an operator has the necessary experience in control of binary distillation towers from their academic training to their professional performance [1], in this context there are limitations that hinder such learning as the economic aspect, since didactic distillation systems cost high amounts of money, also access to these plants is very difficult for safety, integrity of people, environment and equipment [3, 10, 11].

Virtual reality in industry is capable of transmitting information that allows users to have systems similar to real industrial processes [2, 9, 11], using video animations or sounds in order to create applications that simulate training prior to interaction with different industrial plants [2].

The complementary technique for training with virtual reality is Hardware in the Loop, which allows interacting with physical variables within a virtual environment and reducing costs, unnecessary stoppages or breakdowns in industrial processes [5, 6, 10].

© Springer Nature Switzerland AG 2021
L. T. De Paolis et al. (Eds.): AVR 2021, LNCS 12980, pp. 621–638, 2021.
https://doi.org/10.1007/978-3-030-87595-4_45

Virtual reality complemented with the Hardware in the Loop technique provides good results applied in industrial processes, for example, a virtual laboratory with a Hardware in the Loop system for teaching industrial processes [3], another example is the "Amatrol T5552" application of the University of Cauca that is used for industrial processes and control practices within the institution [4].

The present research develops a 3D virtual environment of a binary distillation plant, composed of instruments, equipment and signage based on a real plant. The graphics, animations and sounds are of high quality, making the application pleasant to the user.

The virtual environment has a user-friendly human-machine interface (HMI) where the control menus and the trends of the industrial process variables are located, and the programmable logic controller used for the automatic control is used by means of the Hardware in the Loop technique.

2 Structure of the System

The development of an application in a 3D virtual environment is presented as a proposal for the training of operators of binary distillation tower plants, through the use of 3D animations and sounds controlled by the user from the keyboard. In addition, it allows learning advanced process control topics (Cascade Control), manipulating control constants through the use of an HMI screen, and observing trends.

The Virtual 3D system of a binary distillation tower uses Software and Hardware tools, which allow an interaction between physical variables produced by a DAQ system and animations within the virtual environment. The interaction between the devices and the programs used are shown in Fig. 1.

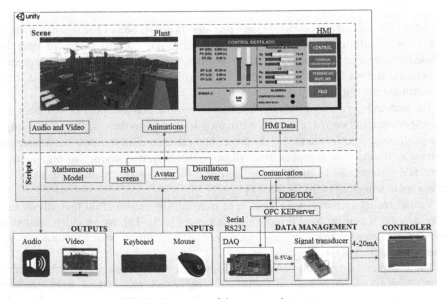

Fig. 1. Structure of the proposed system.

In the input stage, the computer keyboard and mouse are considered; by means of specific keys it will be possible to perform movements throughout the virtual environment as well as certain functionalities such as animations (molecules, control panel, etc.). In addition, the use of the mouse allows users to visualize the scenarios to understand the operation of the plant.

In the scripting stage, the communication between the HMI and the PLC is managed through OPC for automatic process control. The communication is bidirectional and occurs in real time thanks to the "communication" script.

The output stage contains sounds of the virtual plant elements including alarms, and all the animations and the environment are displayed on the screen and can be fully navigated.

3 Virtual Environment

For the development of the virtual environment is considered the diagram of a binary distillation tower, the process starts with the feeding in the middle part of the tower with a liquid called mixture. Inside the tower there are the trays in charge of transferring the energy, at the base of the tower the sediment is concentrated and passes through the reboiler so that the most volatile element ascends to the condenser, here the mixture changes its state to liquid and the distillate is obtained, if the condensed liquid does not

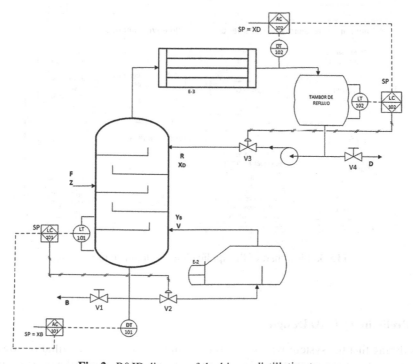

Fig. 2. P&ID diagram of the binary distillation tower.

have the adequate concentration, the reflux drum must resend the mixture to the upper plates of the tower so that the process is repeated as shown in Fig. 2.

Figure 3 shows the diagram describing the design and development process of the virtual environment.

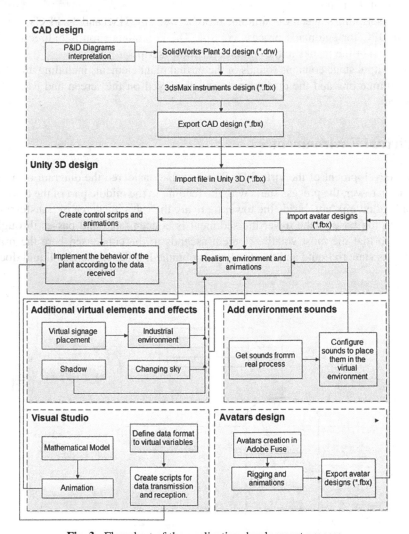

Fig. 3. Flowchart of the application development process.

3.1 Preliminary CAD Design

Considering that the system will allow training in the control of a distillation tower, it is necessary to have a level of detail and realism, to provide these attributes, specialized 3D design programs such as SolidWorks and 3DS Max are used, which have allowed to create and modify elements, equipment and industrial instruments that are part of the distillation plant, in order to improve the user experience, and give the details of each object to obtain a realistic environment, similar to a real plant. Figure 4 shows an instrument designed in the CAD software.

Fig. 4. CAD software design of a level transmitter.

3.2 Unity 3D Design

For the design in Unity 3D, we start in the scene window, where we place all the elements to be part of the plant, we use the 3DS MAX program for the conversion of files from ".drw" to ".fbx" as shown in Fig. 5.

Fig. 5. Unity 3D design of an actuator.

Once the elements with extension ".fbx" are obtained, they are selected from the folder where they are saved and dragged to the UNITY Project window, which are added and displayed in the scene window where they are placed according to the plant design, as shown in Fig. 6.

Fig. 6. 3D design of the distillation tower environment in Unity.

The plant has 3 distillation towers with similar characteristics, the central tower has a cross section throughout its body, so that the distillation process can be observed in greater detail, making it more didactic for the user, as shown in Fig. 7.

Fig. 7. 3D design of the distillation tower in Unity.

Based on the P&ID diagram, the other elements of the plant that make up a binary distillation tower are located, which are the condenser, reflux drum, valves, piping, transmitters, etc. The following result is obtained Fig. 8

Fig. 8. Binary distillation tower design based on the P&ID diagram.

3.3 HMI Design

The operation of the HMI of the Virtual 3D system of a binary distillation tower is focused on being intuitive and easy to use, located in the central part of the distillation tower, it allows the user to make the necessary changes for the automatic control of the process, Fig. 9 shows the structure of the HMI.

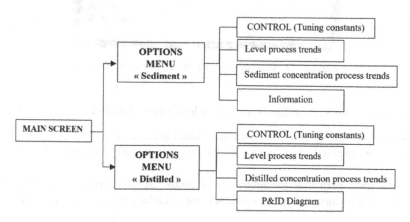

Fig. 9. Distillation tower HMI design flowchart.

Figure 10 shows the two processes (sediment and distillate), the controller tuning parameters for each process, as well as the control variables and essential information for the control of the binary distillation tower process.

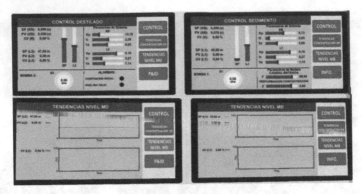

Fig. 10. Main screen of the developed HMI.

The control panel provides information about the P&ID diagram of the binary distillation tower for the user to locate the different areas of the industrial process (distillation tower), as shown in Fig. 11.

Fig. 11. Distillation tower P&ID diagram information.

3.4 Design of the Virtual Environment, Elements and Effects

In this stage, all the details of an industrial plant are added, including a control panel which contains the final control elements, the programmable automaton and the signaling system Fig. 12.

To give more realism to the environment, an industrial environment and details that allow the user to have a better experience were included. Scenarios were developed

Fig. 12. Implementation of elements to improve the detail to the virtual environment.

outside the plant, a parking lot and a landscape with a forest and industries. In addition to implementing effects, shadows and a variant sky, as shown in Fig. 13.

Fig. 13. Implementing effects, shadows, environmental movements to the virtual environment.

3.5 Creation of Environmental Sounds

The environmental sounds of several industrial equipment are created in order to increase the realism of the virtual environment, corresponding to the pumps, condenser and reboiler which are part of the distillation tower. In case the user moves away from the plant, this sound will be diminished.

3.6 Avatar Design

The avatar is obtained from Adobe Fuse, where predefined designs are available, which can be modified in terms of appearance and clothing, to make it more realistic according to the needs or the environment to be used, in this case being an industry, protective clothing is considered: gloves, helmet, boots, etc. as shown in Fig. 14.

Fig. 14. Final design of the avatar.

The animations of the avatar's movements are made in the MIXAMO software, these animations are walking, turning left or right, walking in any direction, these movements are focused on defined points of the avatar's body Fig. 15.

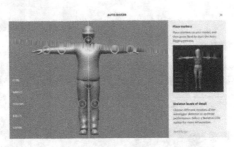

Fig. 15. Movements and animations assigned to the Avatar using MIXAMO software.

For each movement a preview of the movement is obtained to determine if it is in accordance with the needs of the animation, as seen in the movement "walking" presented in Fig. 16.

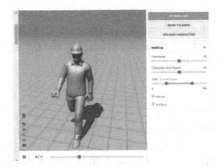

Fig. 16. Preview of the movement "walk".

Once the movements are defined, each of them is downloaded in ".fbx" format, they are added to the avatar script in UNITY and assigned to the necessary keys through programming using Visual Studio.

3.7   Programming in Visual Studio

The programming is done in Visual Studio, within Unity scripts are created which contain the commands for animation, communication and mathematical model of the plant, also an additional program is created for communication between UNITY and the OPC, which is responsible for sending and receiving data to and from the PLC respectively, in Fig. 17 explains the structure of the programming done through scripts in Visual Studio.

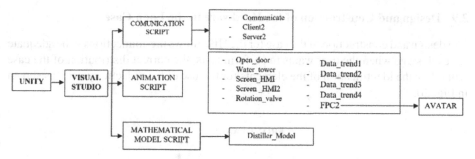

Fig. 17. Flowchart of the scripts developed in unity.

Animation Scripts. In this script there are all the programming commands correspond-ing to the animation of the binary distillation tower, as well as the avatar, besides con-taining the commands that control from the keyboard the actions to be performed by the avatar.

Communication Scripts. In these scripts the communication of all the programming done in Visual Studio with the 3D virtual environment in UNITY is established and in the same way for it to communicate with the OPC through the DLL and DDE. The functionality of the communication scripts is explained in Fig. 18:

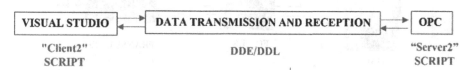

Fig. 18. Communication flowchart between unity and the OPC.

3.8 Signal Acquisition and Conditioning

An Arduino MEGA 2560 is used as DAQ to send signals to the PLC and vice versa, these signals have noise and must be conditioned to decrease the load effect that is produced between the Arduino and the PLC, the signal conditioning presented in Fig. 19 is applied.

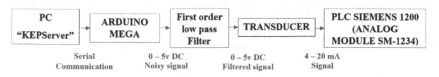

Fig. 19. Signal conditioning flowchart.

3.9   Design and Construction of the Hardware in the Loop Case

The design and construction of the case for the HIL allows the connections to be adequate for each stage when the user wants to perform tests, the correct distribution of the case will allow the identification of the elements for the use of the didactic system, as shown in Fig. 20.

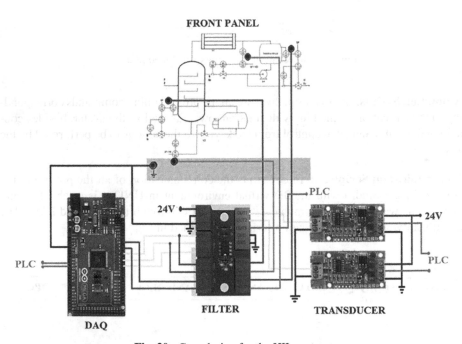

Fig. 20. Case design for the HIL system.

3.10   Control Algorithms Implemented

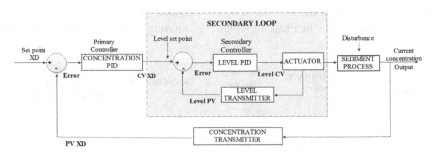

Fig. 21. Block diagram of the cascade control of the base - reboiler assembly.

The cascade control is implemented in two sections of the distillation column called "Reflux drum assembly" where the distillate is obtained and "Base - reboiler assembly" from which the sediment is extracted, as shown in Fig. 21 and Fig. 22 respectively.

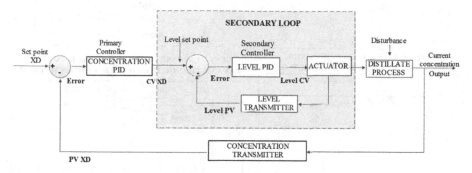

Fig. 22. Block diagram of the cascade control of the reflux drum assembly.

Figure 23 shows the tuning methods implemented in the "base - reboiler assembly" and in the "reflux drum assembly", which allow optimal control at this stage.

"REBOILER BASE" ASSEMBLY

TUNING CONSTANTS FOR TESTS ON THE SECONDARY LOOP

Methods \ Parameters	Kp	TI (s)	Td (s)
FORD	46,65237675	2,06	0,3811
HAY	12,60875047	3,296	0,824
ASTROM	29,63056361	2,06	0,515

TUNING CONSTANTS FOR TESTS ON THE PRIMARY LOOP

Methods \ Parameters	Kp	TI (s)	Td (s)
CHIEN	29,65506477	0,000238	0,000042
MOROS	37,45902919	0,0002	0,000042
ZIEGLER NICHOLS	62,43171531	0,0002	0,00005

BEST RESPONSE CURVE OBTAINED. USING THE HAY METHOD PARAMETERS

"HAY" TUNING METHOD FOR SEDIMENT LEVEL

BEST RESPONSE CURVE OBTAINED. USING THE PARAMETERS OF THE ZIEGLER NICHOLS METHOD

"ZIEGLER NICHOLS" TUNING METHOD SEDIMENT CONCENTRATION

Fig. 23. Implemented tuning methods, and response curves of the controllers in the "base - reboiler assembly".

For the "Reflux Drum Assembly" 3 different tuning methods were implemented in each of its loops corresponding to the level and concentration of the distillate as shown in Fig. 24.

"REFLUX DRUM" ASSEMBLY

TUNING CONSTANTS FOR TESTS ON THE SECONDARY LOOP

Methods \ Parameters	Kp	Ti (s)	Td (s)
FORD	46,65237675	2,06	0,3811
HAY	12,60875047	3,296	0,824
ASTROM	29,63056361	ملف	0,515

TUNING CONSTANTS FOR TESTS ON THE PRIMARY LOOP

Methods \ Parameters	Kp	Ti (s)	Td (s)
CHIEN	4,761651019	0,238	0,042
MOROS	6,014717077	0,2	0,042
ZIEGLER NICHOLS	10,02452846	0,2	0,05

BEST RESPONSE CURVE OBTAINED. USING THE HAY METHOD PARAMETERS

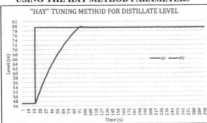

BEST RESPONSE CURVE OBTAINED. USING THE PARAMETERS OF THE ZIEGLER NICHOLS METHOD

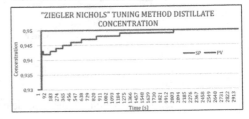

Fig. 24. Implemented tuning methods and response curves of the controllers in the "Reflux drum assembly".

4 Results

The 3D virtual system offers the user a training in the automatic control of a binary distillation tower, the implemented system is presented in Fig. 25.

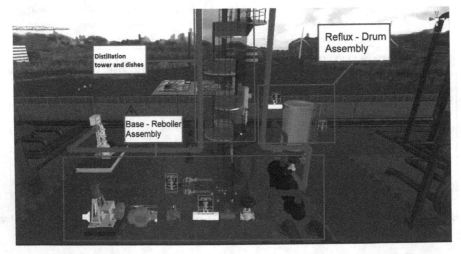

Fig. 25. Final result of the binary distillation tower implemented in Unity 3D.

The developed application starts with a front view of the HMI, which allows the user to enter the tuning constants of the controller and also to observe the response curves of the process, as presented in Fig. 26.

Fig. 26. User's initial position in front of the HMI.

By means of the avatar the user can go to any point of the environment, and with the help of the mouse redirect the view to all the places, to observe the details of the animation of the stages of the process Fig. 27.

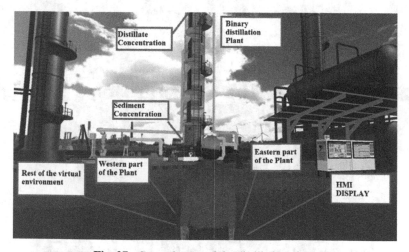

Fig. 27. General parts of the distillation plant.

The details of the animation correspond to the operation of a real distillation tower, so that the user becomes familiar with the plant and knows its stages, as presented in Fig. 28.

Due to the complexity of the system and so that the user can understand the distillation process, an animation is created inside the transparent tower.

The animation starts with the mixture entering the middle of the tower and filling the lower plates, when it reaches the base and depending on the concentration of the sediment, the mixture passes through the reboiler and re-enters the tower as steam.

Fig. 28. Details implemented in the virtual environment.

The vapor rises and passes to the condenser, if the distillate does not have the required concentration the liquid re-enters the tower through the reflux drum, which will fill the upper plates in a descending way to repeat the process. See Fig. 29.

Fig. 29. Sequence of operation of the distillation tower.

In order to demonstrate the performance of the application, the industrial instruments in operation (transmitters and valves, etc.) are presented.

In each image of the industrial elements, the precision and detail can be observed, as well as their performance with respect to the measured and controlled variable. Figure 30.

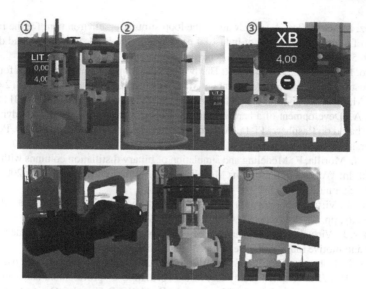

Fig. 30. Operation of the industrial instruments in the virtual environment of the distillation tower.

5 Conclusions

The system implemented by means of the Hardware in the Loop simulation technique, allows the virtualization of a binary distillation tower and the control of the process with the use of a real PLC, which will help the training in automatic control of industrial processes.

The implemented system allows to know the operation of a distillation tower, the behaviour of the transmitters and actuators in a virtual way; for this purpose, the instruments and industrial equipment used in the virtual environment are designed with similar characteristics to real equipment (appearance and physical behaviour).

The operation of the system was validated through the design of PID controllers in the PLC, obtaining a stable control in each stage of the distillation tower (virtual environment).

Acknowledgements. The authors would like to thank the Universidad de las Fuerzas Armadas ESPE for the support for the development of this work, especially the project 2020-PIC-017-CTE "Simulación de proceso industriales, mediante la técnica Hardware in the Loop, para el desarrollo de prácticas en Automatización Industrial".

References

1. Pruna, E., Rosero, M., Pogo, R., Escobar, I., Acosta, J.: Virtual reality as a tool for the cascade control learning. In: De Paolis, L.T., Bourdot, P. (eds.) AVR 2018. LNCS, vol. 10850, pp. 243–251. Springer, Cham (2018). https://doi.org/10.1007/978-3-319-95270-3_20
2. Navarro, J., Vallejo, L.: Virtual Reality under a modular vision of Industry 4.0. In: Los Libertadores University Foundation, pp. 2–3. Los Libertadores University Foundation Bogotá Headquarters (2020)

3. Gómez, M., González, A.: Hardware in the loop simulation environment for the implementation of a virtual laboratory of industrial processes in the PIAI. In: Universidad del Cauca, pp. 49–55. Universidad del Cauca, Popayan (2017)
4. Rosero, B., Gonzales, A., Flórez, J.: Hardware in the loop simulation approach for practices in industrial process control. Colombian Mag. Adv. Technol. 3(special), 103–112 (2021)
5. King, M.: Process Control: A Practical Approach, 1st edn. Wiley, Hoboken (2011)
6. Luna, A.: Development of a hardware-in-the-loop simulator of multivariable dynamic processes based on Raspberry Pi. In: Polytechnic University of Valencia, pp. 16–19. Polytechnic University of Valencia, Spain (2019)
7. Duro, N., Morilla, F.: Modeling and simulation of binary distillation columns with inventory control. In: Workshop in: Systems Modeling and Simulation Methodologies 2001, pp. 2–7. UNED, Spain (2001)
8. Useche, J.: Virtual laboratory for the crude distillation process. In: Nueva Granada Military University, pp. 19–26. Bogotá D.C. (2018)
9. Jimenez, J.: Virtual reality and augmented reality of disassembly and replacement processes in the automotive industry. University of Valladolid, Spain (2018)
10. Velosa, J., Cobo, L., Castillo, F., Castillo, C.: Methodological proposal for use of virtual reality VR and augmented reality AR in the formation of professional skills in industrial maintenance and industrial safety. In: Auer, M.E., Zutin, D.G. (eds.) Online Engineering & Internet of Things. LNNS, vol. 22, pp. 987–1000. Springer, Cham (2018). https://doi.org/10.1007/978-3-319-64352-6_92
11. Laseinde, O., Adejuyigbe, S., Mpofu, K., Campbell, H.: Educating tomorrows engineers: reinforcing engineering concepts through Virtual Reality (VR) teaching aid. In: IEEE International Conference on Industrial Engineering and Engineering Management (IEEM), pp. 1485–1489 (2015)

3D Virtual Environment for Calibration and Adjustment of Smart Pressure Transmitters

Víctor I. Rocha, Kevin R. Rocha, and Edwin P. Pruna$^{(\boxtimes)}$

Universidad de Las Fuerzas Armadas ESPE, Sangolquí, Ecuador
{Virocha,Krrocha,eppruna}@espe.edu.ec

Abstract. This article presents the design and implementation of a 3D virtual environment for the calibration of smart pressure transmitters, in the form of a computer-executable application for the Windows operating system. In the virtual environment, 3D has been integrated with a station of instrumentation and control processes which consists of a closed tank where the level of a liquid is controlled by a PID controller. For the visualization of the physical variables present in the virtual environment, a smart transmitter of differential pressure (level measurement) and a transmitter of absolute pressure is integrated. For the calibration and adjustment of the transmitters, a process calibrator, a manual pump, and pressure modules are integrated, in order to develop the procedure which consists of comparing the measurement of an instrument under test with a standard instrument and finding the error present in the measurements. In the virtual 3D environment, animations and interactions have been integrated in order to make it a more intuitive environment for the user.

Keywords: Virtual process station · Process control · Calibration and adjustment of transmitters · Error in measurements

1 Introduction

At present many systems, processes, laboratories, and conventional teaching media are being virtualized, in order to complement each other with virtual reality and give a greater didactic contribution [1]. The application of virtual reality in teaching-learning processes, whether for education or training, generates many benefits compared to traditional technology. Many applications allow the training of technical personnel making use of the tools of a virtual environment, thus knowing the operation of a machine or device [2, 3].

On the other hand, the calibration of smart pressure transmitters is a very important practice within the area of industrial instrumentation, which consists of comparing the output of an instrument with that of a standard pressure measurement device. This process is performed by generating a common pressure in the measurement circuit for both the device under test and the standard device. Outputs are compared at specific pressure points that are typically in the full-scale range of the device under test. This procedure

© Springer Nature Switzerland AG 2021
L. T. De Paolis et al. (Eds.): AVR 2021, LNCS 12980, pp. 639–654, 2021.
https://doi.org/10.1007/978-3-030-87595-4_46

is performed to ensure that instrument measurements are accurate and that the entire system operates efficiently [4].

In this article, a 3D virtual environment is made in unity software for the calibration and adjustment of smart pressure transmitters, by means of the Hart protocol. The calibration procedure is performed with a Fluke 754 process calibrator. To better understand the calibration and adjustment procedure of a smart transmitter with Hart protocol it is necessary to know the three sections that make up these devices. These sections can be shown in Fig. 1.

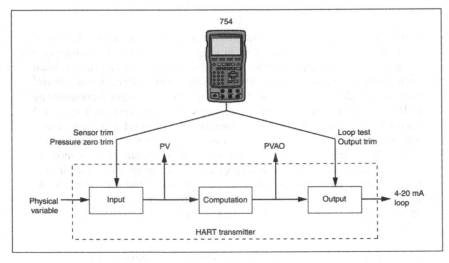

Fig. 1. Block diagram of a Hart transmitter [5].

In the input section, the process variable generates an electrical signal (millivolts, capacitance frequency, etc.) and is converted to a milliamp signal by the transmitter's microprocessor. In the calculation section, a mathematical calculation is performed to pass the process variable to an equivalent value in milliamps which is represented digitally in the instrument. In the output section the signal delivered by the calculation section is converted into a real analog electrical signal (4 to 20 mA) [6].

The sensor adjustment that is made in the transmitter corresponds to the adjustment of the input section (adjustment of the LRV and URV). In output adjustment, the output section is configured (4 to 20 mA), and also the zero pressure adjustment is made, which consists of setting the sensor lower to zero. These three operations are performed in the service menu of the HART mode of the process calibrator [7].

The entire 3D virtual environment, interactions, and animations are developed in Unity 3D software, which is a video game engine designed to create 2D, 3D applications and simulations for computers, consoles, and mobile devices [8].

2 Structure of the System

This section shows the design and implementation of the virtual station didactic instrumentation and process control for the calibration of smart pressure transmitters, modeling of the components of the 3D environment, and implementation of the virtual 3D environment. Figure 2 shows the general outline of the virtual environment developed in Unity 3D.

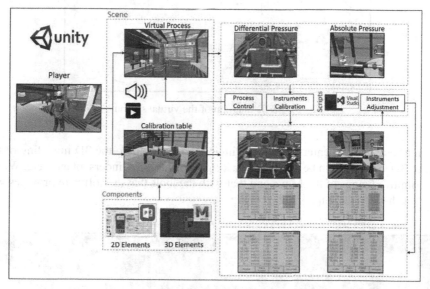

Fig. 2. General scheme of the virtual environment 3D developed.

3 Design of the Virtual Instrumentation and Process Control Station

The virtual instrumentation and process control station is designed under real parameters of a laboratory didactic process, considering the restrictions and main characteristics that guarantee the correct functioning of the virtual environment. Figure 3 presents the P&ID diagram of the virtual instrumentation and process control station, which is used to locate the instruments and devices in the right place within the 3D virtual environment.

The virtual system consists of an industrial smart transmitter for the absolute pressure variable and a second smart industrial differential pressure transmitter for the level variable. The virtual didactic process station consists of the filling of a liquid inside a tank, which will be controlled with a PID controller, calibration equipment such as a process calibrator, a manual pump, and pressure modules are integrated.

3D Modeling of Devices. 3D modeling is a set of mathematical operations to represent an object three-dimensionally. The software to model the equipment and calibration devices, as well as the virtual station was done in Autodesk Maya.

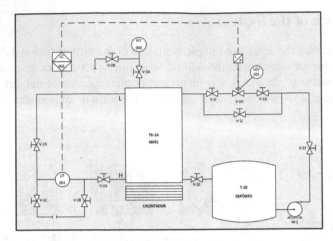

Fig. 3. P&ID diagram of the virtual station.

In Maya, you can enter a reference image to be able to do the 3D modeling of the object. 3D modeling can be started by making from cubes, cylinders, planes, etc. Which are primitive figures of the Maya and that with the tools that the software provides will give the shape to the final 3D object (Fig. 4).

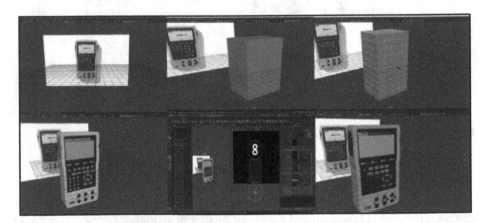

Fig. 4. 3D modeling of computers in Autodesk Maya.

Autodesk Maya software has modeled the different equipment used for the calibration of smart pressure transmitters, as well as some components of the virtual instrumentation station. Some of these 3D objects are shown in Fig. 5.

Implementation of the Virtual Station in Unity 3D. Three-dimensional models built in the Maya software are imported into the Unity 3D software to form the virtual environment; also, other necessary extra components are downloaded from the web and

Fig. 5. Modeling 3D objects in Maya Autodesk software.

integrated into the stage in order to complement and give more realism in the 3D environment. The virtual scenario also uses 2D components (UI, screens, directions, messages, diagrams, etc.).

The implementation of the virtual station is based on the P&ID diagram in Fig. 3. Each three-dimensional model is dragged to the Unity 3D stage, sized and placed according to the previously made design, obtaining a 3D station as shown in Fig. 6.

Fig. 6. Virtual stationing in Unity 3D.

This process has the purpose of controlling the level of a tank and its temperature, that is to say, keeping the process variables to a reference or Set Point that the user has. The level process (Loop 1) consists of a differential pressure transmitter, which will measure the level, and then send a current signal to the controller (PID Control), this, in turn, will send a signal to an actuator (I/P converter) that will drive the final control element (valve). There is also a tank for the deposit of the liquid. There is also an absolute pressure transmitter that is measuring the pressure that is generated in the tank.

To emulate the evolution of the variables, a mathematical model was entered into the programming of the application which is described in Eq. 1.

$$G(s) = \frac{0.9}{2.3s + 1}e^{-1.5s} \rightarrow Level \tag{1}$$

Since the visual programming software study works in the time domain the mathematical model proposed translates into the following equation:

$$\frac{dh(t)}{dt} = \frac{0.9 * x(t - 1.5) - h(t)}{2.3} \rightarrow Level \tag{2}$$

Virtual Absolute Pressure Measurement System. The virtual absolute pressure measurement system consists of the absolute pressure transmitter (PIT), the process intake pipe, and the step valves. This is shown in Fig. 7.

Fig. 7. Virtual system of absolute pressure.

Virtual Differential Pressure Measurement System. The virtual differential pressure measurement system consists of the level transmitter (LIT), the process intake pipes, and the step valves. Figure 8 shows the 3D virtual system.

Fig. 8. Virtual differential pressure system.

For the virtual calibration, a 2D help window is integrated with the necessary instruments (Calibrator, transmitter, hand pump), in which the procedure can be carried out and the information can be visualized in a better way. The window is created using a png image and integrated into unity, then converted to a sprite and added to a canvas-type object (Fig. 9).

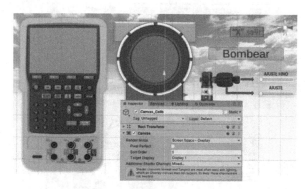

Fig. 9. The window for the calibration of the 2D instrument.

All the screens projected by the calibrator equipment (Fluke 754) during the calibration procedure are also created in png format and integrated into Unity; these images are added to the same canvas when programmed according to the operation of the actual process calibrator (Fig. 10).

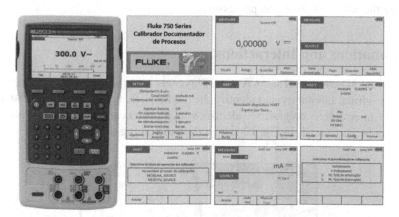

Fig. 10. Creation of screens of the Fluke 754 calibrator equipment.

To interact with the process, user interfaces have been integrated which have been developed as png images initially and then taken to Unity 3D in which the images are formatted so that they can be treated as 3D objects (Fig. 11).

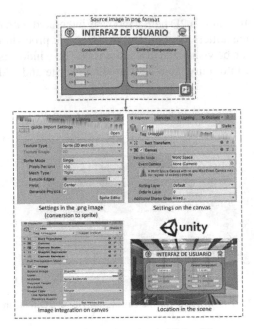

Fig. 11. Virtual station in Unity 3D.

Once you have the image on the Stage, it is integrated into it: selectors for the control mode step, sliders to vary the values of the SetPoint in the automatic control mode and the Control Value in the manual control mode, progress bars, and finally text objects to visualize the values of the Level processes.

4   Animations and Interactions

In the virtual 3D environment, an Avatar (Player) is integrated so that you can navigate within the virtual laboratory and identify the elements that compose it. Indicative messages and an arrow are integrated to identify which object can be interacted with or what action can be performed. In Fig. 12 you can see the taking of the equipment.

Fig. 12. Calibration table.

The animation of the purge of the pipe is performed and the connections of the instruments for calibration are displayed, that is to say, that the instruments appear placed and connected automatically correctly (Fig. 13).

Fig. 13. Animation of valve closure and pipe purging.

The transmitter disconnects from the process and is connected to the calibrator via the gauge's mA terminals and transmitter power cables. The hand pump is connected to the high-pressure socket of the differential pressure transmitter and pressure module. The pressure module is connected to the calibrator communication port 754. Figure 14 shows these connections in the 3D environment.

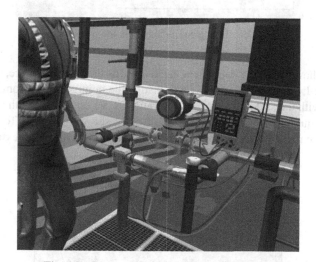

Fig. 14. Connection for transmitter calibration.

For the animations of the pressure modules and transmitters, mathematical models are entered into the programming, these models are described below in Eqs. 3 and 4.

$$\frac{dy(t)}{dt} = \frac{1 * x(t) - y(t)}{0.8} \rightarrow Pressure\ module \tag{3}$$

$$\frac{dy(t)}{dt} = \frac{1.013 * x(t) - y(t)}{1.0} \rightarrow Transsmitter \tag{4}$$

5   Results

It is considered several tests of the application thus obtaining the final application in which the calibrations of the smart pressure transmitters will be performed, below, the procedure to be followed is detailed:

Once inside the virtual environment, head towards the instrument table and stand in front of it, until an indicative message is displayed as shown in Fig. 15, take the computers by pressing the Q key.

Fig. 15. Taking equipment from the work table.

Once you have taken the equipment, head towards the User Interface, place yourself in front of the Level Control parameters; change the control mode from, automatic to manual, and with the slider of the "Control Value" (CV) set a value with which you can get a level of liquid in the tank (PV) around 100 cm as shown in Fig. 16. To vary the value of the CV you can do it directly with the mouse pointer or in turn by pressing F or G.

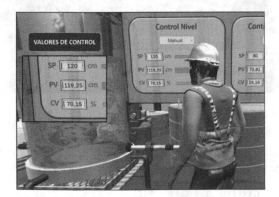

Fig. 16. Change from automatic to manual mode.

Once switched to manual mode, the manual high and low-pressure valves are closed, as well as the bypass valves where the instruments are connected (Fig. 17).

Fig. 17. Opening and closing of valves.

The next step is to purge the pipe before placing the instruments for calibration, for this it is necessary to remove the plugs, press E, and observe the process. You will notice that the plugs are removed and that the pipes are purged as shown in Fig. 18. The placement of equipment is done with the letter Q and these will appear connected.

Fig. 18. Purging of pipes and placement of equipment.

Press the letter Z to display the instruments on the 2D display, proceed to turn on the FLUKE 754 process calibrator by clicking on its power button. It will display a screen as shown in Fig. 19. Press the SETUP key on the process calibrator and enable loop power, you can see that the transmitter will turn on. To finish with this step, click the F4 (Finished) key on the process calibrator (Fig. 19).

Fig. 19. Calibrator ignition and loop feed room.

To communicate with the transmitter, press the hart key on the gauge. The screen in Fig. 20 will be presented. The transmitter parameters are displayed. Press HART again and choose source measurement mode to perform the calibration.

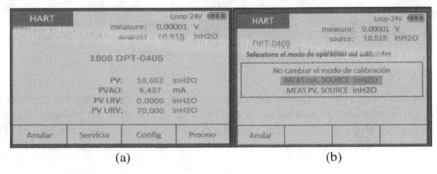

(a)   (b)

Fig. 20. a) Hart communication b) Measurement mode – source.

The next step is to wax the equipment by manipulating the thin-tuning and coarsely adjusted manual pump knobs as shown in Fig. 13. Next, press the CLEAR (ZERO) key (Fig. 21).

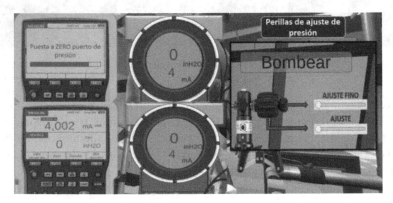

Fig. 21. Wax the instruments.

For the calibration process you select the found value test by clicking on the F1 key you select the instrument option and press enter. The tolerance for calibration is chosen and a manual test will be applied (Fig. 22).

The calibrator will ask you to approach a certain pressure point, for this you will have to click on the PUMP button, which will trigger the manual pump, this is located in the upper right. It will click as many times as necessary to reach that point and proceed to accept it when the value is correct by clicking on the F3 key (Fig. 23).

Fig. 22. Configuration of the calibrator instrument.

Fig. 23. Calibration of the Smart Pressure transmitter.

After finishing with the last calibration point the table will be displayed with all the points and with the respective errors, if any error is not within the tolerance that has been selected you must proceed to make the adjustment of the transmitter (Zero adjustment, Output Adjustment and Sensor Adjustment) (Fig. 24).

		HART mA	Loop 24V	HART	SERVICE	HART mA	Loop 24V
SOURCE		MEASURE	ERROR%			measure: 4,002 mA	
0	inH2O	4,002 mA	-0,013			source: 0 inH2O	
17,501	inH2O	8,054 mA	-0,338	DPT-0405			
35,037	inH2O	12,114 mA	-0,601	Seleccione el SERVICIO de operación para este dispositivo			
52,504	inH2O	16,158 mA	-0,983				
70,004	inH2O	20,21 mA	-1,308	Ajuste ZERO Presión			
52,494	inH2O	16,156 mA	-0,683	Ajuste Salida			
35,008	inH2O	12,107 mA	-0,859	Ajuste Sensor			
17,475	inH2O	8,048 mA	-0,338				
0	inH2O	4,002 mA	-0,013				
Anular	Página Anterior	Página Próx.	Terminado				Terminado

Fig. 24. Calibration table and display of adjustments of the Smart Pressure transmitter.

Once each of the adjustments is made, the calibration is carried out again, thus being able to show if all the points are within the tolerance Once the calibration and adjustment process of the transmitter is completed, the equipment is removed, for this first disable the loop power in the calibrator, turn it off and close the 2D window by pressing X (Fig. 25).

Fig. 25. Disabling loop feeding

Stand in front of the gauge, until the arrow appears as shown in Fig. 26, press Q to remove the equipment.

Fig. 26. Removing equipment from the process

Perform the procedure of enabling the pressure sockets, for this, close the keys of the Bypass, open the key of the low socket, and then the high (Fig. 27).

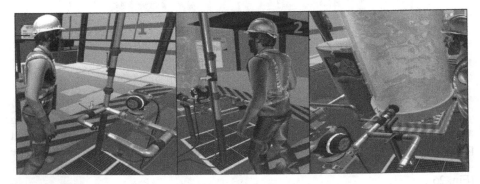

Fig. 27. Enabling the transmitter in the process

As the last step, return control mode to automatic in the User Interface. This concludes the virtual procedure of calibration and adjustment of the differential pressure transmitter in situ (Fig. 28).

Fig. 28. Start-up of the process.

6   Conclusions

The virtual instrumentation and process control station is developed based on real industrial equipment and instruments, which allows emulating the calibration procedures of the transmitters of absolute pressure and differential pressure similar to a real procedure.

The virtual instrumentation and process control station is a low-cost system for the training of professionals in the area of instrumentation since in the design all the stages for the calibration and adjustment of pressure transmitters are considered.

References

1. Enríquez, D.C., Pimente, J.J.A., López, M.Á.H., García, O.S.N.: Didactic use of immersive virtual reality with NUI focused on the inspection of wind turbines. Apertura **9**(2), 8–23 (2017)
2. M. V. A. E. L. R. Angélica De Antonio Jiménez: When and How to use Virtual Reality in Teaching. Revista de Enseñanza y Tecnología, 1–2 (2000)
3. Logitek: Virtualization in industrial plants, pp. 1–5. Stratus
4. Fluke: Fluke Calibration, 25 March 2015. https://la.flukecal.com/products/pressure-calibration. Accessed 30 Mar 2021
5. Fluke Corporation: 754 HART Mode, Everett: Fluke Corporation (2012)
6. Rosetta: Rosetta Technology Solutions. https://rosetta-technology.com/es/aula-tecnica/notas-de-aplicacion/calibracion-instrumentacion-hart. Accessed 30 Mar 2021
7. Fluke Corporation: "Hart Calibration," of 754 Hart Mode, p. 20. Fluke Corporation, Everett (2012)

8. Two Reality: "Two Reality," 21 March 2017. https://www.tworeality.com/la-simulacion-virtual-como-metodo-de-formacion-de-personal/

9. E. G. S. D. F. P.C. T. F.M. R. Jose Ramón Llata García: "Modeling control systems," of Automatic, Creative Commons (2013)

10. A. G. P. Ennys Amaya Isea: "Aplicación para Tanques Cerrados," de Instrumentación Industrial, pp. 66–67. PCI Entrenamiento S.A, Maracaibo (1997)

Systems Engineering Approach for the Development of a Virtual Training Platform: Case Study in the Missile Systems Sector

Giuseppe Di Gironimo[1][(✉)], Sara Buonocore[1], Antonio Fariello[1],
Fabrizio Carpentiero[2], Maria Rosaria Lanza[2], and Andrea Tarallo[1]

[1] Department of Industrial Engineering, JL IDEAS,
University of Naples Federico II, Naples, Italy
{giuseppe.digironimo,andrea.tarallo}@unina.it, {sara.buonocore2,
ant.fariello}@studenti.unina.it
[2] MBDA Italia SpA, Roma, Italy
{fabrizio.carpentiero,maria.lanza}@mbda.it

Abstract. The present work has two main objectives: the realization of a Virtual Training system about assembly operations in two immersive virtual environments and the comparison between the features offered. The first solution proposed is the use of commercial software IC.IDO, produced by ESI Group. It is designed for applications throughout all the PLM, offering support both in the design and production phases, as well as after-sales assistance. At the opposition, the second solution proposed is the use of the Open-source software Unity. This graphics engine has found significant success in gaming field in the recent years, as it allows more flexibility to the developer for the implementation of the features but requires greater competence in terms of programming. The following paragraphs firstly address the path outlined from the collection of customer's requirements to the virtual prototypes' release, following the Systems Engineering approach. Secondly, a benchmark between IC.IDO and Unity's features is illustrated to point out their main differences, strengths and weaknesses.

1 Introduction

Personnel training is a topic theme, especially in the Aerospace sector, which is subjected to particularly stringent tolerances. Personnel must be not only high-qualified, but also adequately trained with respect to the critical issues of a given assembly cycle. Therefore, several companies are currently investing many resources to find an effective and efficient training method, trying to overcome the limits of traditional methods as classroom lectures and on-the-job training. As part of a training class, the participants generally receive paper manuals with textual instructions and any explanatory 2D images. In more advanced cases, users can partially interact with video recordings of the operations or applications for tablets or computers [1]. However, these methods require a considerable effort of imagination to the participants, who are unable to fully understand

© Springer Nature Switzerland AG 2021
L. T. De Paolis et al. (Eds.): AVR 2021, LNCS 12980, pp. 655–669, 2021.
https://doi.org/10.1007/978-3-030-87595-4_47

the geometric and aesthetic characteristics of the components, struggling to recognize their three-dimensionality. These limits are intensified when the object of study is characterized by very low annual production volumes because it becomes strongly difficult to organize on-the-job training sessions. In addition, on-the-job training would require a slowdown or a halt to ongoing activities, causing delays and waste of resources. Once defined the technology and the added value of the project, having already clarified the involved stakeholders, it is fundamental to establish which approach will be applied to achieve the set objectives. In this case, it was found that the best solution was the Systems Engineering approach, as it supports the design team in the path that goes from receiving the customer's needs into a product that fully satisfies them.

2   State of the Art

Over the past thirty years, several experiments have been conducted to verify if there is a significant improvement with the use of Virtual Reality to implement an innovative training system. In the 90s, the research started its long journey with VR[1] technology focusing on its advantages and feasibility. In 1995 a significant project named "VADE"[2] was started by the NIST[3]: a virtual environment for assembly planning and evaluation [2]. The cases analysed were both in a small-scale as a seven parts teleprinter and large-scale assembly as a truck front-axle assembly. Overall, the system allowed real-time collision detection, simulation of dynamic behaviours of the parts held in the user's hand or constrained on the base part, dynamic interactions between the user and the parts. All the participants were mechanical engineers who had knowledge of the problem domain and of VR systems. The system was compatible with several hardware architectures, even if the experiments were primarily based on the use of an HMD[4] to obtain a full-immersion experience. This choice highlighted the difficulty related to a prolonged use of these devices: users were physically tired by the HMD. In fact, in that period, the HMDs with a satisfying level of resolution were cumbersome and heavy. On the other hand, the use of 'fish-tank' VR systems which were lighter could not offer an acceptable level of immersion. However, VADE had strong success and put the basis for many other similar projects. In fact, it was found that, after a necessary period to familiarize with the technology and with a reduced time for the use of the devices, users were fully satisfied with the virtual experience.

The following years, instead, research works became more focused on gesture recognition and haptic devices. In 2005 was released SHARP[5]: a dual-handed haptic interface for training [3, 4]. The system could operate on different VR systems configurations including low-cost desktop configurations, as Barco Baron Powerwall and four or six-sided CAVE[6] systems, allowing users to simultaneously manipulate and orient CAD

---

[1] VR: Virtual Reality.

[2] VADE: Virtual Assembly Design Environment.

[3] NIST: National Institute of Standards and Technology.

[4] HMD: Head Mounted Display.

[5] SHARP: System for Haptic Assembly and Realistic Prototyping.

[6] CAVE: Cave Automatic Virtual Environment. It is a virtual reality space where the walls, the floor and ceiling, act as projection surfaces to create a highly immersive virtual environment.

models to simulate dual-handed assembly operations. It was tested in several industrial applications related to maintenance and training issues, demonstrating promising results for simulating assembly of complex CAD models. SHARP demonstrated a new approach by simulating physical constraints, with collisions detecting accuracy of 0.0001 mm. Despite this, users could not manipulate parts during very low–clearance scenarios with the required precision because of the noise associate with the 3D input devices. For this reason, SHARP itself and many other projects have been focusing on crucial aspects as haptic and force feedback devices, or collision handling. An example is the experiment conducted by Shanghai Civil Aviation College in 2019 [5]. The aim of this work was to implement a Virtual training tool for aircraft maintenance operations that could track the workers' hand movements. The virtual platform selected was Unity; the hardware architecture, instead, consisted in HTC Vive Pro as visor with Leap Motion device mounted on it for hand tracking. Specifically, the system simulated two disassembly cycles of electronic components, as on-the-job training sessions were too difficult to arrange. It was found that this experience helped the users to be more self-conscious during the operations. In addition, it emphasized the fact that nowadays it is necessary to invest more on tracking technologies, not only haptic devices but also full body tracking techniques.

In conclusion, it has been found that a Virtual Training system offers the following advantages:

- User's interaction with the objects in the manual.
- Repetition of the training until satisfactory results are obtained.
- Training sessions execution regardless of work area or specific components' availability, without interfering with ongoing operations.
- User's greater awareness within the environment in terms of postures and devices for safety, without risking any accident [6].
- No permanent presence of qualified instructors, resulting in greater autonomy for users [7, 8].

3 Systems Engineering Approach

Systems Engineering is a multidisciplinary approach used for tackling complex and technologically demanding problems. Firstly, it provides for the choice of the model that will be the entire process' guideline. For the present systems, the model selected is the so-called "V-model", opposed to the "Waterfall model" [9]. Although both well structured, the peculiarity of the "V-model" is that the testing activities take place from the beginning of the project, not downstream of the implementation. It is widely used in the industrial environment, as it allows to recognize any errors much earlier, reducing resource expenditure necessary for the resolution of these. Even though it is considered by the Agile community as too simple and rigid method, it has obvious advantages: each stage is clearly defined and understandable, as well as transparent, optimizing communication between the parties involved and minimizing the risks [10, 11]. The V-model divides the process in three macro-phases: Design, Implementation and Testing. As showed in Fig. 1, the model's V-shape reflects the strict relationship between Design and Testing phases and its descendent/ ascendent trend.

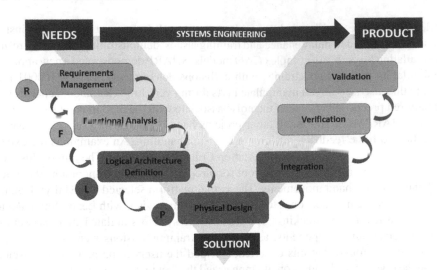

Fig. 1. V-model phases

Following the RFLP[7] path, the model starts with the analysis of the customer's requirements (R), which are secondly translated in functions that the system can offer, evaluating their feasibility (F). At this time, it is extremely useful to carry out a study in the literature to understand if solutions to identical or similar problems have already been implemented. The Design phase consists of the definition of the necessary hardware and software logical architecture (L) and ends with its physical design (P). Across the heart of the model, which is system's Implementation, the closing phase is the system's Validation and Verification. Several test procedures must be conducted to verify the correct functioning of what implemented and the compliance with the required functions: if passed, the virtual or physical prototype can be finally released.

4   Case Study

The case study selected consists in the simulation of some assembly steps of the MCU[8], courtesy of European missile and defence technology manufacturer MBDA S.p.A. This object is a military shelter, with a total weight of about 15 tons, normally mounted on trucks at a height of about 1.5 m. The MCU is designed to work in adverse weather conditions, particularly in hot and sandy areas, with heavy rain. Therefore, each sub-assembly must be electrically independent from the others and capable of working in "stand alone" mode.

Specifically, the simulation in immersive environment has involved the installation of the ACU[9], as it is a good representative of a complex assembly cycle characterized by several operations and different levels of difficulty. The operation manual was provided

---

[7] RFLP: Requirement, Functional, Logical, Physical.

[8] MCU: Mobile Control Unit.

[9] ACU: Air Conditioner Unit.

in digital format, with textual instructions accompanied by snapshots of 3D models and real photos in case of crucial operations. Although already detailed, the manual presents some critical comprehension issues, which are not exceeded by the only enrichment with images. Furthermore, a problem often occurred was the absence of correspondence between the textual instructions and the respective attached images.

4.1 System's Requirements, Functions and Logical Architecture

The first phase of "V-model", as previously described, is the system's Design. Originally, all the customer's requests have been collected and subsequently translated into functional requirements, excluding the ones which were not feasible in the present system. As showed in Table 1, the only remaining features have been organized into five categories described as the fundamental aspects of a Virtual Training system in the current literature [12, 13].

Table 1. Virtual training system's functions required

Category	Functions required
Realism	Perception of depth
Immersivity	Stereoscopic view
Interoperability	Active behaviour towards the objects in the scene
Scalability	Correct sequence of instructions with increasing level of detail
Mnemonic notions	Repetition of one or more operations

Specifically, for each category mentioned:

- Realism is associated with the experience lived by the user and is what allows him/her to feel completely immersed in an alternative reality. Perception of depth is considered the main feature that provides for a satisfying level of realism, in addition to realistic dimensions and colours to be applied to every element of the virtual environment.
- Immersivity is considered the accessibility of both the digital devices used and the virtual spaces. For the first ones, the digital devices must ensure that the user remains interconnected in the system. For the second ones, it is the access capacity that virtual spaces must ensure in terms of freedom in any user's movement. This aspect is fully satisfied thanks to selected hardware architecture, which is detailed in the next paragraphs.
- Interoperability is the ability to interact and exchange information and elements between distinct systems and different platforms in a continuous and as transparent way as possible. This category, for the specific case study, consists in ensuring the simulation of the following actions:

- Manipulation of objects: grasp, move, position and orient the objects.

- Coupling between two components: bring an object closer until it lodges in the seat provided in the assembly.
- Screwing: involves the coupling of a screw and a nut screw.
- Support activities: prepare equipment, wear Personal Protective Equipment, go up and down stairs, etc.

- Scalability is what allows efficient use of the system regardless of the number of users present at the same time. The gradual and successive administration of instructions, as well as the on-off visibility of objects based on their degree of involvement in the specific operation are the main features that define a certain level of scalability of the virtual system. This aspect will be examined deeply in the following description of the logical architecture.
- Mnemonic notions are the complex of various expedients devised to help the memory retain dates, technical terms, chronological lists and other notions that are difficult to associate with each other or to remember. The feature which responds to this category is the possibility to activate the repetition of specific operations to impress them in the user's memory.

The Design process ends with the definition of the software's logical architecture. The one selected is the modular decomposition: the system is divided in several modules, with the aim of creating reusable units [14]. To create a scalable system for other assembly cycles or many other applications, every module must be as more cohesive and less decoupled as possible. Specifically, cohesion measures the functional coherence, which is maximum if the module does one only thing correctly or more things highly interrelated. On the other hand, coupling measures the degree of dependence of a software's modules, which is minimum when there are only a few addictions between the modules, all functionally relevant and necessary. In fact, a software designed with a high level of coupling results difficult to understand, maintain and correct [15]. The development of a software with the highest cohesion and the lowest coupling levels is only ideal, as actually it is a trade-off between these two fundamental aspects. To address this issue, both the modular decomposition approaches have been applied using two different software. The graphics engine Unity has been selected to implement the system with the OOD, meanwhile the opponent FOD has been applied using the industrial platform IC.IDO. Starting from Unity, all the objects used must be reported explicitly, which is time-consuming but also highly reusable, easily allowing localization of changes. As showed in Fig. 2, the logical architecture designed is based on three levels that put the player at the centre. By opening the menu, he/she has two main options: interact with the objects or navigate within the virtual scene. The several Navigation modes designed can offer different experiences to the user, from the classic and more realistic walk to the flying or teleport modes, which are more rapid ways to move within the scene, but less realistic.

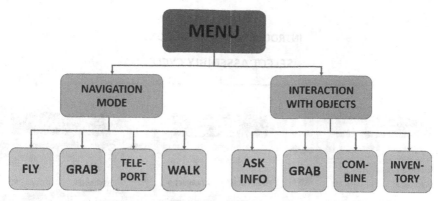

Fig. 2. OOD logical architecture of Virtual Training system

User's interaction consists in basic actions as "Ask info" about the component or "Grab" it, but also more specific as "Inventory" or "Combine". The latter has been designed for the recurrent need of combining two or more components as fastening elements, which is a preliminary action to the assembly itself. The management of an inventory, on the other hand, was designed to allow the user to save the item in a database and recall it at any time via the radial menu.

The commercial software IC.IDO, instead, has been selected to implement the FOD logical architecture, as it allows to add easily new functionalities and create independent modules, despite of the difficulty of establishing a format of interaction between the units developed. The logical architecture consists in several modules, which can be seen as big boxes that are slightly linked to each other but contain many common features. For example, Fig. 3 shows how the first three steps of a specific assembly cycle are structured, providing for the same features for different operations: the simulation of the operations as well as their repetition, the reading of rules and tips, the selection between two experience modes for the same step. Every module quite stands alone, even if the user can interact with all of them in the main[10] of the software, easily switching from a module to another. The selection between "Beginner" and "Advanced" has been introduced to emphasize the advantages of this architecture, which provides for a set of multi-tasking independent modules.

In the same module, the user can simulate every assembly operation in two different modes: Beginner is suitable for those who do not know the cycle, Advanced is for users that already know the main information about the assembly cycle. The Beginner mode has been designed to allow the user to understand the subsequence of the operations and the fundamental movements to be conducted. It is a semi-passive mode that contrasts with the Advanced mode, where the degree of user interaction with the environment increases significantly, as the operations are carried out in first person by the user.

In conclusion, the same case study has been addressed and implemented in two different platform applying two modular approaches. The Object-Oriented system developed in Unity is structured in a set of modules highly specific, but strictly dependent on each

---

[10] Main: Principal part of a software that generally controls the other.

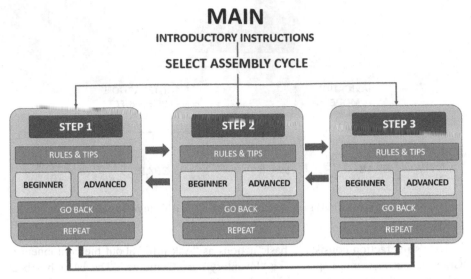

Fig. 3. FOD logical architecture of Virtual Training system

other. On the other hand, the Function-Oriented system implemented in IC.IDO provides for a set of quite independent modules, one of each often involves the same features.

4.2 Implementation Workflow for Physical Design

The heart of the V-Model consists of the system implementation phase which, although it took place in parallel in two different environments, conceptually follows the same workflow, which is presented below:

1. Analysis and modifications of CAD-models: The real work area was faithfully reproduced in the 3D design software SketchUp[11]. Subsequently, the CAD-models of the entire military shelter were viewed, checked and modified using Creo Parametric[12]. Only the components involved the simulation were selected and converted into a suitable format: ".fbx" for Unity and ".stp" for IC.IDO. Finally, the 3D models of equipment and support tools such as trolleys, small parts, tools, etc. were imported.
2. Import and organization of files in the two environments: The 3D models were imported into IC.IDO and Unity respectively and appropriately organized in a clear and recognizable hierarchical structure. Each component has been assigned an initial reference position.
3. Attribution of geometric and aesthetic characteristics: Each component has been attributed aesthetic characteristics as colours and textures to obtain a satisfying level of realism. In addition, preliminary actions as scaling, rotation and translation were carried out on the objects in the scene.

---

[11] SketchUp: 3D modelling software produced by Trimble.
[12] Creo Parametric: 3D modelling software produced by PTC.

4. <u>Creation of Controller-Object interactions:</u> During this step, all objects' offline and online animations have been created. The offline animations consist in the attribution of a discrete number of intermediate positions to be interpolated. For online animation, which are all the movements carried out by the user himself, the paths followed are partially different. In IC.IDO, the components become simulation nodes which simulate objects' mechanical behaviour. The simulation nodes are related to the others through constraints, generated after the snap[13]. On the other hand, in UNITY, characters, properties interface elements or any interactive content must be defined as Game Objects to be involved in simulation [13]. Specifically, they serve as containers for components which can be activated or deactivated by special methods and classes provided by the graphic engine, managed by C# scripts.

5. <u>Creation of User-Controller interactions:</u> In this phase, having defined the animations, it was necessary to manage the succession of these. In both software, the activation of the subsequent instruction was possible by generating the so-called triggers[14]: for each event, the triggering action and the resulting action must be defined. As showed in Fig. 4, the selection of a specific red button causes the activation of the respective instructions.

6. <u>Insertion of dummies and Personal Protective Equipment:</u> The presence of dummies allows the user not only to understand which postures and safety devices are specifically required, but also to recognize himself in them within the scene. The dummies are offered directly by IC.IDO itself, instead of Unity, where external 3D models are imported into the environment.

7. <u>Laboratory tests:</u> The final phase was conducted in immersive mode. It consisted in the selection and configuration of the input devices to allow the user the activation of the menu.

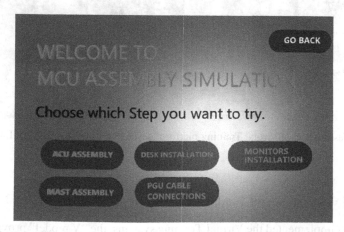

Fig. 4. Example of the assembly operations offered by the Virtual Training system

---

[13] Snap: creation of a constraint when the object reaches the correct position with respect to the target.

[14] Triggers: the singular or multiple actions which determinate a specific event.

4.3 Experimental Set-Up

The selected hardware architecture consists of a workstation and an HMD with tracking system for both IC.IDO and Unity [16]. Workstation was configured with Intel Xeon E5620 Processor, a Memory of 12 GB (6x2GB) 1.333 MHz DDR3 and a 1.5 GB Quadro NVIDIA FX4800 Graphics card. The HMD selected is HTC Vive Pro, a Virtual Reality device developed by HTC and Valve Corporation. Thanks to its Lighthouse technology, the device can support a 360-degree tracking mode in a volume of a few square meters, called "room-scale". Lighthouse, developed by Valve, makes use of base stations that generate laser beams and the photoreceptor sensors scattered on the device and its controllers detect their position in the space, allowing to determine the position and rotation of the tracked object. The device uses two high resolution OLED panels and a 110° field-of-view. HTC Vive runtime supports Microsoft Windows, macOS and GNU / Linux and uses Valve's SDK, Steam VR and OpenVR.

With the same architecture, it is important to point out that only IC.IDO permit a stereoscopic view to all the participants. Unity can currently offer the stereoscopic view only to the player, meanwhile the other participants are forced to witness the session with monoscopic view (Fig. 5).

Fig. 5. Test session of Virtual Training platform developed in Unity, MARTE Laboratory

4.4 V&V: Verification and Validation.

After having implemented the Virtual Training systems, the "V-model" provides for the ascendent and closing phase which precedes the virtual prototype's release. This phase, which consists in the systems' Verification and Validation, has been entirely carried out in CESMA's MARTE Virtual Reality Laboratory, kindly put at disposition from University of Naples Federico II.

The first tests conducted are the so-called UTPs[15]. As you can see in Fig. 6, they have been carried out in both IC.IDO and Unity by the systems' designers themselves. They consist in testing the individual modules developed to verify that the architecture thus conceived can function correctly.

Fig. 6. Example of UTPs conducted within Unity

Once the UTPs have been passed, the Integration Tests have been carried out to verify how the independent units collaborate and communicate with each other, without showing anomalies or errors. Considering the V-shape of the model selected, this kind of tests has the aim of confirming that the functional requirements established have been implemented correctly. The Integration Tests have involved MBDA's experts, who have experienced both the virtual immersive experiences in first and third person. Finally, the Final Users' Test must be conducted to check if the overall requirements have been successfully satisfied, in terms of efficacy and efficiency, with a discrete satisfaction level.

5   Results: Benchmark Ic.Ido-Unity

The benchmark that follows is the result of several interviews to the participants and designers of the virtual immersive experience within IC.IDO and Unity. The Fig. 7 displays an overall comparison between them, highlighting in green the features offered and in red the ones currently not provided. The main differences in terms of features currently offered by IC.IDO and Unity will be explored in the following pages.

- File management: IC.IDO provides for any type of intervention on a CAD model imported into the scene. It allows to combine or separate different geometries and export them in different formats to exploit them even outside the software; this same possibility unfortunately was not found in Unity.

---

[15] UTPs: Unit Test Plans. Verification of a software's single units.

FILES MANAGEMENT	IC.IDO	UNITY
Direct converters CAD models	●	●
Modify and export CAD models	●	●
MENU		
Implement rapid actions	●	●
Customize menu	●	●
NAVIGATION MODE		
Grab World, Fly, Walk, Teleport	●	●
OBJECTS CHARACTERICS		
Define object's rigid body dynamic	●	●
AESTETHIC ASPECTS		
Apply colours/textures	●	●
Create point light (and shadows)	●	●
Import a video in the scene as "animated texture"	●	●
OBTECTS INTERACTIONS		
Collision Handling	●	●
Set picking mode	●	●
Impose constraints	●	●
ANIMATIONS		
Objects animations	●	●
EVENTS MANAGEMENT		
Create actions' triggers	●	●
Insert synthetic audio	●	●
ACTIONS		
Repeat specific operation	●	●
Jump to specific operation	●	●
Active control on mistakes	●	●

DUMMIES	IC.IDO	UNITY
Edit physical chacteristics	●	●
Define kinematic chains and postures	●	●
Create dummy's animations	●	●
Ergonomic analysis	●	●
Save dummy's animations	●	●
COMPATIBLE HARDWARE		
Stereoscopic visualization systems (Powerwall)	●	●
Immersive HMD (Oculus, Vive)	●	●
AR Headset (Microsoft Hololens)	●	●
Optical tracking systems (ART)	●	●
Inertial systems (XSense)	●	●
Finger tracking systems (gloves)	●	●
Finger tracking markerless systems (Leap Motion)	●	●
Tactile systems (MANUS VR)	●	●
Force feedback systems	●	●
JOB EXPORT		
Create session's executable file	●	●
AR applications	●	●
Create session's report	●	●
Creare session's video record	●	●

Fig. 7. Benchmark between IC.IDO and Unity's features

- Menu: It is one of the winning aspects of Unity, as, relying on a high-qualified programmer, it is possible to implement practically any action within the menu. In IC.IDO, this choice is more limited since it is possible to customize the menu in a predetermined list, limit that can be partially overcome if you have access to the software programming code, through the "Script" module.
- Interactions with objects: IC.IDO, thanks to the "Solid Mechanics" module, allows the definition of the dynamics of a rigid body [17]. It is possible to introduce gravity into the scene and impose predefined or customized constraints between two or more objects in the scene: this operation is also one of the necessary steps to make the snap.
- Operations: the repetition of a single operation is a time-consuming function to implement. In IC.IDO, however, it is possible to implement rapidly the repetition of an entire step thanks to the use of "States"[16]: the user can switch to another assembly step activating the respective "State". An active control on the user's errors is currently not implementable in IC.IDO. In Unity, instead, with good programming knowledge, is an achievable feature, showing a clear advantage between this software and IC.IDO.
- Dummies: thanks to the "Ergonomics RAMSIS" module, IC.IDO already provides for a library of mannequins with a well-defined and editable physical characteristics

---

[16] States: IC.IDO's feature that permits to "freeze" and save the entire session or only some aspects of it.

ad age, height, body sizes, nationality [18]. Furthermore, as showed in Fig. 8, it is possible to define kinematic chains that allow to impose several postures. Despite this, dummies' animations are still a critic aspect in IC.IDO, as they are achievable but do not remain in the session after saving.

Fig. 8. Example of dummy in IC.IDO

In Unity, dummies must be imported as a CAD model from other modelling software, with the need to carry out a series of very complex actions to impose a specific posture from building a skeleton to defining its kinematic chain [19].

- Compatible hardware: IC.IDO currently allows an immersive experience both on Powerwall and with helmet, in addition to sensor system for Body Tracking. It is not currently possible, but in the development phase, the use of haptic devices. Its main advantage against Unity is currently the possibility of the stereoscopic view also to the participants in third person. Despite this, Unity is the only one designed also for AR applications.
- Job export: Unity allows to export the session as an executable file, which certainly distinguishes it from IC.IDO. The latter, as commercial software, has a strong dependence on the availability of an adequate license. In contrast to Unity, IC.IDO currently offers to export a video of the session, as well as a report in ".pdf" format to always keep track of the operations performed.
- Time factor: It was found that the development of operations was certainly faster in IC.IDO as it was not necessary to design the basic architecture as well as the basic commands. The designer can concentrate almost directly on the improvement actions, putting the greatest effort on shaping the IC.IDO's pre-built features according to the specific needs. In Unity the preliminary design operations are more complex and took much more time, penalizing the number of cycle operations implemented in the same working hours.

6 Conclusions and Future Works

This paper aims to be a reference point for comparison between commercial and open-source software for VR applications.

The present Virtual Training Systems successfully passed the necessary tests conducted in MARTE Virtual Reality laboratory of CESMA. Both the systems ensure a significant level of realism and a satisfying User-Environment interaction level. All instructions are clearly and correctly administered, as no malfunctions or errors occurred during the test sessions, confirming the achievement of the first set objective. There are already several ideas for subsequent changes to improve the immersive virtual experience, as the insertion of audio and visual feedback, the assignment of a score based on time and errors to stimulate personal improvement, and the insertion of information about moments and forces to be applied.

With reference to the second objective, it was found that a universal choice between IC.IDO and Unity is not possible, as both have strengths and weaknesses. In conclusion, IC.IDO results the best solution in a wider industrial vision. It is a satisfying support tool for every company's department, offering several rapid features but not exploiting a particular flexibility to implement them. However, the significant expenditure for its licence is balanced by reduction of time spent to develop the system's architecture. On the other hand, Unity is preferrable for the implementation of a serious game[17] [20]. It offers the largest freedom and flexibility to implement every feature, with the great advantage of a low expenditure. Despite this, it requires high-qualified personnel about coding and much more working hours to implement the system.

Acknowledgments. The authors thank the University of Naples Federico II and CESMA for having putted at disposition its MARTE Virtual Laboratory to conduct all the necessary tests. A special thanks even to all those people who have actively collaborated to the success of this work, also during this critical pandemic situation. Specifically, thanks to MBDA S.p.A for having supplied, with innovation aims, the case study, ESI Group and Eng. Domenico Coccorese for their significant technical support respectively with IC.IDO and Unity.

References

1. Di Gironimo, G., Mozzillo, R., Tarallo, A.: From virtual reality to web-based multimedia maintenance manuals. Int. J. Interact. Des. Manuf. 7(3), 183–190 (2013)
2. S. Jayaram, U. Jayaram, Y. Wang, H. Tirumali, K. Lyons P. Hart, "VADE: A Virtual Assembly Design Environment", Washington State University and National Institute of Standards and Technology, 1999.
3. Seth A, Su HJ, Vance JM "SHARP: a system for haptic assembly & realistic prototyping". ASME design engineering technical conferences and computers and information in engineering conference, Philadelphia, 2006.
4. Seth A, Vance JM, Oliver JH, "Combining geometric constraints with physics modeling for virtual assembly using SHARP". ASME design engineering technical conferences and computers and information in engineering conference, Las Vegas, 2007.

---

[17] Serious game: games that do not have entertainment as their main purpose, designed primarily for educational purposes.

5. X. Shao, X. Wei, S. Liu, "Research On Aircraft Virtual Assembly Technology Based On Gesture Recognition", Departments of Aviation Maintenance and Aircraft Maintenance, Shanghai Civil Aviation College, 2019.

6. Tarallo, A., Di Gironimo, G., Gerbino, S., Vanacore, A., Lanzotti, A.: Robust interactive design for ergonomics and safety: R-IDEaS procedure and applications. Int. J. Interact. Des. Manuf. **13**(4), 1259–1268 (2019)

7. Di Gironimo, G., Patalano, S., Tarallo, A.: Innovative assembly process for modular train and feasibility analysis in virtual environment. Int J Interact Des Manuf **3**, 93–101 (2009). https://doi.org/10.1007/s12008-009-0066-8

8. Di Gironimo, G., Lanzotti, A.: Designing in VR. Int J Interact Des Manuf **3**, 51–53 (2009). https://doi.org/10.1007/s12008-009-0068-6

9. TutorialsPoint, "SDLC - Waterfall Model", 2018.

10. TutorialsPoint, "Modello V SDLC", 2018.

11. Network Digital 360, "Agile transformation: how way of working changes to deal with digital transformation", 2021.

12. J. D. Dioniso, W. G. Burns III, R. Gilber, "3D Virtual worlds and the metaverse: Current status and future possibilities", 2013.

13. A. Comacchio, V. Dalla Libera, "La Realtà Virtuale come nuovo sistema a supporto dell'azienda competitiva, un'analisi delle opportunità." University Ca' Foscari, Venice, 2016.

14. A. Polini, "Architetture software", Software Engineering course, University of Camerino

15. P. Ciancarini, "La progettazione del software", Software Engineering course, University of Bologna

16. Coding with Unity Channel, https://www.youtube.com/channel/UCUPvKyKhh33gn0VatEjCrcQ

17. Esi Group, "ICIDO 13.2 IDO Solid Mechanics Reference Manual", 2020.

18. Esi Group, "ICIDO 13.2 IDO Ergonomics RAMSIS Reference Manual", 2020.

19. Tutorial Unity 3D https://www.unity3dtutorials.it/

20. Lanzotti, A., Vanacore, A., Tarallo, A., Nathan-Roberts, D., Coccorese, D., Minopoli, V., Carbone, F., d'Angelo, R., Grasso, C., Di Gironimo, G., Papa, S., "Interactive tools for safety 4.0: virtual ergonomics and serious games in real working contexts", (2020) Ergonomics, 63 (3), pp. 324–333.

Virtual System for Industrial Processes:
Distillation Towers

Efren M. Jacome[1](✉), Jaime F. Toaquiza[1](✉), Grace M. Mullo[1](✉),
Víctor H. Andaluz[1,2](✉), and José Varela-Aldás[2](✉) (iD)

[1] Universidad de las Fuerzas Armadas ESPE, Sangolquí, Ecuador
{emjacome3,jftoaquiza,gmmullo,vhandaluz1}@espe.edu.ec
[2] SISAu Research Group, Universidad Tecnológica Indoamérica, Ambato, Ecuador
josevarela@uti.edu.ec

Abstract. In this paper a realistic and intuitive virtual environment of a distillation tower system is developed. The three-dimensional model of the system is based on a real system, which is replicated in Blender software to be later implemented in Unity, in order to simulate its behavior. By showing the evolution of the system, control and monitoring maneuvers are implemented, so that the virtual animation is similar to a real process. The application developed is intended to provide support in the learning process of an operator in the work area.

Keywords: Virtual animation · Control and monitoring · Intuitive

1 Introduction

The constant change of society and the technological revolution that the world is living, makes improvements appear in the techniques and methods implemented in the process of formation of skills to be applied in labor or educational activities.[1].The inclusion of Information and Communication Technologies (ICT's) such as smart boards, video-conferencing, virtual platforms, among others, have allowed a rapid advancement of education, creating in current generations a high dependence on digital products and services to perform daily activities [2].

Due to the pandemic, more and more educational institutions are introducing new teaching methods, which means that engineering students are confronted with real professional situations in the learning process [2]. The use of game simulators in the educational process improves the quality of educational material and enhances the educational effects of the use of innovative pedagogical programs and methods, as it offers teachers additional opportunities to build individual educational trajectories of students [3].

In recent years, technology has shown a great interest in improving methods and skills in training processes in different areas such as education, medicine and especially in industrial processes, thus allowing to increase the experience of operators and instrumentalists at work [4, 5]. Industrial technology has incorporated simulators and programming languages to represent and emulate the operation of different processes

L. T. De Paolis et al. (Eds.): AVR 2021, LNCS 12980, pp. 670–679, 2021.
https://doi.org/10.1007/978-3-030-87595-4_48

in real time, because the maintenance of the operation and maneuvers require significant resources, it is important to mention that by associating these technological tools with the different branches of engineering, great advantages are obtained, for example, in Electromechanical Engineering, allows constant maintenance of calibrations and adjustments of electrical and mechanical components, where the main responsible is the operator to perform these procedures [6].

A virtual environment is an environment in which simulations of activities that are found in everyday life are performed, this is done in order to bring these activities to a controlled environment and analyze in greater depth the stability and robustness of the designed systems, allowing in this virtual test environment, you can experience various disturbances of the system, and thus obtain a complete study of the operation of the system [7]. The advancement of technology has developed computers that allow increasingly realistic and complex simulations in different areas. A virtual environment would be divided into *i) interactive environment* means that the user is "free" to navigate the virtual environment without having programmed the trajectory he/she wishes to move, the system responds according to the user's wishes, this represents that the user can make decisions in "real time" in order to observe the scene from the selected point of view [8]; *ii) implicit interaction* refers to the fact that the user does not have to learn commands or procedures to perform any action in the virtual world; on the contrary, the user performs movements that are natural to those used in the real world to move. It is then sought that the computer adapts to human nature and not the other, thus ensuring that the experience in the virtual environment is as similar as possible to the experience in the real world; and *iii) sensory immersion* refers to the disconnection of the sense of the real world and the connection of this with the virtual world [8].

There are several investigations on virtual systems for industrial processes, in which different control strategies for double effect evaporators are presented, mainly tomato concentrate for commercial use [9, 10]. Another of the fundamental points of this line of research is the focus on the training of workers in different industrial processes. To make the factory of the future a reality, several requirements must be met. It is necessary to continuously train the worker on new and changing technological trends, since the human being is the most flexible entity in the production system [11, 12]. The objective of Industry 4.0 is to integrate machines and operators through networking and information management. It proposes the use of a set of technologies in industry, such as data analytics, the Internet of Things, cloud computing, cooperative robots, and immersive technologies [13, 14].

This work presents the control and virtualization of a distillation tower plant that is widely used in different industrial processes. All the components of the distillation towers are designed from a diagram that is taken as a reference for the creation of the plant in 3D using Blender software. The animation of the plant's own objects is implemented in the UNITY 3D graphics engine. The virtual environment incorporates a control panel that allows to modify the control parameters of the process, as well as to visualize the evolution of the system. Through a bilateral communication between Unity and MATLAB, advanced control algorithms are implemented to control the system in real time.

The stages that make up this work are described as follows: Sect. 2 describes the structure of the system. Section 3 describes the development of the virtual environment in Blender and Unity 3D; the control scheme is detailed in Sect. 4. Section 5 describes the analysis of results; and finally, Sect. 6 describes the conclusions of the work.

2 System Structure

This paper describes the development of an interactive virtual environment for training on distillation tower systems. The virtualization of the plant and the simulation of the industrial process together result in a training tool for new users in a safe environment free of occupational hazards. In addition, the industrial process control is developed through events that occur when the user interacts in the virtual environment, which allows to simulate the process behavior and critical situations that may occur (Fig. 1).

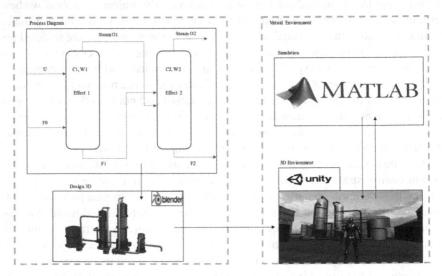

Fig. 1. Virtual environment architecture

The simulation of the process behavior is generated by the mathematical model developed through the analysis of components and variables that act in the behavior of the plant, the exchange of data with MATLAB together with the mathematical modeling produces a reliable behavior of the variables of the virtual environment.

For the creation of the virtual environment begins with the study of the plant diagram, in order to understand each of the parts involved in the process; after finishing the analysis, begins the 3D design in the Blender program where from a real industrial environment begins the modeling and de-sizing of the plant that will later be exported. Once the plant is exported to Unity, the behaviors must be programmed and assigned to each of the elements of the environment. To achieve an effective evolution of the system MATLAB has the function to carry out the control actions and send them to Unity through a bilateral communication.

3 Environment Virtualization

This section describes the process implemented for the virtualization of the distillation towers using Blender, Unity which allows a high degree of immersion for the user (Fig. 2).

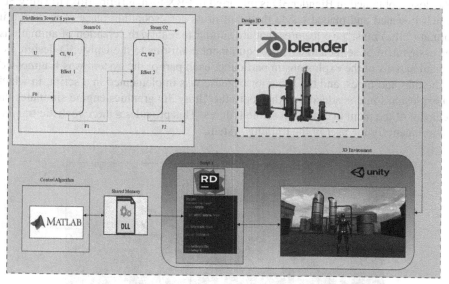

Fig. 2. Virtual system diagram for distillation towers

3.1 Design in Blender Software

The 3D design allows virtualizing the structure of the distillation towers consisting of a system of interconnected piping and industrial equipment to create a double effect. The creation and three-dimensional interconnection of the piping systems and instruments is done using Blender 3D software for the design of virtual environments, as shown in Fig. 3.

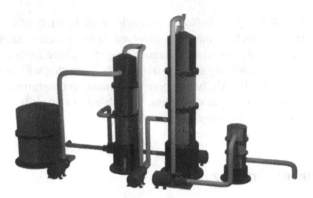

Fig. 3. Distillation tower in blender

3.2 Design in Unity Software

The design obtained in Blender 3D is imported in FBX format (Film Box) to Unity 3D, which is scaled and placed inside the plant in its corresponding place. The design in format (*.fbx) must have features that are similar to reality, the creation of animations, the assignment of sounds to existing equipment conforms to the Unity 3D design. For the animations of the explosions in particular, each part of the system was fragmented, both tanks and pipes, and the behavior of these was implemented in a script, in which an explosion force is added that thanks to the Unity 3D graphics engine simulates the behavior of the plant in case of possible failures. This provides a more realistic training environment for the user of the training system.

Fig. 4. Virtual environment explosion

4 Modeling and Control

Finding equations that describe the behavior of a system is of great importance because through these equations it is possible to describe the behavior of a process and thus know its state at any instant of time. The differential equations are obtained through the study of chemical and physical effects that intervene in a process, in most cases there is a differential equation that governs the behavior of these effects.

The distillation operation basically consists of separating a mixture by difference of composition between a liquid and its vapor, this is the key to know elements. This operation is carried out continuously in the aforementioned distillation towers where a vapor rises from the liquid until it finally exits through the head or highest part of the column, and on the other side the liquid descends until it finally reaches the base.

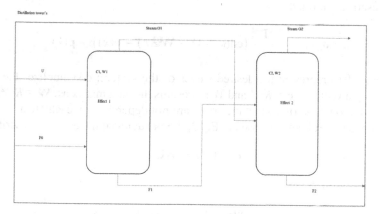

Fig. 5. Distillation column model

The behavior of the system is divided into two effects, in both of which the total mass balance, solute balance and energy balance are analyzed. For didactic purposes the temperature of the second effect is kept constant by the action of the barometric condenser. The system represented in matrix form is presented as follows [15]

$$\begin{bmatrix} \dot{C}_1 \\ \dot{C}_2 \end{bmatrix} = \begin{bmatrix} \frac{k_1}{w_1}C_1 & 0 \\ 0 & -\frac{k_1}{w_2}C_1 + \frac{k_1(1+k_2)}{w_2}C_2 \end{bmatrix} \begin{bmatrix} O_1 \\ O_2 \end{bmatrix} + \begin{bmatrix} \frac{1}{w_1}F_0(C_0 - C_1) \\ \frac{1}{w_2}F_0(C_1 - C_2) \end{bmatrix} \tag{1}$$

$$\dot{c}(t) = \mathbf{H}o(t) + \mathbf{p}(t) \tag{2}$$

where, k_1 and k_2: are positive counters and denote the ratio of the produced flow rate to the steam feed flow rate in both effects.; w_1 and w_2: are the masses of the retained liquid or "level"; F_0: is the initial solution flow; C_0, C_1 and C_2: represents the initial concentration and each concentration in the towers respectively; $\mathbf{p} \in R^{2x1}$: corresponding to the coefficients of the variations of the concentrations; $\mathbf{H} \in R^{2x2}$: corresponding to the coefficients of the concentrations; $\mathbf{o} \in R^{2x1}$: corresponding to the steam flows to the distillation towers.

4.1 Control Algorithm

From the matrix representation of the system, the design of the plant controller is based on the numerical methods tool.

To discretize the system, we start from the Nyquist theorem defining a sampling period T_0 Thus, by discretizing $\mathbf{c}(t)$ becomes $\mathbf{c}(k)$ where k are the samples. Thus, the discretized system is as follows:

$$\dot{\mathbf{c}}(k) = \mathbf{Ho}(k) + \mathbf{p}(k) \tag{3}$$

Given that the state and control action at the instant of time $t(k)$ are known, the state of the system at instant $t(k + 1)$ can be approximated by Euler's method [16] under this consideration it is possible to apply Markov chains, which allows proposing a control law as described in Eq. 4.

$$\mathbf{o}_{ref}(k) = \frac{\mathbf{H}^{-1}}{T_0} \big(\mathbf{cd}(k + 1) - \mathbf{W}\tilde{\mathbf{c}}(k) - \mathbf{c}(k) \big) - \mathbf{p}(k) \tag{4}$$

Where $\mathbf{cd}(k)$ represent the desired values of the system; $\tilde{\mathbf{c}}$ symbolizes the control errors, being a vector of $\tilde{\mathbf{c}} \in R^{2x1}$ and $\mathbf{W}$ represents the gain matrix as: $\mathbf{W} \in R^{2x2}$: which must be a diagonal matrix so that the errors are not dependent on each other.

Using the control law proposed in Eq. 3, the behavior of the errors is described by:

$$\tilde{\mathbf{c}}(k + 1) = \mathbf{W}\tilde{\mathbf{c}}(k) \tag{5}$$

When $k = n$ in Eq. 5

$$\tilde{\mathbf{c}}(n + 1) = \mathbf{W}^n \tilde{\mathbf{c}}(n) \tag{6}$$

If w_{ii} are bounded on the interval $0 < w_{ii} < 1$ the system is globally uniformly asymptotically stable.

5   Analysis and Results

This section presents the experimental results of the virtual environment implemented for the control of an industrial process consisting of 2 distillation towers. For the execution of several simulation or experimentation tests, different situations that may arise were considered; the control algorithm based on numerical methods was implemented using MATLAB software. Meanwhile, the virtual environment and the simulation of the industrial process was implemented in Unity 3D.

For the development of the plant, we used a laptop with the following specifications: i7 eighth generation processor, with a RAM memory of 16 GB and a dedicated video card. These resources allow a fluidity in the development of the virtual application. Based on a real plant, a 3D model is obtained in Blender, which is generated through a three-dimensional geometric modeling process, which is responsible for creating consistent models that can be algorithmically managed in a computer. These models will later be exported to Unity for the simulation of the virtual system.

Once the plant is implemented in Unity using free license assets, different behaviors are programmed to allow the animation of the environment. As shown in Fig. 5.

In addition, it is important to mention that for the simulation of failures, explosions of tanks and pipes were implemented as shown in Fig. 6, these explosions are programmed

Fig. 6. Virtual environment

in a script which triggers them every time there is an error in the process. The main error occurs when there is a non-coherent control value, i.e., outside the limits preset in the model of the plant. Once an explosion is denoted, the controller in MATLAB gives an error, so the system must be reset to return to work and rebuild the towers.

Fig. 7. System failure simulation

Figure 8 shows the evolution of the plant under variations of the desired value, as can be seen. Thus, the code implemented in MATLAB complies with the control requirements, and shows a correct operation for different operating points.

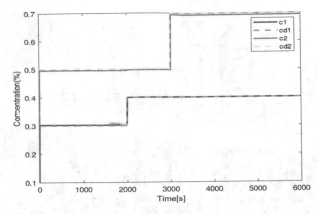

Fig. 8. Plant evolution

6 Conclusions

The development of the Virtual System for Industrial Processes using Unity software provides a very immersive experience in such industrial environment, with the use of MATLAB as a control tool greatly facilitates the management of sending and receiving data between programs, in order to monitor and control the percentage of concentration in the distillate contained in each tower. Finally, the application reflects that the developed 3D environment has components and elements that simulate a real industrial process, showing the correct operation of the mathematical model and the proposed control algorithm, since they allow reaching the desired values entered by the user, in which the errors tend to zero as the system evolves as a function of time.

Acknowledgment. The authors would like to thank the Universidad de las Fuerzas Armadas ESPE; Universidad Tecnológica Indoamérica; SISAu Research Group, and the Research Group ARSI, for the support for the development of this work.

References

1. Reis, M., Gins, G.: Industrial Process Monitoring in the Big Data/Industry 4.0 Era: from Detection, to Diagnosis, to Prognosis. Processes **5**(4), 35 (2017), https://doi.org/10.3390/pr5 030035
2. Quiroga Baquero, L.A., Padilla Vargas, M.A.: The concept of linguistic modes and their application to teaching-learning processes using ICTS. J. Behav. Health Amp Soc. Issues México **6**(1), 9–22 (2014). https://doi.org/10.5460/jbhsi.v6.1.47599
3. Vakaliuk, T.A., Kontsedailo, V.V., Antoniuk, D.S., Korotun, O.V., Mintii, I.S., Pikilnyak, A.V.: Using game simulator Software Inc in the Software Engineering education», ArXiv201201127 Cs, November 2020, Accedido: abr. 08, 2021. [En línea]. Disponible en: http://arxiv.org/abs/2012.01127
4. Araujo, R.T.S., Araujo, M.E.S., Medeiros, F.N.S., Oliveira, B.F.C., Araujo, N.M.S.: Interactive simulator for electric engineering training. IEEE Lat. Am. Trans. **14**(5). 2246–2252 (2016). https://doi.org/10.1109/TLA.2016.7530420

5. Lizcano, P.E., Manchado, C., Gomez-Jauregui, V., Otero, C.: Virtual reality to assess visual impact in wind energy projects. In: Eynard, B., Nigrelli, V., Oliveri, S.M., Peris-Fajarnes, G., Rizzuti, S. (eds.) Advances on Mechanics, Design Engineering and Manufacturing : Proceedings of the International Joint Conference on Mechanics, Design Engineering & Advanced Manufacturing (JCM 2016), 14-16 September, 2016, Catania, Italy, pp. 717–725. Springer, Cham (2017)
6. Valentino, K., Christian, K., Joelianto, E.: Virtual reality flight simulator, vol. 9, n. 1, p. 5 (2017)
7. Govea-Valladares, E.H., Medellin-Castillo, H.I., Ballesteros, J., Rodriguez-Florido, M.A.: On the development of virtual reality scenarios for computer-assisted biomedical applications. J. Healthc. Eng. **2018**, 1–13 (2018). https://doi.org/10.1155/2018/1930357
8. Andaluz, V.H., et al.: Unity3D-MatLab simulator in real time for robotics applications. In: De Paolis, L.T., Mongelli, A. (eds.) AVR 2016. LNCS, vol. 9768, pp. 246–263. Springer, Cham (2016). https://doi.org/10.1007/978-3-319-40621-3_19
9. Miranda, V., Simpson, R.: Modelling and simulation of an industrial multiple effect evaporator: tomato concentrate. J. Food Eng. **66**(2), 203–210 (2005). https://doi.org/10.1016/j.jfoodeng.2004.03.007
10. Runyon, C.H., Rumsey, T.R., McCarthy, K.L.: Dynamic simulation of a nonlinear model of a double effect evaporator. J. Food Eng. **14**(3), 185–201 (1991). https://doi.org/10.1016/0260-8774(91)90007-F
11. Gorecky, D., Khamis, M., Mura, K.: Introduction and establishment of virtual training in the factory of the future. Int. J. Comput. Integr. Manuf. **30**(1), 182–190 (2017). https://doi.org/10.1080/0951192X.2015.1067918
12. Stone, R.: Virtual reality for interactive training: an industrial practitioner's viewpoint. Int. J. Hum.-Comput. Stud. **55**(4), 699–711 (2001). https://doi.org/10.1006/ijhc.2001.0497
13. Roldán, J.J., Crespo, E., Martín-Barrio, A., Peña-Tapia, E., Barrientos, A.: A training system for Industry 4.0 operators in complex assemblies based on virtual reality and process mining. Robot. Comput.-Integr. Manuf. **59**, 305–316 (2019). https://doi.org/10.1016/j.rcim.2019.05.004
14. Myatezh, S.V., Shchurov, N.I., Ivanov, V.V.: Development of methods of structural synthesis for single-phase rectifiers with increased rectified voltage. Russ. Electr. Eng. **89**(5), 350–354 (2018). https://doi.org/10.3103/S1068371218050073
15. Sira-Ramírez, H., Silva-Navarro, G.: On the regulation of a double effect evaporator: a trajectory planning and passivity approach. IFAC Proc. Vol. **32**(2), 2328–2333 (1999). https://doi.org/10.1016/S1474-6670(17)56395-8
16. Lunghi, G., Marin, R., Castro, M.D., Masi, A., Sanz, P.J.: Multimodal human-robot interface for accessible remote robotic interventions in hazardous environments. IEEE Access **7**, 127290–127319 (2019). https://doi.org/10.1109/ACCESS.2019.2939493

Virtual Control of a Perfectly Stirred Reactor for Cyclopentene Production

Daniel D. Amores[1]([⊠]), Edwin P. Lema[1]([⊠]), Lucía D. Guerrero[1]([⊠]),
Víctor H. Andaluz[1,2]([⊠]), Brayan A. García[1]([⊠]), Alex V. Guanopatín[1]([⊠]),
and José Varela-Aldás[2]

[1] Universidad de las Fuerzas Armadas ESPE, Sangolquí, Ecuador
{ddamores,eplema1,ldguerrero1,vhandaluz1,bagarcia,
avguanopatin}@espe.edu.ec
[2] SISAu Research Group, Universidad Tecnológica Indoamérica, Ambato, Ecuador
josevarela@uti.edu.ec

Abstract. This article developed the implementation of a controller for a Perfectly Stirred Reactor (CSTR) for the production of Cyclopentene, through a 3D virtual environment, oriented to the teaching-learning process which allows an immersion to the industrial field. The non-linear process modeling is considered in order to implement a closed loop control algorithm and the simulation of the process through animations in the virtual environment, which is equipped with different elements that faithfully simulate the real process, such as: industrial instrumentation, surround sounds, catastrophic events, etc. Finally, the behavior of the system is validated against the nonlinear controller based on numerical methods with several experimental tests.

Keywords: Virtual reality · Chemical reaction · CSTR reactor

1 Introducción

The advancement of technology has made it possible to solve various problems throughout history and the needs of people, whatever the problem that arises [1]. This has been the case of controller design and simulation techniques since a wrong choice of control structure can impose fundamental limitations on system performance, and especially economic losses in industrial processes [2]. This is the origin of advanced controllers and virtual process representation (VR).

Complex chemical reactions are one of the most important research topics in reaction engineering and thus occupy a privileged place in the academic, research and industrial world. As a result, a large number of alternative solutions have been implemented for any problem that may arise in the future [3, 4]. Over the years, the industries that manufacture chemical products have been updating the processes of elaboration of the products, for this purpose, machinery has been implemented, which have a controlled performance in order to avoid losses in the process [5].

© Springer Nature Switzerland AG 2021
L. T. De Paolis et al. (Eds.): AVR 2021, LNCS 12980, pp. 680–689, 2021.
https://doi.org/10.1007/978-3-030-87595-4_49

CSTR reactors are present in chemical and petrochemical plants due to their perfect agitation characteristic [6]. This type of reactor is widely used in the chemical industry and its design is of utmost importance because it can affect the efficiency of a process [7, 8]. This type of reactor in its ideal configuration is used for most of the reactions in liquid phase, one of its characteristics is that the density change with the reaction is usually very small and can be negligible.

The need to realistically represent the behavior of in-plant industrial control algorithms before implementing them in real life has led to several technological advances in the fields of 3D animation. A large number of industrial processes can be visualized and their behavior can be analyzed in a very practical and intuitive way, and at the same time each of the characteristics of the implemented systems can be observed graphically [9, 10], as well as the behavior of processes within a virtualized environment. Virtual reality (VR) can be described as a set of technologies that allow people to interact with a virtual environment beyond reality [11, 12]. VR leverages informatics technology development and scientific visualization to create a virtual world [13]. The use of VR has become very popular because it offers a high level of realism and immersion, but requires advanced computing technologies capable of processing large amounts of scientific data and graphics [14, 15].

This work presents the simulation of a real process considering a perfectly stirred reactor for the production of cyclopentane, in a Virtual Reality environment. In order to simulate the dynamic behavior of the reactor against the control actions provided by a nonlinear control based on numerical methods, a DLL communication has been implemented to connect the control system and the simulation system (Matlab and Unity). In the latter allowing direct user interaction.

This article is divided into VI sections, including the Introduction, in the second section are detailed: the structure of the system to which the design of each of the components of the system is governed, the third section details the modeling of the process of a CSTR reactor and the design of the nonlinear controller based on numerical methods, In the Fourth Section, the procedure for the virtualization of the CSTR reactor process is detailed, while in the Fifth Section, the results obtained through experimental tests in which the user enters the different reference values with their respective analysis of results are detailed.

2   System Structure

This article points out the design of a controller through a virtual environment of an industrial process to monitor the physical variables of the process, this serves as a reference to know in detail the implemented process. The user can interact with the virtual environment developed, varying different parameters of the main process in order to visualize the events that may occur in different conditions of the plant.

Figure 1 shows the scheme of the present work, which is implemented through the integration of software (Unity-Matlab), both with the purpose of performing the closed-loop control of a CSTR reactor. On the other hand, the scheme consists of a nonlinear controller, which bases its structure and operation on the mathematical model of the process. Using as inputs the references provided by the operator (temperature and

cyclopentene concentration) and these in turn in difference with the signal provided by
the process, enter the controller to generate an equivalent control signal that is sent to the
final control elements (valves). In order to realistically visualize the evolution of the variables that make up the system, it was decided to develop a virtual environment equipped
with different features of the process such as: control panel, HMI, industrial instrumentation, surrounding sounds, personnel locomotion, etc., thus allowing an immersive and
interactive environment for the user. Finally, to communicate bilaterally between the
controller hosted in Matlab software and the process represented by the mathematical
model hosted in Unity, DLL-based communication is used through Shared memory, thus
fulfilling the purpose of closing the process control loop.

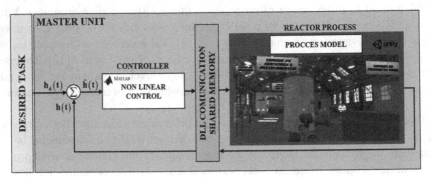

Fig. 1. Esquema del sistema propuesto.

3   Modeling and Control

Within the field of process control modeling and control play very important roles thanks
to the union of these two can be achieved that a process is efficient and robust. And they
are closely related since the mathematical model can be used for the design of advanced
controllers and also for the simulation of the process in order to evaluate the controller,
which is why this section details the mathematical model of the CSTR reactor and the
control strategy used.

3.1   System Model

The CSTR model represents a system consisting of a continuous stirred tank reactor that
simulates the multiple reactions used to obtain cyclo-pentene from cyclopentadylene
[2]. Inside this reactor there are series and parallel reactions between the system input
and the product obtained.

The CSTR reactor process considered for the present article is shown in Fig. 2,
which is formed by a main tank where the necessary chemical reaction is achieved by
controlling the temperature T_k by means of the steam flow that enters by means of a
valve Q, on the other hand, the control of the cyclopentene concentration is achieved by

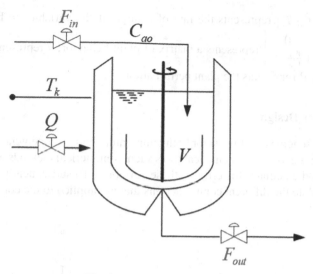

Fig. 2. CSTR reactor process

controlling the inlet flow C_{ao} by means of the flow that passes the valve F_{in} and related to the temperature.

The Cyclopentadilene flow and the heat flow entering the jacket are the inputs of the system and the outputs are the temperature of the reactor jacket and the Cyclopentadilene flow. With these considerations the mathematical model of the reactor is detailed as follows [16].

Cyclopentadilene Balance

$$\frac{d(C_A)}{dt} = \frac{F}{V}(C_{A0} - C_A) - k_1(T)C_A - k_3(T)C_A^2 \tag{1}$$

Cyclopentene Balance

$$\frac{d(C_B)}{dt} = -\frac{F}{V}C_B + k_1(T)C_A - K_2(T)C_B \tag{2}$$

Temperature Mass Balance

$$\frac{d(T)}{dt} = \frac{1}{\rho C_p}\left[k_1(T)C_A(-\Delta H_{RAB}) + k_2(T)C_B(-\Delta H_{RBC}) + k_3(T)C_A^2(-\Delta H_{RAD})\right]$$

$$+ \frac{F}{V}(T_0 - T) + \frac{k_w A_R}{\rho C_p V}(T_k - T) \tag{3}$$

by compactly rewriting Eqs. (1), (2) and (3) we have:

$$\dot{h} = Hv + P \tag{4}$$

where, $\dot{\mathbf{h}} = \begin{bmatrix} \dot{C}_B & \dot{T} \end{bmatrix}$ represents the rate of change of the variables to be controlled;
$\mathbf{H} = \begin{bmatrix} -C_B(t) & 0 \\ T_0 - T(t) & \frac{K_w A_R}{C_\rho \rho V} \end{bmatrix}$ represents a matrix of plant behavior; $\mathbf{v}$ represents the control
actions; finally $\mathbf{P}$ represents the plant perturbations.

3.2 Controller Design

The controller scheme (see Fig. 3) for both temperature and cyclopentene concentration
was made with the use of mathematical tools such as numerical methods which for each
sampling period calculates the error of these variables. To subsequently use this error
signal to calculate the different control actions that are applied to the control valves.

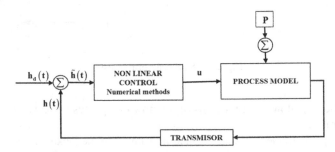

Fig. 3. Control scheme implemented.

In the obtained model (4) it must be discretized using Euler's method, where we
express the derivative (5) of the variables to be controlled as follows:

$$\frac{\mathbf{h}(k+1) - \mathbf{h}(k)}{t_s} = \mathbf{H}(k)\mathbf{v}(k) + \mathbf{P}(k) \tag{5}$$

The evolution of the variables to be controlled after a sampling period can be
determined with the use of the Markov Chain and is defined as follows: $\mathbf{h}(k+1) = \mathbf{h}_d(k+1) - \mathbf{W}[\mathbf{h}_d(k) - \mathbf{h}(k)]$. Based on this, the control law of the present work can
be defined as follows:

$$\mathbf{v}_c(k) = \mathbf{H}^{-1} \frac{[\mathbf{h}_d(k+1) - \mathbf{W}[\mathbf{h}_d(k) - \mathbf{h}(k)] - \mathbf{h}(k)]}{t_s} + \mathbf{P} \tag{6}$$

where, the error is defined as $\tilde{\mathbf{h}} = \mathbf{h}_d - \mathbf{h}$; the process references as $\mathbf{h}_d = [C_{bd} \ T_d]^T$;
t_s as the sampling period and finally $\mathbf{W}$ the gain matrix that allows to compensate the
control errors.

For the stability analysis, the evolution of the discrete control (6) is analyzed in each
of the sampling periods, considering a state of $\tilde{\mathbf{h}}$.

$$\mathbf{W}\left[\tilde{\mathbf{h}}(k)\right] = \tilde{\mathbf{h}}(k+1), \tag{7}$$

$k = 1$,

$$\tilde{\mathbf{h}}_1(2) = \mathbf{W}\left[\tilde{\mathbf{h}}_1(1)\right],$$

$k = 2$,

$$\tilde{\mathbf{h}}_1(3) = \mathbf{W}\left[\tilde{\mathbf{h}}_1(2)\right] = \mathbf{W}^2\left[\tilde{\mathbf{h}}_1(1)\right],$$

$k = 3$,

$$\tilde{\mathbf{h}}_1(4) = \mathbf{W}\left[\tilde{\mathbf{h}}_1(3)\right] = \mathbf{W}^3\left[\tilde{\mathbf{h}}_1(1)\right],$$

$$\tilde{\mathbf{h}}_1(l+1) = \mathbf{W}^n\left[\tilde{\mathbf{h}}_1(1)\right] \tag{8}$$

considered (8) we have that when $0 < \mathbf{W} < 1$, is guaranteed $\tilde{\mathbf{h}}(t) \to 0$ to be asymptotically stable with $m \to \infty$.

4   Virtualization

This section presents the multi-layered scheme for the creation of an immersive and interactive virtual environment that allows the direct interaction of the user with the process and with different instances of instrumentation where it is possible to interact with the variables of the process.

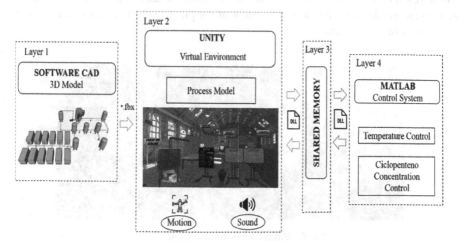

Fig. 4. Process layer diagram

Figure 4 describes the process for the creation of the virtualized environment in the Unity 3D platform and the elements that make up the virtual reality application, which are described in layers: Layer 1, the 3D models are designed considering the layout found in a real industrial process with the use of tools such as Plant 3D that provides functionalities such as checking the concordance between the P&ID diagram and the 3D model to have a virtualized environment as close as possible to the real one, in turn, 3ds Max additional software is used as an intermediary to customize the environments where these objects are located, it also provides robust tools that help to manage animations, texturing, defining an appropriate scale, modifying the position, appropriate orientation through the modeling engines, rendering and changing the CAD model formats to the format admissible by the Unity 3D platform; layer 2, the elements are placed considering the layout of the real CSTR reactor, in which the different animations are included to provide realism to the normal operation and the dangers that can arise when exceeding control limits because the present work has an educational approach which includes raising awareness about the different dangers that can cause the mismanagement of the variables, also including sounds corresponding to the animations so that the environment is immersive; Layer 3, allows communication between layer 2 and 4, in which the variables are exchanged for input to the controller and feedback through the evolution of the plant that in this case is simulated by the mathematical model obtained to close the control loop; Layer 4, the last stage is in the Matlab software in which contains the proposed controllers including both the controller for the temperature and the controller for the concentration of cyclopentene.

5   Experimental Results

In order to analyze and recognize the Cyclopentene production process, the virtual environment was implemented (see Fig. 5), which represents the production of the same, whose results are presented in this section, in which the user will be represented by an avatar that has the ability to move throughout the plant exploring and visualizing each of the parts of the process.

Fig. 5. Virtual environment implemented

Within the industry, industrial instrumentation plays a very important role for control and decision making by the operator in charge of a certain section of the plant. That is why Fig. 6 shows each of the indicators, transmitters and transducers implemented within

Fig. 6. Industrial instrumentation in the virtual environment.

the virtual environment, all of this with the purpose that the operator's experience is as close to reality as possible.

Another way of analyzing and viewing data implemented in the industry are the well-known SCADA systems whose main objective is to provide the operator with information of the process in a supervision room, which displays this information in the form of trends, numerical, alarms, etc. Figure 7 shows the above mentioned as well as a control panel that allows the user to interact with the virtual environment by varying the references of the process through the sliders implemented in the panel.

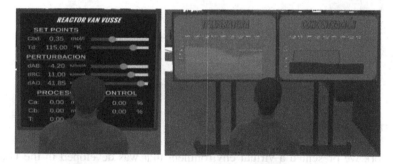

Fig. 7. SCADA system and control panel in the virtual environment

Finally, Fig. 8 shows the control errors and the evolution of the process variables, once the experimental test has been carried out by integrating the software described in this document.

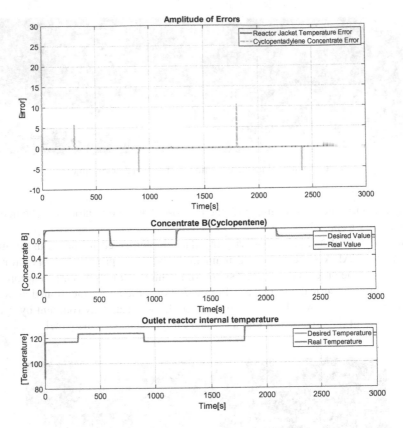

Fig. 8. Control errors and plant evolution.

6 Conclusions

In this work we presented a virtual environment that was developed in the Unity 3D graphics engine, which allows the contribution in the field of teaching-learning in engineering students. This virtual environment is similar to an industrial environment where CSTR reactors are managed, which will help to provide the student an immersive experience in an industrial environment, the use of Matlab as a control tool allows to manage the data received and sent between programs in order to monitor and control the temperature value in the reaction tank and the amount of concentration of cyclopentene in the same reaction tank. The results obtained from the VR application showed that the three-dimensional environment developed is immersive, and has components and elements that resemble a real industrial process; both the mathematical model of the system and the implemented control algorithm work effectively since they allow reaching the set points entered by the user, in which the errors tend to zero as time elapses.

Acknowledgment. The authors would like to thank the Universidad de las Fuerzas Armadas ESPE; Universidad Tecnológica Indoamérica; SISAu Research Group, and the Research Group ARSI, for the support for the development of this work.

References

1. Kaiser, N.M., Flassig, R.J., Sundmacher, K.: Reactor-network synthesis via flux profile analysis. Chem. Eng. J. **335**, 1018–1030 (2018)
2. Trierweiler, J.O., Engell, S.: Controllability analysis via the robust performance number for a CSTR with Van de Vusse reaction. In: 1997 European Control Conference (ECC), pp. 3083–3088. IEEE (1997)
3. Rastegar, S.: Multi Parametric Intelligent Identification and Robust Control Methodologies for Industrial Processes (Doctoral dis-sertation, 00500, Universidade de Coimbra) (2017)
4. Arrieta, O., Vilanova, R., Alfaro, V.M., Moreno, R.: Considerations on PIDController operation: aplication to a continuous stirred tank reactor. In: IEEE International Conference on Emerging Technologies and Factory Automation (ETFA), 2008, Hamburg, Germany, pp.265–272 (2008)
5. Alfaro, V.M., Vilanova, R.: Two-degree-of-freedom proportional integralcontrol of inverse response second-order processes. In: 16th International Conference on System Theory, Control and Computing (ICSTCC) 2012, Sinaia, Romania, pp. 1–6 (2012)
6. Govea-Valladares, E.H., Medellin-Castillo, H.I., Ballesteros, J., Rodriguez-Florido, M.A.: On the development of virtual reality scenarios for computer-assisted biomedical applications. J. Healthc. Eng. 2018, 1–13 (2018). https://doi.org/10.1155/2018/1930357.
7. Folleto del Curso Análisis de Sistemas IE-0409, I-2013: Escuela de Ingeniería Electrica, Universidad de Costa Rica, p. 237
8. Rosas, S.M.: Catalizadores bifuncionales de IR, PT y RH, mono y bimetálicos, soportados en SIO_2-AL_2O_3 para apertura de anillo de decalina (2018)
9. Díaz, H.A.M.: Diseño de un neurocontrolador dinámico (DBP) aplicado a un reactor químico continuo (CSTR). Pontificia Universidad Catolica del Peru-CENTRUM Catolica (Peru) (2011)
10. Aguirre, C.J.M.: Diseño e implementación de cuatro esquemas de control modificados basados en el predictor de Smith en una tarjeta embebida, aplicados a dos modelos simulados que presentan retardo: un tanque de mezclado y un reactor de agitación continua (CSTR) (Bachelor's thesis, Quito, 2019) (2019)
11. The Japanese Society of Pathology: The Japanese Society of Pathology Guideline. The Japanese Society of Pathology, Japan (2015)
12. How Telemedicine Answers Global Pathology Demands (2018). https://proscia.com/blog/2015/07/14/global-crisis-digital-solution
13. Morrison, A.O., Gardner, J.M.: Microscopic image ohotography techniques of the past, present, and future. Arch. Pathol. Lab. Med. **139**(12), 1558–1564 (2015)
14. Yugcha, E.P., Ubilluz, J.I., Andaluz, V.H.: Virtual Training for Industrial Process: Pumping System (2019)
15. Andaluz, V.H., et al.: Unity3D-MatLab simulator in real time for robotics applications. In: De Paolis, L.T., Mongelli, A. (eds.) AVR 2016. LNCS, vol. 9768, pp. 246–263. Springer, Cham (2016). https://doi.org/10.1007/978-3-319-40621-3_19
16. Engell, S., Klatt, K.-U.: Nonlinear control of a non-minimum-phase CSTR. En. In: 1993 American Control Conference, pp. 2941–2945. IEEE (1993)

Virtual Control of a Double Effect Evaporator for Teaching-Learning Processes

Ronald J. Garcés[1]($\boxtimes$), Juan F. Lomas[1]($\boxtimes$), Jessica G. Pilatasig[1]($\boxtimes$),
Víctor H. Andaluz[1,2]($\boxtimes$), Andrea E. Tutasig[1]($\boxtimes$), Alexis S. Zambrano[1]($\boxtimes$),
and José Varela-Aldás[2]($\square$)

[1] Universidad de Las Fuerzas Armadas ESPE, Sangolquí, Ecuador
{rjgarces,jflomas1,jgpilatasig,vhandaluz1,aetutasig,
aszambrano2}@espe.edu.ec
[2] SISAu Research Group, Universidad Tecnológica Indoamérica, Ambato, Ecuador
josevarela@uti.edu.ec

Abstract. This article presents the control and virtualisation of a double effect evaporator plant oriented to teaching-learning processes. A virtual process with similar characteristics to a real one is implemented using CAD tools and the Unity 3D graphic engine, with the aim of simulating the behaviour of an industrial process, specifically, a double effect evaporator; this allows the behaviour of the process to be evaluated and control manoeuvres to be implemented without putting the safety of the operator or the plant at risk. The result is an interactive and immersive virtual environment between the user and the industrial process. The dynamic modelling of the double effect evaporator is incorporated in the virtual environment, so that the virtual animation is similar to a real process.

Keywords: Unity 3D · Double effect evaporator · Virtual environment · Numerical methods

1 Introduction

Evaporation is used to obtain highly concentrated products with low energy impact, as only the first effect requires energy produced in a process outside the evaporator. Within this plant, the vapour produced in the first effect is used to provide energy for the second effect [1–5]. The same principle is applicable as many times as necessary to obtain the desired concentration level, mainly in the sugar industry, evaporators with one to eight effects are used, depending on the heat capacity of the substance and the required flow rate, which is why a double effect evaporator is analysed [3–5].

The double-acting evaporator model is a mathematical model derived from the principle of conservation of energy in conjunction with the law of material balance. The double-acting evaporator is considered to be a non-linear system of the sixth order, there is difficulty in modelling, so it is necessary to assume conditions, e.g., perfect mixing of the substance, no foreign matter in the vapour generated and no vapour retention [6, 7].

© Springer Nature Switzerland AG 2021
L. T. De Paolis et al. (Eds.): AVR 2021, LNCS 12980, pp. 690–700, 2021.
https://doi.org/10.1007/978-3-030-87595-4_50

The proper design of a controller that governs each of the concentration levels of each effect guarantees the optimal operation of the plant. It is important to maintain uninterrupted control of the process to improve the efficiency in the production of concentrated molasses at the output of the second effect [8]. The control parameters include steam flow and the inlet concentration directly at the first effect [9].

Based on advances in virtual reality and global technology, the use of virtual applications can be implemented in the future and the use of real laboratories can be reduced, thus providing more access to training in industrial processes. The multi-platform game engine Unity is used to virtualise real components that favour the study and understanding of the behaviour of various applications, which creates a valuable tool in new teaching methods, representing an improvement in learning for students who do not have access to real systems. [10].

Some researchers predict the growth of distance education in the areas of science, technology, and engineering [11]. In order to improve the methods for industrial training, they propose a virtual didactic tool which is presented as a solution to the latent difficulty of professional training, where one can become familiar with the process and learn from it [12].

As time goes by, process virtualisation is becoming more widespread and is used for different applications. This has allowed a virtual tour of industrial plants and interaction with them, with designs being made based on the characteristics of the real plant [13, 14]. There are some projects where the virtualisation of evaporators used in the sugar industry is presented. In the operation, the molasses-water mixture, the process response and the action of the controller are obtained. The development of these works shows the obvious advantages of using this type of training system, such as the creation of safe situations in critical processes within the plant or the familiarisation of the production stages.

This work presents the implementation of an interactive and immersive virtual environment oriented to the control of a double effect evaporator widely used in the sugar industries. All the components of the evaporation plant are designed from a P&ID diagram that is taken as a reference for the creation of the plant in 3D using computer aided software. The animation of the plant's own objects is implemented in the UNITY 3D graphics engine. The virtual environment incorporates a control panel that allows the process control parameters to be modified and the evolution of the system to be visualised. Through bilateral communication between Unity and MatLab, advanced control algorithms are implemented to control the system in real time. Finally, the operation of the process is shown, allowing the user to observe the behaviour and interact with the plant.

The stages that make up this work are described as follows: Sect. 2 describes the Structured System where the implementation of the virtual environment is specified, the 3D simulation design diagram. The control scheme is detailed in Sect. 3. In addition, it includes the analysis of robustness to disturbances; Sect. 4 describes the analysis of results; and finally, Sect. 5 describes the conclusions of the work.

2 Structured System

The present work is oriented towards the simulation of a virtual environment corresponding to a double effect evaporator commonly used in sugar mills, making use of P&ID diagrams which provide relevant information about the physical and instrumental constitution of the system. The simulation focuses its application on the visualisation of the process allowing the user to interact with a simulated environment representing the evolution of the concentration level in each effect [15].

The behaviour of the process, through the dynamic model, is implemented directly in the Unity 3D graphics engine and through bilateral communication with the Matlab software it allows to simulate the interaction between the plant and the controller algorithm, respectively, and in this way the user can interact with the behaviour of the industrial process [13, 16].

Figure 1 shows the implementation of the virtual environment proposed in this work, the architecture of the virtual system is comprised of two main stages: *i) Creation of the Station*, studies the structure of a real plant with the concatenation of a P&ID diagram which helps to better understand the dimensions and the complete operation of the process, subsequently the CAD design allows the development and virtualisation of the physical structure of the double effect evaporator. Once the 3D plant has been modelled, it is exported in ".fbx" format for its subsequent import into the virtual environment; and *ii) Virtual Environment*, the 3D modelling developed in the CAD tool is imported into the Unity 3D graphic engine where the programming of each object is carried out, a virtual environment is created with Unity's own tools with the help of assets to provide a more user-friendly and realistic environment and an avatar that interacts with the environment. Finally, the shared memories provided by the research group "ARSI" are used to achieve a bilateral communication between MatLab and Unity and consequently simulate the interaction between controller and process, respectively.

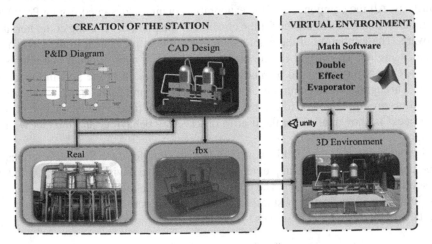

Fig. 1. 3D object construction diagram

Figure 2 shows the diagram of the whole system implemented for the development of the present work, which is made up of four main stages: Virtual Scene, Scripts and Math Software.

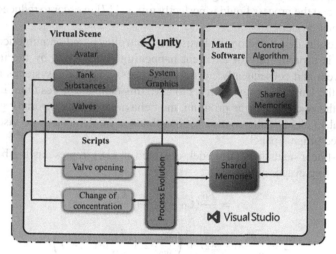

Fig. 2. System diagram.

The VIRTUAL SCENE stage consists of modules necessary to interact with the environment, observe the animation of the process and the results of the simulation. It is subdivided as follows: *(i) Valves*, modifies the opening according to the control actions; *(ii) Tank Substance*, varies the colouring of the evaporator effects depending on the output concentration; *(iii) Avatar*, allows navigation throughout the virtual environment enabling interaction with it; *(iv) System Graphics*, represents graphically, by means of computational modules, the system responses such as: output concentrations, control actions and control errors.

The SCRIPTS stage describes the codes implemented for the animation of 3D objects to obtain the correct functioning of the plant. It is subdivided as follows: *(i) Process evolution*, it is in charge of evolving the system according to the implemented mathematical model, this is the main module of the whole process and it is associated with the secondary modules; *(ii) Concentration Change*, it modifies the colouring of the liquid inside the tanks in the virtual environment depending on the concentration value; *(iii) Valve Opening*, by means of the control actions, animates the movement of the valves in the virtual environment; *(iv) Shared Memories* allows bilateral communication between the SCRIPTS stage and MATH SOFTWARE by sending and receiving data to and from each other; and *(v) Shared Memories* allows bilateral communication between the SCRIPTS stage and MATH SOFTWARE by sending and receiving data to and from the SCRIPTS stage.

The MATH SOFTWARE stage is where the system controller is implemented, it is mainly composed of the module: *(i) Control Algorithm*, the control law of the plant that rectifies the errors is applied; and *(ii) Shared Memories* that fulfils the same operation denoted in the SCRIPTS stage.

3 Control Scheme

A double acting evaporator is considered to be a sixth order non-linear system. This model is simplified by considering conditions such as: There is no heat loss to the environment and the process liquid is perfectly mixed [17] in order to reduce to a second order non-linear system.

The process is developed on the basis of a controller based on numerical methods, where there is a probability of an event happening conditioned by the immediately preceding event and consequently storing the process data in the system's memory. In such a way, the Unity 3D engine allows to save this data and stores them in memories that, during the execution of the program, the behaviour of the evaporator given by the mathematical model and the control actions that are implemented are visualised in a predetermined graphic panel.

The non-linear mathematical model, obtained in [18], represents the behaviour of the double acting evaporator,

$$\dot{x}_1 = \frac{F_0}{w_1}(C_0 - x_1) + \frac{k_1}{w_1}x_1 u \tag{1}$$

$$\dot{x}_2 = \frac{F_0}{w_2}(x_1 - x_2) + \left(\frac{k_2}{w_2}x_2 + \frac{k_1}{w_2}(x_1 - x_2)\right)u \tag{2}$$

where: the inputs to the process, u and C_0, are the vapour flow and inlet concentration, respectively, and the process outputs, x_1 and x_2, are the concentrations of the first and second tank respectively. The constants, F_0 is the solution flow at the process inlet, w_1 and w_2 is the mass of the liquid retained in the first and second tank respectively, k_1 and k_2 static flux constant of the two effects respectively.

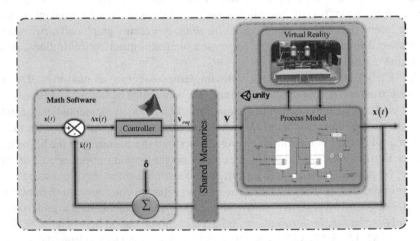

Fig. 3. Control scheme: interaction between MatLab and unity.

Figure 3 shows the implementation in the respective software of each element that makes up the block diagram, emphasising that the controller is in the mathematical software and the process in the virtual environment.

Consider the system described in Fig. 3, where the double-acting evaporator process is defined as:

$$\dot{\mathbf{x}}(t) = \mathbf{H}(\mathbf{x}(t))\mathbf{v}(t) + \mathbf{b}(\mathbf{x}(t)) \tag{3}$$

The non-linear equations of the system described in (1) and (2) are represented in matrix form. Where $\dot{\mathbf{x}}(t) \in \mathbb{R}^{2\times1}$ is the output vector of the process,

$$\dot{\mathbf{x}} = \begin{bmatrix} \dot{x}_1 \\ \dot{x}_2 \end{bmatrix} \tag{4}$$

$\mathbf{H}(\mathbf{x}(t)) \in \mathbb{R}^{2\times2}$ represents the non-constant matrix of the process with respect to the input variables,

$$\mathbf{H} = \begin{bmatrix} \frac{k_1}{w_1}x_1 & \frac{F_0}{w_1} \\ \frac{k_2}{w_2}x_2 + \frac{k_1}{w_2}(x_1 - x_2) & 0 \end{bmatrix} \tag{5}$$

$\mathbf{v}(t) \in \mathbb{R}^{2\times1}$ symbolises the input vector of the process,

$$\mathbf{v} = \begin{bmatrix} u \\ C_0 \end{bmatrix} \tag{6}$$

and $\mathbf{b}(\mathbf{x}(t)) \in \mathbb{R}^{2\times1}$ corresponds to the non-constant vector with independent terms.

$$\mathbf{b} = \begin{bmatrix} -\frac{F_0}{w_1}x_1 \\ \frac{F_0}{w_2}(x_1 - x_2) \end{bmatrix} \tag{7}$$

Under the criteria $t = kT_o$, where T_o is the sampling period, the process can be discretised. Use is made of the Euler method, which is a form of integration denoted in approximation (8),

$$\frac{1}{T_o}(\mathbf{x}(k+1) - \mathbf{x}(k)) \approx \dot{\mathbf{x}}(t) \tag{8}$$

The discretised equation of the process is obtained,

$$\mathbf{x}(k+1) = T_o(\mathbf{H}(\mathbf{x}(k))\mathbf{v}(k) + \mathbf{b}(\mathbf{x}(k))) + \mathbf{x}(k) \tag{9}$$

It is necessary to know the evolution of the variable, under this consideration we use the Markov chains, denoted in (10), which allows us to know the future value knowing previous data.

$$\mathbf{x}(k+1) = \mathbf{x_d}(k+1) - \mathbf{W}\Delta\mathbf{x}(k) \tag{10}$$

where $\mathbf{x_d}(k+1)$ is a vector of desired values at time instant $(k+1)$, $\mathbf{W} \in \mathbb{R}^{2\times2}$ is an adjustable diagonal gain matrix and $\Delta\mathbf{x}(k)$ the vector of control errors, defined as $\Delta\mathbf{x}(k) = \mathbf{x_d}(k) - \tilde{\mathbf{x}}(k)$ being $\tilde{\mathbf{x}}(k) = \mathbf{x}(k) + \delta(k)$ feedback from the control system and $\delta(k)$ disturbances in the sensor measurement.

Therefore, the following control law (5) is proposed which is the output of the controller.

$$\mathbf{v}_{req}(k) = \mathbf{H}^{-1}(\mathbf{x}(k))\left[\frac{1}{T_o}(\mathbf{x_d}(k+1) - \mathbf{W}\Delta\mathbf{x}(k) - \mathbf{x}(k)) - \mathbf{b}(x(k))\right] \quad (11)$$

To perform the robustness analysis of the system, the input of the process is first considered to be the output of the controller, then $\mathbf{v}(k) = \mathbf{v}_{req}(k)$, thus gives the closed-loop equation of the system,

$$\Delta\mathbf{x}(k+1) = \mathbf{W}\Delta\mathbf{x}(k) - \mathbf{W}\delta(k) \quad (12)$$

Table 1 shows the evolution of the closed-loop equation evaluated at the j-th value.

Table 1. Evolution of the closed-loop equation.

k	$\Delta\mathbf{x}(k+1)$	$\mathbf{W}\Delta\mathbf{x}(k) - \mathbf{W}\delta(k)$
1	$\Delta\mathbf{x_i}(2)$	$w_{ii}\Delta x_i(1) - w_{ii}\delta_i(1)$
2	$\Delta\mathbf{x_i}(3)$	$w_{ii}\Delta x_i(2) - w_{ii}\delta_i(2) = w_{ii}(w_{ii}\Delta x_i(1) - w_{ii}\delta_i(1)) - w_{ii}\delta_i(2)$
		$= w_{ii}^2\Delta x_i(1) - w_{ii}^2\delta_i(1) - w_{ii}\delta_i(2)$
j	$\Delta\mathbf{x_i}(j+1)$	$w_{ii}^j\Delta x_i(1) - w_{ii}^j\delta_i(1) - w_{ii}^{j-1}\delta_i(2) - ... - w_{ii}^2\delta_i(j-1) - w_{ii}\delta_i(j)$

It is known that the diagonal of the gain matrix is formed by $w_{ii} = diagonal(w_{11}, w_{22})$ and if a change of variable is made $k = j$ can be described in the evolution at the instant j,

$$\Delta x_i = w_{ii}^j\Delta x_i(1) - w_{ii}^j\delta_i(1) - w_{ii}^{j-1}\delta_i(2) - ... - w_{ii}^2\delta_i(j-1) - w_{ii}\delta_i(j) \quad (13)$$

The gain matrix is considered to be bounded between the values of $0 < w_{ii} < 1$, the limit of the closed-loop equation is applied in time $j \to \infty$, as seen in (14).

$$\lim_{j\to\infty} \Delta x_i = -w_{ii}\delta_i(\infty) \quad (14)$$

Hence, if the perturbation value is bounded, then the Glo-balmente Uniformly Uniformly Stable system.

4   Analysis and Results

This section presents the implementation of a virtual environment in the area of industrial processes, specifically a double effect evaporator, oriented to teaching-learning processes. Figure 4 shows the complete simulation of the operation of the double effect evaporator, which consists of different blocks detailed below.

Figure 5 shows an avatar that allows the user to navigate through the virtual environment consisting of an environment similar to an industrial plant, where the simulated double acting evaporator is located.

Fig. 4. Simulation of a virtual environment.

Fig. 5. Avatar interacting in the virtual environment.

Figure 6 shows the implementation of the double effect evaporator which has the capacity to simulate the behaviour of a real evaporator, as it can represent the variation of the concentration in each of the effects by varying the shade of the substance inside each tank. The higher the concentration, the greater the yellowish hue.

Fig. 6. Double-acting evaporator in operation.

The control panels, shown in Fig. 7, make it possible to modify the process control parameters and to visualise the behaviour of the plant and the controller. It is possible to view graphs of plant responses, control actions and control errors. The output concentrations reach their respective equilibrium point governed by the built-in control law, and as the system evolves, the control errors can be seen.

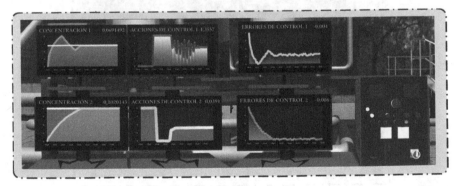

Fig. 7. Control panels.

The animated valves simulate the same operation as real valves, which have a limited angular displacement between zero and ninety degrees depending on the control law, as shown in Fig. 8.

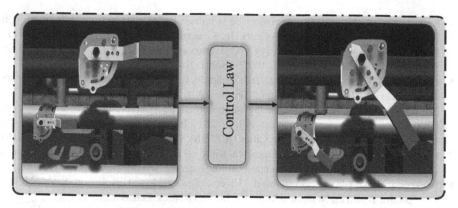

Fig. 8. Control valves.

5 Conclusions

The virtualisation of a double effect evaporator by means of 3D modelling with most of the characteristics present in a real process, allows the user to become familiar with an industrial environment, thus achieving an integral academic and professional development. The option of having a complete plant at the total disposal of the users/students represents a very significant advance in the teaching-learning process, since with a computer with medium-high resources, an interactive environment can be achieved that is easy to access and, above all, very low cost compared to a real system.

The virtual environment implemented allows the implementation of a complete process control system without the need to interact with the real plant, thus reducing possible work accidents due to lack of training, human or mechanical failures that can compromise the integrity of the operator and the plant.

Acknowledgment. The authors would like to thank the Universidad de las Fuerzas Armadas ESPE; Universidad Tecnológica Indoamérica; SISAu Research Group, and the Research Group ARSI, for the support for the development of this work.

References

1. George, S., Kyatanavar, D.N.: Optimization of multiple effect evaporator using fuzzy logic integrated with Taguchi technique. In: 2016 International Conference on Electrical, Electronics, and Optimization Techniques (ICEEOT), Chennai, India, pp. 1415–1419 (2016)
2. Oliden, J., Manrique, Y.J., Ipanaqué, W.: Modelado, simulación y control no lineal de un evaporador para la producción de bioetanol. In: Conferencia CHILENA 2017 de Ingeniería Eléctrica, Electrónica, Tecnologías de la Información y las Comunicaciones (CHILECON), Pucón, pp. 1–6 (2017)
3. Ben-Ali, S.: Modeling of a double effect evaporator: bond graph approach. Chem. Eng. Res. Des. CHERD-3261. **138**, 554–567. Elsevier, Tunisia (2018)

4. Ramanathan, S., Rakshit, D.: Improving the sustainability of wastewater treatment through solar-assisted multiple effect evaporators. In: Gautam, A., De, S., Dhar, A., Gupta, J.G., Pandey, A. (eds.) Sustainable Energy and Transportation. EES, pp. 149–161. Springer, Singapore (2018). https://doi.org/10.1007/978-981-10-7509-4_9

5. Díaz, C.M., Villamizar, E.V., Miranda, H.J., Delgado, E.D.: Study of double acting evaporators In: Engineering, Basic and Agricultural Series, vol. 1. Infometric@, Pamplona (2018)

6. Pan, D., Ning, C.: Mechanism modeling and nonlinear adaptive-predictive control model of multiple evaporator system in a sugar mill, In: 2019 International Conference on Intelligent Transportation, Big Data and Smart Cities (ICITBS), Changsha, China, pp. 528 532 (2019)

7. Símpalo, W.D.: Modeling of a direct current triple effect evaporator for the concentration of sugar solutions. In: School of Agroindustrial Engineering, INGnosis, Chimbote (2016)

8. J. Acosta, V.Andaluz, G.Gonzales de Rivera, J .Garrido,(2019) Energy-Saver Mobile Manipulator Based on Numerical Methods. In: Electronics, Ecuador.

9. Hrama, M., Sidletskyi, V., Elperin, I.: Comparison between PID and fuzzy regulator for control evaporator plants. In: 2019 IEEE 39th International Conference on Electronics and Nanotechnology (ELNANO), Kyiv, Ukraine, pp. 54–59 (2019)

10. González, J., Escobar, J., Sanchez, H., De La Hoz, J., Beltran, J.R.: 2D and 3D virtual interactive laboratories of physics on unity platform. In: 4th International Meeting for Researchers in Materials and Plasma Technology (4th IMRMPT), vol. 935, pp. 23–26, (2017)

11. Porras, A.P., Solis, C.R., Andaluz, V.H., Sánchez, J.S., Naranjo, C.A.: Virtual training system for an industrial pasteurization process. In: De Paolis, L.T., Bourdot, P. (eds.) AVR 2019. LNCS, vol. 11614, pp. 430–441. Springer, Cham (2019). https://doi.org/10.1007/978-3-030-25999-0_35

12. Araujo, R., Araujo, M., Medeiros, F., Oliveira, B., Araujo, N.: Interactive simulator for electric engineering training. IEEE Latin Am. Trans. 14(5), 2246–2252 (2016)

13. Zambrano, J., Bermeo, D., Naranjo, C., Andaluz, V.: Multi-user virtual system for training of the production and bottling process of soft drinks. In: 2020 15th Iberian Conference on Information Systems and Technologies (CISTI), Seville, Spain, pp. 1–7 (2020)

14. Wang, W., Zeng, Z., Ding, W., Yu, H., Rose, H.: Concept and validation of a large-scale human-machine safety system based on real-time UWB indoor localization. In: 2019 IEEE/RSJ International Conference on Intelligent Robots and Systems (IROS), Macau, China, 2019, pp. 201–207 (2019)

15. Andaluz, V.H., Castillo-Carrión, D., Miranda, R.J., Alulema, J.C.: Virtual reality applied to industrial processes. In: De Paolis, L.T., Bourdot, P., Mongelli, A. (eds.) AVR 2017. LNCS, vol. 10324, pp. 59–74. Springer, Cham (2017). https://doi.org/10.1007/978-3-319-60922-5_5

16. Tredinnick, R., Boettcher, B., Smith, S., Solovy, S., Ponto, K.: Uni-CAVE: a unity3D plugin for non-head mounted VR display systems. In: 2017 IEEE Virtual Reality (VR), Los Angeles, CA, USA, pp. 393-394 (2017). https://doi.org/10.1109/VR.2017.7892342

17. Guerrero, M.E., et al.: Fault tolerant control for an evaporator of multiple effect in the sugar industry. In: National Congress of Automatic Control A.M.C.A. Cenidet, Monterrey (2007)

18. Hernandez. Investigation of the behavior of non-linear controllers in a double effect evaporator. In: National Institute for Space Research, ResearchGate, Brazil (2007)

Control of the Malt Mashing and Boiling Process in Craft Beer Production: *Hardware-in-The-Loop-Technique*

Steven I. Pogo$^{(\boxtimes)}$, Jhonatan F. Arias, and Víctor H. Andaluz

Universidad de Las Fuerzas Armadas ESPE, Sangolquí, Ecuador
{sipogo,jfarias5,vhandaluz1}@espe.edu.ec

Abstract. This work presents the design of control algorithms based on mathematical models algebra and PID, for the level and temperature control of a craft beer mashing and brewing plant, which will be designed in an immersive and interactive industrial virtual environment in the Unity 3D graphic engine. The controllers are implemented through the Hardware-in-the-Loop technique in order to allow the implementation of advanced control algorithms in an efficient and safe way. The virtual environment considers 3D models that provide a high level of realism to the process and the possibility of interaction with the user, also avoids the risk of damage to the system or loss of real control elements. For the virtualization of the industrial process, the mathematical model of the plant is considered and finally, the experimental results obtained in the implementation of the controllers through the Hardware-in-the-Loop technique are presented by means of a performance analysis of the same within the industrial process.

Keywords: Temperature control · Level control · Hardware-in-the-Loop · Industrial virtual environments · Virtual reality

1 Introduction

Throughout history, the industry has evolved by leaps and bounds [1], making the concept of automation as essential in modern industry in any field of application, since automatic processes play a fundamental role in the manufacture of a wide variety of products that aim to meet the needs of human beings [2], and nowadays, with the growing need to increase production, guarantee product quality and reduce costs, it is increasingly common to implement automatic systems in artisanal processes through classical and advanced control algorithms [3, 4]. For example, in the production of craft beer, fuzzy controllers have been applied in the malt mashing and boiling stages, by means of various actuators depending on the temperature and time of the process [5].

In the mashing process, automatic controls have also been carried out by controlling and monitoring pH, tank levels and temperature, using specific sensors to measure each of the variables and exchanging data with a PC [6]. Within the mashing process, temperature regulation is essential because the activity of enzymes that generate fermentable sugars

© Springer Nature Switzerland AG 2021
L. T. De Paolis et al. (Eds.): AVR 2021, LNCS 12980, pp. 701–716, 2021.
https://doi.org/10.1007/978-3-030-87595-4_51

depends on this, one of the ways that has been used in the industry to monitor the temperature automatically, for example in [7], is using temperature controllers within a programmable logic controller, as well as in [8], Galileo Intel development and Arduino Mega programming cards have been used, but these cards are not the only ones used to perform this procedure, because in [9] Raspberry Pi cards are also used.

In order to accelerate the algorithm development process for industrial plants, test environments based on the Hardware-in-the-Loop technique have been created [10]. The HIL technique is also used for educational purposes as seen in [11], in order to generate practical experiences eliminating the danger of handling real plants, where the virtual plant controller has been implemented in the same way in embedded cards.

These facts have been the inspiration to propose the implementation of the Hardware-in-the-Loop (HIL) technique for the monitoring and control of craft beer production through an immersive and interactive industrial virtual environment with the user developed in the Unity 3D graphic engine that allows to accelerate the development of control algorithms for real industrial plants and at the same time, that the designed environment allows to be used for educational purposes as it is an interactive environment. For the implementation of the HIL technique, mathematical modeling will be considered to represent the mashing and boiling of malt, with the purpose of implementing advanced control algorithms for the automation of the temperature and level variables of this process.

This document is divided into six sections, including the Introduction. Section 2 presents the development of the virtual environment. Section 3 shows the mathematical modeling of temperature and process level. Section 4 presents the design of the control algorithms. Section 5 shows the results of the implemented virtual system and the developed controllers. Finally, Section 6 presents the conclusions.

2 Virtual Environment

This section presents the industrial process virtualization methodology, which can be divided into four main stages called reference model; 3D modeling; production and integration; and the communication channel, as shown in Fig. 1.

To begin with, a reference model is taken as a starting point in the first stage where characteristics and aspects of a real industrial factory and P&ID diagrams of similar processes are considered, with the objective of making a conceptual design of a mashing and brewing plant for craft beer.

On the other hand, in the 3D modeling process is the design of the MIMO process of mashing and boiling of craft beer, which is developed in Plant 3D software, where the layers are defined for each element (tanks, flanges, pipes, structure, meshes), as well as the dimensions of the design, the structures that contain the tanks to be controlled are also created, the tanks where the mashing and boiling of the wort takes place, the control valves are placed, and the pumps at the outlets of the mashing and boiling tanks, this design has the extension. dwg; once the design is finished, the file is exported in a compact binary format that describes the content of the design data in 3D (AutoCAD native format), finally the 3D model is named and saved.

For exporting FBX type formats you take the native file exported from Plant 3D software and then proceed to open the file in 3ds Max software, which helps to get the

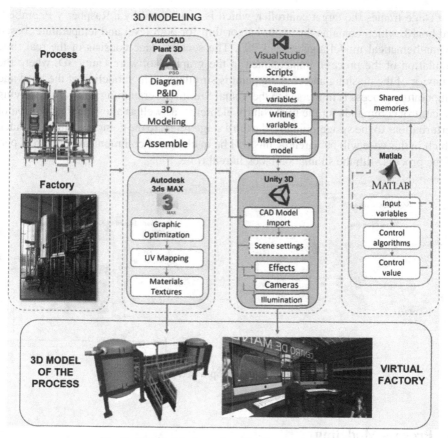

Fig. 1. Industrial plant virtualization methodology

"FBX" file that is recognized by Unity 3D software. Within 3ds Max, once imported, a graphic optimization of the plant is performed by deleting layers and junk figures that are not part of the model, the elements that are part of the layers created in Plant 3D are grouped and assigned a name to make easier its implementation and recognition in Unity, finally an optimization of the textures of the model is performed and the file is saved in FBX format.

Continuing with the virtualization process, you moved on to the stage of integration and production of the 3D virtual environment, in this virtual environment the different characteristics of the process are incorporated, such as heating, liquid filling, exploitations, sounds, textures, among others, making use of the Unity particle system and object-oriented programming in Visual Studio, allowing the virtualized plant to have a greater resemblance to the real plant.

The structure of the bilateral connection between the control board and the Unity software is shown in Fig. 2, which details the three main stages that compose the closed-loop control scheme using the Hardware-in-the-Loop technique, according to [12]. The first stage frames the target controller, which is constituted by a Raspberry Pi embedded board, which contains the control algorithm for both level and temperature, based on mathematical model algebra and PID. The second stage consists of the real time simulation of the process, implemented in the graphic software Unity 3D, where the behavior of the mashing and cooking plant is simulated. The modeling of the level and temperature process is immersed in the Visual Studio programming software, receiving the control commands for the final control elements, as well as allowing the addition of perturbations to the system. Finally, the third stage refers to the communication channel, which in this case will be wireless, this will be in charge of communicating the real part of the process with the simulation block in real time.

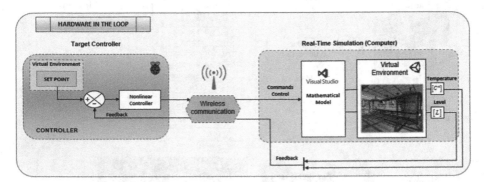

Fig. 2. Hardware-in-the-Loop based control structure.

3 Process Modeling

3.1 Level Model

The leveling process is shown in Fig. 3, consisting of two tanks (Tk1, Tk2), a pump to provide a constant flow for fluid exchange between the tanks, five control valves $a \in R[0 - 1]$ distributed in three adjustable valves (a_1, a_2, a_3) to control the inlet flow of each tank, two solenoid valves ON/OFF (a_4, a_5) that allow one-way flow in the fluid exchange, and a loading valve that allows the fluid to flow in one direction only (a_0) for the system output will also be used to cause disturbances in the stability analysis of the controller.

A continuous and constant inflow is assumed, while the Torricelli theorem is used for the outflow from the tanks, which relates the fluid velocity to the cross-sectional area and its flow is limited by the solenoids valve (EV: a_4, a_5)

$$q_4 = a_4 S_1 \sqrt{2gh_1(t)} \tag{1}$$

$$q_5 = a_5 S_2 \sqrt{2gh_2(t)} \tag{2}$$

where g: gravitational constant; S_1 and S_2: cross-sectional area of each outlet pipe (tanks one and two); h_1 and h_2: height of tanks one and two, respectively.

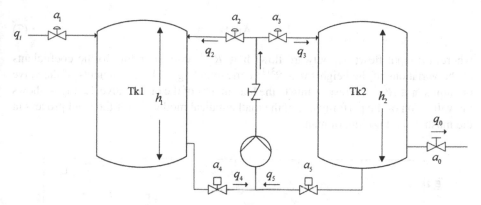

Fig. 3. Maceration and cooking process

For the dynamics of fluids between tanks, the application of the theory of the quantity of motion to a momentum theory as presented in [13]. Where the output velocity of the driving mechanism is equal to the sum of the input velocities (v_i) and output of the driving propeller (v_e), expressed in (3).

$$v_b = \tfrac{1}{2}(v_i + v_e) \tag{3}$$

Multiplying this equality by the cross-sectional area of the pipes gives the pump output flow, this flow is equal to the tank output flow plus the flow provided by the pump.

$$q_b = \tfrac{1}{2}(q_4 + q_5 + K_1 V_1) \tag{4}$$

where $K_1 V_1$: is the pump flow rate which depends on the pump constant K_1 and the voltage supplied to the pump V_1.

The volume variation (m^3) of each tank is affected by the liquid entering and leaving the tank, where the area of the tank bottom is constant (m^2) therefore, the head (m) varies with time depending on the flow rate into and out of the tank.

$$A_1 \frac{dh_1}{dt} = a_1(t)q_i + a_2(t)q_b - a_3(t)q_b \tag{5}$$

$$A_2 \frac{dh_2}{dt} = a_3(t)q_b - a_2(t)q_b - a_0(t)S_3\sqrt{2gh_2(t)} \tag{6}$$

where A_1 and A_2: cross-sectional area of each tank (tanks one and two); the flow and outlet flows are regulated by the control valves, while the process outlet flow is regulated by the loading valve $a_0(t)$.

The mathematical model in Fig. 2 is expressed in the form of a matrix, with the corresponding values of the control valve openings as well as the load valve a_0 denominated with the letter L:

$$
\begin{bmatrix} \dot{h}_1(t) \\ \dot{h}_2(t) \end{bmatrix} =
\begin{bmatrix} \frac{q_i}{A_1} & \frac{q_b}{A_1} & -\frac{q_b}{A_1} \\ 0 & -\frac{q_b}{A_2} & \frac{q_b}{A_2} \end{bmatrix}
\begin{bmatrix} \dot{a}_1(t) \\ \dot{a}_2(t) \\ \dot{a}_3(t) \end{bmatrix} +
\begin{bmatrix} 0 \\ -\frac{s_3\sqrt{2gh_2}}{A_2} \end{bmatrix} [a_0]
$$

$$\dot{\mathbf{h}}(t) = \mathbf{A}\mathbf{u}(t) + \boldsymbol{\eta} \qquad (7)$$

where, q_i: input flow; q_o; outward flow; $\mathbf{h} \in R^{2x1}$: corresponding to the coefficients of the variations of the heights; $\mathbf{u} \in R^{3x1}$: corresponding to the coefficients of the valve openings; $\boldsymbol{\eta} \in R^{2x1}$: corresponding to the load matrix of the outlet valve. La Fig. 4 shows the validation of the performance of the mathematical model (7) for the level process in the mashing and boiling of malt.

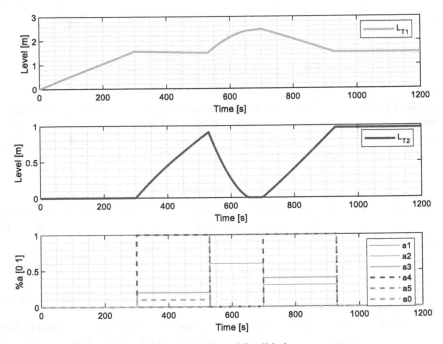

Fig. 4. Level model validation

The tanks start with initial conditions of 0 [m] for each one, from the first second until 300 [s] the valve a_1 is completely open and the others are closed, which fills only Tk1; from 300 [s] to 530 [s] the EV a_4 is enabled for fluid transfer between Tk1 and Tk2 with an opening percentage of 20% for the valve a_3 whereby Tk2 starts to receive fluid from Tk1, from 530 [s] to 700 [s], the valve closes a_1, the EV a_4 and the valve is enabled a_5 with an opening percentage of 60%, this completely empties Tk2 and sends all the liquid to Tk1, then the two EV are enabled and an opening percentage of 30% is given for a_2 and 40% for a_3, for a fluid exchange to take place between the two tanks and the final valve was closed, so the level reached up to that moment is maintained.

3.2   Temperature Model

Steam is an essential part for the different stages of the brewing process and mainly to heat the water where the malt and hops will be dissolved [14]. It is also efficient at transferring heat through condensation, so a shell and tube heat exchanger are used as shown in Fig. 5, to heat the liquid inside the tank and take advantage of the liquid flow to recirculate while heating.

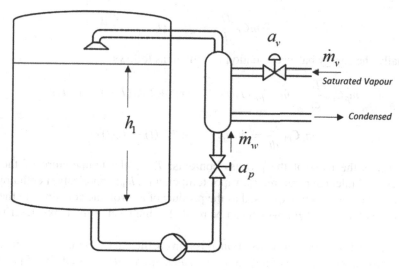

Fig. 5. Heating process with shell and tube heat exchanger

In Fig. 5 the mass flow is defined as $\dot{m}_v$ and as $\dot{m}_w$ for the liquid inlet, in the case of the vapor mass flow it depends on the dynamics of the vapor control valve a_v.

$$\dot{m}_v = a_v(t)K_v\sqrt{\Delta P} \tag{8}$$

in the case of the mass flow of the liquid depends on the flow of the pump that drives the liquid to the exchanger, this flow is regulated by a load valve a_p.

$$\dot{m}_w = a_p(t)K_2V_2 \tag{9}$$

where a_v y $a_p \in R[0-1]$; K_v: valve constant; ΔP: upstream and downstream pressure variation; K_2: pump constant, V_2: voltage supplied to the pump.

The energy balance on the element to which heat is transferred is given by the heat capacity ratio of the fluids involved in the heat exchanger multiplied by the temperature change of that fluid.

$$\dot{Q}_i = \dot{m}C_p(T_i - T_o) \tag{10}$$

where T_i: inlet temperature of the fluid and T_0: outlet temperature, to this is added the heat transferred from the surface through which the hot and cold fluid circulates, the heat transfer rate in a heat exchanger can be expressed by Newton's cooling law [14].

$$\dot{Q}_t = UA_s(T_h - T_c) \tag{11}$$

where U: Convection transfer coefficient; A_s: surface area where the fluids circulate; T_h: Temperature of the hot fluid; T_c: Temperature of the cold fluid; he stored instantaneous energy can be defined as the input energy (Q_i) plus the transferred energy (Q_t). Therefore, the energy balance can be established as follows

$$mC_p\frac{dT}{dt} = Q_i + Q_t \tag{12}$$

Finally, the energy balance equation is defined as follows:

$$m_pC_{pw}\frac{T_0}{dt} = \dot{m}_wC_{pw}(T_i(t) - T_o(t)) + UA_s(T_v(t) - T_o(t)) \tag{13}$$

$$m_vC_{pv}\frac{T_v}{dt} = \dot{m}_vh_{fg} - UA_s(T_v(t) - T_o(t)) \tag{14}$$

where m_p: is the mass of the process contents; T_o: outlet temperature of the heat exchanger; T_i: inlet temperature; T_v: vapor temperature; h_{fg}: vaporization enthalpy; the mass of the process can be expressed as the product of the volume contained in the tank by the density ($m_p = \rho V_{Tk}$), which can be related to the level of the tanks described in (7).

The calculation of the convective transmission coefficient is obtained experimentally and depends on the flow rate of the fluids, the calculation of U is based on [15] and [16] where the analysis is performed for a single-pass heat exchanger, however, the process can be used for multi-pass heat exchangers. A schematic diagram of the heat exchanger is shown in Fig. 6 where the saturated steam enters the shell $\dot{m}_v$ and upon heat transfer by condensation leaves the shell as a liquid due to gravity, while the cold liquid $\dot{m}_w$ passes through the tubes and receives the heat transferred through the pipe walls with an inner radius and an outer radius r_o.

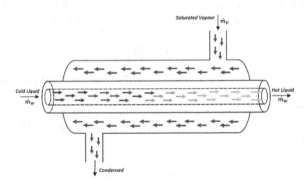

Fig. 6. Shell and tube exchanger Schematic

The area of the heat transfer section is given by:

$$A_s = 2\pi r_oL_t \tag{15}$$

where, L_t is the length of the pipe where the liquid flow circulates.

The general convection heat transfer coefficient U is calculated dynamically using the mechanical conditions of the hot and cold fluids as they enter the heat exchanger, it is important to consider the heat transfer coefficient of the tube H_t and the shell H_s, the convection coefficient for each fluid is calculated by:

$$H = \frac{N_u}{kD_h} \tag{16}$$

where k: is the thermal conductivity of the fluid and its value depends on the temperature of each fluid; D_h: Hydraulic diameter; N_u: Nussel number; it is important that the convective heat transfer coefficient (U) includes the heat conduction coefficient H_c by means of the pipe thickness: $b_t = r_0 - r_i$; and the conductivity coefficient of the pipe material and is calculated as follows:

$$H_c = \frac{k_t}{b_t} \tag{17}$$

Therefore, the overall heat transfer coefficient is determined as follows

$$U = \left(\frac{1}{H_t} + \frac{1}{H_s} + \frac{1}{H_c} \right)^{-1} \tag{18}$$

The Fig. 7 shows the validation of the performance of the mathematical model (13) and (14) for the temperature process in malt cooking and mashing.

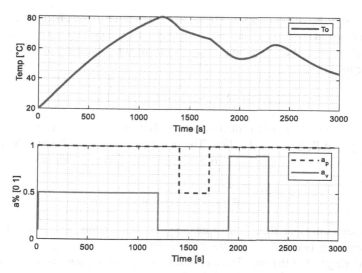

Fig. 7. Temperature model validation

The outlet temperature of the exchanger starts with initial conditions of 20° which is the ambient temperature and the vapor valve a_v is at 50% opening and reaches a temperature of 80 °C, from 1200 [s] the valve is closed by 10% which causes a temperature drop, while the temperature decreases in the range of 1400 [s] to 1700 [s] the disturbance valve a_p closes by 50% which causes the liquid flow is lower so that the temperature begins to decrease with less speed.

4 Controller Design

In this section, the design of a level control algorithm based on mathematical model algebra is presented; on the other hand, PID algorithms are implemented for temperature control. Finally, the performance of the control algorithms in the level and temperature process is analyzed.

4.1 Controller Based on Inverse Behavior of the Process.

The method to be developed using the inverse plant behavior is illustrated in Fig. 8, the plant behavior is obtained from (7).

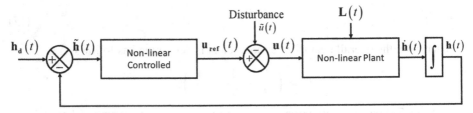

Fig. 8. Control algorithm based on the inverse behavior of the plant

where $\mathbf{h_d}$: is the vector of desired head; $\mathbf{h}$: is the vector of the process head; $\tilde{\mathbf{h}}$: is the vector of error $(\mathbf{hd} - \mathbf{h})$; η: is the vector representing the system load; $\mathbf{u}$: is the vector of the process inputs (valve opening); $\mathbf{u_{ref}}$: is the vector containing the process control actions, defined as

$$\mathbf{u_{ref}}(t) = \mathbf{A}^{-1}\left(\mathbf{K}\tilde{\mathbf{h}}(t) - \eta(t)\right) \tag{19}$$

where $\mathbf{A}^{-1}$: is the inverse of the plant behavior; $\mathbf{K} \in R^{2x2}$ is a fit matrix.

Stability and Robustness Análisis. The behavior of the error $\tilde{\mathbf{h}}$ in the level process for the mashing and boiling of malt is analyzed considering perturbations at the plant input defined as

$$\tilde{\mathbf{u}}(t) = \mathbf{u_{ref}}(t) - \mathbf{u}(t) \tag{20}$$

The disturbances at the plant input may be due to the noise generated in the communication between the controller and the final control element.

Considering (20), (19) and (7) the closed loop equation is determined as follows

$$\dot{\tilde{\mathbf{h}}} = -\mathbf{K}\tilde{\mathbf{h}} + \mathbf{A}\tilde{\mathbf{u}} \tag{21}$$

According to [17], for the stability and robustness analysis, the Lyapunov candidate function $\mathbf{V}\left(\tilde{\mathbf{h}}\right) = \frac{1}{2}\tilde{\mathbf{h}}^{T}\tilde{\mathbf{h}}$, is considered, it is derived as a function of time to determine the evolution of the errors $\dot{\mathbf{V}}\left(\tilde{\mathbf{h}}\right) = \tilde{\mathbf{h}}^{T}\dot{\tilde{\mathbf{h}}}$ therefore, when replacing in (21) we obtain

$$\dot{\mathbf{V}}\left(\tilde{\mathbf{h}}\right) = -\tilde{\mathbf{h}}^{T}\mathbf{K}\tilde{\mathbf{h}} + \tilde{\mathbf{h}}^{T}\mathbf{A}\tilde{\mathbf{u}} \tag{22}$$

for (22) to be negative definite it must be satisfied that $\dot{\mathbf{V}}\left(\tilde{\mathbf{h}}\right) < 0$, therefore

$$\left\|\mathbf{K}\tilde{\mathbf{h}}\right\| > \|\mathbf{A}\tilde{\mathbf{u}}\| \tag{23}$$

when the condition of (23) is fulfilled, the error $\tilde{\mathbf{h}}$ is considered to be bounded by

$$\left\|\tilde{\mathbf{h}}\right\| < \frac{\|\mathbf{A}\tilde{\mathbf{u}}\|}{\lambda_{min}\mathbf{K}} \tag{24}$$

it can be concluded that, when there are disturbances at the input of the plant ($\tilde{\mathbf{u}}$) the error $\tilde{\mathbf{h}}$ is bounded by (24) and the system is stable, where λ_{min}: are the minimum eigenvalues; are the minimum eigenvalues ($\tilde{\mathbf{u}} = 0$) the control error $\tilde{\mathbf{h}}(t) = \mathbf{0}$ when $t \to \infty$, so it is an asymptotically stable system.

4.2 PID Controller

The PID Control is a control strategy that combines proportional, integral and derivative actions, with the objective of correcting the error between the measured value and the desired value or Set Point. The general equation of the PID controller is as follows:

$$u(t) = K_p e(t) + \frac{K_p}{T_i} \int_0^t e(t)dt + K_p T_d \frac{de(t)}{dt} \tag{25}$$

where u and e are the control signal and the control error respectively. The control signal is given by the sum of the proportional term P, integral I and the derivative term D. The tuning parameters of the controller are: the proportional gain K_p, T_i is the integral time and T_d is the derivative time.

5 Experimental Results

This section presents the implementation of the HIL technique for the mashing and boiling process in the brewing process of Fig. 2, where the mathematical model of level and temperature together with the virtual environment is located in the main computer that is characterized by having a Windows 10 operating system, 16 GB of Ram memory, Intel Core i7 processor of tenth generation and 6 GB video card, while the control algorithms are located in the Raspberry PI-4 card, while the bilateral communication between the process and the controller is done through the Xbee wireless modules. The implementation of the Hardware-in-the-Loop technique is shown in Fig. 9.

The Fig. 10 shows the interactive environment with the user, which consists of a control center in the virtual environment, by means of which the process can be controlled through the computer peripherals and the evolution of the variables can be visualized on an HMI interface.

In the development of the virtual environment different features are placed to give greater realism to the implemented process, this is achieved through explosions, irrigation of the liquid in the tanks, movement of the valves, as shown in Fig. 11.

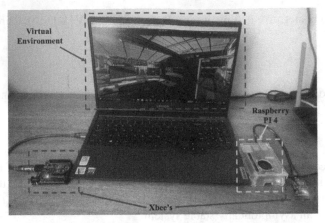

Fig. 9. HIL implementation of mashing and cooking process.

Fig. 10. Command center in the virtual environment.

5.1 Controller Based on Inverse Behavior of the Process

The Fig. 12 shows the performance of the control algorithm based on the inverse behavior of the plant (19), where the behavior of the plant with different values in the desired height vector was evaluated.

From 500 [s] a desired height $h_{d1} = 0.95$[m] and $h_{d2} = 0.7$[m] was entered because the desired value change increases from the previous value for both tanks, the algorithm first fills the T_{k2} up to the desired height once the point is reached proceeds to fill the T_{k1}. To perform a stability analysis of the controller, the load valve a_0 was opened with different values during the process, where the controller compensated the disturbance generated by the load, as a result it is concluded that the control algorithm is uniformly asymptotically stable and for disturbances at the input of the plant ($\tilde{\mathbf{u}}$) greater than 10% in the vector of control actions ($\mathbf{u_{ref}}$) becomes unstable.

Fig. 11. Realism effects in the process.

5.2 Control PID

In the Fig. 13 shows the performance of the PID control algorithm tuned with the Ziegler-Nichols method and the limiting gain.

The process starts with the ambient temperature of 20 °C and a temperature scan is performed, as is common in the process terms the temperature evolution is slow with a percentage of over impulse and steady state error of 1 °C, The Fig. 14 shows the control actions sent by the PID from 950 [s] to 1250 [s] the cold flow load valve is varied, which causes the oscillations to extend for a while until returning to the equilibrium point, which determines the stability of the controller.

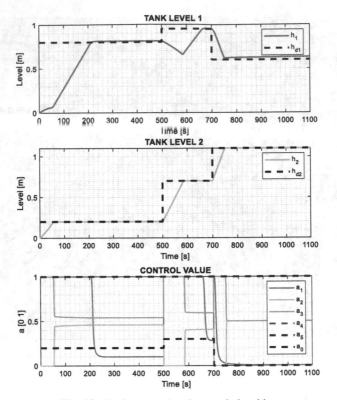

Fig. 12. Performance level control algorithm

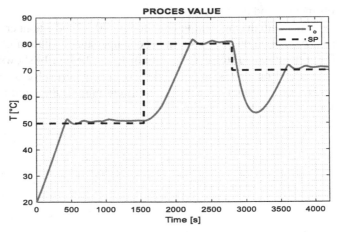

Fig. 13. Performance of the temperature control algorithm

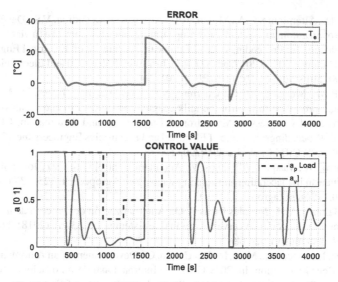

Fig. 14. Evolution of PID controller for the temperature process.

6 Conclusions

Hardware-in-the-Loop is an alternative simulation technique that allows the implementation of advanced control algorithms in processes that present disadvantages due to their high cost or availability. The HIL technique allows to evaluate in real time the behavior of the industrial process, for which it is important to obtain a mathematical model that adequately represents the behavior of the process. The automation of artisanal processes through the application of advanced controllers makes it possible to obtain greater productivity and improve the quality of raw material processing, as in the case of malt mashing and boiling, which requires a scaled temperature control for brewing beer, in addition to achieving product standardization and reducing production costs by significantly reducing raw material losses during the process.

Acknowledgment. The authors would like to thank the Universidad de las Fuerzas Armadas ESPE and the ARSI Research Group for their support in the development of this work.

References

1. Rozo-García, F.: Revisión de las tecnologías presentes en la industria 4.0. Rev. UIS Ing. **19**, 177–191 (2020). https://doi.org/10.18273/revuin.v19n2-2020019
2. González-Filgueira, G., Javier, F., Permuy, R.: Automatización de una planta industrial de alimentación mediante control distribuido. RISTI Rev. Ibérica Sist. e Tecnol. Informação (27), 1–17 (2018). https://doi.org/10.17013/risti.27.1-17, ISSN-e 1696–9895
3. Nieto, E.C.: Manufactura y automatización Manufacturing and automation. Ing. Investig **26**(3), 120–128 (2006). ISSN 0120–5609

4. Oviedo, I.D., Altamirano, C.A., Millan, M.E., Arreaga, N.X., Padilla, V.S.: Development of a prototype of an automatic system for shrimp farming using telecontrol as a viable proposal for small producers. In: Proceedings - 2017 European Conference on Electrical Engineering and Computer Science, EECS 2017, pp. 477–483. Institute of Electrical and Electronics Engineers Inc. (2018). https://doi.org/10.1109/EECS.2017.94

5. Perafan, R.M., Meneses, F.C.G., Guerrero, N.P., Saavedra, J.E., Torres, D.M.: Design of a mechatronic prototype to control the milk coagulation process in cheese making. In: 2020 9th International Congress of Mechatronics Engineering and Automation, CIIMA 2020 - Conference Proceedings. Institute of Electrical and Electronics Engineers Inc. (2020). https://doi.org/10.1109/CIIMA50553.2020.9290323

6. Luján Corro, M., Vásquez Villalobos, V.: Automatic control with fuzzy logic of home-made beer production in maceration and cooking stages. Sci. Agropecu. 1, 125–137 (2010). https://doi.org/10.17268/sci.agropecu.2010.02.03

7. Benitez Baltazar, V.H., Morales Rivas, C.O.: Automatización del proceso de macerado de la malta para la producción de cerveza artesanal. Epistemus 12, 53–61 (2018). https://doi.org/10.36790/epistemus.v12i24.68

8. Rodriguez, L., Vinces, L., Mata, N., Del Carpio, C.: Development of an Automatic Equipment for Craft Beer Maceration. In: 2019 Congreso Internacional de Innovacion y Tendencias en Ingenieria, CONIITI 2019 - Conference Proceedings. Institute of Electrical and Electronics Engineers Inc. (2019). https://doi.org/10.1109/CONIITI48476.2019.8960840

9. Profesional, U., et al.: Instituto Politécnico Nacional, Escuela Superior de Ingeniería Mecánica y Eléctrica (2017)

10. Joaquín Castillo Salinas, D., Pavesi, L.: Proyecto de automatización de planta de cerveza artesanal Easy Brewing. Universidad Andrés Bello (2017)

11. Jorque, B.S., Mollocana, J.D., Ortiz, J.S., Andaluz, V.H.: Mobile manipulator robot control through virtual hardware in the loop. In: Rocha, Á., Adeli, H., Dzemyda, G., Moreira, F., Ramalho Correia, A.M. (eds.) WorldCIST 2021. AISC, vol. 1365, pp. 80–91. Springer, Cham (2021). https://doi.org/10.1007/978-3-030-72657-7_8

12. Ortiz, J.S., Palacios-Navarro, G., Andaluz y, V.H., Guevara, B.S.: Marco basado en la realidad virtual para simular algoritmos de control para tareas de asistencia robótica y rehabilitación a través de una silla de ruedas de pie. Sensores 21(15), 5083 92021)

13. Streeter, V.L.: Mecanica de los fluidos. Mc Graw-Hill, DF. Mexico (1970)

14. Más información sobre el vapor | Spirax Sarco. https://www.spiraxsarco.com/learn-about-steam, Accessed 11 Aug 2021

15. Çengel, Y.A.: Transferencia de calor y masa un enfoque practico. McGraw-Hill, México, D.F. (2007)

16. Bastida, H., Ugalde-Loo, C.E., Abeysekera, M., Xu, X., Qadrdan, M.: Dynamic modelling and control of counter-flow heat exchangers for heating and cooling systems. In: 2019 54th International University Power Engineering Conference UPEC 2019 – Proceedings, pp. 1–6 (2019). https://doi.org/10.1109/UPEC.2019.8893634

17. Bonilla, E., Rodriguez, J., Acosta y, J., Andaluz, V.: Teaching and learning virtual strategy for the navigation of multiple-UAV. In: 15th Iberian Conference on Information Systems and Technologies (CISTI) (2020)

Virtual Training System for Robotic Applications in Industrial Processes

Erick B. Cobo$^{(\boxtimes)}$ and Víctor H. Andaluz

Universidad de Las Fuerzas Armadas ESPE, Sangolquí, Ecuador
{ebcobo,vhandaluz1}@espe.edu.ec

Abstract. This work presents the development of a virtual reality training system applied to industrial robotics and oriented to the teaching learning processes. The system considers a manipulator anthropomorphic industrial robot of 6DOF to perform autonomous object manipulation tasks in two virtual environments. The virtual environments are developed in the graphic engine Unity3D, the environment exchanges information with MATLAB by shared memory to execute position and trajectory control algorithms for the operating end of the manipulator robot. The virtual training system connects whit an Android mobile app that considers the following control panel functions: articular coordinate system, velocity configuration and dead man switch. Finally, evaluations of the developed virtual environments, the mobile application and the control algorithm are carried out to guarantee the usability of the virtual training system in the teaching-learning processes.

Keywords: Virtual reality · Manipulator robot · Trajectory and position control · Mobile app

1 Introduction

Industrial processes have evolved over the years due to improvements and development in: productivity, product standardization, reduction of production costs and the application of new technologies related to the Industry 4.0 [1]. The Industry 4.0 includes different digital technologies in conventional industry in order to increase productivity and efficiency using the Internet of things to supervise industrial processes in real time to allow decentralized decision making [2]. The most relevant technologies in the Industry 4.0 are: *i) Cloud Computing,* is an intelligent and programmable tool that allows users to access to different services and repositories to obtain and share large quantities of information [3]; *ii) Big Data,* consists of the analysis of large amounts of data to transform them into information or knowledge [4]; *iii) Robotics,* is an engineering branch that combines knowledge of electronics, mechanics, mathematics and control to build machines that perform repetitive or dangerous work faster and more efficiently than humans [5]; *iv) Immersive Technologies,* these are technologies that allows user interaction with digital recreated worlds, the most important are: Augmented reality "AR" that allows to add graphic information to the real world using technologic devices [6], and

L. T. De Paolis et al. (Eds.): AVR 2021, LNCS 12980, pp. 717–734, 2021.
https://doi.org/10.1007/978-3-030-87595-4_52

Virtual Reality "VR", is an immersive technology that provides simulated experiences in 3D environments projected by specialized glasses [7].

It is evident that Augmented Reality and Virtual Reality systems are widely used in industrial applications. Using AR systems in human-robot collaborative object manipulation tasks reduces the risk and time to perform the work [8]. User performance in robot programming improves when AR is used in educational training systems [9]. VR systems facilitates the development of industrial Mechatronics systems by allowing prototype testing analysis [10]. Creating a digital bidirectional robot twin to program the robot in the same HMI as the real one using VR, enables performance and security tests in the simulation before the implementation of the program in the real robot [11]. An automotive assembly environment in VR is a useful tool for collaborative product design because it allows the users to identify and solve problems in the process in order to decrease manufacturing costs [12]. An application of VR environments in the industry for the ship pipeline system assembly helps the operators to identify the most efficient assembly sequence for the process [13]. The previously described works shows that the AR and VR systems applied to industrial processes generate a big interest in the scientific community because it allows the users to interact with simulated industrial robotics systems in order to decrease operation risks and increase productivity.

Actually, due to Covid-19 lockdown restrictions the students do not have access to the laboratories in their Universities, this affects directly to the teaching-learning processes. Immersive technologies are a viable and accessible option for users to interact with simulated environments. For what is described it is proposed the development of an immersive and interactive system that allows free access to virtual environments to boost the teaching-learning processes. This work considers the development of two virtual environments: *i) Industrial Robotics Virtual Laboratory,* where the user can handle a 6DOF industrial manipulator anthropomorphic robot using a mobile application for Android with wireless connection to the environment that includes the following control panel functions: articular coordinate system, velocity configuration and dead man switch in order to learn and recognize the movement characteristics and restrictions of the manipulator robot; *ii) Industrial Virtual Environment,* that allows the user to implement autonomous control tasks for the robot in industrial environments. This environment considers a palletizing robotic cell that interchanges data by shared memory with the mathematic software MATLAB in order to perform position and trajectory control tasks to manipulate boxes that came from a conveyor belt. Performance tests of the control algorithm will be carried out in this environment and also, users can develop their own control algorithm for the industrial robot in order to carry out performance and functionality tests.

This document is divided in five sections including the Introduction. Section 2 presents the System Structure and the mathematic modeling of the manipulator robot. Section 3 shows the development of the Virtual Training System, the Control Algorithm design and the Robot Control Panel development. Section 4 presents the performance results of the Virtual Training System and the controller developed. Finally, conclusions are presented in Section 5.

2 System Structure

Robotics oriented VR environments are a viable alternative to boost teaching-learning processes in a didactic and entertaining way. Applying Robotics in VR environments allows the users to visualize and understand the characteristics and functionalities of industrial robots without the need to purchase real robots. Using industrial robots in VR reduces the risk of using real robots for inexperienced users and allows the users to do performance and functionality tests in virtual environments that are similar to a real one. Therefore, a Virtual Reality Training System that includes a 6DOF industrial manipulator anthropomorphic robot will be carried out. The industrial manipulator robot to use is the ABB-IRB 140, which can be used for many industrial applications such as: palletizing, welding, assembly, classification, among others [14].

In order to perform the manipulation tasks desired for the industrial manipulator robot, in Fig. 1 is presented the system proposed in this work, which considers a closed loop advanced control algorithm to define the position and trajectory of the operating end of the industrial robot.

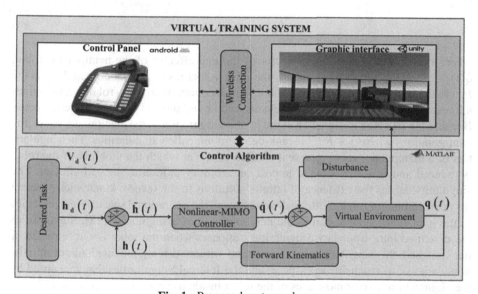

Fig. 1. Proposed system scheme.

The proposed Virtual Training System contains: the graphic interface developed in Unity3D, the control panel mobile app developed in Android Studio and the control algorithm implemented in MATLAB. It is necessary to obtain the mathematic model of the manipulator robot in order to apply it to the control algorithm. The controller uses the kinematic model of the robot to define the articular movements. The kinematic model of a manipulator robot defines the position of the end-effector as a function of its joint configuration, or the operational coordinates of the manipulator robot as a function of its generalized coordinates [15].

$$\mathbf{q} \mapsto \mathbf{h} = f(\mathbf{q}).$$

The forward kinematic model is obtained by the Denavit-Hartenberg parameters (DH), which represents the translation and orientation of the manipulator robot by using articular transformation matrices. The complete homogenous transformation matrix $^0\mathbf{T}_n$ of the manipulator robot can be calculated as a string of the individual articular transformation matrices $^{n-1}\mathbf{A}_n$ [16]

$$^0\mathbf{T}_n =^0 \mathbf{A}_1^1\mathbf{A}_2...^{n-1}\mathbf{A}_n \tag{1}$$

where n represents the amount of DOF of the manipulator robot. The position and orientation vector of the end-effector of the manipulator robot

$$\mathbf{h} = \left[h_x, h_y, h_z, h_\alpha, h_\beta, h_\gamma\right]^T \tag{2}$$

is obtained from the homogenous transformation matrix.

The instantaneous kinematic model describes the derivative of the end-effector position of a manipulator robot as a function of the derivative of the robotic arm configuration [17]

$$\dot{\mathbf{h}}(t) = \mathbf{J}(\mathbf{q})\dot{\mathbf{q}}(t) \tag{3}$$

where $\dot{\mathbf{h}}(t) \in R^m$ is the velocity vector of the end effector of the manipulator robot, $\dot{\mathbf{q}}(t) \in R^n$ is the vector that contains the joint velocities of the robot, and $\mathbf{J}(\mathbf{q})$ is the Jacobian matrix of the manipulator robot. The Jacobian matrix of a robotic arm defines a linear mapping between the joint velocity vector and the end-effector velocity vector. Because the Jacobian is a function of the joint configuration of the manipulator robot, the configurations where $\mathbf{J} \in R^{m \times n}$ is rank-deficient are called singularities. The singularities of a manipulator robot represent configurations at which the mobility of the robot is reduced and is not possible to impose an arbitrary motion to the end-effector. The singularity causes the existence of infinite solutions in the inverse kinematics problem for the manipulator robot. With small velocities in the operational space, large velocities in the joint space shall appear in the neighborhood of a singularity [18]. Singularities are classified into: Boundary Singularities, appears when the robot is out retracted or out stretched, this singularities can be avoided without driving the manipulator into the boundaries of its reachable workspace; and the Internal Singularities that are caused by the alignment of two or more axes of the robot inside its reachable workspace [17].

3   Training Virtual Environment

In this Section it is presented the Training Virtual Environment and the Control Algorithm development. Figure 2 presents the proposed scheme for the Training Virtual Environment, which is developed in the graphic engine Unity3D. The training system contains: *i) External Resources,* that considers the CAD models of the environment that are developed in the Inventor software, post processed in 3DS-Max, and exported in (.fbx) format to be compatible with the graphic engine; *ii) Graphics Engine,* contains all of the graphic resources used in the environment, and the scripts that are the code lines that configures all of the system elements; *iii) Controller,* contains the control algorithm developed in the mathematical software MATLAB and the communication between the mathematical software and the graphics engine. The Unity3D-MATLAB communication is performed by using the dynamic link library (DLL) to assign a shared memory between both software's, in order to exchange data to implement the control algorithm developed in MATLAB [18, 19]; *iv) Virtual Devices,* that considers the input and output devices to allow the immersive experience to the user.

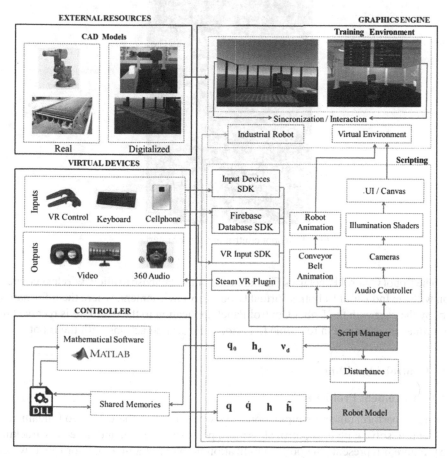

Fig. 2. Proposed virtual environment scheme.

Furthermore, it is important to emphasize the functionality of the Cellphone input device, because it contains the Robot Control Panel application. The Robot Control Panel is developed in Android Studio. In the application the user can define the movement of each joint of the robot and its velocity. Figure 3 shows the Robot Control Panel user interface.

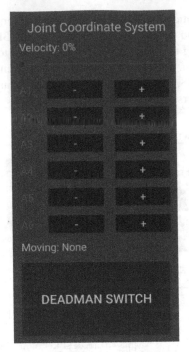

Fig. 3. Robot control panel user interface.

The Robot Control Panel uses Firebase Real-time Database to allow wireless connection with the Industrial Robotics Virtual Laboratory environment, where the information sent by the user with the Robot Control Panel application to the database is received by the virtual environment in real time to perform the desired actions with the robot.

3.1   Control Algorithm

3.1.1   Movement Problems

In order to perform object manipulation tasks with the robot, there are two fundamental problems to solve with the control algorithm: point stabilization and trajectory tracking [15]. Figure 4 represents the point stabilization problem of a manipulator robot, which consists in moving the end effector of the robot to a fixed target location that is defined by the desired position and orientation of the end effector of the robot

$$\mathbf{h_d} = \left[h_{dx}, h_{dy}, h_{dz}, h_{d\alpha}, h_{d\beta}, h_{d\gamma} \right]^T. \tag{4}$$

The desired position and orientation are constant values, so the desired velocity for point stabilization is

$$\mathbf{v_d}(t) = \dot{\mathbf{h}}_{\mathbf{d}}(t) = 0. \tag{5}$$

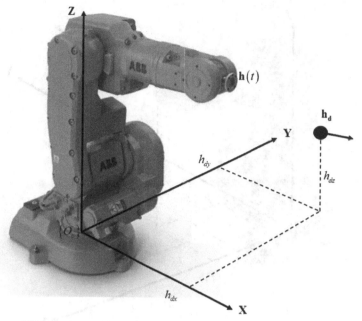

Fig. 4. Point stabilization problem for the manipulator robot represented in the world framework $\{O_O, X, Y, Z\}$.

The point stabilization problem consists in finding a closed loop control law, where the position and orientation errors are [17]

$$\tilde{\mathbf{h}}(t) = \mathbf{h_d} - \mathbf{h}(t), \tag{6}$$

hence

$$\lim_{x \to \infty} (\mathbf{h_d}(t) - \mathbf{h}(t)) = 0. \tag{7}$$

The second problem for the object manipulation with the robot is the trajectory tracking, which consists in following a desired time-varying trajectory and its derivative that describes the desired velocity [15]. This desired trajectory is independent of the instantaneous position of the robot. The desired trajectory for the manipulator robot is defined by a vector

$$\mathbf{h_d}(t) = \left[h_{dx}(t), h_{dy}(t), h_{dz}(t), h_{d\alpha}(t), h_{d\beta}(t), h_{d\gamma}(t) \right]^T. \tag{8}$$

The desired velocity $\mathbf{v_d}(t)$ is the time derivative of $\mathbf{h_d}(t)$, i.e., $\mathbf{v_d}(t) = \frac{d}{dt}\mathbf{h_d}(t)$.

Figure 5 shows the trajectory tracking problem of a manipulator robot, which should consider the position and orientation of the operating end of the manipulator robot $\mathbf{h}(t)$ and the desired positions $\mathbf{h_d}(t)$ and velocities $\mathbf{v_d}(t)$ for the operating end, in order to achieve

$$\lim_{x \to \infty} (\mathbf{h_d}(t) - \mathbf{h}(t)) = 0. \tag{9}$$

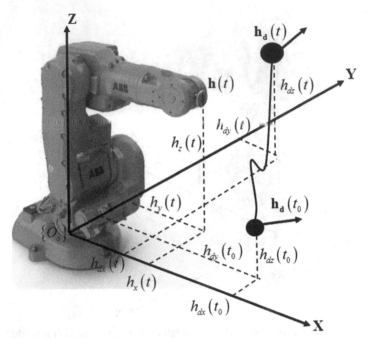

Fig. 5. Trajectory tracking problem for the manipulator robot represented in the world framework $\{Oo, X, Y, Z\}$.

3.1.2 Proposed Control Law

To solve the point stabilization and trajectory tracking problems with the manipulator robot, it is proposed a feedback control law that considers the requirements of both problems to perform manipulation tasks with the robot. The controller considers the redundancy characteristics of the manipulator robot to perform the control actions. The control algorithm uses the minimal norm solution, in order to reach the target with a small number of movements [17]. The controller is developed in MATLAB, and uses the inverse differential kinematics method in order to achieve the desired tasks by saturating the position and orientation errors $\tilde{\mathbf{h}}(t)$ to calculate the articular velocities with the following control law:

$$\dot{\mathbf{q}}_{\mathbf{ref}} = \mathbf{J}^{-1}(\mathbf{q})\left(\mathbf{v_d} + \mathbf{K}\tanh\left(\tilde{\mathbf{h}}\right)\right) \tag{10}$$

where $\dot{\mathbf{q}}_{\mathbf{ref}}(t)$ is the robot joint angular velocity vector, $\mathbf{J}^{-1}(\mathbf{q})$ is the inverse Jacobian matrix of the manipulator robot and $\mathbf{K}$ is the definite positive diagonal gain matrix. The proposed control law considers the redundancy characteristics of the manipulator robot. The minimal norm solution is used for the design of the controller that means that the manipulator robot will follow the desired task at any time with the smallest number of possible movements. The tanh(.) function is proposed to perform analytical saturations for the velocities of the manipulator robot [20].

3.1.3 Stability and Robustness

Using the kinematic model of the manipulator robot (3), the proposed control law (10) and considering the errors caused by the disturbance applied to the system

$$\dot{\tilde{q}} = \dot{q}_{ref} - \dot{q} \tag{11}$$

and also considering that the desired velocity is $v_d = \dot{h}_d$ and the end effector velocity errors are $\dot{\tilde{h}} = \dot{h}_d - \dot{h}$ the resultant closed loop equation is

$$\dot{\tilde{h}} = -K \tanh\left(\tilde{h}\right) + J\dot{\tilde{q}}. \tag{12}$$

Using the candidate Lyapunov function $V\left(\tilde{h}\right) = \frac{1}{2}\tilde{h}^T\tilde{h}$ for the stability analysis, and replacing the closed loop equation in its time derivate $\dot{V}\left(\tilde{h}\right) = \tilde{h}^T\dot{\tilde{h}}$ the resultant expression is [15]

$$\dot{V}\left(\tilde{h}\right) = -\tilde{h}^T K \tanh\left(\tilde{h}\right) + \tilde{h}^T J\dot{\tilde{q}}. \tag{13}$$

To be negative definite the Eq. (13) should accomplish $\dot{V}\left(\tilde{h}\right) < 0$, then.

$$\left\| K \tanh\left(\tilde{h}\right) \right\| > \left\| J\dot{\tilde{q}} \right\|, \quad \text{so,} \tag{14}$$

$$\left\| \tilde{h} \right\| < \frac{\left\| J\dot{\tilde{q}} \right\|}{\lambda_{min}(K) \tanh(k_{aux})} \quad \text{with } 0 < k_{aux} < 1 \tag{15}$$

where $\lambda_{min}(K)$ are the minimum auto-values and considering that if $\dot{\tilde{q}} = 0$ then $\tilde{h} \to 0$ when $t \to \infty$ for which it can be concluded that the system is asymptotically stable for the point stabilization and trajectory tracking problems.

4 Experimental Results

This section presents the experimental results of both of the virtual training environments, the control algorithm and the Robot Control Panel application. The hardware used for the tests of the virtual environment and the control algorithm is a mid-range computer that contains (4th generation Intel Core I7 processor, 8 GB DDR3 RAM and 64-bit Windows 8.1 operating system); and for the Robot Control Panel it is used an Android cellphone with Snapdragon 720G processor and 6 GB RAM. The experimental results are divided in two parts. The first part considers the Industrial Virtual Environment tests, where the control algorithm is applied to perform manipulation tasks using different point stabilization locations. The second part contains the Industrial Robotics Virtual Laboratory and the Robot Control Panel performance tests, where the user can define the desired joint values for the manipulator robot in the environment. Lately the usability of the virtual environment will be presented.

4.1 Industrial Virtual Environment Tests

The Industrial Virtual Environment tests, considers a palletizing robotic cell, where the robot performs box manipulation tasks. Considering the point stabilization problem for the manipulation tasks are defined five desired positions and fixed orientations that will be reached by the end-effector of the robot, in order to perform the desired manipulation task avoiding crashes with the other objects in the virtual environment. The initial conditions for the robot joints are $\mathbf{q_0} = [\,0 \;\; \frac{\pi}{9} \; -\frac{\pi}{6} \; \frac{\pi}{18} \; \frac{\pi}{12} \quad \frac{\pi}{18}\,][rad]$ Figure 6 presents a box palletizing sequence performed by the manipulator robot in the virtual environment.

Fig. 6. Manipulator robot performing palletizing tasks.

To confirm the proper functionality of the robot in the palletizing application in Fig. 7 will be shown the position and orientation errors of the end-effector of the robot.

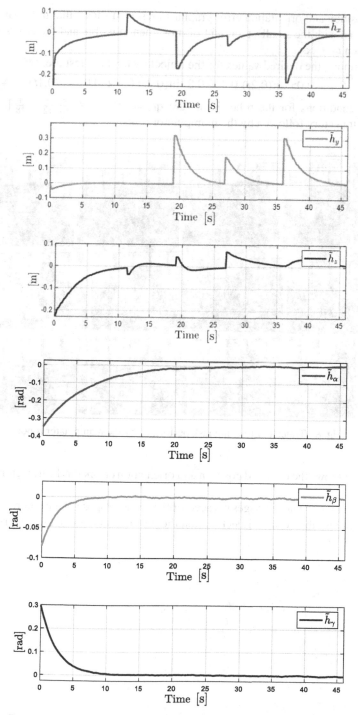

Fig. 7. Time graphics of the robot end-effector position and orientation errors.

The position and orientation error graphics presented shows that the desired task is accomplished with the smallest amount of movement possible and the errors converge to zero when $t \to \infty$.

Furthermore, the desired values for the trajectory tracking test are.

$$\mathbf{h_d} = \begin{bmatrix} 0.4 + 0.05\sin(0.2t) & 0.4 + 0.2\sin(0.2t) & 0.4 + 0.05\sin(0.1t) & 0 & \frac{\pi}{4} & 0 \end{bmatrix} \text{ and}$$

the initial conditions for the robot joints are $\mathbf{q_0} = [0 \ \frac{\pi}{9} \ -\frac{\pi}{6} \ \frac{\pi}{18} \ \frac{\pi}{12} \ -\frac{\pi}{18}]$. Figure 8 shows the trajectory followed by the manipulator robot.

Fig. 8. Trajectory tracking task performed by the manipulator robot.

Figure 9 shows the obtained position and orientation errors for the trajectory tracking test.

As seen in the previous images it's accomplished the propose of the controller because the robot follows the desired trajectory and the position and orientation errors converge to zero.

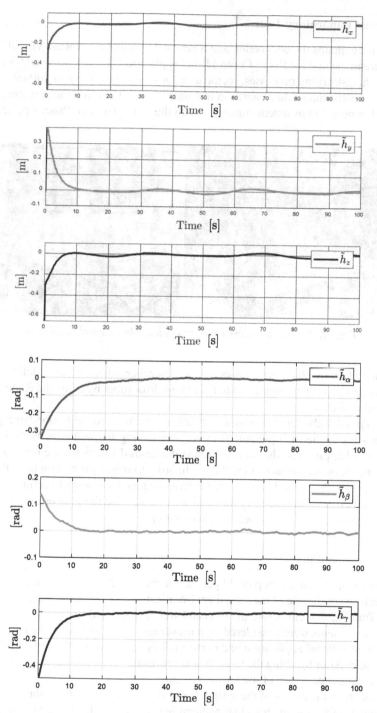

Fig. 9. Position and orientation errors of the trajectory task performed by the robot.

4.2 Virtual Laboratory Tests

This section contains the connection and functionality tests between the Virtual Laboratory Environment and the Robot Control Panel application. This environment is oriented to the teaching-learning processes, so, the user can observe the most important variables of the robot performance in a canvas in real time. Figure 10 shows the performance test of the Laboratory Environment connected with the Robot Control Panel Application.

Fig. 10. Virtual laboratory environment and robot control panel tests.

Figure 11 shows the performance of the controller when the user defines desired angles q_d for the joint configuration of the manipulator robot by using the Robot Control Panel application.

The Virtual Laboratory Environment allows the user to understand the physical characteristics of the manipulator robot without buying the real one. With the Robot Control Panel application the user can define the desired values for the robot joints and observe the robot performance in real time. In order to send information from the Robot Control Panel to the Virtual Laboratory Environment the user needs to define the desired velocity and click simultaneously the dead man switch and the plus or minus button of the joint to move, so the robot performs the action.

4.3 System Usability

There was considered a group of 20 people for the usability tests in order to measure the experience in the use of the virtual environment. All of the participants installed the Virtual Training System before the tests and were capacitated in the use of the system. For the experiments were considered joint movement tasks defined by the users with the Robot Control Panel application and performed by the robot in the Virtual Laboratory environment. After finishing the tests, the experimental group carried out a usability test to measure the acceptance of the virtual system.

The degree of usability of the system is calculated by using one of the most popular questionnaires for usability tests in the scientific community, this is the System Usability Scale (SUS) [21, 22]. The questionnaire consists in a quiz that has positive and negative statements. The questions were adapted for the proposed Virtual Training System and

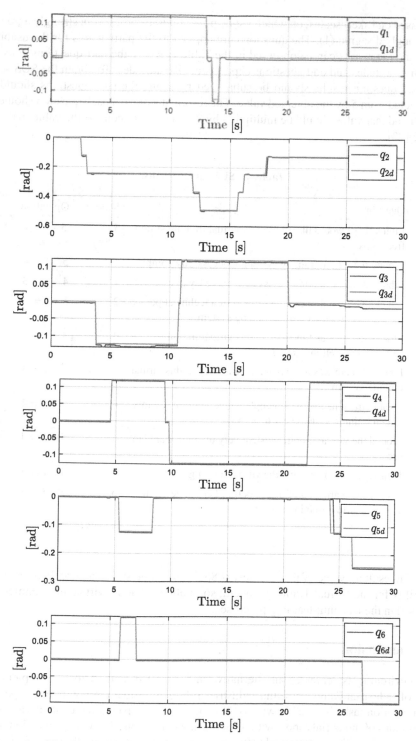

Fig. 11. Performance time graphics of the robot joint movements.

it's based on Likert scales, on which the response options varies from strongly agree (5) to strongly disagree (1). The questionnaire applied to the participants for the usability tests and the results can be observed in the Table 1, where the pair questions consider negative attitudes and odd questions express positive attitudes. To obtain the SUS score the odd question results should be subtracted by 1 and the pair questions should be subtracted from 5 by the obtained value. The resultant scores of each question should be added and that value should be multiplied by 2.5 in order to convert the value to 0–100 range [23].

Table. 1. SUS survey results.

N°	Question	Score	Operation
Q1	I think that I would like to use this virtual training system frequently	5	5 - 1 = 4
Q2	I found the virtual training system unnecessarily complex	1	5 − 1 = 4
Q3	I thought the virtual training system was easy to use	4	4 − 1 = 3
Q4	I think that I would need the support of a technical person to be able to use this virtual training system	2	5 − 2 = 3
Q5	I found the various functions in this virtual training system were well integrated	4	4 − 1 = 3
Q6	I thought there was too much inconsistency in this virtual training system	1	5 − 1 = 4
Q7	I would imagine that most people would learn to use this virtual training system very quickly	4	5 − 1 = 4
Q8	I found the virtual training system very uncomfortable to use	1	5 − 1 = 4
Q9	I felt very confident using the virtual training system	4	4 − 1 = 3
Q10	I needed to learn a lot of things before I could get going with this virtual training system	3	5 − 3 = 2
		TOTAL	34 × 2.5 = 85

The resultant value of the SUS test is 85%, this value shows an excellent degree of usability for the Virtual Training System; so, it allows that the virtual environment can be used in the teaching-learning processes.

5   Conclusion

VR environments serves as an alternative and effective method for the implementation of Industrial Robotics, using industrial robots in virtual environments to perform manipulation tasks is a viable way to allow users to understand the characteristics and restrictions of industrial robots without acquiring real robots. The interconnection of VR environments with mathematical software's using shared memory, allows implementing and testing control algorithms for manipulator robots in real time. The implementation of numerical methods in closed loop controllers allows performing manipulation tasks with industrial robots in virtual environment with the possible less movements to perform the action. However, the synergy between VR environments and control algorithms in mathematical software's are a viable way to boost teaching-learning processes in the scientific community.

Acknowledgements. The authors would like to thank the Universidad de las Fuerzas Armadas ESPE and the ARSI research group for the support in the development of this work.

References

1. Stankovski, S., Ostojić, G., Baranovski, I., Babić, M., Stanojević, M.: The impact of edge computing on industrial automation. In: Proceedings of the 2020 19th International Symposium INFOTEH-JAHORINA (INFOTEH), March 2020, pp. 1–4 (2020)
2. Lasi, H., Fettke, P., Kemper, H.-G., Feld, T., Hoffmann, M.: Industry 4.0. Bus. Inf. Syst. Eng. 6(4), 239–242 (2014). https://doi.org/10.1007/s12599-014-0334-4
3. Mirashe, S.P., Kalyankar, N.V.: Cloud Computing (2010). arXiv:1003.4074 [cs]
4. Ranjan, J., Foropon, C.: Big data analytics in building the competitive intelligence of organizations. Int. J. Inf. Manag. 56, 102231 (2021). https://doi.org/10.1016/j.ijinfomgt.2020.102231
5. Tresa, M., Francina, S., Jerlin Oviya, V., Lavanya, K.: A study on internet of things: overview, automation, wireless technology, robotics. Ann. Roman. Soc. Cell Biol. 2021, 6546–6555 (2021)
6. Atici-Ulusu, H., Ikiz, Y.D., Taskapilioglu, O., Gunduz, T.: Effects of augmented reality glasses on the cognitive load of assembly operators in the automotive industry. Int. J. Comput. Integr. Manuf. 34, 487–499 (2021). https://doi.org/10.1080/0951192X.2021.1901314
7. Araiza-Alba, P., et al.: The potential of 360-degree virtual reality videos to teach water-safety skills to children. Comput. Educ. 163, 104096 (2021). https://doi.org/10.1016/j.compedu.2020.104096
8. Newbury, R., Cosgun, A., Crowley-Davis, T., Chan, W.P., Drummond, T., Croft, E.: Visualizing Robot Intent for Object Handovers with Augmented Reality (2021). arXiv:2103.04055 [cs]
9. Radu, I., Hv, V., Schneider, B.: Unequal impacts of augmented reality on learning and collaboration during robot programming with peers. In: Proceedings of the ACM on Human-Computer Interaction, vol. 4, p. 1822. ACM Digital Library (2021). https://doi.org/10.1145/3446568
10. Gausemeier, J., Berssenbrügge, J., Grafe, M., Kahl, S., Wassmann, H.: Design and VR/AR-based testing of advanced mechatronic systems. In: Ma, D., Fan, X., Gausemeier, J., Grafe, M. (eds.) Proceedings of the Virtual Reality & Augmented Reality in Industry, pp. 1–37. Springer, Heidelberg (2011). https://doi.org/10.1007/978-3-642-17376-9_1
11. Arnarson, H., Solvang, B., Shu, B.: The application of virtual reality in programming of a manufacturing cell. In: Proceedings of the 2021 IEEE/SICE International Symposium on System Integration (SII), January 2021, pp. 213–218 (2021)
12. Ma, D., Zhen, X., Hu, Y., Wu, D., Fan, X., Zhu, H.: Collaborative virtual assembly operation simulation and its application. In: Ma, D., Fan, X., Gausemeier, J., Grafe, M. (eds.) Proceedings of the Virtual Reality & Augmented Reality in Industry, pp. 55–82. Springer, Heidelberg (2011). https://doi.org/10.1007/978-3-642-17376-9_3

13. Fan, X., Yang, R., Wu, D., Ma, D.: Virtual assembly environment for product design evaluation and workplace planning. In: Ma, D., Fan, X., Gausemeier, J., Grafe, M. (eds.) Proceedings of the Virtual Reality & Augmented Reality in Industry, pp. 147–161. Springer, Heidelberg (2011). https://doi.org/10.1007/978-3-642-17376-9_9

14. Almaged, M.: Forward and inverse kinematic analysis and validation of the ABB IRB 140 industrial robot. J. Mech. Eng. Technol. (JMET) **9**, 1–20 (2017)

15. Andaluz, V., Roberti, F., Toibero, J.M., Carelli, R.: Adaptive unified motion control of mobile manipulators. Control. Eng. Pract. **20**, 1337–1352 (2012). https://doi.org/10.1016/j.coneng prac.2012.07.008

16. Corke, P.I.: A simple and systematic approach to assigning denavit-hartenberg parameters. IEEE Trans. Rob. **23**, 590–594 (2007). https://doi.org/10.1109/TRO.2007.896765

17. Siciliano, B., Sciavicco, L., Villani, L., Oriolo, G.: Robotics: Modelling, Planning and Control (2009). https://doi.org/10.1007/978-1-84628-642-1

18. Andaluz, V.H., et al.: Unity3D-MatLab simulator in real time for robotics applications. In: De Paolis, L.T., Mongelli, A. (eds.) AVR 2016. LNCS, vol. 9768, pp. 246–263. Springer, Cham (2016). https://doi.org/10.1007/978-3-319-40621-3_19

19. Carvajal, C., Méndez, M., Torres, D., Terán, C., Arteaga, O., Andaluz, Víctor. H.: Autonomous and tele-operated navigation of aerial manipulator robots in digitalized virtual environments. In: Paolis, L.T.D., Bourdot, P. (eds.) AVR 2018. LNCS, vol. 10851, pp. 496–515. Springer, Cham (2018). https://doi.org/10.1007/978-3-319-95282-6_36

20. Ortiz, J.S., Palacios-Navarro, G., Andaluz, V.H., Guevara, B.S.: Virtual reality-based framework to simulate control algorithms for robotic assistance and rehabilitation tasks through a standing wheelchair. Sensors (Basel) **21**, 5083 (2021). https://doi.org/10.3390/s21155083

21. Sauro, J., Lewis, J.: When designing usability questionnaires, does it hurt to be positive?, pp. 2215–2224 (2011)

22. Salvendy, G.: Handbook of Human Factors and Ergonomics. John Wiley & Sons, Hoboken (2012). ISBN 978–1–118–12908–1

23. Borsci, S., Federici, S., Lauriola, M.: On the dimensionality of the system usability scale: a test of alternative measurement models. Cogn. Process. **10**, 193–197 (2009). https://doi.org/10.1007/s10339-009-0268-9

Author Index

Printed in the United States
by Baker & Taylor Publisher Services